D0205438

INTRODUCTION TO
CAMBODIAN

INTRODUCTION TO
CAMBODIAN

JUDITH M. JACOB

Lecturer in Cambodian
School of Oriental and African Studies

LONDON
OXFORD UNIVERSITY PRESS
BOMBAY   KUALA LUMPUR
1968

Oxford University Press, Ely House, London W.1

GLASGOW   NEW YORK   TORONTO   MELBOURNE   WELLINGTON
CAPE TOWN   SALISBURY   IBADAN   NAIROBI   LUSAKA   ADDIS ABABA
BOMBAY   CALCUTTA   MADRAS   KARACHI   LAHORE   DACCA
KUALA LUMPUR   HONG KONG   TOKYO

Printed in England by Stephen Austin and Sons, Ltd., Hertford

TABLE OF CONTENTS

PART III   GRAMMAR AND TRANSLATION

CONTENTS

PREFACE

It was during a fifteen months' study leave in Cambodia financed by the School of Oriental and African Studies, London University, that most of the material used in this book was gathered. The field notes were put into the shape of a course during several successive years of teaching at the School. Encouragement to publish the course came from Professor E. J. A. Henderson, Head of the Department of South East Asia and the Islands. The small but increasing number of requests for information on the language which have come to me from various parts of the world in the last year or two provided a further stimulus to make the course available to a wider public than the students attending at the School.

I am greatly indebted to the work of Professor Henderson. The phonetic transcription of the language and the analysis of the syllable-structure worked out by her form the basis of those used and presented here.

To the School my very real thanks are due for making everything possible: the original study leave, the recent recording of the exercises in the book and finally, publication of the book, of which the full cost has been met by the Publications Committee.

Many Cambodians, during the course of several years, have helped me and have indirectly contributed to the writing of this book. The three who have contributed directly, however, are Mr. Veng Heng, who worked as my informant for a year in Phnom Penh and prepared several of the passages used as exercises in the book, Mr. Sieng Kim Houn who very kindly checked the sentences, wrote some passages and did the tape-recordings of all the exercises at the School, and Mr. Sum Sorel, who has checked all the keys and sentences used as examples in the text of the work and has also helped in extending and re-recording some exercises and illustrative material.

Copies of the tape-recordings may purchased at £4 4s., post-free. Requests for copies, *together with the remittance*, should be addressed to Mrs. J. M. Jacob, School of Oriental and African Studies, University of London, W.C.1. They are not available from the publisher.

J. M. J.

October, 1965

GENERAL INTRODUCTION

Over five and a half million people in Cambodia speak as their mother-tongue the language called Cambodian or Khmer. The language is a member of the Mon-Khmer language family which includes many languages and dialects spoken in Burma and Malaya as well as in Cambodia.

Cambodians vary in their speech habits as much as speakers of any other languages. Thus there are dialectal differences in the speech of Cambodians native to Siem Reap or Battambang or various other areas of Cambodia, as compared with the speakers in Phnom Penh. Well-educated Cambodians use many French words; they tend to adopt a formal, reading style of speech rather easily if they become serious or didactic. They then reveal a consciousness of the writing and of Sanskrit and Pali loanwords and give a pronunciation based on the spelling. The Cambodian language read in this heavy-going style is very different indeed from the lively language of rapid speech. The present course is aimed to introduce the student to both the spoken and written language. The style of speech described is that heard among the educated people of Phnom Penh.

It is appreciated that even among the comparatively small public who wish to learn Cambodian or learn something about it there is a great diversity of aims and conditions of study. My students and those enquiring about the language have included people of both European and Asian language backgrounds, people who have had phonetic training and those who have not, and people who hoped to obtain the help of a Cambodian teacher and some who were far removed from such help. For the sake of those with no phonetic training the attempt has been made to describe sounds in terms of British English or French. To meet the needs of the students with no teacher keys to all exercises have been given and tape-recordings of all exercises have been made: it is nevertheless to be emphasized that the task of the student working on his own will be very difficult. Since there may be people who wish to learn something about the language without learning the script, the course is so arranged that it may be followed entirely in transcription. It is partly owing to this arrangement and partly in order to cut down costs and facilitate printing that the orthography is confined to two places in the book, Part I, Lessons 5–13 and Part IV. It is hoped that this will not cause the student or teacher to forget it.

It is strongly recommended that the student should work through the Lessons in the order in which they are presented with the exception of Lessons 6–13 on the orthography. Most students will be learning this eventually but it may be assimilated gradually. Students who have no previous experience of phonetics or of South East Asian languages may have to spend rather a long time practising the lessons of pronunciation. This may be conveniently combined with some practice in drawing and learning the characters for individual consonants or vowels which are being pronounced. No attempt should be made to write the complete syllables which are given for pronunciation in Lessons 1–4 since these happen to be difficult and unsuitable for the beginner. It is suggested that the student should certainly have gained some knowledge of the script by the time he begins Part II and that he should be able to turn all the exercises for Lessons 14–18 into script from transcription or *vice versa* before proceeding to Lesson 19.

When Part II is being worked through with a teacher it is probably desirable to use some reading material in addition to the exercise. The Cambodian School Readers[1] are difficult for the foreigner but some parts of them can be used, with a great deal of help from the teacher, during the study of Part II so as to provide some relief from the constant introduction of new grammar. The first few passages in Part III are in fact easier than such reading matter but it is intended that by the time he reaches Part III the student should be fully prepared to examine the grammar of every sentence in the Cambodian passages. He will be at this stage only after completing Part II.

The course contained in this book has been worked through, with additional reading and translation passages, both by students registering for six months' intensive study and by students spending a year or more at the rate of 2–4 hours per week of class-work and 4–6 hours per week of preparation in term-time.

---

[1] See Bibliography, Part VII.

PART I

PRONUNCIATION AND ORTHOGRAPHY

The variety and unfamiliarity of the Cambodian sounds may cause some dismay, no matter how they are presented. Unfortunately there is no short cut to Part II, since words cannot be distinguished and remembered unless at least some idea of their pronunciation has been gained. The consonants, vowels and diphthongs are presented in Lessons 1 to 3 and word-forms in Lesson 4. The syllables used are not necessarily Cambodian words but they involve no non-Cambodian sounds. The sounds are introduced gradually a few at a time in separate paragraphs, beginning with those which are least difficult for the English-speaking student. Each paragraph begins with a description of the pronunciation of the new sounds. For the sake of the student who is working without a teacher and who is not familiar with phonetic symbols, an indication is also given for each sound of the nearest equivalent in British English or French. It must be emphasized that this is only a very rough guide. The numbers which have been given to each sound refer to Lesson 5 where a complete résumé of the sounds and their pronunciation is given in this numerical order, together with an indication of how each sound may be written in the orthography.

The student who has a teacher or the tape-recordings may not need to use the descriptions of the articulation of the sounds at all. The descriptions are followed by lines of practice syllables. These are identical with those which will be found on the tape-recordings. The student who does not have the recordings should practise these syllables, if possible with a Cambodian teacher or assistant. Lesson 5 will prove useful to the Cambodian helper since it links the transcription and the orthography.

At the end of most paragraphs the word 'dictation' is written. This indicates that a dictation of eight to twelve words, appropriate to the study of the paragraph, is given on the tape-recordings. The key to these dictations will be found in Part V and might of course be useful to a teacher wishing to give dictation and not using the tape.

The orthography is divided into several lessons but it is appreciated that it may be tackled in various ways. The student may for example learn some vowel-signs while practising the sounds in the earlier lessons. Some progressive exercises in the use of the script are given in Lesson 10, for which the keys will be found by reference to Part V.

LESSON 1

FIRST REGISTER VOWELS AND DIPHTHONGS WITH INITIAL AND FINAL CONSONANTS

1.1. *The two registers*

There are two series of vowels and diphthongs in Cambodian, which will be called the first and second 'registers'. Second register vowels and diphthongs are marked by a grave accent in the transcription used in this book; first register vowels and diphthongs are left unmarked. The vowels and diphthongs of the two registers are articulated differently from each other with the exception of *uɔ/ùːɔ*, *uɔ/ùɔ* and *iɔ/ìɔ*. The Cambodians themselves are sometimes confused about these diphthongs in some words, not knowing to which register they belong and therefore not knowing which spelling to use. There is potentially a distinction of voice quality in the utterance of the vowels and diphthongs of the two registers, those of the first register being pronounced with a clear, 'head' voice and a certain degree of tension and those of the second with a breathy, 'chest' voice and a comparatively relaxed utterance. This difference of voice quality will, however, not be heard in the speech of all speakers. It may be heard occasionally in the speech of some speakers and is then most easily noted in syllables uttered in isolation.

The vowels and diphthongs of both registers, the initial and final consonants and the various types of native word-forms are described and presented below, in 34 paragraphs, with lines of syllables or words for pronunciation practice. The paragraphs are divided into four groups, forming the first four lessons but the numbering of the paragraphs is continued from 1 to 34 throughout the four lessons so that they match the numbered paragraphs announced on the tape-recordings.

1.2. *Recorded paragraphs 1–6*

1. *Initial consonants n, m, y, r, l, s and h. Vowels ɔː, aː, oː and eː*

n (9)[1] Post-dental nasal. cf. English n in 'no'.

m (10) Bilabial nasal. cf. English m in 'man'.

y (11) Palatal semi-vowel, vigorously articulated. cf. English y in 'yard'.

r (14) Frictionless continuant in the speech of Phnom Penh. cf. English r in 'rose'. In Battambang a one-tap uvular *r* is heard and elsewhere a rolled *r*.

l (12) Post-alveolar lateral. cf. English l in 'look'.

s (5) Voiceless, post-dental sibilant. cf. English s in 'see'.

h (6) Aspirate. cf. English h in 'hard'.

ɔː (18) Open rounded back vowel. cf. American o in 'hot', pronounced with slight lip-rounding and with length (as length-mark, ː, indicates).

aː (20) Open unrounded mid (neither front nor back) vowel. cf. French a in 'patte' with length or Yorkshire pronunciation of vowel-sound in 'cart'.

oː (27) Mid to close, back though slightly centralized vowel. cf. French vowel in first syllable of 'sauter'.

eː (32) Unrounded half-close slightly centralized front vowel. cf. vowel in English 'hay' or vowels in French 'été'.

  (i) **nɔː mɔː yɔː rɔː lɔː sɔː hɔː**[2]
  (ii) **naː maː yaː raː laː saː haː**
  (iii) **noː moː yoː roː loː soː hoː**
  (iv) **neː meː yeː reː leː seː heː**
  (v) Contrast **nɔː noː naː neː mɔː moː maː meː**
Dictation.[3]

---

[1] Numbers in parentheses refer to Lesson 5 where the descriptions of the sounds are summarized and an indication of their orthography is given.

[2] Recorded passages are printed throughout in bold letters.

[3] See introduction to Part I.

2. *Final consonants, ŋ, n, m, y, l and s*

ŋ (71) Velar nasal. cf. the final consonantal sound in English 'bang'.

n (73) Alveolar nasal. cf. English final consonant in 'can'.

m (74) Bilabial nasal. cf. English final consonant in 'him'.

y (75) Palatal semi-vowel. cf. English final sound in 'boy'.

l (76) Post-alveolar lateral semi-vowel of fairly dark resonance. cf. English final consonant in 'haul'.

s (69) Voiceless sibilant. cf. English final consonant in 'mass'. It is only in a careful reading style, however, that this written final consonant is kept separate from written final h (see paragraph 4 below). Both written s and h may be pronounced as *s, h* or *h* with *s* offglide.

(i) saːŋ   saːn   saːm   saːy   saːl   saːs
(ii) haːŋ   haːn   haːm   haːy   haːl   haːs
(iii) Contrast saːŋ soːŋ   soːm soːm   haːl hoːl   haːy hoːy   loːy loːy   seːm saːm
Dictation.

3. *Short vowels ɔ, a and o*[1]

ɔ (19) Very open rounded back vowel. cf. American o in 'hot' with slight lip-rounding.

a (21) Unrounded open vowel, slightly more front than *aː*. cf. a in French 'patte' or in Yorkshire 'cat'.

o (26) Fairly open back vowel with quite strong lip-rounding. cf. French vowel in 'sauter' without length.

(i) nɔŋ   lɔm   mɔs   hɔl   yɔŋ   rɔm   sɔl
(ii) naŋ   man   yay   ral   lam   sas   haŋ
(iii) noŋ   mon   yom   roy   los   soŋ   hom
(iv) Contrast nɔːŋ nɔŋ   saːm sam   hoːl hol   maːy may
(v) Contrast nɔŋ noŋ   lɔs los   sol sɔl   rom rɔm
Dictation.

4. *Final consonant h*

h (70) Aspirate. cf. English h in 'hat' but used as a final consonant. Written final h is kept separate from written final s only in a most careful reading style; it is always preceded by a vowel which is pronounced short.[2]

(i) nɔh   mah   yoh   rɔh   lah   soh
(ii) Compare nas nah   sos soh   los lɔh

5. *Short vowel e*[1]

e (22) Unrounded half-close front vowel. cf. English e in 'yet'.

(i) neh   meh   yeh   reh   leh   seh   heh
(ii) Contrast neːs neh   meːs meh   reːs reh
Dictation.

---

[1] Short vowels do not occur in native Cambodian words without a final consonant following them. When a Cambodian needs to pronounce a short vowel with no consonant following it, as here in the title of this paragraph, he closes the vowel with a glottal stop (78) or, sometimes, with *k*. This will be heard on the tapes in the announcement of the vowels of paragraph 3 as 'ɔʔ, aʔ and oʔ' and will be heard again in the announcement of the short vowels in paragraphs 5, 14, 17, 19, 21 and 22 below.

[2] Final *s* and *h* are kept separate here because they can be different in the careful pronunciation of isolated words. It is also useful to maintain a link between transcription and the spelling.

6. *Initial consonants k, c, t and p*

k (1) Voiceless unaspirated velar plosive. cf. English hard c in 'cook'.
c (2) Voiceless unaspirated palatal plosive. cf. English ch in 'chat'.
t (3) Voiceless unaspirated post-dental plosive. cf. English t in 'tank'.
p (4) Voiceless unaspirated bilabial plosive. cf. English p in 'post'.

Careful practice is required to ensure that no aspiration (*h*) occurs between these consonants and the following vowel. In most kinds of English c, t and p are aspirated in the words, 'cook', 'tank' and 'post'. *k, c, t* and *p* are to be contrasted with the same consonants aspirated in pairs of words, e.g. *kat, khat, cat, chat,* etc.[1]

(i) kɔː kaː koː keː kɔːŋ kaːn koːm keːs
(ii) cɔː caː coː ceː cɔːy caːl coːŋ ceːm
(iii) tɔː taː toː teː toːl taːs toːm teːm
(iv) pɔː paː poː peː pɔːm paːy poːs peːl

Dictation.

LESSON 2

FIRST REGISTER VOWELS AND DIPHTHONGS WITH INITIAL AND FINAL CONSONANTS (CONTINUED)

2.1. *Recorded paragraphs 7–15*

7. *Final consonants k, c, t and p*

k (65) Voiceless velar occlusive. cf. English final consonant in 'back'. Occurs in free variation with glottal stop, ʔ (78). cf. English dialect final consonant in 'biʔ' (for 'bit').
c (66) Voiceless palatal occlusive. cf. English final sound in 'such', pronounced, however, in a clearcut way so that no slurring (affrication) follows the contact.
t (67) Voiceless alveolar occlusive. cf. English final consonant in 'bat'.
p (68) Voiceless bilabial occlusive. cf. English final consonant in 'cup'.

These four final consonants are very different from the nearest English sounds since the release of contact is usually inaudible. Vowels preceding a palatal final are affected by a palatal onglide. Thus *bac* is heard as [*baic*].

(i) sak saːk nɔk nɔːk mok moːk leːk
(ii) mac maːc toc toːc kac kaːc tec
(iii) cɔt cɔːt kot koːt rat raːt ceːt
(iv) kɔp koːp cap caːp sop soːp neːp
(v) Contrast mɔk mɔt mɔp   noːk noːt noːp   hok hoc hot hop

Dictation.

8. *Diphthongs uːə and iə*

uːə (28) Falling diphthong starting from a well-rounded close back vowel and moving towards a more open vowel; in open syllables this has a tendency to be accompanied by uvular friction; in closed syllables the final point of articulation is a central half-open vowel. cf. English diphthong in 'truer'.

---

[1] See Lesson 4.3.

6

iə (31) Unrounded falling diphthong starting from a close front vowel and moving towards a more open central vowel. cf. English diphthong in 'here'.

(i) suːə huːə kuːə cuːə puːəs huːəc cuːəl tuːən
(ii) siə hiə kiə ciə ciəs piəc niəl tiən

9. *Diphthongs aə and ae*

aə (29) Unrounded falling diphthong starting from an open vowel similar to *a* (21) and moving towards a half-close, slightly centralized back vowel. cf. English vowels in 'fatter' without the consonant 't', and pronounced smoothly one after the other.

ae (33) Unrounded falling diphthong starting from an open vowel, more front than *a* (21) and moving towards a closer front vowel. cf. English vowels in 'adept' without the consonant 'd' and pronounced smoothly one after the other.

(i) saə haə kaə caə laəs kaət saəc kaən
(ii) sae hae kae cae laen taek saem kaep
(iii) Contrast laəŋ laeŋ caət caet naən naen haəp haep
(iv) Contrast naː naə nae neː taː taə tae taːy tay taəy paə pae pay
    haəy hay haːy
Dictation.

10. *Diphthongs ao and au*

ao (35) Falling diphthong starting from an open unrounded vowel, slightly more back then *a* (21) and moving towards a closer back vowel with lip-rounding. cf. English diphthong in 'how' but without proceeding to so close a final point.

au (36) Falling diphthong starting from an open vowel similar to *a* (21) and moving towards a close back vowel, pronounced either with rounded lips or with lips in position for the vowel ʋ (as in the pronunciation of the English vowel in 'put') with bilabial closure. cf. English diphthong in 'how'. *au* is never followed by a final consonant.

(i) nao mao yao rao kaoŋ maok saol haoy caom paoc kaot
(ii) nau mau yau rau lau sau hau kau cau tau pau
(iii) Contrast nao nau mao mau rao rau lao lau
(iv) Contrast kɔːŋ koːŋ kaoŋ noːy noːy naoy
(v) Contrast laəŋ laoŋ haəy haoy kaəp kaop raəm raom
Dictation.

11. *Initial consonants ŋ, ɲ and v*

ŋ (7) Velar nasal. cf. English ng in 'song' used as an initial consonant.
ɲ (8) Palatal nasal. cf. English ni in 'onions'.
v (13) Labial semi-vowel, weakly articulated; sometimes realized as bilabial w or labio-dental ʋ. cf. English v in 'very' with weak articulation.

(i) ŋoː ŋaː ŋoː ŋeː ŋuːə ŋiə ŋaə ŋae ŋao ŋau ŋoːŋ ŋoŋ ŋaːk ŋak
(ii) ɲoː ɲaː ɲoː ɲeː ɲuːə ɲiə ɲaə ɲae ɲao ɲau ɲeːs ɲeh ɲaək ɲaom
(iii) voː vaː voː veː viə vaə vae vao vau vaːn van vaːy vay
(iv) Contrast nas ŋas ɲas nal ŋal ɲal nɔk ŋɔk ɲɔk
Dictation.

12. *Final consonants ɲ and v*

ɲ (72) Palatal nasal. cf. English ni in 'onions'.

v (77) Labio-dental (or sometimes bilabial) semi-vowel, accompanied by velarization. When oː occurs before v it loses the lip-rounding, in the speech of Phnom Penh, because of the lip-spreading for the v; the resulting vowel + final may be heard as [əu] and may sound to the student like the diphthong ɤu (60).[1] cf. English final sound in 'cove' with weak articulation.

   (i) laːɲ saːɲ haːɲ maːɲ saɲ soːɲ seɲ toɲ ruːəɲ
   (ii) saːv haːv paːv caːv seːv kaev ɲiəv coːv
   (iii) Contrast kaːŋ kaːɲ kaːn kaːm   saŋ saɲ san sam   loːŋ tuːəɲ som
   (iv) Contrast sao sau saːv   lao lau laːv   kaːv kao kau   hao haːv
   Dictation.

Note. All final consonants have now been introduced.

13. *Initial consonants d, b and ʔ*

d (15) Voiced post-alveolar implosive. cf. English d as in 'do'.[2]

b (16) Voiced bilabial implosive. cf. English b in 'bat'.[2]

ʔ (17) Weak glottal plosive. Occurs in English when a word beginning with a vowel and stressed on the first syllable is pronounced with a harsh, constricted voice, e.g. '*Any*one can do it!'.

   (i) dɔː daː doː deː duːə diə daə dae dao dau dɔːŋ dɔk dom dal
   (ii) bɔː baː boː beː buːə biə baə bae bao bau baːn beːs biət baok
   (iii) ʔɔː ʔaː ʔoː ʔeː ʔuːə ʔiə ʔaə ʔae ʔao ʔau ʔoːm ʔɔːk ʔaət ʔaːc
   (iv) Contrast daːn baːn ʔaːn   duːəl buːəl ʔuːəl
   Dictation.

14. *Vowels and diphthongs ɤ,[3] ɤy and ɤː*

ɤ (24) Fairly back half-close unrounded vowel. cf. English vowel in 'bird' pronounced short.

ɤy (23) Unrounded falling diphthong starting from a half-close central vowel and moving towards a close front unrounded vowel. cf. English vowels in 'surfeit' without the consonant 'f' and pronounced smoothly one after the other. ɤy is never followed by a final consonant.

ɤː (25) As for 24 but with length. cf. English vowel in 'bird'.

   (i) sɤk sɤŋ sɤn sɤp sɤm sɤl sɤs hɤŋ kɤt cɤŋ vɤk pɤn
   (ii) kɤy ŋɤy cɤy ɲɤy dɤy tɤy pɤy bɤy mɤy rɤy lɤy sɤy hɤy
   (iii) kɤː cɤː tɤː dɤː pɤː bɤː ŋɤː nɤː mɤː sɤːt sɤːp bɤːt
   (iv) Contrast kay kɤy   cay cɤy   tay tɤy   day dɤy
   (v) Contrast sɔk sak sɤk   hɔn han hɤn
   Dictation.

---

[1] oːv is not pronounced [əu] on the tape recording of this paragraph, but this pronunciation may be heard, for example, in the word troːv in the recording of Exercise 21 A 1.

[2] English d and b, which are not imploded consonants, are not at all satisfactory as guides to the Cambodian pronunciation. English speakers sometimes use an imploded b when imitating the sound of water coming out of a bottle in spurts (bubububu).

[3] See footnote to paragraph 3 above.

15. *Diphthong ɯə*

ɯə (30) Unrounded falling diphthong starting from a fairly close, unrounded back vowel and moving towards a more open central vowel. The second vowel is like English a in 'about'; the first cannot be compared with any sound in the better-known European languages. The exclamation of disgust, 'ugh!', is by some English speakers pronounced with a similar vowel (ɯ) but other speakers use a vowel closer to ɤː. The vowel ɯ is articulated by maintaining the tongue position for 'oo' while spreading the lips.

(i) kɯə cɯə tɯə pɯə ŋɯə ɲɯə nɯə mɯə rɯə lɯə sɯəŋ bɯəŋ dɯəŋ

(ii) Contrast sɤː sɯə hɤː hɯə bɤː bɯə nɤː nɯə
Dictation.

Note. All the vowels and diphthongs of the first register have now been introduced.

2.2. *Exercise for pronunciation, dictation or writing practice*

1. ɔː/oː. kɔːŋ hoːŋ doːn dɔːŋ tɔːk ʔoːn kɔːm sɔŋ hoːɲ cɔːŋ
2. Length. kɔt kɔːt bak kɔːk saɤ deːk seh kɔːŋ leːp
3. ɔː/ɔ/oː/o. kɔːt ton bɔŋ koːn sɔŋ toːk ʔɔːk mɔŋ hoːp sɔk
4. ɔ/a/o. kon sap kɔp kɔl kat cok dɔk bɔn nok
5. ɔ/ɤ/a. bal tɤn lɤk kɔh sɤm pan rɤm cɔŋ kat
6. uːə/ao. kuːət haok ʔuːəm laom ruːəc haoc tuːən laon
7. iə/eː. kiək ɲeːp tiəm leːŋ diək deː riəp ceːk
8. aə/ae. daəm saen paəm ʔaək laəŋ kaət haəy caet
9. aː/aə/ae. paː daə laek mae kaət saəm haeŋ ɲaːl
10. ae/ay/aːy. day maet ʔaɤy yaɤŋ laeŋ kay caek maːn
11. aə/ao/au. caə nau sao hau paə lao dau haə
12. aəy/aoy/ay/aːy. saəy baɤy baoy laəy cay daoy kay
13. au/aːv/ay/aːy. haɤy ʔaːv pay bau kaɤy lay mau raːv
14. ɲ/ŋ/v. ɲat ɲaek vaɤy ŋaok voːp ɲɤm ŋɔːm ɲom
15. ɤ/aə/ɤy. haəm sɤk nɤm caə rɤy baək paəy dɤy

LESSON 3

SECOND REGISTER VOWELS AND DIPHTHONGS WITH ALL CONSONANTS

3.1. *Recorded paragraphs 16–23*

The accent serves to distinguish sounds which are represented by the same symbol but which are articulated differently, e.g. first register oː and second register òː which is closer; it is also helpful when the transcription is to be turned into the orthography, since two different sets of consonants are used to indicate the two registers.

16. *The diphthongs ùːə and ìə/ìːə*

ùːə (51), ìə (54) and ìːə (43). The articulation of ùːə and ìə is as for uːə and iə on the first register; only the voice-quality[1] can potentially distinguish them. ìə and ìːə are pronounced alike in the speech of Phnom Penh. They are distinguished in the transcription for two reasons, (i) because they are

---

[1] See Lesson 1.1.

written with different symbols in the Cambodian script and it is convenient to be able to turn script into transcription and *vice versa* without confusion; (ii) because to the north and south of Phnom Penh the diphthong written ìːə has a less close starting point than that written ìə.

(i) kùːəŋ   cùːəŋ   tùːəŋ   pùːəŋ   yùːəŋ   rùːəŋ   lùːəŋ   kùːək
(ii) kìəŋ   cìəŋ   tìəŋ   pìəŋ   rìəŋ   lìəŋ
(iii) lìːəŋ   mìːən   hìːən   lìːən   pìːəŋ   rìːəy   lìːəy   vìːəl

17. Vowels ì,[1] ìː, ù[1] and ùː

ì (45) Short close unrounded front vowel. cf. English i in 'bit'.
ìː (46) Close unrounded front vowel. cf. English vowel in 'beat'.
ù (49) Short close back rounded vowel. cf. English vowel in 'put'.
ùː (50) Close back rounded vowel. cf. English vowel in 'boot'.

(i) cìh   nìh   mìh   rìh   lìh
(ii) cìː   tìː   pìː   lìː   sìː   ɲìː   rìː   rìːk   cìːk   mìːŋ   lìːŋ
(iii) kùk   cùc   tùk   pùk   lùŋ   sùc   pùh   yùm   kùy   pùn
(iv) kùː   cùː   tùː   pùː   rùːŋ   pùːc   mùːs   lùːɲ
(v) Contrast kùːəs kùs kùː   tùːən tùn tùː   pùːəs pùh pùːc
(vi) Contrast rìh rìːə rìː   tìh tìːə tìː
Dictation.

18. Vowels èː and ɛː

èː (55) Half-close unrounded front vowel. cf. French vowels in été.
ɛː (57) Half-open unrounded front vowel. cf. English vowel in 'let', pronounced with length.

(i) kèː   cèː   tèː   pèː   ŋèː   ɲèː   cèːs   pèːk   lèːŋ   tèːp
(ii) pɛː   rɛː   mɛː   lɛː   vɛːk   pɛːt   mɛːn   nɛːl
(iii) Contrast kèː kɛː   pèːŋ pɛːŋ   lèːk lɛːk   mèː mɛː
(iv) Contrast seː kèː   ce: cèː   deːk tèːp   keːl pèːl
(v) Contrast seːp lèːp nɛːp   ceːs tèːs vɛːs
Dictation.

19. Vowels è[1] and èy

è (56) Short half-close unrounded front vowel. Articulation as for 55 with short duration.

èy (58) Unrounded falling diphthong starting from a half-close unrounded front vowel and moving towards a close unrounded front vowel. cf. English vowel sequence in 'payee', but with prominence given to the first element and the second element shorter.

(i) rèh   lèh   vèh   ɲèh   tèɲ   mèɲ   lèc   cèɲ   tèh
(ii) cèy   tèy   pèy   nèy   lèy   rèy   kèy   mèy
(iii) Contrast cèːs cèh   tèːs tèh   mèːs mèh
(iv) Contrast keh kèh   teh tèh   tec tèc   mec mèc   ceɲ tèɲ   deɲ mèɲ
Dictation.

---

[1] See footnote to paragraph 3 above.

20. *Vowels ɔ: and ò:*

ɔ: (41) Half-open centralized back vowel with lip-rounding. It is particularly difficult to describe in terms of familiar sounds of English, French, German, etc., the variety of 'o' vowels in Cambodian. ɔ: may be attempted by pronouncing English vowel in 'saw' with rounded lips.

ò: (59) Half-close rounded back vowel; similar in articulation to o: (27) but less centralized.

  (i) kɔ̀: cɔ̀: tɔ̀: pɔ̀: yɔ̀:k lɔ̀:ŋ ɲɔ̀:y mɔ̀:m
  (ii) kò: cò: tò: pò: yò:k lò:ŋ kò:m
  (iii) Contrast kɔ̀:k kò:k cɔ̀:k cò:k yɔ̀:k yò:k
  (iv) Contrast kɔ̀: kò: kù: mɔ̀:k lò:k tù:k lò:p lò:p lù:p
  (v) Contrast kɔ:k kɔ̀:k dɔ:ŋ tɔ̀:ŋ dɔ:p lɔ̀:p
  (vi) Contrast ko:t kò:t so:m rò:m ho:p lò:p to:c pɔ̀:c
Dictation.

21. *Short diphthongs ùə, ɔ̀ə and ɛ̀ə*[1]

ùə (42) Falling diphthong starting from a rounded close back vowel and moving towards a more open central vowel. cf. English diphthong in 'sure'. This diphthong is of short duration as compared with all other diphthongs except ɔ̀ə and ɛ̀ə. It must be particularly contrasted with ù:ə in which the first element is considerably longer in duration.

ɔ̀ə (27a) and ɛ̀ə (27b). These diphthongs are in complementary distribution, ɔ̀ə occurring before all finals except k, ŋ, h and ʔ, while ɛ̀ə occurs only before these. ɔ̀ə is a falling diphthong starting from a back rounded half-open vowel, closer than ɔ (19) and moving to a central open vowel with less lip-rounding. cf. English diphthong in 'more'.

ɛ̀ə is a falling diphthong starting from a front half-open unrounded vowel and moving towards a more central vowel. cf. the diphthong heard in English 'there'.

  (i) kùət rùət pùət lùət cùəŋ ŋùəŋ tùəh lùək
  (ii) kɔ̀əp rɔ̀əp cɔ̀əp ŋɔ̀əp tɔ̀ən mɔ̀ət pɔ̀əs rɔ̀əl
  (iii) cɛ̀ək tɛ̀ək rɛ̀ək lɛ̀ək pɛ̀əŋ mɛ̀əŋ tɛ̀əh rɛ̀əh
  (iv) Contrast pù:ək pùək lù:ət lùət kù:əŋ kùəŋ cù:əl cùəl
  (v) Contrast pùh pùəh tùŋ tùəŋ tùk cùək lùt lùət mùn mùən
  (vi) Contrast rɛ̀:k rɛ̀ək tɛ̀:ŋ tɛ̀əŋ cɛ̀:k lɛ̀ək vɛ̀:s vɛ̀əh
  (vii) Contrast rɔ̀:p rɔ̀əp kɔ̀:l kɔ̀əl cɔ̀:m cɔ̀əm pɔ̀:t pɔ̀ət
Dictation.

22. *The vowels, ù*[1] *and ù:, and the diphthong, ùə*

ù (47) Short close back unrounded vowel. For pronunciation guide see paragraph 15 above, where a description of the first element in the diphthong, ùə, is given.

ù: (48) Close back unrounded vowel. Articulation as for ù but with length.

ùə (53) Articulation as for uə (30), potential voice quality being the only difference between the two.

---

[1] See footnote to paragraph 3 above.

  (i) kŭɪt cŭɪt tŭɪt pŭɪt nŭɪŋ mŭɪm tŭɪp vŭɪl
  (ii) kɯ̀ɪ: cɯ̀ɪ: rɯ̀ɪ: lɯ̀ɪ: yɯ̀ɪ:t tɯ̀ɪ: pɯ̀ɪ: mɯ̀ɪ:
  (iii) kɯ̀ɪə ŋɯ̀ɪə cɯ̀ɪə tɯ̀ɪə kɯ̀ɪəy ŋɯ̀ɪək rɯ̀ɪəŋ nɯ̀ɪəm
  (iv) Contrast yɯ̀ɪ: yɯ̀ɪə kɯ̀ɪ: kɯ̀ɪə rɯ̀ɪ: rɯ̀ɪə lɯ̀ɪ: lɯ̀ɪə
  (v) Compare bɯɪəŋ pɯ̀ɪəŋ sɯɪəŋ cɯ̀ɪəŋ tɯɪə cɯ̀ɪə
Dictation.

23. *Vowel ɤ̀: and the diphthong ɤ̀u*

ɤ̀: (52) Half-close back unrounded vowel. cf. English vowel in 'bird'; the Cambodian vowel is pronounced further back. Compared with ɤ and ɤ:, ɤ̀: is slightly closer.

ɤ̀u (60) Falling diphthong starting from a half-close unrounded back vowel similar to ɤ̀: and moving towards a close back vowel with either lip-rounding or labialization. cf. English vowels in 'her book' with no 'b', pronounced smoothly one after the other.

  (i) kɤ̀: cɤ̀: tɤ̀: pɤ̀: lɤ̀:k cɤ̀:ŋ ɲɤ̀:c hɤ̀:ɲ
  (ii) kɤ̀u cɤ̀u tɤ̀u pɤ̀u nɤ̀u ɲɤ̀u mɤ̀u rɤ̀u
  (iii) Contrast tɤ̀: tɤ̀u nɤ̀: nɤ̀u pɤ̀: pɤ̀u lɤ̀: lɤ̀u
  (iv) Contrast bɤ̀:t pɤ̀:t mɤ:n mɤ̀:n lɤ: lɤ̀:
  (v) Contrast lɯ̀:əs lɯ̀ɪəŋ rɯ̀:əy rɯ̀ɪəy tɯ̀:ən tɯ̀ɪən pɯ̀:ə pɯ̀ɪə
  (vi) Contrast kɯ̀ɪh kɯ̀ɪ: kɤ̀: lɯ̀ɪŋ lɯ̀ɪ: lɤ̀: rɯ̀ɪk rɯ̀ɪ: rɤ̀:s
Dictation.

Note. All the vowels and diphthongs of the second register have now been introduced.

3.2. *Exercise for pronunciation, dictation or writing practice*

1. *ɪ:/ì/ìə. rìəl rìh rì:k lɯ̀:ɲ lɯ̀əŋ hì:ŋ mìən mì:ɲ rìəŋ rìən pì:v pìəv lìh cìəs*
2. *ɯ̀:ə/ɯ̀:/ɯ̀ə. pɯ̀:əŋ pɯ̀:ŋ pɯ̀əh pɯ̀h tɯ̀:c sùc lɯ̀:əm lɯ̀əŋ lɯ̀:ŋ tɯ̀:l tɯ̀:əl tɯ̀əl tɯ̀l pɯ̀əs*
3. *ŭ/ɯ̀:ə/ɔ̀ə. kɔ̀əm lɯ̀h tùm pɔ̀əl pɯ̀:əl lɯ̀əh kɔ̀ət tɯ̀:ət rɯ̀:əm kɯ̀ət nɔ̀əm rùm lɯ̀ŋ*
4. *ɛ̀:/è/ɛ̀:/ì:ə. tè: kèc pèy lɛ̀:ŋ nì:əy mè:ŋ rèŋ rɛ̀:k nèy cì:əy rɛ̀:*
5. *ɛə/ɛ̀:/ɛ̀:/è. tɛ̀ək pɛ̀:k lɛ̀:k pɛ̀:t cɛ̀:k cɛ̀əŋ tɛ̀:n rɛ̀əh tɛ̀h kɛ̀:*
6. *ɔ:/ɔ̀:/ɯ̀:/ɯ̀:ə. rɔ̀:ŋ lɯ̀:əŋ mɔ̀:n pɯ̀:t yɯ̀:əc lɯ̀:ɲ kɔ̀: rɔ̀:l pɯ̀:əl kɔ̀:p*
7. *ɯ̀/ɯ̀ə/ɤ̀:/ɔ̀:/ɯ̀:ə. lɯ̀əŋ lɔ̀:m lɤ̀:p sɤ̀:m sùm kɯ̀t nɯ̀əy rɯ̀:əy*
8. *pɤ̀u cɤ̀: mɤ̀:l tɤ̀u ŋɤ̀:p lɔ̀:p rɔ̀:y rɯ̀əy*
9. *kɔ̀ət ŋɔ̀:y rɔ̀əl tɯ̀əl pɔ̀:l tɤ̀:p cɯ̀ə mɔ̀ət*

LESSON 4

WORD-FORMS

4.1. *Extended initial sequences*

In practising the initial consonants, vowels and diphthongs and final consonants, the student has already met the simplest Cambodian word-form, the monosyllable consisting of simple initial consonant, vowel or diphthong and final consonant (which may be absent); this may be represented as CV(C). The initial element of the Cambodian syllable may, however, be complex or extended;[1] it may consist of a sequence of two consonants, or

---

[1] To use the term introduced by Professor E. J. A. Henderson in The Main Features of Cambodian pronunciation, *B.S.O.A.S.*, 1952, pp. 149–174.

three or even four. Between certain types of consonant occurring in this
way no sound at all occurs; one may compare the two consonants which
occur together at the beginning of the English words, 'print' and 'small'.
When certain other types of consonant occur together as an initial sequence,
aspiration (marked h) occurs between them; this is particularly the case
with occlusives, k, c, t, p, followed by a liquid or nasal. Between yet other
kinds of initial consonants occurring in sequence a vowel (marked $ə$) occurs.
In a reading style of speech this vowel is a long $ɔː$ or $ɔ̀ː$[1] but in rapid speech
it is rather like English a in 'about'. The aspiration and the short vowel are
represented as h and $ə$ respectively in the transcription. Examples of all
kinds of monosyllables, simple and extended, are given below.

4.2. *Monosyllables with simple initial consonant, CV(C), recorded
paragraph 24*

24. (i) bɔːŋ pɔ̀ːŋ kɔŋ kùəŋ haet pɛ̀ːt sɔːt ŋùːt haoc ròːc

4.3. *Monosyllables with 2-place initial sequence, recorded paragraphs 25–29*

With no intervening sound between the consonants, CCV(C).

25. (i) kraːp craən treːk pram krɔ̀ən crùːk trùːŋ prùːəy srah mrɛ̀c
    Dictation.

26. (i) khɔː chɔː thɔː phɔː khaː chaː thaː phaː khat chùː phok thùm[2]
    (ii) Contrast[3] kɔː khɔː cɔː chɔː tɔː thɔː pɔː phɔː kan khan kɔ̀ː khɔ̀ː
    can chan cìːə chìːəm taː thaː tùm thùm paəŋ phaəŋ
    Dictation.

27. (i) kdaːm cbas tbiət pdɤy mdɔːŋ lbaeŋ sdok mtɛ̀ːs spɔ̀ən stùŋ
    (ii) kŋaok mɲlə mnɛ̀ək lŋùəŋ lmɔ̀ːm sŋat smaː smaok
    (iii) pyùːə myaːŋ lvìːə svaː slɔːt ʔvɤy kʔɔːm lʔɔː sʔoy sʔaːt mkak
    mcas mhoːp lhoŋ
    Dictation.

With aspiration between the consonants, ChCV(C).

28. (i) khcat chkae thklːəp khmae phkɔ̀əp chnam thnùː phɲaə khlaː
    phlèːŋ chlɤ̀y thlɛ̀ək phtɤl phsɤt phʔaem chvèːŋ thvae
    Dictation.[4]

With a short vowel between the consonants, CəCV(C).[5]

29. (i) kəkaːy kəklːət cəcɔːk cəcɛ̀ːk dədael təteh tətùːəl bəbuːəl pəpok
    pəplːəl ŋəŋùt ɲəŋùm nənɔ̀ːl məmlːəl rəkaː rəŋlːə rəyɛ̀əh rəlùət
    ləlɔ̀ːk səseː(r)
    Dictation.

---

[1] Following the spelling, see Lesson 10.2.

[2] h is here a functioning consonant and not a feature of the junction.

[3] Particular attention should be paid to this contrast; it should be borne in mind that,
in English, plosive initials, e.g. k, t, p, are usually aspirated.

[4] This dictation contains a word ending in $ɔːv$, in which the pronunciation [əu] is heard.
See note to paragraph 12.

[5] On the tape recordings the word-forms occurring in paragraphs 29 and 30 are pronounced
in a formal reading style. The short vowel, represented by $ə$ is heard as $ɔ$ or $ɔ̀$, according to
the syllabary register of the written consonant which is pronounced immediately before it.
This formal style is discussed in Lesson 5.5.

4.4. *Monosyllables with 3-place initial sequences, recorded paragraph 30*

Here the nature of the consonants is such that ə always occurs as a feature of one junction, while the other is marked by either aspiration or no sound.

30. (i) CCəCV(C) krəʔoːp krəcɔ̀əm crəmoh crəlùək trəsɔk prəɲap prəlùm
　　 srəlaɲ trənɔ̀əp
　 (ii) CəCCV(C) kəkrɤt kəkrɛ̀əŋ cəcrɔ̀ːk tətrɛ̀ːt pəpreh pəpriːəy səsraəm
　 (iii) CəCCV(C) kəkhop kəkhɔ̀ː təthɛ̀ək ləkhaon pəphɔŋ məkhaːŋ[1]
　 (iv) CəCCV(C) kəkʔiək pəphʔak[2] kəkhlɤ̀ːɲ[2] pəploŋ pəphɲaoɲ[2]
Dictation.

4.5. *Restricted disyllables, recorded paragraphs 31–32*

One type of disyllable is composed in its simplest form of two sequences of consonant-vowel-consonant but is restricted in that the vowel in the first syllable may be only ə, ùə or ù and that the final consonant of the first syllable is always a nasal. The second syllable is usually a simple mono-syllable but may be a monosyllable with 2-place initial sequence. They may be represented formulaically as CvN-C(C)V(C), where v stands for the restricted vowel possibility and N for the nasal. The first syllable lacks stress in comparison with the second, in a colloquial speech style.

31. (i) kɔŋve: kɔŋkaep sɔmpùət kɔntɛ̀ːl kùmrùp cɔŋʔiət cɔntɔ̀əs cùənlɔ̀ː
　　 cɔmlaek
　 (ii) dɔŋhaəm dɔndaəm tùəŋkùh tùənsaːy tùmlɔ̀əp bɔɲceɲ bɔntec
　　 pùəŋrìːk sɔŋkat sɔŋsay ʔɔmbaɲ cùəɲcram bɔŋkhos bɔmphlùː
Dictation.

A second type of disyllable is even more restricted than the above since the final consonant of the first syllable is always *m* and the initial consonant of the second is always *n*; formula: Cvm-nV(C). Again, in colloquial speech, the first syllable lacks stress in comparison with the second.

32. (i) kɔmnaət kùmnɔ̀ː cɔmnaek cùmnùm tùmniəm bɔmnoːŋ pùmnɔ̀ːl
　　 sɔmnaəc ʔɔmnaoy
Dictation.

4.6. *Full disyllables, recorded paragraphs 33–34*

These are composed of two simple words, or forms having the structure of simple words (i.e. any of the structures described above) and are usually one of the following:—[3]

Ordinary compounds, of which both parts also occur alone.

33. (i) **rətèh-phlɤ̀ːŋ chɤ̀ː-kùs yùən-hɔh daəm-tnaot**

Reduplicative compounds, of which one part usually occurs also alone.

---

[1] *h* is here a functioning consonant and not a feature of junction.
[2] *h* is here a feature of the junction between consonants.
[3] There are, however, some disyllabic words which are not known to be of foreign origin and which cannot be shown to be compounds, e.g. *kaːrɔŋ* 'bag', *siəvphɤ̀u* 'book'. These are not hyphenated in the transcription. They tend to be pronounced with lack of stress on the first syllable and shortening of a long open vowel in the first syllable. These two features occur also in the colloquial pronunciation of disyllabic loanwords, e.g. *saːlaː* 'hall', and *baːraŋ* 'French', which may be realized as [*salaː*], [*baraŋ*].

34. (i) rì:əy-mì:əy kme:ŋ-kma:ŋ mɛ̀:n-tɛ̀:n khsɤk-khsu:əl tətrɛ̀:t-tətrò:t
bu:əŋ-su:əŋ prəɲap-prəɲal smaok-krò:k

Dictation.

Note. All native Khmer word-forms have now been introduced.[1]

LESSON 5

RÉSUMÉ OF PRONUNCIATION WITH ORTHOGRAPHY

Lesson 5 is chiefly a résumé of the descriptions of pronunciation given in Lessons 1–4.[2] With each sound the various ways in which it may be written in the orthography are indicated. The lesson may be used as a means of revision of the pronunciation and transcription, as an introduction to the orthography[3] or as a place of reference for checking the link between the transcription and the orthography.[4]

5.1. *The initial consonants*

Note. The symbols differ according to the register of the following vowel or diphthong.

1. *k.* Voiceless, unaspirated velar plosive. cf. English c in 'cook'. ក for 1st register; គ for 2nd register.

2. *c.* Voiceless, unaspirated palatal plosive. cf. English ch in 'chat'. ច for 1st register; ជ for 2nd register.

3. *t.* Voiceless, unaspirated post-dental plosive. cf. English t in 'tank'. ត for 1st register; ទ for 2nd register.

4. *p.* Voiceless, unaspirated bilabial plosive. cf. English p in 'post'. ប for 1st register; ព for 2nd register.

5. *s.* Voiceless, post-dental sibilant. cf. English s in 'see'. ស for 1st register; ស for 2nd register.

6. *h.* Aspirate. cf. English h in 'hard'. ហ for 1st register; ហ for 2nd register.

7. *ŋ.* Velar nasal. cf. English ng in 'song'. ង for 1st register; ង for 2nd register.

8. *ɲ.* Palatal nasal. cf. English ni in 'onions'. ញ for 1st register; ញ for 2nd register.

9. *n.* Dental nasal. cf. English n in 'no'. ន for 1st register; ន for 2nd register.

10. *m.* Bilabial nasal. cf. English m in 'man'. ម for 1st register; ម for 2nd register.

---

[1] Apart from the comparatively small number of trisyllabic compounds, such as *chɤ̀:-pɛ̀ək-ʔa:v* (wood/hang on/dress) 'coat-hanger'.

[2] Some extra notes on rapid colloquial forms will be found in Lesson 5.6.

[3] For the student who has a teacher. The student working on his own would find it easier to begin learning the orthography from Lessons 6–11.

[4] Certain extra features of the transcription, such as underlining and accents over consonant signs, will be observed in Lessons 5–11.3 in the transcription of a few words; these features are explained in Lesson 11.4.

11. *y*. Palatal semi-vowel, vigorously articulated. cf. English y in 'yard'. ꞵ for 1st register; ꞵ for 2nd register.

12. *l*. Post-alveolar lateral. cf. English l in 'look'. ꞵ for 1st register; ꞵ for 2nd register.

13. *v*. Labial semi-vowel, weakly articulated; sometimes realized as bilabial w or labio-dental v. cf. English v in 'very' with weak articulation. ꞵ for 1st register; ꞵ for 2nd register.

14. *r*. Frictionless continuant in the speech of Phnom Penh. cf. English r in 'rose'. In Battambang a one-tap uvular r is heard and elsewhere a rolled r. ꞵ for 1st register; ꞵ for 2nd register.

15. *d*. Voiced, alveolar implosive. cf. English d in 'do'.[1] ꞵ for 1st register; occurs with 2nd register vowel or diphthong following only rarely and in words of foreign origin; is then written ꞵ.

16. *b*. Voiced bilabial implosive. cf. English b in 'bat'.[1] ꞵ for 1st register; occurs with 2nd register vowel or diphthong following only rarely and in words of foreign origin; is then written ꞵ.

17. *ʔ*. Weak, glottal plosive. Occurs in English when a word beginning with a vowel and stressed on the first syllable is pronounced with a harsh, constricted voice. e.g. '*Any*one can do it!' ꞵ for 1st register; ꞵ for 2nd register.

5.2. *The first register vowels and diphthongs in syllabary order*

The vowels and diphthongs here given include, in accordance with Cambodian tradition, the so-called 'vowels', *om, ɔm, am* and *ah*. For convenience the short vowels, *ɔ, a* and *e*, which are not recited in the syllabary, are inserted; *ɔ* and *a* follow the long vowel of similar articulation. The vowel-symbols depend on the initial consonant. For the 1st register, this must be either a 1st register consonant (i.e. a consonant which has the vowel *ɔː* and not *ɔ̀ː* in the syllabary)[2] or a 2nd register consonant converted to 1st register by means of the sign ″. When a new vowel-symbol is given below or when reference is made to a vowel-symbol it is presented with the vowel-base, ꞵ. It happens that ꞵ is the orthographic symbol for the initial glottal stop but it is also the traditional way to present the vowel-signs. Further examples of a vowel-sign are given with other initial consonants.

18. *ɔː*. Open, rounded back vowel. cf. American o in 'hot', with slight lip-rounding and pronounced with length. Any 1st register consonant, having no other vowel-sign written with it, bears the implication that this vowel will be pronounced immediately after it. e.g. ꞵ *ʔɔː*, ꞵ *cɔː*. This vowel, and its counterpart on the 2nd register, *ɔ̀ː*, are often referred to as the 'inherent vowels' because they are implicit in the written consonant.

19. *ɔ*. A very open, rounded back vowel. cf. American o in 'hot' with slight lip-rounding. The short inherent vowel. Written (i) like the long

---

[1] English d and b, which are not imploded consonants, are not at all satisfactory as guides to the Cambodian pronunciation. English speakers sometimes use an imploded b when imitating the sound of water coming out of a bottle in spurts (bubububbu).
[2] See Lesson 7.2.

16

inherent vowel but with either a short mark over the final consonant, e.g. ꞩ *ʔɔt* or final *anusvara*, e.g. ꞩ *ʔɔm*; or, in an Indian borrowing, final syllable, with no *saŋŋɔːksaŋŋaː*,[1] e.g. ꞩ *sɔŋ*, ꞩ *bɔt* or (ii) with ꞩ and final *visarga*, e.g. ꞩ *kɔh*.

20. *aː*. Unrounded, open vowel, mid (neither front nor back). cf. Yorkshire pronunciation of 'cart'. Written ꞩ, e.g. ꞩ *kaːc*.

21. *a*. Unrounded, open vowel, slightly more front than *aː*. cf. Yorkshire a in 'cat'. Written (i) ꞩ either with a short mark over the final consonant, ꞩ *kat*, or with final *anusvara*, ꞩ *kam*, or (ii) with the inherent vowel and final *visarga*, ꞩ *kah*, or (iii) in Indian loanwords, final syllable, with the inherent vowel and the *saŋŋɔːksaŋŋaː*, e.g. ꞩ *can(t)*.[2,3]

22. *e*. Unrounded, half-close front vowel. cf. English e in 'yet'. Written ꞩ or ꞩ before palatal finals (*c* and *ɲ*), e.g. ꞩ *tec*, ꞩ *ceɲ* and before final *h*, ꞩ *teh*, ꞩ *keh*. This vowel is also the pronunciation of ꞩ in open 1st register syllables in Indian loanwords. e.g. ꞩ *kereyaː*.

23. *ɤy*. Unrounded, falling diphthong starting from a half-close central vowel and moving towards a close front unrounded vowel. cf. the English sequence of vowels which occur in 'surfeit' but with no consonant f between them and pronounced smoothly one after the other. Written ꞩ, e.g. ꞩ *dɤy*.

24. *ɤ*. Fairly back, half-close, unrounded vowel. cf. English vowel in 'bird'. Usually written ꞩ in Khmer words before final *k*, *ŋ* and *m*, e.g. ꞩ *dɤk*; ꞩ in Khmer words before other finals, e.g. ꞩ *sɤn* and in closed syllables of Indian loanwords, e.g. ꞩ *cɤt(t)*.

25. *ɤː*. Fairly back, half-close, unrounded vowel, pronounced with length. cf. English vowel in 'bird'. Written ꞩ, e.g. ꞩ *bɤːt*.

26. *o*. Fairly open back vowel with quite strong lip-rounding. cf. French o in 'bonne'. Written ꞩ, e.g. ꞩ *coh*.

27. *oː*. Mid-close, back though slightly centralized vowel. cf. French vowel in first syllable of 'sauter'. Written ꞩ, e.g. ꞩ *koːn*. When *v* follows, the sequence is pronounced [əu] by many speakers, and thus resembles *ɤu* (60) though the latter has a closer starting point.

28. *uːə*. Falling diphthong starting with a well-rounded close back vowel and moving towards a more open vowel; in open syllables this has a tendency to be accompanied by uvular friction. In closed syllables the final point of articulation resembles that of the diphthongs *uə* and *iə*, 30 and 31, being a central, half-open vowel. cf. English diphthong in 'truer'. Written ꞩ, e.g. ꞩ *suːən*.

---

[1] See footnote 4, p. 15.

[2] In the final syllable of an Indian loanword with two written final consonants, however, the short inherent vowel is usually pronounced *a/ɛə* ~ *ɔə*, whether or not the *saŋŋɔːksaŋŋaː* is written.

[3] Unpronounced characters are given in parentheses. See Lesson 11.4.

29. *aə*. Unrounded, falling diphthong starting from an open vowel similar to *a* (21) and moving towards a half-close, slightly centralized back vowel. cf. Northern English vowels in 'fatter' without the consonant t, and pronounced smoothly one after the other. Written เ◌ิ, e.g. เบิก *baək*.

30. *uə*. Unrounded falling diphthong starting from a fairly close, unrounded back vowel and moving towards a more open central vowel. The second vowel is like English a as in 'about'; the first cannot be compared with any sound in the better known European languages. The exclamation of disgust, 'Ugh!' is by some English speakers pronounced with a similar vowel, *u*, but other speakers realize it by using a vowel closer to *ɤː* (25). The vowel *u* is articulated by maintaining the tongue position for 'oo' while spreading the lips. Written เ◌ือ, e.g. เตือ *tuə*.

31. *iə*. Unrounded falling diphthong starting from a close front vowel and moving towards a more open central vowel. cf. English diphthong in 'here'. Written เ◌ีย, e.g. เสีย *siət*.

32. *eː*. Unrounded half-close, slightly centralized front vowel. cf. English vowel in 'hay' or French vowels in 'été'. Written เ◌, e.g. เอก *ceːk*.

33. *ae*. Unrounded falling diphthong starting from an open vowel more front than *a* (21) and moving towards a closer front vowel. cf. English vowels of the word 'adept', pronounced smoothly one after the other with no consonant d in between. Written แ◌, e.g. แบบ *baep* or, in Indian loanwords, แ◌, e.g. แขต *khaet(t)*.

34. *ay*. Unrounded falling diphthong starting from an open vowel similar to *a* (21) and moving towards a close, unrounded front vowel. cf. English 'I'. Written ไ◌, e.g. ได *day* or, in Indian loanwords, by means of inherent vowel with *saɲɲòːksaɲɲaː* and final *y*, e.g. สมัย *samay*.

35. *ao*. Falling diphthong starting from an open, unrounded vowel, slightly more back than *a* (21) and moving towards a closer back vowel with lip-rounding. cf. English diphthong in 'how', but without proceeding to so close a final point. Written เ◌า, e.g. เกา *caol*.

36. *au*. Falling diphthong starting from an open vowel similar to *a* (21) and moving towards a close back vowel pronounced either with rounded lips or with lips in υ position, with bilabial closure. cf. English diphthong in 'how'. Written เ◌า, e.g. เกา *cau*.

37. *om*. Pronounced as *o* (26) with final consonant *m* (74). Written ◌ํ, e.g. กํ *kom*.

38. *ɔm*. Pronounced as *ɔ* (19) with final consonant *m* (74). Written ◌ํ, e.g. บ *cɔm*.

39. *am*. Pronounced as *a* (21) with final consonant *m* (74). Written ◌ำ, e.g. ดำ *dam*.

40. *ah*. Pronounced as *a* (21) with final consonant *h* (70). Written ◌ะ, e.g. บะ *pah*.

5.3. *The second register vowels and diphthongs in syllabary order*

The vowels and diphthongs here given include, in accordance with Cambodian tradition, the so-called 'vowels', *ùm, ɔ̀əm, ɛ̀əm* and *ɛ̀əh*. For convenience *ùə, ɛ̀ə* ∼ *ɔ̀ə* and *è*, which are not recited in the syllabary, are inserted, following *ɔ̀ː, ìːə* and *èː* respectively. All the symbols given below for the vowels and diphthongs depend on the initial consonant being either a 2nd register consonant, i.e. a consonant which has the inherent vowel *ɔ̀ː* and not *ɔː* in the syllabary[1] or a 1st register consonant converted to 2nd register by means of the sign ⌣. The vowel-base, ឣ̃, which is pronounced as initial glottal stop, is used below as a means of writing the vowel symbols. An example of each character in a word is added.

41. *ɔ̀ː*. Half-open, centralized back vowel with lip-rounding. May be attempted by pronouncing English vowel in 'saw' with closely-rounded lips.[2] Any 2nd register consonant, having no other vowel-sign written with it, bears the implication that this vowel will be pronounced immediately after it. e.g. ឣ̃ *ʔɔ̀ː*, ល *lɔ̀ː*. This vowel may be referred to as the 'inherent' vowel of a 2nd register consonant.

42. *ùə*. A falling diphthong starting from a rounded close back vowel and moving towards a more open central vowel. cf. English diphthong in 'sure'. This diphthong is of short duration as compared with all other diphthongs except *ɔ̀ə* and *ɛ̀ə* (44a and b). It must be particularly contrasted with *ùːə* in which the first element is considerably longer in duration. Written (i) as the long inherent vowel, but with a short mark over the final consonant, e.g. គ̆ ់ *kùət* or in an Indian loanword final syllable, with no *saɲɲòːksaɲɲaː*,[3] e.g. ពល *pùəl* or (ii) with ើ and final *visarga*, e.g. ពោះ *pùəh*.

43. *ìːə*. In the speech of Phnom Penh there is no difference in articulation between this diphthong and the one written ើ *iə* or ើ *iə*. Both are falling unrounded diphthongs starting from a close front vowel and moving towards a more open central vowel. It is convenient to transcribe them differently, however.[4] cf. English diphthong in 'here'. Written ី, e.g. លៀន *lìːən*.

44. The short diphthongs *ɔ̀ə* (44a) and *ɛ̀ə* (44b) are in complementary distribution, *ɔ̀ə* occurring before all final consonants except *k, ŋ, h* and the glottal stop[5] and *ɛ̀ə* occurring before these final consonants. *ɔ̀ə* is a falling diphthong starting from a back half-open rounded vowel (closer than *ɔ* (19)) and moving towards a more central open vowel with less lip-rounding.

---

[1] See Lesson 7.2.
[2] It is particularly difficult to describe in terms of familiar sounds of English, French, etc., the variety of 'o' vowels of Cambodian.
[3] And, usually, a single written final consonant.
[4] Moreover, to the North and South of Phnom Penh there is a distinction between them. The diphthong written ើ／ើ has a closer starting point than the one written ី.
[5] The glottal stop occurs only as a variant of final *k* in native Khmer words but it occurs frequently in Indian loanwords to close syllables where the vowel is the written inherent (pronounced as *a/ɛ̀ə-ɔ̀ə*) and there is no final consonant.

cf. English diphthong in 'more'. èə is a falling diphthong starting from a front half-open unrounded vowel and moving towards a more central vowel. cf. the diphthong heard in standard Southern English 'there'. Written (i) ẫ either with a short mark over the final consonant, e.g. គាត់ kɔ̀ət, ដាក់ cèək; or with final *anusvara*, e.g. ង៉ា nɔ̀əm or with final *anusvara* plus ង, e.g. ទាង tèəŋ. (ii) with the inherent vowel and either the *sappò:ksappa:*, e.g. រ ដ្ឋ rɔ̀ət(th) or with final *visarga*, e.g. ទះ tèəh; or, in Indian loanwords where a glottal stop must close the syllable, with inherent vowel only. e.g. ជលៈ cèəlèətì: (cèəʔlèəʔtì: represents the realization more accurately).

45. ĭ. Short close unrounded front vowel. cf. English vowel in 'bit'. Written (i) ẫ, e.g. ជិះ cĭh. (ii) (exceptionally) ឥ as in ឥឹះ nĭh.

46. ì:. Close unrounded front vowel. cf. English vowel in 'beat'. Written ẫ, e.g. ជីក cì:k.

47. ŭ. Short close back unrounded vowel. For pronunciation guide see diphthong uə (30). Usually written ẫ in Khmer words before k, ŋ and m, e.g. នឹង nŭŋ; ẫ in Khmer words before other finals, e.g. ជុត cŭt and in closed syllables of Indian loanwords, e.g. ចុត្ត mŭt(t).

48. ŭ:. Close back unrounded vowel as 47 with length. Written ẫ, e.g. គឺ kŭ:.

49. ŭ. Short close back rounded vowel. cf. English vowel in 'put'. Written (i) ẫ, e.g. កុក kŭk ធុំ thŭm. (ii) with the inherent vowel of any 2nd register consonant either before final p with a short mark over it, e.g. ជុប chŭp, or with final *anusvara*, e.g. នុំ nŭm.

N.B. The above two ways of writing ŭm serve to distinguish in writing one or two pairs of homonyms, e.g. ទុំ tŭm 'to perch' and ទុំ tŭm 'to be ripe'.

50. ŭ:. Close back rounded vowel. cf. English vowel in 'boot'. Written ẫ, e.g. ជូត cù:t.

51. ŭ:ə. Articulation as for u:ə (28), potential voice quality being the only difference between the two diphthongs. Written ẫ, e.g. មួក mù:ək.

52. ɤ̀:. Half-close back unrounded vowel. cf. English vowel in 'bird', but the Cambodian vowel is pronounced further back. Written ើ, e.g. ឃើង yɤ̀:ŋ.

53. ùə. Articulation as for uə (30), potential voice quality being the only difference between the two diphthongs. Written ឿ, e.g. លួន lùəŋ.

54. ìə. Articulation as for iə (31), potential voice quality being the only difference between the two diphthongs. Written ៀ, e.g. រៀន rìən. Identical, in the speech of the capital, with ì:ə (43), see footnote to 43.

55. è:. Half-close unrounded front vowel. cf. French vowels in 'été'. Written េ, e.g. ពេក pè:k.

56. è. Short, half-close unrounded front vowel. Articulation as for 55 with short duration. Written ⒤ or ⒤ before palatal finals (*c* and *ɲ*) (ⒼⓊ *tèc*, ⒤ⓅⓂ *pèɲ*) and ⒤ before final *h*, ⒤ⓈⓈ *rətèh*.[1]

57. *è:*. Half-open front unrounded vowel. cf. English vowel in 'let', pronounced with length. Written ⒤, e.g. ⒤Ⓤ *lè:ɲ*.

58. *èy*. Unrounded falling diphthong starting from a half-close unrounded front vowel and moving towards a close unrounded front vowel. cf. English vowel-sequence in 'payee' but with prominence given to the first element and the second element shorter. Written either ⒤, e.g. ⒤Ⓢ *nèy* or, in Indian loanwords, with the inherent vowel and *saɲɲò:ksaɲɲa:* and final *y*, e.g. ⒤Ⓤ *cèy*.

59. *ò:*. Half-close rounded back vowel. Similar in articulation to *o:* (27) but less centralized. Written ⒤Ⓘ, e.g. ⒤ⓊⓀ *lò:k*.

60. *ŭu*. Falling diphthong starting from a half-close unrounded back vowel, similar to (52) and moving towards a close back vowel with either lip-rounding or labialization. cf. English vowels in 'her book', with no b. Written ⒤Ⓘ, e.g. ⒤Ⓟ *pŭu*.

61. *ùm*. Pronounced as *ù* (49) with final consonant *m* (74) ⒤, e.g. ⒤ *cùm*.

62. *ɔəm*. Pronounced as *ɔə* (44a) with final consonant *m* (74). This is a special realization of ⒤ in the syllabary; elsewhere the spelling is ⒤Ⓘ, e.g. ⒸⒾ *pɔəm*.

63. *èəm*. Pronounced as *èə* (44b) with final consonant *m*. This is a special realization of ⒤Ⓘ in the syllabary; elsewhere *èə* does not occur before *m* (see under 44).

64. *èəh*. Pronounced as *èə* (44b) with final consonant *h*. Written with the inherent vowel and *visarga*, ⒤Ⓢ, e.g. ⓉⓈ *tèəh*.[2]

5.4. *The final consonants*

65. *k*. Voiceless velar occlusive.[3] cf. English final consonant in 'back'. Occurs in free variation with the glottal stop (78). Written Ⓚ, e.g. ⓊⓀ *bɔ:k*. In Indian loanwords Ⓐ Ⓚ Ⓤ and Ⓚ also occur as the final consonant or consonants, in writing; the pronunciation is *k*.

66. *c*. Voiceless palatal occlusive.[3,4] cf. English final sound in 'such', but pronounced in a clearcut way so that no slurring (affrication) follows the contact. Written Ⓞ, e.g. ⒶⓄ *ka:c*. In Indian loanwords Ⓠ Ⓠ Ⓠ Ⓠ Ⓠ Ⓙ and Ⓠ also occur as the final consonant or consonants in writing; pronunciation is *c*.

67. *t*. Voiceless alveolar occlusive.[3] cf. English final consonant in 'bat'. Written Ⓚ, e.g. ⓊⓀ *cɔ:t*. In Indian loanwords Ⓩ Ⓩ Ⓡ Ⓡ Ⓤ Ⓦ Ⓦ and Ⓐ also occur as the final consonant or consonants in writing; the pronunciation is *t*.

---

[1] Does not occur with other finals, except in so far as *èy* (58) may be regarded as *è* with final *y*.

[2] Sometimes spelt ⒤Ⓘ in older dictionaries and texts.

[3] The release of contact is usually inaudible.

[4] Vowels preceding a palatal final are affected by a palatal on-glide. Thus *bac* is heard as [*baic*].

68. *p*. Voiceless alveolar occlusive.[1] cf. English final consonant in 'cup'. Written ប, e.g. ករប *carp*. In Indian loanwords ក and គ occur as the final consonants in writing; the pronunciation is *p*.

69 and 70. *s* and *h* finals. It is only in a careful reading style that these consonants are still kept separate; *s* is pronounced as the final consonant in English 'mass' and *h* as English h (but in final position). They are written ស, e.g. ឡូស *ⁱoːs*, and ះ, e.g. ចុះ *coh*, respectively. (ស្ may occur in Indian loanwords.) The colloquial pronunciation for any of the written consonants may be either *h*, *s* or *h* with *s* off-glide, [*hˢ*].

71. *ŋ*. Velar nasal. cf. the final consonantal sound in English 'bang'. Written ង, e.g. ហាង *haːŋ* and, to shorten ា or ៅ, ង, e.g. កាង *taŋ*. In Indian loanwords ង្ង ង្គ and ង្គ្រ also occur as final consonants in writing; the pronunciation is *ŋ*.

72. *ɲ*. Palatal nasal. cf. English ni in 'onions'. Written ញ, e.g. មិញ *mèɲ*. In Indian loanwords ញ្ញ also occurs as a final consonant sequence in writing; the pronunciation is *ɲ*.

73. *n*. Alveolar nasal. cf. English final consonant in 'can'. Written ន, e.g. ករន *caːn*. In Indian loanwords ណ ណ្ណ ណ្ឌ ន្ត ន្ធ and ន្ទ also occur as the final consonant or consonants in writing; the pronunciation is *n*.

74. *m*. Bilabial nasal. cf. English final consonant in 'him'. Written ម, e.g. ស្ម *soːm* and, as a device to shorten the inherent and ា ៅ vowels, °, e.g. ចុំ *com*, កំ *kam*. *m* is also written ° when it occurs as a final consonant after the vowel *o* (see 37) or *u* (see 61). In Indian loanwords ម្ម ម្ព and ម្ភ occur as the final consonant or consonants in writing; the pronunciation is *m*.

75. *y*. Palatal semi-vowel. cf. English final sound in 'boy'. Written យ, e.g. លុយ *lùy*. In Indian loanwords, យ្ occurs as a final consonant sequence; the pronunciation is *y*.

76. *l*. Post-alveolar lateral semi-vowel, of fairly dark resonance. cf. English final consonant in 'haul'. Written ល, e.g. ហាល *haːl*. In Indian loanwords, ល្ល occurs as a final consonant sequence; the pronunciation is *l*. There are a few words in which the realization *l* occurs for written *r*, e.g. ⸢ប្រាំពីរ *prampùl*, ចុរ *coːl*, កណ្ដុរ *kɔndol*, ហូរ *hɤl*.

77. *v*. Labio-dental (or sometimes bilabial) semi-vowel, accompanied by velarization. When *oː* occurs before *v* it loses the lip-rounding because of the lip-spreading movement for the *v*; the resulting vowel may be compared with *ɤː* (25) and the vowel plus final *v* may be compared with *ɤu* (60), with, however, the first register more open *ɤ*. cf. English final sound in 'cove', with weak articulation. Written រ, e.g. កាវ *kaːv*.

Note. Many words have a written final r (រ). e.g. ហេរ *haə(r)*,[2] ដេរ *daə(r)*. Usually this is not pronounced.[3]

---

[1] The release of contact is usually inaudible.
[2] (r) indicates that the consonant is present in the spelling but not in the pronunciation.
[3] In Battambang final r (a uvular R in that area) is pronounced.

78. *ʔ.* Glottal stop. This occurs (i) as a variant of final *k* and (ii) as a means of closing an open syllable of which the vowel is short. The latter feature has been mentioned in connection with the announcement of the short vowels on the tape-recordings, as in paragraph 5 of Lesson 1. In connected speech it occurs in the closing of open short syllables in Indian loanwords.[1] cf. the sound occurring in some English dialects as a variant of a final plosive, e.g. 'biʔ', dialect variant of 'bit'. Final glottal stop occurring as a variant of *k* is written by the same symbol, ក. When it occurs as a means of closing a short open syllable, it has no representation in the script.

5.5. *The pronunciation of word-forms*

1. CV(C). The pronunciation of monosyllables with simple initial is provided for when the student has worked through the initial consonants, vowels and diphthongs and final consonants.

2. CCV(C). Where a 2-place initial sequence has no sound occurring between the consonants, no difficulty in pronunciation should be experienced. We have a few similar sequences in English, e.g. 'print', 'clamp'. It should be mentioned that when *k*, *c*, *t* or *p* occur with *h* in second place the sequence is pronounced as an aspirated occlusive and written with one symbol, e.g. ខ *khɔː*. Otherwise, the second consonant is written by means of a subscript consonant, e.g. ក្ឌ *kdry*. Sometimes when an imploded consonant, i.e. *b* or *d* occurs in second position, as in *kbaːl*, *sdok*, the preparation for the implosion causes a lapse of time between the pronunciation of the first and second consonants which reminds one of the sequences in which a short neutral vowel occurs, see 4 below.

3. ChCV(C). Aspiration between the consonants is usually noted in the Cambodian spelling, the first consonant being an aspirated occlusive symbol, e.g. ឃ្កត់ *khcat*. There are words, however, which are not spelt with the aspirated symbol and in which, in the pronunciation of most speakers, aspiration occurs. It is, e.g. usual for aspiration to occur in pronouncing any occlusive followed by any nasal or liquid, yet the word *plaek* is spelt with a non-aspirated symbol.

4. CəCV(C) and CCəCV(C) or CəCCV(C). The short neutral vowel which occurs between two consonants is represented in the Cambodian spelling by the inherent vowel, e.g. កកាយ *kɔːkaːy*, ធ្ងឹត *ŋɔːŋùt*, [ក្រពើ *krɔːpɤ̀ː*. In poetry a long vowel may be heard, when the first written syllable is required as a metric syllable. In speeches and other semi-literary forms of speech, a careful *ɔ* or *ɔ̀* of some length may be heard. In colloquial speech, however, the vowel is of such short duration that the representation *ə* seems adequate.

5. In restricted disyllables the vowel represented by the short inherent vowel in the script (and pronounced *ɔ*, *ùə* or *ù* according to context) is again given great prominence in poetry if the syllable is required as a metric syllable. In colloquial speech it may either be reduced as far as length and

---

[1] See Lesson 12, No. 9.

stress are concerned but retain the character of the vowel, or it may be realized as *ə*.

6. Compound words or full disyllables are written as two simple words; the orthography does not indicate that they are more closely connected than any other two words; spaces occur only between clauses and sentences in the Cambodian script. e.g. ស្រះផ្លើង *rətèh-phlɤ̀ːŋ*.

5.6. *Variant forms of words in rapid colloquial speech*

Certain kinds of word-form may be pronounced in more than one way in rapid colloquial speech, e.g. the word written កំណត់ may be heard pronounced as written (*kɔmnat*) or may have the colloquial variant *kənat*. The student needs to be prepared, therefore, to hear and interpret such forms. They occur as follows:—[1]

1. *Extended monosyllables CəCVC*

(i) Where *r* is in 1st place *ʔ* may occur as a variant of it, e.g. *rəlùət* or *ʔəlùət, rənaː(r)* or *ʔənaː(r)*.

(ii) Where homorganic imploded consonants are concerned, the first may be realized as an occlusive, e.g. *bəbɔː(r)* or *pəbɔː(r)*, *dədael* or *tədael*.

(iii) Where the initial sequence consists of two sibilants *t* may occur as a variant of the first, e.g. *səsɔː(r)* or *təsɔː(r)*, *səseː(r)* or *təseː(r)*.

2. *Restricted disyllables*

(i) If the 1st syllable begins with an occlusive or *s* (and the initial consonant of the 2nd syllable is not the same consonant) a variant form may occur in which the vowel of the 1st syllable is realized as *ə* (instead of *ɔ, ùə* or *ù*) and the final nasal consonant of the 1st syllable is absent. Thus the words *kɔndaːl, kùmnɔ̀əp, cɔmbaŋ, cùmtìːəv, tùmnèɲ, sɔmnaːp* and *sɔndaek* have the colloquial variants *kədaːl, kənɔ̀əp, cəbaŋ, cətìːəv, tənèɲ, sənaːp, sədaek*.[2] Where an imploded consonant is the initial consonant of the 1st syllable, a voiceless occlusive of similar articulation is heard in the variant form, e.g. *dɔndɤ̀ŋ* or *tədɤ̀ŋ*, *bɔŋʔuːəc* or *pəʔuːəc* (cf. *bəbɔː(r)* or *pəbɔː(r)* in 1 (ii) above).

A further variant of restricted disyllables of this kind will be heard, in which *r* occurs between the two 'initial' consonants, e.g. *srənaːp, prəʔuːəc* and *krənat* occur as variants of *sɔmnaːp, bɔŋʔuːəc* and *kɔmnat*. These forms, however, are felt by Cambodians educated in the study of their own language to be less acceptable than the forms without *r*. This is probably due to the fact that the colloquial variant with *r* has the same form as another word-form, the extended monosyllable with 3-place initial sequence, and its use, therefore, suggests ignorance of the spelling.

(ii) Where a restricted disyllable has either (i) the glottal stop as its first

---

[1] The examples which follow are recorded on the tapes. See Part VII, Appendix 4.

[2] The initial sequences here involved (*kd, kn, cb, ct, tn, sn, sd*) are marked by aspiration or no sound when they occur in words of the form CCVC. They are therefore recognizable to the ear as colloquial variants of restricted disyllables when they occur, as here, with the vowel *ə* marking the junction.

consonant or (ii) the same consonant (occlusive or *s*) as the initial consonant of both syllables, a variant colloquial form occurs with the form: syllabic nasal-CVC, e.g. *ʔɔntùəŋ* or *n̥tùəŋ*, *ʔɔmbaŋ* or *m̥baŋ*, *kɔŋkaep* or *ŋkaep*, *cùəpcù:n* or *n̥cù:n*, *cùəpcì:ŋ* or *n̥cì:ŋ*, *sɔnsaəm* or *n̥saəm*.[1]

LESSON 6

METHOD OF WRITING THE CHARACTERS

6.1. *General principles*

When writing the characters:—

(i) Procedure is from left to right and from below to above as far as possible. Where there is a small circle at the left or lower left of a character, one starts with this.

(ii) Characters or parts of characters are written as far as possible without taking the pen from the paper.

(iii) Certain upper elements in the make-up of the characters are quite separate from the rest, although typescript and some print does not make this clear. Others are attached. All are drawn after the lower parts.

(iv) Short cross-strokes are added last.

(v) In writing the characters which, though spoken after the consonant, are placed before it, e.g. ร *e:*, one must think ahead.

6.2. *Writing individual characters*

1. The following characters should be practised beginning from the left and without moving the pen from the paper:—

Consonants ៵[2] ៜ ញ[3] ʊ ៖ ៈ ឈ ៩ ៦ ៣ ៱

Subscript consonants ្ក[4] ្ខ ្ត ្ស ្ច ្ឈ ្ឆ ្ឃ ្គ ្ម ្ន ្ដ ្ឌ ្ស[5] ្ញ ្ត ្ន ្ឱ ្ឍ

Vowels ◌ុ ◌ូ ◌ៅ[6]

Sanskrit initial vowel-signs ៖ ឫ ឭ ឦ ៣[7]

Numerals ១ ៦ ៧ ០

Punctuation marks ។ ៗ

Diacritics ◌់ ◌៉ ◌៊ ◌៌ ◌៍ ◌៌

---

[1] The phonetic symbol ,, used here and in Lesson 43, implies syllabification of the consonant. This might be represented in another way as [*nn*], [*mm*], etc., a continued nasal sound.

[2] Lowest line last.

[3] Lowest line is drawn last and is attached, in hand-writing.

[4] The Cambodian symbol, *O*, 'zero', is used, here and in the following lessons on the orthography, to indicate the position which will be occupied in the writing of words by a consonant-symbol. The normal position of a subscript vowel- or consonant-sign may thus be clearly seen.

[5] Proceed as for writing the letter *u*.

[6] Attached to the preceding character. See Lesson 8.1.

[7] Proceed as when writing the arabic numeral 3, finishing with the line at the left.

The following require a fractional lift of the pen:—

Consonants ᯯ ᯮ ᯯ

Subscript consonants ᯚ ᯛ[1]

Vowel (part only) ᯝ[2]

Numeral ᥑ

2. The following characters should be written starting at the bottom:—

Consonants ᥲ ᥳ ᥴ

Subscript consonants ᯚ ᯛ ᯜ ᯝ ᯞ

Vowel ᥶ (parts only) ᯟ ᯠ

3. The following characters are written in two parts. Each part is to be written from left to right.

(i) Consonants with ~ above, added after lower part:

ᥑ ᥒ ᥓ ᥔ ᥕ ᥖ

Sanskrit initial vowel-sign, similarly written ᥗ

(ii) These characters are written starting from the middle at the left with a straight downstroke, carrying through to mid-right. The upper curling part is added last and is attached to the lower.

Consonants ᥘ ᥙ ᥚ ᥛ

Sanskrit initial vowel-signs ᥜ ᥝ ᥞ ᥟ

(iii) For the following characters the 'hook' at the top left corner is added after the main part has been drawn:—[3]

Consonants ᥠ ᥡ ᥢ ᥣ

(iv) These characters are written in two steps:—

Consonants ᯡ ᥥ

Vowels ᯢ ᯣ

Sanskrit initial vowel-signs (short strokes 2nd) ᥦ ᥧ

4. Characters written in three steps:—

Consonants ᥨ ᥩ

Subscript consonant ᯤ

Sanskrit initial vowel-signs ᯥ ᥬ

5. Character written in four steps:—

Sanskrit initial vowel-sign ᥭ

---

[1] In hand-writing these subscript consonants resemble their respective main characters and therefore need a lift of the pen after the drawing of the first 'hook' (absent in the printed form).
[2] Attached to the preceding character. See Lesson 8.1.
[3] All other 'hooks' form part of an up-stroke, e.g. ᯯ ᯮ ᯯ ᯰ

6. Characters for which one starts exceptionally from the right, but doing the lower part first where possible:—

Subscript consonants ្គ ្ឌ ្ង ្ឡ

Vowels ឹ ឺ ើ ឿ

Numerals ៦ ៤ ៧ ៥ ៨

Diacritic ៊

7. Characters for which one starts with a downstroke:—

Subscript consonants ្ឆ ្ល

Vowel ុ

Diacritic ់ ៎

LESSON 7

THE CONSONANTS

7.1. *The Cambodian orthography*

This was derived from the Indian script used for Sanskrit. Very few of the characters now resemble their Indian counterparts but certain Indian features have been retained, such as the order in which the syllabary is presented in school-books, dictionaries, etc., and the use of some diacritics. The Cambodians gradually added new vowel-signs and diacritics to the Sanskrit syllabary, because the Cambodian vowel-system is more complex than that of Sanskrit. The consonant-system of the Indian syllabary, however, having complete sets of symbols for voiced and unvoiced occlusives which are not needed for Cambodian, provided a means of writing the vowels and diphthongs of the two Cambodian registers.

7.2. *The consonants*

These are set out below in the traditional way as presented to school children in Cambodia. The Sanskrit equivalents are given in parentheses for the student's reference.

Consonants in syllabary order (reading from left to right)

ក *kɔː* (k)	ខ *khɔː* (kh)	គ *kɔ̀ː* (g)	ឃ *khɔ̀ː* (gh)	ង *ŋɔ̀ː* (ṅ)
ច *cɔː* (c)	ឆ *chɔː* (ch)	ជ *cɔ̀ː* (j)	ឈ *chɔ̀ː* (jh)	ញ *ɲɔ̀ː* (ñ)
ដ *dɔː* (ṭ)	ឋ[1] *thɔː* (ṭh)	ឌ *dɔ̀ː* (ḍ)	ឍ *thɔ̀ː* (ḍh)	ណ *nɔː* (ṇ)
ត *tɔː* (t)	ថ *thɔː* (th)	ទ *tɔ̀ː* (d)	ធ *thɔ̀ː* (dh)	ន *nɔ̀ː* (n)
ប *bɔː* (p)	ផ *phɔː* (ph)	ព *pɔ̀ː* (b)	ភ *phɔ̀ː* (bh)	ម *mɔ̀ː* (m)
យ *yɔ̀ː* (y)	រ *rɔ̀ː* (r)	ល *lɔ̀ː* (l)	វ *vɔ̀ː* (v)	
ស *sɔː* (s)	ហ *hɔː* (h)	ឡ *lɔː* (ḷ)	អ *ʔɔː* (initial short a)	

It will be observed that the pronunciation of each consonant is given with the inherent vowel *ɔː* or *ɔ̀ː*. This indicates the register appropriate to

---

[1] Or the more old-fashioned form ឋ.

the consonant. According to its register in the above table, a consonant will be described as a 'first register consonant' or a 'second register consonant' from now onwards, although a consonant may also be converted to the opposite register when required. If the first five rows of the consonants are studied in columns reading downwards it will be seen that the registers of the consonants are regular with one exception, ណ, *nɔː* in the last column. Rows six and seven are uniform if studied from left to right. The two series of vowels and diphthongs, those of the first register and those of the second, are written with the same set of vowel-symbols; the required register and articulation is indicated by the initial consonant; if this is a first register consonant the vowel-symbol has first register and its first register articulation; if it is a second register consonant the vowel-symbol has second register and its second register articulation. Thus the vowel-symbol ◌ា is pronounced *aː* with a first register initial and *ìːə* with a second register initial. A glance at the two lists of vowel-symbols given below in Lesson 8 with first register ស and second register ង respectively will make this quite clear.

7.3. *Conversion to the other register*

The syllabary provides occlusives, aspirated[1] and unaspirated, for both registers. By the use of ណ *nɔː* as a first register consonant and ន *nɔ̀ː* as a second register consonant, *n* is provided for on both registers. Similarly ឡ *lɔː* and ល *lɔ̀ː* provide first and second register *l*. Other consonants are converted to the other register, when required, by means of the diacritics ◌̊ (*mùːsekətɔ̀ən(t)*) and ◌̈ (*trɤ̀ysap̀(ì)*). Thus, in the word យាង *yìːəŋ*, យ has its syllabary register but in the word យ៉ាង *yaːŋ*, it has first register; in the word សូរ *sòː(r)* ស has its syllabary register but in the word ស៊ូ *sùː* it has second register; in the word ឥ *ʔɤy* ឥ has its syllabary register but in ឥ៊ *ʔ̀ìː* it has second register. When the register of an initial consonant, other than ស, has to be changed and a vowel-sign has to be placed above it, an alternative form of ◌̊ and ◌̈ is used (◌ុ), e.g. ្រ្ *vɤy*, ស៊ូ *sìː*. A special use of the *mùːsekətɔ̀ən(t)* indicates that ប is to be pronounced *pɔː* and not *bɔː* (when initial *p* is required on first register). e.g. បន *bɔn*, ប៉ន *pɔn*, ប្រ *brɤy*, ប៉្រ *prɤy*.

7.4. *Final consonants in Khmer native words*

Only some of the consonants occur as final consonants in native words. These are:—

ក	*k*	ច	*c*	ត	*t*	ប	*p*
ង	*ŋ*	ញ	*ɲ*	ន	*n*	ម	*m*
យ	*y*	ល	*l*	វ	*v*	ស	*s*

---

[1] In Cambodian these symbols represent a sequence of sounds which are best treated as two successive consonants, *k* + *h*, *t* + *h* and *p* + *h*. Only in this section of the book are the symbols referred to as 'consonants'. Elsewhere, the written form is called an 'aspirated occlusive symbol'; the pronunciation is described as an 'aspirated occlusive', but structurally each represents a 2-place initial sequence.

ร r occurs in the spelling of many native words but is not normally pronounced, e.g. ເຮ̃ร *daə(r)*, ໄບร *bae(r)*, ຫร *hoː(r)*. The *r* is written in the transcription in parentheses to facilitate the task of turning transcription into script.

Final *h* is written with the *visarga*, ៖, e.g. ຕ៖ *coh*.

Final *m* may be written with the *anusvara*, ◌ំ, as shown in Lesson 8.3.

LESSON 8

THE VOWELS

8.1. *The vowel-signs*

These are set out here in the order in which they are recited by school children. The short vowels, *ɔ/ùə*[1,2] (19 and 42),[3] *a/èɔ ~ ɔ̀ɔ* (21 and 44 a and b) and *è* (56) have no place in the syllabary. The way they are written is explained below in 8.3. and the order in which they occur in dictionaries is given in Lesson 13.

The vowel-signs in syllabary order (reading down each column separately)

First register vowels with អ	Second register vowels with អ̃
អ *ʔɔː*	អ̃ *ʔɔ̀ː*
អា *ʔaː*	អា̃ *ʔìːə*
អិ *ʔe*[4]	អិ̃ *ʔì*[5]
អឹ *ʔɤy*	អឹ̃ *ʔì̀ː*
អី *ʔɤ*	អី̃ *ʔừ*
អឺ *ʔɤː*	អឺ̃ *ʔừː*
អុ *ʔo*	អុ̃ *ʔừ*
អូ *ʔoː*	អូ̃ *ʔừː*

[1] The sloping line, here as elsewhere, is used to separate 1st and 2nd register vowels which are written with the same symbol.

[2] From here onwards, the term 'vowel' will be applied without distinction to the sounds which have been described, for the purpose of clarifying the pronunciation, as either vowels or diphthongs in preceding lessons.

[3] Numerals in parentheses refer to Lesson 5.

[4] អិ is pronounced *e*, as in the syllabary, only before a palatal final consonant or *h*, e.g. តិច *tec*, តិះ *teh*, or in open syllables of Indian loanwords, e.g. 2nd syllable of ក្រិតេយ្យុស *kɤtteyùəs*. Where it occurs with a final consonant other than *c*, *ɲ* or *h*, it is pronounced *ɤ*, e.g. កិន *kɤn*, ចិត្ត *cɤt(t)*.

[5] អិ̃ is pronounced *ì*, as in the syllabary, only before final *h*, e.g. ជិះ *cìh*, or in Indian loanwords in open 2nd register syllables, e.g. 1st syllable of ពិធី *pìthìː*. Where it occurs with a final consonant other than *h*, it is normally pronounced *ừ*, e.g. គិត *kừt*, មិត្ត *mừt(t)* except before palatals where it is *è*.

First register vowels with ស		Second register vowels with ស̃	
ស៊	ʔuːə	ស̃៊	ʔùːə
ៈស	ʔaə	ៈស̃	ʔɤ̀ː
ៈស	ʔuə	ៈស̃	ʔùə
ៈស	ʔiə	ៈស̃	ʔìə
ៈស	ʔeː[1]	ៈស̃	ʔèː[1]
ៈស	ʔae	ៈស̃	ʔɛ̀ː
ៈស	ʔay	ៈស̃	ʔèy
ៈសិ	ʔao	ៈស̃ិ	ʔòː
ៈសិ	ʔau	ៈស̃ិ	ʔɤ̀u
ស	ʔom	ស̃	ʔùm
ស	ʔɔm	ស̃	ʔɔ̀əm[2]
សិ	ʔam	ស̃ិ	ʔɛ̀əm[2]
សៈ	ʔah	ស̃ៈ	ʔɛ̀əh

The vowel-signs, ា *and* ៗ

ា is attached to the consonants as follows:—

(i) For consonants of which ⌃ forms part of their normal construction (i.e. not counting its possible use to convert them to second register), ⌃ is modified and joined to ា, e.g. ភ ព ភ.

(ii) For consonants which have a 'hook' at the right-hand top corner, like ឃ *yɔ̀ː* and ស *ʔɔː*, the 'hook' is modified and the character is joined to ា, e.g. ឃា សា ឡា.

ឋ is a special case: ឋ + ា = ឰ.

(iii) Otherwise, ា is attached at the appropriate level, e.g. បា ភ ថ ឋ ឋ.

ៗ is joined to the consonants in the same way, e.g. ៈបៗ *cau,* ៈសៗ *ʔau,* ៈទៗ *tɤ̀u.*

8.2. *The Sanskrit initial vowel signs*

These are given here with Sanskrit equivalents in parentheses:—

ឥ ʔe, ɤ or ʔì (i)	ឯ ʔae (e)	ឫ rù̆ (ṛ)
ឦ ʔɤy or ʔìː (ī)	ឰ ʔay (ai)	ឬ rù̆ː (ṝ)

---

[1] ៈស/ៈស̃ are pronounced *eː/èː,* as in the syllabary, before all final consonants except palatals and *h.* Before these they are pronounced short, e.g. ៈសក *deṇ,* ៈសឡ *lèc.*

[2] These pronunciations occur only in the syllabary. Elsewhere ស̃ is pronounced *ʔùm* and ស̃ិ *ʔɔ̀əm.*

ꩱ¹ *ʔo* or *ʔù* (u)   ៣³ *ʔao* (o)   ឮ *lù* (ḷ)

ꩱ² *ʔoː* or *ʔùː* (ū)   ៵⁴ *ʔau* (au)   ឮ *lùː* (ḹ)

It will be seen that in Khmer the vowel-signs given in the first two columns are pronounced with initial glottal stop preceding the vowel and that they duplicate the following: ឥ ឦ ឧ ឩ ឰ ឱ ឲ ឳ. The last four signs represent in Khmer initial *r* or *l* with *ù* or *ùː* which also could be written otherwise: ឫ ឬ ឭ ឮ. These symbols occur in the spelling of some native words, e.g. ឯ *ʔae*, 'at, to', ឱពុក *ʔoːpùk*, 'father', ឬ *rùː*, 'or', as well as in Indian loanwords, e.g. ឯក *ʔaek*, 'one, principal', ឫស្សី *rùsʳy*, 'hermit'. In many Sanskrit and Pali words the first column of vowel-signs have, without the addition of any diacritic, the second register pronunciations, *i, iː, u, uː*, which one may assume are nearer to the original Indian realizations, e.g. ឥស្វរ *ʔiːsvara*.

8.3. *The* anusvara, 'bɔntɔk' *and* visarga *and the writing of short vowels*

The Sanskrit syllabary provided for the occurrence of a short a, written as the inherent vowel in Sanskrit, and a long a, written by means of the vowel-sign from which Cambodian ា has developed. In Cambodian both these devices are used to write long vowels, *ɔː/ɔːʳ*[5] being written by means of the inherent vowel and *aː/ìːə* by means of ា. The short vowels, *ɔ/ùə* and *a/èə* ~ *ɔə*, may be written by the same means (*ɔ/ùə* as the inherent vowel and *a/èə* ~ *ɔə* as ា), but they are marked short by the occurrence of either the *anusvara* or the '*bɔntɔk*'. The *visarga* is discussed here too, since it also has a shortening effect on the preceding vowel and provides a further way of writing the vowels *ɔ/ùə* and *a/èə*, when they occur before *h*.[6]

1. *Anusvara.* When the final consonant of the syllable is *m* and the short inherent vowel or short ា/ា is required to precede it, the *anusvara*, ំ, is used instead of ម, as a means to indicate this shortening. e.g. កំ *kɔm*, ប៉ *cɔm*, កាំ *kam*, ប៉ាំ *cam* (contrast កម *kɔːm*, បម *cɔːm*, កាម *kaːm*, បាម *caːm*); គំ *kɔəm*, ជំ *cɔəm* (contrast គាម *kìːəm*, ជាម *cìːəm*).

When the final consonant of the syllable is *ŋ* and short ា/ា is required to precede it, the *anusvara* is used with ង, instead of ង alone, as a means to indicate the shortening. e.g. កាំង *kaŋ*, ចាំង *caŋ*, គាំង *kèəŋ*, ជាំង *cèəŋ* (contrast កាង *kaːŋ*, ចាង *caːŋ*, គាង *kìːəŋ*, ជាង *cìːəŋ*). Contrast also the writing of the short inherent vowel with final *ŋ*; for this, the '*bɔntɔk*' is used.

---

[1] An alternative form of this, used when it is 2nd register, is ꩱ.
[2] Alternative form, ꩱ.
[3] Alternative form, ៵.
[4] Alternative form, ៵.
[5] The sloping line separates 1st register vowels from 2nd.
[6] Not *ɔə*, since *ɔə* does not occur before *h*.

2. *'bɔntɔk'*. This sign, ', placed over the final consonant, shortens the preceding vowel, e.g. កត់ *kɔt*, ចប់ *cɔp*, គក់ *kùək*, ជង់ *cùəŋ* (contrast កត *kɔːt*, ចប *cɔːp*, គក *kɔ̀ːk*, ជង *cɔ̀ːŋ*); កាត់ *kat*, ចាប់ *cap*, គាក់ *kɛ̀ək*, ជាត់ *cɔ̀ət* (contrast កាត *kaːt*, ចាប *caːp*, គាក *kìːək*, ជាត *cìːət*). The *'bɔntɔk'* is thus used to write the short inherent vowel before consonants other than *m* and *h* and short អា/អ៊ា before consonants other than *m*, *ŋ* and *h*.

The *anusvara* and *'bɔntɔk'* are also connected with the writing of *ù* before labial consonants (*p* and *m*), since the written short inherent vowel on the second register, occurring before *p* or *m*, is pronounced *ù* instead of *ùə*. e.g. គប់ *kùp*, ទប់ *tùp*, គំ *kùm*, ជំ *cùm*. *ùə* does not occur in pronunciation before these final consonants. There are thus two ways of writing *ù* before *m*, អ៊ំ and អ៊ុំ. There is at least one pair of homonyms distinguished in writing by these alternative spellings: ទំ *tùm*, 'to perch', and ទុំ *tùm*, 'to be ripe'.

3. *Visarga.* ហ is never written as the final consonant in a native word. The *visarga*, ះ, is used instead. When the *visarga* is the written final consonant the preceding vowel is pronounced short. The vowel-sign, អេ/អ៊េ, occurring before the *visarga*, represents short *e/è* instead of long *eː/èː*, and other vowel-signs which occur before the *visarga* represent, in this context, completely different vowels. Those vowel-signs which occur before the *visarga* with special realizations are given here:—

(i) Written inherent vowels are realized as *a/ɛ̀ə* according to the register.

(ii) អោ/អ៊ោ are realized as *ɔ/ùə* respectively.

(iii) អេ/អ៊េ are realized as *e/è* respectively.

(iv) អើ is realized as *ɤ*.

(v) អ៊ែ is realized as *è*.

The following examples have parallel forms with written final s for comparison. It will be remembered that written s may be realized as *h*, but words having written s will retain the usual pronunciation of the vowel:—

(i) ប៉ះ *pah*, ទះ *tɛ̀əh*, វស *vɔ̀ːs*, លស *lɔ̀ːs*

(ii) កោះ *kɔh*, គោះ *kùəh*, បោស *baos*, ទោស *tòːs*

(iii) កេះ *keh*, ទេះ *tèh*, កេស *keːs*, ទេស *tèːs*

(iv) and (v) are very rare. The following occurrences, in disyllabic words, may be noted: ចង្កើះ *cɔŋkɤh*, with the parallel form, (ច្រឡើសបើស *crəlaəs-baəs*, and សែះពផ្លែះ *sèh-pəphlèh*, for which no parallel form has been found.

Note. Where a short vowel has its own sign, it occurs before *visarga* as before other final consonants, e.g. ចុះ *coh*, ពុះ *pùh*, តិះ *teh*, ជិះ *cìh*. After អុ/អ៊ុ, *m* is written with the *anusvara*, e.g. *kom* កុំ.

4. Summary of the orthography of all short vowels in Khmer words:—[1]

ɔ. Inherent vowel with *anusvara* or '*bɔntɔk*'. ເກ with *visarga*.

ùə. Inherent vowel with '*bɔntɔk*'. ເຮ̃ກ with *visarga*.

a ກ with *anusvara* or '*bɔntɔk*'. Written inherent vowel with *visarga*.

èə ຮ̃ກ with '*bɔntɔk*'. Inherent vowel with *visarga*.

ɔ̀ə ຮ̃ກ with *anusvara* or '*bɔntɔk*'.[2]

e ຮ̃ before *c, ɲ* or *visarga*. ເຮ̃ before *visarga*.

ì ຮ̃. Occurs only before *visarga*.

è ຮ̃ before *c, ɲ*. ເຮ̃ before *c, ɲ* and *visarga*.

ɤ ຮ̃ before *k, ŋ* and *m*. ຮ̃ before other final consonants. ເຮ̃ before *visarga*, rarely.

ù ຮ̃ before *k, ŋ* and *m*. ຮ̃ before other final consonants.

o ຮ̃.

ù ຮ̃. Alternative before *m* is inherent vowel and *anusvara*. Alternative before *p* is inherent vowel and '*bɔntɔk*'.

LESSON 9

SUBSCRIPT CONSONANTS

9.1. *The subscript forms of the consonants*

The ordinary form of the consonant is given at the left, in each case, and the subscript form is given with o as a dummy consonant, to show the position of the subscript in relation to whatever consonant may be needed in the normal position.

ក ្ក	ឩ ្ឩ	ត ្ត	យ ្យ	ឋ ្ឋ
ខ ្ខ	ឈ ្ឈ	ថ ្ថ	រ ្រ	ឍ ្ឍ or ្ឍ [3]
គ ្គ	ញ ្ញ	ទ ្ទ	ឡ ្ឡ	
ឃ ្ឃ	ដ ្ដ	ធ ្ធ	ឝ ្ឝ	ឯ ្ឯ
ង ្ង	ឋ ្ឋ	ន ្ន	ស ្ស	ឳ ្ឳ
ច ្ច	ឌ ្ឌ	ប ្ប	្	
ឆ ្ឆ	្	ផ ្ផ	ហ ្ហ	

---

[1] For Indian loanwords see Lesson 12.

[2] The word, ញ្រ *ɲɔə(r)*, 'to tremble', is apparently an exception here. It seems to be a native word but, perhaps because its final consonant is unpronounced *r*, it is written, like a loanword, with the inherent vowel and the *saɲɲɔ̀:ksaɲɲa:* (see Lesson 11).

[3] The first of these subscript forms is used everywhere except in a Pali word in which ញ is subscript to another ញ; this is written ញ្ញ. When ញ has to have a subscript consonant below it, the lower part of the character, ្, is omitted, e.g. ញ្ច *ɲc*.

A subscript consonant cancels the inherent vowel of the consonant written above it and is itself pronounced immediately after that consonant and before the vowel, e.g. ផ្ការ *phkaː*, ស្គរ *skɔː*, ល្មម *lmɔːm*. The register of the vowel is determined by a rule. In order to state this rule and the extensions of it, which are needed for the determination of the register in the orthography of more complex words, it is convenient to divide the consonants as follows:—

1. Strong consonants: occlusives, *s* and the glottal stop. Note, however, that the glottal stop is of very restricted occurrence in the initial complexes and does not behave like the other strong consonants in one of the word-forms which will be discussed below.

2. Weak consonants: liquids, nasals and *h*.

The register of the vowel is the syllabary register of the second consonant, unless (i) the second consonant is weak and (ii) the first consonant is strong. When both conditions (i) and (ii) are fulfilled, the register is that of the first consonant-symbol.

Examples

2nd consonant determines the register in the following:—

Consonants of the initial conjunct sequence are both strong: ស្គរ *skɔː*, ស្ទឹង *stùŋ*, ច្បាស់ *cbas*, ខ្ពស់ *khpùəs*, ខ្ទម *khtùm*, ថ្ពល់ *thpɔəl*, ក្បែរ *kbae(r)*.

Consonants of the initial conjunct sequence are both weak: ម្លូរ *mlùː*, ម្ហូប *mhoːp*, ល្ហង *lhoŋ*, ម្រេច *mrèc*, ល្វីរ *lvìːə*, ល្មម *lmɔːm*, ម្លិះ *mlìh*.

Consonants of the initial conjunct sequence are in the order weak-strong: ល្បែង *lbaeŋ*, ម្ចាស់ *mcas*, ល្ទ្ធរ *lʔɔː*, ម្សៅ *msau*, ល្កក់ *lkak*, ម្ទេស *mtèːs*, ល្ព្រៅ *lpr̀u*.

1st consonant determines the register in the following:—

Consonants of the initial conjunct sequence are in the order strong-weak: ឆ្មារ *chmaː*, ខ្លា *khlaː*, ក្រូច *kroːc*, ផ្លូវ *phloːv*, ឈ្ញញ *chɲaŋ*, ខ្មោច *khmaoc*, ព្រះ *prùh*.

9.2. *Conventions applying to the writing of initial conjunct consonant sequences*

1. When two strong consonants occur in a conjunct consonant sequence (i.e. one written subscript to the other) the first or upper one is usually the first register symbol. (It is the second consonant in this context which is actually determining the register.) e.g. ផ្គប់ *phkɔəp*, ត្បាញ *tbaːɲ*, ស្ពាន *spɔən*.

2. When *l* is required as the first consonant of a conjunct sequence it is always written ល (not ្ល), e.g. ល្ទ្ធរ *lʔɔː*, ល្មម *lmɔːm*, ល្ហង *lhoŋ*.

3. ប with a subscript consonant is pronounced *p*, e.g. ប្រប់ *prap*, ប្ដ្រ *pdr̀y*, ប្ន *plɔːn*.

34

4. *h* does not occur as a subscript consonant below an occlusive. When *h* is the second consonant of a CC sequence and an occlusive is the first, an aspirated occlusive symbol is used, e.g. ផង *phɔːŋ*, ឈរ *chɔː(r)*.

5. Subscript ឌ is the same as subscript ត. It has the form ្ត. Where the first consonant is not an aspirated occlusive, no confusion arises; the pronunciation of the subscript is *d*, e.g. ស្ដប់ *sdap*, ប្ដ្រ *pdry*. Where the first consonant is an aspirated occlusive confusion may arise and spellings must be memorized, e.g. ផ្ដេស-ផ្ដាស *phdeːs-phdaːs*, ផ្ដល *phtyl*.

6. When *n* is required as a subscript consonant in a Khmer native word it is always ្ន (not ្ណ).[1]

7. ហ្ម ហ្ល ហ្វ *(h)m, (h)l* and *(h)v* are a means of writing *m, l* and *v* on the first register, instead of using the diacritic ″. The device is of Thai origin and is chiefly used in the spelling of words which have been borrowed from Thai. e.g. ហ្មង *(h)mɔːŋ*, ហ្លួង *(h)luːəŋ*, ហ្វង *(h)vɔːŋ*.

8. In newspapers, etc., for the spelling of foreign names, ហ is used with any required subscript consonant as a device to indicate that the subscript consonant is voiced, e.g. ហ្គ represents hard *g* in 'de Gaulle' and ហ្ស represents soft *g* in 'Algérie'.

LESSON 10

THE ORTHOGRAPHY OF THE VARIOUS TYPES OF NATIVE KHMER WORD-FORM

10.1. *CVC monosyllable with simple initial consonant*

The orthography of this word-form has been indirectly described in Lessons 7 and 8, e.g. កូន *koːn*, កាត់ *kɔət*, ចំ *cɔm*.

10.2. *Monosyllable with 2-place initial sequence*

CCVC (where no sound occurs between the two consonants of the sequence). If the first consonant is an occlusive and the second the aspirate, the syllabary provides aspirated occlusive symbols for all instances: e.g. ខំ *kham*, ខោ *khòː*, ឆប់ *chap*, ឈឺ *chùː*, ថោ *thoː*, ធុំ *thùm*, ផាយ *phaːy*, ភាយ *phiːəy*. Otherwise the second consonant is subscript to the first and the first, if it is an occlusive, is an unaspirated one, e.g. ក្រាប *kraːp*, ប្រា *praə*, ក្ដ្រ *kdry*, ស្ប្ *spùː*, ឡ្វ្រ *lvry*, ម្យ្រង *myaːŋ*.

ChCVC (where aspiration occurs between the two consonants of the

---

[1] Except in the spelling of a very few colloquial words such as *ponnɣŋ* ប៉ុណ្ណឹង, 'so, like this'.

sequence). Here the first consonant is usually an aspirated occlusive,[1] e.g. ផុត *phyo:t*, ឆ្មប *phli:əm*, ថ្កប់ *thkap*, ខ្ពុស *khpùəs*.

CəCVC (where a short central vowel (ə) occurs between the two consonants of the sequence). Here the second consonant is written to the right of the first consonant, e.g. កកាយ *kəka:y*. This should, according to the implications of the script, represent *kɔ:ka:y* and in poetry this is a possible realization if the metre requires two syllables. In reading style a shorter inherent vowel and in colloquial speech a minimal vowel-sound occurs between the two consonants. e.g. ប៉ុប៉ុក *pəpok*, រនាត *rəni:ət*, រហូត *rəho:t*. The register is that of the second consonant. The rule is in fact as for initial conjunct consonant sequences, but the strong-weak order of consonants does not occur; when a strong consonant is followed by a weak one in a native word the junction is marked either by no sound or by aspiration. Where the two consonants are homorganic, they are written with the same symbol, e.g. កកាយ *kəka:y*, ជៃជក *cəcè:k*, លលោក *ləlɔ:k*, ននាល *nəni:əl*, សសិត *səsɤt*.

10.3. *Monosyllable with 3- or 4-place initial sequence*

1. With *r* in second place. *r* is written subscript to the first consonant and the third consonant is written to the right of them. When the first and third consonants are strong, the first symbol is a first register consonant, whatever the third may be. e.g. ប្រកន់ *prəkan*, ត្រសក់ *trəsɔk*, ស្រទាប់ *srətɔəp* ត្រពាំង *trəpèəŋ*. The register is determined by the third consonant. When the third consonant in such a sequence is weak, the register of the vowel is determined by the first consonant (which is always a strong consonant). e.g. ក្រហោម *krəho:m*, ទ្រហឹង *trəhùŋ*, ត្រងិល *trəŋɤl*, ទ្រងីង *trəŋɤ̀:ŋ*, ប្រញាប់ *prəɲap*, ត្រញុំង *krəɲù:ŋ*, ច្មុះ *crəmoh*, ស្រយុត *srəyot*, ប្រវែង *prəvaeŋ*, ក្រវាត់ *krəvɔət*. The strong consonant is thus dominating both the weak consonants.

When the third consonant is *n* or *l*, for which the table of consonants provides a symbol on both registers, the appropriate symbol is used.[2] In such a word the first consonant must also have the appropriate register. e.g. ច្រណែន *crənaen*, ស្រណុក *srənok*, ទ្រនិង *trənùŋ*, ប្រឡាក់ *prəlak*, ស្រឡាញ់ *srəlaɲ*, ព្រលឹម *prəlùm*.

---

[1] There are, however, some words, such as *knoŋ* ក្នុង and *tnaot* ត្នោត which have no aspiration marked in the spelling but which may be heard pronounced with aspiration.
[2] Modern practice is referred to here. Old texts and dictionaries may not have 1st register *n* or *l* when appropriate.

2. With *r* in third place. The first two consonants are written side by side; *r* is written subscript to the second consonant. Two homorganic consonants, written side by side have the same register, i.e. although the second determines the register, the first is made to match it, e.g. ក[ក៊ត *kəkrɤt*, ជ៎[ជក *cəcrɛːk*, ១ត[១ត *tətrèːt*, សៃ[សឲ *səsraəm*.

3. With *h* in third place. The second and third consonants are written with a single symbol, the aspirated occlusive. If the first consonant is an occlusive or *r*, the two consonant symbols are written side by side; otherwise the second symbol is subscript. e.g. ក៩ឋ *kəkhop*, កឈ *kəkhɔː*, ១ភាក *təthìːak*, ាខ្ឈ *rəkhop*, but ២ឌ *mkhaːŋ*, ាឈន *lkhaon*. It will be observed that when the aspirated occlusive is written to the right of the homorganic (unaspirated) occlusive, they are written with symbols of the same register.

4. With various other consonants in third place. All the examples have an occlusive as first consonant and the second reduplicating it; in some cases the second consonant is written with the aspirated occlusive symbol because aspiration is required between it and the last consonant, e.g. កៃក្ឬ]ក *kəkʔiək*, ថៃផ្ធឋ *pəphʔaep*, ថ ឋ្ឌ *pəploŋ*, កៃឈ្ឍ៣ *kəkhlɤ̀ːɲ*, ថៈផ្ក *pəphtək*, ថៃ ផ្ឈ៣ *pəphlaoɲ*, ថៃ ផ្ឍក *pəphʔaːk*.

5. 4-place sequences occur very rarely: [ថៈឈ្ឬន *prəchlùəh*, [ថៈផ្យ *prəthoy*, [ថៈឈ៩ *prəcheh*, [ថៈផ្ថ *prəthop*.[1]

In all these types of monosyllable with 3- or 4-place initial the principle contained in the rule given for the register in words having initial conjunct consonant sequences is applicable, in that a preceding strong consonant dominates one or even two succeeding weak consonants but does not dominate a succeeding strong consonant.

10.4. *Restricted disyllables*

1. First syllable: consonants. The initial consonant is written in the normal position. When the final consonant (always a nasal) is *ŋ*, *ɲ* or *n* it must be written to the right of the initial consonant. When it is *m*, it may be ឲ, placed to the right, or it may be the *anusvara*, placed above.

2. Second syllable: consonants. The initial consonant is written subscript to the nasal (except when this is written with the *anusvara*) and the final consonant is written to the right of the nasal, e.g. សឲ្fក *səmbɔːk*, កញក *kəɲcɔːk*.[2]

3. First syllable: vowel. The vowel of the first syllable is written as the long inherent (except when the *anusvara* is used) but it is pronounced by

---

[1] In the last three examples *h* is functioning as a consonant in its own right; in the first, it is a feature of junction.

[2] The nasal and a following occlusive are mostly written as homorganic consonants; thus if *k* follows, *ŋ* precedes; if *c* follows, *ɲ* precedes; if *t* follows, *n* precedes and if *p* or *b* follows, *m* precedes.

convention as if it were the written short inherent vowel (ɔ on the first register, ùə on the second register, except before a labial final, where it is ù). No shortening device is required. If the vowel of the second syllable is to be short inherent (or ù before *p*, *m*) this would be indicated in the writing in the usual way, e.g. សម្ម *sɔmɲɔm*, កន្លល់ *kɔɲvɔl*.

4. Second syllable: vowel. When this needs a vowel-sign (i.e. when it is any vowel other than the inherent) this sign is placed in the position which is normal for it, above, below, left or right of the nasal + subscript, e.g. ជន្ឌ្រ *dɔŋkoːv*, បង្កើត *bɔŋkaət*, បង្កៀង *cɔŋkiəŋ*, កំហែន *kɔŋhaen*, បង្កោម *cɔŋkaom*, សង្កេត *sɔŋkeːt*, បង្ហាញ *bɔŋhaːɲ*.

5. *Anusvara* used as final *m* of first syllable. This alternative way of writing the final consonant of the first syllable when this is *m* causes the initial consonant of the second syllable to be placed to the right of the first consonant, e.g. សំបក *sɔmboːk*, កំពង់ *kɔmpùəŋ*, បំបើង *cɔmbaəŋ*, ទំពិរ *tùmpìːə*, លំដាប់ *lùmdap*, បំអែត *cɔmʔaet*.

6. When the initial consonant of the second syllable is a weak consonant the register of the vowel is determined by the first consonant of the first syllable unless this is the glottal stop.[1] Compare បង្ហាន់ *cɔŋhan*, ទំហំ *tùmhùm*, ចំងាយ *cɔmɲaːy*, ទំងន់ *tùmŋùən*, សំព្រៅ *sɔmpau*, ចំណែក *cɔmnaek*, ពំនោល *pùmnòːl*, សំយុង *sɔmyoŋ*, ពន្យល់ *pùənyùəl*, បំរើ *bɔmraə*, គំរប់ *kùmrùp*, បន្លោះ *cɔnlɔh*, ទំលាប់ *tùmlɔəp*, បង្វិល *bɔŋvɤl*, ជំវៀញ *cùmvèɲ*, អរ្ថ *ʔɔnlɤː*, អរ្កិក *ʔɔŋrèːk*.

When the *anusvara* is used as final *m* of the first syllable and the initial of the second syllable is *n* or *l*, for which the table of consonants provides a symbol on both registers, the appropriate symbol is used. In such a word, the first consonant of the first syllable also has the appropriate register, e.g. ដំណាក់ *dɔmnak*, សំណោច *sɔmnaəc*, អំណាច *ʔɔmnaːc*, ទំនៀម *tùmnìəm*, ចំលង *cɔmlɔːŋ*, សំឡាប់ *sɔmlap*, ទំលុះ *tùmlùh*.

When the initial of the second syllable is some other liquid or nasal the register is still determined by the first syllable initial but there is no choice of symbol for the second syllable, e.g. សំរាប់ *sɔmrap*, ចំងាយ *cɔmɲaːy*.

7. ស and ណ. When the initial consonant of the second syllable is ដ *d*, it is distinguished from ត *t* (of which the subscript form is the same) by the use of ណ to represent *n*, the final consonant of the first syllable, instead of ស, e.g. បន្ទូ *bɔntec*, ប៉ុន្ទែ *pontae*, but កណ្ដាល *kɔndaːl*, អណ្ដូង *ʔɔndoːŋ*. Where no ambiguity arises ស is used, e.g. កន្ទុយ *kɔntùy*.

<hr>

[1] It is in this word-form that the glottal stop does not behave according to its class as a strong consonant.

8. When the second syllable has a 2-place initial sequence this may be:—

(i) an occlusive and aspirate, written with the aspirated occlusive symbol, e.g. កន្ធ្រក *kɔnthʏk*, បន្ខុស *bɔŋkhos*.

(ii) an occlusive and *r*, e.g. កន្ត្រៃ *kɔntray*, ប្រ្ក្រ័ប *bɔŋkrùp*.

(iii) an occlusive and *l*, e.g. បំភ្លេ *bɔmphlèc*, បំភ្លឺ *bomphlùː* (with aspiration, occurring between *p* and *l*, noted in the spelling).

Summary of the principles involved in the choice of symbols for writing initial sequences

(i) The initial complex of a Cambodian word-form may be written as a conjunct sequence (CCVC with soundless or aspirated junction); or as a sequence of two consonants side by side (CəCVC) or as a conjunct sequence followed by a single consonant (CCCVC) or a single consonant followed by a conjunct sequence (CCCVC and restricted disyllables). In all cases the rule applies that the register of the vowel is determined by the symbol whose pronunciation occurs immediately before the vowel, unless (*a*) this is a weak consonant and (*b*) a strong consonant precedes it in the sequence. When conditions (*a*) and (*b*) are fulfilled the register is that of the strong consonant.

(ii) Two consonants of the initial sequence, appearing side by side are made to conform to the register of the vowel as follows:—(*a*) If the second is *n* or *l* it has the register appropriate to the vowel, which may in fact be determined by the first consonant. (*b*) If both consonants are homorganic occlusives they are written with symbols of the same register. This applies even when one is aspirated.

(iii) When two strong consonants occur in the sequence, the first has first register (except when, as in (ii) above, it is conforming to the register of a following homorganic consonant).

10.5. *Full disyllables*[1]

Here two complete word-forms, each written like one or other of the types of word described in 1–4 above, are normally written one after the other with no indication that they belong together. In the Cambodian orthography they are indistinguishable from a succession of two words, since spaces do not occur between words. In the transcription a hyphen is used if the word is a compound;[2] otherwise it is written as one unhyphenated word, e.g. រទេះភ្លើង *rətèh-phlʏːŋ*, 'train'; ទ្រេតទ្រោត *tətrèːt-tətròːt*, 'swaying to and fro'; ឪពុក *ʔoːpùk*, 'father'; សៀវភៅ *siəvphʏu*, 'book'.

It is assumed that the student will recognize in the transcription words having the form of restricted disyllables and will write them in accordance

---

[1] A small number of trisyllabic compound words and a greater number of trisyllabic foreign borrowings occur. Indian loanwords are discussed in Lesson 12 and Lesson 48.6.

[2] See Lesson 48 for a full definition of compounds as treated in this book.

with the rules stated above without further indication in the transcription. Hyphenated forms he will know to write as though the components were separate words. Two further points must be made in connection with unhyphenated disyllables and polysyllables.

(i) A comparatively small number of native disyllabic or trisyllabic words are written irregularly with an initial consonant of the second or third syllable subscript to the final consonant of the preceding syllable, i.e. on the pattern of restricted disyllables, e.g. ប៉ុន្តែ *pontae*, ឥឡូវ្នេះ *ʔɤylo:vneh*, សប្បាយ *sɔpba:y*. These will be indicated in the transcription by means of the diacritic ͡, e.g. *po͡ntae*.

The student will, therefore, write an unhyphenated native disyllable as two separate syllables unless such indication is given.[1]

(ii) The general principle on which depend the rules for the determination of the register in extended monosyllables and restricted disyllables, i.e. that a weak consonant, or even a succession of weak consonants, is over-ruled by a preceding strong consonant, applies to full disyllables, of which the two syllables do not occur also as separate words, e.g. *ba:raŋ* បារាំង, *ka:roŋ* ការុង, *po͡nma:n* ប៉ុន្មាន.

10.6. *Exercises in the use of the script*[2]

Turn script into transcription and transcription into script in the following:—

1. Consonants, aspirated or unaspirated, with inherent vowel.

ព ញ ផ ង ភ ត គ ឆ ធ យ យ ស ឡ ថ ដ ជ
ម ប អ រ ហ ល ខ វ ប ក ន ទ ណ ឈ

kɔ̀: kɔ: cɔ: chɔ: tɔ: thɔ̀: phɔ̀: khɔ̀: yɔ̀: chɔ̀: lɔ̀: sɔ: hɔ: nɔ: bɔ:
mɔ̀: ʔɔ: ŋɔ̀: khɔ: ɲɔ̀: tɔ̀: nɔ̀: pɔ̀: rɔ̀: vɔ̀: lɔ: cɔ̀: dɔ: thɔ: phɔ:

2. Consonants with vowel-signs. No change of register from 'syllabary' register.

តា ចួ ជី ធុ ឡើ សឿ បោ ទឹ រេ ពា ភេ កៀ ញិ ណោ ហា លា

ka: co: kɔ̀: ŋì:ə cù:ə ɲɛ̀: daə na: tau tì: nì:ə bɯə pìə mɔ̀:
yù:ə rì:ə lɔ̀: vù: sɔ: ha: laə ʔao

Aspirated occlusive symbols.

ឆេ ធៃ សេ ផៅ ភឿ ឈុ ខៀ ថឹ ឃើ

kha: chɔ: thì:ə khɔ̀: phao thù: chì: phɤy taə phɤ̀:

---

[1] This statement does not apply to Indian loanwords. See Lesson 11.4, No. 5.

[2] The keys to the first part of each exercise will be found in Part V, Keys; the keys to the second part of each exercise will be found in Part IV, Orthography.

3. Use of õ and ö̈.

រ៉ ៤៉ា ហ៉ យ៉ា ម៉ឺ ៤ើ៉ រ៉ឺ

paː yoː mʁy sìː vaː paə hìːə ʔùː rao

4. Use of final consonants.

ផែរ រាយ ហ្ញុប លាត ផែហល រ្ញុ កាស គម ៤្រពាស ៤ើប ១ុក

ម៤ ៗn បាឡ ១ញ្ញ ផែន

kɔːk caːv tùːl saːp lùh saːm caːs lìːən sok tùk pùh pùːəɲ rìəl lìːŋ haə(r)

Vowel-signs for *ay, èy, au* and *ʁu* mixed in with *y* and *v* final consonants.

៤ើ៉ ផាយ ក្ញាវ៉ កា៉វ ៤ៅ៉ ផៃ បាយ

kay kaːy kau pʁu kìːəv cìːəy cay cau cʁu caːv daːv dau cèy

5. Sanskrit initial vowel-signs and the 'cerebral' consonants other than ដ and ណ.

ឯ ឫ ឧ ଓ ឋត អរ ញ ଓន

6. The short vowels, ɔ/ùə and a/èə, mixed with long inherent vowel and long អា.

គ៉ា សង៉ បំ កំ កាច ផាច់ ៤ាំ រាត់ រាយ លាច វ៉ា៤

រ៤ សាំ៤ ផាក៉ បត់ ៤ំ

cɔːk cùm kɔk caːŋ cay daːt cat bɔːŋ bɔŋ haːm ham baŋ kah lah sɔm kɔːk kùək cìːət cèək cɔət tìːəp tɔən pɔːŋ pɔəm pɔət nas rìːəy rèəy rɔəl dɔm tɔk

7. Short vowels and *visarga*.

៤្រពាៈ ច្ព៉ ៤ៈ ៤ៅកាៈ ឡ្ញៈ ៤ៅៈ ប៉ៈ ផ៤៉ៈ ៤ៅៈ

dɔh kɔh bah kùəh rìh tèəh pùh tah keh

8. Mixed *CVC*.

ប៉ូក ផាក៉ ៤ៅៈ ៤ៈ លប់ ៤ៅ៉ម ផាំ ៤ៅៈ ៤្ញាក៉ រ៉ៈ សក៉ ហ៉ុប សៈ

kòːk laːn kɔŋ sʁːp seh pùːə(r) mèək tɔːŋ dɔh lùəy rèəh nìːəm rɔəm cam pak saəc

9. *CCVC* and subscript consonants.

(i) 2-place sequence written by means of a single consonant-symbol:—

ផាប់ ៤ត ឩច ៤ើម ល្ញុក ៤ៅៅ

thaəp khos thùː(r) chìːəm phùː phaoŋ chap

(ii) Single consonant initial written by means of a consonant plus subscript consonant (in occasional loanwords):—

ហ្ញុយ ៤ល្ញៅ ហ្ញុប

(iii) 2-place initial sequence written by means of a consonant with sub-script consonant. (*CCVC* with no intervening sound.)

រ្ល៉ា ស្ងួន ស្ដាប់ ព្យុះ

dbxt   lhoŋ   kda:m   pyùh

With nasal or liquid in 2nd place:—

ក្រាប ស្វា ក្រៃ ស្លាប់ ស្រុក ព្លាញ

craən   sva: krù: trap   srɔk   pla:ɲ

ChCVC:—

ឆ្លាញ ខ្មោ ផ្លាត ឈ្លី ខ្មៅ

chlak   thmɔ: phla:s   chlì: khmau

CəCVC:—

ជៃជក រួួត ទៅទ លលក សរសោះ

pəpɔ:k   dədael   nəniəl   rədɔ:k

10. *CCCVC.* 3-place initial consonant sequences.

With *r* in 2nd place:—

ប្រទះ ក្រពើ ស្រទំ ក្រដាស

prəsɔp   srəpò:n   trəcèək   prədap

With *r* in 2nd place and nasal, liquid or *h* in 3rd place:—

ច្រមុះ ច្រមូល ត្រឡប់ ព្រហៀន ក្រឡែ

crəŋùək   trənaot   prəlùp   srəmaoc   krəla:

With *r* in 3rd place:—

ក្រាត ជ្ជក ទៅ្រ្ទត ប៉្រ្រះ

cəcrùl   tətrèək   səsrxp   pəprì:əy

With other consonants in 3rd place:—

ប៉្ដក សស្ដាក់ រដុយ គយឹក

kəklʔa:k   səslao   rəche:ŋ   pəphŋak

11. Restricted disyllables.

បង្កាប់ ជប្ចន ចង្កក់ សនុំ

dəŋkak   kɔpcas   tùəntèŋ (with ឥ)   pùənlɔ:k

With *anusvara:*—

សំអាប់ រំពេច ជំពាញ កំពត

tùmpè:k   rùmcù:əl   kəmbaɲ   cəmbɔk

With *anusvara* and liquid or nasal following:—

អំណោយ   គំនិត   សំនៅ   សំឡ្វែន

bɔmnɔːŋ   cɔmlak   sɔmrap   cùmnɔ̀ən

With ណ្ឌ or ន្ឌ:—

ដណ្ឌ   អវណ្ឌត   បន្ឌ្រា   សណ្ឌែក

bɔntɤŋ   ʔɔndaək   bɔntùːl   sɔndaek

With 2-place initial sequence in second syllable:—

បង្ខោក   ករៀ]រ   បផ្ឆ្លាន   បផ្ឆ្របូ

sɔŋkhòːk   tùəntrìːəm   bɔmphlɛ̀əŋ   bɔŋkhɤt

LESSON 11

NUMERALS, DIACRITICS AND PUNCTUATION MARKS; THE TRANSCRIPTION

11.1. *The numerals*

១	២	៣	៤	៥	៦	៧	៨	៩	០
1	2	3	4	5	6	7	8	9	0

e.g. ៨ 8, ១៧ 17, ៥៤៣ 543, ៦០២៩ 6,029

11.2. *Diacritics and two special consonants*

័ លេខអស្ដា *leːk(h) ʔasdaː*.[1] This is used in the spelling of two words which consist of one character, an occlusive and its inherent vowel. The diacritic prevents confusion with a longer word, e.g. ក៏ *kɔː*, ដ៏ *dɔː*, either of which fairly common particles might be thought to be part of the following word since there are no spaces in writing between words.

់ កាកបាទ *kaːkbaːt*. Some exclamations and other colloquial words are written with this sign above, e.g. ចាស *cah* (particle which occurs in women's speech to introduce a reply or indicate an affirmative answer), នេះ *neh*, 'here!, hey!', ឬ៉ [nə] or [ŋ] (particle which occurs at the end of a question in colloquial speech).

៑ សញ្ញាកសញ្ញា *saŋɲòːksaɲɲaː*. This diacritic is used to indicate that the written inherent vowel is to be pronounced as though it were short អា/អ៊ា, e.g. ខណ្ឌ *khan(d)*, ពាទ *pɔ̀ət*, សម័យ *samay*. Where it occurs with second

---

[1] The uses of underlining, accents over consonant-signs, the sign +, etc. in the transcription of certain words is explained in 11.4.

register and a following ឧ, however, the sequence of vowel and final consonant are pronounced like ើ្យ, èy, e.g. ជឹយ cèy.

◌̊ or ◌̊ របា.ត rəba.t. This is a superscript r; it occurs in Indian loanwords
but is not pronounced. The consonant below it is not pronounced either, if
the written form of the word ends with the two consonants, e.g. ធ៌ម thɔə(rm),
ពណ៌ pɔə(rn).

◌̊ ទណ្ឌឃាត tɔəndəkhì.ət. This sign is placed over a character which is not
to be pronounced or have any effect on the pronunciation of the preceding
consonant or vowel, e.g. ភូមិ phùːm(i), ប្រយោជន៍ prəyaoc (+ n).[1] The sign is
not used to delete subscript final consonants, however; these are usually not
pronounced, e.g. សុក្រ sok(r), រ័ត្ថ rɔət(th). These unpronounced characters
occur in the writing of loanwords, which tend to be as nearly as possible
transcribed into Cambodian.

ឝ, ś, is used in learned treatises to represent the Sanskrit palatal sibilant.
ឞ, ṣ, is used in learned treatises to represent Sanskrit cerebral s.

11.3. *Punctuation*

A space is used to indicate a break in sense of the kind for which we use
a comma, semi-colon or even a full stop.

។ ខណ្ឌ khan(ḍ). A full stop. It often occurs only at the end of several
sentences.

៕ គោមូត្រ kòːmoːt(r). A final stop sign used, though with less frequency
in modern books, to mark the very end of a chapter or book.

៘ la.[2] This means 'etc.'.

ៗ លេខទោ leːk(h) tòː. This sign indicates that the previous word, or sometimes the previous two words, are to be repeated, e.g. មួយ ៗ mùːəy-mùːəy,
ដោយឡែក ៗ daoy-laek daoy-laek. Only the sense of the passage tells the
reader whether one or two words is to be repeated.

11.4. *The transcription*

The transcription has a twofold aim: to provide a reliable guide to the
pronunciation and at the same time to indicate the spelling. The transcription
used in this book is based on that evolved by Professor E. J. A. Henderson.[3]
Some small changes and additions to the vowel-symbols have been made,
which arose out of the needs of students. Thus aʏ, av and ẁə, which tended

---

[1] See footnote 1, p. 43.
[2] This syllable, used as a name for the sign, is an abbreviation of the Pali word, *peyyāla*,
of which it is the last syllable. It is pronounced [laʔ], being subject to the conventions which
apply to the pronunciation of Indian loanwords. See Lesson 12, No. 9.
[3] E. J. A. Henderson. 'The Main features of Cambodian pronunciation', *B.S.O.A.S.*, 14,
1952, pp. 149–74.

to be misread by students with no phonetic training, have been changed to
ɑə, au and *ùə*. To avoid confusion, ᾑ/ᾑᵌ[1] have been transcribed *u:ə/ù:ə*.
The initial glottal stop and the length in open vowels are always noted to
remind the student constantly of these features. The transcription *ì:ə*

distinguishes the diphthong written ᾑ from that written ᾑᾑ] (transcribed *ìə*).

In some parts of Cambodia a distinction is heard in the pronunciation of
the two diphthongs.[2]

In order to clarify several ambiguities of Cambodian spelling, certain
additional diacritics and conventions have been devised and will be used
from here onwards. These are:—

1. ¨ to indicate that the vowel thus marked, or the diphthong of which
the first letter is thus marked, is written with ᾑ where this could not otherwise be known, e.g. in native words in which the short vowel *e* occurs before a

palatal final. Contrast *cëɲ* ᾑᾑ, *mrĕc* ᾑᾑᾑ, with *tèɲ* ᾑᾑ, *tec* ᾑᾑ. The diacritic
is not used in the transcription of words in which ᾑ is pronounced short in
accordance with the orthographic rules set out in Lesson 8, e.g. *seh* ᾑᾑ:.
It is, however, used in Indian loanwords and will be used in the special
cases to be treated in the next lesson, in which the vowel ᾑ is pronounced
as though it were *ʔae/ɛ:*, e.g. *häet(o)* ᾑᾑᾑ, *pè:t(y)* ᾑᾑᾑ.

2. — to indicate that the vowel or diphthong thus underlined
(ᾑ, *ùə, ɑ, ɛ̀ə, ɔə, ù* or ᾑ in an Indian word) is written as the long inherent
vowel, e.g. *phɔl* ᾑᾑ, *nìmùən(t)* ᾑᾑᾑ. The underlining will not be used for
native words in which by regular convention a long inherent vowel in the
spelling is pronounced short, e.g. *kɔnda:l* ᾑᾑᾑ.

3. ′ to indicate in the transcription of Indian loanwords that the vowel
or diphthong thus marked (*á, ɔ́ə, ɛ́ə* or *é*) is written with the inherent vowel
and the *saɲɲò:ksaɲɲa:*. Where ′ is used, the second register sign ˋ, if needed,
will be transferred to the initial consonant, to facilitate printing, e.g.
cèy ᾑᾑ, ᾑᾑ *pɔ́əì(ìh)*.

4. ₍ to indicate that *ù* before *p* or *m* is written with the vowel-symbol ₍
and not by means of the short-mark, *bɔntɔk*, over the final consonant.
Contrast *tùm* ᾑᾑ, *tùm* ᾑᾑ, *hùp* ᾑᾑᾑ, *chùp* ᾑᾑᾑ.

5. ⌒ to indicate the unexpected instances of a consonant being written
subscript to another, e.g. *poɲma:n* ᾑᾑᾑ, *sɔpba:y* ᾑᾑᾑ. These words have
the form of native full disyllables but are not written in the usual way, i.e.
as though each syllable was a separate word.[3] There are two further types
of word in the orthography of which it is expected that the second consonant in a medial consonantal sequence will be written subscript to the first.

---

[1] The sloping line is used here as elsewhere to separate 1st and 2nd register vowels which
are written with the same symbol.
[2] In such dialects the diphthong transcribed *ì:ə* has a more open starting point and greater
relative length of the initial vowel. See Lesson 5.3, note to 43.
[3] See Lesson 10.5.

These types are (i) the Cambodian restricted disyllable and (ii) Indian loanwords. It is assumed that the student will recognize these types of word in the transcription, the first from its precise form[1] and the second from its non-Cambodian form and the presence of extra diacritics, and that he will, without any reminder, write any second medial consonants as subscripts, e.g. *kɔŋkaep* កំផែប, *paɲca* បញ្ច.

6. Words derived from Sanskrit or Pali often retain in the spelling, at the end of the word, consonant- or vowel-signs which are not pronounced in the modern Khmer form, e.g. ភូម *phùːm*. Similarly an aspirated occlusive may still be written as the final consonant although pronounced unaspirated or a cerebral occlusive will be the spelt final although the pronounced final is a dental occlusive, e.g. មុខ *mùk*, បុណ្យ *bon*. Such words are transcribed with these unpronounced elements written in parentheses, *phùːm(i)*, *mùk(h)*, etc. Where a consonant occurs of which the transcription would not indicate the orthography, a dot below, for cerebral consonants, and the second register accent, `, for written sonant symbols, are used from here onwards so as to show what the spelling should be, e.g. បុណ្យ *boṇ(y)*, កុដ *koṭ(e)*, សុទ *sol*, ពុល *pùl(h)*, ពុម *pùm(ph)*. These devices are applied also to medial consonants in a few words in order to indicate the spelling without misrepresenting the pronunciation. Thus the unpronounced *s* in *vɔ(s)saː* វស្សា, *kèːhɔ(s)thaːn* គេហស្ឋាន are placed in parentheses, while ឆ and ិ in វិច្ឆិ *vicchiːə* and ពុទ្ធ [កាឆ *pùlthiːəsɑkraːc* respectively are indicated by the second register sign.

Unpronounced consonants which are not written subscript to the last pronounced consonant are indicated in parentheses with a plus sign. This applies chiefly to *n*, *ṇ* and *y* in Indian words ending in *ana*, *aṇa* and *aya*, e.g. [ប្រយោជន៍ *prəyaoc(+n)*. *prəyaoc(n)* would wrongly suggest that ន was subscript to ជ.

The method thus applied to Sanskrit and Pali words is used for Cambodian words which have final written *r*, e.g. ដើរ *daə(r)*, វេរ *vèː(r)*, ហោរ *hoː(r)*.

7. ' is used over a letter in the transcription to indicate that the *tɔ̀əṇḍɑkhìːət* occurs in the orthography over the character represented by that letter, e.g. [ប្រយោជន៍ *prəyaoc(+n̊)*. Sometimes a word may be correctly spelt with or without the *tɔ̀əṇḍɑkhìːət*, e.g. *phùːm(i)* may be spelt ភូម or ភូម.

8. The convention has been adopted that initial glottal stop with vowel or diphthong represents an Indian initial vowel sign (i.e. in the case of vowels for which there is an Indian vowel sign),[2] e.g. *ʔae* ឯ, *ʔoːpùk* ឪពុក.

---

9. It is assumed that the rule for the spelling of *r*/*ŭ* is operating (i.e. that the vowel is written ◌ before *k*, *ŋ* and *m* and otherwise ◌).[1]

10. It is assumed that the orthographic convention for determining the register (i.e. that a strong consonant over-rules one or more succeeding weak ones) is operating in disyllables and polysyllables, both Cambodian[2] and Indian. Thus *saːlaː* is to be interpreted as សាលា and not សាឡា. In the comparatively rare cases where the first syllable has a strong first register consonant and the second syllable has a cerebral *n* or *l* in the spelling, it is therefore necessary to indicate, by means of a dot below the *n* or *l*, that a cerebral symbol is required, since by convention ន or ល would equally have first register, e.g. កាណត់ *kaːṇoːt*, កាឡរ *kaːḷry*.

There are further, less common, irregularities of Cambodian spelling, such as the pronunciation of final written *r* as *l* in a few words, or exceptions to the (Cambodian) guide rule stipulating that ◌ occurs before ñ, ḍ and ṭ, and ◌ before other consonants. In some naturalized Indian loanwords ñ is pronounced *d*, e.g. ចេតិយ *ceːdry*. There are also completely isolated instances of irregular spelling such as *thom* ធំ. It was felt, however, that enough diacritics had been added to the transcription. Such spellings as these have therefore been appended in a list in Part IV 2. The words are marked with an asterisk at their first, and sometimes second appearance in Part II or III and at all occurrences in the vocabulary, Part VI.

A final addition to the transcription is the hyphen, which, as has been explained in Lesson 10.5, is used to indicate the components of disyllabic or polysyllabic words which have been found, by methods set out in Lesson 48, to be compounds.

LESSON 12

INDIAN LOANWORDS: THE INTERPRETATION OF THE ORTHOGRAPHY IN RELATION TO THEM

Certain conventions apply to the pronunciation of Indian loanwords in Cambodian, although no hard and fast rules can be stated. The chief conventions are given in this lesson, together with a few other points which arise out of the naturalization of Indian words in the Cambodian language context. Most features are presented by means of examples followed by a statement of the point to be observed. The Sanskrit or Pali source word is given in parentheses. Its meaning is not necessarily the same as that which the Cambodian loanword now has.

1. បាទ *baːt* (pāda)[3] 'yes' (male speaker), គុណ *kùṇ* (guṇa) 'gratitude'.

As with native Khmer words, initial vowels have their usual Khmer register after occlusives and s and a final written consonant is pronounced with no inherent vowel following it.

---

[1] See Lesson 8.3, footnote.
[2] i.e. Cambodian disyllables of which the two syllables do not occur also as separate words.
[3] Sanskrit and Pali words are transcribed according to normal practice; the length mark indicates a long vowel.

2. បុណ្យ *boṇ(y)* (puṇya) 'festival', មុខ *mùk(h)* (mukha) 'face, front'.
Note that only the first of the final written consonants is pronounced in Khmer.

3. ការ *ka:(r)* (kāra) 'work', ទ្វារ *tvì:ə(r)* (dvāra) 'door', ឧទរ *ʔùtɔ̀:(r)* (udara) 'stomach'.
As with native Khmer words, final r is not pronounced.

4. Indian inherent vowel, 'a', in final syllables.

(i) ផល *phɔl* (phala) 'fruit', កល *kɔl* (kala) 'ruse', គោរព *kò:rùp* (gaurava[1]) 'to respect', ពល *pùəl* (bala) 'force'.
When there is only one written final consonant, the pronunciation of the vowel is usually as for short Khmer inherent (i.e. *ɔ* for first register, *ùə* for second register, except for *ù* before labials).

(ii) កម្ម *kam(m)* (kamma) 'action', ទ្រព្យ *trɔ̀əp(y)* (dravya) 'goods', ភក្ត្រ *phĕək(tr)* (vaktra) 'face'.
Where there are two or more written final consonants, the pronunciation of the vowel is usually as for short Khmer អៈ, i.e. *a* (first register), *ɔ̀ə~ɛ̀ə* (second register).

5. Indian cerebral consonants, as in បុណ្យ *boṇ(y)* (puṇya) 'festival', អណ្ឌ *ʔɔṇdɛ̀ə* (aṇḍa) 'egg'.
These are usually retained in the spelling but are pronounced initially as *d* (both Indian ṭ and ḍ), *th* (both Indian ṭh and ḍh) and *n* (ṇ); in final position they are pronounced as *t* (Indian ṭ, ṭh, ḍ, ḍh) or *n* (ṇ); they are given the register appropriate to them from the Khmer syllabary.

6. Indian p is pronounced *p* in unnaturalized words, e.g. បត្នី *patanì:* (patanī) 'wife'. In naturalized words it is pronounced *b*, e.g. បុណ្យ *boṇ(y)* (puṇya) 'festival'.

7. The *anusvara* is retained in spelling and pronounced *ŋ* in unnaturalized words, e.g. ជិតំ *cìtaŋ* (jitaṃ) 'victory', ទុក្ខំ *tùkkhaŋ* (dukkhaṃ) 'trouble', នបុំសក *nèəpoŋsaka*[2] (napuṃsaka) 'neuter'. In naturalized words the *anusvara* is pronounced as in Cambodian native words, e.g. សំបត្តិ *sɔmbat(te)* (sampatti) 'goods'.

8. ស្នេហា *snäeha:* (snehā) 'love', ខេត្ត *khäet(t)* (khetta) 'province' (ខេត្រ *khaet(r)* from Sanskrit kṣetra also occurs).
The vowel អែ is pronounced *ae* after a first register consonant.

9. ជលធិ *cèəʔ-lèəʔ-tì:*[3] (jaladī) 'sea', កិរិយា *keʔ-reʔ-ya:* (kiriyā) 'behaviour', ឥរិយា *ʔeʔ-reʔ-ya:* (iriyā) 'manner', សុចរិត *soʔ-caʔ-rɤt* (sucarita) 'good behaviour,' កិត្តិយស *kɤt-teʔ-yùəs* (kittiyasa) 'reputation', ភរិយា *phèəʔ-rìʔ-yì:ə* (bhariyā) 'wife'.

---

1 Sanskrit and Pali *v* are often ព (*p*) in Khmer.

2 Note that this word, not being a naturalized word, retains the pronunciation of final inherent vowel, contrary to the convention explained in 1.

3 Syllables are separated by a hyphen for the sake of clarity, where desirable, in this lesson only.

Short vowels in open syllables are followed in formal style by a glottal stop. The written long inherent vowel, which represents Indian short a, is given the Khmer short pronunciation (ɛə, not ɔə, for second register before glottal stop).[1] Indian i has the syllabary realizations e and i according to register. In rapid colloquial style ə is heard instead of a, ɛə and e in unstressed syllables and the glottal stop is not usually heard in either stressed or unstressed syllables:—

cèạlɔ̣tìː, kerɔ̣yaː, ʔerɔ̣yaː, socɔ̣rʌt, kʌttɔ̣yùəs, phɛ̀ərìyìːə.

10. Indian i in closed syllables.

(i) ចិត្ត cʌt(t) (citta) 'heart', សិស្ស sʌs(s) (sissa) 'pupil', លិង្គ lʌŋ(k) (liṅga) 'liṅga', អធិប្បាយ ʔạ-thìp-baːy (adhippāya) 'to explain'.
The pronunciation is ʌ or i according to register.

(ii) However, in the final syllable of some words, there is an alternative pronunciation ù for ìː:—សមាជិក sạmaːcìk or sạmaːcùk (samājika) 'member'. In other cases only ù is heard, e.g. ពិនិត្យ pìnùt(y) (vinicchaya) 'to scrutinize', ជីវិត cìːvùt (jīvita) 'life'.

11. ធីតា thìːdaː (dhītā) 'daughter', តន្ត្រី dʌntrʌy (tantrī) 'music', ពិតាន pìdaːn (vitāna) 'ceiling'.
A single initial ត is often pronounced d.

12. កុមារី koʔ-maː-rʌy (kumārī) 'girl', សាលា saː-laː (sālā) 'hall', សុចរិត soʔ-caʔ-rʌt (sucarita) 'good behaviour', ឥរិយា ʔeʔ-rìʔ-yaː (iriyā) 'behaviour', ហោរា hao-raː (horā) 'augury'.
A syllable or series of syllables having liquid or nasal initial consonants may have first register if the initial consonant of the syllable which precedes them is a first register occlusive, s or h. The aspirate, h, however, may itself be over-ruled by a preceding second register consonant. e.g. ព្រហស្បតិ prạhɔ̀əs(p+tè) (prahaspati) 'Thursday', ព្រហារ prɔ̣hìːə(r) or វិហារ vihìːə(r) (vihāra) 'temple'.

Note. In compound words of which both parts occur separately as Cambodian words, the influence just described does not extend from the first component to the second. e.g. កិត្តិយស kʌtte/yùəs (kittiyasa) 'renown', បុប្ផានារី boppha:/nìːərìː (puphānāri) 'flower-like maiden'.

13. ហុត hùt (huta) 'to sacrifice', ករុណា kạrùṇaː (karuṇā) 'pity', អណូ ʔạnùː (aṇū) 'small, fine'.
Indian u and ū have second register in Khmer except where there is an initial first register occlusive or s.

---

[1] The realization aʔ or ɛə of the written long inherent vowel is sometimes represented in dictionaries by the diacritic, ː, e.g. ជ:ឡ:ទ cèəʔlèəʔtìː.

14. បក្សី *ḅạk-sᵳy* (paksī) 'bird', វត្ថុ *vɔ̀ɔt-tho* (vatthu) 'thing'.

The written long inherent vowel, which represents Indian short a, is given, except as under 4 (i) above, the pronunciation of shortened កា (i.e. *a/ɛ̀ə~ɔ̀ə* according to register). This was stated under 9 above as applying to open syllables; it applies to closed syllables also. When, however, the Indian word resembles in form a Khmer restricted disyllable, at least to the extent of having an inherent vowel followed by a nasal consonant in the first of its two syllables, it may be pronounced in accordance with Khmer rules, e.g. វង្ស *vùəŋsaː* (vaṃsa) 'family'. Moreover, when *ɔ̀ə~ɛ̀ə* would be required before a palatal final (not an acceptable sequence in Khmer) the vowel is pronounced instead as first register *a*. e.g. មច្ឆា *mạc-chaː* (macchā) 'fish', រជ្ជកាល *rạccèəkaːl* (rajjakāla) 'reign'.

15. ណ, ṇ, in Indian words is treated as follows:—

(i) When it has no written vowel sign for which it acts as base, i.e. when it has the inherent vowel, it bears its syllabary value of first register, e.g. វណ្ណ *vɔ̀ɔnnạ* (vaṇṇa) 'writing'.

(ii) When it has a written vowel for which it acts as base, it normally has second register, e.g. មណី *mèənìː* (maṇī) 'jewel' (this may be changed to first register by a first register consonant in a preceding syllable in naturalized words, however).

16. យាត្រា *yìːə-traː* (yātrā) 'to go', អាជ្ញា *ʔaːc-ɲaː* (ājñā) 'permission', បក្សី *ḅạk-sᵳy* (paksī) 'bird', បុត្រី *ḅot-trᵳy* (putrī) 'daughter'.

Generally speaking, if two medial consonants are suitable as a Khmer initial sequence they are so used (e.g. *yìːə-traː*). If not, they are pronounced in separate syllables (e.g. *ʔaːc-ɲaː*). If a short vowel precedes the conjunct consonants, the first consonant is in any case used, if suitable, to close that syllable (e.g. *ḅạk-sᵳy*). This process has led to the reduplication of the first consonant after a short vowel if the two consonants are an entirely suitable Khmer initial sequence (e.g. *ḅot-trᵳy* putrī).

17. សម័យ *sạmáy* (samaya) 'time', ភយ *p̣héy* (bhaya) 'to fear', ជ័យ *čéy* (jaya) 'victory'.
Indian -aya is pronounced *ay* (first register), *èy* (second register).

18. ភូមិ *p̣hùːm(ì)* (bhūmi) 'village', ហេតុ *hӕt(o)* (hetu) 'cause', កុដិ *koṭ(e)* (kuṭi) 'hut'.
Short final vowels have been dropped in pronunciation, in words which have become naturalized. The resulting words in these examples are monosyllables.

19. ជីវិត *čiːvùt* (jīvita) 'life', ពិបាក *p̣ibaːk* (vipāka) 'difficult', វិស័យ *vìsáy* (visaya) 'refuge', និទាន *nìtìːən* (nidāna) 'to relate', ប្រាកដ *praːkɔ̀t* or

prəkət (prakaṭa, prākaṭa) 'fixed, determined', សាហារ *ʔaːhaː(r)* (ahāra) 'food'.

Short final vowels have been dropped; the resulting words are disyllables.

20. Indian short vowels in unclosed syllables have been dropped:—

(i) ក្លិង្គ *klɤŋ(k)* (kaliṅga) 'Indian', ក្បត់ *kbɔt* (kapaṭa) 'to betray', សបថ *sbɔt(h)* (śapatha) 'to swear', ប្រុស *pros* (puruṣa) 'male'.

Here trisyllables have been reduced to monosyllables in Khmer.

(ii) ឧបាសក *baːsɔk* (upāsaka) 'layman', អធិបតី *thìpdɤy* (adhipati) 'leader', ប្រទេស *prətèːs* (paradesa) 'country'.

Here 4-syllabled words have been reduced to disyllables in Khmer.

(iii) បរិភោគ *bərephòːk* (paribhoga) 'to eat', បតិបត្តិ *prədɤybat(te)* (pratipatti) 'to conform', អនុញ្ញាត *ʔanùɲɲaːt* (anujñāti) 'to grant permission', អភិសេក *ʔaphìsäek* (abhiseka) 'to anoint'.

Here 4-syllabled words have been reduced to trisyllables, as is more usual.

21. ប្រយោជន៍ *prəyaoc(+n̊)* (prayojana) 'use' (n.), លក្ខណ៍ *lèak(kh+n̊)* (lakkhaṇa) 'endowment, natural qualities', ព្រាហ្មណ៍ *prìːə(h)m(+n̊)* (brāhmaṇa) 'Brahmin'.

Indian -ana, -aṇa have been dropped, though the n or ṇ is still present in the spelling.

22. បុណ្យ *bon̊(y)* (puṇya) 'festival', គុណ *kùn* (guṇa) 'good deed', ប្រុស *pros* (puruṣa) 'man',[1] ក្លិង្គ *klɤŋ(k)* (kaliṅga) 'Indian', សបថ *sbɔt(h)* (śapatha) 'to swear', ប្រទេស *prətèːs* (pradesa) 'country', ប្រាកដ *praːkɔt* (prākaṭa) 'fixed', សម្បត្តិ *sɔmbat(te)* (sampatti) 'goods', ជីវិត *cìːvùt* (jivita) 'life', រក្ស *rɛ̀aksaː* (rakṣā) 'to look after'.

These are examples of loanwords which are indistinguishable in pronunciation from native words of various forms.

23. Compare លោភ *lòːp(h)* (lobha) 'greed', ល្មោភ *lmòːp(h)* (h) 'to be greedy', សបថ *sbɔt(h)* (śapatha) 'to swear', សំបថ *sɔmbɔt(h)* 'oath', ទោស *tòːs* (dosa) 'wrong' (n.), បន្ទោស *bəntòːs* 'to scold', ឃោរ *khòː(r)* (ghora) 'to be awful', ឃោរឃៅ *khòː(r)-khɤ̀u* 'to be horrifying'.

Here are instances of Cambodian prefixation, infixation and reduplication[2] being applied to Indian loanwords.

---

[1] Another form of this borrowing, បុរស *borɔs*, occurs with the meaning 'man'.

[2] For which see Lessons 44, 45 and 46 respectively.

LESSON 13

DICTIONARY ORDER

The order in which words will be found in the Cambodian dictionary[1] is as follows.[2] The consonants follow each other in syllabary order[3]; thus all words with initial ក are given, with their vowels in syllabary order[4] before the words having initial ខ. The following words are therefore in dictionary order: ក *kɔː*, ក្ម *koː*, កុំ *kom*, កេ្ខ *khao*, កោ *kòː*, ហើ *khɔəm*, គ *ŋìːə*. The final consonants of words having the same initial and vowel must be in syllabary order too, e.g. ចួន *cuːən*, ចួប *cuːəp*, ចែត *chaet*, ចែប *chaep*.

Short ɔ/ùə and a/èə~ɔ̀ə written with the *bɔntɔk* are given after the long vowels which are spelt with the same vowel symbol, e.g. ចង់ *cɔ̀ːŋ*, ចង់ *cùəŋ*, ជាត *cìːət*, ជាត់ *cɔ̀ət*. Words which have these short vowels written with the *anusvara*[5] come in syllabary position at the end of the other vowels, e.g. ត្រូ *tr̀u*, ទះ *tèəh*, ទុំ *tùm*, ទុំ *tùm*. A word whose initial consonant is converted to the other register is given after a word of the same spelling having the syllabary register, e.g. ញញ *ɲùːp*, ញញ្ញញ *ɲoːɲ-ɲaːɲ*.

Words having a 2-place initial sequence with no sound or with aspiration between the consonants are written by means of subscript consonants. These come in the section concerned with the first of these consonants, following all the words written with the single consonant symbol. The dictionary order of the consonants which are subscript is maintained, together with that of the vowels which occur with each subscript, e.g. តិច *tec*, តាង *taŋ*, តះ *tah*, ត្យោក *tɲaok*, ត្នោត *tnaot*, ត្បក *tbɔːk*, ត្បាញ *tbaːɲ*, ថប *thɔp*, ថ្នល់ *thnɔl*, ថ្នក់ *thnak*, ថ្លង់ *thlɔŋ*.

Words having a 3-place initial sequence come in the position appropriate to their consonants, e.g. the words *trəhùŋ* and *prəlɔːŋ* in the following list: ទុំ *tùm*, ទ្រ *trɔː*, ទ្រង *trùəŋ*, ទ្រហុង *trəhùŋ*, ទ្រុង *trùŋ*, ប្រក *prɔk*, ប្រលង *prəlɔːŋ*, ប្រប *prap*.

Where the short neutral vowel, ə, occurs between consonants of an initial sequence and the consonants occur side by side, e.g. បប៊ុល *bəbuːəl*, it must be remembered that the long inherent vowel is written between the consonants; *bəbuːəl* comes therefore after បក *bɔːk* and before ពន *baːn*.

---

[1] វចនានុក្រមខ្មែរ *vèəcanaːnùkrɔm khmae(r)*. Dictionnaire cambodgien, Tome 1, k–m, Phnom Penh, 1938, Tome 2, y–a, 1943. 2nd edition, Phnom Penh, 1951.

[2] In the vocabulary, Part VI, the order is slightly changed, because the presentation of words in transcription in dictionary order makes the process of looking up words unnecessarily complicated.

[3] See Lesson 7.2.　　　　　[4] See Lesson 8.1.　　　　　[5] See Lesson 8.3.

Similarly, restricted disyllables come before words having the same initial with the vowel សា, unless they are written with the *anusvara*: បង្ *bɔːŋ*, បង្កុ *bɔŋkɔː*, បរណ្ដ *bɔndau*, ពទ *baːt*, but ស្ពាល *baol*, ប៉្ពុល *bɔmpùl*, ប៉្ព្រោត *bɔmpròət*, ប៉្ព្លុ *bɔmphlùː*.

Full disyllables are written usually as two separate words, e.g. សៀវភៅ *siəvphɤ̆u*, កៅរី *kau?ry*. Some, which are written in the transcription with the diacritic, ⌢, linking two medial consonants, are written on the lines of restricted disyllables:—ដុះ *dɔːc=neh*, ប៉ុន្តែ *pontae*, ប៉ុន្មាន *ponmaːn*.

In the Cambodian dictionary, words beginning with ប៉ *pɔː* are given separately after all those beginning with ប *bɔː*, i.e. after *bah*, but before words beginning with ប and a subscript consonant. With them are included words from Sanskrit and Pali in which initial ប is pronounced as if it were ប៉.

With the exception of ឫ *rù*, ឬ *rùː*, ឭ *lù* and ឮ *lùː*, words having the Sanskrit initial vowel symbols are included in the place which they would occupy if written with the vowel base and ordinary vowel signs; the following are therefore in dictionary order: ឥត *?ɤt*, ឥន្ *?ɤn(ɨr)*, ឯង *?oŋ*, ឧបមា *?opama ː*, ឧស *?oːs*. Sanskrit and Pali loanwords which had an initial vowel are spelt with the initial vowel signs. Some Cambodian words are spelt with the initial vowel signs too, e.g. all words beginning with *?r* and many words beginning with *?o, ?ae* and *?ao*. Cambodian words beginning with *?oː* and *?ry* are spelt ឧ and ឥ. In this book, any word of this kind which is not spelt with an Indian initial vowel sign, will be entered in the special spellings list in Part IV. ឫ *rù* and ឬ *rùː* come at the end of all words beginning with រ, e.g. រះ *rèəh*, ឫស្ស *rùssɤy*, ឬ *rùː*. ឭ *lù* and ឮ *lùː* come at the end of the section for ល.

Two diacritics, ៗ and ៝ or ៓, which will be found in the spelling of certain Indian loanwords, need mention here. A word in which ⌣ occurs is entered after a word of similar spelling without the sign, e.g. ដ *cɔː* comes before ដ *cɔə*. ៝ or ៓ is unpronounced but represents an *r*; thus ធម៌ *thɔə(rm)* is found where one would expect it if it were spelt ធ, after ធរាង *thɛərèəmiːən*.

Dictionaries compiled by J. Guesdon[1] and S. Tandart[2] before the appearance of the Cambodian dictionary referred to above have slightly different word-orders. The former has the consonants arranged as though ឥ came first, while words with initial ប៉ are placed after words with the same spelling but with no ៝.

---

[1] Joseph Guesdon, *Dictionnaire cambodgien–français*, Paris, 1930, 2 vols.
[2] S. Tandart, *Dictionnaire cambodgien–français*, Phnom Penh, 1935, 2 vols.

PART II

GRAMMAR AND EXERCISES

INTRODUCTION TO PART II

Cambodian sentence-structure is introduced in Part II, beginning with the simplest sentences and a limited number of word-categories and building up step by step. Exercises for translation from Cambodian to English and English to Cambodian form part of most lessons; exceptions are lessons such as 22 (numerals) which consists entirely of material to be learned by heart; some lessons have more than one exercise. The Cambodian sentences in the exercises are intended to be used as a graded series of exercises in pronunciation too. The student will gain the maximum practice from them if he hears the tape-recordings and records his own pronunciation in the spaces provided.

Many students will find that they can work rapidly through the first five lessons of Part II, particularly if they are familiar with another South-East Asian language. It is suggested, however, that at this stage students who are to learn the orthography should be perfecting their knowledge of its rules. Teachers and students are reminded that the exercises and the keys to them are given in orthography in Part IV and that it is therefore possible to work in script, using the transcription only where necessary to read examples and consult the vocabularies.

A vocabulary of new words is given for each exercise in Part II. The words are presented in the order in which they will be required as the exercise is done. Occasionally this principle is disregarded in order to put all words of one kind together (e.g. numerals in Lesson 10 and colours in Lesson 14). Sentences used in the text, to illustrate new grammar, contain extra vocabulary but, since translations are given for all such sentences, the vocabulary should be readily understood. All words introduced in Parts II and III, whether in examples or exercises, will be found in the vocabulary, Part VI. The reader is reminded that an asterisk marks the first occurrence of a word of which the irregular spelling cannot be deduced from the transcription. A list of the spellings of asterisked words will be found in Part IV. These spellings should be memorized at their first occurrence.

The keys to the exercises, which are given in Part V, may be used as revision exercises, being translated in reverse, after the completion of work on a further one or two lessons.

It is suggested that the Cambodian School Reader[1] might be used during the study of Part II. It will provide extra practice in reading the orthography and it has two advantages as reading material, that its sentences are comparatively simple and that the elementary subject matter contains basic everyday vocabulary.

---

[1] See bibliography, Part VII.

LESSON 14

SIMPLE STATEMENTS

14.1. *Intonation*

In Lessons 14–24, sentences will be used which should be pronounced with one of the two basic intonation tunes associated with a plain, unemotional, fairly slow style of speech. The tunes will be referred to as 'sentence-tunes 1 and 2'.

Sentence-tune 1 (a) and (b)[1]

The tune for straightforward statements, affirmative or negative, such as those described in this lesson, is characterized by a steep fall to low level (\\) on the last syllable:—

1.(*a*) *khɲom tə̀u.* (\\)[2] I am going.
    khɲom tə̀u phtèəh. (\\) I am going home.
    khɲom mùn tə̀u phtèəh tèː. (\\) I am not going home.

1.(*b*) Sometimes the sentence subject (the first noun in these sentences), may be slightly emphasized by being pronounced with rising pitch (‚) and followed by a slight pause (‖):—
    khɲom (‚‖) nə̀u phtèəh tùːlìːəy. (\\) I live in a roomy house.

In later sentences a word or series of words may be emphasized by the rise + pause; the degree of emphasis may be measured by the steepness of the rise, the height of the pitch reached and the length of the pause.

All the sentences in Exercises 1–7 should be practised with sentence-tune 1.(*a*) or 1.(*b*).

14.2. *Affirmative statements*

Straightforward statements may be composed of a sequence of noun and verb (**n v**) or a sequence of noun, verb and noun (**n v n**). In Lessons 14–17, sentences other than replies are basically of this pattern, with some elaboration of the noun element and with some particles introduced. The word-order is as for simple English statements, subject-verb, with object or destination in third place, e.g. *khɲom*[3] *nə̀u,* 'I am staying'; *khɲom nə̀u phtèəh,* 'I am staying at home'; *khɲom tèɲ phtèəh,* 'I am buying a house'. This basic sentence pattern will be referred to as **'sentence-form I 1.'**

Exercise 1

Nouns.[4] *ʔɔːpùk*[5] father *laːn* car *mdaːy* mother *mhoːp* meal *bɔːŋ* elder brother or sister *phtèəh* house, home *pʔoːn* younger brother or sister

---

[1] Illustrated specifically on the tape recordings. See Part VII, Appendix 4.
[2] Signs indicating intonation will always be placed in parentheses following the syllable to which they apply.
[3] *khɲom* is regarded as a pronoun; these are classed with nouns, as a limited sub-class, and represented by **n**.
[4] In the vocabularies of new words which are given for each exercise in Part II, the words are presented, within their grammatical groups, in the order in which they are required for doing the exercise. All vocabulary will also be found in Part VI.
[5] The vowel in the first syllable of this word has, in the speech of many speakers, the diphthongized pronunciation [əu] which is characteristic of the pronunciation of *oː* with final *v*. See footnote to Lesson 2.1, paragraph 12, line ii. re the realization of *oːv*.

lbaeŋ game   *khɲom*[1] I   *saːlaː-rìən* school   *taː* grandfather, old man   *tùː* cupboard

Verbs.[2] *cìh* to mount, to get into, onto, to ride in, on   *thvɤ̀ː* to do, to make   *nɤu* to remain, to be at, in   *lèːŋ* to play   *tɤu* to go

A.1. ʔoːpùk cìh laːn. 2. mdaːy thvɤ̀ː mhoːp. 3. bɔːŋ nɤu phtɛ̀əh. 4. pʔoːn lèːŋ lbaeŋ. 5. khɲom tɤu saːlaː-rìən. 6. taː thvɤ̀ː tùː. 7. pʔoːn tɤu. 8. khɲom nɤu.

B.1. The[3] old man is playing a[3] game. 2. Mother is going home. 3. (My)[4] elder brother/sister is making the meal. 4. Father is staying. 5. (My) younger brother/sister is going to school. 6. Father is making a cupboard. 7. I am getting into the car. 8. Grandfather is going.

14.3. *Attributive verbs,* v

The English sequence, verb 'to be' plus adjective (e.g. 'is small') must be translated into Cambodian by a verb, e.g. *phtɛ̀əh tɔːc*, 'The house is small'. Such verbs are not usually followed by a noun and are often followed immediately by the adverbial particles, *nas*, 'very' and *pèːk*, 'too much'. They will be called attributive verbs while most other verbs will be called operative verbs. Adverbial particles are abbreviated to **a**; the overall pattern for sentences in Exercises 2 and 3 in which the verbs are attributive is: **n v (a).**

Exercise 2

Verbs. **thom*[5] to be big, tall   *tɔːc* to be small   *cas* to be old, to be grown up   *thmɤy* to be new   *kmeːŋ* to be young,   to be beautiful, nice, lovely, good   *lʔɔː* to be large and roomy *tùːlìːəy*

A.1. bɔːŋ thom. 2. pʔoːn tɔːc. 3. taː cas. 4. laːn tɔːc. 5. lbaeŋ thmɤy. 6. khɲom kmeːŋ.

B.1. The school is new. 2. Father is small. 3. (My) elder brother/sister is grown-up. 4. The cupboard is beautiful. 5. The house is roomy. 6. I am tall.

Exercise 3

Nouns. *mìːŋ* aunt   *pùː* uncle
Verbs. *kdau* to be hot   *mìːən* to have
Particles. **a.** *nas* very   *pèːk* too much, too

A.1. tùː lʔɔː nas. 2. bɔːŋ tɤu saːlaː-rìən. 3. mìːŋ nɤu phtɛ̀əh. 4. mhoːp kdau pèːk. 5. pùː mìːən laːn. 6. taː cìh laːn.

B.1. I have a cupboard. 2. (My) younger brother/sister is very tall. 3. Mother is staying at the house. 4. I am too hot. 5. The car is very new. 6. Aunt is making the meal.

---

[1] See footnote 3, p. 58.
[2] See footnote 4, p. 58.
[3] English definite and indefinite articles are not translated into Cambodian except in special circumstances. See Lesson 44, Ex. 55 A, (3).
[4] Parentheses indicate that the enclosed word should not be translated.
[5] For spelling of asterisked forms, see list, Part IV.

14.4. *Noun with attribute* (*noun-verb,* **nv**)

An attributive verb may follow a noun in close junction (i.e. in a close-knit phrase). e.g. *khɲom mìːən phtèəh toːc,* 'I have a small house'. *toːc* here occurs in close junction with the word *phtèəh.* The form of such a sentence may be represented as **n v nv** and regarded as a development of **n v** (**n**) (which is a formula representing either **n v** or **n v n**).

Exercise 4

A.1. pʔoːn lèːŋ lbaeŋ thmᵣy. 2. mìːŋ thvᵣ̀ː mhoːp kdau. 3. ʔoːpùk thvᵣ̀ː tùː thom. 4. pùː mìːən laːn lʔɔː. 5. khɲom tᵣu saːlaː-rìən toːc. 6. taː nᵣu phtèəh tùːlìːəy.

B.1. Aunt has a new house. 2. The old man is getting into a big car. 3. Elder brother/sister goes to a big school. 4. (My) younger brother has a small cupboard. 5. The house is very small. 6. Uncle has a roomy car.

14.5. *Noun with attribute* (*noun-noun,* **nn**)

A noun may have another noun following it in close junction expressing possession and therefore translating English possessive adjective, e.g. 'my' and ''s' as in 'John's'. e.g. *phtèəh khɲom toːc pèːk,* 'My house is too small'. *ʔoːpùk thvᵣ̀ː tùː taː,* 'Father is making grandfather's cupboard'. The first sentence may be represented as **nn v** (**a**) and the second as **n v nn**. They are regarded as further developments of **n v** (**n**).

Exercise 5

Nouns. *vìːə* he, she, they (familiar)   **nèək* you (to equal)

A.1. ʔoːpùk khɲom nᵣu phtèəh. 2. bɔːŋ vìːə tᵣu saːlaː-rìən. 3. pʔoːn nèək toːc nas. 4. phtèəh pùː tùːlìːəy. 5. ʔoːpùk vìːə cas nas. 6. saːlaː-rìən khɲom lʔɔː.

B.1. Aunt's car is very small. 2. Their house is too big. 3. (My) younger (sister)'s school is very nice. 4. His uncle is going home. 5. Father's cupboard is too small. 6. Your mother is tall.

Exercise 6

Nouns. *bɔːŋ-pros* elder brother   *bɔːŋ-srᵣy* elder sister   *pʔoːn-pros* younger brother   *pʔoːn-srᵣy* younger sister   *bɔːŋ-pʔoːn* brothers and sisters, relatives   *ʔoːpùk-mdaːy* parents, father and mother
Verbs. *khᵣ̀ːɲ* to see.

A.1. khɲom khᵣ̀ːɲ ʔoːpùk khɲom. 2. ʔoːpùk-mdaːy mìːən phtèəh thom. 3. bɔːŋ-pʔoːn vìːə nᵣu phtèəh. 4. bɔːŋ-srᵣy nèək tᵣu saːlaː-rìən. 5. pʔoːn-pros khᵣ̀ːɲ tùː thmᵣy. 6. phtèəh thmᵣy lʔɔː nas.

B.1. Your parents are at home. 2. His elder brother has a big car. 3. The big cupboard is new. 4. My younger sister sees you. 5. Their brothers and sisters go to school. 6. The old man is making a new cupboard.

14.6. *Negative statements*

Negative statements are formed by the use of the pre-verbal particle, **p.v.p.** *mùn,* 'not', which immediately precedes the verb. e.g. *khɲom mùn tᵣu saːlaː-rìən,* 'I am not going to school'. **n pv** (**n**).[1] The final phrase particle, **f.**,

---

[1] **p** (= particle) is adequate to indicate the pre-verbal particle in sentence analyses since the position of the symbol, immediately before the verb, shows that it is the pre-verbal particle.

tè:, 'indeed, (not) at all', may be used to give emphasis to the negation. It comes after the nouns and verbs of the sentence-form. e.g. *khɲom mùɯn nɤ̌u*, 'I'm not staying'. *khɲom mùɯn nɤ̌u tè:*, 'I'm *not* staying'. *mì:ŋ mùɯn nɤ̌u phtèəh*, 'Aunt isn't at home'. *mì:ŋ mùɯn nɤ̌u phtèəh tè:*, 'Aunt is *not* at home'. The above four sentences may be represented as **n pv (n) (f)**.

Note. tè: occurs less frequently and rather idiomatically as an intensifier of affirmative statements. It will also be met in the next lesson with the sense 'or not?' in the formation of questions.

Exercise 7

Nouns. *phsa:(r)* market   *trɤy* fish   *trɤy-ŋìət* dried fish
Verbs. *cùɯt* to be near   *tèɲ* to buy   *lùək* to sell
Particles. *mùɯn* **p.v.p.** not   *tè:* **f.** indeed, (not) at all

A.1. vì:ə mùɯn tɤ̌u phsa:(r) thom. 2. phtèəh khɲom mùɯn cùɯt phsa:(r) tè:. 3. mda:y mùɯn tèɲ trɤy tè:. 4. p?o:n-pros khɲom lùək trɤy-ŋìət. 5. bo:ŋ-srɤy vì:ə mùɯn l?o: tè:. 6. khɲom mùɯn mì:ən bo:ŋ-p?o:n tè:.

B.1. The old man's house is not big. 2. The elder brother's school is not at all big. 3. Your parents are not going-in (*cìh*) the car. 4. I am not buying dried fish. 5. The big cupboard is not nice. 6. (His) uncle *isn't* selling his car.

LESSON 15

SIMPLE QUESTIONS AND ANSWERS; NOUN WITH ATTRIBUTE; TRANSLATION OF 'YOU'

15.1. *Sentence-tune 2 (a) and (b)*[1]

Sentence-form I composes a straightforward question if followed by the final phrase particle, *tè:*, or the two final phrase particles, **rùː tè:* used together in this order and pronounced with sentence-tune 2. This tune is characterized by a rise from mid to high level (´) on the last syllable:—

2.(*a*) *nèək tɤ̌u phsa:(r) tè: (´)*? Are you going to the market?
      nèək tɤ̌u phtèəh rùː tè: (´)? Are you going home?

2.(*b*) Again, as in 1.(*b*), the sentence subject may be emphasized by separation (rise in pitch with following pause) but in questions this is not usual unless the sentence subject is expressed in several words.

Note. In Cambodian there is no alteration of the word-order for questions.

Exercise 8

Nouns. *bɔntùp* room   *kɔntè:l* mat
Particles. **f.** *tè:?* not?   **rùː?* or   **rùː tè:?* or not?

A.1. vì:ə nɤ̌u bɔntùp vì:ə rùː tè:? 2. nèək mì:ən kɔntè:l l?o: tè:? 3. mì:ŋ mùɯn tèɲ trɤy to:c tè:. 4. mho:p kdau rùː tè:? 5. bo:ŋ-p?o:n nèək nɤ̌u phtèəh tè:? 6. ?o:pùk mì:ən kɔntè:l tè:?

B.1. Do you sell dried fish? 2. Is the nice mat in your room? 3. Do you see his parents? 4. Their younger brother goes to a beautiful school. 5. Is uncle's house big? 6. Has she a new car?

---

[1] Illustrated specifically on the tape recordings. See Part VII, Appendix 4.

15.2. *Responding particles,* r[1]

In polite conversation a respectful reply, made to equals, elders and 'betters', should be introduced by the appropriate responding particle. For male speakers this is *baːɪ̀*; for female speakers it is *cah. No idea of affirmation need be conveyed by these particles, e.g. *ʔoːpùk nèək nỳu ʔae naː* (')? (= where) Where is your father? *cah* (.),[2] *ʔoːpùk nỳu phtèəh* (\\). Father is at home (r, **n v n**). The responding particles may, however, convey alone an affirmative answer,[3] e.g. *ʔoːpùk nèək nỳu phtèəh tèː* (')? Is your father at home? *baːɪ̀* (\\). Yes.

A negative answer, given politely is as follows:—

pʔoːn tỳu phsaː(r) tèː (')? Are you going to the market, younger brother? *baːɪ̀* (.) *tèː* (\\). No.

This is a complete polite answer but it would be possible also to add '*khɲom mùn tỳu tèː.*' An abrupt answer would be '*tèː*' alone.

It is possible in informal speech to use a responding sentence in which no subject is expressed, since this has been mooted[4] in the question sentence. e.g. *pʔoːn nỳu phtèəh tèː? baːɪ̀ tèː, mùn nỳu phtèəh tèː*. 'Is younger brother/ sister at home?' 'No, he/she isn't.'

If, however, one is speaking about someone to whom or about whom one should show respect or if one wishes to speak formally and very politely one would express the subject. In referring to a grandparent, uncle or father, for example, one would express the subject and if one wished to use a pronoun as subject the pronoun would be *kɔ̀ət* (see Exercise 9) and not *vìːə*.

Exercise 9

Nouns. *bɔŋʔuːəc* window   *kɔ̀ət* he, she, they (respectful)
Verb. *kmìːən = mùn mìːən*
Responding particles. **r**. *baːɪ̀* (male speakers), *cah (female speakers)

A.1. ba:ɪ̀ tèː, bɔntùp khɲom kmìːən bɔŋʔuːəc thom tèː. 2. cah tèː, ʔoːpùk-mdaːy mùn nỳu phtèəh tèː. 3. pùː thvỳː tùː tèː? baːɪ̀, kɔ̀ət thvỳː tùː. 4. bɔːŋ cìh laːn ʔoːpùk rùː tèː? baːɪ̀. 5. laːn vìːə thmɤy tèː.? cah, thmɤy.

B. Sentences 1–3 to be translated as for male speakers replying; 4–5 as for female speakers replying. 1. Have you a big room? No, my room is small. 2. Is aunt going to market? Yes. 3. Does the old man go in the car? Yes. 4. Is the meal hot? Yes, it is very hot. 5. Is uncle making a big cupboard? No, he is not making a cupboard at all.

15.3. *Noun with attribute (noun-numeral-numeral coefficient,* **nxc**)

A numeral, **x**, may follow the noun in close junction, e.g. *phtèəh pìː(r)*, two houses. In certain kinds of counting a numeral coefficient, **c**, follows the numeral, also in close junction. This is generally the case when human beings

---

[1] Their intonation, discussed in this section, is illustrated specifically on the tape recordings. See Part VII, Appendix 4.

[2] Responding particles, preceding a reply, are uttered with a tune separate from the sentence-tune, either on a rather low, level note, short and unstressed, (.) or, when more lively reply is intended, on a note falling from mid level (ˌ).

[3] In this case they bear a complete sentence-tune (\\).

[4] i.e. 'introduced'.

are counted. Any noun which refers to human beings, e.g. *bɔːŋ*, *taː*, etc., will, if followed by a numeral, be followed after that by the numeral coefficient, *nèak*, 'person'. *poñmaːn*, 'how much, how many' and *craən*, 'much, many' behave like numerals and are therefore also classed as **x**, e.g. *bɔːŋ poñmaːn nèak?* **nxc** 'How many elder brothers/sisters?' *bɔːŋ-srɤy pìː(r) nèak* **nxc** 'Two elder sisters'. *mnèak*, a word which has to be classed as a particle, since it is neither verb, noun, numeral nor numeral coefficient, nor divisible into two independent parts, is used for 'one person'; *mùəy nèak*, of which it is a contraction, is not used. e.g. *pùː mnèak*, 'one uncle'. The following sentence illustrates the use of a numeral in a complete sentence:—

khɲom mìːən tok pìː(r) **n v nx** I have two tables.

Exercise 10

Nouns. *tok table   *cau* grandchild
Verb. *dɤŋ* to know
Numerals. one *mùəy* two *pìː(r)* three *bɤy* four *buːən* five *pram* six *pram-mùəy* seven *prampùl eight *pram-bɤy* nine *pram-buːən* ten *dɔp* how much, how many *poñmaːn* *craən* much, many
Numeral coefficient. *nèak* person. This word is spelt as the transcription indicates and is thus distinguished from *nèak 'you'.

A.1. **pʔoːn nèak mìːən phtèəh poñmaːn?**[1] **baːt̚, vìːə mìːən phtèəh pìː(r). 2. nèak mìːən bɔːŋ-pʔoːn poñmaːn nèak? cah, khɲom mìːən bɔːŋ bɤy nèak. 3. ʔoːpùk nèak mìːən bɔːŋ-pʔoːn poñmaːn nèak? baːt̚, khɲom mùm dɤŋ tèː. kɔ̀ət mìːən craən nèak.**[2] **4. nèak mìːən tok poñmaːn? baːt̚, khɲom mìːən tok pìː(r). 5. taː mìːən cau poñmaːn nèak? baːt̚, mìːən pram nèak. 6. mìːŋ tèɲ trɤy poñmaːn? kɔ̀ət tèɲ buːən.**

B. Translate 1–3 as for male speaker replying and 4–6 as for female. 1. How many grandchildren has uncle? He has two. 2. How many cupboards has mother? One.[3] 3. How many fish have you? Five. 4. How many tables have they? Three. 5. How many brothers and sisters has he? I don't know. 6. How many aunts have you? Many.

15.4. *The translation of 'you'*

The noun, *nèak*, and other words which will be introduced later, may be translated as 'you' and may translate 'you' when a grown-up is addressed on friendly terms of equality. The words *taː*, *mìːŋ*, *bɔːŋ*, *pʔoːn*, *ʔoːpùk*, *mdaːy* and other similar 'titles' are, however, normally used to translate English 'you' when grandfather, aunt, elder sibling, younger sibling, father, mother, etc., are being addressed. Thus the question asked in A.6 of Exercise 10 has the following alternative translation, 'How many fish are you buying, aunt?'. Only the context, provided here in the answer (by the word *kɔ̀ət*, 'she'), but absent in an exercise consisting of isolated sentences, can show whether in

---

[1] Questions in which *poñmaːn* occurs do not need *tèː?* or *rùː tèː?* at the end, since *poñmaːn* is itself a question-word.

[2] It will be noted that in some of the responding sentences the numeral, and numeral coefficient if required, are used without the noun, which is already mooted by the question.

[3] In a responding sentence in informal speech it is possible for just a keyword such as 'one' to be given, but a more polite formal sentence would resemble those given in Exercise 10 A.

such sentences aunt is being spoken about in the third person or addressed. There is no ambiguity in the question in A.2 of Exercise 10, since *nèək* is always 'you', but only the context can clarify A.5. The student should offer alternative translations from now on, where these are possible.

Exercise 11

A.1. mìːŋ mìːən bɔːŋ poñmaːn nèək? 2. taː khr̀ːɲ laːn khɲom tèːP 3. cau tr̀u saːlaː-rìən tèːP 4. nèək dɤŋ tèːP 5. pPoːn tèɲ kɔntèːl tèːP 6. Poːpùk nèək nɤ̀u phtèəh tèːP

B.1. Are you making the meal, mother? 2. Is uncle making a cupboard?
3. Do you know, grandfather? 4. Elder brother, are you staying at home?
5. Are you buying dried fish, aunt? 6. Is aunt going to market?

Lesson 16

Noun Construct; Translation of 'I'

16.1. *The noun construct,* **N**

We have seen that a noun may function alone (*phtèəh*, **n**, 'a house, the house'), or may be closely followed by an attributive verb (*phtèəh thom*, **nv**, 'a/the big house'), or by another noun (*phtèəh taː*, **nn**, 'grandfather's house'), or by a numeral (*phtèəh bry*, **nx**, 'three houses'), or by a numeral and numeral coefficient (*mənùs(s)* (= man) *buːən nèək*, **nxc**, 'four men'). It is possible for a noun to be followed by more than one such attribute. e.g. *mənùs(s) thom bry nèək* (**nvxc**) 'three tall men'; *cau khɲom pram nèək* (**nnxc**) 'my five grandchildren'; *phtèəh thom thmry* (**nvv**) 'a big new house'; *bɔntùp tɔːc mùːəy*, **nvx**, 'one little room'; *bɔːŋ pìː(r) nèək khɲom* (**nxcn**) 'my two elder siblings'.

The order in which attributes occur is not fixed; a numeral, for example, with its classifier if required, may come before or after an attributive verb, a noun before or after either, etc.

16.2. *The post-nominal particles,* **post n.p.**, **nìh, *nùh and Pae-tìət*

Words which are neither nouns, verbs, numerals nor numeral coefficients are particles of various kinds. Several particles have been met already: the adverbial particles, **a.**, *nas*, and *pèːk*; the pre-verbal particle, **p.v.p.**, *mùn*; the final phrase particles, **f.**, *tèː* and *rùː*; the responding particles, **r.**, *baːt* and *cah*. The particles *nìh*, 'this, these'; *nùh*, 'that, those', and *Pae-tìət*, 'other', usually occur as the last word in the closely knit sequence which follows the noun, e.g. *mənùs(s) thom nùh*, 'that tall man/those tall men'. (Only the context can show which is intended.) *mənùs(s) thom bry nèək nìh*, 'these three tall men'; *bɔntùp nìh*, 'this room, these rooms'; *bɔntùp khɲom mùːəy nìh*, 'this one room of mine'; *phtèəh tɔːc Pae-tìət*, 'other small houses'; *phtèəh thmry khɲom nùh*, 'that new house of mine'.

16.3. *A formulaic representation of the noun construct*

The kinds of word-sequences described in 1 and 2 above will be called noun constructs and will be represented as **N** at the top level of sentence analysis. At the lowest level of analysis a symbol represents each word, e.g.

cau khɲom pìː(r) nèək nùh **N** [1]   those two grandchildren of mine
nnxcp

Exercise 12

Nouns. *mɔən* fowl   *sac-crùːk* pork   *koːn* child   *koːn-pros* son   *koːn-srʋy* daughter   *slʋk-tnaot* leaf of sugar-palm   *sboːʋ* thatch
Verbs. *thlay* to be dear, expensive   *prɔk* to be roofed with

A.1. mìːŋ tèɲ mɔən thom buːən nùh tèːʔ 2. nèək khʋ̀ːɲ sac-crùːk nùh rùː tèːʔ thlay nas! 3. pù: mìːən koːn poñ̃maːn nèəkʔ baːṭ, kɔ̀ət mìːən bʋy nèək. 4. phtɛ̀əh ʔae-tìət prɔk slʋk-tnaot tèːʔ baːṭ tèː, prɔk sboːʋ. 5. phtɛ̀əh taː mìːən bɔŋʔuːəc poñ̃maːnʔ baːṭ, mìːən pìː(r). 6. taː tèɲ sac-crùːk nìh rùː tèːʔ tèː, thlay nas.

B.1. How many fowls have you, uncle? 2. His younger sister is buying pork. 3. My two sons go to that big new school. 4. I have three uncles. You have four aunts. 5. Are you buying the other dried fish, younger sister? 6. Grandfather's two elder sisters are staying at this house.

16.4. *Sentence intonation*

The longer sentences which are now being introduced often need to be pronounced as two phrases,[2] the first noun construct being uttered with rising pitch and followed by a pause and the rest of the sentence being pronounced with the tune appropriate to it (statement tune or question tune). The rise to mid-level characterizes the pronunciation of the last or only syllable of the noun construct. Previous syllables, if any, may be stepped downwards from a moderately high note (¯).

e.g. *bɔːŋ*(¯)-*pros khɲom* (,|) *tʋ̀u saːlaː-rìən nùh* (\). My elder brother goes to that school.
khɲom (,|) *tʋ̀u saːlaː-rìən thom nùh* (\). I go to that big school.
koːn (¯) *pìː(r) nèək nùh* (,|) *tʋ̀u saːlaː-rìən rùː tèː* (') ? Are those two children going to school?

Exercise 13

Nouns. *nèək-bɔmraə* servant   *sac* flesh, meat
Verbs. *thaok* to be cheap   *praə* to use, to use the services of, to have (servants)   *cam* to wait for   to summon *hau*   to go in (= ride in) *cìh*

A.1. nèək-bɔmraə pìː(r) nèək nùh tʋ̀u phsaː(r). 2. vìːə tèɲ sac-crùːk thaok. 3. sac thaok nìh mùm lʔɔː tèː. 4. ʔoːpùk-mdaːy khɲom mùm praə nèək-bɔmraə tèː. 5. tùː thom nùh lʔɔː nas! 6. bɔːŋ-pʔoːn nèək cam nèək tèːʔ

B.1. Father is summoning those three servants. 2. The two children are waiting for their aunt. 3. Is that big house roofed with thatch? 4. Does uncle go in that little car? 5. These two pigs are not at all dear. 6. Is uncle's father waiting for you? No, he is going to his daughter's house.

---

[1] Post-nominal particles, like pre-verbal particles, may be represented in sentence analyses by **p**, since their position in the analysis indicates their nature.
[2] The term 'phrase' is used to mean any part of the sentence which is separated from the rest by pause and rise in pitch. Sentence-tunes 1.(*b*) and 2.(*b*), which are involved here, are illustrated specifically on the tape recordings. See Part VII, Appendix 4.

16.5. *The translation of 'I'*

The words *taː, mìːŋ, ʔoːpùk, mdaːy*, etc., which may often represent English 'you', if grandfather, aunt, etc., are being addressed, may also represent English 'I' when the speaker is speaking to someone who actually is a grandchild, nephew, etc., or is of suitable age to be so addressed in friendly conversation.

e.g. *taː tŗu phtèəh rùː tèː? baːt̯, taː tŗu phtèəh.* Are you going home, grandfather? Yes, I am going home.

Only the context can show that grandfather is addressed and replying. The words could equally mean, 'Is grandfather going home? Yes, he is'.

Exercise 14

Nouns. *sɔmpùət* material, sarong　*pòə̯(rŋ)* colour　*khao* trousers　*ʔaːv* dress, blouse, shirt　*khao-ʔaːv* suit　*dɔːn* grandmother
Verbs. *srəlaɲ* to like, love　*krəhɔːm* to be red　*sliək* to wear below the waist　*pèək* to wear above the waist or on feet and legs　*sliək-pèək* to wear in general, to wear (a suit)　*sɔː* to be white　*khmau* to be black　*lùəŋ* to be yellow　*khiəv* to be blue　*baytɔːŋ* to be green　*baːraŋ* to be European, French

Alternative translations may be offered for some of the sentences.

A.1. mìːɲ tèɲ sɔmpùət rùː tèː? cah, khɲom srəlaɲ pòə̯(rŋ) krəhɔːm nùh. 2. bɔːŋ sliək khao sɔː tèː? tèː, bɔːŋ sliək khao khmau. 3. pùː pèək ʔaːv thlay. 4. dɔːn mìːən ʔaːv sɔː tèː? cah, dɔːn mìːən ʔaːv sɔː pìː(r). 5. pʔoːn sliək-pèək khao-ʔaːv baːraŋ rùː tèː? baːt̯ tèː, pʔoːn sliək sɔmpùət. 6. sɔmpùət nih thlay nas. taː mìːən sɔmpùət thaok rùː tèː? baːt̯ tèː, khɲom kmìːən sɔmpùət thaok tèː.

B.1. Is uncle wearing those white trousers? No, he is wearing a sarong. 2. Aunt, are you going to the big market? No, I am going to the little market. 3. Are you buying that yellow material, mother? Yes. 4. Does your elder brother wear European suits? No, he wears a sarong. 5. One grandson is wearing a blue shirt. One is wearing black trousers. 6. Does his mother wear a red dress? No, she does not.

LESSON 17

VERB CONSTRUCT; ADVERBIAL CONSTRUCT; TRANSLATION OF 'IT'

17.1. *The verb construct,* **V**

All the words, which, in the sentences used so far, come after the noun construct, between the pre-verbal particle, e.g. *mùn*, if it occurs and any adverbial or final phrase particle, e.g. *nas, pèːk, tèː* which occurs are termed the verb construct. This may consist only of the main verb (i.e. the verb before which a pre-verbal particle may occur) or of the main verb + a second noun construct. A noun construct may thus itself be part of the verb construct. The overall pattern for sentence-form I, including all the components so far introduced, may be expressed as follows:—

Responding particle	Noun construct	Pre-verbal particle	Verb construct	Adverbial particle	Final phrase particle
r	N	p	V	a	f
baːì	n	mùn	v	nas	tèː
	nv		vN		
cah	nn } p		n		
	nxc,		nv } p	pèːk	rùː
	etc.		nn		
			nxc,		
			etc.		

17.2. *Independent noun constructs*

A noun construct which forms the sentence-subject and may be separated as one phrase when the sentence is pronounced as two phrases, will be termed an independent noun construct, in contrast to the dependent noun construct which occurs as part of the verb construct.

17.3. *Expressions of time, manner, place and circumstance*

These may be composed as follows:—

1. They may be adverbial particles, **a**.

e.g. *sʔaek* tomorrow **ʔʋyloːʋ*, **ʔʋyloːʋ=nìh* now *phlìːəm* immediately *rùəy-rùəy* constantly *bɔntec* a little *mkhaːŋ* at one side *mdɔːŋ-mdɔːŋ* sometimes.

2. They may be adverbial constructs, **A**. These consist of a word or series of words similar to a noun construct, preceded by a pre-nominal particle. The following are pre-nominal particles of frequent occurrence:—

pìː from (of place or time), at (of time) *knoŋ* in *ʔae*[1] at, to (a place), as to *ʔɔmpìː* about, concerning *nʋu* at *nʋu-cùt* near *taːm* along *daoy* along, by *kraom* under *lʋ̀ː* on *kraoy* behind *nʋu-mùk(h)* in front *mùn* before (of time)

e.g. *pìː saːlaː-rìən* from school *nʋu phtèəh* at home *kraom tok* under the table.

3. They may be adverbial constructs of a limited type of construction in which the particle is often absent but before which one may often be used without altering the meaning of the sentence or its construction. Such expressions usually consist of a noun such as *thŋay*, 'day', *yùp*, 'night', *prùk*, 'morning', *lŋìːəc*, 'afternoon', *khaːŋ*, 'side', *tìː* or *kɔnlaeŋ*, 'place', followed by a post-nominal particle, such as *nìh*, 'this', *nùh*, 'that', *naː*, 'some, any', *naː?*, 'which?', *meɲ* or *mèɲ*, 'last, previous, just past'.[2]

e.g. *thŋay nìh* today, *kɔnlaeŋ nìh* in this place, *tìː naː* at, in some, any place, *khaːŋ naː?* which side, on which side?, *yùp meɲ* last night, *prùk nìh* this morning, *lŋìːəc naː* some, any afternoon.

---

[1] *ʔae*, 'at', refers to places at some distance from the speaker; *nʋu* may be used to refer to the place where the speaker is.

[2] *meɲ* is usually used to refer to short periods of time, such as 'night', 'day', 'morning'.

The following pairs of sentences demonstrate the possibility of using a pre-nominal particle with such expressions:—

thŋay nìh khɲom tɤ̀u kɔmpùəŋ caːm.
nɤ̀u thŋay nìh khɲom tɤ̀u kɔmpùəŋ caːm. } I am going to Kompung Cham today.

thŋay nùh khɲom tɤ̀u kɔmpùəŋ caːm.
pìː thŋay nùh khɲom tɤ̀u kɔmpùəŋ caːm. } I went to Kompung Cham that day.

khaːŋ nùh nèək khɤ̀ːɲ phtèəh thom mùːəy.
ʔae khaːŋ nùh nèək khɤ̀ːɲ phtèəh thom mùːəy. } On that side you see a large house.

Expressions such as *thŋay nìh, yùp meɲ* may be further catalysed as adverbial constructs and not nominal constructs by their occurrence in the position following the verb construct, e.g.

khɲom mùn tɤ̀u kɔmpùəŋ caːm thŋay nìh tèː. I am not going to Kompung Cham today.

An independent noun construct does not occur in this position.

17.4. *Sentence-form I expressed as a formula*

This may now be expressed formulaically in the most economical way as **N V**, since **N** and **V** are its only essential components. Sentences may include one or more expressions of time, place, manner or circumstance, occurring in the positions indicated below and particles occurring in their appropriate positions.

(r) (A/a) N (ᴘ)V (A/a) (f)

e.g. *baːt, nɤ̀u phnùm-pèɲ nèək khɤ̀ːɲ phtèəh thmɤy craən nas.* Yes, in Phnom Penh you see very many new houses.

      r, **A　N V**　　a
      r, **ᴘN n vN**　　a
      r, **ᴘn n vɴvx** a

17.5. *Sentence-tunes 1 (c) and 2 (c)*[1]

An adverbial construct occurring in the first position indicated above may be pronounced as a separate phrase. In a sentence such as the above, sentence-tune 1 (*b*) would thus be used:—

baːt (,) *nɤ̀u phnùm-pèɲ* (,|) *nèək khɤ̀ːɲ phtèəh thmɤy craən nas* (\).

In many of the sentences which will soon be met, however, there will be a need to pause after both **A** and **N**,

e.g. *pìː thŋay nùh* (,|) *bɔːŋ-pros khɲom* (,|) *mùn tɤ̀u saːlaː-rìən tèː* (\).[2]
From that day, my elder brother did not go to school.

This tune, and its counterpart in the question tune, will be called 'sentence-tune 1 (*c*)' and '2 (*c*)' respectively.

---

[1] Illustrated specifically on the tape recordings. See Part VII, Appendix 4.
[2] The signs used to indicate intonation might seem to suggest that the tunes for two phrases such as the first two phrases in this sentence are identical; in fact, there would be some variation of pitch and tune.

17.6. *The translation of 'it' and 'they' with reference to objects*

vìːə may be used to translate 'it' and 'they' when reference is made to animals but for objects Cambodians prefer to repeat the noun to which reference is made or make no reference.

e.g. That boat is very nice. Yes, uncle is buying it.

tùːk nùh lʔɔː nas! baːt, pùː tèɲ tùːk nùh.

Do you see that boat? Yes, I see it.

nèək khɤ̀ːɲ tùːk nùh tèː? baːt, khɲom khɤ̀ːɲ.

The use of *nùh* in a reply, as in the first example, gives the sense 'the one already mentioned'. *nùh* is used similarly in narratives to refer a second time to a character or object where in English we have 'the', e.g. *taː nùh*, 'the old man (whom we have mentioned already) . . . '.

Exercise 15

Nouns. *sìəvphɤ̀u* book *srok* country *srok-phùːmìːə* Burma *kmuːəy* nephew, niece *kmuːəy-pros* nephew *kmuːəy-srɤy* niece *srok-sìəm* Siam *thŋay* day *yɤ̀ːŋ* we

Verbs. *mɤ̀ːl* to look at, read *phùːmìːə* to be Burmese **ʔɔŋklèːs* to be English *sìəm* to be Siamese *yùːən* to be Vietnamese *mɔ̀ːk* to come

Particles pre n.p. *knoŋ* in *ʔɔmpìː* about *pìː* from, at (of time) *lɤ̀ː* on in front of *nɤu-mùk(h)* a. **ʔɤyloːv* now *sʔaek* tomorrow immediately *phlìːəm*

A.1. *ʔoːpùk nɤu knoŋ bɔntùp. kɔət mɤ̀ːl sìəvphɤ̀u ʔɔmpìː srok-phùːmìːə.*
2. *kmuːəy-srɤy khɲom mùːn tɤu srok-ʔɔŋklèːs tèː. kɔət nɤu knoŋ srok-sìəm.*
3. *thŋay nìh bɔːŋ-srɤy nèək pèək ʔaːv lʔɔː nas.* 4. *ʔɤyloːv yɤ̀ːŋ mɔ̀ːk pìː srok-yùːən. sʔaek yɤ̀ːŋ tɤu srok-sìəm.* 5. *yɤ̀ːŋ kmìːən sìəvphɤ̀u baytoːŋ nìh knoŋ saːlaː-rìən yɤ̀ːŋ tèː.* 6. *sɔmpùət phùːmìːə nèək nɤu lɤ̀ː tok thmɤy.*

B.1. Does grandmother live in that big white house? No, she lives in this house. 2. Uncle has many books about England. Are they in his room? Yes, they are in (his) little cupboard. 3. Are you going to the market immediately, elder brother? Yes, I am. 4. Mother is buying that expensive red material from Siam. It is very nice. 5. Do you see the white material on the table? It is very cheap. 6. Are you buying that black material in front of the white material, aunt? No, it is very dear.

17.7. *The context of time; past, present and future*

The Cambodian verb does not change its form to convey any idea of time. The sentence, *vìːə tɤu phsaːr)*, may have to be translated as 'He went to market', 'He is going to market' or 'He will go to market', according to the context. Sometimes the situation itself makes the context clear. When, for example, someone trips over an unseen object and falls, an English comment might be, 'He didn't see it'. In Cambodian this would be *'mùn khɤ̀ːɲ!'*. A particle, e.g. *sʔaek*, 'tomorrow', or an adverbial construct, e.g. *yùp meɲ*, 'last night', is sufficient to establish the time context. e.g. *sʔaek khɲom tɤu phtèəh vìːə.* 'Tomorrow I shall go to his house'. *yùp meɲ pùː tɤu phtèəh pɛ̀ːt(y).* 'Last night uncle went to the hospital'. Once the context is established, further indications of time are unnecessary. e.g. *pìː msɤl mìːŋ tɤu phsaːr).* *kɔət khɤ̀ːɲ sɔmpùət sìəm lʔɔː pɔɲtae mùn tèɲ tèː.* 'Yesterday aunt went to the market. She saw (some) lovely Siamese material but she didn't buy it'.

The pre-verbal particle, *nùŋ*, conveys the idea of futurity or intention and may thus establish a context of time. e.g. *khɲom nùŋ mɤ̀ːl siəvphɤ̌u nùh ʔɔmpìː srok khmae(r)*. I intend to read/shall read that book about Cambodia. *nùŋ* may occur in conjunction with an expression of time. e.g. *sʔaek khɲom nùŋ tèɲ laːn nùh*. Tomorrow I intend to/shall buy that car.

Exercise 16

Nouns. *yùp* night *cao(r)* thief *phtɛ̀əh-pɛ̌ːt̀(y)* hospital *lŋìːəc* afternoon *msɤl* (usually used either with *pìː* preceding or *meɲ* following) yesterday *chnam* year *phìːəsaː* language *tùːk* boat *pèːl* time *kèː* one, people, someone, he, she, they   morning *prùk* week *ʔaːtùt(y)*

Verbs. *coːl* to enter *suːə(r)* to ask a question *tɤ̀u suːə(r)* to go to visit *chùː* to be ill *rìən* to learn *baːraŋsaes* to be French *ŋìət* to be dried and salted

Particles. **post n.p.** *meɲ* (or *mèɲ*) just past, last   **a.** *mnɛ̀ək* alone, one person *bɔntec* a little

Expression. *bɔntec tìət* soon, a little later   from time to time, sometimes *yùː(r)-yùː(r) mdɔːŋ*

A.1. **yùp meɲ cao(r) mnɛ̀ək coːl phtɛ̀əh taː. kɔ̀ət mùn dɤŋ tèː.** 2. **khɲom nùŋ tɤ̀u suːə(r) mìːŋ khɲom knoŋ phtɛ̀əh-pɛ̌ːt̀(y) lŋìːəc nìh. kɔ̀ət chùː: pìː msɤl.** 3. **chnam nìh cau nùŋ rìən phìːəsaː: baːraŋsaes.** 4. **bɔntec tìət pùː nùŋ tèɲ tùːk mùːəy.** 5. **pèːl nùh bɔːŋ-srɤy nɛ̀ək chùː: bɔntec.** 6. **knoŋ tìː nìh kèː mùn lùək trɤy-ŋìət tèː.**

B.1. This morning I shall buy those two books about Siam. 2. Their grand-children didn't enter the house that day. 3. Did the three thieves enter the house from that side? 4. From that day her younger brother has been (= stayed) in this hospital. 5. We have visited him from time to time. 6. Yesterday that old man was selling fish here.

LESSON 18

INTERROGATIVE WORDS

18.1. *Interrogative expressions of fixed position*

In direct questions some expressions which translate English 'why ...?' come before the independent noun construct and others, like those which translate English 'how ...?', 'when ...?' and 'where ...?', come at the end of the sentence. They are in fact mostly either adverbial particles or adverbial constructs and are thus occupying appropriate positions.

mëc . . . . ?		
mdëc . . . . ?	(colloquial)	why ...?
mëc-*kɔː . . . . ?		
mdëc-*kɔː . . . . . . ?		

häet(o)-ʔvɤy-baːn-cìːə (formal, literary) why, for what reason?

. . . . *pìː-prùəh ʔvɤy?*	for what reason?
. . . . *daoy häet(o) ʔvɤy?*	

.... *ya:ŋ mëc?* (colloquial)
.... *ya:ŋ do:c-mdëc?* (formal, literary and colloquial) } how, by what means?
.... *do:c-mdëc?*

....*ʔɔŋkal?* (colloquial)
.... *ka:l na:?* (formal, literary and colloquial) } when ....?

.... *pì: ʔɔŋkal?* (colloquial)
.... *pì: ka:l na:?* (formal, literary and colloquial) } when ....? (in the past)

.... *na:?* where ....?
....*ʔae na:?* where, to what place ....?
.... *nɤu-ʔae na:?* where, in what place ....?

e.g. *mëc-kɔ: vì:ə nɤu phtèəh thŋay nùh?* Why did he stay at home that day?
pù: tɤu na? Where is uncle going?/Where are you going, uncle?
nèək mò:k phnùm-pěɲ pì: ʔɔŋkal? When did you come to Phnom Penh?
vì:ə tha: do:c-mdëc? What (lit. how?) does he say?
mì:ŋ cìh yùən(t)-hɔh ka:l na:? What time do you board the plane, aunt?

Exercise 17

Nouns. *lò:k* sir, Mr., you (polite, formal)　*lò:k-krù:* teacher (polite for speaking to or about the teacher)　*phnùm-pěɲ* Phnom Penh　*yùən(t)-hɔh* aeroplane　*kɔmpùəŋ-ca:m* Kompung Cham　place *kɔnlaeŋ*　steamer *kɔpal*
Verbs. *ceh* to know, to know how　to put *dak*　to get *ba:n*　to be .... still *nɤu*
Particles. **m.** *mëc-*kɔ:* why　**a.** *bɔntec-bɔntu:əc* to a small extent, just a little　**pre n.p.** *nɤu-ʔae* at　*ʔae* at, to　*pì:* from (time and place), at (past time)　**post n.p.** *meɲ* just past, last
Expressions. *pì: ʔɔŋkal* when (in the past)

A.1. *mëc-kɔ: lò:k-krù: tɤu sa:la:-rìən thŋay nih? thŋay nih yɤ:ŋ mùm rìən tè:.*
2. *ta: mì:ən phtèəh nɤu-ʔae na:? ba:t, khɲom mì:ən phtèəh ʔae phnùm-pěɲ.*
3. *lò:k ceh phì:əsa: ba:raŋsaes rùɤ: tè:? ba:t, khɲom ceh bɔntec-bɔntu:əc.*
4. *nèək tɤu srok-siəm do:c-mdëc? ba:t, khɲom cìh yùən(t)-hɔh.* 5. *mì:ŋ cɔl phtèəh-pě:t(y) pì: ʔɔŋkal? cah, mì:ŋ cɔl pì: prɤk meɲ.* 6. *pì: msɤl meɲ pù: nèək cìh tù:k. kɔət tɤu na:? cah, pù: tɤu kɔmpùəŋ-ca:m.*

B.1. Why is grandmother still in hospital? Do you know, uncle? 2. Where did you put those books? In that cupboard of uncle's. 3. How did he come from England? Did he come by (= *cìh*) aeroplane? 4. When will those four grandchildren visit their grandmother? 5. How shall I get a place in that school? 6. For what reason does that steamer come to Kompung Cham from Phnom Penh?

18.2. *Interrogative words which form part of a noun construct or adverbial construct*

English 'who/whom?' and interrogative adjectives 'which/what?', are translated by means of post-nominal particles following a noun.[1] 'How many' is translated by the numeral, *pɔɲma:n:*—

---

[1] This is the case, too, with the expressions, *ya:ŋ mëc* and *ka:l na:*, in Lesson 18.1 above, but these differ from the constructs discussed here in having a fixed position in the sentence.

.... nèək naː .... ?	Who, Whom .... ?
.... siəvphỳu naː .... ?	Which book(s) .... ?
.... siəvphỳu naː-mùːəy .... ?	Which (one) book .... ?
.... siəvphỳu naː-khlah .... ?	Which (several) books .... ?
.... häet(o) ʔvʀy .... ?	What reason .... ?
.... häet(o) ʔvʀy-mùːəy .... ?	What reason .... ?
.... häet(o) ʔvʀy-khlah .... ?	What reasons .... ?
.... mənùs(s) poñmaːn nèək .... ?	How many men .... ?
.... ʔvʀy .... ?	
.... sʔʀy .... ?	What .... ?
.... ʔʀy .... ?	

In English the question word comes first. Thus both 'who' (subject) and 'whom' (object) have first place in the sentence. e.g. Who saw him? Whom did he see? In Cambodian the same order is maintained as in a statement (subject-verb-object). e.g.

nèək naː khỳːɲ vìːə? Who saw him?
vìːə khỳːɲ nèək naː? Whom did he see?
siəvphỳu naː thmʀy? Which books are new?
vìːə tèɲ siəvphỳu naː-mùːəy? Which book is he buying?
kɔ̀ət mìːən kaː(r) ʔvʀy knoŋ tìː nìh? What business has he here?
mənùs(s) poñmaːn nèək mòːk phtèəh? How many men are coming to the house?
lòːk khỳːɲ mənùs(s) poñmaːn nèək? How many men do you see?
vìːə mìːən ʔvʀy /sʔʀy/ʔʀy knoŋ phtèəh? What has he in the house?
vìːə dak siəvphỳu knoŋ tùː naː? In which cupboard did he put the book?

Exercise 18

Nouns. *khsae* string *tùː-kroŋ* city, town *koːn-sʀs(s)* pupil *thnak* level, class in school Vietnamese *yùːən*
Verbs. *boŋrìən* to teach *tha:* to say
Particles. **post n.p.** *naː-mùːəy* which? (sing.) *naː-khlah* which? (plur.)
Expression. *yaːŋ naː* how?

A.1. kè: lùək khsae ʔae naː? 2. nèək na: tʀu tìː-kroŋ prùk nìh? 3. knoŋ saːlaː-rìən nùh kè: boŋrìən phìːəsa: ʔoŋklèːs yaːŋ naː? kè: praə siəvphỳu naː-khlah? 4. prùk meɲ nèək khỳːɲ nèək na: knoŋ tìː-kroŋ? 5. lòːk-krùː mìːən koːn-sʀs(s) poñmaːn nèək knoŋ thnak nìh? 6. yùp meɲ cao(r) poñmaːn nèək coːl phtèəh pùː?

B.1. Which students are learning French this year? 2. Whom did your father visit in hospital yesterday? 3. What (= how) did the teacher say about your son? 4. How many books did you buy this morning, grandson? 5. Who saw the teacher in the city yesterday? 6. Which house is that Vietnamese selling now?

Exercise 19

Noun. *kmeːŋ* young person, child *doːn-taː* grandparents, grandfather and grandmother
Verbs. *ceɲcʀm* to bring up, keep, nourish to write *sɔse:(r)

A.1. kmeːŋ khmae(r) lèːŋ lbaeŋ naː-khlah? 2. bɔːŋ mòːk pìː srok-siəm pìː ʔoŋkal? 3. phtèəh pʔoːn cùt phsaː(r) rùː tèː? 4. khɲom kmìːən trʀy-ɲlət thŋay nìh tèː.

5. lɲìːəc nìh doːn-ta: lòːk tr̀u na:? 6. ʔoːpùk vìːə ceɲc̆r̆m koːn pram nèək yaːŋ doːc-mdĕc?

B.1. How many students has this teacher in his class? He has ten. 2. Has he written other books about Cambodia? I don't know. 3. When will you wear that new blue shirt, grandfather? 4. Which steamer are you going by (go by = cìh), sir? 5. Why is that yellow dress expensive? It isn't at all nice. 6. How many pigs does your grandmother keep? Three.

LESSON 19

COMPOUND PRE-VERBAL PARTICLES; INITIATING VERBS

19.1. *Compound pre-verbal particles*

Pre-verbal particles precede the verbs immediately. The ones which have been introduced so far have been simple words (*mùn* and *nùŋ*). Four other such particles, **kɔː*, *pùm*, *dael* and *ʔɔt* will be included here for convenience; all the other particles given below are compound words.

*kɔː so, therefore, accordingly
pùm not (literary and may occur in any of the compounds where *mùn* occurs)
dael already; has/have at some time in the past
ʔɔt, ʔr̆t not (colloquial)
mùn-dael never (in past or present)
mùn-mèːn not really, not in fact
mùn-tɔ̀ən not yet
mùn-soːv hardly; (with attributive verb) not very
ceh-tae 1. always, constantly. 2. still (in spite of something). (Usually the first meaning is with an attributive verb and the second with an operative verb.)
cɔmnam-tae, taeŋ-tae, rèːŋ-tae, rəmèːŋ-tae usually, habitually
kan-tae, rùt-tae increasingly (*kan-tae* is more colloquial)
sr̆ŋ-tae almost all, almost always, almost altogether (not colloquial)
soi-tae all, without exception
craən-tae mostly, usually, nearly all
kɔmpuŋ-tae in the middle of, just now
str̀ː-tae, str̀ː-tae-nùŋ on the point of
krɔ̀ən-tae only just, hardly
tr̀ːp-tae, tr̀ːp-tae-nùŋ, tr̀ːp-nùŋ have just, just a moment ago
srap-tae immediately, suddenly
kùəŋ-tae continually, still
mùk(h)-tae, mùk(h)-cìːə probably
hiəp-tae nearly, almost
nr̆u-tae continually, still
troːv-tae absolutely must
prəhael-cìːə perhaps
doːc-cìːə as though

e.g. *khɲom ʔɔt tr̀u.* I'm not going.
kɔnlaeŋ nìh ceh-tae krəkhvɔk. This place is always dirty.
khɲom tr̀ːp-tae-nùŋ coːl phtèəh. I have just come into the house.
ʔoːpùk mùn-dael tr̀u srok siəm. Father has never been to Siam.

73

mì:ŋ kɔmpùŋ-tae mỳ:l siɘvphỳu. Aunt is reading a book at the moment/ is in the middle of reading a book/is reading a book just now.

ʔo:pùk ʔɔt ceh phì:ɘsa: *klɣŋ(k̀) tè:. Father doesn't know the Indian language.

dɔl ʔa:tùt(y) kraoy mì:ŋ mùk(h)-tae nùŋ sru:ɘl khlu:ɘn. Next week, aunt will probably be better.

Exercise 20

Nouns. *ʔɔksɔ:(r)* writing, alphabet *khmae(r)* a Cambodian *phlo:v* street people *mɘnùs(s)* celebration *boŋ(y)* letter *sɔmbot(r)* Paris *pa:rì:s* England *srok-*ʔɔŋklè:s*

Verbs. *slap* to die *thvỳ: ka:(r)* to work *sru:ɘl* to be comfortable, well *cëɲ* to go out *prɘlɔ:ŋ* to sit for an examination to be naughty *ka:c* to be wicked *kho:c* to set fire to *dot* to send *phɲaɘ*

Particle. **pre n.p.** *nỳu-lỳ:* on, 'in' (street)

A.1. **chnam nùh cau khɲom stỳ:-tae slap.** 2. **lò:k cɔmnam-tae thvỳ: ka:(r) knoŋ bontùp na:ʔ** 3. **nὲɘk dael tɤu kɔmpùɘŋ ca:m tè:ʔ ba:t̀, dael.** 4. **lò:k mùn-so:v sru:ɘl tè:.** 5. **mda:y cëɲ pì: phtὲɘh. cao(r) pì:(r) nὲɘk srap-tae co:l bontùp.** 6. **mì:ŋ mùn-dael tɤu srok-siɘm tè:.** 7. **ko:n-sɤs(s) mnὲɘk krɔɘn-tae ceh ʔɔksɔ:(r).** 8. **knoŋ thnak nìh kme:ŋ tɤ-p-tae-nùŋ prɘlɔ:ŋ.** 9. **mdëc-kɔ: cau ceh-tae chù:ʔ** 10. **nɤu phtὲɘh, khmae(r) craɘn-tae sliɘk sɔmpùɘt.** 11. **knoŋ phsa:(r), trɤy-ŋlɘt taeŋ-tae thaok.** 12. **sɔmpùɘt lʔɔ: nùh sot̀-tae thlay.**

B.1. He is in the middle of building a new house. 2. Uncle hasn't gone to the market yet. 3. Which pupils are constantly playing in the street? 4. Why are those young boys increasingly naughty? 5. What is their aunt doing just now? 6. Which book have you just read, grandfather? 7. We usually see Mr. Kae in this road. 8. These people are not really wicked. 9. All the Cambodian students go to this celebration in Paris. 10. I have just seen our teacher in the town. 11. That old man was on the point of setting fire to this house. 12. They have never been to England this year at all. 13. This boy doesn't yet know the alphabet. 14. We absolutely must send this letter to Paris.

19.2. *Close verbal sequences* ($v \to v$) *and the full verb construct,* **V**

In Lesson 17.1. the verb construct, **V**, was described as consisting of **v** or **vN**. The formula will now be extended slightly. A small number of verbs are regularly used immediately before another verb with no possibility of the occurrence of another noun or other word in between. e.g. *khɲom cɔŋ tɤu* 'I want to go'. Verbs fulfilling this function will be called 'initiating verbs' and will be represented formulaically as $v \to$. The sequence of verbs, $v \to v$ will be referred to as a 'close verbal sequence'. Any pre-verbal particle which is needed occurs before the initiating verb.[1] e.g. *khɲom mùn cɔŋ tɤu.* 'I don't want to go'. The formula $(v \to)v(N)$ represents in detail the full verb construct possibilities. At the top level of sentence analysis, the construct is still represented by **V**. e.g. *khɲom cɔŋ tɤu pos(te).* 'I want to go to the post office'.

N	V
n	$v \to vN$
n	$v \to vn$

---

[1] Thereby making it the main verb of the sentence. See Lesson 17.1.

19.3. *Initiating verbs*

The following verbs may fulfil this function:—

cɔŋ to wish to

prɔːm to agree to

tətùːəl (id.)

khɔm to try hard to

lɔː to try to

hìːən to dare to

ʔaːc to have the power to, to dare to

prəsɔp to be clever at, to be good at

pùːkae (id.)

ʔɔɲcɤ̀ːɲ to invite to

tɤ̀u to go to

mɔ̀ːk to come to

taeŋ to have the habit of —ing

cùt to be near (in time) to

taŋ to set to, begin to

phdaəm to begin to

cap to begin to

coːl to go in to

cëɲ to go out to

chùp to cease to

lèːŋ (id.)

rìən to learn to

thlɔ̀əp to be used to, accustomed to

ceh to know how to

chap to be quick to

troːv to have to

sɔmrap to be used for

prəɲap to be in a hurry to

rəvùəl to be busy —ing

kùt to think of —ing

baːn to have already (+ English past participle) e.g. *baːn thvɤ̀ː* 'have done' or English past tense

sɔːm to ask to

ʔaːnɤt to be so kind as to

Exercise 21

Nouns. *kon* film   *nìːəŋ* young lady, Miss, young Mrs.   *kae* Kê (proper name) *lòːk-pùː, lòːk-mìːŋ*, etc. uncle, aunt, etc. (more polite than *pùː, mìːŋ*, etc.) *srok-*ʔaːmeːrìːk* America   grandson *cau-pros*

Verbs. *baːraŋsaes* to be French   *coːl cɤt(t)* to like   to put away *tùk* to drive (a car) *baək*   to catch *cap*

Particle. in (village, town, city, etc.) *nɤu* pre n.p.

A.1. nèək na: cɔŋ mɤ̀ːl kon nìh? mdaːy khɲom cɔŋ mɤ̀ːl kon nìh sʔaek. thŋay nìh kɔ̀ət troːv nɤu bontùp kɔ̀ət. 2. pèːl nùh nìːəŋ mùm baːn pèək ʔaːv khìəv tèː. 3. mdaːy rəvùəl thvɤ̀ː kaː(r) knoŋ phtɛ̀əh. 4. ʔoːpuk taeŋ-tae cìh laːn. 5. cau kae prəsɔp rìən phìːəsaː baːraŋsaes tè? 6. lòːk-krùː khɲom chùp nɤu phtɛ̀əh nìh. 7. khɲom baːn mɤ̀ːl kon baːraŋsaes nùh. 8. lòːk-mìːŋ troːv tɤ̀u kroŋ phnùm-pèɲ rùː tè? 9. sɔmpùət sɔː nìh sɔmrap thvɤ̀ː ʔaːv. 10. koːn yɤ̀ːŋ sɔːm lèːŋ lbaeŋ nùh. 11. mɛ̌c-kɔː cau khɔm rìən phìːəsaː ʔɔŋklèːs? cau kùt tɤ̀u srok-ʔaːmeːrìːk tèː? 12. khɲom coːl cɤt(t) tèɲ sɔmpùət lùrəŋ nùh. 13. bɔːŋ lòːk cɔŋ mɤ̀ːl kon khmae(r) nùh tèː? 14. lòːk prəɲap tɤ̀u na:?

B.1. We want to buy (some) green material. This material is too dear. 2. Did the mother agree to live in this house? 3. He is not used to working in the city. 4. Yes, one has to wear a suit here. 5. He does not dare to go to that house. 6. Where did you put the cheap shirt? 7. This cupboard is used for putting away Mr. (. . . .)'s suits. 8. The two sons do not know how to drive the car. 9. These books are used for learning English. 10. They are not used to catching fish. They do not know how to do (it). 11. Your grandson is quick at learning. 12. Why do you wish to go to France, uncle? 13. My niece is thinking of learning English. 14. Whom do you have to visit at the hospital, father?

19.4. *Compound pre-verbal particles preceding initiating verb + verb*

In Exercise 2 the close verbal sequences were preceded only by the simple verbal particle, *mùn*. The following exercise consists entirely of sentences in which compound pre-verbal particles precede the initiating verb.

Exercise 22

Nouns. *ba:rɤy* cigarette **ʔa:me:rì:kaŋ* an American Chinese *cɤn* shop *tiəm* Verbs. *cùək* to smoke *nìyì:əy* to speak

A.1. nì:əŋ mùn-tɔ̀ən ceh cùək ba:rɤy. 2. ʔa:me:rì:kaŋ ceh-tae cɔŋ tèɲ sɔmpùət siəm nìh. 3. ʔo:pùk yɤ̀:ŋ taeŋ-tae rəvùəl səse:(r) sɔmbot(r). 4. ko:n mùn-so:v hì:ən co:l bɔntùp ta: tè:. 5. mì:ŋ sɤŋ-tae nùŋ prɔ̀:m tɤ̀u srok ba:raŋ. 6. ko:n-sɤs(s) nùh sot-tae khɔm rìən phì:əsa: ʔɔŋklè:s.

B.1. Aunt doesn't really want to live in that village. 2. The thief suddenly rushed to get into the car. 3. The Chinese usually try to buy those shops. 4. I have just asked to read that English book. 5. Uncle had never learned to speak Cambodian. 6. He hardly knew how to write the alphabet.

Lesson 20

Minor Verbs and their Uses

20.1. *Minor verb constructs*

A small number of verbs, which express lexically the idea of motion or position, are regularly used to perform a minor function. They form minor verb constructs (← **v**) which follow the main or major verb construct **V**.

e.g. *vì:ə yɔ̀:k sɔmbot(r) tɤ̀u*. He took the letter away.   **N V ← v**

                                            n vN v

                                            n vn v

The minor verbs are used after a major verb which expresses the idea of 'setting in motion' without specifying the direction. They are relatively unstressed (unless they are the last syllable of the sentence) and are dependent lexically and grammatically on the preceding major verb construct; the minor verb construct is therefore represented by ← **v**.

20.2. *Sentence-tune in relation to minor verbs*

In past sentences it has been possible to pause and begin a new phrase after an independent noun construct or an adverbial construct. In sentences having two verb constructs a phrase may end immediately before the second verb, e.g.

vì:ə tèɲ sìəvphɤ̀u nìh (,|) ʔaoy khɲom. He bought these books for me ('to give' me).[1]

20.3. *Minor verbs*

The following verbs may fulfil the minor verb function:—

tɤ̀u to go	*coh* to go down
mɔ̀:k to come	*laəŋ* to rise up

---

[1] This sentence is recorded as an example of sentence-tune 1 (*b*). See Part VII, Appendix 4.

cëɲ to go out
coːl to go in
kraom to be under
lɤ̀ː to be on
taːm
daoy} to follow, to go along
doːc to be like
cùt to be near
chɲaːy to be far

nɤ̌u to stay, to be at
cìːə to be, to be as
ʔaoy to give
cùːn to offer
dɔl to arrive
trɔɲ to move directly towards
kraoy to be behind, to be after (of time)

Note. These verbs may be used as main verbs (i.e. having the position of verb in a sentence of the pattern of sentence-form I and being preceded by any pre-verbal particle which occurs).

e.g. *ʔoːpùk dɔl phtèəh.* Father has arrived home.
chmaː coh pìː dəəm-chɤ̀ː. The cat came down from the tree.
mənùs(s) nùh cìːə krùː. That man is a teacher.[1]
vìːə laəɲ cùəndaə(r). He is mounting the stairway.

Sentences illustrating the use of minor verbs (usually translated by a preposition in English)

e.g.

khɲom yɔ̀ːk sɔmbot(r) tɤ̌u pos(te). I am taking the letter to the post office.
vìːə yɔ̀ːk sìəvphɤ̌u mɔ̀ːk khɲom. He brought the book to me.
khɲom yɔ̀ːk tok nìh coːl phtèəh. I am taking this table into the house.
khɲom nɔ̀əm koːn cëɲ pìː saːlaː-rìən. I took (= led) the child out of the school.
khɲom phɲaə sɔmbot(r) tɤ̌u lòːk. I sent the letter to you.
lòːk phɲaə sɔmbot(r) mɔ̀ːk khɲom. He sent a letter to me.
vìːə trəlɔp pìː phsaː(r) mɔ̀ːk phtèəh. He came back home from the market.
vìːə trəlɔp pìː tìː nìh tɤ̌u phtèəh. He is returning home from here.
khɲom tèɲ sìəvphɤ̌u nìh cùːn lòːk. I am buying this book for you.
vìːə thvɤ̌ː kaː(r) cìːə krùː. He works as a teacher.
vìːə thvɤ̌ː kaː(r) nɤ̌u phtèəh. He works at home.
khɲom tɤ̌u taːm phloːv thnɔl. I am going by the main road.
lòːk rùt-tae chùː laəɲ. He is becoming more and more ill.

20.4. *The translation from English of the verbs of motion and position*

'to' May be i. *tɤ̌u* or *mɔ̀ːk* according to position of speaker ('to' someone else than the speaker or 'to' some place away from the speaker is *tɤ̌u*; 'towards' the speaker is *mɔ̀ːk*). If in doubt use *tɤ̌u*. ii. *dɔl* if the sense is 'as far as, right up to'.

'for' May be *ʔaoy* (familiar) or *cùːn* (polite). *ʔaoy khɲom* always, because one speaks of oneself; *cùːn lòːk* always, because one is polite in referring to another person as *lòːk* and *cùːn* matches the degree of politeness. If in doubt use *ʔaoy*.

'at' After verb of movement, arriving, etc., use *dɔl*; otherwise use *nɤ̌u* (or *ʔae*, the particle met in Lesson 17.3).

'in' or 'into', 'out' *coːl*, *cëɲ*

'down', 'up' and 'along' are respectively *coh*, *laəɲ* and *taːm*, *daoy*.

'as' may be *cìːə*.

---

[1] For this use of *cìːə* see Lesson 36.1.

In some instances there is no preposition in the English translation. e.g. the English verb 'return' represents the entire sequence, *trələp . . . . mɔ̀:k*. In English the alternative way of expressing 'to return' differs from the Cambodian in the word-order. Compare

to come back　　*trələp . . . . mɔ̀:k*
to go back　　　*trələp . . . . tɤu*
to come out　　　*cəɲ . . . . mɔ̀:k*

Similarly the English expressions composed of verb 'to go/come' and adverb ('in, out, up, down', etc.) are translated into Cambodian by the verbs *co:l, cəɲ, laəŋ, coh*, etc., with *tɤu/mɔ̀:k* as minor verbs. Here there is often no noun following the minor verb, e.g.

He went into the room. *vì:ə co:l bəntùp tɤu*.
He is coming into the room. *vì:ə co:l bəntùp mɔ̀:k*.
He came up the hill to the house. *vì:ə laəŋ phnùm mɔ̀:k phtèəh*.

Often the English does not express in any way the Cambodian *tɤu* or *mɔ̀:k*:—

e.g. He sent the letter. *vì:ə ba:n phɲaə səmbot(r) tɤu*.
　　They ran into the house. *vì:ə rùət co:l phtèəh mɔ̀:k*.

One must remember to use a verb of motion too in sentences like the following.

He hurried home ('to hurry' *prəɲap*, with no idea of direction). *vì:ə prəɲap tɤu phtèəh* or, if the speaker is at home, *vì:ə preɲap mɔ̀:k phtèəh*.

Note. Minor verb constructs in sentence analysis. The minor verb construct may be entered in the detailed analysis in the same way as **A/a** though only in the second position open to **A/a**. The analysis would now be presented as (**r**) (**A/a**) **N** (**p**)**V** (**A/a/v**) (**f**).[1]

20.5. *Indirect object*

The indirect object of the major verb may be expressed by means of one of the minor verbs, *tɤu* or *mɔ̀:k*.

e.g. *khɲom ʔaoy siəvphɤu tɤu nèək*. I give you the book.
　　nèək ʔaoy siəvphɤu mɔ̀:k khɲom. You give the book to me.

It may equally be expressed by a succession of noun constructs with no minor verb, especially if there is no idea of motion in the major verb.

e.g. *lò:k nìh bəŋrìən khmae(r) khɲom*. This gentleman is teaching me Cambodian.
　　mì:ŋ nùəŋ bəɲha:ɲ phlo:v nèək. Aunt will show you the way.

Exercise 23

Nouns. *hɤp* trunk　*krè:* bed　*thɔ:t-tok* drawer (in table)　*kəɲcəp* parcel *tha:s* tray　typewriter *ma:sì:n-ʔəŋkùlì:le:k(h)*[2]　staircase *cùəndaə(r)*
Verbs. See those given in the list of minor verbs above. *rùət* to run　*dəɲ* to pursue　to bring a person *nɔəm*　to arrive *mɔ̀:k . . . . dəl*　to show *bəɲha:ɲ*.

---

[1] Some forms which are minor verbs are also pre-nominal particles, e.g. *nɤu* and *cì:ə*. When these occur after the main verb they may be construed as either minor **v.** + **N** or **pre n.p.** + **N**. When they occur before it they must be construed as **pre n.p.** + **N**.
[2] *le:k(h)* spelt *lè:k(h)*.

A.1. hʏp nɛ̀ək nʏ̀u kraom krɛ̀: khɲom. 2. ʔaːv nìːəŋ baytoːŋ nùh doːc ʔaːv lòːk-srʏy. 3. mənùs(s) mnɛ̀ək troːv mòːk taːm khɲom. 4. sʔaek lòːk nùɨŋ yòːk sɔmbot(r) nìh cĕŋ pìː thɔːt-tok. 5. cao(r) rùət cĕŋ pìː bɔntùp. 6. lòːk dĕŋ vìːə dɔl kɔnlaeŋ naːʔ 7. nɛ̀ək naː phɲaə kɔɲcɔp nùh mòːkʔ 8. nìːəŋ baːn dak thaːs kaː(h)veː lʏ̀ː tok toːc.

B.1. Your French books are behind the typewriter. 2. We sent three letters to your uncle. 3. They bought those books for the pupils of this class. 4. How shall I send this parcel to England? 5. Why did you bring that man into the house? 6. The four sons will arrive tomorrow. 7. They are coming up the staircase now. 8. Who took the tray into grandfather's room? 9. Who gave you that letter, grandson? 10. Their uncle showed us the cupboard.

LESSON 21

MAJOR VERBAL SEQUENCES

21.1. *Sentence-form I 2; major verbal sequences,* **V V**

So far each sentence has had one major verb construct, preceded by any pre-verbal particle or particles which occurred in the sentence. In sentence-form I 2 there is a sequence of two major verb constructs. e.g.

khɲom tʏ̀u phsaː(r) tèɲ trʏy. **N V V** I am going to market to buy fish.
  n vn vn

kmeːŋ sɔ̀ɓaːy lèːŋ lbaeŋ nùh. **N V V** The children are happy playing
  n v vN that game.
  n v vnp

Between the two verb constructs is a third position (i.e. in addition to the positions at the beginning and end of the sentence as in sentence-form I 1) where an adverbial construct or adverbial particle may occur and a second position where a minor verb construct may occur.[1] The formula is therefore:—
(r) (A/a) N (p)V (A/a/v) V (A/a/v) or basically **N V V**, e.g. *vìːə cɔŋ tʏ̀u krɔŋ lɔndɔn sʔaek cìh yù̀ən(t)-hɔh.* They want to go to London tomorrow by aeroplane. **N V a V** The second major verb usually receives stress, in
  n vvN a vN
  n vvnn a vn
contrast to a minor verb. The succession of verbs in the two verb constructs is termed a 'major verbal sequence'.

Many kinds of construction which form part of English grammar are represented in Cambodian by major verbal sequences:—

1. Operative Verb—Attributive Verb. English verb + adverb.[2]

e.g. *caːp* **yùm pìːrùəh.** The sparrow *chirps delightfully.* ('sparrow'/'to weep, cry, call'/'to be beautiful to hear')
  vìːə tʏ̀u rəhás. He *goes quickly.* (*rəhás* 'to be quick')

---

[1] It is not, however, until Lesson 37 that sentences with more than two verb constructs, major or minor, are used.

[2] Sometimes a sequence of operative verb and attributive verb does not lend itself to translation by English verb and adverb; e.g. *bat kdau* (lose/to be hot) 'become less hot', *baek phlùː* (to break (intr.)/to be light) 'become light'.

chkae **prùh khlaŋ** *nas*. The dog *barks* very *loudly*. ('dog'/'to bark'/'to be
strong, to be loud'/'very')

kmeːŋ **lèːŋ sɔp͡baːy**. The children *play happily*. (*sɔp͡baːy* 'to be happy')

vìːə **yùəl cbas**. He *understands clearly*. ('he'/'to understand'/'to be clear')

khla: **mùt** *day* **chùː.** The tiger *has cut* its paw *badly*. ('tiger'/'to be cut'/
'hand, arm'/'to be ill')

vìːə **ʔoŋkùy sɲiəm**. They *sit quietly*. (*sɲiəm* 'to be silent')

2. Two operative verbs.

(i) English verb . . . . present participle.

cau **t̮u** *phsaː(r)* **taːm**[1] *rətèh*. The little boy *went* to market *following* the cart.
(*taːm* 'to follow')

nèək **ròːk** *khɲom* **mìːən** *kaː(r)* *ʔvɤy?* (Lit. you *seek* me *having* work what?)
What is your business with me?

(ii) English: two successive actions, expressed by two finite verbs, linked
by 'and'.

vìːə **deːk lùək**. He *lay* down and *slept*. (*deːk* 'to lie down'; *lùək* 'to fall asleep')

lòːk-krùː **baək** *siəvphɤu* **mɤ̀ːl** *tùmp̀ɔ̀ə(r)*. The teacher *opened* the book and *read*
the page. (*tùmp̀ɔ̀ə(r)* 'page')

taː **yò̀ːk** *dɔːŋ-*p̀ak̂kaː **sɤase:(r)** *sɔmbot(r)*. The old man *took* a pen and *wrote*
the letter.

(iii) English verb followed by infinitive expressing purpose.

kɔ̀ət **t̮u** *phsaː(r)* **tèŋ** *trɤy*. She *went* to the market *to buy* fish.

vìːə **phɲaə** *sɔmbot(r)* **ʔoɲcɤ̀ːɲ** *phɲìəv*. He *sends* the letter *to invite* the guests.

yɤ̀ːŋ **t̮u** *tìː* *kroŋ* **mɤ̀ːl** *kon*. We *go* to town *to see* films.

kè: **yò̀ːk** *bɔnlae* **slɔ:** *sɔmlɔ:*. She *takes* vegetables *to make* the stew. (*bɔnlae*
'vegetable'; *slɔ:* 'to stew'; *sɔmlɔ:* 'stew')

Note. The above references to English grammar are made chiefly in order
to help the student with translation from English. The three divisions under 2
should not be regarded as absolutely clearcut. The sentence, '*vìːə deːk lùək*'
for example, might represent, according to context, either 'He lay down
and slept' or 'He lay sleeping'.

Exercise 24

Nouns. *lìːə* donkey *day* hand, arm *sìːklo:* 'cyclo' *mèː* chief *khùm*
  district *bɔŋ(y)* fête, festival *phùːm(ì)* village *kɔntèːl* mat *siəm* a
  Siamese, Thai *srok-khmae(r)* Cambodia *phloːv* *ʔaːkaːs* air(way) *kɔɲcròːŋ*
  fox *kɔ:* neck song *cɔmriəŋ* prison *kùk* basket *kɔɲcɤ̀:* matter *sĕckdɤy*
  cloth *sɔmpùət* design *kbac* boy *kmeːŋ-pros*
Verbs. *sɔp͡baːy* to be happy *bɔk* to wave *tbaːɲ* to weave *rəhás* to be quick
  praə to use *cùːt* to wipe, to clean *criəŋ* to sing *pìːrùəh* to be melodious
  rùət to run *dëɲ* to pursue *lò:t* to jump *kham* to bite *nìyìːəy* to speak
  khlaŋ to be loud, strong to take (people) *nɔ̀əm* to put in (prison) *dak*
  to tell, inform *prap* (self or person to or about whom one speaks familiarly),
  cùmrìːəp (person to or about whom one speaks formally) to put away
  tùk to escape with one's life *rùːəc cì:rvùt*

---

[1] *taːm* is here a major verb with stress.

A.1. cau mɔ̀:k phtɛ̀əh yɤ̀:ŋ cìh lì:ə. 2. khɲom mùm-soːv sɔp̄baːy thvɤ̀: kaː(r) knoŋ tì: nìh tèː. 3. nɛ̀ək bok day hau sìːkloː. 4. mèː khừm baːn ʔəɲcɤ̀ːɲ lòːk-krùː mɔ̀:k phtɛ̀əh. 5. taː nùh cɔŋ tɤu mɤ̀ːl boɲ(y) knoŋ phùːm(ì) yɤ̀:ŋ sʔaek. 6. doːn nɛ̀ək tbaːɲ kontèːl rəhás nas. 7. lòːk-srɤy praə nɛ̀ək-bəmraə cùːt phtɛ̀əh tèːʔ 8. koːn lòːk soṫ-tae criəŋ pìːrùəh nas. 9. siəm buːən nɛ̀ək nùh baːn mɔ̀:k srok-khmae(r) taːm phloːv ʔaːkaːs. 10. vìːə rùət dëɲ cao(r). 11. kɔɲcròːŋ lòːt kham kɔː mɔ̀ən. 12. kmeːŋ nùh nìyìːəy khlaŋ pèːk.

B.1. The children were happy singing songs. 2. He wanted to buy a book to learn French. 3. The village chief took the thief to put him in prison. 4. Aunt weaves baskets to sell in the market. 5. He sent a letter informing us about that matter. 6. The pupils put away their books very happily. 7. She learned to weave cloth making designs. 8. I am buying material to make two shirts. 9. The five boys went to the house and told the village chief. 10. Four people got into those two boats, and escaped with their lives. 11. That servant sings well. 12. What do you want (say 'use') me to do, sir?

21.2. *Note on sentence analysis*

Sentences have now been introduced which are composed of the same kind of word sequence but which should be analysed differently, e.g.

vìːə cap trɤy toːc. He is catching small fish.

N	V
	vN
n	vnv

vìːə cap trɤy lùək. He is catching fish to sell.

N	V	V
	vN	v
n	vn	v

The following exercise of sentences similar to the above should be used for analysis as well as for translation and pronunciation practice.

Exercise 25

Nouns. *tùːk* boat *baːy* rice *nɛ̀ək-srae* farmer *sroːv* paddy *dɤy* earth, ground (rice-)seed *krɔ̀əp (sroːv)* fork *cɔːp*

Verbs. *dam* to cook *chɲaŋ* to be tasty *dɔːk* to uproot to be heavy *thɲùən* to prepare *rìəp* to sow *saːp* to dig *cìːk* to be long *vèːŋ*

A.1. kmeːŋ mnɛ̀ək baːn yɔ̀:k sombot(r) tɤu. 2. ʔoːpùk mùm tèɲ tùːk thom tèː. 3. mìːŋ dam baːy cùːn lòːk rùː tèːʔ 4. mdaːy khɲom thvɤ̀ː mhoːp chɲaɲ nas. 5. nɛ̀ək-srae dɔ̀:k sroːv cëɲ pìː dɤy. 6. lòːk cìh laːn thmɤy.

B.1. I have seen that big parcel. It is not too heavy. 2. The farmer is just now preparing the ground to sow the rice-seed. 3. He took a fork to dig the earth. 4. The Cambodian farmers use heavy forks. 5. He wrote a long letter to his teacher. 6. We want to sell the old house.

LESSON 22

NUMERALS

22.1. *Cardinal numbers*

The terms from which all the numbers are composed are the following:—

mùːəy one	*dɔp* ten	*rɔːy* hundred
pìː(r) two	*-dɔndɔp* -teen	*pɔ̀ən* thousand
bɤy three	*mphèy* twenty	*mɤːn* ten thousand
buːən four	*saːmsɤp* thirty	*saen* hundred thousand
pram five	*saesɤp* forty	*lìːən* million
*prampùːl seven	*haːsɤp* fifty	*kaoṭ(e)* ten million
	hoksɤp sixty	
	cɤtsɤp seventy	
	paetsɤp eighty	
	kausɤp ninety	

N.B. zero = *sɔːn(y)* **v.**

The above terms are, with the exception of *sɔːn(y)* and *-dɔndɔp*, simple words and numerals. Other numerals are either compounds formed from these elements or more than one word.

The whole system may be conveniently arranged as follows:—[1]

1–9	10–19		20–29
	dɔp		*mphèy*
mùːəy	*mùːəy-dɔndɔp*	or *dɔp-mùːəy*	*mphèy-mùːəy*
pìː(r)	*pìː(r)-dɔndɔp*	*dɔp-pìː(r)*	*mphèy-pìː(r)*
bɤy	*bɤy-dɔndɔp*	*dɔp-bɤy*	*mphèy-bɤy*
buːən	*buːən-dɔndɔp*	*dɔp-buːən*	*mphèy-buːən*
pram	*pram-dɔndɔp*	*dɔp-pram*	*mphèy-pram*
pram-mùːəy	*pram-mùːəy-dɔndɔp*	*dɔp-pram-mùːəy*	*mphèy-pram-mùːəy*
prampùːl	*prampùːl-dɔndɔp*	*dɔp-prampùːl*	*mphèy-prampùːl*
pram-bɤy	*pram-bɤy-dɔndɔp*	*dɔp-pram-bɤy*	*mphèy-pram-bɤy*
pram-buːən	*pram-buːən-dɔndɔp*	*dɔp-pram-buːən*	*mphèy-pram-buːən*

30–39	40–49	50–59	60–69
saːmsɤp	*saesɤp*	*haːsɤp*	*hoksɤp*
saːmsɤp-mùːəy	*saesɤp-mùːəy*	*haːsɤp-mùːəy*	*hoksɤp-mùːəy*
saːmsɤp-pìː(r)	*saesɤp-pìː(r)*	etc.	etc.
etc.	etc.		

70–79	80–89	90–99	100–109
cɤtsɤp, etc.	*paetsɤp*, etc.	*kausɤp*, etc.	*rɔːy* or *mùːəy-rɔːy*
			mùːəy-rɔːy mùːəy
			mùːəy-rɔːy pìː(r)

200 *pìː(r)-rɔːy* etc., 300 *bɤy-rɔːy* etc., 400 *buːən-rɔːy* etc.
500 *pram-rɔːy* etc., 600 *pram-mùːəy-rɔːy* etc., 700 *prampùːl-rɔːy* etc.
800 *pram-bɤy-rɔːy* etc., 900 *pram-buːən-rɔːy* etc.
1,000, 2,000 etc. *mùːəy-pɔ̀ən, pìː(r)-pɔ̀ən*, etc.
10,000, 20,000 etc. *mùːəy-mɤːn, pìː(r)-mɤːn*, etc.
100,000, 200,000 etc. *mùːəy-saen, pìː(r)-saen*, etc.
1,000,000, 2,000,000 etc. *mùːəy-lìːən, pìː(r)-lìːən*, etc.
10,000,000, *mùːəy-kaoṭ(e)*, 20,000,000, *pìː(r)-kaoṭ(e)*

---

[1] Only the final syllable of each word receives full stress, e.g. *mphèy-pram-'bɤy*.

It will be observed that every number up to 100 is shown as a single word, simple or compound. Each of the 'hundreds' (100, 200, etc.) is also a single compound word, *mùːəy-rɔ̀ːy*, *pìː(r)-rɔ̀ːy*, etc., but when these are followed by another number (as in 101, 250, 634) the whole number is a sequence of two words, *mùːəy-rɔ̀ːy mùːəy*, *pìː(r)-rɔ̀ːy haːsʏp*, *pram-mùːəy-rɔ̀ːy saːmsʏp-buːən*. The thousands, tens of thousands, millions and billions are similarly each one compound word (e.g. 1,000, *mùːəy-pɔ̀ən*, 50,000, *pram-mʏːn*). If, however, these are followed by lesser numbers, the whole number is composed of more than one word (e.g. 55,061 *pram-mʏːn pram-pɔ̀ən hoksʏp-mùːəy*; 1,004,320 *mùːəy-lìːən buːən-pɔ̀ən bʏy-rɔ̀ːy mphèy*). The criterion by which the words were established was the potentiality of the occurrence of a pause and rise in pitch.[1] Such a phenomenon marks the end of a word. In slow style one can say *mùːəy-rɔ̀ːy haːsʏp-mùːəy* with a rise on the *rɔ̀ːy* but a rise would not be possible on any other syllable. The sequence may thus be divided into two words, (**xx**).

In colloquial speech *mùːəy* in its capacity as a multiplier, i.e. occurring before *rɔ̀ːy*, *pɔ̀ən*, *mʏːn*, *saen*, *lìːən* and *kaot̪(e)* has the alternative form, *mə:—mərɔ̀ːy*, *məkaot̪(e)*.

The numeral class, **x**, is established by reference to the following characteristic:—that a numeral may follow immediately the word *cɔmnuːən*, 'number' and the word *t̪ìː*, 'place' (for the latter see below *re* ordinal numbers).

Two words, *poňmaːn?* 'how many?' and *craən*, 'many', are members of the numeral class thus established in addition to the words which represent utterances of the various combinations of the figures 0–9.

22.2. *Ordinal numbers*

These are formed by the use of the word *t̪ìː* 'place' preceding the numeral. e.g. *t̪ìː pram* 'fifth', *t̪ìː hoksʏp-mùːəy* 'the 61st'. Used in conjunction with a noun, the ordinal takes the second position, *chnam t̪ìː bʏy* 'the third year'.

LESSON 23

THE PROCESS OF COUNTING AND THE NUMERAL COEFFICIENTS

23.1. *The process of counting*

Numerals may be used alone, e.g. *mùːəy*, *pìː(r)*, *bʏy*, *buːən*, 'one, two, three, four'. A steep fall in pitch on the last syllable of each numeric item is then usual, e.g. *mùːəy-rɔ̀ːy* (‚|) *haːsʏp-pram* (\).

When numerals are used in grammatical relation with other words, one or more of the following three items may be involved:—

(i) a headword. This expresses the subject to which reference is made in the numeration. It is usually a noun but may be a verb.
(ii) a numeral.
(iii) a numeral coefficient.

Numeral coefficients, **c**, are catalysed by their occurrence immediately after the numeral in close junction, e.g. *mənùs(s) buːən nèak*, 'four men'

---

[1] Some compound numerals are recorded on the tapes. See Part VII, Appendix 4.

(mankind four persons), *bɤy thŋay*, 'three days', *ʔɔŋkɔː(r) pram cìːəl*, 'five baskets of husked rice' (husked-rice five baskets). *nèək, thŋay* and *cìːəl* are numeral coefficients.

In numeration, only the numeral is indispensible. It is convenient to postulate a numeral construct, **X**, which may consist of a number only (**x(x)**) or a numeral followed by a numeral coefficient (**x(x)c**). The numeral construct has in effect been introduced already (15.3), as a possible part of the noun construct, but without its being given a separate term or formula. Such a sequence of words as the two examples above, *mənùs(s) buːən nèək* and *ʔɔŋkɔː(r) pram cìːəl* would now be recorded formulaically as **N** and the third

$$\begin{array}{c} nX \\ nxc \end{array}$$

example, *bɤy thŋay*, as **X**

$$xc.$$

In first reference, there are the following possible constructions involving a numeral construct:—

1. Noun headword with numeral construct, either **N** or **N . . . . X**

$$\begin{array}{ccc} nX & & \\ nx/xc & n & x/xc \end{array}$$

2. Verb headword with numeral construct, **V . . . . X**

$$\begin{array}{cc} v & x/xc \end{array}$$

3. No headword. Numeral construct alone, **X**

Numeration will be examined from the point of view of these three constructions:—

1. *Noun headword with numeral construct*

(i) Some nouns may be followed by a numeral without a following numeral coefficient. In such cases the numeration takes place with direct reference to the noun, which represents a countable substance or object. e.g. *chkae bɤy*, 'three dogs', *siəvphɤu pìː(r)*, 'two books', *tok buːən*, 'four tables'. (**N**, in all cases).

$$nx$$

(ii) Other nouns are normally in careful speech or written style followed by numeral and coefficient (see list 1 below, Lesson 23.2.). In such cases the numeration refers directly to the coefficient and only indirectly to the headword. e.g. *koːn bɤy nèək*, 'three children' (child three persons), *sdäc bɤy prὲəh-ʔɔŋ(k̇)*, 'three kings' (king three eminent bodies). In colloquial speech these numeral coefficients are not used at all regularly. *koːn bɤy* and *sdäc bɤy* may equally well be heard; the kind of numeration then resembles the first.

(iii) Quite a large proportion of the numeral coefficients refer lexically to shapes (list 2 below). There is again direct reference to **x** and indirect reference to **n**. e.g. *baːrɤy pìː(r) daəm*, 'two cigarettes' (cigarette two trunks), *smau bɤy *səsay*, 'two blades of grass' (grass two sinews). Where the noun represents an uncountable substance, a numeral coefficient is essential but otherwise (e.g. with 'cigarette') the numeration may equally take place without the numeral coefficient.

(iv) A large proportion of numeral coefficients refer lexically to quantities, measurements or containers (list 3 below). When these are used numeration again takes place with direct reference to the numeral coefficient and indirect reference to the noun-headword. e.g. *ʔɔŋkɔː(r) pram cìːəl*, 'five baskets of rice', *skɔː(r) bʀy nìːəl*, 'three pounds of sugar' (sugar three pounds). There is no possibility here of using **nx** only.

(v) Some numeral coefficients (list 4 below) refer lexically to the manner of presentation of a commodity (if man-made) or the manner of growing (if natural). e.g. *sɑtraː mùːəy khsae*, 'a bundle (lit. 'string') of palm-leaves', *dɔːŋ pìː(r) cɔŋkaom*, 'two clusters of coconuts', *phlèːŋ mùːəy sɔmrap*, 'a set of musical instruments' (lit. 'a set of music').

(vi) Some numeral coefficients refer lexically to pairs and groups of people or animals (see list 5). e.g. *dɔmrʀy mùːəy (h)voːŋ*, 'a herd of elephant', *siəm mùːəy pùːək*, 'a group of Siamese'.

(vii) A few numeral coefficients refer lexically to items, kinds, examples, in a general way (list 6). e.g. *laːn pìː(r) yaːŋ*, 'two types of car', *dɔmloːŋ bʀy baep*, 'three kinds of potato'.

2. *Verb headword with numeral construct*

A verb sometimes has a grammatical relationship with a numeral construct which follows. Numeral coefficients which may occur in this context are given in list 7 below. e.g. *vìːə pɔ̀ət phnùm bʀy cùm.* 'He went round the Phnom three times' (lit. 'three rounds'). *vìːə sraek pìː(r) mɔ̀ət.* 'He called out twice' (lit. 'two mouths'). *vìːə soːt(r) bʀy cɔp.* 'He recited three times' (lit. 'three get-to-the-ends'). The above sentences all conform to the pattern, **N V X**.

3. *No headword; numeral construct used alone*

Numeral constructs are used alone, without any headword at all, in expressions relating to time, space and money. e.g. *bʀy maoŋ*, 'three hours', *pìː(r) kìːloːmaet(r)*, 'two kilometres'. *dɔp rìəl haːsʀp seːn*, 'ten riel fifty cents'. The numeral coefficients which apply here are given in list 8.

Note. The above statements under 1, 2 and 3 apply to sentences of first reference, i.e. when a subject is first mooted. In second reference (by the same speaker or in a response) a headword need not be present. e.g. *cau dael khʀːɲ tìːəhìːən yùːən nʀu kɔnlaeŋ nìh tèː? baːt, khʀːɲ pram nèək.* 'Did you see Vietnamese soldiers here, young fellow?' 'Yes, I saw five'. *lòːk mìːən koːn-pros tèː? baːt, mìːən pìː(r) nèək.* 'Have you any sons, sir?' 'Yes, I have two'.

23.2. *Numeral coefficients; representative lists 1–8*

1. *Used with noun headwords of which the lexical reference is to human beings*

nèək laymen and women of all ages and ordinary social rank
prèəh-ʔɔ̀ɲ(k̊) royal persons
ʔɔ̀ɲ(k̊) clergy
rùːp people from philosophical point of view, characters in books, etc.

2. *Used with noun headwords of which the lexical reference is to substances or objects formed by nature or by man into certain characteristic shapes*

*sɑsay long sinewy thing, blade, strand
dom lump or piece

krɔəp seed, pill
phaen disc, tablet
sɔnlɤk leaf, sheet
daəm trunk (of tree)
tuːə upright object, letter, character in play, person

3. *Used with noun headwords of which the lexical reference is to measurable substances, as indicated below*

(i) Capacity (solids); specific measurements
cìːəl small, meshed basket with narrow neck and handle; capacity: $\frac{1}{2}$ bushel
tau a bushel
kɔŋcɤ̀ː large basket; capacity: 1 bushel
kɔntaŋ basket containing $\frac{1}{4}$, $\frac{1}{3}$ or $\frac{1}{2}$ bushel
baːv sack of meshed china-grass or bark-cloth; capacity: 100 lbs. of raw cotton
thaŋ zinc barrel; capacity: 2 bushels
kaːroŋ hemp sack; capacity: 3 bushels
dɤk a man-load
rətèh a cartload
N.B. 4 *cìːəl* = 1 *thaŋ*, 20 *thaŋ* = 1 *dɤk*, 4 *dɤk* = 1 *rətèh*

(ii) Capacity (solids); unspecific measurements
hao small box
hɤp trunk
prəʔɔp box
slaːp-prìːə spoon
vèːk ladle
caːn plate
chnaŋ metal cooking pot
phaəŋ earthenware basin, etc., etc.
This list could be augmented by the addition of all words which express lexically the idea of a container.

(iii) Capacity (liquids)
kʔɔːm pitcher: $\frac{3}{4}$ pint
thoː pitcher with a stopper
pìːəŋ tall earthenware pitcher for water
khap earthenware jar for water with same size base and top, with lid
pan teapot
dɔːp jar
thnaŋ node of bamboo
pèːŋ cup
pèːŋ-cɔːk a very small cup
kɔnsiəv kettle

(iv) Weight
cdao(r) lingot
dɔmlɤŋ ounce
haːp 60 kilograms
cìː 3·75 grams
coŋ 30 kilograms

nìːəl 1 'lb' (600 grams)
kìːloː kilo

N.B. 10 *cìː* = 1 *dəmlɤŋ*, 16 *dəmlɤŋ* = 1 *nìːəl*, 50 *nìːəl* = 1 *coŋ*, 2 *coŋ* = 1 *haːp*

(v) Number

dəmbɔː(r) a foursome, four (used for counting fruit and vegetables)
phloːn forty (used for counting fruit and vegetables)
slɤk[1] four hundred (used for counting fruit and vegetables)

(vi) General measurements

kənlah half
cəmhiəŋ half (especially of a symmetrically-shaped object)
kùmnɔː(r) heap
kəmnat cut piece

4. *Used with a noun headword of which the lexical reference is to natural or man-made phenomena handled or presented in a special way*

trənaot skewer ⎫
cəŋkak large skewer ⎪
dəmbot small skewer ⎬ of meat or fish, as sold
cəmriək lengthwise section ⎪
kəntùy tail ⎭

kəndap sheaf ⎫
contìːəs small bundle ⎬ of paddy, cane, etc.
bac large bundle ⎭

trəbɔːk wrapper, packet
caːn 'plate' (of wax)
srak stack (of tablets of sugar)
kùəl trunk of tree (with branches removed) ⎫
hùp log (i.e. bark and branches removed) ⎬ of wood
crɔːŋ criss-cross pile ⎭
kùm(p̌) clump
cùənlùəŋ trellis (on which pepper trees are grown)
cəŋkaom cluster
kəmrɔːŋ garland
kbaːl head, pair (of horns)
cùːə(r) row
rùət tier
khsae a bundle (of palm-leaf manuscripts) ⎫
kan a book ⎪
kùmpìː collection ⎪
tùmpɔ̀ə(r) a page ⎪
cùmpùːk chapter ⎬ of books and papers
phìːək part ⎪
kbaːl volume ⎪
krɔ̀ːp file ⎪
cbap copy ⎪
pùm(p̌h) sheet ⎭

___
[1] This word is not now commonly used.

hoŋ reel
cɔŋvaːɣ skein
tbɔːŋ 5-yard length
kɣy loomful, 20-yard length
kaːlɣy set of 20 sarong-lengths
} of thread and materials

sɔmrap set, necessary parts or equipment

5. *Used with a noun headword of which the lexical reference is to people or animals grouped together*

pùːək group
thnak class (school, etc.)
cɔmnaek type, class (social)
vùəŋ circle, group (N.B. *phlèːŋ mùːəy vùəŋ*, 'orchestra' (lit. 'music one circle'); *lkhaon mùːəy vùəŋ*, 'a theatrical company' (lit. 'theatre one circle')
(h)voːŋ herd
kùː pair
nùm team, yoke (of buffalo, oxen).

6. *Used with a noun headword of which the lexical reference may be to objects*

(i) Any objects, ideas or persons

baep kind, sort
mùk(h) item, course of a meal, kind
yaːŋ kind, way, method
prəkaː(r) item

(ii) Particular objects

hoːpɔ̀ən honour, degree of rank (military), e.g. *sak(te) pram-buən hoːpɔ̀ən*, 'insignia of nine honours'
pɔ̀ən (colloquial form of *hoːpɔ̀ən*)
*pyaŋcɔ̯nè̯ə syllable (used with *pùːək(y)* 'word' as headword)
khnɔːŋ item (lit. 'back') (colloquial only; used with *phtèəh*, 'house' as headword)

7. *Used with a verb as headword*

mɔ̀ət cry, call, utterance
cùm turn, round
tùk round of boxing match
cɔp going-through-to-the-end
kambɣt stroke of the knife
ʔɔnlùːŋ stroke of a mallet

8. *Used without any headword*

(i) Lexical reference to time

nìːətìː
mìːnùt
} minute
maoŋ hour
thŋay day
ʔaːtùt(y) week
khae month
chnam year

khuːəp year's cycle
prèəh-və(s)saː year as spent by clergy
phlèːt moment
rùmpĕc moment
dɔːŋ time, occasion

(ii) Lexical reference to space or place

thnɔ̀əp finger's width
cɔmʔaːm handspan
hat(th) cubit
kaːŋ width across outstretched arms
pyìːəm distance equal to two yards
mìːlìːmaet(r) millimetre
sɔŋtìːmaet(r) centimetre
deːsìːmaet(r) decimetre
*kìːlɔːmaet(r) kilometre
kɔnlaeŋ place, e.g. *sɔŋ phtèəh pìː(r) kɔnlaeŋ*, to build houses in two places

(iii) Lexical reference to money

seːn cent
rìəl riel

23.3. *Sentences, divided into three groups, according to their grammatical construction, illustrating the use of the numeral coefficients*

1. *Noun headword*

No coefficient. *sìːkloː tr̆u taːm phloːv thom mùːəy.* The cyclo-pousse went along a certain main road.
saːlaː-rìən thom nùh mìːən tvìːə(r) buːən. The big school has four entrances.
taː mìːən tùːk pìː(r). The old man owns two boats.

List 1. *bɔːŋ khɲom pìː(r) nèək tr̆u mɤ̀ːl kon.* My two elder brothers (and/or sisters) have gone to see the film.
pùː mìːən cau-srɤy poñmaːn nèək? How many grand-daughters have you, uncle?

List 2. *khɲom troːv leːp thnam bɤy krɔ̀əp.* I have to take (swallow) three pills.
ʔoːpùk mìːən daəm-tnaot buːən daəm. Father has four sugar-palms.

List 3. *nìəŋ nùŋ yɔ̀ːk tùːk-tae mùːəy pèːŋ cùːn mìːŋ.* She (the young lady) will bring a cup of tea for you, aunt.
khɲom tɤ̆ːp-nùŋ tèɲ tùːk-tnaot mùːəy thnaŋ. I have just bought a 'node' of toddy.

List 4. *taː kɔmpùŋ-tae tèɲ mlùː pìː(r) trəbɔːk.* Grandfather is just buying two packets of betel.
cau nùŋ tèɲ soːt(r) lùəŋ mùːəy cɔŋvaːy ʔaoy dɔːn tèː? Will you buy a skein of yellow silk for me, grandson?

List 5. *prìəp mùːəy kùː nɤ̆u cùːt phtèəh khɲom.* A pair of pigeons lives near my house.
khɲom khɤ̆ːɲ kòː mùːəy nùm ʔoːs nɛ̀əŋkɔ́əl thom. I saw a team of oxen pulling a large plough.

List 6. *yร̀:ŋ ba:n tətù:əl tì:ən mho:p bɤy mùk(h).* We had a three-course meal.
nὲək-srok thvร̀: səmpùət pì:(r) ya:ŋ. The people of the district make two kinds
of material.

2. *Verb headword*

List 7. *khmae(r) pì:(r) nὲək dal mù:əy tùk.* The two Cambodians boxed
one round.

3. *No headword*

List 8. *khɲom ba:n cam pì:(r) maoɲ.* I have waited two hours.
siəvphร̀u nùh thlay dɔp rìəl. That book costs ten riel.

23.4. *Numeral construct as attribute*

Sometimes a **X** used with a noun headword is not quantitative lexically
but attributive.

e.g. *siəvphร̀u 200 tùmpว̀ə(r)* a 200-page book (not '200 pages of a book')
tok bu:ən crùŋ a four-cornered table (not 'four corners of a table')

23.5. *Syntactical positions of the numeral construct*

When it occurs as part of a noun construct the numeral construct does
not present new syntactical material. When it occurs separately from its
noun headword or with a verb headword or with no headword it may occupy
any of the positions in the sentence-form which an adverbial construct or
adverbial particle may occupy:—

Sentence-form I 1 (r), (A/a/**X**) N (p)V (A/a/v/**X**) (f) or
Sentence-form I 2 (r), (A/a/**X**) N (p)V (A/a/v/**X**) V (A/a/v/**X**) (f)

More than one of the items, **A**, **a** and **X** may occur in one position but not
more than one **V**. No fixed order within the series can be stipulated. There is
a convention as to the order in which the constructs occur in the following
case, however, where two numeral constructs occur together,

e.g. *khɲom tro:v lè:p thnam mù:əy thŋay pì:(r) dɔ:ŋ.* I have to take (lit.
'swallow') the medicine twice a day.
vì:ə lùək səmpùət nìh mù:əy kɤy ha:sɤp rìəl. He sells this material at
fifty riel a twenty-yard length.

The universally applicable yardstick (length of time or material, etc.)
against which measurement takes place usually comes first and the variable
(number of items, price, etc.) comes second.

When *mnὲək*,[1] 'one person, each', is used, however, the opposite is the case.
vì:ə cù:n kɔmrɔ:ŋ-phka:(r) tɤu nὲək-krù:, pì:(r) bɤy kɔmrɔ:ŋ mnὲək. 'They
offered garlands of flowers to the teachers, two or three each'.

Exercise 26

Nouns. *tùk-tae* tea *dɤy* land *seh* horse *srɤy* woman *ba:rɤy* cigarette
lò:k-sɔ̀ŋ(kh) monk *sa̱tra:* manuscript *sro:v* paddy king *sdäc* palace

---

[1] *mnὲək,* it will be remembered, is a particle, not a numeral plus numeral coefficient.
See Lesson 15.3.

rìːə̀c-vèəŋ abbot *cau-ʔaŧthìkaː(r)* monastery *vɔ̀ɔ̯t(t)* coconut *doːŋ* market-garden *cɔmkaː(r)* pepper-tree *mrĕc* cucumber *trəsok* train *rətèh-phlʏ̀ːŋ* pills = medicine (*thnam*, **n**) **x** pills (*krɔ̀əp*, **c**)

Verbs. *bɔndaoy* to be long *ʔaːyù* to be aged *tɔ̀ːt* to read (of monks) *prəlɔːŋ* to sit for an examination *cɔ̀əp* to stick, to pass an examination *thlèək* to fall, to fail an examination *daə(r)* to walk to eat (polite, of other people) *pìsaː* to take, swallow *lèːp*

Numeral Coefficients. *pɛ̀ːŋ* cupful *pyìːəm* length measurement (= 2 yards) *ʔɔ̯ŋ(k̆)* person, monk **kìːloːmaet(r)* kilometre *haːp* weight measurement (= 60 kilograms) *rìəl* riel *cɔŋkak* skewer time *dɔːŋ* collection of manuscripts *kùmpìː* half (of a symmetrically-shaped object) *cɔmhìəŋ* trellis *cùənlùəŋ* volume *kbaːl* minute *mìːnùt* hour *maoŋ* forty (of fruit or vegetables) *phloːn* pill *krɔ̀əp*, with *thnam*, medicine, as noun headword.

Particles **a.** *tìət* more once *mdɔːŋ*

A.1. kɔ̀ət baːn cùːn tùrk-tae mɔ̀ːk yʏ̀ːŋ, mùːəy pɛ̀ːŋ mnɛ̀ək. 2. koːn-pros khɲom mùm-tɔ̀ən prəlɔːŋ coːl thnak tìː bʏy tèː. 3. dʏy khɲom bɔndaoy dɔp pyìːəm. 4. ʔʏyloːvᵊnìh lòːk mìːən seh poῆmaːn? baːt̆, khɲom mìːən mphèy. 5. knoŋ thnak tìː pìː(r) koːn-sʏs(s) craən-tae ʔaːyù prampùl chnam. 6. mùːəy chnam tìət khɲom tʏu srok-ʔɔŋklèːs. 7. srʏy nùh baːn cùːn baːrʏy pìː(r)-dɔndɔp daəm mɔ̀ːk khɲom! 8. lòːk-sɔ̯ŋ(k̆h) pìː(r) ʔɔ̯ŋ(k̆) nùh craən-tae tɔ̀ːt saɯtra: pèːl lɲìːəc. 9. cau pìː(r) nɛ̀ək tʏ̀ːp-nùŋ prəlɔːŋ. mnɛ̀ək krɔ̀ən-tae cɔ̀əp mnɛ̀ək thlèək. 10. vìːə mùm prɔ̀ːm daə(r) pìː(r) kìːloːmaet(r) tìət. 11. sroːv mùːəy haːp thlay dɔp rìəl. 12. trʏy nìh thlay poῆmaːn rìəl? baːt̆, mùːəy cɔŋkak pìː(r) rìəl.

B.1. Eighteen pupils took the examination this year. Ten passed. 2. We go to see my grandmother three times a month. 3. Three kings have lived in this palace. 4. The abbot has two collections of manuscripts in the monastery. 5. Will you have (= eat) half a coconut? My father has just bought forty! 6 (*a*)[1] Where do I buy smoked fish? (*b*) Here, (sir). How many skewers? (*a*) How much is a skewer? (*b*) Five riel a skewer, (sir). 7. In this market-garden, I have four trellises of pepper-trees. 8. In the first class thirty pupils learn English. 9. The old gentleman is used to going in a cyclo-pousse once a week. 10. Mr. — sent four cucumbers to the abbot. 11. We usually have to wait two or three minutes for your train. Today we waited two hours! 12. Why did aunt take those two pills today?

LESSON 24

CLAUSES, COMPOSITE SENTENCES AND MARKERS

24.1. *Definition of clauses, composite sentences and markers*

Sentences have so far been pronounced as either one, two or three phrases. A rise in pitch (,) plus potential pause (|) before the second phrase are the features which characterize this separation of one part of the sentence from others. From now onwards the term, 'clause', will be used to designate any series of words which may be analysed as composing one of the sentence-forms I 1 or I 2 or further ones considered below. All the sentences so far

---

[1] Here, as elsewhere, (*a*) and (*b*) indicate different speakers.

used have been simple sentences consisting of one clause, even though they may have been pronounced as two phrases. We come now to composite sentences consisting of two clauses. These may be pronounced as two phrases.[1]

e.g. *nèək tร̆u phtèəh nèək* (ˌ|) *khɲom tร̆u phtèəh khɲom.* (If) you go to your house, I shall go to mine.

N	**V**	**N**	**V**
n	vN	n	vN
n	vnn	n	vnn

lò:k-pa: thvร̆: yaːŋ mëc (ˌ|) *khɲom kɔː mùn prɔ̀ːm.* Whatever[2] you do, father, I shall not consent.

N	**V**	**A**	**N**	**ppV**
n	v	np	n	ppv

ʔaɲ thvร̆: cìːə prəpùən(ih) ʔaeŋ (ˌ|) *ʔaeŋ sok(h) cร̆t(t) tèː?* (If) I become your wife, will you be pleased?

N	**V**	**A**	**N**	**V f**
n	v	pnn	n	vN f
			n	vn f

The beginning of a clause may be marked by the occurrence of a clause-marking particle or 'marker', **m**. e.g. *baə nèək tร̆u phtèəh nèək* (ˌ|) *khɲom tร̆u phtèəh khɲom.* The translation is as for the first sentence above but the style is less colloquial and vivid.

    khɲom tร̆u phtèəh pì:-prùəh nèək cɔŋ tร̆u. I am going home because you want to go.

N	**V**	**m**	**N**	**V**
n	vN	m	n	v → v
n	vn	m	n	vv

24.2. *List of markers*

The student is advised to read the following through carefully, learn one way of translating each English conjunction, adverb, etc., and then use the list for reference. The words meaning 'why?' met in 18.1 are also markers.

1. Those for which the general translation is 'if'.

   baə [General word. Will replace any of the others, but without giving the precise meaning which each of the others has.]
   kaːl-baə if, when, whenever, if (as now turns out to be the case), if (as may be expected)
   baə-sร̆n-naː ⎱ if by some possible chance (and it is a definite
   baə-sร̆n-naː-cìːə ⎰ possibility)
   prəsร̆n-baə ⎱
   baə-prəsร̆n-cìːə ⎰ if by any chance (but it is unlikely)
   prəsร̆n-cìːə supposing (a most unlikely supposition, but just suppose)
   kaːl-naː-baə if ever, whenever

---

[1] This is illustrated on the tape recordings. See Part VII, Appendix 4.
[2] See Lesson 33 for this translation of *yaːŋ mëc*.

baə-ka:l-na: if at any time, present or future [For past use *ka:l-baə*.]
baə . . . . mùn if . . . . not, unless
lɤ̀:k-tae⎫
kom-tae⎭ unless, without, apart from, except that ⎱if . . . . not, unless

2. Those for which the general translation is 'when'.

ka:l when [May refer to a time different from that of the other clause.]
ka:l-dael⎫
pè:l
pè:l-dael ⎬ at the time when, on the occasion when, as
krì:ə-dael [Slightly more formal.]⎭
ka:l-na: when at any time, whenever, if ever
lùh at the time when (and only then, not before) (past, present and future)
lùh-tae only if, only when (and not before)
lùh-tra:-tae when and only when; if, and only if; if and when
dɔl when (in the future)
dɔl-ka:l-na: at some time in the future when
dɔl-pè:l-dael at the (future) time when
tɔ̀əl-tae by the time that, when

3. *pè:l-na:-dael* every time that ⟶ whenever

4. *knoŋ-pè:l-dael*⎫
   nɤ̀u-pè:l-dael⎭ during the time that ⟶ while

5. *dɔl*⎫
   tɔ̀əl-tae
   tɔ̀əl-dɔl ⎬ until ⎱until
   tɔ̀əl-tae-dɔl⎭
   dɔl-pè:l-dael until the occasion when, until such time as

6. *mùn-nùŋ* at some time before (but not necessarily between now, or the time referred to, and then, some future time)⎫
   tùmrɔ̀əm⎫ during the time which will, or was to, elapse ⎬before
   tùmrɔ̀əm-dɔl⎭ between the time of speaking, or time of reference, and some future time⎭

7. *kraoy* following (a minor step in a narrative)⎫
   kraoy-pì: following (a specific event)⎭ after

8. *taŋ-pì:* since

9. Those for which the general translation is 'so . . . . that (not)', expressing purpose.

   Ɂaoy so that [*Ɂaoy* may only be used when the purpose expressed in its clause is either for the benefit of or by the command or permission of the person designated by the independent **N** (subject) of the first clause. cf. *Ɂaoy* **v.** 'to give; to have (someone) do . . . .'.]
   mùn-Ɂaoy⎫ so that . . . . not [As with *Ɂaoy* the benefit or command by the subject of the first clause is suggested. *kom-Ɂaoy* conveys a
   kom-Ɂaoy⎭ stronger sense of purpose or compulsion than *mùn-Ɂaoy*.]

daəmbɤy-ʔaoy
daəmbɤy-mùn-ʔaoy
daəmbɤy-nùŋ-mùn-ʔaoy
daəmbɤy-kom-ʔaoy

[Same sense as *ʔaoy*, *mùn-ʔaoy*, and *kom-ʔaoy* respectively but slightly more emphasis. cf. English 'in order that' as contrasted with 'so that'. These words may occur as markers of a 1st clause in a sentence whereas *ʔaoy*, *mùn-ʔaoy* and *kom-ʔaoy* may occur as markers only of second clauses.]

daəmbɤy-nùŋ
daəmbɤy

so that, having in mind the intention that [May introduce 1st or 2nd clause, like the above words formed with *daəmbɤy*. Do not suggest benefit to or order by subject.]

10. *tɔəl-tae* up to the point that   so that (result)

11. *prùəh*
    pìː-prùəh
    dbɤt
    daoy-saː(r)
    daoy-häet(o)

[All may occur as markers of either a 1st or 2nd clause. The two latter have a more emphatic meaning, 'for the reason that . . . .'.]

    prùəh-tae
    häet(o)-tae

just because, it was because . . . . (that) [The clause for which these words occur as markers must come first]   because

12. *baːn-cìːə*   1. May occur as marker of a 1st clause, 'the reason why . . . . '. 2nd clause then has *prùəh* or *pìː-prùəh* as marker, translated 'is that, is because . . . .'.

           2. May occur as marker of a 2nd clause, 'and that is why'. 1st clause may have one of the markers, *prùəh*, etc., but need not.   wherefore

13. *tùəh*
    tùəh-cìːə
    tùəhbɤy   even if

    dbɤt
    dbɤt-tae   although
    thvɤy-dbɤt-tae

[Used with or without *kɔː-daoy*, f., at the end of the clause. The possibility is made more remote by the presence of *kɔː-daoy*.]   although

14. *dael* who, which; of, at, in whom, which   who

15. *ʔaoy-tae* provided that   so long as

16. *(rùː)* . . . . *rùː* (either) . . . . or

17. *thaː* [The more commonly used of the two. May follow either a verb whose lexical reference is to speech or a verb whose lexical reference is to thought.]
    cìːə [May follow only a verb whose lexical reference is to thought.]   that

18. *tae*
    pontae
    *kɔː-pontae

[These are arranged in order of emphasis, *tae* being the least emphatic.]   but, however

19. *haəy-nùŋ*   and

20. *taːm* } according to what, as

21. *kùː* as follows, that . . . ., that is, i.e., viz.

22. **kɔː* then, so, accordingly, therefore

23. *sʏm* then, then only [Usually precedes an exhortation or suggestion.]
tʏ̀ːp then next after fulfilment of a condition, then and not before
rùːɔc then, after that, and
rùːɔc-haɔy then after that
haɔy and, and then [Next step in story.] } then

24. *srap-tae* immediately, suddenly, thereupon

25. *prɔhael-cìːɔ* perhaps, it is possible that

26. *mùk(h)-cìːɔ* probably

27. *taɔ* [A question follows.] tell me, ... ?

28. *coːl* (spelt *coːr*) [Precedes a command, uttered to a person whom one addresses familiarly.] } come now please . . . .

29. *coh-baɔ* [Introduces a new suggestion or an appeal to the hearer to consider one's view.] } what if . . . . ?

24.3. *Occurrence of markers in simple and composite sentences*

These markers generally speaking operate, in an initiating context, only in composite sentences, i.e. they introduce a clause which depends on the occurrence in the same sentence of another clause. Some (**kɔː, taɔ, rùːɔc, haɔy, rùːɔc-haɔy, srap-tae*) may, however, occur at the beginning of separate sentences, linking them with what has gone before. A few (*coːl, prɔhael-cìːɔ, mùk(h)-cìːɔ, kom-ʔaoy* and *mùn-ʔaoy*[1]) may introduce a new subject and sentence.

24.4. *Sentence-tune; emphasis of markers*

It has been suggested[2] that emphasis may be given by means of the rise + pause (ˌ|). Some markers are emphasized in this way, by being separately phrased (especially **kɔː-pontae, pontae, tae, prùɔh, pìː-prùɔh, rùːɔc, haɔy* and *rùːɔc-haɔy*).[3]

e.g. *vìːɔ tèɲ skɔː(r)* (ˌ|) *rùːɔc* (ˌ|) *vìːɔ trɔlɔp tʏ̀u phtèɔh.*
He bought the sugar and then went back home.

On the other hand, when the first word of a phrase is to be emphasized this can also be done by means of a fall in pitch with no pause following it:—
vìːɔ tèɲ skɔː(r) (ˌ|) *rùːɔc* (\) *vìːɔ trɔlɔp tʏ̀u phtèɔh.*
This method is always used with *tʏ̀ːp* and *sʏm.*

e.g. *khɲom tʏ̀u phtèɔh* (ˌ|), *tʏ̀ːp* (\) *khɲom tʏ̀u sùːɔ(r) mìːɲ.*
I'm going home and then I'll go and see aunt.

---

[1] In this context *kom-ʔaoy* and *mùn-ʔaoy* have the meaning 'let . . . . not'.
[2] See Lesson 14.1.
[3] Emphasis of markers is illustrated specifically on the tape recordings. See Part VII, Appendix 4.

24.5. *Sentence-forms in composite sentences*

The sentence-forms have been based on sentences which may occur in initiating contexts. Responding or following up sentences can not be taken as examples of sentence-forms. Sometimes in a composite sentence one clause acts as the initiating clause for the other, not necessarily the one which comes second, e.g. *thvə̀ː kaːr(r) rùːɔc haəy, lòːk trɔlɔp tɤ̀u phtèəh vèɲ.* 'When he had finished working, Mr. — went back home'. *lòːk* is mooted in the second clause and therefore can be absent from the first. Sometimes one clause is interrupted by another, e.g. *khɲom, baə tɤ̀u kɔmpùəŋ caːm, nùŋ səseːr(r) sɔmbot(r) tɤ̀u cau.* 'If I go to Kompung Cham I'll write to you'. *siəvphɤ̀u nùh, dael nèək tèɲ pìː msʏl, bat tɤ̀u haəy!* 'That book, which you bought yesterday, has disappeared!' These first clauses would therefore be regarded as analysable as sentence-forms, since *nèək* and *lòːk* could be used in the appropriate places and thus make the clauses complete; the sentences can then be analysed as composite sentences.

24.6. *Sentences illustrating the use of the markers listed in* **24**.2

1. *baə phlìəŋ kèː troːv cὶh sὶːkloː.*
   If it rains one has to go by cyclo.
   kaːl-baə nèək cɔŋ baːn rəbɔs nùh, mdëc mùʼn tèɲ?
   If you wanted to have those things, why didn't you buy them?
   baəːsʏn-naː   }
   baə-sʏn-naː-cὶːə }*phlìəŋ, khɲom mùʼn tɤ̀u suːə(r) mùʼt(t)-sɔmlaɲ khɲom tèː.*
   If it rains I shall not go to see my friend.
   prɔsʏn-baə   }
   baə-prɔsʏn-cὶːə }*khɲom troːv chnaot, khɲom nùʼŋ tèŋ laːn.*
   If I were to win the lottery, I would buy a car. (I have a ticket but the chance is slight.)
   prɔsʏn-cὶːə khɲom troːv chnaot, khɲom nùʼŋ tèŋ laːn.
   Suppose I were to win a lottery, I would buy a car. (I have not even bought a ticket.)
   kaːl-naː-baə kèː tɤ̀u lèːŋ mὸət sɔmoï(r) kèː ɲam mhoːp sɔmoï(r).
   Whenever they go to the seaside, they eat sea-food (*lèːŋ* 'to amuse oneself at, in'; *mὸət sɔmoï(r)* 'sea-side'; *ɲam* 'to eat').
   baə-kaːl-naː: nèək mɔ̀ːk bat-dɔmbɔːŋ, nèək ʔɔɲcɤ̀ːɲ-mɔ̀ːk suːə(r) khɲom.
   If you ever come to Battambang, do come and see me.
   baə vὶːə mùʼn səseːr(r) sɔmbot(r) mɔ̀ːk khɲom, khɲom nùʼŋ khʏŋ nùʼŋ vὶːə.
   If he doesn't write a letter to me, I shall be angry with him.
   lɤ̀ːk-tae khɲom krὶn bɔntec khɲom sok(h)-sₐp̄baːy.
   Apart from a little fever, I am well. (*krὶn* 'to be feverish'; *sok(h)-sₐp̄baːy* 'to be well')
   kom-tae khɲom cùːəy vὶːə, kèː troːv ʔɔŋkùy thvʏ̀ː mùːəy yùp.
   If I hadn't helped him he would have had to sit and do it all night.

2. *kaːl khɲom tɤ̀u dɔl kɔnlaeŋ nùh, khɲom prətèəh khʏ̀ːɲ pùəs mùːəy.*
   When I got to the place I happened to see a snake. (*prətèəh* 'to meet with, happen to')

ka:l po:lǐ:s tr̆u dəl kɔnlaeŋ nùh, cao(r) ba:n cĕɲ phot tr̆u.
When the police got to the place, the robber had already escaped.
   (*phot* 'to be free')

ka:l-dael mì:ŋ cìh yùən(t)-hɔh, mì:ŋ ba:n bɔk day mɔ̀:k yr̆:ŋ.
As aunt stepped onto the plane she waved to us.

pè:l yr̆:ŋ tr̆u mɤ̀:l kon, yr̆:ŋ ba:n cù:əp nùŋ mùt(t)-sɔmlaɲ yr̆:ŋ mnɛ̀ək.
When we went to see the film we met a friend of ours.

*pè:l-dael ⌉lò:k rɔ̀ət(th)-mùəntr̆y coh pì: lɤ̀: kɔpal-hɔh, mənùs(s) craən nɛ̀ək
kri:ə-dael⌋ ba:n sraek, 'cĕy-yò:(c)!'*
When the minister got off the plane, many people called out, 'Hurrah!'

*ka:l-na: yr̆:ŋ ba:n tr̆u kɔnlaeŋ nùh, yr̆:ŋ ba:n cù:əp nùŋ lò:k-ta:
mdɔ:ŋ-mdɔ:ŋ.*
Whenever we have gone there we have met the old gentleman from time
   to time.

lùh vì:ə prəlɔ:ŋ cɔ̀əp, tr̆:p vì:ə co:l sa:la:-thom ba:n.[1]
When he passes his examination he will be allowed to go to the University.

lùh-tae nɛ̀ək mì:ən lìkhɤt-chlɔ:ŋ-daen, tr̆:p kè: ʔaoy tr̆u srok-ʔɔŋklɛ̀:s.
Only if you have a passport will they allow you to go to England.
   (*lìkhɤt-chlɔ:ŋ-daen* 'passport, letter-to cross-border')

lùh-tra:-tae vì:ə khɔm rìən, tr̆:p vì:ə prəlɔ:ŋ cɔ̀əp.
If, and only if, he studies hard will he pass the examination.

*ʔaeŋ tro:v cam nr̆u tì: nìh dəl khɲom mɔ̀:k vèɲ.
dəl-ka:l-na: ʔaeŋ thom, ʔaeŋ nùŋ thvɤ̀: ka:(r) do:c ʔo:pùk.*
When you are big you will work like me.

dəl-pè:l-dael kè: thvɤ̀: bɔɲ(y) co:l chnam, yr̆:ŋ nùŋ tr̆u siəm-rì:əp.
When the New Year Festival is celebrated, we shall go to Siem Reap.

tɔ̀əl-tae kɔ̀ət baək thɔ:t-tok tr̆:p kɔ̀ət dɤŋ tha: kɔ̀ət bat prak.
When he opened the drawer he knew that he had lost some money.

3. *pè:l-na:-dael kɔ̀ət mɔ̀:k su:ə(r) lò:k-ta:, lò:k-ta: sɔpba:y cɤt(t) nas.*
   Every time he comes to see grandfather, grandfather is delighted.

4. *knoŋ-pè:l-dael⌉
   nr̆u-pè:l-dael ⌋kɔ̀ət lè:ŋ lbaeŋ nr̆u phtèəh khɲom, phtèəh kɔ̀ət cheh.*
   While he was playing a game at my house, his house caught fire.

5. *ko:n-ʔaeŋ tro:v nr̆u cam tì: nìh*
   tɔ̀əl-tae⌉
   tɔ̀əl-dəl ⌉khɲom mɔ̀:k vèɲ.
   tɔ̀əl-tae-dəl⌋
   You must stay here until I come back.

khɲom tùk cɔmnr̆y phʔaem nùh dəl-pè:l-dael bɔ:ŋ-pʔo:n mɔ̀:k su:ə(r) yr̆:ŋ.
I am putting away these sweet things (to eat) until the relatives come to
   see us. (*cɔmnr̆y* 'food'; *phʔaem* 'to be sweet')

---

[1] For *ba:n* as a 2nd position main verb, with the meaning 'can', see Lesson 30.

6. *mùn-nùŋ prəlɔːŋ yɔ̀ːk saɲɲaːbạt(r) nɤ̌u saːlaː-thom, nèək troːv mìːən lĭkhɤt phseːŋ-phseːŋ.*
Before sitting for a degree at the University, you have to have various certificates. (*saɲɲaːbạt(r)* 'certificate', here 'degree'; *lĭkhɤt* 'official letter', here 'certificate')

tùmrɔ̀əm phɲiəv mɔ̀ːk yɤ̌ːŋ mìːən pèːl ɲùːt tùk.
We have time to have a shower before the guests arrive. (*ɲùːt* 'to go under water')

tùmrɔ̀əm-dɔl yừạn(t)-hɔh coh yɤ̌ːŋ mìːən pèːl ɲam phèːsạcèə.
Before the plane lands we have time to have a drink.

7. *kraoy khɲom mɔ̀ːk dɔl, khɲom tɤu cùmrìːəp-suːə(r) lòːk-srɤy.*
After I arrived I went to say 'hello' to Mrs. —.

kraoy-pìː cùːn mùt(t)-sɔmlaɲ kɔ̀ət laəŋ rətèh-phlɤ̌ːŋ, kɔ̀ət nɔ̀əm prəpừạn(th) kɔ̀ət tɤu pìsaː baːy.
After seeing his friend onto the train, he took his wife (out) to a meal.

8. *taŋ-pìː kèː sɔŋ saːlaː-thom nùh haəy, kɔːn-sɤs(s) craən mɔ̀ːk rìən.*
Since they built the University, many students have come to study. (*haəy* f. 'to completion'. See next Lesson).

9. *kɔ̀ət baːn phɲaə sɔmbot(r) pìː(r) bɤy thŋay mùn, ʔaoy nèək-bɔmraə rìəp bɔntùp cùːn phɲiəv mnèək.*
He sent a letter two or three days before so that the servant would prepare a room for a guest.

khɲom thvɤ̌ː kaː(r) ʔaoy baːn cɔmnèŋ craən.
I work so as to have plenty of profit.

kèː dak taːraŋ haːm mənùs(s) mùn-ʔaoy dəə(r) lɤ̌ː smau.
They put up notices forbidding people to walk on the grass.

kèː troːv dak baːv khsac cùmvèɲ cùəɲcèəŋ kom-ʔaoy lùː sɔː(r).
They have to put sacks of sand round the walls, so as not to hear the sound. (*cùmvèɲ* 'round')

daəmbɤy-ʔaoy kɔːn-srɤy tɤu tətùːrəl bɔːŋ kɔ̀ət nɤ̌u cɔmnɔːt yừạn(t)-hɔh, ʔɔːpùk phɲaə sɔmbot(r) tɤu kɔːn-srɤy nùh.
So that his daughter would go and meet her brother at the airport, the father sent her a letter.

daəmbɤy-mùn-ʔaoy   ⎱*chùː knoŋ pèːl rədoːv rəŋìːə kèː troːv prɔŋ-*
daəmbɤy-nùŋ-mùn-ʔaoy⎰   *prəyát(n) cìːə dəraːp.*
One has to take care always so as not to be ill in the cold season. (*rədoːv* 'season'; *rəŋìːə* 'cold'; *cìːə dəraːp* 'always')

daəmbɤy-kom-ʔaoy lùː sɔː(r) kèː troːv dak baːv khsac cùmvèɲ cùəɲcèəŋ.
In order not to hear the noise, they have to put sand-bags round the walls.

ʔɔːpùk ʔaoy khɲom tɤu srok-ʔɔŋklèːs daəmbɤy-nùŋ⎱*khɲom rìən phìːəsaː*
daəmbɤy   ⎰*ʔɔŋklèːs.*
My father is letting me go to England so that I shall learn English.

10. *krùː baːn tèəh kmeːŋ nùh ɣaːŋ khlaŋ tɔ̀əl-tae kmeːŋ nùh duːəl.*
The teacher hit the boy so hard that he fell. (*tèəh* 'to hit with the flat of the hand')

11. *khɲom mùn baːn tr̃u thvỳː kaː(r) pìː msʏl* { *prùəh* / *pìː-prùəh* / *dbʏt* / *daoy-saː(r)* / *daoy-häet(o)* } *khɲom chùː.* or

{ *prùəh* / *pìː-prùəh* / *dbʏt* / *daoy-saː(r)* / *daoy-häet(o)* } *khɲom chùː pìː msʏl baːn-cìːə khɲom mùn baːn tr̃u thvỳː kaː(r).*
I didn't go to work yesterday because I was ill.

{ *prùəh-tae* / *häet(o)-tae* } *phlìəŋ, baːn-cìːə khɲom mùn baːn mɔ̀ːk ʔaoy tɔ̀ən pèːl-vèːlìːə.*
It was because of the rain that I did not come on time. (*tɔ̀ən* 'to catch, be in time for')

12. *baːn-cìːə khɲom mùn baːn tr̃u thvỳː kaː(r), pìː msʏl, prùəh khɲom chùː.*
The reason why I did not go to work yesterday was that I was ill.

pìː msʏl vìːə bɔ̃rephòːk cɔmnʏɣ-ʔaːhaː(r) ʔaːkrɔk baːn-cìːə vìːə chùː ʔʏloːv.
Yesterday he ate some bad food and that is why he is ill now. (*bɔ̃rephòːk* 'to eat'. General polite word)

13. { *tùəh* / *tùəh-cìːə* / *tùəhbʏɣ* } *koːn khɲom kaː(r) kɔː-daoy, khɲom nùŋ nʏu phtèəh nìh cìːə dəraːp.*
Even if my daughter were to get married I should always live in this house. (*kaː(r)* 'to marry')

{ *tùəh* / *tùəh-cìːə* / *tùəhbʏɣ* } *nèək kmìːən kaː(r) ʔvʏɣ,[1] nèək ʔɔŋcr̃ːŋ mɔ̀ːk lèːŋ phtèəh khɲom.*
Even if you have no[1] particular business, do come and visit me at my house.

{ *dbʏt* / *dbʏt-tae* / *thvʏɣy-dbʏt-tae* } *koːn khɲom kaː(r) kɔː-daoy, khɲom nùŋ nʏu phtèəh nìh cìːə dəraːp.*
Although my daughter may marry, I shall always stay in this house.

{ *dbʏt* / *dbʏt-tae* / *thvʏɣy-dbʏt-tae* } *koːn khɲom kaː(r), khɲom nùŋ nʏu phtèəh nìh cìːə dəraːp.*
Although my daughter is getting married, I shall always stay in this house.

---

[1] See Lesson 32 for this use of negation plus question word.

14. *khɲom khə̀ːɲ mənùs(s) nùh dael lòːk-krùː baːn nìyì:əy pì: msɤl.*
I see that man about whom the teacher spoke yesterday.

15. *ʔaoy-tae nèək khəm rìən, nèək prəlɔːŋ nùŋ cɔ̀əp.*
So long as you study hard, you will pass the examination.

16. *(rùː) kèː thvə̀ː srae rùː kèː dam dəmnam nɤu phù:m(ì) nìh.*
(Either) they grow rice or they have plantations in this village. (*srae*
'rice-field'; *dam* 'to plant'; *dəmnam* 'plant').

17. *krùː prap khɲom thaː kmeːŋ nùh prəlɔːŋ cɔ̀əp.*
The teacher told me that this boy will pass the examination.

khɲom smaːn cì:ə kmeːŋ nùh prəlɔːŋ cɔ̀əp.
I think that this boy will pass the examination.

18. *kmeːŋ-pros nùh cɔŋ tɤu rìən nɤu srok-baːraŋ pon̄tae* }
tae
*kɔː-pon̄tae } *ʔoːpùk-mdaːy mùn prɔ̀ːm.*
That young man wants to go to France to study but his parents will not
agree (to it).

19. *nèək-bɔmraə nɤu phtèəh khɲom cù:t tok haəy-nùŋ lì:əŋ caːn.*
The servant at my house dusts the tables and washes the dishes.
(*lì:əŋ* 'to wash')

20. *taːm khɲom smaːn, kèː mùn srəlaɲ rɔ̀ət(th)-mùəntrɤy nùh tèː.*
In my opinion, people don't like the minister. (*smaːn* 'to think, guess')

21. *caːŋ-(h)vaːŋ baːn kat sĕckdɤy rùːəc haəy[1] kù: siəm troːvʔaoy prèəh-vìhì:ə(r)*
tɤu khmae(r) vèɲ.
The chairman had already decided the matter as follows, that the Thais
had to give the temple back to the Khmers. (*kat sĕckdɤy* 'make a legal
decision, decide'. Literally 'cut the matter')

22. *lòːk ʔaoy khɲom mərɔ̀ːy rìəl, kɔː khɲom mì:ən prak doː(r) cù:n lòːk.*
If you give me a hundred riels then I have the change for you. (*doː(r)* to
give change, give in exchange)

23. *cam bɔntec, sɤm ʔaeŋ tɤu!*
Wait a moment and then go!

tɔ̀əl-tae kɔ̀ət baək thɔːt-tok, tɤ̀:p kɔ̀ət dɤŋ thaː kɔ̀ət bat prak.
When he opened the drawer he knew that he had lost the money.

khɲom thvə̀ː nìh haəy, rùːəc khɲom tɤu phtèəh.
I shall do this and then go home.

kmeːŋ mɤ̀:l tùmpɔ̀ə(r) mù:əy tìət, rùːəc-haəy vì:ə bɤ̀ siəvphɤu.
The child read one more page and then closed the book.

mì:ŋ baːn tèɲ ʔɤyvan nùh (,|) haəy trəlɔp mɔ̀:k phtèəh vèɲ.
Aunt bought the things and then returned home.

---

[1] *haəy*, f., is discussed in the next Lesson. *rùːəc*, 'to finish', occurring as a 2nd position main
verb is discussed in Lesson 30.

24. *kraoy yʌ̀ːŋ cëɲ pìː phtèəh haəy, srap-tae cao(r) coːl lùːəc.*
After we had left the house, a thief immediately went in and stole (some things).

25. *prəhael-cìːə sɔmbot(r) khɲom tʌ̀u mùn dɔl.*
Perhaps my letter didn't get there.

26. *mùk(h)-cìːə sɔmbot(r) khɲom tʌ̀u mùn dɔl.*
It looks as though my letter didn't arrive.

27. *taə kroŋ bat-dɔmbɔːŋ nʌ̀u-ʔae naː?*
Where is Battambang?

28. *coːl ʔaeŋ mʌ̀ːl tùmpɔ̀ə(r) mùːəy tìət!*
Come on, read one more page!

29. *coh-baə nèək prəlɔːŋ thlèək? nèək troːv prəlɔːŋ mdɔːŋ tìət.*
What if you do fail? You'll have to sit for the examination again.

Exercise 27

Nouns. *bat-dɔmbɔːŋ* Battambang *dʌy* earth *kaːroŋ* bag *sɔmbot(r)* letter *prèy-nə̀kɔ̀ː(r)* Saigon **ʔʌyvan* things, luggage **kə̀naʔ-*prə̀cìːəthìpdʌ̀y(y)* Democratic party dog *chkae* school bell *skɔ̀ː(r)* (literally 'drum') soldier *tìːəhìːən* relatives *bɔːŋ-pʔɔːn* Water Festival *bon(y) ʔom tùːk* Europe *srok-baːraŋ*

Numeral coefficient. *dom* piece

Verbs. *thɲùən* to be heavy *cëɲ pìː* to leave *lùːəc* to steal *smaːn* to guess, think, be of the opinion *chnèəh* to win *pìsaː baːy* to eat (of other person in polite conversation) to bark *prùh* to hear *lùː* to 'ring' (literally 'beat') *tùːŋ* to be on fire *cheh* to meet (= to meet together) *cùːəp knìːə*

Particles. See Lesson 24.2 for markers

Expressions. another, other (sing.) *mùːəy tìət* by boat *taːm tùːk*

A.1. *taŋ-pìː khɲom mɔ̀ːk bat-dɔmbɔːŋ khɲom chùː bɔntec.* 2. *tùəhbʌy koːn-sʌs(s) nìh khɔm rìən, vìːə nùŋ mùn ceh craen tèː.* 3. *bɔːŋ-pros khɲom prəlɔːŋ bʌy doːŋ, pontae kə̀ət ceh-tae thlèək.* 4. *vìːə baːn dak dʌy mùːəy dom nùh daəmbʌy-ʔaoy kaːroŋ thɲùən.* 5. *baə-prəsʌn-cìːə sɔmbot(r) nùh mùn baːn mɔ̀ːk dɔl, ʔoːpùk nùŋ mùn cëɲ pìː prèy-nə̀kɔ̀ː(r) thŋay nìh tèː.* 6. *knoŋ-pèːl-dael lòːk-srʌy mɔ̀ːk suːə(r) khɲom ʔae phtèəh cao(r) mnèək coːl phtèəh lòːk-srʌy lùːəc ʔʌyvan craən.* 7. *taːm khɲom smaːn, kə̀naʔ-prə̀cìːəthìpdʌ̀y(y) nùŋ mùn chnèəh tèː.* 8. *mdaːy baːn thvʌ̀ː mhoːp, rùːəc kə̀ət cëɲ tʌ̀u phsaː(r).* 9. *khɲom cɔŋ mʌ̀ːl sɔmbot(r) dael mdaːy phɲaə pìː srok-sìəm.* 10. *kaːl-naː-baə lòːk mɔ̀ːk kompùəŋ-caːm mdɔːŋ tìət, lòːk troːv pìsaː baːy ʔae phtèəh khɲom.*

B.1. Twenty-three children took the examination and nineteen passed. 2. Either the dog did not bark, or I did not hear it. 3. Did you say that their house was near the big market, sir? 4. When the teacher rings the bell (lit. 'beats the drum'), the children will come out. 5. That man told me that my house was on fire. 6. After the village chief arrived, the soldiers left the house. 7. The room is very spacious but we shall not put another cupboard (in it). 8. The relatives came to Phnom Penh to see the Water Festival but they stayed three weeks! 9. When they go to Europe, will they wear sarongs sometimes? 10. After the two men had met at his house, he left Kompung Cham by boat.

LESSON 25

FINAL PHRASE PARTICLES; NOTE ON DIRECT QUESTIONS

25.1. *Definition of final phrase particles*

Two particles labelled 'final phrase particles' have been introduced already; these are *tèː* and *rùː*. Their function may now be described as occurring at the end of phrases (which very often coincide with the end of clauses).

e.g. *khɲom mùn tr̆u tèː,* (,|) *baə nèək mùn tr̆u.* I am not going if you are not.

25.2. *List of final phrase particles,* ꝼ

1. *thaː* (\) 'that'. Followed by direct or lively indirect speech.

2. *tèː*. With *mùn* or some other negative pre-verbal particle preceding, 'at all'. In an affirmative statement, often with *tae*, 'only', preceding, 'indeed'. May simply add emphasis.

3. *tèː*, or the sequence, *rùː tèː*, at the end of a question, forms a blunt question, requiring the answer, 'yes' or 'no'. 'or not?'

4. *rùː* 'perhaps, isn't that so?' Occurs at the end of a question, forming a much less forceful, more tentative question than *tèː*, or *rùː tèː*, when the sentence is pronounced with a straightforward question tune. Given a sentence-tune consistent with a more excited style of speech, with stress on a key word, *rùː* may help to convey sarcasm or surprise.

5. The sequence *tèː rùː* may occur at the end of either an affirmative or a negative clause. It suggests that the speaker has a definite idea of what answer he will receive. 'surely?' 'isn't that so?' 'then?' Like *rùː*, *tèː rùː* may convey sarcasm or surprise when the sentence is uttered with a tune associated with an excited speech style.

6. *dvŋ* occurs especially in the sequence, *tèː dvŋ?* at the end of a question, with the meaning, 'do you know?'

7. *taə*, especially in the sequence, *tèː taə*, forms an exclamation of considerable surprise. 'So . . . . after all!' 'So . . . . , then!'

8. *laəy* 'at all'. Reinforces a negation usually but may also add emphasis to an affirmative clause. Occurs in slightly contradictory or argumentative statements. The verb *nr̆u* often precedes *laəy* when the sense is 'not yet'.

9. *sɔh* at all. Reinforces a negation more strongly than *tèː*. Is often used preceding *laəy*.

10. *tìət* 'further, again, more'.

11. *saot* 'moreover, in addition, too'.

12. *phɔːŋ* 'too, as well'. May link two constructs or two sentence-forms but need not.

hɔːŋ Literary form of *phɔːŋ*.

13. *dae(r)*. 'too, also, even so'. May also simply add emphasis, suggesting that a fact is so, in spite of something, e.g. in spite of what the other person has said to the contrary.

14. *vèɲ* 'back again, again, tracing the same path over again'. (Contrast *tìət*, which may mean 'again' in the sense of 'adding yet another time, once more'.)

15. *haəy* 'already'. Often no word is needed in English to translate *haəy*, because the perfect or pluperfect tense in the English is conveying the idea

of completion which *haəy* conveys in the Cambodian. The sequence *haəy rùː* at the end of a question forms a polite enquiry, 'Has . . . . (yet/already)'? See *rùː* in 4. above.

16. . . . . *kɔː-daoy 'even if' (referring to what precedes).

17. . . . . *kɔː-daoy . . . . *kɔː-daoy. Emphasizes one pos-
    sibility as against another.
    . . . . *kɔː-baːn . . . . *kɔː-baːn. Occurs when listing
    possibilities, potential only.
    . . . . *kɔː-mìːən . . . . *kɔː-mìːən. Occurs when listing
    definite alternatives.
    . . . . *kdɤy* . . . . *kdɤy*. Definite alternatives, usually
    a list of single words.

    'either . . . . or'
    'whether . . . . or'

18. *coh!* 'Off you go and . . . . !'
19. *sɤn!* 'get on with it immediately!'
20. *tɤu!* 'go on, do!' Occurs at the end of a command, pronounced with a steep fall in pitch.
21. *mɤːl* 'perhaps, it is possible'.
22. *mɔːk* 'forth up to now' [1]
    tɤu 'forth from then'
    tɔː-mɔːk 'continually until now'
    tɔː-tɤu 'continually from then'
    tɔː-tɔː-mɔːk 'all the time from
    rìəŋ-mɔːk   then until now'
    tɔː-tɔː-tɤu 'all the time from
    then'

    usually occur after *pìː* and a stated time or date

mɔːk and its compounds suggest continuation right up to the time of speaking; this may be intimated by use of the perfect tense in English. *tɤu* and it compounds may refer to a time which was completed before the time of speaking.

23. *tɤu-tìət* 'longer', of time.

25.3. *Order of occurrence of final phrase particles*

Some of the above are regularly used together with others in a fixed word-order:—*sɔh laəy* 'at all', *tɤu coh* 'go on, then!' Others, not so regularly used together, nevertheless have a fixed word-order when they do occur in sequence. A question word or *tèː taə* come last. *kɔː-baːn*, *kɔː-daoy*, *kɔː-mìːən* and *kdɤy* come last except that they may be followed by *dae(r)*. *vèɲ*, *tìət*, *naː*, *tèː* come before *sɔh*, *laəy*, *phɔːŋ*, *hɔːŋ*. *thaː* comes at the end; it has been met already as a marker (compare also *haəy* which may be a marker or a final phrase particle). *thaː*, as a final phrase particle, is uttered with a steep fall and followed by a pause, while *haəy*, occurring as a final phrase particle, forms part of a rising intonation tune before a pause.

25.4. *Sentences illustrating the use of final phrase particles*

Phrases which may occur in the kinds of sentence used so far and within the limits of the sentence-tunes so far introduced may be described as follows:—

---

[1] Not used until Lesson 35.

(i) Simple sentence (consisting, that is, of one clause) pronounced as one phrase.

(ii) Simple sentence consisting of one clause, of which part is pronounced as one phrase and the rest is pronounced as a second phrase.

(iii) Composite sentence, consisting of two clauses, each pronounced as a phrase.

The following sentences illustrate the use of final phrase particles in phrases such as those described above in (i), (ii) and (iii).[1]

(i) *lò:k-kru: cɔŋ tỷu kɔmpùəŋ-ca:m dae(r).* 'The teacher wants to go to Kompung Cham too.'

(ii) *siəvphỷu nùh saot (‚|) kɔ: mùun l?ɔ: mỷ:l tè: taə!* 'That book's not worth reading either, then!'

(iii) *ka:l-na: cau səse:(r) sɔmbot(r) rù:əc haəy (‚|) khɲom nùŋ yɔ:k sɔmbot(r) tỷu dak pos(te).* 'When you have finished writing the letter, I will take it to the post.'

The following sentences illustrate the use of all final phrase particles listed in 25.2.

1. *kè: su:ə(r) khɲom tha: (\) nèək nỷu phù:m(ì) na:?*
   They asked me, 'Which village do you live in?'

2. *khɲom mùun dɤŋ tè:.*
   I don't know.

   khɲom mì:ən tae pì:(r) tè:.
   I have only two.

3. *nèək tỷu tè:* or *nèək tỷu rù: tè:?*
   Are you going?

4. *?o:pùk khɤŋ nùŋ khɲom rù:?*
   Is my father angry with me?

5. *lò:k nỷu phtèəh tè: rù:?*
   Mr. — is at home isn't he? Surely Mr. — is at home?

   lò:k mùun nỷu phtèəh tè: rù:?
   Mr. — isn't at home, is he?

   ?aeŋ kmì:ən phnè:k (‚) tè: rù: (')?[2]
   Haven't you got *eyes*, then?

6. *yỷ:ŋ tro:v tỷu kɔnlaeŋ nìh tè: dɤŋ?*
   Is this the place we have to go to, do you know?

7. *nèək mùun prò:m tỷu mỷ:l kon cì:ə-mù:əy-nùŋ khɲom tè: taə?!*
   You refuse to go to see the film with me, then?!

   khɲom sma:n tha: krəhɔ:m tè: taə!
   I thought it was *red*! (and now I see that it is not.)

8. *khɲom mùun dɤŋ rùəŋ nìh laəy.*
   I don't know this story at all! (You seem to think I do . . . .)

---

[1] These sentences are recorded. See Part VII, Appendix 4.
[2] This sentence is recorded on the tapes. See Part VII, Appendix 4, 'Emphasis of one word.'

koːn-sɤs(s) nù̀ŋ mùùn coːl cɤt(t) nù̀ŋ krùː nìh sɔh laəy!
The students will not like this teacher at all! (I disagree with you.)

khɲom mùùn-tɔ̀ən baːn tətùːrəl sɔmbot(r) nɤ̆u laəy.
I have not yet received the letter. (You seem to think I have.)

9. *thŋay nìh tìət vìə mùn prɔ̀ːm tɤ̆u phtὲəh sɔh!*
On that day again he refused to go home!

10. *vìːə thvɤ̀ː haəy thvɤ̀ː tìət, tɔ̀əl-tae khɲom khɤ̆ŋ.*
He did it again and again until I lost my temper.

ʔaeŋ troːv khɔm thvɤ̀ː kaː(r) tìət.
You must work harder./You must make more effort with your work.

11. *mənùs(s) nùh saot kɔː mùn baːn mɔ̀ːk dae(r).*
That man, too, didn't even come.

12. *khɲom soːm phɲaə kɔɲcɔp nìh phɔːŋ.*
I would like to send this parcel too, please.

13. a.[1] *khɲom tɤ̆u phsaː(r).* b. *khɲom tɤ̆u dae(r).*
a. I'm going to the market. b. So am I.
Contrast the answer, *khɲom tɤ̆u phɔːŋ,* I would like to go too (i.e. if I may).

a. *mìən nɤ̆u sɔl ʔɔŋkɔː(r) rùː tὲː?* Is there any husked rice left?
b. *baːt, nɤ̆u sɔl ʔɔŋkɔː(r) dae(r).* Yes, there *is.*

14. *ʔoːpùk trəlɔp mɔ̀ːk phtὲəh vèɲ.*
Father is coming back home.

15. *kaːl-naː kɔ̀ət baːn ʔɔŋkùy haəy, tɤ̀ːp kèː ʔaoy sɔmbot(r) nùh tɤ̆u kɔ̀ət.*
When he had sat down, they gave him the letter.

kɔ̀ət baːn phɲaə sɔmbot(r) haəy rùː?
Has he sent the letter?

16. *tùəhbɤy koːn khɲom kaː(r) kɔː-daoy, khɲom nù̀ŋ nɤ̆u phtὲəh nìh.*
Even if my daughter were to get married I should live in this house.

17. *ʔaeŋ tɤ̆u mɤ̀ːl kon kɔː-daoy, tɤ̆u daə(r) lèːŋ kɔː-daoy, khɲom kɔː tɤ̆u phtὲəh ʔɤylɔːv.*
Whether you go to see a film or go for a walk, I shall go home now.

lòːk cìh yùə̀n(t)-hɔh tɤ̆u taːm vìːə kɔː-baːn (,|), khɲom baək laːn tɤ̆u taːm vìːə kɔː-baːn.
It would be possible for you to get on a plane and follow him or for me to drive after him.

lòːk tèɲ khsae ʔae phsaː(r) kɔː-mìən, ʔae haŋ mùːəy kɔː-mìən.
You can buy string either at the market or at a store, sir.

yɤ̀ːŋ nù̀ŋ cùːəp knìə nɤ̆u phtὲəh nèək kdɤy rùː nɤ̆u phtὲəh khɲom kdɤy.
We will meet either at your house or at mine.

khɲom thvɤ̀ː nìh kdɤy nùh kdɤy, kèː kɔː sok(h) cɤt(t) dae(r).
Whatever I do, he agrees to it.

18. *ʔaeŋ tɤ̆u lèːŋ coh!*
Off you go and play now!

---

[1] Here, as elsewhere, a. and b. indicate two different speakers.

19. *mɔːk thvɤ̀ː nìh sɤn!*
    Come and do this (this minute)!

20. *mɤ̀ːl siəvphɤ̀u tɤ̀u!*
    Go on, read (your) book!

21. *vìːə mùn dɤŋ tèː mɤ̀ːl?*
    Perhaps he doesn't know?

22. *pìː thŋay nùh mɔːk, pʔoːn-srɤy khɲom chùːr.*
    From that day my sister has been ill.

    pìː thŋay-ʔɔŋkìːə(r) nìh tɤ̀u, kèː chùp thvɤ̀ː kaː(r) nɤ̀u maoŋ pram.
    From Tuesday onwards, they will stop work at five o'clock.

    pìː chnam nùh tɔː-mɔːk, sdäc khmae(r) nɤ̀u phnùm-pè̌ɲ.
    From that year onwards, Cambodian kings have lived at Phnom Penh.

    pìː chnam nùh tɔː-tɤ̀u, sdäc siəm nɤ̀u tì-kroŋ nùh.
    From that year onwards, Thai kings lived in that city.

    pìː pèːl nùh tɔː-tɔː-mɔːk } *sdäc khmae(r) baːn nɤ̀u phnùm-pè̌ɲ.*
        rìəŋ-mɔːk
    Since that time, Cambodian kings have always lived in Phnom Penh.

    pìː chnam nùh tɔː-tɔː-tɤ̀u, sdäc saoy rìːəc nɤ̀u phnùm-pè̌ɲ.
    From that year onwards the kings have ruled the kingdom continually
    at Phnom Penh.

23. *kɔ̀ət mùn prɔ̀ːm thvɤ̀ː kaː(r) tɤ̀u-tìət tèː.*
    He refuses to work any longer.

25.5. *Difference in time*

In sentences consisting of two clauses there may be a difference in time
between the occurrences expressed by the two main verbs. This may be
made more explicit by the use of *baːn* or *nùŋ*, e.g.

lòːk nìyìːəy thaː kɔ̀ət nùŋ mɔ̀ːk thŋay nìh. Mr. — said that he would come
today.

khɲom baːn phɲaə sɔmbot(r) mùn-nùŋ khɲom dɤŋ dɔmnɤŋ nìh. I had sent the
letter before I heard this news.

A further note on this subject is given in connection with indirect questions
in Lesson 29.

Exercise 28

Nouns. *prəlùm̀* dawn   **kauʔɤy* chair   abbot *cau-ʔaìthìkaː(r)*   India *srok-
klɤŋ(k)

Verbs. *trəlɔp* to turn round   *trəlɔp . . . . mɔ̀ːk* to come back   *trəlɔp . . . . tɤ̀u*
to go back   to decide *dac cɤt(t)*   to intend (see under particles)   to consider *kùt*

Particle. intend to *nùŋ* p.v.p.

For final phrase particles see list above

Exclamation. *ʔao!* oh!

A.1. *mìːŋ trəlɔp pìː srok-siəm mɔ̀ːk vèɲ haəy rùː?* 2. *ta: baːn thvɤ̀ː kaː(r) pìː
prəlùːm haəy ʔɤylòːvᵇnìh kɔ̀ət tro:v bɔɲhaəy kauʔɤy nìh phoːŋ.* 3. *ʔao! doːn ʔɤt*

chừ: tè: taəʔ pì: msɤl kɔ̀ət baːn coːl phtɛ̀əh-pɛ̌ːt̀(y)! 4. nɛ̀ək tɤu bat-dombɔːŋ cìh rətèh-phlɤ̀ːŋ thŋay nìh kɔː-baːn, khɲom cìh laːn sʔaek kɔː-baːn. 5. khɲom mùm khɤ̀ːɲ konlaeŋ naː: lʔɔ: sɔh laəy! 6. nìːəŋ mùm prɔ̀ːm cùːt phtɛ̀əh tìət tè:.

B.1. The teacher said that my grandson isn't learning French at all! 2. I should like to (= want to) know if you decide to leave Phnom Penh, sir. 3. At that shop they sell materials from India too. 4. Mr. —'s uncle has come back to his home already. 5. What are you going to do in Phnom Penh tomorrow? I'm going to buy some things and go to see some friends as well. 6. The abbot intends to consider the matter further.

25.6. *Notes on the formation of various kinds of direct question*

The two new uses of the final phrase particles *rùː* and *tèː* introduced in this Lesson (i.e. *rùː* occurring alone and the sequence *tèː rùː*) will increase the student's flexibility in framing questions considerably. The opportunity is taken here of summarizing the styles of question which have been introduced so far and of anticipating, i.e. in 3 (iii) below, one question form which will be met in the next Lesson.

All the styles of question have the following characteristics:—

1. The sentence-form is unchanged (i.e. the word-order is not altered to form a question).

2. The question tune is needed (').

3. One of the following is needed:—

    (i) a question word or phrase. See Lesson 18.

    (ii) a question-forming final phrase particle. *tèː* or *rùː tèː* forms a blunt interrogation, 'Is this so or not?' *rùː* forms a polite question, 'Is it the case that . . . . ?' *tèː rùː* suggests that the speaker thinks he knows the answer, 'Surely . . . . ?'

    (iii) *rùː* occurring as a marker with a clause following.[1]

    A particularly common form of this is *rùː nɤu* 'or does there remain (time)', e.g. Has he come (yet)? *kɔ̀ət mɔ̀ːk dɔl haəy rùː nɤu?*

    In colloquial speech *rùː ʔɤy* and *rùː ʔeh* occur at the end of questions, suggesting surprise or indignation, e.g.

    nɛ̀ək mùn thvɤ̀ː dɔːcᵊneh rùːʔɤy? You surely didn't do it that way, did you? (not really expecting an answer).

    nɛ̀ək mùn thvɤ̀ː dɔːcᵊneh rùːʔeh? You don't mean to say you did it that way, do you? (demanding an explanation).

Exercise 29

Nouns. scissors *kɔntray*

Verbs. *tətùːəl* to receive, meet *thvɤ̀ː tɔ̀ːs (kèː)* to punish (a person) to be terrified *phùt-phéy* to hide *lɛ̀ək* to die *slap* to deceive *bɔɲchaot*

Particles **a.** *dɔːcᵊneh* thus, like this together with, with, in company with *cìːə-mùːəy-nù̀ŋ* **pre n.p.**

---

[1] The sequence *rùː ʔeh*, which is included here, might preferably be analysed as a compound final phrase particle since *ʔeh* does not seem to occur alone, except as a verb, *ʔeh* 'to scratch'.

A.1. kè: mùm-tɔ̀ən tù:ŋ skɔ̀:(r) tè: rừ:ʔ 2. ka:l-na: bo:ŋ-pʔo:n nɛ̀ək mɔ̀:k mɤ̀:l boŋ(y) ʔom tù:k, nɛ̀ək nùŋ tɤ̀u tətù:əl ʔae kɔ̯pal rừ: tè:ʔ 3. yɤ̀:ŋ ba:n cừ:əp knì:ə haəy rừ:ʔ 4. mì:ŋ nɛ̀ək mừm ba:n dac cɤ̀t(t) tèɲ phtɛ̀əh thmɤ̀y nùh tè: rừ:ʔ 5. lò:k-krừ: cɔŋ thvɤ̀: tò:s ko:n-sɤ̀s(s) ka:c nùh rừ:ʔ

B.1. When you went into father's room, you didn't see my scissors did you? 2. If I go by train will uncle go with me? 3. Ever since his grandfather died he has been ill, hasn't he? 4. Even if she had stolen the book she wouldn't be terrified like this, would she? 5. You didn't hide that letter so as to deceive him, did you?

Lesson 26

Sentence-form II; Commands and Impersonal Use of Verbs

26.1. *Sentence-form II 1 and II 2; initiating sentences with no independent noun construct*

Up to now, when there has been no noun construct before the first verb construct,[1] it has been in a responding sentence (which need not represent a sentence-form). e.g.

Initiating sentence	*Responding sentence*
ʔo:pùk nɤ̀u ʔae na:?	*nɤ̀u phtɛ̀əh.*

Initiating sentences will now be introduced which have no independent noun construct. This produces two new sentence-forms, which, however, in other respects resemble the preceding two:—

Sentence-form II 1. V   In full (r), (m) (A/a/X) V (A/a/v/X) (f)

Sentence-form II 2. V V In full (r), (m) (A/a/X) V (A/a/v/X) V (A/a/v/X) (f)

Two kinds of grammatical function take place within this framework: the expression of commands and the expression of actions without reference to any agent (impersonal verbs).

26.2. *Commands*

1. affirmative. e.g. *yɔ̀:k siəvphɤ̀u mɔ̀:k khɲom!* 'Bring the book to me' (**V V**). *co:l bɔntùp!* 'Go into the room!' (**V**).

2. negative. A negative command is formed by means of the pre-verbal particle, *kom*. e.g. *kom tɤ̀u!* 'Don't go!' *kom sraek!* 'Don't shriek!' (**V**). *kom rɔ̀:k rùəy cɔmʔɔ:k vì:ə!* 'Don't look for ways of mocking him!' (**V V**).

A command may be made less abrupt however by the use of sentence-form I. e.g. *ʔaey kom thvɤ̀: nìh!* 'Don't you do this!' (**N V**). *ko:n kom prừ:əy!* 'Don't be miserable, child!' (**N V**). *cau kom tɤ̀u prap krù:!* 'Don't go and tell the teacher, young fellow!' (**N V V**).

26.3. *Impersonal use of verbs*

This may be illustrated by examples divided on lexical grounds as follows:—

1. Verbs which may be lexically connected with the weather.

e.g. *rəɲì:ə nas!* It's very cold! (**V**)

trəcɛ̀ək lmɔ̀:m. It's just cool enough ('to be fresh'/'to be just right') (**V V**)

---

[1] i.e. no noun construct other than those incorporated into verb constructs. See Lesson 17.2.

2. Verbs which may be lexically connected with the passage of time.

e.g.[1] *dɔl maoŋ haəy*. It is already time. (It has arrived at the hour already.) (**V**)

huːəs maoŋ haəy. It is past the time already. (It has passed beyond the time already.) (**V**)

nɤ̆u bɤy mìːnùt tìət. Three more minutes! (There remain three minutes more.) (**V**)

dɔl maoŋ haəy rùː nɤ̆u? Is it time yet? (Has it arrived at the hour already or does there remain (time)?) 2 clauses **V + V**

3. Verbs which may be lexically connected with general accidental or natural events (breaking, growing, catching fire, falling).

e.g. *cheh phtèəh*. Fire breaks out in the house (**V**) (*cheh* 'to catch fire').

baek pèːŋ. A cup was broken (*baek* 'to break' (intr.) *pèːŋ* 'cup').

duːəl dɔːp. A jar fell over (*duːəl* 'to fall over', *dɔːp* 'jar').

For verbs which fit into 1 and 2 above, there is no alternative means of expression; for many verbs of this third lexical category, however, sentence-form I may be used:—*phtèəh cheh, dɔːp duːəl*. The style is then less vivid.[2]

Many verbs belonging lexically to this category must retain the word-order verb-noun which is in fact verb-object (subject not expressed).

e.g. *lùː sɔː(r) khlaŋ*. There was a loud sound.

thŭm klɤn *krəʔɔːp. There was a pleasant scent. (*thŭm* 'to smell', *klɤn* 'scent', **krəʔɔːp*, 'having a pleasant scent').

4. Verbs which introduce possibilities, necessities, happenings, etc.

e.g. *mìːən phtèəh mùːəy nɤ̆u cùt khaːŋ phloːv*. There is a house at the side of the road (**V V**).

troːv bɔːŋ tɤ̆u saːlaː-rìən. It is necessary for elder brother to go to school (**V V**).

troːv kom-ʔaoy phɤ̆k tùk krəkhvɔk. It is essential not to drink dirty water. (2 clauses **V + V**).

nɤ̆u dɔːŋ mùːəy phloːn. There remain 40 coconuts (**V**).

haːm mùn-ʔaoy cùək baːrɤy. It is forbidden to smoke. (*haːm* 'to forbid'. 2 clauses **V + V**).

thŋay nùh cùːən cìːə laːn khoːc. It happened that the car broke down that day. (*cùːən* 'to happen', *khoːc* 'to go wrong'. 2 clauses **V + N V**).

Exercise 30

Nouns. *ʔaeŋ* you (familiar, to inferior or to child) *ʔaɲ* I (familiar) *phlìəŋ* rain *suːən* garden *prəlùp* dusk *klɤn* smell *phkaː* flower *khae* month *kmuːəy* nephew, niece *phlɤt* fan *rùəŋ* story, event *prèy* forest *prəlùm* dawn *sɔː(r)* sound *sat(v)-haə(r)* bird *nùm* cake *rose* *phkaː-kolaːp* door *tvìːə(r)* plate *caːn* tray *thaːs* tile *kbuəŋ* roof *dɔmbòːl* temple **vihìːə(r)*

Verbs. *laəŋ* to climb up, go in, come in (the house) *thlèək* to fall *sraek* to cry out *thlɔŋ* to be deaf *thŭm* to smell (tr.) **krəʔɔːp* to have a pleasant

---

[2] In the first examples under 3 the subject-verb order is inverted. We are concerned here, however, only with the occurrence or non-occurrence of an independent noun construct, potentially pronounced as a separate phrase in the sentence.

scent   *kdau* to be hot   *trəcèək* to be fresh, cool   *ʔaːnɤt* to be so kind as to
bɤt to shut, to turn off (electrical appliances)   *kaət* to be born, to arise,
to happen   *plaek* to be different, interesting   *nìtìːən* to relate (a story),
to tell   **lùː* to hear   *sol* to remain, to be left over   *ʔɔɲcɤ̀ːɲ* please do
to go for a walk *daə(r)-lèːŋ* to be past (of time) *huːəs* to be late *yùːt*
to be cold *rəɲìːə* to be broken, to break (intr.) *baek* to be dented *pìəc*
Particles. *sɤn* f. go on, do it now!   *mùn* pre n.p. before   *coh* f. do!

A.1. ʔaeŋ laəŋ phtèəh sɤn! ʔ<u>a</u>ɲ coŋ nìyìːəy cìːə-mùːəy-nùŋ ʔaeŋ phlìːəm. 2. pìː
msɤl meɲ thlèək phlìəŋ mɔ̀ːk craən. 3. kmeːŋ kom sraek! krù: mùm-mèːn
thlɔŋ tèː. 4. knoŋ suːən lòːk kae pèːl prəlùp thùm klɤn phka: krəʔoːp nas.
5. khae nih kdau nas pèːl yùp. 6. kmuːəy kom daə(r) rəhás doːc⌐neh! mìːŋ mùn
coŋ tɤu dəl mùn maoŋ tèː. 7. knoŋ bontùp nih trəcèək nas. nìːəŋ ʔaːnɤt bɤt
phlɤt ʔaoy khɲom. 8. thŋay nih kaət rùəŋ mùːəy plaek. khɲom nùŋ nìtìːən
tɤu lòːk-srɤy. 9. knoŋ prèy nih pèːl prəlùm lùː soː(r) s<u>a</u>t(v)-haə(r) craən.
10. nɤu sol nùm pìː(r) dom tìət. nèək ʔɔɲcɤ̀ːɲ pìsa: mùːəy coh!

B.1. Take those two books to Mr. Kê! 2. It is already past the hour! We must
not arrive late! 3. I don't want to go for a walk. It is too hot today.
4. Rain is falling already; we must hurry and call a cyclo-pousse. 5. There
was a sound of children crying behind the house. 6. Don't buy the smoked
fish in the big market, younger (sister). It's too dear there. 7. There was
a scent of roses in the room but I didn't see any flowers at all. 8. Do sit
here! It is cold near the door. 9. Three plates were broken and the tray
was dented! 10. A tile fell from the roof of the temple.

LESSON 27

VOCABULARY AND GRAMMAR OF THE PROCESS OF TELLING THE TIME, EXPRESSING THE DATE, ETC.

27.1. *Vocabulary*

Numeral coefficients

Time divisions: *nìːətìː* or *mìːnùt* minute   *maoŋ* hour, o'clock   *thŋay* day
ʔaːtùt(y) week   *khae* month   *chnam, khuːəp* year   *s<u>a</u>kraːc* century.
Parts of the day: *prəlùm, phlùː* dawn   *prùk* morning   *thŋay, thŋay*
trɔŋ late morning and lunch-time   *rəsìəl* early afternoon (noon to 2 p.m.)
lŋìːəc afternoon and early evening (2 p.m. to dusk)   *prəlùp* dusk   *yùp*
dark, night.

Nouns

Names of the days of the week: *thŋay-c<u>a</u>n(t)* Monday   *thŋay-ʔɔŋkìːə(r)*
Tuesday   *thŋay-pùt(h)* Wednesday   *thŋay-pr<u>ə</u>h<u>ɔ̀ə</u>s(p + tè)* Thursday
thŋay-sok(r) Friday   *thŋay-sau(r)* Saturday   *thŋay-ʔaːtùt(y)* Sunday.
Names of the months: *khae-mè<u>ə</u>k<u>a</u>raː* January   *khae-komphè<u>ə</u>* February
khae-mìːnìːə March   *khae-mèːsaː* April   *khae-ʔos<u>a</u>phìːə* May   *khae-mìthonaː*
June   *khae-k<u>a</u>kdaː* July   *khae-sɤyhaː* August   *khae-k<u>a</u>ɲɲaː* September
khae-tolaː October   *khae-vìccheka:* November   *khae-thnù:* December.

The following names of the months, which are in accordance with the Candagati system, are little used now: *mì:rək̀(h)* January–February *phọlkùn* February–March *cäet(r)* March–April *vìsa:k(h)* or *pìsa:k(h)* April–May *cè:s(ìh)* May–June *ʔa:sa:ḷ(h)* June–July *sra:p̀(+ ṇ)* July–August *phọ̀ɔtrè̀əbọ̀l* August–September *ʔạssoć* September–October *kạtdɤk* October–November **mìkè̀əse:(r)* November–December *bos(s)* December–January.

Parts of the lunar month: *khnaət* period of the waxing moon *rənò:c* period of the waning moon.

Names of the years: 1. *chnam-cù:t* rat 2. *chnam-chlo:v* ox 3. *chnam-kha:l* tiger 4. *chnam-thɔh* hare 5. *chnam-rò:ŋ* dragon 6. *chnam-msaɲ* serpent 7. *chnam-məmì:* horse 8. *chnam-məmè:* goat 9. *chnam-vò:k* monkey 10. *chnam-rəka:* cock 11. *chnam-cɔ:* dog 12. *chnam-kol* pig.

The names of the cycles, *-sák* of 12 years. These are counted by means of Sanskrit numerals. 1. *ʔaekasák* 2. *tò:sák* 3. *trɤysák* 4. *cạtva:sák* 5. *paɲcạsák* 6. *chɔ:sák* 7. *sạptạsák* 8. *ʔạṭṭhạsák* 9. *nùppè̀əsák*. 10. *sɔmrɤtthìsák* (the completing cycle).

Names of the Eras. *pùlthè̀əsạkra:ć* Buddhist Era. *krì:stạsạkra:ć* Christian Era.

Verbs. *khvah* to lack *hu:əs* to pass *nɤ̀u* to remain *dɔl* to arrive at *kaət* to wax (of moon) *rò:c* to wane (of moon).

27.2. *Stating clock-time*

The precise hours of the clock are expressed in the form of a noun construct (nx). e.g. *maoŋ bɤy* '3 o'clock', *maoŋ pì:(r)-dɔndɔp* '12 o'clock'. The construct is often followed by the word *haəy*, e.g. *maoŋ pì:(r) haəy*. 'It is two o'clock (already).'

To form a question about the time one needs the question numeral, *ponma:n*, e.g. *maoŋ ponma:n?* or *maoŋ ponma:n haəy?* 'What time is it?' (Answer: *maoŋ* x *haəy*.) When questions about clock time are made more precise, the words *dɔl*, *hu:əs* and *nɤ̀u* are used, in the impersonal way discussed in Lesson 26.3, e.g. *dɔl maoŋ bu:ən haəy rù: nɤ̀u?* 'Is it 4 o'clock yet?' (has it got to 4 o'clock yet or does there remain time?) Possible answers to this are: '*dɔl maoŋ haəy*' or '*hu:əs maoŋ haəy*' or '*nɤ̀u*'. ('It is' or 'It's past the hour' or 'Not yet'.)

When the number of minutes to or past the hour are to be expressed the words *nùŋ* 'with, and', and *khvah* 'to lack' are used, followed by a numeral construct. *maoŋ bɤy nùŋ pram nì:əti:*. 'It's five past three.' *maoŋ pram-mù:əy khvah dɔp mì:nùt*. 'It's ten to six'. *maoŋ mù:əy-dɔndɔp nùŋ pram-dɔndɔp nì:əti:*. 'It's a quarter past eleven.' *maoŋ prampùl nùŋ sa:msɤp nì:əti:*. 'It's half past seven.' There is no word for a quarter of an hour. Half an hour may be expressed by *kɔnlah* as well as by *sa:msɤp nì:əti:*, e.g. *dɔl maoŋ pram-bɤy kɔnlah haəy rù: nɤ̀u?* 'Is it half past eight yet?'

A numeral construct expresses length of time without reference to the clock. *vì:ə ba:n cam bɤy chnam*. He waited three years. *nɤ̀u tae mù:əy mì:nùt tìət tè!* There is only a minute left! *nɤ̀u* (the pre-nominal particle) is used when one wishes to say 'at — o'clock', e.g. *vì:ə mò:k su:ə(r) khɲom nɤ̀u maoŋ bɤy*. He is coming to see me at 3 o'clock.

111

27.3. *The date*

The date is expressed as follows in a newspaper,

thŋay-ʔɔŋkìːə(r) pram-mùːəy ròːc khae-phɔ̀ɔtrèəbɔ̀ chnam-khaːl cɑtvaːsák pùtthɛ̀əsakraːc̀ pìː(r) pɔ̀ən pram-ròːy pram, troːv nùŋ thŋay tìː pram-buːən-dɔndɔp kaŋŋaː məpɔ̀ən pram-buːən-ròːy hoksɤp-pìː(r). Tuesday the 6th of the waning moon, month of August–September, year of the tiger, fourth cycle, Buddhist Era, 2505, coinciding with the 15th day of September, 1962.

In less formal contexts dates and times are expressed as follows,

thŋay-pùl(h) tìː pram mìːnìːə[1] on Wednesday, the 5th March
pìː thŋay-cɑn(l) dɔl thŋay-sok(r) from Monday to Friday
pìː ʔaːtùt(y) mùn last week
ʔaːtùt(y) nìh this week
ʔaːtùt(y) kraoy next week
pìː khae-thnùː from December
khae-mɛ̀əkaraː in January
dɔl khae-mìːnìːə in March (yet to come)
khae mùn last month
chnam nìh this year
khae-kaŋŋaː kraoy next September
knoŋ chnam məpɔ̀ən pram-buːən-ròːy hoksɤp-buːən in 1964

Exercise 31

Nouns. *häet(o)* reason   *krùː-pɛ̀ːl(y)* doctor   cinema *ròːŋ-kon*
Verbs. *saəc* to laugh   *krùn* to have a fever   *khlìːən* to be hungry   to be American *ʔaːmeːrìːkɑŋ*   to rest *tətùːəl tìːən dɔmneːk* to be asleep *lùək* to put on (electric appliances) *baək*   to be necessary *troːv*
Particles. *knìːə* a. together   and *haəy-nùŋ* m.   all *tɛ̀əŋ-ʔɔs* a. post n.p.
Expression. —*ʔɤy*—!/—*ʔɤːy*—! How . . . . !

A.1. pɛ̀ːl prùk dɔl maoŋ pram-bɤy khvah pram-dɔndɔp nìːətì: lòːk-krùː tùːŋ skɔ̀ː(r) tɔ̀əl-tae koːn-sɤs(s) coːl saːlaː-rìən tɛ̀əŋ-ʔɔs knìːə. 2. knoŋ kɔnlaeŋ nìh, tùəh-cìːə huːəs maoŋ pìː(r)-dɔndɔp yùp kɔː-daoy, lùː: soː(r) mənùs(s) craən nɛ̀ək saəc taːm phloːv. 3. mìːən häet(o) mùːəy tìət baːn-cìːə khɲom mùm cɔŋ tɤu thvɤ̀ː kaː(r) ʔae kɔmpùəŋ caːm, pìː-prùəh khɲom tɤ̀ːp-nùŋ tèŋ phtɛ̀əh nɤu phnùm-pèɲ. 4. rətèh-phlɤ̀ːŋ cèŋ maoŋ poɲmaːn? baːt̀, cèŋ tɤu maoŋ prampùl prùk. tɤu dɔl bat-dɔmbɔːŋ maoŋ poɲmaːn? baːt̀, tɤu dɔl maoŋ pram-mùːəy lɲìːəc. 5. lòːk krùn pìː ʔaːtùt(y) mùn pontae lòːk mùm prɔ̀ːm hau krùː-pɛ̀ːt̀(y) tèː. 6. thŋay-pùt̀(h) khɲom cèŋ pìː phtɛ̀əh pìː prəlùm tɤu cap trɤy. dɔl maoŋ pram-mùːəy lɲìːəc khɲom trəlɔp mɔ̀ːk phtɛ̀əh vèɲ. khlìːən ʔɤy khlìːən!

B.1. While heavy rain was falling we waited in the temple. 2. Don't come on Thursday; we are going to see an American film at the new cinema. 3. Although it was already seven o'clock, the old man and his son had not yet finished the chair. 4. Mr. Kê usually rests in the early afternoon but I don't think he is asleep. 5. If my elder sister goes to study in England in October she will stay four years. 6. In April it will be very hot! It will be necessary to put the fan on at night.

---

[1] In such a context, the month names, not compounded with *khae*, occur as numeral coefficients.

LESSON 28

SUMMARY OF GRAMMATICAL TERMS USED IN LESSONS 14–27 WITH DEFINITIONS

Noun, **n.** A noun is a word which may occur immediately following pre-nominal particles (q.v.) e.g. *ta:* 'old man', *khnom* 'I', *tù:* 'cupboard'.

Verb, **v.** A verb is a word which may occur immediately following pre-verbal particles (q.v.) e.g. *rìən* 'to learn', *nỷu* 'to remain', *chù:* 'to be ill'.

Numeral, **x.** A numeral is a word which may occur after the words, *cɔmnuːən* 'number' or *tì:* 'place' (*tì: mùːəy* 'first'). Each numeral, with the exception of *craən* 'many' and *ponmaːn* 'how many' (which behave like numerals in other ways and are therefore included in this category) represents a written figure, 1–9 or 0 in one of its positions as a unit, ten, hundred, thousand, etc. e.g. *mùːəy-rɔ̀ːy* 'a hundred', *pram-bỷy* 'eight', *hoksỷp* 'sixty'.

Numeral coefficient, **c.** A numeral coefficient is a word which occurs after a numeral in close junction. e.g. *nèək* 'person', *rìəl* 'riel'.

Dependent particles, **p.** A dependent particle may be one of several types:—

(i) Pre-nominal particles, **pre n.p.** These are words such as *pì:* 'from' (of place), 'from, at' (of time), *ʔae* 'at, to', *knoŋ* 'in'. They may precede noun constructs immediately and thus form adverbial constructs (**A**) which may occur in several different positions in the various sentence-forms and may be pronounced with separate phrasing in the sentence-tune (i.e. may be cut off by rise + pause (,|).

(ii) Post-nominal particles, **post n.p.** These are words such as *nìh* 'this, these', *nùh* 'that, those', *khlah* 'some'. They may be the last word in a noun construct.

(iii) Pre-verbal particles, **p.v.p.** These are words such as *mùn* 'not', *nùŋ* (future), *ceh-tae* 'constantly' and other compound particles given in Lesson 19. They precede the main verb immediately.

Independent particles. These are words which are not nouns, verbs, numerals or numeral coefficients and which have no specific relationship with other words of these categories or any other categories in the utterance. Many of them occur alone as complete utterances (i.e. in responses) and, when occurring with other words in a sentence, may be pronounced with separate phrasing in the intonation tune, i.e. may be cut off by rise + pause. There are several types:—

(i) Responding particles, **r.** These may occur as whole utterances, or complete sentences in responses. They then have the intonation-tune appropriate to a question or statement. Alternatively, when they are not complete utterances, and when they are not to be given emphasis, they may be pronounced either on a fairly low note without stress (.) or with a fall from mid level (,), preceding a complete sentence, e.g. *cah* (.), *vìːə nỷu phtèəh* (\). 'Yes, he is at home.' When the responding particle is used with *tè:* (e.g. *baːt tè:*. 'No'), it is an instance of the second alternative since *tè:* may form a whole (responding) sentence on its own.[1]

---

[1] The intonation of responding particles is illustrated on the tape recordings. See Part VII, Appendix 4.

(ii) Adverbial particles, **a.** These occur in one or more of the three positions indicated for sentence-form I (see below). e.g. *nas* 'very', *sʔaek* 'tomorrow'.

(iii) Final phrase particles, **f.** These occur at the end of a phrase. See below for 'phrase'. More than one final phrase particle may be present. e.g. *tèː* '(not) . . . . at all', 'indeed', *tìət* 'more, again'.

(iv) Markers, **m.** These occur at the beginning of a clause. e.g. *baə* 'if', *prùəh* 'because'.

Noun construct, **N.** This is either a noun with no other word occurring in close junction with it or a noun closely followed by one or more of the following, (i) a verb (usually attributive), (ii) another noun, (iii) a numeral with numeral coefficient if required, (iv) a post-nominal particle (which is normally the last word in the sequence).

Verb construct, **V.** This is either (i) a verb (operative or attributive) with no noun following it in close junction and no initiating verb preceding it in close junction or (ii) a verb followed by a noun construct in close junction or (iii) a verb preceded by an initiating verb in close junction or (iv) a verb both followed by a noun construct and preceded by an initiating verb in close junction.

A minor verb construct (← **v**) is one composed like **V** but with a minor verb and no possibility of the occurrence of an initiating verb as **v.** It follows a major verb construct.

Adverbial construct, **A.** This is a noun construct preceded by a pre-nominal particle. A limited form of the adverbial construct occurs with no pre-nominal particle, but in such cases the same adverbial construct may occur in the same sentence with a pre-nominal particle as well as without it, with no change of meaning. In sentence-forms it has three possible positions.

Numeral construct, **X.** This consists of one or more numerals, forming a number, followed, if required, by a numeral coefficient: **x(x)(c)**. It may occur as part of a noun construct. When it occurs independently it may occupy the same range of sentence-positions as an adverbial construct.

Close verbal sequence. This consists of an initiating verb followed by a verb in close junction.

Major verbal sequence. This term is applied to the two major verbs of a sentence in which two major verb constructs occur.

Sentence-form I 1. **N V** or (**r**) (**m**) (**A/a/X**) **N** (**p**)**V** (**A/a/v/X**) (**f**)

,,   ,,   I 2. **N V V** or (**r**) (**m**) (**A/a/X**) **N** (**p**)**V** (**A/a/v/X**) (**p**)**V** (**A/a/v/X**) (**f**)

,,   ,,   II 1. **V** or (**r**) (**m**) (**A/a/X**) (**p**)**V** (**f**)

,,   ,,   II 2. **V V** or (**r**) (**m**) (**A/a/X**) (**p**)**V** (**A/a/v/X**) (**p**)**V** (**A/a/v/X**) (**f**)

Sentence-tune 1 (*a*) . . . . (\\)

,,   ,,   1 (*b*) . . . . (,|) . . . . (\\)

,,   ,,   1 (*c*) . . . . (,|) . . . . (,|) . . . . (\\)

,,   ,,   2 (*a*) . . . . (′)

,,   ,,   2 (*b*) . . . . (,|) . . . . (′)

,,   ,,   2 (*c*) . . . . (,|) . . . . (,|) . . . . (′)[1]

---

[1] The sentence-tunes are specifically illustrated on the tape recordings. See Part VII. Appendix 4.

Phrase. A phrase is part of a sentence separated from the other part or parts by a pause occurring before and after it and by a rise in pitch occurring on the last syllable (unless it is the last phrase in a statement, when a fall is required). A phrase has no direct relationship with the sentence-forms. It may consist of one independent particle, one construct or several, a whole sentence-form, etc.

LESSON 29

INDIRECT QUESTION

29.1. *Usage and structure of indirect questions*

Direct speech is preferred to indirect in Cambodian and is used colloquially wherever possible; it is only in formal written language, e.g. newspaper reporting, that sustained passages of reported speech may be found. It is sometimes necessary, however, in colloquial speech to report an isolated statement or question. Here we are concerned with the limited sphere of reported speech in which indirect questions occur.

The sentence consists of two clauses. In the first clause there is a verb expressing the lexical idea of questioning or knowing. In the second clause there is a question particle, noun or construct, occurring in the same position as in a direct question.

The first clause may always be followed by *thaː*; it then resembles an indirect statement, except for the absence in indirect statement of a question word in the second clause. Compare:

Indirect statement. *khɲom mùn baːn dɤŋ thaː kɔ̀ət kɔmpùŋ-tae səseː(r) sɔmbot(r)*. I didn't know he was in the middle of writing a letter.

Indirect question. *khɲom mùn baːn dɤŋ thaː kɔ̀ət tɤ̀u naː tèː*. I didn't know where he was going.

It is always safe to use *thaː* in indirect questions since it is always correct. The student will, however, hear or read sentences in which *thaː* is absent, e.g. often after *dɤŋ* in the first clause. He will also meet sentences in which *cìːə*, m., introduces the second clause; in such cases *thaː* is usually absent. Sometimes he will hear *thaː* pronounced clearly as f., i.e. with falling pitch and with a following pause; in other utterances it may have neither of these characteristics and will therefore be catalysable as m.[1]

When a question clause is preceded by a verb expressing the idea of questioning, e.g. *suːə(r)*, 'to ask', the Cambodian preference for direct, lively speech may be clearly seen. Thus where we in English would say 'I asked my friend where he was going', a Cambodian would be likely to choose to use direct speech, i.e. to quote the exact words spoken, *khɲom baːn suːə(r) sɔmlaɲ khɲom thaː 'ʔaeŋ tɤ̀u naː?'*

An indirect question used in translating this sentence produces a very prosaic style, more suited to the written language, *khɲom baːn suːə(r) sɔmlaɲ khɲom thaː kɔ̀ət tɤ̀u naː*. The Cambodian has a means of enlivening such a sentence by using the particle, *taə*. It may follow *thaː* or, with even

---

[1] See lists of **m.** and **f.** in Lessons 24 and 25.

greater liveliness, be used without *thaː*. A combination of features of direct and indirect speech is found here in that when *taə* is used the sentence intonation tends to be that of direct question, with rising pitch at the end. *khɲom suːə(r) səmlaɲ khɲom (thaː) taə kèː tʀ̈u naː?* This is still classifiable as an indirect question because of the use of *kèː*, 3rd person pronoun, and not *ʔaeɲ* or *nèək*.

If the first clause is negative and the last word of the second clause is a question word, the particle *tèː* is usually present at the end of the whole sentence. Its occurrence helps to establish that the sentence is not a direct question. e.g. *kəət mùːn baːn prap khɲom thaː kəət tʀ̈u naː tèː.* He didn't tell me where he was going.

29.2. *Sentences illustrating uses of question words in indirect questions*

Using question words of fixed position

1. *khɲom mùn dʀŋ häet(o)-ʔvʀy-baːn-cìːə pùː prùːəy cʀt(t) tèː. (prùːəy, prùːəy cʀt(t) 'to be sad, miserable').*
   I don't know why uncle is miserable.
   khɲom baːn suːə(r) lòːk-pùː thaː mëc-kɔː kəət prùːəy.
   I asked uncle why he was sad.
   khɲom nù̀ŋ suːə(r) pùː thaː kəət prùːəy cʀt(t) pìː-prùəh ʔvʀy.
   I shall ask uncle why he is miserable.
   khɲom mùn dʀŋ kəət prùːəy cʀt(t) daoy häet(o) ʔvʀy.
   I don't know why he was miserable.

2. *khɲom mùn dʀŋ kèː thvʀ̀ː kəntèːl nìh yaːŋ doːc-mdëc tèː.*
   I don't know how they make these mats.
   khɲom kùt thaː taə kèː thvʀ̀ː kon nìh yaːŋ mëc.
   I wonder how they made this film.

3. *khɲom mùn dʀŋ lòːk nù̀ŋ mɔ̀ːk kəmpùəŋ-caːm kaːl naː tèː.*
   I don't know when he will come to Kompung Cham.
   khɲom suːə(r) lòːk thaː lòːk baːn mɔ̀ːk kəmpùəŋ-caːm pìː ʔɔŋkal.
   I asked him when he had come to Kompung Cham.

4. *lòːk mùn baːn thaː kəət tʀ̈u naː tèː.*
   Mr. — didn't say where he was going.
   khɲom mùn dʀŋ kmeːŋ nù̀h mɔːk pùː naː tèː.
   I don't know where that child comes from.

Using question words of variable position

1. *khɲom mùn dʀŋ rətèh-phlʀ̀ːŋ naː tʀ̈u bat-dəmbɔːŋ tèː.*
   I don't know which train goes to Battambang.
   khɲom baːn suːə(r) lòːk-krùː thaː kəət praə siəvphʀ̈u naː-khlah.
   I asked the teacher which books she used.

2. *khɲom baːn prap kəət thaː khɲom baːn khʀ̀ːɲ siəvphʀ̈u ʔvʀy-mùːəy nʀ̈u-knoŋ thɔːt-tok.*
   I told him which book I had seen in the drawer.
   kəət baːn prap khɲom thaː kəət ceh phìːəsaː ʔvʀy-khlah.
   He told me what languages he knew.

3. *vìːə nùəŋ prap khɲom thaː nèək thvɤ̀ː sʔɤy.*
He will tell me what you do.

4. *khɲom mùn dɤŋ thaː nèək naː tèɲ siəvphɤ̀u nìh tèː.*
I don't know who bought this book.

khɲom baːn suːə(r) ʔoːpùk thaː kɔ̀ət baːn ʔɔɲcɤ̀ːɲ nèək naː mɔ̀ːk.
I asked the father whom he had invited (to come).

nèək nùh suːə(r) khɲom thaː taə phtèəh nèək naː cheh.
That person asked me whose house was on fire.

5. *khɲom mùn dɤŋ thaː phtèəh poñmaːn cheh tèː.*
I don't know how many houses caught fire.

lòːk suːə(r) taː thaː kɔ̀ət mìːən daəm-tnaot poñmaːn daəm.
Mr. — asked the old man how many sugar-palms he had.

6. An indirect question which it would be convenient to include here but which does not quite fit the above description, since the question word is not needed in the indirect form, is that based on the direct question with *tèː?* as the question word. e.g. Direct question. *lòːk tɤ̀u tèː?* 'Are you going?' Indirect question. *khɲom suːə(r) thaː lòːk tɤ̀u rùː mùn tɤ̀u.* 'I asked him whether he was going (or not).' *khɲom baːn suːə(r) nèək nùh baə kɔ̀ət cɔŋ tɤ̀u rùː mùn cɔŋ.* 'I asked him whether or not he wanted to go.' Occasionally *baə* is used after a negative verb in the first clause, e.g. *khɲom mùn dɤŋ baə vìːə tɤ̀u rùː mùn tɤ̀u tèː.* 'I don't know whether he is going or not.'

29.3. *Constructs of fixed position*

Constructs such as *kaːl naː, yaːŋ naː* or *pìː-prùəh ʔvɤy, daoy häet(o) ʔvɤy* are composed of nouns (*kaːl, yaːŋ, ʔvɤy, häet(o)*) either preceded by a pre-nominal particle (*pìː-prùəh, daoy*) or followed by a post-nominal particle (*naː, ʔvɤy*) or both. It happens that *ʔvɤy* and *naː* are themselves question words and that these constructs could have been presented under the same divisions as they are (*kaːl naː*, e.g. = 'which time'?). They are illustrated separately in the two groups of sentences given above for two reasons, first because these constructs (*kaːl naː*, etc.) have a fixed position whereas *ʔvɤy* and *naː* with the nouns which precede them have not and second because the arrangement is convenient from the point of view of translation.

29.4. *The use of nùəŋ and baːn in indirect questions*

One must remember that if the context makes the sequence of events clear no *nùəŋ* or *baːn* need be used, e.g. *khɲom suːə(r) cau thaː vìːə thvɤ̀ː yaːŋ mëc.* 'I'll ask grandson how he did this.' (speaker moving towards grandson; broken gate indicating past action). If an indication of time relation is needed, *nùəŋ* and *baːn* have their usual effect on the main verb in the first clause and the following effect on that in the second clause:—

nùəŋ. The verb relates to the future *in comparison with the verb in the first clause.*

baːn. The verb relates to the past *in relation to the verb in the first clause.*

Absence of *nùəŋ* or *baːn* in an uncertain context suggests that the verbs relate to the same time. e.g. *khɲom baːn suːə(r) taː thaː kɔ̀ət nùəŋ thvɤ̀ː nìh ka:l na:*. 'I asked grandfather when he would do this.' The action may have been finished by the time the speaker said the sentence but it was in the future at the time the question was asked. *khɲom ba:n dʁŋ tha: kɔ̀ət (ba:n) thvʁ̀: nìh pì: ʔɔŋkal*. 'I knew when grandfather had done this.' *pì: ʔɔŋkal* refers to the past and, in conjunction with the context in which the sentence would be spoken, would probably make use of *ba:n* unnecessary. If *ya:ŋ mĕc* is substituted for *pì: ʔɔŋkal* ('I knew how grandfather had done this') *ba:n* could be used to make the time relation of grandfather's action very clear.

Exercise 32

Nouns. *nɛ̀ək-thɛ̀ək-sì:klo:* (person-kick-cyclo) cyclo-driver　　*phtɛ̀əh-sɔmnak* hotel　*tùmpɔ̀ə̀(r)* page　*la:n-chnù:əl* bus　money *prak*

Verbs. *rò:k-sì:* to earn a living　*cùmrì:əp* to inform, to tell (polite alternative for *prap* when superior is informed) *pyì:əba:l* to look after　*so:m* to ask a favour, to ask to do, please may . . . . *ʔɔŋcʁ̀:ɲ-tʁu* to go (of respected persons) *bat* to disappear　to have dinner *bɔrephò:k̓* to wonder *kùt* to keep *tùk*

A.1. nɛ̀ək-thɛ̀ək-sì:klo: nùh nùŋ prap khɲom tha: mì:ən phtɛ̀əh-somnak nʁu-ʔae na:. 2. khɲom mùm dʁŋ cì:ə kɔ̀ət rò:k-sì: thvʁ̀: ka:(r) ʔvʁy tè:. 3. cau tro:v cùmrì:əp lò:k-krù: tha: cau ba:n mʁ̀:l tùmpɔ̀ə̀(r) na:-khlah. 4. ta: mùm-tɔ̀ən dʁŋ tha: la:n-chnu:əl nùŋ mò:k dɔl phnùm-pěɲ maoŋ pom̃a:n tè:. 5. pì: ʔa:tùt(y) mùn mda:y khɲom chừ: ya:ŋ khlaŋ. bə:ŋ-srʁy khɲom cɔŋ pyì:əba:l kɔ̀ət nʁu phtɛ̀əh. krù:-pě:t̓(y) kɔ: prap tha: tro:v thvʁ̀: ʔvʁy-khlah. 6. khɲom so:m su:ə(r) lò:k-srʁy taə lò:k-srʁy nùŋ ʔɔɲcʁ̀:ɲ-tʁu su:ə(r) lò:k-do:n ʔɔŋkal. 7. nɛ̀ək-bɔmraə nùh mùm prɔ̀:m tha: kɔntray lò:k-srʁy bat tʁu na: tè:. 8. lò:k-krù: mùm-dael prap khɲom tha: mì:ən ko:n-sʁs(s) pom̃a:n nɛ̀ək nʁu thnak tì: pì:(r) tè:. 9. so:m ʔaoy nì:əŋ prap khɲom tha: dɔl maoŋ pram-bʁy haəy rừ: nʁu. 10. khɲom cɔŋ cùmrì:əp lò:k-srʁy tha: mĕc ba:n-cì:ə khɲom mùm ba:n tʁu su:ə(r) kɔ̀ət nʁu phtɛ̀əh-pě:t̓(y).

B.1. I asked Mr. — what countries he would like to visit (= go to see). 2. They will ask me whether I want to have dinner at home tonight. 3. Please tell me where this train is going to. 4. That gentleman did not want to tell me whom he visited in Phnom Penh. 5. I shall ask uncle when he will be coming to Kompung Cham. 6. We wondered what else the girl's younger brother would do, next morning. 7. They did not say how the burglar entered the room. 8. I asked my grandson why he was sad this morning. 9. Madam did not say how many people there were in the house. 10. The thief knew where Mr. — kept his money.

LESSON 30

'SECOND POSITION' MAIN VERBS

30.1. *Major verbal sequence, **V V**, with main verb in second place*

In the kind of major verbal sequence which was met in Lesson 21 the main verb (i.e. the verb before which the negative pre-verbal particle would occur if needed) was the first of the two verbs, e.g. *vì:ə mùn ʔɔŋkùy səse:(r) sɔmbot(r) tè:*. 'He isn't sitting writing letters.' *mì:ŋ ʔɔt tʁu kɔmpùəŋ-ca:m su:ə(r) lò:k-pù: tè:*. 'Aunt isn't going to Kompung Cham to visit uncle.'

The kind of open sequence which is now introduced has the second verb as its main verb. Pre-verbal particles other than the negative ones may occur before either the first or the second verb.

e.g. *lòːk ceh-tae ròːk siəvphɤu mùn khɤ̀ːɲ.* Mr. — can never find the book. (Mr. — constantly looks for the book, doesn't find/see).

30.2. *The 'second position' main verbs*

It is convenient to divide the verbs which may be 'second position main verbs' into three categories, based on lexical meaning, as follows:—

1. Verbs which may be second in a sequence where the two verbs are lexically comparable with each other, the first expressing the idea of an action and the second expressing the idea of its completion or result. The second verb is very often negative. The following are pairs of verbs of this category:—

ròːk to look for	*khɤ̀ːɲ* to see	(*ròːk—[1]khɤ̀ːɲ* to find)
nùk to rack one's brains, to think about	*khɤ̀ːɲ* to see	(*nùk—khɤ̀ːɲ* to realize, to come to a conclusion)
mɤ̀ːl to look at	*khɤ̀ːɲ* to see	(*mɤ̀ːl—khɤ̀ːɲ* to observe)
sdap to listen	*lùː* to hear	(*sdap—lùː* to hear (intentionally))
cak to stab at	*mùt* to be pierced at the surface	(*cak—mùt* to inflict a stab-wound)
rìən to learn	*ceh* to know	(*rìən—ceh* to know by learning, to have learned)
tətùk to be wet	*còːk* to be soaked	(*tətùk—còːk* to be wet through)
cìəs to avoid	*phot* to be free from	(*cìəs—phot* to escape from, to get free from)
kap to strike with pointed weapon	*cak* to stab (at)	(*kap—cak* to stab, to attack with a dagger)
kùt to think,	*khos/troːv* to be wrong/right	(*kùt—khos/troːv* to be wrong/right)
smaːn to guess	*khos/troːv* to be wrong/right	(*smaːn—khos/troːv* to guess wrongly/ rightly)
kùt to think, ponder	*khɤ̀ːɲ* to see, perceive	(*kùt—khɤ̀ːɲ* to realize, conclude, solve a problem)

e.g. *vìːə sdap lòːk-krùː mùn lùː tèː.* He listens to the teacher, doesn't hear him/He can't hear the teacher.

lòːk-srɤy baːn kùt sëckdɤy nìh troːv. You were right about this, madam.

lòːk smaːn mùn khos. You guessed right/were not wrong, sir. Your guess wasn't wrong, sir.

cao(r) kap mcas-phtèəh mùn cak. The thief struck at the householder did not pierce/The thief attacked the householder (with a knife) but did not stab him to death.

2. Where the idea of achievement or failure needs to be expressed and no special word is lexically suitable for position 2, one of the following verbs is used:—*baːn* 'to be able, to have the possibility', *mùn baːn* 'to be unable',

---

[1] The dash indicates that the two verbs thus joined may occur as a major verbal sequence.

kaət 'to manage, to be able', *mùn kaət* 'to be unable',[1] *rùːɔc* 1. 'to have finished' 2. 'to achieve, get through to the end, be able', *mùn rùːɔc* 'to be unable', *mùn-tɔ̀ən rùːɔc* 'to have not yet finished'.

e.g. *pì: ʔaːtùt(y) mùn lòːk tร̆u kɔmpùəŋ-caːm mùn rùːɔc pì:-prùəh laːn lòːk khoːc.* Last week Mr. — $\begin{Bmatrix} \text{didn't} \\ \text{couldn't} \end{Bmatrix}$ manage to go to Kompung Cham because his car broke down.

khɲom thvร̆ː kaː(r) mùn-tɔ̀ən rùːɔc. I haven't finished work yet.

khɲom tร̆u siəm-rìːəp nùŋ nèək mùn baːn pì:-prùəh troːv nร̆u phtèəh pyìːəbaːl mdaːy khɲom. I can't go to Siemreap with you, because I must stay at home and look after my mother.

lòːk thvร̆ː kaː(r) thŋay nih mùn kaət pì:-prùəh kɔ̀ət mùn sruːəl khluːən. Mr. — can't work today because he isn't well.

Note. baːn is more widely used than *kaət* or *rùːɔc*. Its use here must not be confused with *baːn,* (initiating verb) 'to have already' or *baːn,* 'to get, to obtain'. The three uses may be illustrated by the following sentences:—

mìːŋ baːn prap khɲom thŋay mùn nùh. Aunt told me the day before that.

nèək baːn koːn poňmaːn nèək haəy? How many children have you (got) (already)?

mìːŋ prap khɲom mùn baːn tèː. Aunt can't tell me.

There are many contexts in which the translations of *baːn* may overlap, although the three usages are distinct, e.g. (*a*)[2]*ʔɔpcร̆ːɲ nèək tร̆u daə(r)-lèːŋ cìːə-mùːəy-nùŋ khɲom?* (*b*) *tèː khɲom mùn baːn tร̆u tèː, prùəh khɲom mùn sruːəl khluːən.* 'Would you like to go for a walk with me?' (*daə(r)-lèːŋ* 'to go for a walk') 'No, I can't go because I'm not very well'.[3] The construction is as for 'I have not gone' (which is impossible in this sentence). The difficulty is most easily understood by thinking of *baːn* in all difficult contexts as 'to get (the chance)', 'to get (a result)'.

3. Sometimes a verb which has no connection lexically with the idea of achievement or completion may be the main verb in position 2. The inversion of main verb/verb order in the **V V** construction may in fact apply to any appropriate sequence of verbs.

e.g. *nèək-srae bɔɲhoː(r) tùk mùn-tɔ̀ən baːn pěɲ srae tèəŋ-ʔɔs nùh tèː.* The farmer is irrigating (his ricefields) but has not yet finished (lit. 'got full') them all.

nìːəŋ nùh slɔː sɔmlɔː mùn dak mtèːs tèː! She makes soup without putting seasoning in!

nร̆u srok kdau kèː baok khao-ʔaːv mùn bac yɔ̀ːk tùk pùh tèː. In hot countries they wash clothes without (bothering to take) hot water (lit. 'boiling water').

nìːəŋ nùh beh phkaː-kolaːp mùn kat phkaː rìːk tèː. She is gathering roses, not cutting the full-blown flowers/She isn't cutting the fully-open flowers, as she gathers the roses.

---

[1] There is a slight preference for the use of this word when physical possibility is referred to, e.g. 'cannot reach—because not tall enough'.

[2] Here, as elsewhere, (*a*) and (*b*) indicate two different speakers.

[3] *khɲom tร̆u mùn baːn tèː* is equally possible.

krùːəsaː(r) khmae(r) ɲam baːɣ mùn praə cɔŋkɣh tèː. Cambodian families do not use chopsticks to eat rice.

The effect of the position of the negative on the meaning of a sentence may be seen from the following:—

kɔ̀ət criəŋ pìːrùəh nas. He sings beautifully.
kɔ̀ət mùn criəŋ pìːrùəh tèː. He does *not* sing beautifully.
kɔ̀ət criəŋ mùn pìːrùəh. He sings, but not well./He's not much of a singer.

The verb *khaːn*, 'to miss', is very often used as a second position main verb with negation, as follows:—

baə pʔoːn thvɣ̀ː nùh, bɔːŋ nùŋ cùmrìːəp lòːk-taː mùn khaːn. If you (younger brother) do that, I shall tell grandfather without fail.

Exercise 33

Nouns. *mùt(t)-sɔmlaɲ* friend   *cɣ̀ːŋ* leg, foot   *rəbɔs* thing, object   *kòː* ox   *vìtyù* radio   *kaːsaet* newspaper   *mùk(h)* face   police *poːlìːs*   motor-boat *kaːnoːt*   girl *kmeːŋ-srɣy*   name *chmùəh*

Verbs. *ʔoːs* to pull along   *pìbaːk* to be difficult   *kùt—khɣ̀ːɲ* to solve a problem   *nìmùən(t)-tɣ̀u* to go, walk (of monks)   *nìmùən(t)-taːm* to go along (of monks)   *tɔ̀ən* to catch, to catch up with   *tətùk* to be wet   *còːk* to be soaked   *lèːŋ* to play, to be amused   *lèːŋ phtɛ̀əh* to visit (people socially)   *thlɔŋ* to be deaf   *srɔːk* to abate   to follow (in pursuit) *dëŋ taːm*   to be small (in height) *tìːəp*   to find *rɔ̀ːk—khɣ̀ːɲ*   to pronounce *ʔaːn*

Particle. *rɔ̀əl* **pre n.p.** every

Expressions. *yaːŋ rəhás* quickly   *häet(o) nìh haəy baːn-cìːə* that is the reason why   *mùn ʔɣy tèː* that's all right, not at all   *sɔp(v) thŋay* nowadays   on the radio *taːm vìtyù*

A.1. **cau tɣ̀u lèːŋ phtɛ̀əh mùt(t)-sɔmlaɲ cau mùn baːn tèː. cau daə(r) mùn kaət pìː-prùəh chùː cɣ̀ːŋ.** 2. **cao(r) pìː(r) nɛ̀ək cëŋ tɣ̀u taːm bɔŋʔuːəc haəy cih laːn tɣ̀u yaːŋ rəhás.** 3. **rəbɔs thŋùən nas. kòː ʔoːs rətèh mùn rùːəc.** 4. **sĕckdɣy nùh pìbaːk nas. taː kùt mùn khɣ̀ːɲ tèː.** 5. **lòːk-sɔŋ(kh) buːən ʔɔŋ(k) nùh baːn nìmùən(t)-tɣ̀u mùn tɔ̀ən laːn-chnùːəl, häet(o) nìh haəy baːn-cìːə lòːk nìmùən(t)-taːm phloːv.** 6. **mùn ʔɣy tèː! khao-ʔaːv khɲom tətùk mùn-soːv còːk tèː.** 7. **rɔ̀əl thŋay-ʔɔŋkìːə(r) mùt(t)-sɔmlaɲ khɲom pìː(r) bɣy nɛ̀ək mɔ̀ːk lèːŋ phtɛ̀əh khɲom nɣu maoŋ pram-mùːəy kɔnlah mùn khaːn.** 8. **sɔp(v) thŋay taː thlɔŋ bontec. kɔ̀ət sdap vìtyù mùn lùː tèː.** 9. **ʔoːpùk mɣ̀ːl kaːsaet mùn-tɔ̀ən rùːəc. nɛ̀ək troːv cam bontec, tɣ̀ːp nɛ̀ək mɣ̀ːl baːn.** 10. **nìːəŋ nùh krùn yaːŋ khlaŋ; mùk(h) nìːəŋ ceh-tae krəhɔːm mùn srɔːk.**

B.1. Grandmother couldn't find the book about the temple. 2. He looked at the suit but didn't see that it was torn. 3. One hears too many children shouting here. I can't hear you at all. 4. The wicked man chased after the old soldier but failed to catch him. 5. I can't eat because I am ill. 6. Grandmother can't see the boats because she is too small. 7. If the police had followed the thieves in a motor-boat they would have caught them up without fail. 8. Where can I buy English newspapers? 9. I asked the child why her clothes were soaking wet but she couldn't speak at all. 10. We heard on the radio where they found the plane but I can't pronounce the name of the place. (= I say the name of that place not correctly.)

Lesson 31

Grammatical Context 1; Translation of 'Some'

31.1. *Question words and indefinite words*

Many of the question words which have been used in forming direct and indirect questions may have different lexical meanings from those met so far. They may be used to express indefiniteness, having in English translation the value of 'some' and 'any', with and without stress. These meanings depend on the grammatical context in which the words occur. In this and the next three lessons the occurrence of question words in four different contexts will be discussed. A table summarizing all the uses of question words will be found in Lesson 34, pp. 134–5. Certain other words of which the lexical meaning is similar to that of question words in a given context are included in the notes on that context and will be referred to as 'indefinite words'.

31.2. *Grammatical context 1*

The question word occurs in an affirmative context. The translation is 'some', 'something', etc., without stress. e.g. *khɲom troːv thvɤ̀ː ʔvɤ̀y mùn nùŋ cëɲ pìː bùyroː.* 'I have to do something before leaving the office.' The affirmative context may be either a complete simple sentence in which no negative pre-verbal particle occurs or a clause within a composite sentence (in which another clause may be negative) or sometimes merely a construct preceding a negative main verb. A clause made indefinite by the presence of the marker, *baə*, 'if', or *kaːl-naː*, 'when', would not provide a context in which the meaning 'some', etc., could occur. (See below, Grammatical context 2.)

A word of warning is required about the use of question words in grammatical context 1. They are all direct question words and tend to be understood as such. One risks being misinterpreted if one forms an initiating statement using a question word, unless one chooses the question word carefully and frames the sentence carefully. In a reply, i.e. in a mooted context, the sense 'some' is much more easily conveyed. Thus the sentence, *mìːən rəbɔs ʔvɤy-khlah knoŋ hɤp nìh*, even though pronounced with the intonation of a statement would probably be taken as the question, 'What is in this trunk?' if it were an initiating sentence. If it were preceded and mooted by a question such as, *kèː yɔ̀ːk rəbɔs cëɲ pìː hɤp buːən nùh haəy rùː nɤ̀u?* 'Have the things been taken out of those four trunks yet?', then the sentence would be interpreted as 'There are some things in this one'. If one needs to initiate a statement of this kind, one must choose a more positive way of doing it. e.g. *khɲom smaːn thaː mìːən rəbɔs ʔvɤy-khlah knoŋ hɤp nìh.* 'I think there are some things in this trunk.'

The question words, especially *ʔvɤy* and its compounds, imply a vagueness which is not necessarily implied by English 'some'. They are nearer to the English 'some or other' (with the possibility of being followed by 'but I don't know what exactly . . . .') In English we may say only 'some' and still imply this degree of vagueness, e.g. *'There's some book on the subject* (but I don't know either the title or author)'. This is the kind of situation in

122

which to use a question word in grammatical context 1. English 'some' may also be very positive, as in the sentence, 'Some do this, some do that.' The indefinite words, listed 31.4 below are required to translate 'some' in such a case.

Where English 'some' is merely a plural or 'partitive' form of the indefinite article, Cambodian uses only the noun, e.g. 'I bought some sugar/some books'. *khɲom baːn tèɲ skɔː(r)/siəvphɤ̀u.*

English 'some' with stress will be referred to under Grammatical context 4.

31.3. *Question words in grammatical context 1*

The following notes are intended as a guide to the use of question words which may occur in context 1.

ʔvɤy[1] **n.** 'something'. The use of this word in this context is limited by the fact that it tends to refer to abstract things such as 'something to do, something to tell', as in the example given above. It is safer, when referring to a literal object, to say *rəbɔs ʔvɤy-mùːəy,* using *ʔvɤy-mùːəy,* **post n.p.** (see below).

ʔvɤy[1] **post n.p.** 'some'. Like *ʔvɤy* **n.** this word tends to refer to abstract things. If applied to concrete objects it indicates the most extreme indefiniteness; *ʔvɤy-khlah* and *ʔvɤy-mùːəy* are more positive in that they indicate that one knows at least that the object is singular or plural. e.g. *khɲom dɤŋ thaː kɔ̀ət troːv thvɤ̀ː kaː(r) ʔvɤy.* 'I know he has some work/some piece of work or other to do.'

ponmaːn **x.** 'some, a certain (but limited) number', 'just a few'. This word may be used with a noun headword only, in this context. If used with a verb headword it is understood to form a direct question. e.g. *mìːən sɔl mənùs(s) ponmaːn nèək nɤ̀u-knoŋ phùːm(ì) nìh.* 'There are a few people left in this village.'

naː-mùːəy **post n.p.** 'some' (sing.). Used with reference to people,[2] countries, places and abstract ideas rather than to objects. *ʔvɤy-mùːəy* is usually used with reference to objects. e.g. *khɲom tɤ̀u nɤ̀u kɔnlaeŋ naː-mùːəy taːm mɔ̀ət səmoɬ(r).* 'I am going to live somewhere by the sea.'

ʔvɤy[3]*-mùːəy* **n.** 'something'. May be used with reference to objects of a very vague nature. e.g. *mìːən ʔvɤy-mùːəy nɤ̀u knoŋ hɤp nìh kɔː-ponɬae khɲom mùn dɤŋ cìːə ʔvɤy tèː.* 'There is something in this trunk but I don't know what it is.' It is safer to use '*rəbɔs ʔvɤy-mùːəy*'.

ʔvɤy[3]*-mùːəy* **post n.p.** 'some' (sing.). Used with reference to objects rather than to people, countries or ideas. e.g. *lòːk troːv kaː(r) rəbɔs ʔvɤy-mùːəy dael nɤ̀u knoŋ tùː.* 'Mr. — needs something which is in the cupboard.' *nɤ̀u dɤŋ nìh kèː lèːŋ lbaeŋ ʔvɤy-mùːəy.* 'On this piece of ground they play some game or other.'

naː-khlah **post n.p.** 'some' (plur.). Like *naː-mùːəy* this word is used with reference to people, places and abstract ideas rather than to objects. *ʔvɤy-khlah* is usually used with reference to objects. e.g. *khɲom baːn nìyìːəy cìːə-mùːəy nèək naː-khlah dae(r) knoŋ pèːl prəcùm nìh ponɬae khɲom*

---

[1] Or, as indicated in Lesson 18, *sʔɤy* or *ʔɤy.*
[2] No numeral coefficient is used after *mùːəy* in this compound.
[3] Or *sʔɤy* or *ʔɤy.*

phlĕc chmùəh. 'I did talk to some people at that meeting but I forget their names.'[1]

ʔvɤy²-khlah **n.** 'some things'. Like *ʔvɤy* this word tends only to be used to refer to abstract things, such as things to do. Literal 'things' are *rəbɔs ʔvɤy-khlah.* (See *ʔvɤy-khlah,* **post n.p.**) e.g. *khpom troːv thvɤ̀ː ʔvɤy-khlah mùn-nùŋ cĕŋ pìː bùyroː.* 'I have some things to do before I leave the office.'

ʔvɤy-khlah **post n.p.** 'some' (plur.) *khpom smaːn thaː mìːən sɔmbot(r) ʔvɤy-khlah nɤ̆u knoŋ hɤp nùh.* 'I think there are some letters in that trunk.'

Note that the question word, *naː,* does not occur in this context.

31.4. *Indefinite words*

The following words are not question words; they are included here because their translation involves the words, 'some, a certain', etc. They occur with these meanings in contexts which are not specifically affirmative, e.g. in indefinite clauses.

kèː **n.** 'someone, one, people, they'. e.g. *mìːən kèː cɔŋ suːə(r) lòːk-srɤy.* 'There's someone to see you, madam.'

khlah **n.** 'some people' *khlah kèː thvɤ̀ː nìh, khlah kèː thvɤ̀ː nùh.* 'Some people (they) do this, some that.'

khlah **post n.p.** 'some' (plur.). e.g. *mìːən koːn-sɤs(s) khlah nɤ̆u-knoŋ thnak nìh dael rìən phìːəsaː baːraŋsaes.* 'Some students in this class learn French.' Note that *khlah* suggests a positive statement, while *poñmaːn,* which is more difficult to use correctly, suggests 'some, but only a few'.

ʔvɤy-ʔvɤy³ **n.** 'something or other', 'some things or other'. Used alone this word suggests abstract things to do or say, etc. e.g. *mùt-sɔmlaŋ khpom troːv thvɤ̀ː ʔvɤy-ʔvɤy mùn-nùŋ cĕŋ tɤ̆u phtèəh.* 'My friend has some thing or other to do before going home.' If followed by the adverbial construct, *cìːə craən, ʔvɤy-ʔvɤy* may be more easily used with reference to actual objects. e.g. *mìːən ʔvɤy-ʔvɤy cìːə craən nɤ̆u-knoŋ hɤp nìh.* 'There are various things in this trunk.'

ʔvɤy-ʔvɤy³ **post n.p.** 'some or other' (suggests plurality). e.g. *doːn ceh-tae səseːr(r) sɔmbot(r) ʔvɤy-ʔvɤy.* 'Grandmother is always writing letters of some sort or other.'

naː-naː **post n.p.** 'of various kinds'. This word is used more in literature than in the colloquial language. e.g. *mìːən sat(v)-haə(r) prèy baep naː-naː dael mìːən pɔ̀ə(rn) khiəv, lùəŋ, krəhɔːm doːc pɔ̀ə(rn) nìh dae(r).* 'There are wild birds of various kinds which are (coloured) blue, yellow and red like these colours too/like this.'

cuːən-kaːl ⎫
cuːən-naː ⎬ **a.** 'sometimes'. The first two words are more common than
mdɔːŋ-mdɔːŋ ⎭

the last, which has rather the meaning 'from time to time'. e.g. *cuːən-kaːl cau mɔ̀ːk suːə(r) lòːk-taː.* 'He comes sometimes to see his grandfather.' A useful phrase which may be used to translate 'sometimes' when it means 'every now and then' is *yùː(r)-yùː(r) mdɔːŋ.*

---

[1] Note the effect of *dae(r)*: 'I did talk . . . . ', i.e. in spite of not now remembering names. See Lesson 25.2.

[2] See footnote 3, p. 123.

[3] Or *ʔɤy-ʔɤy* or *sʔɤy-sʔɤy.*

Exercise 34

Nouns. *baːraŋ* French (the language), Frenchman, European   *poːliːs* police   *rùəŋ* story, incident   *bɔntùp-tətùːəl-phɲiəv* sitting-room (*tətùːəl* to receive, *phɲiəv*, guest)   thing *rəbɔs*   kind *baep*   cinema *ròːŋ-kon*

Verbs. *baːraŋ* French, European   *yùəl sɔ̀p̀(t)* to dream   *cuːəp* to meet   *dam* to plant, grow   to discuss (a matter) *kùt (kaː(r))*   to guard *cam*

Particles. *tɛ̀əŋ-ʔɔs* **post n.p.** all   *doːc-cìːə* **pre n.p.** like   *knìːə* **a.** together, each other, reciprocally   *mùn-nùŋ* **m.** before

Expression (occurring as a phrase, particularly at the beginning or end of a sentence). *mỳːl tỳu* probably, do you think so?

A.1. koːn-sɤs(s) tɛ̀əŋ-ʔɔs rìən phìːəsaː baːraŋ rùː? tèː, mìːən koːn-sɤs(s) poñmãːn nèək dae(r) dael mùm rìən phìːəsaː baːraŋ. 2. yùp meŋ khɲom ceh-tae yùəl sɔ̀p̀(t) khỳːɲ ʔɤy-ʔɤy doːc-cìːə mənùs(s). 3. khɲom dɤŋ thaː mìːən bon(y) ʔɤy-mùːəy knoŋ vòət(t) nih. (This is an indirect statement.) 4. mənùs(s) poñmãːn nèək nùh ceh baːraŋ. 5. prəhael-cìːə thŋay naː-mùːəy yỳːŋ nùŋ cùːəp knìːə tìət mỳːl tỳu. 6. mənùs(s) khlah thlɔ̀əp mỳːl kon mùːəy ʔaːtùt(y) bɤy doːŋ. 7. krùː prap koːn-sɤs(s) thaː mìːən srok naː-khlah dael kɛ̀ː mùm dam sroːv tèː. 8. poːliːs baːn prap thaː cao(r) nùh, mùn-nùŋ slap, baːn nìyìːəy ʔvɤy-khlah ʔɔmpì rùːəŋ nih. 9. mìːən kɔŋcɔp ʔvɤy knoŋ bɔntùp-tətùːəl-phɲiəv. khɲom mùm dɤŋ kɔŋcɔp nùh mɔ̀ːk pì naː tèː. 10. lòːk-taː ceh-tae ʔaoy yỳːŋ thvỳː kaː(r) ʔɤy-ʔɤy.

B.1. Someone told me where you would be sitting. 2. I would like to discuss something with you, Mr. —. 3. Do you know where my things are? No, I don't but there are some things on the table. 4. He has already bought a certain number of Vietnamese books. 5. My young brother sometimes writes to our mother in Cambodia. 6. That girl has some story or other to tell Mrs. —. 7. At the market there are fish of various kinds but they are very dear. 8. There is someone to guard the cinema at night. 9. I think you have something to tell me, haven't you, grandson? 10. Does Mrs. — (still) live in that house? No, but there are some things (of hers) in the house.

LESSON 32

GRAMMATICAL CONTEXT 2 ((i) AND (ii)); TRANSLATION OF 'ANY'

32.1. *Grammatical context 2 (i) and (ii)*

Two contexts are discussed together here because of the translation value, 'any . . . .' pronounced without stress, which they both convey to the question word or indefinite word. The contexts are (i) a negative clause and (ii) an indefinite clause. Many question words occur with the meaning 'any' in both contexts. A few of the indefinite words listed under grammatical context 1 occur with the meaning 'any' in context 2 (ii).

(i) A negative pre-verbal particle makes the clause (or the whole sentence if it is a simple sentence) negative. e.g. *khɲom mùn khỳːɲ nèək naː tèː.* 'I don't see anybody.'[1]

---

[1] Or, of course, 'I see no-one'. This alternative English translation of 'not . . . . any' applies throughout.

(ii) A clause may be made indefinite by the use of a marker such as *kaːl-naː*, 'when', *kaːl-naː-baə*, 'if', and other words composed with *baə*. Such a marker may be absent; absence of any marker makes a clause indefinite or conditional. e.g. *nèək khɤ̀ːɲ nèək naː, ʔaːnɤt prap khɲom*. 'If you see anyone, please tell me.' The marker, *dael*, may also produce an indefinite context, when it expresses a condition on which the rest of the statement depends and refers to the question word, e.g. *khɲom sʔɔp nèək naː dael thvɤ̀ː nùh*. 'I dislike anyone who does that' (i.e. 'if he does that').

The lexical meaning, 'any . . . . ' is thus expressed by the combination of the negative particle or indefinite marker or absent marker with the question word or indefinite word within one clause; the whole sentence may consist of more than one clause.

32.2. *Question words in grammatical context 2 (i) and (ii)*

naː **n.** 'anywhere'

(i) *khɲom mùn tɤu naː tèː*. I'm not going anywhere.

(ii) *baə nèək tɤu naː, prap khɲom*. Tell me if you go anywhere.

naː **post n.p.** 'any'. This word is applied to people, places and ideas rather than to objects. As in direct questions, *naː* **post n.p.** occurs with *kaːl, yaːŋ, kɔnlaeŋ* and *nèək*; in the present contexts the meanings are then 'any time', 'anyhow',[1] 'anywhere', 'anyone', respectively.

(i) *lòːk-krùː nìh mùn praə siəvphɤu naː tèː*. This teacher doesn't use any books.

lòːk taː mùn prɔ̀ːm cìh laːn nèək naː tèː. The old gentleman won't go in anybody's car.

(ii) *baə-prəsɤn-cìːə khɲom tɤu srok-ʔɔŋklèːs kaːl naː, khɲom nùŋ tɤu cìh kɔpal-hɔh*. If ever I go to England I shall go by plane.

naː in an indefinite clause is often referred to in the other clause by *nùh*.

The English translation is then 'whoever, whatever' rather than 'any'.

e.g. *lòːk-krùː rɤ̀ːs nèək naː, nèək nùh nùŋ mɤ̀ːl siəvphɤu*. 'Whoever is chosen by the teacher will read the book.'

ʔvɤy[2] **n.** 'anything'

(i) *kɔ̀ət ʔɔt thaː ʔvɤy tèː*. He didn't say anything.

kmìːən ʔvɤy nɤ̀u-lɤ̀ː tok. There's nothing on the table.

(ii) *baə lòːk cɔŋ baːn ʔvɤy, ʔɔɲcɤ̀ːɲ prap khɲom*. If you want anything, do tell me.

ʔvɤy[2] **post n.p.** 'any'. This word is used for literal objects rather than for people, places or ideas.

(i) *knoŋ-pèːl-dael khɲom nɤu srok khmae(r), khɲom mùn cɔŋ mɤ̀ːl kon ʔaːmèːrìkaŋ ʔvɤy tèː*. While I am in Cambodia I don't want to see any American films.

(ii) *baə vìːə khɤ̀ːɲ rəbɔs ʔvɤy vìːə ceh-tae cɔŋ tèɲ*. If he sees anything he always wants to buy (it).

---

[1] *yaːŋ naː* = 'in any way, at all, to any degree', and not 'by any method'.
[2] Or *sʔɤy* or *ʔɤy*.

cau coːl cʁt(t) ɲam cɔmnʁy-ʔaːhaː(r) ʔvʁy dael phʔaem. Grandson likes to eat any food which is sweet.

poɲmaːn **x.** 'to any extent, any great number, many'.

(i) *phtèəh lòːk mùn chɲaːy poɲmaːn tèː.* Mr. —'s house isn't very far/ isn't any distance at all.

(ii) *baə mìːən *viət-mìɲ poɲmaːn nèək tìət nʁu-knoŋ phùːm(ì) nìh, yʁːŋ troːv cap pùːək tèəŋ nìh tʁu thvʁ̀ː tòːs.* If there are any Viet Minh still in this village, we have to capture them all and take them for punishment.

naː-mùːəy **post n.p.** 'any', '(not) . . . . a single', '(not) . . . . a'

(i) *knoŋ tiəm nùh kmìːən ʔaːv baːraŋsaes naː-mùːəy.* There's not a French blouse in the shop.

(ii) *baə mìːənʔaːv baːraŋsaes nʁu-knoŋ tiəm nùh, khɲom cɔŋ tèɲ.* If there is a French blouse in the shop, I want to buy (it).

ʔvʁy[1]-mùːəy **n.** 'anything'. The presence of *mùːəy* in this compound word makes it more specific than *ʔvʁy*, and more difficult to use. It is rather 'any particular thing (of several particular things)'. It may occur when specified in some way by the context.

(i) *khɲom mùn khʁ̀ːɲ ʔvʁy-mùːəy dael khɲom pèɲ cʁt(t).* 'I don't see anything I like.' Here the clause introduced by *dael* makes 'anything' more specific.

(ii) *baə nèək khʁ̀ːɲ ʔvʁy-mùːəy nʁu knoŋ suːən, prap khɲom.* 'If you see anything in the garden, tell me.' Here the context of situation makes 'anything' more specific. Something or someone suspicious had been reported in the garden.

ʔvʁy[1]-mùːəy **post n.p.** 'any' (sing.). Used with reference to literal objects rather than to people, and particularly used with the noun, *rəbɔs*.

(i) *kmìːən rəbɔs ʔvʁy-mùːəy nʁu-knoŋ bɔntùp nùh pìː-prùəh kèː troːv baos sɔmʔaːt.* There isn't anything in that room/There's not a single thing in that room because it has to be cleaned. (*baos*, to sweep, *sɔmʔaːt*, to clean).

(ii) *baə nèək khʁ̀ːɲ sat(v) ʔvʁy-mùːəy, nèək prap khɲom phɔːŋ baːn tèː?* If you see any animal could you tell me?

The three question words which are compounded with *khlah*, *naː-khlah*, **post n.p.** and *ʔvʁy-khlah*, **n.** and **post n.p.**, are too positive in their lexical meaning, suggesting a definite, known plurality, to occur in the negative context. They may be found in an indefinite context, however, if qualified by a descriptive clause. This helps to justify the use of *khlah*, which suggests 'particular, certain' things.

naː-khlah **post n.p.** 'any' (plur.)

(ii) *baə mìːən mənùs(s) naː-khlah knoŋ phùːm(ì) yʁ̀ːŋ dael taː nùh mùn skɔ̀əl, khɲom chɲɔl nas.* I shall be very surprised if there are any people in our village whom that old man doesn't know.

ʔvʁy-khlah **n.** 'anything' (referring to several things), 'any things'

(ii) *baə mìːən ʔvʁy-khlah dael nèək troːv kaː(r), sɔːm nèək prap khɲom tʁu!* Please tell me if there is anything/if there are any things you need.

---

[1] Or *sʔʁy* or *ʔʁy*.

ʔvɤy-khlah **post n.p.** 'any' (plur.)

(ii) *baə mìːən rəbɔs ʔvɤy-khlah dael lʔɔː cìːəŋ *thɔ̰̀əm-mədaː, sɔːm kɔːn tèɲ.* If there are any things which are specially attractive, please buy them. (*lʔɔː cìːəŋ thɔ̰̀əm-mədaː,* 'good exceeding usual').

Note. It is not possible to use a question word as part of an independent noun construct followed by a negative verb to translate 'not . . . . any', 'No . . . . ', etc. Thus one cannot translate 'No-one said that' directly, word for word, into Cambodian. The question word must follow the introductory verb, *kmìːən,* used impersonally: *kmìːən nèək naː thaː nùh.*

32.3. *Indefinite words in grammatical context 2 (ii)*

ʔvɤy-ʔvɤy **n.** 'anything', 'any things'
baə mìːən ʔvɤy-ʔvɤy dael nɤ̀u praə baːn, troːv ʔaeŋ tùk ʔae kɔŋlaeŋ nùh. If there are any things which may still be used, you must put them there.[1]

ʔvɤy-ʔvɤy **post n.p.** 'any at all' (plur.)
baə mìːən rəbɔs ʔvɤy-ʔvɤy dael cɔmlaek, sɔːm prap khɲom. If there are any things which are special/If there are any interesting things, please tell me.

naː-naː **post n.p.** 'any at all, any of any kind' (plur.)
baə mìːən rəbɔs naː-naː dael nèək pèɲ cɤt(t) nɤ̀u srok-ʔɔŋklèːs, sɔːm nèək tèɲ phɲaə khɲom phɔːŋ. If there are any things in England that you like please buy them and send them to me!

kèː, khlah, cuːən-kaːl, cuːən-naː, and *mdɔːŋ-mdɔːŋ,* although they are indefinite words, giving no precise information as to which person or persons or what times are referred to, are nevertheless too positive in meaning to occur with the translation value of 'any'. They do occur in indefinite clauses, as was mentioned under grammatical context 1, but require the translation 'some'. e.g. *baə mìːən kèː mɔːk suːə(r) khɲom mdɔːŋ-mdɔːŋ, khɲom sɔ̰pbaːy cɤt(t).* 'If someone comes to see me now and again, I'm happy.' Contrast the translation of a question word in this context:—*baə mìːən nèək naː mɔːk phtèəh, prap khɲom.* 'Tell me if anyone comes to the house.'

Exercise 35

Nouns. *yìːəy* old lady　*dɔmlay* value　*thɔːt-tok* drawer (of table)　*tbɔːŋ* jewel　*prədap-prədaː* tool　sailing-boat *tùːk-kdaoŋ*　river *tùənlèː*　parcel *kɔɲcɔp*
Verbs. *troːv kaː(r)* to need　*skɔ̀əl* to know (persons), to recognize　*lèək* to hide *baək (laːn)* to drive (a car)　*cùːn* to offer, give a lift　*vay* (spelt *vìːəy*) to hit to be angry *khɤŋ*
Particle. outside, apart from *krau-pìː* **pre n.p.**
Expression. *ʔaoy praːkɔ̰t* thoroughly, properly

A.1. *kɔ̀ət mùm baːn thaː: ʔɤy tèː.* 2. *srok-ʔɔŋklèːs mùm chɲaːy poɲ̃maːn pìː: srok-baːraŋ tèː rùɯ?* 3. *khɲom ʔaoy yìːəy nùh rəbɔs ʔvɤy dael khɲom mùm troːv kaː(r).* 4. *baə nèək mìːən rəbɔs ʔvɤy-ʔvɤy mìːən dɔmlay, sɔːm ʔaoy nèək tùk rəbɔs nùh knoŋ thɔːt-tok.* 5. *khɲom mùm skɔ̀əl koːn-sɤɤs(s) naː knoŋ thnak nìh dael ʔaːc thvɤ̀ː doːcᵊneh tèː.* 6. *kmìːən kɔnlaeŋ naː dael yɤ̀ːŋ lèək tbɔːŋ nìh*

---

[1] This sentence needs to be mooted by the context of situation, e.g. the speaker and the addressee might be sorting out old things.

baːn tèː. 7. ʔaeŋ thv̀ːː kaː(r) ʔɤy-ʔɤy, troːv thv̀ːː ʔaoy praːkɔ̀t. 8. nɛ̀ək cɔŋ tɤu konlaeŋ naː, khɲom bəək laːn cùːn nɛ̀ək tɤu konlaeŋ nùh. 9. nɛ̀ək naː vay kèː, kèː nùŋ vay nɛ̀ək nùh vèɲ. 10. kmìːən prədap-prədaː somrap thv̀ːː suːən[1] ʔvɤy-mùːəy nɤu-knoŋ suːən nùh.

B.1. I can't see anybody's luggage here. 2. There are not many sailing boats on the river today. 3. Her brother (younger) doesn't play any games at all. 4. No-one knows who did it. 5. That Siamese family did not want to go anywhere by train. 6. If you (grandson) take any things out of that drawer, I (grandmother) shall be very angry. 7. There are no tools of any kind in uncle's house. 8. The old man likes to stay at home. He refuses to go anywhere. 9. I didn't see any parcels there. 10. That abbot has never been anywhere outside Kompung Cham.

LESSON 33

GRAMMATICAL CONTEXT 3; TRANSLATION OF 'ANY' WITH
MODERATE EMPHASIS

33.1. *Grammatical context 3*

The sentence consists of two clauses. The first clause, in which a question word occurs, is an indefinite clause.[2] This may be introduced by *baə*, by a marker which is a compound of *baə*, by *tùəh, tùəhbɤy* or *tùəh-cìːə* or it may have no marker at all.[3] The second clause has either the marker *kɔː* or the pre-verbal particle *kɔː*. The translation of the question word is 'whatever, wherever', etc., or 'any', pronounced with moderate stress. e.g. *lòːk tɤu naː, khɲom kɔː tɤu dae(r)*. 'Wherever you go, sir, I shall go too.'/'You may go anywhere, sir, I shall go too.' The final particle *dae(r)* occurs very frequently in the second clause. Sometimes the translation required is 'too', sometimes 'even so, still'; sometimes no word seems suitable in English. The indefinite words introduced in Lesson 31 do not occur with the emphatic meanings discussed in this lesson.

33.2. *Question words in grammatical context 3*

mëc **a.** 'however'; (after *thaː*) 'whatever, anything'
    mdaːy thaː mëc, koːn nɨh kɔː mùn sdap. Whatever the mother says this child doesn't listen.

mëc **post n.p.** 'however, whatever'. Restricted to use with *yaːŋ*.
    nɛ̀ək-bomraə thv̀ːː rəbiəp yaːŋ mëc, kɔː kɔ̀ət mùn pɛ̌ɲ cɤt(t) dae(r). However the servant does it, he isn't satisfied.

doːc-mdëc **a.** 'however', 'anyhow'
    koːn khɔm thv̀ːː kaː(r) doːc-mdëc, kɔː ʔɔːpùk mùn sə̀pbaːy cɤt(t). However hard I work, you are not pleased, father.

---

[1] The sequence, *somrap thv̀ːː suːən* is grammatically the equivalent of an attributive verb here.

[2] See notes on grammatical context 1 and 2 for indefinite clauses.

[3] The further indefinite context described for grammatical context 2, in which a clause introduced by *dael* refers to the question word, cannot receive emphasis as described here, but may be emphasized in the way described under grammatical context 4.

129

naː **n.** 'wherever', 'anywhere'
baə rìːəc-kaː(r) bɔɲcùːn khɲom tr̃u naː, khɲom kɔː nùŋ troːv tr̃u kɔnlaeŋ nùh.
Wherever the government sends me, I shall have to go.

naː **post n.p.** 'whichever', 'any' (Or, with *nɛ̀ək, kaːl, kɔnlaeŋ, yaːŋ,* 'whoever, whenever, wherever, however')
baə nɛ̀ək prəcùm r̃ːs nɛ̀ək naː, nɛ̀ək ʔae-tìət kɔː troːv bɔh chnaot ʔaoy.
Whoever the meeting chooses, the rest must vote for him.
sɔmlaŋ mɔ̀ːk phtɛ̀əh khɲom kaːl naː, kɔː cùːəp nùŋ khɲom daǝ(r). Whatever time you come to my house, you will find me there.

ʔvɤy **n.** 'whatever', 'anything'
bɔːŋ thaː ʔvɤy, pʔoːn kɔː mùn sdap dae(r). Whatever you say, I shall not listen.

ʔvɤy **post n.p.** 'whatever', 'any . . . .'
mdaːy thvɤ̀ː mhoːp ʔvɤy, ʔoːpùk kɔː pìsaː dae(r). No matter what food mother prepares, father eats it.

poñmaːn **x.** 'whatever number, however much', 'to any extent', etc.
lòːk mɔ̀ːk maoŋ poñmaːn, kɔː kɛ̀ː nùŋ baək tvìːə cùːn. Whatever time you come, the door will be opened to you, sir.

naː-mùːəy **post n.p.** 'whichever', 'any' (sing.)
pdɤy tr̃u srok naː-mùːəy, prəpùən(ìh) kɔː tr̃u cìːə-mùːəy. Whichever country the husband goes to, the wife will go with him.

ʔvɤy-mùːəy **n.** 'whatever', 'anything'
kmeːŋ khɤ̀ːɲ ʔvɤy-mùːəy nr̃u knoŋ bɔntùp nəŋùt, kɔː srap-tae rùət cëɲ!
If the children see anything in a dark room they immediately come rushing out!

ʔvɤy-mùːəy **post n.p.** 'whatever', 'any' (sing.)
ʔaeŋ cɔŋ thvɤ̀ː kaː(r) ʔvɤy-mùːəy, kɔː troːv prap khɲom. If you want to do any kind of work, you must let me know.

naː-khlah **post n.p.** 'whichever', 'any' (plur.)
ʔaeŋ troːv kaː(r) sìəvphr̃u naː-khlah, ʔoːpùk kɔː nùŋ tèɲ ʔaoy. If you need any books, father will buy them for you.

ʔvɤy-khlah **n.** 'whatever', 'anything' (plural; suggests 'whatever tasks').
nɛ̀ək troːv thvɤ̀ː ʔvɤy-khlah, khɲom kɔː nùŋ cùːəy thvɤ̀ː. Whatever (things) you have to do, I will help you.

ʔvɤy-khlah **post n.p.** 'whatever', 'any' (plur.)
baə mìːən rəbɔs ʔvɤy-khlah, kɔː ʔaeŋ troːv yɔ̀ːk tr̃u taːm. Whatever things you have, you must take with you.

Exercise 36

Nouns. *pìːək(y)* word   *nùh* there   **sɑmaːcùk* member
Verbs. *ʔaːn* to pronounce, read aloud   *yɔ̀ːk* to take (here = buy)   *yùm* to cry   *cùːəy* to help   **thɔ̀ə̀m-məda:* to be usual   *phlìəŋ* to rain   to be satisfied   *troːv cɤt(t)*   to be pleased *sok(h) cɤt(t)*

A.1. *krù: ʔaːn pìːək(y) ʔɤy-mùːəy, sɤs(s) kɔː ʔaːn pìːək(y) nùh taːm.* 2. *sɔmpùət nìh thlay poñmaːn, kɔː khɲom yɔ̀ːk dae(r).* 3. *lòːk praə khɲom thvɤ̀ː ʔɤy, khɲom kɔː mùn prò:m thvɤ̀ː dae(r).* 4. *nɛ̀ək srəlaɲ sɔmpùət naː-mùːəy, khɲom kɔː srəlaɲ sɔmpùət nùh dae(r).* 5. *nɛ̀ək tr̃u naː, khɲom kɔː tr̃u nùh dae(r).*

6. krùː thaː thvɤ̀ː ʔvɤy, koːn-sɤɤs(s) kɔː thvɤ̀ː taːm. 7. tùəhbɤy ʔoːpùk vay koːn nùh doːc-mdĕc, koːn nùh kɔː mùm yùm dae(r). 8. mdaːy thvɤ̀ː mhoːp ʔɤy-mùːəy, koːn kɔː nùɳ cùːəy thvɤ̀ː dae(r). 9. bɔːɳ thvɤ̀ː kaː(r) nìh doːc-mdĕc, khɲom kɔː thvɤ̀ː doːc thɔ̰̀əm-mədaː. 10. phlìəɳ doːc-mdĕc, khɲom kɔː tɤu.

B.1. Wherever you are staying, Mrs. —, I shall come to visit you, without fail. 2. Whoever said that doesn't know anything about it. 3. Wherever the son goes the mother goes too! 4. Whoever the teacher chooses must read the story aloud. 5. Whatever kind of radio our parents buy, the children will be pleased. 6. Whatever book the teacher has I shall buy too. 7. Whatever you are doing, (niece), I shall help you. 8. However many kilometres you go (walk) I shall follow you. 9. Whatever I do, he is not satisfied. 10. Whoever the members choose, we shall be pleased.

LESSON 34

GRAMMATICAL CONTEXT 4; TRANSLATION OF 'ANY' WITH FULL EMPHASIS

34.1. *Grammatical context 4*

A question word occurs in the same clause as, and usually preceding, the final phrase particle, *kɔː-daoy*, or, less commonly, the final phrase particle, *kɔː-baːn*. The translation may be stated briefly as 'what*ever*, wher*ever*', etc., or '*any* . . . .'. Stressed 'some . . . .' is, however, also a possibility and various English phrases such as 'I don't care when', 'it doesn't matter who', 'whatever you like' may be translated simply by the use of grammatical context 4.

The whole sentence may consist of only one clause, e.g. *taː deːk lùək kɔnlaey naː kɔː-daoy*. 'Grandfather can sleep *any*where.'/'No matter where he is, grandfather falls asleep!'

The sentence may consist of two clauses, between which a strong interdependence exists. This may be outlined as follows:—

Clause 1 . . . . *ever* . . . . , clause 2, even so/still/nevertheless . . . . e.g. *lòːk chùː ʔɤy kɔː-baːn, khɲom cɔɳ suːə(r) lòːk phlìːəm*. What*ever* may be the matter with Mr. —, I still want to see him immediately. *nèək tɤu naː kɔː-daoy, khɲom nɤu tùː nìh*. I don't care where you are going, I am staying here.

The particle *kɔː-daoy* is sometimes not immediately following the question word. The emphasis is then less strong and is in fact affecting the whole clause instead of being concentrated on the question word. Compare

nèək naː kɔː-daoy thvɤ̀ː nùh, kɔː kèː nùɳ troːv tòːs dae(r).
It doesn't matter *who* did this, he will be punished.
nèək naː thvɤ̀ː nìh kɔː-daoy, kèː nùɳ troːv tòːs dae(r).
Who*ever* did this will be punished.

It was stated above that *kɔː-baːn* is less common than *kɔː-daoy* in this context. The latter is of general application ('however it may be') while *kɔː-baːn* suggests 'so far as it affects me, the speaker, *any* . . . .'. e.g. *ʔaeɳ tɤu naː kɔː-baːn, ʔoːpùk mùn thaː ʔvɤy*. Go where you like. I shall say nothing. *koːn nìh thvɤ̀ː ʔvɤy kɔː-daoy, ʔoːpùk mùn thaː ʔvɤy*. It doesn't matter what this child does, the father says nothing.

34.2. *Intonation pattern*

The intonation patterns which were introduced earlier and which have been applicable to all sentences used so far may be used here but, in order to achieve the greatest emphasis to the question word, either a steep fall or a slight rise followed by a steep fall is required on the last syllable of the question word after which the pronunciation of the rest of the clause is at or near low level and with very little stress, e.g. *taː deːk lùək kaːl naː* (′\) *kɔː(.)-daoy(.).* If a further phrase follows *kɔː-daoy* or *kɔː-baːn*, a slight rise will be heard during the second syllable of the final phrase particle.[1]

Note. In emphatic sentences of other kinds (i.e. not incorporating question words) which will be discussed in a later lesson,[2] emphasis may be gained by a change from the usual word-order; a word or construct which needs emphasis comes first, e.g. *kmeːŋ nùh, khɲom ʔɔt skɔəl sɔh.* 'I don't know *that* boy at all.' Grammatical context 4 may occur in combination with a word-order of this kind. e.g. *kɔnlaeŋ naː kɔː daoy, lòːk cɔŋ tr̀u.* 'Mr. — wants to go, wherever it is.' *doːc-mdëc kɔː-daoy, khɲom thvr̀ː nùh.* 'I shall do it *somehow.*'/ 'I don't know *how*, but I shall do it.' Contrast the position occupied by *kɔnlaeŋ* and *doːc-mdëc* in a question: *lòːk cɔŋ tr̀u kɔnlaeŋ naː? khɲom thvr̀ː nùh doːc-mdëc?* In order to have natural examples of all the question words in this emphatic context it has been found necessary to anticipate in one or two sentences the occurrence of this word-order. Such examples are footnoted.

34.3. *Question words in grammatical context 4*

mëc **a.** 'however'; (after *thaː*) 'whatever'

> *krùː thaː mëc kɔː-daoy, koːn-sʀs(s) kɔː mùn sdap.* Whatever the teacher says, the children don't listen.

> *nèək thvr̀ː mëc kɔː-baːn.* Do it how you like.

(yaːŋ) mëc (*mëc* **post n.p.**) 'in whatever way', 'however'

> *prəpùən(ìh) thvr̀ː kaː(r) pìbaːk yaːŋ mëc kɔː-daoy, pdʀy kɔː thvr̀ː mùn dʀŋ.* However hard the wife works, the husband pretends not to know.

> *kɔ̀ət thvr̀ː kaː(r) yaːŋ mëc kɔː-baːn, khɲom kɔː mùn yùəl khos ʔvʀy tèː.* I see no wrong in his working just as hard as he likes.

doːc-mdëc **a.** 'in whatever way', 'however'

> *khɲom troːv-tae thvr̀ː nùh tùəhbʀy doːc-mdëc kɔː-daoy.* I must do it somehow./It doesn't matter how, but I must do it.

> *nèək thvr̀ː doːc-mdëc kɔː-baːn.* You may do it how you like.

naː **n.** 'wherever', 'anywhere'

> *ʔaeŋ tr̀u naː kɔː-daoy, khɲom mùn tr̀u cìːə-mùːəy.* You may go where you like! I'm not going with you!

> *nèək tr̀u naː kɔː-baːn, khɲom mùn rəvùəl dɔl nèək tìət tèː.* Go where you like! I am not concerned with you any more.

naː **post n.p.** 'whichever', 'any'

> *nèək nr̀u kɔnlaeŋ naː kɔː-daoy, khɲom nùŋ mɔ̀ːk suːə(r).* Wherever you live I shall come to visit you.

---

[1] These features of intonation have been recorded on the tapes. See Part VII, Appendix 4.
[2] Lesson 38. A further sentence-form is involved.

nèak ?aoy khɲom siəvphɤ̀u naː kɔː-baːn. I don't mind *which* book you give me.

?vɤy **n.** 'whatever', 'anything'

nèak thvɤ̀ː ?vɤy kɔː-daoy, kɔː-poñtae dɔl maoŋ troːv mɔ̀ːk cùːəp nùŋ khɲom mùn khaːn. You may do what you like, but at the (agreed) time, you must come to meet me without fail.

nèak nìyɤ̀əy ?vɤy kɔː-baːn, kɔ̀ət mùn ceh khɤŋ tèː. You may say what you like. He doesn't know how to be angry./He's never angry.

?vɤy **post n.p.** 'whatever', 'any'

khɲom kùː kùmnùː ?vɤy kɔː-daoy, lòːk-krùː kɔː mùn sɔp̂baːy cɤt(t) dae(r). Whatever drawing I do, the teacher isn't pleased.

?aey kùː kùmnùː ?vɤy kɔː-baːn dae(r). You may draw *any* picture/anything you like.

poñmaːn **x.** 'however much', 'however many'

cɔmŋaːy poñmaːn kɔː-daoy, yɤ̀ːŋ kɔː nùŋ tɤu dae(r).[1] Whatever the distance, we shall still go.

nèak ?aoy thlay chnùːəl ?aːv poñmaːn kɔː-baːn. You may give me whatever you like for making the shirt.

naː-mùːəy **post n.p.** 'whichever', 'any' (sing.)

sɔmlaŋ tèŋ sɔmpùət naː-mùːəy cùːn prəpù̀ən(ìh) kɔː-daoy, prəpùən(ìh) sɔmlaŋ nùŋ sɔp̂baːy cɤt(t). Whichever material you buy for her, your wife will be pleased.

sɔmlaŋ tèŋ sɔmpùət naː-mùːəy cùːn prəpù̀ən(ìh) kɔː-baːn, prəpùən(ìh) sɔmlaŋ nùŋ sɔp̂baːy cɤt(t). Buy whichever material you like for your wife. She will be pleased.

?vɤy-mùəy **n.** 'whatever', 'anything'

nèak tèŋ ?vɤy-mùːəy ?aoy khɲom kɔː-daoy, khɲom nùŋ treːk-?ɔː(r). Whatever you buy for me I shall be delighted.

nèak tèŋ ?vɤy-mùːəy ?aoy koːn khɲom kɔː-baːn, khɲom mùn thaː ?vɤy tèː. You may buy what you like for my child, I shall not say anything.

?vɤy-mùːəy **post n.p.** 'whatever', 'any' (sing.)

nèak-tlok lèːŋ rùəŋ ?vɤy kɔː-daoy, khɲom kɔː coːl cɤt(t) mɤ̀ːl. Whatever act the comedians do I enjoy it.

nèak cɔŋ tɤu mɤ̀ːl rùəŋ kon ?vɤy-mùːəy kɔː-baːn. sräc tae[2] *cɤt(t) nèak.* It doesn't matter what film you want to go and see. It's a matter of (personal) taste.

naː-khlah **post n.p.** 'whichever', 'any' (plur.)

krùː praə siəvphɤ̀u naː-khlah kɔː-daoy, khɲom nùŋ mùn tèŋ tèː. I don't care which books the teacher uses; I'm not going to buy them.

nèak praə mɔnùs(s) naː-khlah kɔː-baːn. sräc tae[2] *nèak rɤ̀ːs.* It doesn't matter which people you use/employ. It's entirely a matter for your choice.

---

[1] See Lesson 38 for the emphatic word-order here used.

[2] 'depends only on . . . . '. For *tae*, g. see Lesson 36.

Uses of question words

Question word		Direct or Indirect Question	G.C.1	G.C.2		G.C.3	G.C.4
				a. Negative	b. Indefinite		
ʔɔŋkal	**a.**	when	—	—	—	—	—
mdëc-kɔː } *mëc-kɔː* } *häet(o)-ʔvʁy-baːn-cìːə*	**m.**	why	—	—	—	—	—
mëc } *mdëc* }	**m.**	why	—	—	—	—	—
	a.	how, why; what (after *thaː*)	—	—	—	anyhow, however; whatever (after *thaː*)	*any*how, howe*ver*; whate*ver* (after *thaː*)
(with *yaːŋ*)	**p.n.p.**[1]	how	—	—	—	anyhow, however	in *any* way, howe*ver*
doːc-mdëc	**a.**	how	—	—	—	anyhow, however	in *any* way, howe*ver*
naː	**n.**	where	—	anywhere	anywhere	anywhere, wherever	*any*where, where*ver*
	p.n.p.	which (interrogative adj.)	—	any	any	any, whichever	*any*, which*ever*
ʔvʁy	**n.**	what (interrogative noun)	something	anything	anything	anything, whatever	*any*thing, whate*ver*
	p.n.p.	what (interrogative adj.)	some or other	any	any	any, whatever	*any*, whate*ver*

poʔma:n	**x.**	how much, how many	a certain (but limited) number	any great number; (not) much, many	any great number; to any extent	however much, many; to whatever extent	*any number; to any extent; however much, many*
nɑ:-mɪ:ɾəy	**p.n.p.**	which (sing.) (interrogative adj.)	some (sing.); a certain	any (sing.); (not) a single	any (sing.)	any, whichever (sing.)	*any, whichever (sing.)*
ʔʋxy-mɪ:ɾəy	**n.**	what (sing.)[2] (interrogative noun)	something	anything	anything	anything, whatever	*anything, whatever*
	p.n.p.	what (sing.) (interrogative adj.)	some (sing.)	any (sing.); (not) a single	any (sing.)	any, whatever (sing.)	*any, whatever (sing.)*
nɑ:-khlɑh	**p.n.p.**	which (plur.) (interrogative adj.)	some (plur.)	—	any (plur.)	any, whichever (plur.)	*any, whichever (plur.)*
ʔʋxy-khlɑh	**n.**	what (plur.)[3] (interrogative noun) what things	some things	—	anything (plur.); any things	anything, whatever (plur.); any things	*anything, whatever (plur.); any things*
	p.n.p.	what (plur.) (interrogative adj.)	some (plur.)	—	any (plur.)	any (plur.)	*any, whatever (plur.)*

[1] = **post n.p.** in this table.
[2] i.e. referring to a single object or piece of work, etc.
[3] i.e. referring to several objects or pieces of work.

135

ʔvʋy-khlah **n.** 'whatever', 'any things', 'anything'. Suggests a plurality which is not always present in an English translation.

nèǝk troːv thvɤ̀ː ʔvʋy-khlah kɔː-daoy, troːv-tae thvɤ̀ː nìh mùn. Whatever you may have to do, you must certainly do this first.

nèǝk ʔaoy vìːǝ thvɤ̀ː ʔvʋy-khlah kɔː-baːn, kɔː-poñtae soːm nèǝk ʔaoy vìːǝ chùp nɤ̌u vèːlìːǝ pèːl baːy. By all means have him do anything you like but please have him stop at lunch/dinner-time.

ʔvʋy-khlah **post n.p.** 'whatever', 'any' (plur.)

rǝbɔs ʔvʋy-khlah kɔː-daoy, troːv kèː dot caol.[1] The things will have to be burnt, whatever they are. (*dot* to set fire to, *caol* to throw away).

nèǝk thvɤ̀ː mhoːp ʔvʋy-khlah kɔː-baːn. You may do whatever dishes you like.

Exercise 37

Nouns. *svaːy* mango   *nèǝk-srʋy* Mrs., madam (less elevated than *lòːk-srʋy*) subject (of study) *vìccìːǝ* engine *maːsìːn* patient *nèǝk-cùmŋùː* evening (if time stated) *lŋìːǝc*, (if not) *yùp*

Verbs. *kɔt* to note down   *haǝy* to finish   *tɔ̀ǝn* to be in time   to elect *rɤ̀ːs-taŋ* to bargain *tɔː thlay*   to pay *bɔŋ prak*   to be a soldier *thvɤ̀ː tìːǝhìːǝn*   to repair *thvɤ̀ː*   to go (of machine, engine) *daǝ(r)*   to inject *cak*   to be well *cìːǝ*

Particle. *tèǝŋ-ʔɔs* **a.** all

Expressions. *cìːǝ nèc(c)* always   carefully *daoy sëckdʋy prǝyát(n)-prayaeŋ*

A.1. khɲom kɤ̀t tɤ̀u srok khɲom. khɲom tɤ̀u thŋay na: kɔː-baːn. 2. svaːy nìh mɔ̀ːk pì: srok na: kɔː-daoy, khɲom coːl cɤ̌t(t) tèǝŋ-ʔɔs. 3. nèǝk troːv-tae kɔt s?ʋy kɔː-daoy nɤ̌u-pèːl-dael vìːǝ nìylːǝy. 4. mdaːy mɔ̀ːk pèːl na: kɔː-daoy, koːn mìːǝn kɔnlaeŋ cùːn cìːǝ nèc(c). 5. nèǝk-srʋy ʔɔɲcɤ̌ːɲ-mɔ̀ːk lèːŋ phtèǝh khɲom pèːl na: kɔː-baːn. 6. nèǝk thvɤ̀ː yaːŋ na: kɔː-daoy ʔaoy tae chap haǝy. 7. doːc-mdëc kɔː-daoy, ʔaeŋ troːv thvɤ̀ː ʔaoy tɔ̀ǝn mùn pèːl yùp nìh. 8. nèǝk thvɤ̀ː ʔvʋy kɔː-baːn, khɲom nɯ̀ŋ mɯ̀n tha: ʔʋy tèː. 9. mìːŋ tèɲ sìǝvphɤ̌u na:-mùːǝy ʔaoy kmuːǝy kɔː-baːn dae(r). 10. thlay poñmaːn kɔː-daoy, khɲom kɔː tèɲ.

B.1. Which*ever* hospital you go into they will look after you carefully. 2. No matter what subject he studies he will pass his examinations. 3. What*ever* hour of the day Mr. — comes, we are always pleased to receive him. 4. You can say anything you like; we shall not elect him. 5. How*ever* much (in whatever way) he bargains, I shall not pay 50 riels. 6. Which market shall I go to, madam? Go to which*ever* you like. 7. It doesn't matter whose son you are you have to be a soldier. (The son of whomso*ever* must . . . .). 8. They may repair this car how they like, the engine won't go. 9. What*ever* medicine the doctor may inject, this patient will not be well. 10. You must come to meet me at seven o'clock this evening *some*how or other. (For '*some*how or other', translate 'how*ever*' at the beginning of the sentence.)

---

[1] See Lesson 38 for the emphatic word-order here used.

Exercise 38 (covering the material of Lessons 31–34)

Nouns. **ʔɤyvan* luggage   *tùk-dɔh-kò:* milk   shop-keeper *mcas-haːŋ*   old lady
   lòːk-yìːəy relations *bɔːŋ-pʔoːn* administration *rìːəc-kaː:(r)*
Verbs. *sʔɔp* to hate   *thvɤ̀ː baːp* to harm   *plaek* to be different, interesting
Numeral coefficient. *kɔmpoŋ* tin
Pre-nominal particle. *doːc* like
Expression. for many years *poñmaːn chnam tɤ̀u haəy*

A.1. poñmaːn chnam tìət tèː,[1] khɲom nùŋ thvɤ̀ː kaː:(r) rɔ̀ːk-sìː doːc ʔoːpùk
   khɲom dae(r). 2. kmìːən lòːk-krù: naː-mù:əy sɔh dael baːn mɤ̀:l siəvphɤ̀u
   tèəŋ-ʔɔs nùh. 3. ʔoːpùk sʔɔp nèək naː: dael tɔː thlay ʔɤyvan pèːk. 4. nèək naː:
   thvɤ̀ː baːp kèː yaːŋ naː:, kèː thvɤ̀ː baːp nèək nùh vèɲ yaːŋ nùh dae(r). 5. mìːŋ
   tɤ̀u cìh yùən(t)-hɔh kaːl naː: kɔː-baːn, kmuːəy cùːn mìːŋ tɤ̀u kɔnlaeŋ cɔmnɔːt.
   6. vìːə cɔŋ tɤ̀u kɔnlaeŋ naː-mù:əy dael vìːə tɤ̀u pìː(r) bɤy chnam mùn nùh.
   7. mìːən ʔɤy-khlah nɤ̀u-knoŋ phsaː:(r) trɤy nìh? kmìːən sʔɤy plaek tèː. 8. a.[2] ʔaeŋ
   tèɲ tùk-dɔh-kò: ʔaoy khɲom mù:əy kɔmpoŋ. b. tùk-dɔh-kò: baep naː:? a. baep
   naː: kɔː-daoy.

B.1. There are some shopkeepers here who sell Vietnamese goods. 2. There
isn't a single person that I know in this village. 3. When the old lady came
in, Mr. — didn't say anything. 4. That old lady hasn't any relations at all.
5. I can hardly hear at all, because for many years I have been deaf.
6. No-one entered our house from mid-day until dusk. 7. My husband will
have to go to whatever country the administration chooses. 8. Those
things are somewhere in the house but I can't find them.

Lesson 35

Uses of Pre-nominal Particles

35.1. *List of pre-nominal particles*

In Lesson 17.3 pre-nominal particles were introduced. A more complete list
is given here including several compounds. Many of the simple words belong
to two or more word categories; in such cases the other usages are indicated
here.

pìː from (time and place); at (past time); about, concerning
taŋ-pìː, tɔː-pìː ever since
rùːəc-pìː after
kaːl-pìː at, on (of time, date)
ʔɔmpìː about, concerning, out of (e.g. made out of)
ʔae at, to, as for
nɤ̀u-ʔae at
ʔae-cɔmnaek, cɔmnaek (**n.c.** also), *rìː-ʔae* (lit.) with regard to, as to, as for
cɔmnaek-khaːŋ, khaːŋ (**n.** also) on the part of
nɤ̀u (written *nùːv*) with, and⎫
nìːə with, and, of   ⎭ (lit.)

---

[1] *tèː* is used idiomatically here to round off the limiting effect of *poñmaːn*. It is used similarly
after *tae*, see Ex. 39 A.5 and Lesson 47, Ex. 59 A, (12) and note to latter.
[2] Here, as elsewhere, a. and b. indicate different speakers.

mùk(h) (**n.** also), *nỷu-mùk(h)* in front of
*ʔaep, *nỷu-cùt* near
kan (**v.** also) towards
cùt-dɔl almost (of time and place)
cùmvèɲ round
mɔːk-dɔl by (of future time, e.g. 'by next week')
dɔl (**v.** also) until, as far as; towards (of feelings)
rəhoːt-dɔl until, all the time until, as far as
rəhoːt-mɔːk-dɔl all the time until
*rùː[1] (**m.** and **f.** also) or
haəy-nùŋ[1] (**m.** also) and, with
tèəŋ together with, all
prɔːm-tèəŋ[1] (**m.** also) and, at the same time as, together with
nùŋ[1] (**p.v.p.** also) with (= by means of), and
rəbɔs[1] (**n.** also) of, belonging to
cùːəs (**v.** also), *cùmnùːəs* (**n.** also) instead of
knoŋ (**a.** also) in
nỷu-knoŋ in
lỷː (**v.** also) on
kraom (**v.** also) under
nỷu-kraom under
kraoy (**v.** also) behind, after (of time and place)
trɔŋ (**v.** also) directly on, towards
mùn (**a.** also) before (of time)
taːm (**v.** and **m.** also) following, by, along
daoy (**v.** also) along
doːc (**v.** also) like
doːc-cìːə (compound **v.** also) like
*ʔaoy[1] (**v.** and **m.** also) for; (with following attributive **v.**) in a — manner
cìːə[1] (**v.** and **m.** also) as, being; (with following attributive **v.**) in a — manner
cìːə-mùːəy, *cìːə-mùːəy-nùŋ* together with
cìːəŋ[1] (**a.** also) in excess of, exceeding, to a greater extent, more
rɔəl[1] every (mostly of time and place)
rɔəl-tae absolutely every (mostly of time and place)
sɔp̀(v)[1] (**v.** also) every (mostly of time and place)
krùp̀[1] (**v.** also) every (mostly of time and place)
ʔɔs[1] (**v.** also) the whole of, all the (sing. unit of time)

The uses of these particles are threefold:—(i) They occur with ordinary nouns (catalysing them as such). (ii) Some are used in conjunction with certain final particles (*tỷu*, *mɔːk*, *tɔː-tỷu*, *tɔː-mɔːk*, etc.). (iii) They act as *ad hoc* nominalizers of words of other categories (verbs, numerals, adverbs) and even of miniature sentences. These usages are illustrated below.

(i) With ordinary nouns

ʔae khɲom, khɲom mùn cɔŋ tỷu. As for me, I don't want to go.
ʔae-cɔmnaek lòːk, kɔət mùn prɔːm tèː. As to Mr. —, he doesn't agree.

---

[1] Treated separately below.

rəho:t-mɔ̀:k-dɔl thŋay nìh, vì:ə chù: ya:ŋ khlaŋ. $\begin{cases} \text{Until this very day} \\ \text{Right up to today,} \end{cases}$ he has been very ill.

taŋ-pì: ʔa:tùt(y) nùh, mda:y chù:. Ever since that week, the mother has been ill.

pʔo:n ba:n t̃ru cùmnù:əs bɔ:ŋ. His younger brother went instead of him.

rù:əc-pì: chnam nùh, srok yɤ̀:ŋ thvɤ̀: sɔŋkrì:əm. After that year our country was at war.

vì:ə mɔ̀:k dɔl mùn khɲom. He arrived before me.

dɔl khae thnù:, yɤ̀:ŋ nùŋ mì:ən pè:l tùmnè:. By December we shall have some free time.

nùŋ, rù:, haəy-nùŋ, prɔ̀:m-tɛ̀əy and *rəbɔs,* form an adverbial construct with a following noun which may follow a noun construct immediately. This introduces a new position for **A**, when it follows an independent noun construct. It is discussed in Lesson 37.3. e.g. *khɲom haəy-nùŋ mda:y khɲom t̃ru tì:-kroŋ.* My mother and I[1] went to town.

(ii) The final phrase particles *t̃ru, mɔ̀:k, tɔ:-t̃ru, tɔ:-mɔ̀:k, tɔ:-tɔ:-t̃ru, tɔ:-tɔ:-mɔ̀:k,* given in Lesson 25 are used in conjunction with some of the pre-nominal particles.

taŋ-pì: khae kaɲɲa: t̃ru, yɤ̀:ŋ nɤ̀u phtɛ̀əh nùh. From September onwards (but not necessarily all the time until the moment of speaking) we lived in that house.

pì: khae kaɲɲa: mɔ̀:k, yɤ̀:ŋ nɤ̀u phtɛ̀əh nùh. From September onwards we have lived in that house (and still do).

mù:əy sɔntùh tɔ:-mɔ̀:k, lò:k du:əl slap. A moment later he fell dead.

pì: thŋay nìh tɔ:-t̃ru, lò:k nùŋ sru:əl khlu:ən. From today onwards, you will be better.

pì: thŋay nùh $\begin{cases} tɔ:-tɔ:-t̃ru \\ tɔ:-tɔ:-mɔ̀:k, \end{cases}$ *kmì:ən nɛ̀ək na: khɤ̀:ɲ vì:ə sɔh.* From that day ever onwards, no-one ever saw him at all.

(iii) The following are regarded as *ad hoc* nominalizations of words otherwise primarily catalysed as belonging to various other categories. The resulting sequence of words is an adverbial construct.

ceh mɔ̀:k pì: rìən, mì:ən mɔ̀:k pì: rɔ̀:k. (Proverb) Knowledge comes from learning, having comes from seeking.

mì:ən mnùs(s) mɔ̀:k cì:ə craən. People came in numbers.

vì:ə nùŋ t̃ru cì:ə mù:əy. He will go too (together with (you)).

khɲom t̃ru cì:ə rəhás. I shall go quickly. (in a quick manner).

nɛ̀ək tro:v thvɤ̀: ka:(r) pì: sʔaek tɔ:-t̃ru. You must work from tomorrow onwards.

The nominalizing process may be applied to constructs or miniature sentences too, e.g.

vì:ə t̃ru cì:ə mùn kha:n. He is going for certain/without fail. (lit. 'as, in a manner do-not-miss').

vì:ə slap nùŋ pùəs cɤk. He died of a snake bite. (lit., with the-snake-bit).

---

[1] Note that in Cambodian 'I' comes first.

35.2. *Comparison; use of cìːəŋ*

The pre-nominal particle, *cìːəŋ*, 'in excess (of), exceeding, to a greater extent than' is used in an adverbial construct in making comparisons, when the person or object compared is mentioned:—

nìːəŋ nìh lʔɔː cìːəŋ nìːəŋ nùh. This girl is prettier than that one.

ʔɔːpùk yùəl cìːəŋ koːn. Father understands better than you, child.

kɔ̀ət baːn səseː(r) sìəvphɤ̀u craən cìːəŋ lòːk. He has written more books than Mr. —.

bɔːŋ-srɤy khɲom crìəŋ pìːrùəh cìːəŋ nìh. My (elder) sister sings better than this.

khɲom coːl cɤt(t) mɤ̀ːl kon baːraŋsaes cìːəŋ kon ʔaːmeːrìkaŋ. I prefer to see French films to American.

The superlative is expressed by using *cìːəŋ* with *kèː*.

e.g. *nìːəŋ nìh lʔɔː cìːəŋ kèː.* This girl is the most beautiful (beautiful exceeding anyone).

kɔ̀ət baːn səseː(r) sìəvphɤ̀u craən cìːəŋ kèː. He has written the most books.

khɲom coːl cɤt(t) mɤ̀ːl kon baːraŋ cìːəŋ kèː. I prefer French films to any.

bɔːŋ coːl cɤt(t) nɤ̀u phtèəh cìːəŋ tɤ̀u mɤ̀ːl kon. My brother would rather stay at home than go to see a film.

mùn is used with *kèː* in a similar way, when 'first' in time, is to be expressed, e.g. *khɲom mɔ̀ːk dɔl phtèəh mùn kèː.* I arrived home first. *kɔ̀ət tèɲ laːn mùn kèː.* He was the first to buy a car.

The adverbial particle *cìːəŋ* is used in making comparisons, without mentioning the person or thing compared, e.g.

nìːəŋ nìh lʔɔː cìːəŋ. This girl is prettier.

kɔ̀ət baːn səseː(r) sìəvphɤ̀u craən cìːəŋ. He has written more books.

bɔːŋ-srɤy khɲom crìəŋ pìːrùəh cìːəŋ. My sister sings better/is a better singer.

nèək-srɤy nùŋ coːl cɤt(t) mɤ̀ːl kon ʔaːmeːrìkaŋ cìːəŋ tèː? Would you prefer to see an American film?

LESSON 36

USES OF SOME COMMON VERBS AND PARTICLES; GENERAL DEPENDENT PARTICLES

36.1. *Uses of cìːə*

The word-form, *cìːə*, needs four dictionary entries:—**v.** 'to be', **v.** 'to be well', **pre n.p.** (i) 'as, being', (ii) 'in a — manner', **m.** 'that'. The second use is straightforward and the last two have been met already; an example of each is given here:—

mdaːy nèək cìːə rùː tèː? Is your mother well?

khɲom mìːən khmae(r) mnèək cìːə krùː. I have a Cambodian as my teacher.

khɲom mùn dɤŋ cìːə mìːən phlìəŋ mɔ̀ːk craən poɲɲɔh tèː! I didn't know heavy rain like that had fallen!

cìːə, **v.** 'to be' may be used when two nouns are linked by it, e.g.

nèək nìh cìːə mcas phtèəh. This man is the householder.

khɲom cìːə krùː-boŋrìən. I am a teacher.

nìːəŋ nùh cìːə koːn-srɤy lòːk. That girl is Mr. —'s daughter.

cìːə has a special sense when it occurs as the first verb in a major verb construct preceded by a negative pre-verbal particle; the second verb is usually an attributive verb. *cìːə* in this context expresses a personal opinion, differing from that of a previous speaker, e.g.

a. *kɔ̀ət ʔɔs kɔmlaŋ!* b. *kɔ̀ət mùun cìːə ʔɔs kɔmlaŋ tèː!*
a. He's tired! b. He doesn't seem tired to me!
a. *sɔmpùət nìh lʔɔː nas.* b. *sɔmpùət nùh mùun cìːə lʔɔː tèː.*
a. This material is nice. b. I don't think so.

These replies, without the word *cìːə* would also be correct, but would imply a flat contradiction, not an opinion.

cìːə forms several compounds:—*dɔːc-cìːə*, **p.v.p.** 'as though', **v.** 'to seem as if'; *prɔhael-cìːə*, **m. p.v.p.** 'perhaps'; *mùk(h)-cìːə*, **m. p.v.p.** 'probably'. e.g.

dɔːc-cìːə lòːk-sryy mùun sruːəl khluːən. You seem to be not very well, Mrs. —.
prɔhael-cìːə rèəŋ phlìəŋ haəy. Perhaps the rain has stopped.
nèək mùk(h)-cìːə nùuŋ mùun tɔ̀ən rɔtèh-phlỳːŋ. You're going to miss your train. (You will probably not catch your train.)

The verb, *kùː*, is used like *cìːə*, 'to be', in linking two nouns but has the lexical meaning, 'to be in essence, to be by nature', e.g. *nìh kùː ʔvry? nìh kùː phkaː-thmɔː.* 'What's this?' 'It's coral.' *kùː* is also used to introduce a list, e.g. *vìːə rìəp-cɔm rɔbɔs phseːŋ-phseːŋ, kùː rɔnɔ̀əp, nḕəŋkɔ̀əl, cɔːp, cìːə daəm.* 'They were getting various things ready, such as rakes, ploughs, spades, etc.'

It is possible for two words otherwise catalysed as nouns to be apparently linked as though by *cìːə* or *kùː* without any verb at all being used, e.g. *thŋay nìh thŋay ʔry?* 'What day is it today?' *thŋay nìh thŋay ʔaːtùt(y).* 'It's Sunday.' *kɔ̀ət mèːmaːy.* 'She's a widow.' *sʔry phkaː-thmɔː?* 'What is coral?' *nèək na: mcas rɔbɔs nìh?* 'Whose are these things?' *nìh rɔbɔs khɲom.* 'These are my things.' These are regarded as *ad hoc* verbalizations of nominal constructs cf. the *ad hoc* nominalizations of words otherwise catalysed as belonging to other categories discussed above in Lesson 35.1. Pre-verbal particles are used with the above noun constructs in the following sentences, thus catalysing them as verbs:—*thŋay nìh mùun-mèːn thŋay ʔaːtùt(y) tèː.* 'It isn't Sunday today!' *nìh sɔl-tae rɔbɔs khɲom.* 'These things are all mine.' *nìh mùun-soːv phkaː-thmɔː tèː.* 'This is hardly coral.' *prɔhael-cìːə saːraːy.* 'Perhaps it's seaweed.' *kɔ̀ət sɔl-tae mèːmaːy.* 'They are all widows.'

36.2. *Uses of ʔaoy*

The word-form *ʔaoy* also needs several dictionary entries:—**v.** 'to give, to let, to have (someone do something for one)', **m.** 'so that, so as to', **pre n.p.** (i) 'for', (ii) 'in a — manner'. The following sentences illustrate their uses:—

lòːk-krùː ʔaoy nùm nìh mɔ̀ːk khɲom. The teacher gave me this cake.
ʔaɲ mùun ʔaoy ʔaeŋ dɑə(r)-lèːŋ. I don't let you go for walks.
lòːk ʔaoy kèː yɔ̀ːk ʔryvan tỳu. Mr. — is having his luggage taken away.
khɲom khɔm thvỳː kaː(r) ʔaoy ʔoːpùk khɲom sɔpbaːy crt(t). I am working hard so that my father will be pleased.
ʔoːpùk tèŋ sìəvphỳu ʔaoy khɲom. Father buys books for me.
cau rùət tỳu saːlaː-rìən ʔaoy rɔhás. The little boy ran quickly to school.

36.3. *Uses of ʔɔs, tὲəŋ, rɔ̀əl, sɔ̀p̀(v), krùp and tὲəŋ-ʔɔs*

ʔɔs 'all' (+ sing. noun), 'the whole of'. Used chiefly in connection with time and with a numeral construct following (and thus nominalized). e.g. *ʔɔs mùːəy yùp*, 'the whole of one night, all night, all the night'. *ʔɔs pìː(r) thŋay*, 'the whole of two days, for two full days'. Also used with *pèːl-vèːlìːə*, e.g. *ʔɔs pèːl-vèːlìːə*, 'the whole of the time'.

tὲəŋ 'with, together with, including all'.

    e.g. *kɔ̀ət tɤ̀u tùː-krɔŋ tὲəŋ bɤy nèək.* ⎫ They went to the town,
                                   ⎬   all three of them.
            tὲəŋ pìː(r) nèək. ⎭ both of them.

    kɔːn-sɤs(s) prəlɔːŋ cɔ̀əp tὲəŋ dɔp nèək. All ten students passed the exam.
    yɤ̀ːŋ rùp laːn baːn tὲəŋ ŋìːəy. We can push the car easily (all easily, with ease).
    dɔmrɤy rùət tɤ̀u tὲəŋ (h)voːŋ. The elephants ran away, the whole herd.

rɔ̀əl, 'all' (+ plur. noun), 'every'. Used with a following noun and especially in connection with time and place but also used with *knìːə* (*rɔ̀əl knìːə* 'all together') and other words implying 'persons'. e.g. *rɔ̀əl dɔːŋ* 'every time', *rɔ̀əl nìːətìː* 'every minute', *rɔ̀əl chnam* 'every year', *rɔ̀əl pèːl-vèːlìːə* 'every time', *rɔ̀əl kɔnlaeŋ* 'every place'.

sɔ̀p̀(v) and *krùp*. These words have very limited uses. It is enough at this stage to recognize the five adverbial constructs given here:—*sɔ̀p̀(v) dɔːŋ* (= *rɔ̀əl dɔːŋ*) 'every time'; *sɔ̀p̀(v) ʔɔnlɤ̀ː* = *krùp kɔnlaeŋ* = *rɔ̀əl kɔnlaeŋ* 'every place, each place'. *krùp knìːə* = *rɔ̀əl knìːə* 'all together'. *sɔ̀p̀(v) thŋay* has, however, the unexpected meaning 'nowadays', 'these days' and not, like *rɔ̀əl thŋay*, 'every day'. Both *sɔ̀p̀(v)* and *krùp* are verbs as well as pre-nominal particles. Together they form a compound verb 'to be all, complete, without exception'.

tὲəŋ-ʔɔs, 'all'. This word has two functions:—

(i) post-nominal particle. Its position may vary in relation to that of any other post-nominal particle, e.g. *nìh* or *nùh* occurring with the same noun construct.

    e.g. *kɔːn-sɤs(s)* ⎰ *nùh tὲəŋ-ʔɔs* ⎱ *tɤ̀u kɔmpùəŋ caːm.* All the students have gone
                  ⎱ *tὲəŋ-ʔɔs nùh* ⎰   to Kompung Cham.
      cau baːn mɤ̀ːl siəvphɤ̀u ⎰ *tὲəŋ-ʔɔs nùh.* ⎱ (My) grandson has read all those
                      ⎱ *nùh tὲəŋ-ʔɔs.* ⎰ books.

(ii) adverbial particle

  mnùs(s) nùh tɤ̀u kɔmpùəŋ caːm ⎰ *tὲəŋ-ʔɔs knìːə.* Those men have all gone to
                              ⎱ *tὲəŋ-ʔɔs.*   Kompung Cham.
  yɤ̀ːŋ mɤ̀ːl sɔmpùət nùh, dael mɔ̀ːk pìː srok siəm tὲəŋ-ʔɔs. We saw all those sarongs which came from Thailand.

Note. *tὲəŋ-laːŋ* is a more literary counterpart of *tὲəŋ-ʔɔs*. It is used in exactly the same way, except that *tὲəŋ-laːŋ* is preferred at the very end of a noun construct; *nìh*, *nùh*, etc., must precede it.

    To translate 'all, every' with wide coverage in generalizations, *sɔl-tae* (**pre n.p.**) should be used, e.g. *mnùs(s) nùh sɔl-tae khcùl.* 'These men are all lazy.' *nɤ̀u srok nùh, mnùs(s) krɔː sɔl-tae khlìːən.* 'In that country the poor people all starve.' *tὲəŋ*, discussed immediately above, is used to translate 'all' in 'all three persons', 'all twelve of them', etc. However, as a very general guide, one may say that *rɔəl* is used to translate 'all, every' and *ʔɔs* 'the whole of' in connection with time; otherwise *tèəŋ-ʔɔs* and *sɔl-tae* may be used.

36.4. *General dependent particles*

tae, prəhael, sɔːm͡bɤy and **dɔː* are dependent, like pre-nominal and pre-verbal particles, in that they must precede another word to which they are closely bound. They are 'general' particles in the sense that the word they precede need not belong to a specific category (verb, noun, numeral, etc.). They lack stress in comparison with the word on which they are dependent. They do not affect the rest of the sentence grammatically in any way. Contrast pre-nominal particles, which form, with noun constructs, a different kind of construct; or the pre-verbal particle, *mùn*, which indicates the main verb and profoundly alters the meaning of the sentence. The meaning and use of *tae, prəhael, sɔːm͡bɤy* and *dɔː* are as follows:—

tae, 'only, not more than', e.g. *vìːə tətùːrəl tìːən tae tùk-dəh-kòː.* 'He is taking (i.e. 'eating and drinking') only milk.' *mìːən tae khɲom nɤu phtèəh.* 'There's only myself at home.' *khɲom dael tɤu srok sìəm tae pìː(r) dɔːŋ.* 'I have only been to Siam twice.' *khɲom khɤːɲ kmeːŋ-pros tae bɤy nèək.* 'I see only three boys.' *taː daə(r) tae yùːt-yùːt.* 'Grandfather walks only very slowly.'

prəhael, 'about'. This particle is usually confined to use with numerals. e.g. *khɲom baːn khɤːɲ tìːəhìːən prəhael dɔp nèək.* 'I saw about ten soldiers.' *nɤu prəhael dɔp nìːətìː tìət!* 'About ten minutes more!'

sɔːm͡bɤy, 'even', e.g. *kaːl vìːə kaː(r), sɔːm͡bɤy ʔoːpùk mùn tɤu.* 'When he got married, even his father didn't go!'

**dɔː*, 'the one which, the . . . .'. This particle is used in formal and literary language. It links an attribute to the noun, giving a little emphasis to the whole construct. e.g. *cɔmriəŋ dɔː pìːrùəh nùh,* 'that delightful song'.

Exercise 39

Nouns. *krùːəsaː(r)* family   *srok-cèəpon* Japan   *samáy* period, time   *kaː(h)veː* coffee   *knìːə* we, they (pronoun)   *ʔɔŋkɔː(r)-vɔ̀ət(t)* Angkor Vat   *rìːəc* kingdom   money *prak*   *srɤy-srɤy* women (plur.)[1]

Verbs. *chlaːt* to be clever   *pìnùt(y)-mɤːl* to scrutinize   *bɔmrɔŋ nùŋ* to set one's mind on   *hat* to practise   *rɔ̀əm* to dance   *tùən-phlùən* to be supple   *thvɤ̀ː* to do, to make, to do the work of   *saoy* to rule   to talk *niyìːəy* to be quiet *sŋìəm*

Expression. a lot *craən* **x**.

Note. For pre-nominal particles see previous pages.

A.1. ʔae-cɔmnaek lòːk-pùː, kɔ̀ət chlaːt cìːəŋ kè: knoŋ krùːəsaː(r) rəbɔs yɤ̀ːŋ. 2. pì: thŋay nùh rəhoːt-mɔ̀ːk-dɔl thŋay nìh, poːlìːs pìnùt(y)-mɤ̀ːl mənùs(s) tèəŋ-ʔɔs dael coːl knoŋ phtèəh vìːə. 3. nèək tɤu cìh kɔpal kɔː-baːn cìh laːn kɔː-baːn, khɲom nùŋ tɤu dɔl mùn nèək. 4. taŋ-pì: thŋay nùh mɔ̀ːk, khɲom bɔmrɔŋ nùŋ tɤu srok-cèəpon mùm khaːn. 5. koːn-sɤs(s) nùh hat rɔ̀əm rɔ̀əl thŋay, pon͡tae mì:ən tae pì:(r) nèək tè: dael ceh rɔ̀əm yaːŋ tùən-phlùən.[2]

---

[1] See Lesson 46 for this plural form.
[2] For use of *tè:*, see Ex. 38 A.1 and Lesson 47, Ex. 59 A (12) and note to latter.

6. yùə̯n(t)-hɔh sạmáy thmʀy tʀu baːn mùːəy maoŋ cìːəŋ mùːəy pɔ̀ən kìːloːmaet(r). 7. khmae(r) khlah coːl cʀt(t) pìsaː kaː(h)veː cìːəŋ tùk-tae. 8. ʔoː-pùk nìːəŋ thvʀ̀ː krùː-pě̤ːt̤(y) nʀ̀u phnùm-pě̤n prəhael dɔp chnam haəy. 9. mùk(h)-cìːə nɛ̀ək troːv ʔaoy nɛ̀ək-bɔmraə cùːt phtɛ̀əh mùn. 10. knìːə rɔ̀ːk tboːŋ nùh krùp kənlaeŋ ʔʀt khʀ̀ːɲ. 11. mùt(t)-sɔmlaɲ cau nù̀ŋ tʀu ʔɔŋkɔː(r)-vɔ̀ə̯t(t) ʔɔs mùːəy ʔaːtùt(y). 12. pì chnam nùh tɔː-tɔː-mɔ̀ːk tìət, sdäc khmae(r) sot̤-tae saoy rìːə̀c nʀ̀u phnùm-pě̤n.

B.1. The thieves took the jewels from the cupboard, together with the money which was in a drawer. 2. From Monday of last week until Friday of next week, Mr. — is in Saigon. 3. The shopkeeper told the police that he had not seen any boys in the shop that afternoon. 4. At home my brother talks a lot but at the office he is very quiet. 5. Why does your friend have a house so near the Phnom? (= near the Phnom like this). 6. By next Saturday I shall have earned a living for a whole week! 7. As for grandfather, he left Phnom Penh and went to Battambang. 8. The house belonging to your grandmother is nearer to Kompung Cham. 9. Would you please write this letter instead of me? I don't know this person at all. 10. The gentleman said he would stay sitting in the same place until I came back. 11. From the third day onwards, give Mrs. — only one pill per day. 12. Under the house was a place where the women wove cloth.

LESSON 37

SENTENCE-FORMS I AND II AND THE ANALYSIS OF LONGER SENTENCES

The full possibilities which were opened up by the introduction of minor and second major verbal constructs have not been seen in practice in sentences which have been used since. Before proceeding to these longer sentences, there are a few points to be elaborated.

37.1. *Use of several initiating and minor verbs together*

In Lessons 19 and 20 respectively initiating verbs and minor verbs were introduced. These have been used in sentences since then but only one of each has occurred in one sentence. Often, however, two or even more initiating or minor verbs occur together, e.g.

khɲom kùt cɔŋ tʀu lèːŋ phsaː(r). I would rather like to go and spend some time in the market.

kùt cɔŋ tʀu (thinking of wanting to go)   N   V   V

                              n   v   v   v   vN

                                     vn

*sạt(v)-*kɔndol rùə̯t mɔ̀ːk pìː kənlaeŋ nìh cĕɲ.* The rat came running out from this place.

rùə̯t mɔ̀ːk . . . . cĕɲ v ← v ← v.   N V ← v   A ← v

                                 n v   v pN   v

                                   pnp

37.2. *Limitations of minor verb construct*

In Lesson 21.1 when the second major verb construct was introduced, it was pointed out that this could have a pre-verbal particle or an initiating verb before it. The minor verb construct is limited in these respects; its full formula is only **vN**. A verb of motion or position which is used with an initiating verb or a pre-verbal particle receives stress and for this reason alone would be regarded as a verb of a major verb construct.

37.3. *Further position which* **A**, **a** *or* **X** *may occupy*

Sentences which have been used up to this point have not had adverbial constructs, adverbial particles or numeral constructs occurring between the independent noun construct and the first major verb construct.[1] This is, however, a possibility, particularly in colloquial speech. e.g.

mnùs(s) pìː(r) nèək nùh pìː msɤl mèn tɤu phsaː(r) thom. 'Those two men, yesterday, they went to the big market.'   **N   A   V**

                                                    nxcp   pnp   vN

                                                              nv

yùːən nùh tèəŋ pìː(r) nèək knìːə baːn mòːk suːə(r) lòːk. Those Vietnamese — both of them — came to see Mr. —.   **N   A   a   V**

                                                    pN   v   v   vN

                                                    np   pxc   a   v   v   vn

37.4. *Occurrence of more than two verb constructs*

In Lessons 20 and 21 sentences were introduced in which the first verb construct was followed either by a minor verb construct or by a second major construct. In sentences used since then, there have been no more than two constructs in one sentence, either a major and a minor or two **major**. In the following sentences, there are two major and one minor verb constructs:—

Independent **N**	*Major* **V**	*Minor* **v**	*Major* **V**
1. —	*coːl*	*tɤu*	*suːə(r).*
2. *khɲom*	*soːm phɲəə phkaː-thmɔː*	*tɤu*	*prəkèːn lòːk.*

Independent **N**	*Major* **V**	*Major* **V**	*Minor* **v**
3. —	*rùɲ sìːkloː*	*coːl*	*mòːk.*
4. *kɔət*	*dɔːk*	*yɔːk thmèɲ*	*cèɲ.*

Translations of the above sentences: 1. Go in and ask! 2. I would like to send the coral to you, sir, (to monk). 3. Push the cyclo in here! 4. He pulled the tooth out.

37.5. *Sentences with three major verb constructs*

Each verb is stressed to some extent and potentially each verb construct may begin a new phrase.

Independent **N**	*Major* **V**	*Major* **V**	*Major* **V**
1. *vìːə*	*cèː(r)*	*vay*	*haːm kɔːn.*
2. *vìːə*	*cok cɤ̀ːŋ*	*cok day*	*prùːəy cɤt(t) nas.*
3. *koːn-sɤs(s) nùh*	*khɔm yɔːk cɤt(t)*	*tùk-dak*	*sdap krùː.*
4. —	*kom *khsɤp*	*prap*	*nìyìːəy bɔntec-bɔntec cùt trəciək.*

---

[1] Except in 35.1, *nùŋ* and *həəy-nùŋ*, forming adverbial constructs.

Translations of the above sentences: 1. He rebukes, beats and restricts the children. 2. He has a bad leg and a bad arm and is very miserable. 3. Those pupils try to give their minds to listening to the teacher (= try to take their minds to put them to listen). 4. Don't tell (the others) by whispering. (Don't whisper to inform, speaking a little, near the ears.)

37.6. *Sentences having three or more major verb constructs, with or without minor ones*

A suitable way of phrasing the sentences is indicated by the sign, (,|). The verb constructs contained in each sentence are noted in parentheses at the end of the sentence.

nὲǝk nùh (,|) *chὸːŋ* (,|) *cap day* (,|) *soːm lừːǝ.* (**V V V**). The man extended his hand, seized (the other's) hand and said goodbye.

vìːǝ cìh krǝbⱴy (,|) *tùːl sroːⱴ* (,|) *bɔː(r) tⱴu.* (**V V V ← v**). He got on to the buffalo with the paddy on his head and rode off.

kmeːŋ lὲːŋ sɑǝc sɔpbɑːy. (**V V V**). The children were playing and laughing happily.

vìːǝ rὸːk-sìː thⱴừː kɑː(r) ʔvⱴy mùn bɑːn. (**V V V**). He wasn't able to earn his living by doing any work.

nìːǝŋ vùǝŋvèːŋ (,|) *rὸːk pùm khⱴừːⱴ.* (**V V V**). She was bewildered and couldn't find (the way).

cao(r) dɑǝ(r) mὸːk (,|) *khⱴừːⱴ poːlìːs cap pⱡɔːn.* (**V ← v V V**). The thief walked towards (them) and saw the police catch his brother.

mìːǝn phlìǝŋ thlὲǝk mὸːk crɑǝn (,|) *pὲŋ srae tὲǝŋ-ʔɔs hɑǝy.* (**V V ← v V**). Rain fell in great quantities, spreading over the whole ricefield.

Sentences such as the above which have three or more major verb constructs are regarded as being further extensions of sentence-forms I and II. Their basic formula would be:—

Sentence-form I 3   **N V V V**
Sentence-form II 3   **V V V**

37.7. *Grammatical relationships between the nouns and verbs involved in a sequence of major verb constructs*

Within one clause, the subject of the first verb construct may not be the subject of the second. It is frequently the case that the dependent noun construct which forms part of the first verb construct is the subject of the second major verb. e.g. *khⱡom khⱴừːⱴ mnùs(s) mnὲǝk dɑǝ(r) taːm phloːⱴ.* 'I see someone walking along the road.' *khⱡom hau kɔːn tⱴu cùːⱹp lὸːk.* 'I'll call (my) son/daughter to go and meet Mr. —.' *pùǝs cⱴk khlɑː slap.* 'The snake bit the tiger to death' (contrast the same words uttered as two vivid clauses, *pùǝs cⱴk* (,|), *khlɑː slap.* 'The snake bit and the tiger was dead').

In Lesson 21.2 it was pointed out that **nvnv** might have to be analysed as **N V** or as **N V V**, since the second verb might be used attributively with the preceding noun, e.g. *khⱡom tὲn trⱴy thom.* 'I bought a big fish.' Usually verbs used attributively are attributive verbs (which *dɑǝ(r)*, *cùːⱹp* and *slap* are not). If there is any doubt, the test may be carried out of referring to the last **nv** as a noun construct in a new sentence, e.g. *trⱴy thom nùh* .... will work, but *mnùs(s) dɑǝ(r) nùh* will not.

A third verbal construct may refer back again to the first noun construct, e.g. *khɲom hau koːn tɤu cùːəp lòːk mùn baːn.* 'I can't call my son/daughter to go and meet Mr. —' or it may continue to refer to the new one, e.g. *yɤ̀ːŋ khɤ̀ːɲ nìːəŋ nùh daə(r) tɤu knoŋ suːən-phkaː(r) ʔɔŋkùy nɤu-kraom mlùp daəm-chɤ̀ː.* 'We saw the girl go into the garden and sit down in the shade of the trees.'

Another possibility, disconcerting for English speakers, is a similar lack of reference to the original 'subject' when there is nevertheless no noun present to cause it, e.g. when someone is trying to light damp matches, *khɲom kùs mùn cheh!* 'I am striking (them but they) don't light.' The *chɤ̀ː-kùs* are mooted by the context of situation.

The first verb construct sometimes refers to an action which has never or will never take place. This fits in with English in e.g. *khɲom tɤu mùn baːn.* 'I can't go' but seems different in e.g. *yɤ̀ːŋ kaː(r) koːn hau phɲiəv tèəŋ-ʔɔs haəy.* 'We have invited all the guests for the wedding of our daughter.' ('We, marrying our daughter, invited . . . . ').

LESSON 38

SENTENCE-FORM III AND SUMMARY OF USES OF SENTENCE-FORMS I AND II

38.1. *Sentence-form III,* **N N V . . . .**

Sentence-form III has two independent noun constructs. Otherwise it closely resembles the other sentence-forms.

Among the pre-nominal particles are several which help to emphasize the sentence subject, within the framework of sentence-form I (*ʔae, cɔmnaek, cɔmnaek-khaːŋ,* 'as to', 'with regard to', etc.), e.g.

ʔae taː, kɔ̀ət mùn prɔ̀ːm tɤu tèː. As for grandfather, he won't go.
A   N   p   V   f

Emphasis may also be given without using an adverbial construct in sentences constructed with two independent noun constructs. e.g.

lòːk (ˌ|) kɔ̀ət cën tɤu *bùyroː haəy. Mr. — has gone off to the office.
N   N   V   v   f

yùːən buːən nèək nùh (ˌ|) vìːə cìh yù̀ən(t)-hɔh tɤu prèy-nəkɔ̀ː(r). Those four
N   N   V   v
Vietnamese have gone to Saigon by air.

The degree of emphasis depends on the pitch reached and amount of pause. It can be very slight. A rise to mid level with a slight pause in the following sentence would merely make the subject explicit: *khɲom (ˌ|) khɲom mùn prɔ̀ːm thvɤ̀ː tèː.* 'Me? I don't agree to do it.' A steep rise to high level, followed by a distinct pause, however, would give more emphasis to the subject: '*I* don't agree to do it.' ('The others may, but I don't').

38.2. *Emphasis of sentence object*

Without any apparent grammatical difference, sentence-form III may equally be used to throw into prominence what would otherwise be the dependent noun construct, i.e. the sentence object. Here, there is considerable emphasis. Sentences with similar meaning but without emphasis are given alongside emphatic examples for comparison.

Emphatic	*Unemphatic*
siəvphv̌u nùh (,|)*, khɲom mv̌:l cɔp haəy.*	*khɲom mv̌:l siəvphv̌u nùh cɔp haəy.*

I have read *this* book/this book already.

cùəɲcèəɲ (,|) *khɲom lì:əp pɔ̀ə(rɲ) bayto:ɲ.*	*khɲom lì:əp cùəɲcèəɲ pɔ̀ə(rɲ) bayto:ɲ.*

I am painting the *walls*/the walls green.

sɔmpùət nùh (,|) *khɲom lùək ʔɔs haəy.*	*khɲom lùək sɔmpùət nùh ʔɔs haəy.*

I have sold *that* material/that material completely.

With *kè:* as subject:—

Emphatic	*Unemphatic*
trvy nìh (,|) *kè: chʔaə(r) lv̌: rùmɲv̌:k phlv̌:ɲ.*	*kè: chʔaə(r) trvy nìh lv̌: rùmɲv̌:k phlv̌:ɲ.*

This fish/This fish has been roasted over the embers.

phlae-chv̌: nùh (,|) *kè: lùək thlay nas!*	*kè: lùək phlae chv̌: nùh thlay nas!*

Those fruit/Those fruit are being sold very dear.

phtèəh nùh (,|) *kè: sɔɲ ʔɔmpì: ʔvt̥(th).*	*kè: sɔɲ phtèəh nùh ʔɔmpì: ʔvt̥(th).*

This house/This house was built of brick. (They built *this*/this house of brick.)

38.3. *Sentence topic and emphasis*

Sometimes the verb is used impersonally and the independent noun construct is not the object in the non-emphatic version, e.g.

bɔmpùəɲ cèɲ tùk. cèɲ tùk pì: bɔmpùəɲ. 'The pipe is dripping.' (The pipe there comes out water/There comes out water from the pipe.)

nèək nùɲ krù:ə-sa:(r) nèək, mì:ən mnùs(s) ponma:n nèək? mì:ən mnùs(s) ponma:n nèak nv̌u-knoɲ krù:ə-sa:(r) nèək? 'You and your family, how many people are there?' 'How many people are there in your family?'

vì:ə bat ʔvy? bat ʔvy rəbɔs vì:ə? 'What has he lost?' 'What of his is lost?'

In the following, the verb is not impersonal, but the independent noun construct is not the object: *phlo:v-thnɔl, cak kausù:. kè: cak kausù: nv̌u lv̌: phlo:v-thnɔl.* The main road is being made. They pour tar macadam on the main road.

In the next, sentence-form III is properly represented but only one of the independent noun constructs is the subject or object.

krù: nìh, phnè:k mùn pù:kae. phnè:k krù: nìh mùn pù:kae. This teacher has poor eyesight.

In these last sentences, the independent noun construct represents neither the subject nor the object, but a general sentence topic, the chief point of interest in the sentence.

Both the independent noun construct in sentence-form I and the first independent noun construct in sentence-form III might also be regarded as sentence topics rather than as sentence subject and sentence object. The latter terms have been used, chiefly because of their general familiarity but, since no formal criteria distinguish the independent noun construct occurring in sentence-form I from that occurring in sentence-form III, a term less suggestive of grammatical form might be more acceptable.

Special position of the marker in sentences with emphasis

A marker sometimes occurs after the first or only independent noun construct, e.g.

lòːk nìh, mëc-kɔː lòːk chùp thvɤ̀ː kaː(r) haəy? Why has *Mr.* — stopped work already?

tok nìh, kom-ʔaoy kèː yɔ̀ːk cën! Don't let anyone take *this table* out!

An emphatic form of question has this feature; it consists of a construct containing a question word followed by the marker, *dael*, which is in turn followed by the rest of the sentence-form, e.g.

nèak naː dael thvɤ̀ː nùh? Who did that? Who was it who did that?

siəvphɤ̀u naː-mùːəy dael nèak baːn tèɲ pìː msɤl? Which book did you buy yesterday?

ʔvɤy dael nɔ̀əm ʔaoy nèak khɤŋ mleh? Whatever made you so cross?

38.4. *Translation of the English passive voice*

It may have been observed that in several of the above sentences the passive voice was used in the English translation. There is no special form of the verb or use of particle in Cambodian to form a passive voice. It is usually necessary in translation from English to turn the passive form round to the active, using as subject, where necessary, 'one' or 'they', and then to translate.

e.g. I was seen by the teacher. The teacher saw me. *lòːk-krùː khɤ̀ːɲ khɲom.*

This man was elected by the laymen. The laymen elected this man. *ʔobaːsɔk rɤ̀ːs taŋ nèak nìh.*

He was seen yesterday. Someone saw him yesterday. *kèː khɤ̀ːɲ vìːə pìː msɤl meɲ.*

Rice is sold here. They sell rice here. *kèː lùək ʔɔŋkɔː(r) knoŋ kɔnlaeŋ nìh.*

Note, in passing, other possibilities in sentences in which the passive occurs in English:—

The boy was run over and killed by a bus. *kmeːŋ slap nùŋ laːn-chnuːəl kɤn.*

Children are not allowed in here. *haːm mùn-ʔaoy kmeːŋ cɔːl kɔnlaeŋ nìh.*

When the object of the action is of more interest than the action itself, sentence-form III is used, *ʔɔŋkɔː(r), kèː lùək knoŋ kɔnlaeŋ nìh.* Rice is sold here. Sometimes the author of the action is unknown and of so little interest that even *kèː* is absent; this may occur when the object comes before the verb, e.g.

phtèəh nìh sɔŋ ʔompìː chɤ̀ː. This house is built of wood.

sɔmpùət nìh tbaːɲ taːm kbac thmɤy. This material was woven with a new design.

With reference to the absence of *kèː* in these sentences, it is common for *kèː* meaning 'one', 'they', 'you' to be absent in other grammatical contexts too.

e.g. *thvə̀ː ʔɤy-ʔɤy, thvə̀ː ʔaoy praːkɔt.* If you do a thing, do it properly.

> *sɔŋ phtèəh.* They're building a house. (Spoken as an initiating sentence by a person observing the builders.)

Where *kèː* is absent, the sentences given above resemble those having sentence-form I.

cf.   *khɲom tɤu cìːə-mùːəy-nuŋ nèək.* I am going with you.

> *phtèəh sɔŋ ʔɔmpìː chɤ̀ː.* The house is built of wood.

38.5. *Summary of the uses of sentence-forms I and II*

It is convenient here to summarize the uses of the sentence-forms introduced earlier.

Sentence-form I **N V**

This is constantly used to express:—

(i) subject + verb + object, e.g. *ʔɔːpùk vay cao(r).* 'Father hit the thief.' The validity of the word-order is seen by comparing *cao(r) vay ʔɔːpùk.* 'The thief hit father.'

(ii) subject + verb + destination, e.g. *khɲom tɤu phtèəh.* 'I am going home.'

(iii) subject + verb + sphere of reference, e.g. *khɲom chùː kbaːl.* 'I have a head-ache.' (I am ill as to the head), *lòːk sruːəl khluːən.* 'He is well.' (He is comfortable as to the body.) (Compare also *mùt day* 'to be cut as to the hand, to have a cut hand'; *cok cɤ̀ːŋ* 'to be hurt as to the foot, lame'; *sɔpbaːy cɤt(t)* 'to be happy at heart, glad'; *prùːəy cɤt(t)* 'to be sad at heart, sad'; *kao(r) sɔk* 'to be shaved as to the head, to have a shaven head'; *lùəŋ tùk* 'to be drowned in water, drowned'; *lìːəp pɔ̀ə(rn) khiəv* 'to be painted with the colour blue, to be painted blue'; *prɔk kbuəŋ* 'to be roofed with tiles'.)

To these uses is now added a fourth:—

(iv) object + verb, e.g. *phtèəh sɔŋ nuŋ ʔɤt(th).* The house is built of bricks. (The house, unexpressed subject, build of bricks.) No difference in intonation or pause marks this sentence off grammatically from a sentence such as *khɲom səseː(r) nuŋ dɔːŋ-pakkaː.* I write with a pen. Yet the word-order, noun-verb, implies in Cambodian, as in English, the relationship subject-verb, as was shown in (i) above. In order to understand how a basic word-order meaning can be overthrown in this way, it is necessary to consider lexical meaning. It is entirely because the house cannot do the action of building that the order, house-build, can be tolerated. The object-verb order is particularly common with verbs expressing the idea of creating in contexts where one is not interested at all in the creator, e.g.

ʔaːv nùh deː(r) yaːŋ lʔɔː. That blouse is sewn beautifully.

spìːən nùh lìːəp haəy. That bridge has already been painted.

The same construction is possible, however, with verbs which do not express the lexical idea of creation, provided that the collocation between them and the noun is well-established.

e.g. *dɤy rùŋ kap mùn mùt.* One hacks at hard earth without breaking the surface.

dɤy sʔɤt kap mùn crɤu. One digs into sticky earth but not deeply.

(These sentences would be good translations of English 'You can't break the surface of hard earth easily' and 'You can't dig deep into sticky earth'.)

sɔmdɤy nìh sdap mùn soːv pìːrùəh. One listens to this talk but it's not pleasant to hear. (It's not nice to hear talk like this.)

khsae nùh kat mùn dac. One can't cut this string. (One cuts at this string, without its breaking.)

chɤːkùs mùːəy prəʔɔp nùh kùs mùn cheh. These matches in this box (lit. 'this box of matches') don't light when you strike them.

kdaːr troːv mìːən vèːŋ rùː khlɤy? Do (we) need long or short planks?

Sentence-form II **V**

While **N V** (sentence-form I) is the normal form for expressing (i) subject + action or state (as in *lòːk tɤu haəy.* 'Mr. — has already gone.' *lòːk tìːəp nas.* 'Mr. — is very small.'). (ii) object + action done by unknown agent in whom one is not interested (*phtèəh sɔŋ ....*) it is not a favourite word-order for subject + action of an accidental or natural kind, not brought about by any known or unknown agent. Sentence-form II is the normal form here (as in *cheh phtèəh,* 'the house is on fire.'), *rəbaək twìːə(r)* 'The door is open.'

The uses of sentence-form II may be summarized, in terms of the present discussion, as (i) verb + object, e.g. *yòːk siəvphɤu mɔːk!* 'Bring the book!' (ii) verb + sphere of action, e.g. *dɔl maoŋ haəy.* 'It's time!' *cheh phtèəh.* 'The house is on fire!' (There is a fire in respect of the house).

Exercise 40

Nouns. *lòːk-pros* husband (polite term often used by wife of own husband) self *khluːən*　　*pdɤy* husband (general word)　　*kèːhə(s)thaːn* building *ʔɤṭ(ṭh)* brick　　*srok-*ʔɔŋklèːs* England　　evening-at-dusk *pèːl prəlùp* elephant *dɔmrɤy*　　mountain stream *stùŋ*　　north *khaːŋ-cɤːŋ*　　minister *rɔəṭ(ṭh)-mùəntrɤy*　　prince *prèəh-ʔɔ̯ŋ(k̊)-mcas*　　New Year Festival *bon(y)* *coːl chnam*　　America *srok-*ʔaːmeːrìːk* Verbs. *lɤːk* to lift　*cak sao(r)* to bolt　*cùt* to be close　*krùk-krùk* clank to irrigate *bɔŋhoː(r) tùk coːl*　to have a drink (animals) *phɤk tùk*　to work hard *khɔm thvɤ̀ː kaːr* to plot *rùːəm kùmnùt nùŋ*　to capture *cap-cɔːŋ* to celebrate *thvɤ̀ː*　old (and plural) *cas-cas*[1]　new (and plural) *thmɤy-thmɤy*[1] Particle. *rəhoːt-dɔl* pre **n.p.** all the way to Expression. by sea *taːm cɤ̀ːŋ tùk*

A.1. *ʔɤyvan nùh, khɲom lɤːk mùn rùːəc.* 2. *lòːk-pros, kɔ̀ət chùː yaːŋ khlaŋ.* *yɤ̀ːŋ troːv-tae nɤu sɲiəm.* 3. *kɔntèːl nùh, lòːk-yìːəy tba:ŋ khluːən ʔaeŋ.* 4. *srɤy*

---

[1] See Lesson 46 for plural meaning of reduplicated forms.

nùh, pì:(r) bɤy khae mùn, pdɤy slap tɤu. 5. kè:hə(s)tha:n thmɤy nùh, sɔŋ nùŋ ʔɤt(ṭh) tɛ̀əŋ-ʔɔs. 6. tvì:ə(r) nìh, cak sao(r) haəy kɔ: bɤ̀t mùm cὺt dae(r). 7. lò:k nùh, co:l mɔ̀:k pos(te) phɲaə kɔɲcɔp mù:əy tɤu srok-ʔɔŋklè:s. 8. nὲək na: kɔ:-daoy, lò:k kɔ: mùm prɔ̀:m tətὺ:əl prὺk nìh dae(r). 9. cao(r) cìh tὺ:k-kdaoŋ nìh tɤu na:, po:lì:s nùŋ cìh ka:ɲo:t tɤu ta:m dae(r). 10. la:n nìh, bɔ:(r) tɤu, lὺ: so:(r) krὺk-krὺk.

B.1. Ever since last year *this* land has been irrigated. 2. Every evening at dusk those elephants come all the way to this mountain stream to have a drink. 3. His nephew said he would prefer to go in the sailing boat rather than in the steamer. 4. No-one in this village locks ('shoots the bolt of') the door at night. 5. That shopkeeper is said to be the happiest man in Kompung Cham. 6. The husband—he's working very hard nowadays as a doctor in the north. 7. The minister knew that some people were plotting to capture the prince. 8. Next week, from Tuesday until Thursday, the New Year Festival will be celebrated. 9. We all prefer the old buildings in that city to the new. 10. All *this* luggage I'm sending to America by sea.

PART III

GRAMMAR AND TRANSLATION

INTRODUCTION TO PART III

In each of the ten lessons of Part III a new grammatical topic such as prefixation or exclamations is discussed. This is followed by one or more translation exercises of continuous prose. The exercises do not have a close connection with the new grammatical subject with which they are associated in the lesson. It would have been possible to place all the exercises together at the end of the ten lessons. It was felt, however, that their distribution among the lessons, as nearly as possible as in Part II, might encourage the student to continue both to study the new material and to do the exercises!

Each of the exercises consists of a reading passage,[1] followed by notes, and a short passage on a similar subject for translation from English. The passages are presented in the transcription with numerals dividing them into sections, to facilitate reference to the notes. The notes have the threefold purpose of (i) referring the student back or forward to the lesson in which a pertinent grammatical point is treated, (ii) helping occasionally with translation, since all new words have now to be looked up in the vocabulary, Part VI, and (iii) presenting marginally new material, such as the developed attribute in the noun construct.

By the time he has worked through Part II the student will probably have read many continuous passages in books such as the Cambodian School Reader. The first five or six passages in Part III will seem very short and easy to him in comparison with his other reading. These exercises contain material, however, which was met only towards the end of Part II and are intended as examples of constructions and sentence-forms; the methods of analysis used in Part II may be applied to all sentences which will be now encountered in the exercises or in reading.

As he begins Part III the student should be ready for wider reading than the school reader. A general course would include Cambodian stories such as those contained in *Recueil des contes et légendes cambodgiens*[2] and passages from novels and newspapers. The student working without a teacher will find the task of looking up new words from his general reading both laborious and discouraging; the list of dictionaries given in the bibliography in Part VII is intended to be as helpful as possible.

LESSON 39

RESPONDING PARTICLES, INITIATING PARTICLES, PRONOUNS AND TITLES

39.1. *Responding and initiating particles*

Up to this lesson the only responding particles introduced have been *baːt* and *cah*, and no initiating particles have been introduced; the words used to translate 'I' and 'you' have been either

---

[1] Of which the orthography is given in Part IV.
[2] Fasc. 1–5, Phnom Penh, 1963.

(i) the words or titles expressing genuine kinship or

(ii) the kinship terms used to persons of appropriate age or

(iii) the familiar *ʔaeŋ* or polite *nèək-srʏy*[1] or very respectful *lòːk/lòːk-srʏy, loːk-krùː,* etc., with *khɲom* to translate 'I'.

More responding particles will now be added, such as *ʔaə* used by a superior to an inferior and in Lesson 40 **kənaː* used by a layman to a monk. With these words, however, should be associated not only a word to translate 'you' but also a different word for 'I'. There are also a few pairs of words, given in Lesson 40, which translate 'go, come, eat, tell', etc., with reference to inferior or superior respectively. When one is speaking to royalty, there is a new set of particles, in addition to the responding particles. These are initiating particles (i), used in the same position and with the same kinds of intonation patterns as responding particles but occurring when the speaker initiates a conversation. Thus the sentence, 'I would like to go to Kompung Cham instead of you', initiating a conversation to a high-ranking male prince would, spoken by a male speaker, be,

soːm-trùəy-prèəh-mèːttaː-praos (= initiating particle), *tùːl-prèəh-bɔŋkùm-cìːə-khɲom* (= pronoun, 'I'), *coːl cʏt(t) tʏu kɔmpùəy caːm cùmnùːəs sɔmdäc* (= title, 'you').

This is the fringe of a special vocabulary, the *rìːəc-sap̱(t)* or royal vocabulary, for which the Cambodians themselves have a special book of reference. All personal possessions, parts of the body, actions etc. of the King or Queen have a special name, mostly derived from Sanskrit. There is a similar but less extensive vocabulary for things connected with monks. It is not proposed here to deal with the special vocabularies but to provide the initiating and responding particles and the pronouns and titles required when one is speaking to or about royalty, monks and laymen of varying ranks and ages. The lexical field of reference of other pronouns and titles including several which have been met and used frequently is also summarized below in Lesson 41.

39.2. *Pronouns*

It was stated in Lesson 14.2 (footnote) that pronouns are a sub-class of nouns. They are distinguished from other nouns by having the following characteristics:—

(i) They do not have the full noun construct possibilities; they are not used with an attributive verb in close junction.

(ii) They cannot be followed by the pre-nominal particle, *rəbɔs,* and a second noun as in *taː rəbɔs khɲom,* my grandfather.

(iii) They are constantly used in second reference to previous nouns, which might, like nouns associated with particular numeral coefficients, be shown to belong lexically to certain classes.

The following words are pronouns: *ʔaɲ, khɲom, yʏːŋ, ʔaeŋ, vìːə, kɔət, kèː, knìːə, khlah.*

---

[1] *nèək,* the word which one would expect to be the male counterpart of *nèək-srʏy* is both male and female and is used by people on equal terms with each other.

39.3. *Titles*

These are nouns which either (i) are kinship terms, e.g. *ta:* grandfather, *mì:ŋ* aunt, or (ii) are used to express the relative social positions which are valid between people, e.g. *lò:k*, 'Mr., sir', *sɔmdäc*, 'Prince, Your Highness'. The latter are used frequently in composition either with the former or with *pros*, *srɤy*, or with proper names, e.g. *lò:k-pros mnèək*, 'a gentleman', *lò:k sɔmrɤt*, 'Mr. Samret', *nì:əŋ mənì:*, 'Miss Mani', *lò:k-mì:ŋ*, 'you' to elder female (polite and friendly).

Titles are frequently used instead of a first or second person pronoun in Cambodian where only a pronoun would be acceptable in English. For many situations there is no pronoun; the titles, *lò:k, nèək* and their compounds are used instead. These gaps in the pronominal system, as compared with European languages, will be seen by reference to the table below.

39.4. *ʔa: and mnɔ̀əl*

Two words, *ʔa:* and *mnɔ̀əl*, which belong to the category of exclamations, **e**, discussed below in Lesson 43, are treated here, because they are closely connected in usage with pronouns and titles. *ʔa:* acts like a title in occurring chiefly in composition with proper names. Its connotation is derogatory or very familiar. It occurs particularly when a servant is being called by name, e.g. *ʔa: baen!* 'Baen!' It may occur in connection with names of objects, when the speaker is exclaiming and grumbling about them, e.g. *ʔa: phka:-thmɔ: nùh!* 'That (piece of) coral! (which always has to be moved every time I dust the table)'. *mnɔ̀əl* is similarly used preceding a noun, but in this case the noun is usually itself a title, e.g. *mnɔ̀əl lò:k nèək*, 'all of you ladies and gentlemen', *mnɔ̀əl nì:əŋ*, 'all of you ladies'. *mnɔ̀əl* is particularly used at the beginning of a speech and always in a religious context.

39.5. *Table of terms of address for laymen* (pp. 158–9)

The responding particles, pronouns and titles in the table may be used by an adult male or female person, Cambodian or foreign, of fairly good social background, in addressing laymen and laywomen of various relative age and social position. Alternative terms are listed with commas between, except for male/female alternances which are separated by a stroke. Titles are placed in parentheses.

Exercises 41–43

The three passages are intended to be studied in close succession. Although they are easy to understand, they involve sentence constructions introduced in Lesson 38. It will be observed that in connected passages in Cambodian a subject, or sentence topic is not repeated unless it is necessary for comprehension. A *khan(ʔ)*[1] is used to mark the end of a short section which may comprise several short sentences, cf. (1)–(4) of Exercise 41 A and (1)–(2) of Exercise 43 A.

---

[1] See Lesson 11.3.

Status of person addressed or to whom reference is made relative to speaker	Style	Responding particle	1st person	2nd person	3rd person
Inferior		ʔaə, ʔŭː	ʔaɲ pl. yɤ́ːŋ, knìːə	ʔaeŋ	vìːə
Equal		baːt/*cah	khɲom pl. yɤ́ːŋ	(lɔ̀ːk, nɛ̀ak/lɔ̀ːk-srɤy, nɛ̀ak-srɤy, nɛ̀ak)	kɔ̀at, kèː
Superior		baːt/*cah	khɲom, khɲom-baːt/nìːəŋ-khɲom pl. yɤ́ːŋ, yɤ́ːŋ-khɲom	(lɔ̀ːk/lɔ̀ːk-srɤy, nɛ̀ak-srɤy)	kɔ̀at,[2] (lɔ̀ːk)
Younger (a child)	familiar	ʔaə, ʔŭː	ʔaɲ pl. yɤ́ːŋ	ʔaeŋ	vìːə
	formal	baːt/*cah	khɲom pl. yɤ́ːŋ	(nìːəŋ)	(nìːəŋ-prɒs/nìːəŋ-srɤy)
Younger (but adult)	familiar	ʔaə, ʔŭː	ʔaɲ pl. yɤ́ːŋ	ʔaeŋ	vìːə
	formal	baːt/*cah	khɲom pl. yɤ́ːŋ	(nɛ̀ak/nìːəŋ)	kɔ̀at,[2] nɛ̀ak/nìːəŋ, lɔ̀ːk

Of equal age	tɛə, tɛ̀.	pl. yə̀:ŋ, knə̀:ə	(lɔ̀:ŋ)	kè:
formal	ba:t/*cah	khɲom pl. yə̀:ŋ	(lɔ̀:k, nɛ̀ək/nɛ̀ək)	kə̀t, kè:
Older — familiar	ʔaə, ʔù:	ʔaɲ pl. yə̀:ŋ	(pù:/mì:ŋ)	vì:ə
Older — formal	ba:t/*cah	khɲom pl. yə̀:ŋ	(lɔ̀:k-pù:/lɔ̀:k-mì:ŋ)	kə̀ət,² (lɔ̀:k)
Elderly¹ — familiar	ʔaə, ʔù:	ʔaɲ pl. yə̀:ŋ	(ta:/yì:əy)	kə̀ət
Elderly¹ — formal	ba:t/*cah	khɲom pl. yə̀:ŋ	(lɔ̀:k-ta:/lɔ̀:k-yì:əy)	kə̀ət,² (lɔ̀:k), (lɔ̀:k-ta:/lɔ̀:k-yì:əy)

159

¹ When the speaker's age is such that the elderly person addressed might suitably be addressed as 'uncle/aunt' rather than 'grandfather/grandmother', the same titles would be used as those given in the above section (under 'Older').

² kə̀ət, used alone, is not quite respectful enough for these contexts, but, if preceded by a title, it may be used with respect, e.g. lɔ̀:k-ta:, kə̀ət . . . .

Exercise 41 A

phtɛ̀əh cau heːŋ

(1)[1] phtɛ̀əh cau heːŋ thvɤ̀ː ʔompì: chɤ̀ː (2) prɔk slɤk-tnaot (3) sɔŋ lɤ̀ː cɔntùəl (4) mìːən tvìːə(r) mùːəy haəy nùŋ bɔŋʔuːəc bɤy toːc-toːc. (5) khmae(r) mùm thvɤ̀ː tvìːə(r) bɔŋʔuːəc craən tèː. (6) kè: laəŋ phtɛ̀əh taːm cùəndaə(r). (7) nɤ̀u-knoŋ phtɛ̀əh mìːən bɔntùp pìː(r) (8) tù: mùːəy (9) haəy-nùŋ tok thom mùːəy. (10) nɤ̀u-knoŋ phtɛ̀əh kmìːən kauʔɤy nùŋ krè: tèː. (11) kè: deːk lɤ̀ː kɔntèːl kraːl lɤ̀ː rənìːəp.

(5) *tvìːə(r) bɔŋʔuːəc* **N** has been met in connection with the expression of **nn**

possession, as in *phtɛ̀əh khɲom*, my house. It is also the analysis of title plus proper name, as in *cau heːŋ*. Here it is the analysis required for a **N**, consisting of two nouns forming a list.

(6) *taːm*, v., **pre n.p.** Here minor **v**. Only in the most unusual circumstances could it receive stress here and be a major **v**. A form which is both ← **v** and **pre n.p.** can only be catalysed as **pre n.p.** when the **A** comes before the **V**, e.g. *taːm mɔ̀ət tùənlèː mìːən phtɛ̀əh craən*. Along the river there are many houses. Similarly, *lɤ̀ː* in *lɤ̀ː rənìːəp* (11) is catalysable as ← **v**.

Exercise 41 B

Is the roof of your house made of palm-leaves? No, our house has a tiled roof.

Exercise 42 A

phtɛ̀əh cau heːŋ (tɔː)

(1) phtɛ̀əh cau heːŋ mìːən rəbɔːŋ bɔŋkɔ̀ːl rùssɤy pɔ́ət(th) cùmvèɲ. (2) nɤ̀u-knoŋ rəbɔːŋ nùh mìːən daəm ceːk doːŋ slaː. (3) nɤ̀u kiən mìːən kraol kɔ̀ː. (4) nɤ̀u-kraom mlùp daəm-svaːy mìːən trùŋ crùːk haəy-nùŋ trùŋ mɔ̀ən (5) nɤ̀u-mùk(h) phtɛ̀əh mìːən kmeːŋ lèːŋ sɔp̂baːy.

(1) *phtɛ̀əh cau heːŋ* and *rəbɔːŋ bɔŋkɔ̀ːl rùssɤy*. In both sequences **N** = **nnn**.

Exercise 42 B

(To be translated as between equals of the same sex.)

What animals do you keep in your enclosure? We keep several pigs and hens. What is the fence made of? It is made of bamboo.

Exercise 43 A

phsaː(r) knoŋ phùːm(ì) cau heːŋ

(1) phsaː(r) knoŋ phùːm(ì) cau heːŋ prɔk kbuɹəŋ mìːən səsɔŋ(r) ʔɤt̪(th) (2) cɔmhɔː ʔɤt cùəɲcèəŋ. (3) nɤ̀u phsaː(r) nùh nèək-srok dak tùmnèɲ lùək. (4) phsaː(r) mìːən prəvaeŋ pram-bɤy maet(r). (5) tətùŋ prəhael mphèy maet(r) (6) caek cìːə craən lvèːŋ. (7) knoŋ lvèːŋ mùːəy mìːən cɤn lùək sac-kɔ̀ː. (8) nɤ̀u lvèːŋ mùːəy tlət mìːən srɤy lùək trɤy ʔɔŋkùy caoŋ-haoŋ (9) dak kɔɲcɤ̀ː pìː mùk(h). (10) mìːən

---

[1] In previous exercises the separate sentences were numbered. From this exercise onwards the numbers mark short sequences which are not necessarily whole sentences. They are enclosed in parentheses to indicate that the text is not interrupted at the place where they occur and they need not be copied in translation. Their use is exclusively to facilitate reference to the notes to the passages.

trɤy rɔs, trɤy srɔs, trɤy ŋɔ̀əp, trɤy-ɲlət, trɤy chʔaə(r). (11) kɔnlaeŋ lùək sac haəy nùŋ trɤy nih kè: baos lì:əŋ rɔ̀əl thŋay.

(1) *phsa:(r) knoŋ phù:m(ì) cau he:ŋ.* Comparatively rare occurrence of **N** (independent) followed by **A** before **V**. Here, however, **A** is attributive and may not therefore occur in other positions which are usually possible for **A**.

(6) and (7) *lvè:ŋ* is used in two functions, **c** in (6) and **n** in (7).

Exercise 43 B

Where does your father put the things to sell? In this section on the right. It is not very clean now but it will be washed soon.

LESSON 40

SPECIAL RELIGIOUS AND ROYAL VOCABULARY

40.1. *Table of terms of address for monks*

The following terms are used by a layman or laywoman when speaking to a monk and by a monk speaking to a layman or laywoman. Titles are again given in parentheses.

Speaker	*Responding particle*	*1st person*	*2nd person*
Layman or laywoman	kɔrùna:, *kəna:	khɲom-kɔrùna:, khɲom-*kəna:	(lò:k-sɔ̰ŋ(k̀h))
Monk	pɔ̀:(r) or, to more elevated person, cɔmraən-pɔ̀:(r)	ʔa:tma:	(as for layman)

Note. The following are a few common words from the special vocabulary relating to monks: 'to give' (to a monk), *prəkè:n;* 'to eat' (of monk eating), *chan;* food (of monks), *cɔɲhan;* 'to go, come' (of monk going, coming), *nìmùən(t)-tɤu, nìmùən(t)-mɔ̀:k;* 'to sit, stay', *kùəŋ;* greeting (from a monk), *thva:y prèəh pɔ̀:(r).*

40.2. *Table of royal vocabulary* (pp. 162–3)

These terms are required by various ranks of person when speaking to the King or Queen and other members of the royal family. In this table parentheses are used to indicate syllables which may be absent unless the speaker wishes to present himself as very humble in relation to the royal person addressed. Where more than one word is given for one situation, the possibilities are given in order of formality (i.e. the first word is the most elevating to the person addressed). The most formal word is used in full in writing.

Exercise 44 A

(1) **phnùm do:n-pèɲ**

(2) **nɤu tì:-kroŋ phnùm-pèɲ** (3) **mì:ən phnùm mù:əy mì:ən vɔ̰ət(t) taŋ nɤu-lɤ̀: phnùm nùh** (4) **dael cì:ə lùmʔɔ:(r) dɔl tì:-kroŋ.** (5) **prəhael-cì:ə mì:ən phnùm nih haəy** (6) **ba:n-cì:ə kè: hau tha: phnùm-pèɲ rəho:t-mɔ̀:k-dɔl sɔ̰p(v) thŋay nih.** (7) **nɤu phnùm nih kha:ŋ-lec[1] prèəh-*vìhì:ə(r) chiəŋ kha:ŋ-tbo:ŋ** (8) **mì:ən *ce:dɤy mù:əy thom** (9) **dael khpùəs srəlah pì: mɛ̀:k chɤ̀: phse:ŋ-phse:ŋ. nɤu**

---

[1] Spelt *lèc* but pronounced *lec*.

	Initiating particles (**i**)	Responding particles (**r**)	1st person pronouns	2nd person pronouns or titles[1]
Monks' words				
To King or Queen		*thvaːy-prèəh-pɔ̀ː(r)*	*ʔaːtmaːphìːəp̀*	*prèəh-kərùnaː-*[2]*-cìːə-ʔɔɲ(k̀)-mcas(-cìːvùt)*
To *sɔmdäc* and *prèəh-ʔɔɲ(k̀)-mcas*		*thvaːy-prèəh-pɔ̀ː(r)*	*ʔaːtmaːphìːəp̀*	*trùəɲ-prèəh-kərùnaː-pìseːs*[3]
To *nèək-ʔɔɲ(k̀)-mcas*		*thvaːy-prèəh-pɔ̀ː(r)*	*ʔaːtmaːphìːəp̀*	*trùəɲ* (male) or *mcas* (female)
Men's words				
To King or Queen	*(soːm-trùəɲ-)prèəh-mèːtta-praos*	*prèəh-kərùnaː-thlay-pìseːs* or *(prèəh-)kərùnaː-pìseːs*	*tùːl-prèəh-bɔɲkùm-cìːə-khɲom*	(King) *prèəh-kərùnaː-cìːə-ʔɔɲ(k̀)-mcas-cìːvùt-lɤ̀ː-tboːɲ* or *prèəh-ʔɔɲ(k̀)-mcas(-ksatraː)* or *mcas-ksatraː* (Queen) *prèəh-kərùnaː-cìːə-ʔɔɲ(k̀)-mcas-cìːvùt-lɤ̀ː-tboːɲ* or *prèəh-ʔɔɲ(k̀)-mcas-ksatrɤyaːnìː* or *(prèəh-ʔɔɲ(k̀))-mcas-ksatrɤy*
To high-ranking male *sɔmdäc*	*(soːm-trùəɲ-)prèəh-mèːtta-praos*	*(prèəh-)kərùnaː-pìseːs*	*tùːl-prèəh-bɔɲkùm-cìːə-khɲom*	*lʔoːɲ-thùːlìː-prèəh-baːt̀* or *trùəɲ-prèəh-kərùnaː-pìseːs*
To other *sɔmdäc* or *prèəh-ʔɔɲ(k̀)-mcas*	*soːm-trùəɲ-mèːtta-praos*	*(prèəh-)kərùnaː-pìseːs*	*tùːl-bɔɲkùm-cìːə-khɲom*	*trùəɲ-prèəh-kərùnaː-pìseːs* or *prèəh-ʔɔɲ(k̀)-mcas*
To *nèək-ʔɔɲ(k̀)-mcas*	*soːm-mèːtta-praos*	*kərùnaː-pìseːs*	*tùːl-bɔɲkùm*	*trùəɲ* (male), *nèək-ʔɔɲ(k̀)-mcas* (female)

To King	kra:p-tù:l	(prèah-)pɔ̀:(r)-cì:ə-mcas	khɲom-mcas	prèah-kərùnà:-cì:ə-ʔɔɲ(k̀)-mcas-cì:vu̇ɨt-lɨ̀ɨ-tbo:ɲ or prèah-ʔɔɲ(k̀)-mcas(-cì:vu̇ɨt-lɨ̀ɨ-tbo:ɲ)
To Queen	kra:p-tù:l	(prèah-)mɛ̀:-cì:ə-mcas	khɲom-mcas	Same as for King
To high-ranking female *somdäc*	kra:p-tù:l	tavù:ə̀l-prèah-rì:ə̀l-sɑvɑnxy(ŷ)-cì:ə-mcas or mɛ̀:-cì:ə-mcas	khɲom-mcas	kraom-prèah-ba:t
To female *somdäc* of ordinary rank	kra:p-tù:l	(prèah-)mɛ̀:-cì:ə-mcas	khɲom-mcas	kraom-prèah-ba:t
To female *prèah-ʔɔɲ(k̀)-mcas*	kra:p-tù:l	mɛ̀:-mcas	khɲom-mcas	kraom-prèah-ba:t
To female *nèak-ʔɔɲ(k̀)-mcas*	kra:p-tù:l	mɛ̀:	khɲom-mcas	nèak-ʔɔɲ(k̀)-mcas
To male *somdäc* and *prèah-ʔɔɲ(k̀)-mcas*	kra:p-tù:l	pɔ̀:(r)-mcas	khɲom-mcas	kraom-prèah-ba:t
To male *nèak-ʔɔɲ(k̀)-mcas*	kra:p-tù:l	pɔ̀:(r)	khɲom-mcas	trìəɲ

[1] The following are titles: *prèah-ʔɔɲ(k̀)-mcas*, *nèak-ʔɔɲ(k̀)-mcas*, *prèah-ʔɔɲ(k̀)-mcas-ksɑtry*, *prèah-ʔɔɲ(k̀)-mcas-ksɑtrya:ni:*.

[2] *kəna:* may be heard as an alternative to *kərùna:* in all compounds.

[3] *ʁìe:s* may be heard as an alternative to *pìee:s* in all compounds.

163

kha:ŋ-cɤ̀:ŋ (10) pì: daəm mì:ən trùŋ khla:-rəkhɤn, khla:-thom, khla:-khmŭm nùŋ nɤ̀u kha:ŋ-tbo:ŋ mì:ən kɔnlaeŋ kè: ceɲc̆ɤm krəpɤ̀:, sva:, pùəs, praəs, nùŋ mì:ən sạt(v) phse:ŋ-phse:ŋ tìət. (11) ʔɤylo:v-nih, rì:əc̆-ka:(r) yɔ̀:k rəbɔs nih cëɲ ʔɔs haəy (12) nɤ̀u tae tì:-kɔnlaeŋ bɔntec-bɔntu:əc.

(1) The *phnùm* of Phnom Penh, a small hill in the centre of the city, is said to have been named after an old lady, Daun Penh. The temple on the Phnom is said to have been built to house a statue of the Buddha which had been carried on to the Phnom by flood water and was found by Daun Penh.

(2)–(3) Repetition of *phnùm* not offensive to the Cambodian ear.

(10) *mì:ən kɔnlaeŋ kè: ceɲc̆ɤm krəpɤ̀:, sva:* . . . . The clause, *kè: . . . . praəs* may be regarded in either of two ways, 1. as an ordinary clause (which might well have been introduced by the marker, *dael*) or 2. as a 'downgraded' clause functioning merely as an attribute of *kɔnlaeŋ*, cf. the attributive use of **A** in Exercise 41 A, (1).

(11) *prèəh-vìhì:ə(r)* in (7) and *rì:əc̆-ka:(r)* here are instances of compounds based on Indian loanwords in which the Indian word-order is maintained. See Lesson 48. *ʔɔs* is here a verb.

Exercise 44 B

What is the name for a place where animals are kept, such as lions and tigers, etc.? It is called a zoo. Why do they no longer have a zoo near the Phnom? Perhaps it was because a wide road was needed here and there was no room for (no place to put) a zoo, any longer (more).

Exercise 45 A

(1) ka:(r) thvɤ̀: trɤy-ɲìət

(2) kè: yɔ̀:k trɤy-rɔs rù:: trɤy phse:ŋ-phse:ŋ mɔ̀:k yɔ̀:k srəka: cëɲ haəy vèəh pùəh crìək cì:ə bu:ən cùmrìək. (3) cù:ən-ka:l kè: kat kba:l caol haəy kè: yɔ̀:k trənùŋ-khno:ŋ cëɲ dae(r). (4) kè: bok ʔɔmbɤl ʔaoy lʔɤt (5) yɔ̀:k tɤu prəlak trɤy haəy kè: tram tùk prəhael bɤy bu:ən maoŋ. (6) kè: yɔ̀:k mɔ̀:k lì:əŋ tùrk ha:l thŋay prəhael pì:(r) bɤy thŋay (7) rù:əc ha:l lɤ̀: ska:k.

(1) *thvɤ̀:* is not an attributive verb; it is an operative verb, with an object here expressed, *trɤy-ɲìət*. It is not a main verb in this sentence, however; no pre-verbal particle could occur with it here; it is pronounced in the same phrase with *ka:(r)*. The whole **V** is used attributively, cf. the **A** in Exercise 43 A. The relationship between it and the **n**, *ka:(r)*, is therefore not that of **V** to **N** subject, but that of attributive verb to **n** in a noun construct; this is another instance of a developed **N**. *ka:(r)*, 'work, matter', *sĕckdɤy*, 'subject, matter' and *rùəŋ*, 'incident, story' are all used constantly in this way, with a **V** or even a **N** and **V** following in close sequence, e.g. *ka:(r) sɔŋ phtèəh*, the work of building a house, *sĕckdɤy pùəs cɤk*, the matter of the snake biting.

(2) *trɤy-rɔs rù:: trɤy phse:ŋ-phse:ŋ. rù::* is here to be construed as **pre n.p.** forming an **A** with the following two words. Note *phse:ŋ*, 'different', *phse:ŋ-phse:ŋ* (plural) 'of various sorts'. See Lesson 46.

cì:ə bu:ən cùmrìək. A temporarily nominalized **X**. See Lesson 37.

(3) v . . . . v and v . . . . ← v.

(4) *ʔaoy lʔɤt*. Capable of two different analyses. 1. *ʔaoy* **m.** *lʔɤt* **v.** 'so that it is fine'. 2. *ʔaoy* **pre n.p.** *lʔɤt* **v.**, temporarily nominalized, 'in a fine way, to a fine degree'.

(5) *bɤy buːən maoŋ*. With alternative numerals, Cambodian does not usually use *rùː*, cf. (6) *pìː(r) bɤy thŋay*.

Exercise 45 B

Please will you tell me what kind of fish that is over there, put in the sun to dry? Yes, it is called *rɔs*. When *rɔs* fish and other kinds of fish have been in the sun for two or three days, we call them smoked fish.

Exercise 46 A

(1) krùːəsaː(r) rəbos cau heːŋ

(2) *taː*   nɤu-knoŋ krùːəsaː(r) cau mìːən mənùs(s) poñmaːn nɛ̀ək?

(3) *cau*   baːt̀, khɲom mùm dɤŋ tèː! prəhael-cìːə prampùl nɛ̀ək.

(4) *taː*   ʔao! cau mùm dɤŋ poññɤŋ! cau mìːən ʔoːpùk-mdaːy tèːʔ

(5) *cau*   baːt̀, khɲom mìːən.

(6) *taː*   cau mìːən bɔːŋ-pʔoːn tèːʔ

(7) *cau*   baːt̀, khɲom mìːən bɔːŋ-pros bɤy nɛ̀ək, bɔːŋ-srɤy pìː(r) nɛ̀ək nùŋ pʔoːn-pros mnɛ̀ək.

(8) *taː*   cìː-doːn-cìː-taː cau nɤu cìːə-mùːəy cau rùː tèːʔ

(9) *cau*   baːt̀ tèː, poñtae ʔoːpùk khɲom ceñcɤm kmuːəy-srɤy mnɛ̀ək.

(10) *taː*   doːcᵊneh cau mìːən ʔoːpùk-mdaːy, bɔːŋ-pʔoːn pram-mùːəy nɛ̀ək nùŋ kmuːəy mnɛ̀ək, kùː pram-buːən nɛ̀ək tɛ̀əŋ-ʔɔs.

(11) *cau*   baːt̀ tèː! taː phlɛ̀c khɲom!

(12) *taː*   ʔao! ʔɔɲcɤŋ mìːən dɔp nɛ̀ək.

(3) *baːt̀*. Polite use of *baːt̀*. No answer 'yes' here. *prəhael-cìːə* is **m.** here, introducing a responding clause of limited construction (**X** only).

(4) and (11) The exclamation *ʔao* is discussed in Lesson 43.

(7) As in English, a list in Cambodian may be given with no joining word until the last item, e.g. *bɔːŋ-pros . . . . pʔoːn-pros mnɛ̀ək*; this is to be analysed as **N N A**. cf. also the list in (10). In both cases the potential division into separate phrases marks them as separate constructs.

(8) Both *cìːə-mùːəy* and *cìːə-mùːəy-nùŋ* are **pre n.p.** and mean 'together with'.

Exercise 46 B

Have you any brothers and sisters? (Translate and answer for yourself.) How many people live in your house? (Translate and answer for yourself.)

Lesson 41

Additional Notes on Terms of Address

Terms of address in Cambodian vary from one area to another and from one family to another. Some additional notes are given below concerning the uses of some words which were given in the table in Lesson 39 and introducing a few other words which may be met.

1. *1st person pronouns*

ʔaɲ, khɲom. khɲom is always a safe and polite word for the foreigner to use except to monks and royalty.

khɲom-baːɫ and *niːəŋ-khɲom*, 'I'. These words are used by men and women respectively when speaking to a superior, as the table indicates, but one may also hear *prɛ̀əh-baːɫ-tiːən* and *khɲom-prɛ̀əh-baːɫ* or their more colloquial forms, *prəbaːɫ-tiːən* and *khɲom-prəbaːɫ* spoken by servants to their masters.

yɤ̀ːŋ. Generally speaking, *khɲom* is singular and *yɤ̀ːŋ* is plural. *yɤ̀ːŋ* may, however, be used by one person about himself and therefore have singular meaning, provided that the context helps to make the meaning clear. It follows from this that, where there might be a lack of clarity, *khɲom* would be used for the singular. *yɤ̀ːŋ tɛ̀əŋ-ʔɔs kniːə* would make a plural meaning explicit.

yɤ̀ːŋ-khɲom. The two words may be used together to mean 'we' when the speaker wishes respectfully to point to the fact that he is one of the group referred to: 'I and the others'.

2. *2nd person pronoun and titles used to translate 'you'*

ʔaeŋ. *ʔaeŋ* is used, as the table indicates, to children and to other people whom one may treat with familiarity. The word-form, *ʔaeŋ*, occurs with a different meaning as a **post n.p.** in combination with terms of address. See Lesson 42.1.

khluːən is used when friends of equal age are talking together.

kɔət is used as a 2nd person singular pronoun between friends.

pùː and *mìːŋ* are used in addressing one's relatives or servants older than oneself, or persons with whom one may have a slightly familiar relationship established by the situation, e.g. to a shopkeeper (not necessarily older than oneself). One may note in passing that certain Chinese words are used as titles for shopkeepers who are Chinese or Vietnamese, *hìːə* (male), *cae* (female). *thao-kae* is used for a prosperous shopkeeper of any race. *lòːk-pùː*, *lòːk-mìːŋ* are very formal and polite. They would be used by children to a grown-up visiting the family or by younger men and women to older ones to whom they may be introduced.

In towns one may hear other words for *pùː* and *mìːŋ*, used in addressing middle-aged persons, *ʔom* or *ʔom-pros*, *ʔom-srɤy* and in various parts of the country *mìːə* is used instead of *pùː*. Strictly within the family *pùː* and *mìːŋ* refer to the younger brother and sister of either parent and *ʔom* (*pros* or *srɤy*) is the elder brother or sister of either parent.

lòːk, *lòːk-srɤy*. *lòːk* is used to any person whom one should address formally, e.g. to one's superior in the office, to an Excellency and to a stranger. It is used between equals (male) who speak formally to each other, e.g. people working together in an office or school. Men who are good, close friends may use *lòːk* to each other. Women, speaking formally to each other may use *lòːk-srɤy* or *nɛ̀ək-srɤy* depending on the status of the woman addressed. A stranger of similar age to oneself may be quite politely addressed as *nɛ̀ək-srɤy*. An elderly wife of a man whose position is important must be addressed as *lòːk-srɤy*. A much younger woman would be addressed as *niːəŋ*, or, if over twenty, as *nɛ̀ək* or *nɛ̀ək-srɤy*. Personal names are used only when needed for clarity, as for example in the 3rd person.

nɛ̀ək and *niːəŋ*. Women friends use *nɛ̀ək* to each other; men may use *nɛ̀ək* to each other or may retain the more formal *lòːk*.

nèək is the word to use to address formally boys of 13–20, after which they could be *lò:k* formally.

nèək is used among friends of both sexes together; it is also used by husband and wife, though *bɔ:ŋ*/*?o:n* are more affectionate. *nèək* may be used to men servants, women shopkeepers. It may be used to the younger members of the master's family by servants if the household is a friendly, informal one.

nèək is both familiar and polite; it is applicable to both male and female. *nèək* is combined not only with *srvy* and *mì:ŋ*, but also with *nì:əŋ*. Thus a man-servant in a friendly household would address a young lady of the house as *nèək-nì:əŋ*. In connection with the use of *nèək* and its compounds for speaking to women, it may be observed that slightly more familiar terms may be used in speaking to women than would be suitable for their menfolk. e.g. *nèək-srvy* is formal for a woman to whom one speaks in the street but *lò:k*, not *nèək*, must be used for a man addressed in the same circumstances. A nephew may address his uncle and aunt as *lò:k-pù:*, *nèək-mì:ŋ*. *lò:k-mì:ŋ* is possible for an aunt he knows less well (but is otherwise reserved for older women met on friendly but formal terms); *nèək-pù:* would not be possible.

nì:əŋ. Young women servants aged 8 to 20 are addressed as *nì:əŋ*; from 20 to 30 they are addressed as *nèək* and later as *mì:ŋ*. *nì:əŋ* is also the formal word used for addressing girls and young women up to 20 years old of any rank. It may also be used to address children up to 13 of both sexes, politely yet affectionately.

bɔ:ŋ, *p?o:n* and *?o:n*. *bɔ:ŋ* and *p?o:n* are used much more among brothers and sisters than are the personal names belonging to each. *bɔ:ŋ* (wife to husband) and *?o:n* (husband to wife) are used whether or not their respective ages coincide with the meanings of *bɔ:ŋ* and *p?o:n*.[1] *bɔ:ŋ* may be used by men to address a manservant, even if he is younger than they are, until he is old enough to be called *pù:*; women address a manservant as *pù:* rather than *bɔ:ŋ*, whatever his age. Alternatively he may be addressed very familiarly as *?a:* (+ his proper name) or, in households where very friendly relations are found, as *nèək*. In modern usage *bɔ:ŋ* also occurs as a term of address for either sex in friendly groups of people of approximately the same age.

3. *3rd person pronouns*

vì:ə is familiar and therefore is used to translate 'he', 'she', 'it' and 'they' when the reference is to animals as well as when reference is to servants, and the younger members of one's family with whom one is very familiar. *vì:ə* is used when one refers to people whom one does not know personally but about whom one is unfavourably impressed, e.g. the manager of a poor restaurant; a theatrical company which one does not admire; someone who does something stupid, etc. *vì:ə* is also used with reference to things but only with a derogatory sense and in a careless style of speech (and never in writing).[2]

---

[1] To which the word *?o:n* is related.
[2] The student has been encouraged to repeat a noun if he needed to refer to a thing. See Lesson 17.6.

kèː is used to refer to objects or people, male or female, singular or plural. It is less familiar than *vìːə* but not so respectful as *lòːk*. It is used when the identity of the person is not known as well as when it is known.

kɔ̀ət is used to refer to people, male and female, singular and plural. It is no more formal and elevated than *kèː* but suggests that the person referred to is known as an individual. Where royalty is concerned, the title of the individual person is used, e.g. *sɔmdäc*, 'His Highness', or *lòːk* may rather familiarly be used for a 3rd person reference.

knìːə. This word is used in a familiar style of speech for both 1st person singular and 3rd person singular and plural. It may occur with these senses only as an independent noun construct, however. When it occurs after the verb it occurs as *knìːə* a. with the meaning 'together, each other'. *knìːə-yɤ̀ːŋ* is used as a 1st person plural pronoun.

Note. The following words are alternatives, to be used according to the degree of politeness or formality with which one wishes to address a person. Where English has a similar distinction, a stroke separates the alternative translation.

Familiar	*Formal*	
tɤ̀u	*ʔɔɲcɤ̀ːɲ-tɤ̀u*	to go
mɔ̀ːk	*ʔɔɲcɤ̀ːɲ-mɔ̀ːk*	to come
prap	*cùmrìːəp*	to tell/to inform
⎰ *sìː* (very familiar)		
⎰ *ɲam* (homely)		to eat, drink/to dine,
⎰ *tətùːəl tìːən*	*pìsaː*	lunch, have a drink
⎱ *bərephòːk*		
⎰ *deːk*		
⎱ *tətùːəl tìːən dɔmneːk*	*sɔmraːn(t)*	to rest

Exercise 47 A

(1) **phnùm-pèɲ thŋay bɤy khae mèːsaː 1964**

(2) **sɔmlaɲ!**

(3) **thŋay nìh cìːə thŋay ʔaːtùt(y)** (4) **yɤ̀ːŋ nùŋ bəbuːəl sɔmlaɲ daə(r)-lèːŋ komsaːn(t) taːm mɔ̀ət tùənlèː** (5) **haəy-nùŋ mɤ̀ːl kon daəmbɤy-ʔaoy sɔ̱ɒbaːy cɤt(t).**

(6) **häet(o) nìh khɲom soːm ʔɔɲcɤ̀ːɲ sɔmlaɲ mɔ̀ːk cùːəp nùŋ khɲom nɤu phtɛ̀əh khɲom thŋay rəsiəl maoŋ buːən kom khaːn.**

(7) **suːəsdɤy!**
    sɔmlaɲ!

(6) Analysis of whole sentence:—

häet(o) nìh	khɲom	soːm ʔɔɲcɤ̀ːɲ sɔmlaɲ		mɔ̀ːk cùːəp nùŋ khɲom
A	**N**	**V**		**V**	**A**
np	n	v→	vn	v→	v	pn

nɤu phtɛ̀əh khɲom	thŋay rəsiəl	maoŋ buːən	kom khaːn.
A	**A**	**A**	**V**
pnn	nn	nx	pv

There is a change of subject (see Lesson 37.7) and four **A** separating the second **V** from the third, but the sentence is basically **N V V V**.

The limited **A** might be supplied with suitable **pre n.p.** as follows:

daoy häet(o) nǐh, nɤ̆u thŋay rəsiəl, nɤ̆u maoŋ buːən.

The particle preceding the last verb is **kom**, not **mŭm. kom** has been presented as the particle to be used in negative commands. It does not, however, have quite the exclusive sense, 'do not'. It may be used with **ʔaoy** in **kom-ʔaoy** (instead of **mŭm-ʔaoy**) 'so as not to', when there is a certain amount of exhortation in the utterance; here the writer is urging the other to be there without fail. **mŭm** is possible but **kom** is more urgent.

Exercise 47 B

Battambang, 3rd January, 1964

Dear —,

I would like to invite you to meet me at the — store at 8 o'clock in the evening on the tenth of this month to have dinner.

Yours sincerely,

Exercise 48 A

(1) phnŭm-pèŋ thŋay bɤy khae-mèːsa: 1964

(2) mɔ̀ːk rùəs-saːrɯ̀ən cìːə tǐː rəlŭk

(3) cìːə yùː(r) khae haəy (4) yɤ̆ːŋ mŭm-dael baːn cùːəp pìːək̂(y) səmdɤy rùː: mŭk(h) rəbɔs somlaɲ ʔaeŋ sɔh. (5) taŋ-pǐː baek knǐːə mɔ̀ːk prəhael-cìːə buːən pram khae haəy (6) rùː: mùːəy somlaɲ baek cɤt(t) ʔɔmpǐː yɤ̆ːŋ? (7) baːn-cìːə mŭm khɤ̆ːɲ phɲaə sombɔt(r) mɔ̀ːk sɔh? (8) yɤ̆ːŋ mŭm baːn dɤŋ tǐː-kɔnlaeŋ somlaɲ ʔaeŋ ʔaoy pùɹt praːkɔ̀t. (9) tɤ̆ːp-tae suːə(r) kèː dɤŋ thaː: (10) somlaɲ ʔaeŋ cёɲ pǐː prёy-nəkɔ̀ː(r) tɤu nɤ̆u paːrìːs. (11) sɔ̀p̣(v) thŋay somlaɲ ʔaeŋ sok(h)-sɔp̂baːy tèː rùːʔ (12) rùː: mùːəy mìːən sёckdɤy tùk(h) yaːŋ naːʔ (13) baə somlaɲ ʔaeŋ baːn sёckdɤy sok(h) haəy yɤ̆ːŋ mìːən cɤt(t) treːk-ʔɔː(r) nas. (14) rɔ̀ːk ʔvɤy priəp-phtùm kmǐːən. (15) cɔmnaek-khaːŋ khɲom vèɲ (16) sok(h)-sɔp̂baːy tèː.

(17) sɔːm tətùːəl daoy mèːtrɤyphǐːəp̣.

(2) *mɔ̀ːk*, 'to'. *cìːə tǐː rəlŭk*. **A.** 'as an indication of the (writer's) missing (the other)'.

(3) *cìːə yùː(r) khae haəy*. **A.** *yùː(r)* 'to be long (of time)' has a noun in the object position. cf. *yùː(r) chnam tɤu*, 'after a number of years'. *cìːə* hardly adds anything to *yùː(r) khae haəy*, except by making it clear that it is subordinate to the rest of the sentence.

(4) *yɤ̆ːŋ* may be used for *khɲom* 'I' between very close friends, in speech or writing. *cùːəp*. Here used like *prətèəh*, 'to come across'.

(5) *prəhael-cìːə* may be taken as **m.** or **p.v.p.**; in either case the sentence has a **X** operating as its verb.

(6) and (12) *rùː: mùːəy*. *mùːəy* is often used twice, *mùːəy . . . . mùːəy* 'the one . . . . the other'. Here it expresses 'another point', 'another possibility', although the first possibility is not directly expressed in words; it is implied in the preceding sentences and is, in effect, 'You have not yet written in all these months'. The second possibility is 'You don't intend to write because you are no longer friendly'. In (12) the possibilities are clear.

(12) Here *tùk(h)* and *sok(h)* are nouns, but the combination with *sёckdɤy* makes more of them.

(13) *mì:ən cʏt(t) tre:k-ʔɔ:(r) nas.* A useful if rather formal way of expressing pleasure, e.g. *khɲom mì:ən cʏt(t) tre:k-ʔɔ:(r) nas ba:n cù:əp nùŋ lò:k,* 'I am very pleased to have met you'.

(15) *vèɲ,* f. 'in return', 'returning to the subject of (what precedes)'.

(16) *tè:.* Here adding emphasis to an affirmative sentence (see Lesson 14.6).

Exercise 48 B

Dear *He:ŋ,*

My sister and I were sorry that we could not attend the fête last Saturday and so we missed seeing you. It is so long since we met. Could you call to see us one afternoon?

Yours sincerely,

Exercise 49 A

(1) phnùm-pèɲ thŋay bʏy khae mè:sa: 1964

(2) khɲom so:m cùmrì:əp mò:k lò:k thom (3) tì: cat ka:(r) nèy krom phsa:y domnʏŋ lʔo: so:m tì:ən crì:əp.

(4) khɲom mùm ba:n mò:k phtɔəl khlu:ən khɲom (5) prùəh thŋay nìh khɲom mùn-so:v sru:əl khlu:ən (6) ceh-tae vùl-mùk(h) chù: kba:l.

(7) häet(o) nìh khɲom so:m cbap chùp thvʏ: ka:(r) pì:(r) thŋay (8) tùmrɔəm-dɔl khɲom sru:əl khlu:ən laəŋ vèɲ. (9) so:m mè:tta: daoy sëckdʏy ʔɑnùkrùəh.

(10) sëckdʏy kù:ə(r) pùm kù:ə(r) so:m ʔɑ̀phéy tò:s.

(5) and (6) This clause has three major verbs, *sru:əl, vùl* and *chù:.*

(8) This clause has a **V** and a **v**.

(10) *sëckdʏy* here forms a noun construct, conveying an abstract idea. There is no noun formed from *kù:ə(r).* The Khmer love of opposites and parallels leads to the inclusion in this well-used phrase of one illogical item. *sëckdʏy kù:ə(r)* should not need forgiveness.

Exercise 49 B

Dear Sir,

I am writing to inform you (I ask to inform you) that my son will not be able to work today since he has a fever. I hope he will be able to work next week.

Yours faithfully,

Lesson 42

Translation of 'Self'; Further Use of Titles

42.1. *khlu:ən and ʔaeŋ and the translation of 'self'*

1. The reflexive 'oneself', 'himself', etc. (object of the verb of which the subject refers to the same person) is translated simply by the noun, *khlu:ən,* 'body, person', as in the following, *rìəp khlu:ən* 'to prepare oneself, get oneself ready', *dʏŋ khlu:ən* 'to be aware' (to know oneself), *sru:əl khlu:ən* 'to be well (to be well as to the body)'. e.g. *vì:ə rìəp khlu:ən.* 'He gets ready.' *khɲom rìəp khlu:ən haəy.* 'I have got ready, I am ready.' *kɔət mùn dʏŋ*

khluːən tèː. 'He isn't aware (of it).' *yɤ̀ːŋ sruːəl khluːən tèəŋ-ʔɔs.* 'We are all well.' *daoy khluːən,* 'according to persons', is used as follows:—*vìːə tɤ̀u phtèəh daoy khluːən.* 'They went to their respective homes'/'They went each to his own home.'

2. The noun *khluːən* may also precede a pronoun or title to express 'myself' 'yourself', etc. e.g. *khluːən khɲom,* 'myself'; *khluːən vìːə* 'him-, her-, itself, themselves'. *khluːən lòːk* 'Mr. — himself'; *khluːən kɔ̀ət* 'him-, her-, themselves'; *khluːən yɤ̀ːŋ* 'ourselves'.

The words, **nn**, form an adverbial construct, of the limited type described in Lesson 17.3. Its position after the verb construct precludes its being analysed as a noun construct, since an independent noun construct does not occur after a verb construct and it may be shown that it is not the dependent noun construct which forms part of the verb construct; it is possible for it to follow this dependent construct, e.g. *cau baːn səseː(r) sɔmbot(r) khluːən cau.* 'The grandson wrote the letter himself.' *khɲom cɔŋ tɤ̀u pos khluːən khɲom.* 'I want to go to the post myself.'

3. Alternatively *ʔaeŋ* (here a post-nominal particle) may follow *khluːən.* The sequence, **np**, *khluːən ʔaeŋ* is again analysed as an adverbial construct; it may be used with reference to any pronoun or title, e.g. *khɲom thvɤ̀ː nìh khluːən ʔaeŋ mùən baːn tèː.* 'I can't do this myself.' *lòːk cɔŋ mɤ̀ːl kɔnlaeŋ nùh khluːən ʔaeŋ.* 'Mr. — wants to have a look at the place himself.' *ʔaeŋ,* the post-nominal particle, may follow any noun, e.g. *khɲom mùən baːn khɤ̀ːɲ cao(r) nùh ʔaeŋ tèː.* 'I didn't catch sight of the thief himself.' It often follows a term of address, emphasizing that that particular person is being addressed. e.g. *nèək ʔaeŋ tɤ̀u naː?* 'And where are *you* going?' *khɲom cɔŋ nìyìːəy cìːə-mùːəy-nùŋ cau ʔaeŋ.* 'I want to speak to *you.*'

42.2. *Titles used in a form of address*

Initiating and responding particles may be either (i) uttered entirely at low pitch or (ii) uttered with a fall in pitch to low level on the last syllable.[1] Responding particles may also occur with a rise on the last syllable, expressing a questioning or encouraging reaction on the part of the speaker. Another kind of utterance which may have these three characteristics occurs when a title or proper name is spoken, not as a part of a clause but separately, to call the attention of the person addressed or simply as an allusion to the fact that the person is being addressed. This happens even when the title occurs in the clause as well as outside it.[2]

e.g. *pìː thŋay nìh tɤ̀u, saːruən (.), khɲom ʔaoy saːruən cùːt phtèəh.* From today onwards, Saroeun, I want you to clean the house.

lòːk (ˌ), khɲom tɤ̀u phtèəh *ʔɤylòːv. Sir, I am going home now.

A title used as a form of address at the end of a question may be pronounced with a rise in pitch.

pùː tɤ̀u naː ('), mìːŋ (ˌ)? Where is Uncle going, Aunt?

---

[1] See Lesson 15.2.
[2] Sentences with a title used as a form of address are recorded in Exercise 51 A, (6), (8) and (10).

Exercise 50 A

(1) maːsìːn-ʔɔŋkùlìːleːkh[1]

(2) kaːl-pìː thŋay mùːəy khae-mìthonaː chnam mùːəy-pɔ̀ən pram-buːən-rɔ̀ːy hoksʁp-pìː(r) khɲom troːv coːl rìən vay maːsìːn ʔɔ̀ksɔː(r). (3) nʁu-knoŋ kɔnlaeŋ rìən mìːən tok pìː(r) cùːə(r) mìːən krùː srʁy cìːət(e) yùːən mnɛ̀ək nùŋ sʁs(s) cìːə craən nɛ̀ək. (4) khɲom coːl tʁu suːə(r) cìːə phìːəsaː khmae(r) thaː, 'mìːən sɔl kɔnlaeŋ rùː tèːʔ khɲom cɔŋ coːl rìən dae(r)' (5) srʁy nùh chlaəy thaː, 'kɔnlaeŋ cɔŋʔiət nas. baə nɛ̀ək cɔŋ rìən, rìən baːn tae pèːl prùk mùːəy maoŋ nùŋ lɲìːəc mùːəy maoŋ.' (6) khɲom kɔː sok(h) cʁt(t) haəy kèː ʔaoy khɲom kɔt chmùəh tìː-lùmnʁu nùŋ bɔŋ prak pìː(r)-rɔ̀ːy rìəl mùn. (7) pèːl khɲom coːl rìən, khɲom pìbaːk cʁt(t) nùŋ day khɲom nas prùəh day khɲom rùŋ mùm-tɔ̀ən stɔ̀ət. (8) cùːən-kaːl vay ʔɔ̀ksɔː(r) mùːəy tuːə vay tɛ̀əŋ mrìːəm pram. (9) ʔʁyloːvˉnìh khɲom ceh vay krɔ̀ən-baə haəy. dɔl khae kraoy khɲom nùŋ prəlɔːŋ yɔ̀ːk saɲɲaːbat(r) cɛ̀ɲ thvʁ̀ː kaː(r) knoŋ kɔnlaeŋ naː-mùːəy mùm khaːn.

(3) *mìːən sɔl kɔnlaeŋ*. Impersonal use of *mìːən* with *sɔl* as second major verb, 'is there left over . . . . ?' *sɔl* tends not to be used alone; it is frequently met with *nʁu* (*nʁu sɔl*).

(5) *pèːl prùk mùːəy maoŋ*, **nnxc**, to be construed not as **N**, but as **A X**. Contrast *tok pìː(r) cùːə(r)* in (3) above, **N** . *lɲìːəc mùːəy maoŋ* similarly is **a X**.

                    nxc

(6) *sok(h) cʁt(t)*. cf. *dac cʁt(t)* 'decide', *prùːəy cʁt(t)* 'miserable', *coːl cʁt(t)* 'like', **v**, and, in (7) below, *pìbaːk cʁt(t)* 'depressed'. *chmùəh tìː-lùmnʁu* 'name and address'; no 'and' in the Cambodian, as often.

(7) *rùŋ mùm-tɔ̀ən stɔ̀ət. stɔ̀ət* is a second position main verb with **p.v.p.**

(9) Four major verbs: *prəlɔːŋ . . . . yɔ̀ːk . . . . cɛ̀ɲ → thvʁ̀ː . . . . khaːn. naː-mùːəy* occurs here in grammatical context 1, since it precedes not follows the negative verb.

Exercise 50 B

My friend is learning typing at that school. He says it is very difficult to get a place. It is very crowded. He had to put down a deposit of three hundred piastres too!

Exercise 51 A

              (1) tèɲ sɔmbot(r) laːn-chnùːəl

(2) *nɛ̀ək-lùək-sɔmbot(r)*	lòːk ʔɔɲcʁ̀ːɲ-tʁu naːʔ
(3) *lòːk sɔmrʁt*	ʔʁː, khɲom cɔŋ tʁu kɔmpùəŋ-caːm nʁu maoŋ mùːəy kɔnlah thŋay trɔŋ nìh.
(4) *nɛ̀ək-lùək-sɔmbot(r)*	lòːk cɔŋ baːn baŋ naːʔ
(5) *lòːk sɔmrʁt*	khɲom cɔŋ baːn khaːŋ mùk(h) cùrt *soː(h)vɔ̀ə(r).
(6) *nɛ̀ək-lùək-sɔmbot(r)*	ʔao! nʁu sɔl kɔnlaeŋ nìh mùːəy, lòːk. lòːk ʔaːc nùŋ yɔ̀ːk baːn.
(7) *lòːk sɔmrʁt*	(h)nʁŋ haəy. taə, thlay poñmaːnʔ
(8) *nɛ̀ək-lùək-sɔmbot(r)*	haːsʁp-pram rìəl, lòːk.
(9) *lòːk sɔmrʁt*	ʔao! khɲom mìːən tae krədaːs mùːəy-rɔ̀ːy rìəl tèː.

---

[1] *leːk(h)* spelt *lèːkh*.

(10) *nèək-lùək-sɔmbot(r)*   mùm ʔʁy tèː, lòːk! khɲom mìːən doː(r) cùːn lòːk baːn.
(11) *lòːk sɔmrʁt*   ʔʁː, maoŋ poṁmaːn baːn laːn tʁu dɔl kɔmpùəŋ-caːmʔ
(12) *nèək-lùək-sɔmbot(r)*   baːt, prəhael-cìːə maoŋ bʁy kɔnlah rùː buːən.

(1) No *kaː(r)*, *sëckdʁy* or *rùəŋ* to introduce the title. Any of these would have been possible but the Cambodian writer preferred the verb alone. Here it may be translated by a verbal noun, 'buying'.

(2) *nèək* + verb. One Cambodian way of expressing the agent. Compare English, '-er'. e.g. reader *nèək-mʁːl*, writer, *nèək-səseː(r)*. This noun-forming device is alive, whereas the infix, **m**, which used to be a live agent-former is now found only in existing words, see Lesson 45.

(5) **soː(h)vɟə̀(r)*. For French loanwords, as for Sanskrit and Pali, there is a convention that consonants which are present in the spelling are represented in the Cambodian spelling, whether or not they are pronounced in either pronunciation. e.g. *r* at the end of this word and at the end of *kìːloːmaet(r)*, and *te* at the end of *pos(te)*.

(6) *kɔnlaeŋ nìh mùːəy*, **N X**. *kɔnlaeŋ mùːəy nìh*,   **N** would also have been
                n p x   **n x p**
possible.

(6) and (8) *lòːk* as a form of address. See 2 above. *ʔaːc nùŋ yɔːk baːn*. *ʔaːc* is usually met in its capacity as an initiating verb, 'have the power to, be able to, dare to'. It is very often used in conjunction with *baːn*, giving, from the English point of view, an extra 'can', which becomes an embarrassment in the process of translation. Here *ʔaːc* is further reinforced by the following *nùŋ*, 'to, with the intention of', which merely acts as a stronger link with the verb, '*yɔːk*'. The latter is a construction which may be met with other initiating verbs, e.g. *kùt nùŋ thvʁː* instead of *kùt thvʁː*. (See Exercise 54, (2).)

(7) *(h)nʁŋ haəy*. A very popular colloquial phrase, 'That's it! Exactly! Of course!' *taə* **m.**, introducing a question.

(9) *tae*. **g.**, as in Exercise 50, (5) but here, as often, it is used in conjunction with *tèː*. There is no negation but the limiting idea expressed by *tae* is confirmed by *tèː*. *krədaːs mùːəy-rɔ̀ːy rìəl*, **N** with attributive not quantitative **X** included.

(10) *mùn ʔʁy tèː*. Another common colloquial phrase, cf. (7) above. 'That's all right! Not at all!'

(11) *baːn*. Here used as a major verb in first position, with its essential meaning, 'get'.

Exercise 51 B

Is it possible to go to Siem Reap by bus nowadays?
Yes, sir. There's a bus every day.
How much does it cost?
120 riel, sir.
I should like to go tomorrow. Is there a seat left?
Yes, there is one seat left at the back, sir.
Good! I'll have that one. What time does the bus set off?
At 7 o'clock in the morning, sir.

LESSON 43

EXCLAMATORY PARTICLES

A large proportion of exclamatory particles,[1] e., occur always at the beginning of an utterance. Like responding particles, these may either 1. be uttered with no stress and low or mid level pitch (usually then followed by a sentence) or 2. be uttered with a complete sentence-tune and not necessarily followed by any further utterance.

Examples of such exclamatory particles:—

ʔeːp! 'Hey there!'

nɛ̀ː (followed by proper name or title) draws attention of hearer, e.g. *nɛ̀ː kɔːn!* 'Children!'

mnɔ̀əl (followed by proper name or title), e.g. *mnɔ̀əl lòːk nɛ̀ək,* 'Ladies and gentlemen, ... ' (literally 'all of you people, superior and equal').

ʔeː! 'hurrah!'

ʔìː, yìː or *yèː!* 'well!' (expressing surprise).

ʔay-yaː! 'help! crash!'

vɔː, vɔːs-vaːs 'shoo! be off!'

ʔao! 'oh!' (expressing surprise but of a slighter nature than that expressed by *ʔìː*).

hay-yùː hay-yùː! (uttered in time to rowing strokes in boat-race).

rùp! 'off! go!' (at the beginning of a race).

ʔay-yoːy! 'ooh! ouch!' (exclamation of pain).

rɔ̀əp! or *hɔ̀əp!* 'stop! wo!'

ʔɤː 'er' (expressing hesitation).

Other exclamatory particles occur in various positions in the sentence, as follows:—

ʔaː precedes a noun, with very familiar and derogatory meaning, e.g. when calling a servant who should be nearby, but is not. *ʔaː baen!* 'Baen!' It may also precede the name of an object with which one is annoyed.

ʔɤːy or *ʔaəy* 'ah!' 'oh!' 'hail!' 'hello'. Occurs after the title of the person addressed. e.g. *bɔːŋ ʔaəy!* 'ah! my friend!' This usually occurs in narratives.

ʔɤy or *ʔɤːy* or *ʔɤy *kɔː* occur between two reduplicated words,[2] e.g. *kdau ʔɤy kdau!* 'How hot it is!' *sɔk ʔɤːy sɔk!* 'What a lot of hair!' *phlìəŋ ʔɤy *kɔː phlìəŋ!* 'What a lot of rain!'

vɤːy or *vɤy* may occur at the beginning or end of a sentence. It calls the attention (familiarly) of other people, e.g. *vɤːy kɔːn!* 'Children!' (summoning them), *mɤ̀ːl nùh vɤːy!* 'Look!'

(h)nə is realized as [nə], [nɔ] or [n̩].[3] It is written *(h)nɔ*, with the *kaːkbaːl* over it. It occurs at the end of a sentence or phrase, expressing doubt, admiration or surprise.

---

[1] Some of these are illustrated on the tape recordings. See Part VII, Appendix 4.
[2] See Lesson 47.2.
[3] The phonetic symbol ˌ implies syllabification of the consonant. This might be represented in another way as [nn], a continued n.

e.g. *vì:ə mɔ̀:k neh¹ (h)nə?* Is he coming *here*, then? *siəvphʳu (h)nʳŋ² (h)nə? This* book? *lʔɔ: nas (h)nə!* Marvellous!

Exercise 52 A

lkhaon khmae(r)

(1) **nʳu kroŋ phnùm-pèɲ** mì:ən lkhaon khmae(r) bʳy kənlaeŋ, rò:ŋ thmo: mù:əy, rò:ŋ phsa:(r) sì:-lʳp mù:əy, nùⁿ rò:ŋ phsa:(r)-kap-kò: mù:əy. (2) **pè:l** yùp maoŋ pram-bʳy nʳu-mùk(h) rò:ŋ krùp lkhaon tὲəŋ-ʔɔs mì:ən mənùs(s) craən nas, khlah lùək cɔmnʳy phse:ŋ-phse:ŋ, khlah tèɲ sɔmbot(r) lkhaon, khlah su:ə(r) knì:ə tha:, 'kè: lè:ŋ rùɨəŋ ʔʳy?' khlah nìyì:əy knì:ə pì: rùɨəŋ ʔvʳy phse:ŋ-phse:ŋ lù:̀ so:(r) trəhùⁿ-ʔʳ:ŋ-kɔ:ŋ. (3) **dɔl maoŋ** pram-bu:ən nὲək-lè:ŋ-phlè:ŋ-lkhaon kè: lè:ŋ phlè:ŋ kùmnɔ̀əp prὲəh kɔrùⁿa: rù:əc haəy, kè: cap lè:ŋ rùɨəŋ phse:ŋ-phse:ŋ tɔ:-tʳu. (4) **nὲək-mʳ:l** khlah nìyì:əy knì:ə tha: 'lkhaon sräc nùⁿ nὲək-tlok. baə nὲək-tlok mùⁿ-so:v kɔmplaeŋ tè:, mùⁿ lʔɔ: mʳ:l tè:.' (5) **khlah** tha: 'ʔa̱ɲ mʳ:l lkhaon mùⁿ-so:v cam rùɨəŋ sɔh.' nὲək tiət, 'ʔa̱ɲ mùⁿ co:l cʳt(t) mʳ:l lkhaon rò:ŋ thmo: tè:. ʔa̱ɲ co:l cʳt(t) mʳ:l lkhaon rò:ŋ phsa:(r)-kap-kò:, prùəh srʳy-srʳy lʔɔ:-lʔɔ: nas haəy crìəŋ pì:rùəh phɔ:ŋ.'

(1) *lkhaon khmae(r) bʳy kənlaeŋ.* Attributive **X**, of kind mentioned in Lesson 23.4. Use of *mù:əy* is typical of Cambodian style; could be translated, 'one, the — theatre, two, the — theatre and three, the — theatre' but the Cambodian is not nearly so heavy-going as that. The *mù:əy* in each case just singles out the theatre to which it is applied and makes the short list of three items crisp and clear; it thus gives a very slight emphasis to each one. *phsa:(r) thmɔ:, phsa:(r) sì:-lʳp, phsa:(r) kap-kò:.* Three verb constructs are here used attributively with the noun *phsa:(r): thmɔ:, sì:-lʳp* and *kap kò:.* A sequence, noun + attributive verb used attributively, may be turned into a sentence form by a change of intonation, e.g. *phsa:(r) thmɔ:* (\). 'The market is of stone.' This would be more natural if the post-nominal particle were used after the noun (*phsa:(r) nùh thmɔ:*) and two phrases were used:— *phsa:(r) nùh (ˌ|), thmɔ:* (\). This procedure may be applied to the other cases here:—*phsa:(r) nùh (ˌ|) sì:-lʳp.* 'In this market, (they) do petty-thieving'; *phsa:(r) nùh (ˌ|) kap kò:* 'In this market (they) kill oxen'. The last two sentences are of the type discussed in Lesson 38.4. On semantic grounds, one might class the first and second sequences as proper names, the 'Stone Market' and the 'Petty Thieves' Market'. The third sequence, which is of more general and common occurrence, has been treated as a compound. One might substantiate this distinction by the following illustration:— *phsa:(r) nùh, kè: hau tha: phsa:(r) thmɔ:.* 'This market is called the Stone Market'. *phsa:(r) nùh kè: hau tha: phsa:(r) sì:-lʳp.* 'This market is called the Petty Thieves' Market'. *phsa:(r) nùh kùː phsa:(r)-kap-kò:* 'This is a meat-market'.

(2) *krùp* **pre n.p.** The **A** thus formed with *lkhaon* is attributive to *rò:ŋ* and is therefore itself within an **A**, *nʳu-mùk(h) . . . . tὲəŋ-ʔɔs.* There are many

---

¹ *neh* and *nɔh* are colloquial words meaning the same as *tì: nìh* and *tì: nùh,* 'here' and 'there' respectively.
² *(h)nʳŋ* is a colloquial **post n.p.** meaning 'this, about which speaker and hearer know'. *nìh* on the other hand indicates a physically present object to which the speaker can point.

words with the meaning 'all' and it is a common occurrence for more than one to be used as here.

khlah. nìh, nùh and *khlah* which have been met and used as post-nominal particles up to now are capable of being catalysed as nouns also. In this function, they have the restricted usage associated with pronouns (see Lesson 39.2).

phse:ŋ-phse:ŋ 'various' (and numerous), *phse:ŋ* 'different'. See Lesson 46 *re* effect of reduplication on meaning.

sɔmbot(r) is used for all kinds of tickets as well as for letters.

knì:ə. **a.** or **n.** Could be either here.

rùəŋ ʔvʁy phse:ŋ-phse:ŋ. Both *ʔvʁy* 'some' and *phse:ŋ-phse:ŋ* 'various' serve to indicate that the speaker thinks of *rùəŋ* as being definite, plural but unspecified. It is perhaps impossible to give in translation a word for each word; the English plural is itself serving to translate part of the meaning of the Cambodian.

lù:. Impersonal use. See Lesson 26.

Exercise 52 B

We might go to the theatre this evening. You're not tired, Uncle? No, I'm not tired! Which theatre shall we go to?

That depends on you. You choose, Uncle, because you are visiting Phnom Penh. I am always here. I can go to a show any evening.

No. You know the theatres better than I do. Which show do you like best? I like the Stone Theatre best. The comedians are very funny.

Well then, we'll go to the Stone Theatre.

Exercise 53 A

(1) knoŋ rò:ŋ lkhaon

(2) yùp meɲ bo:ŋ ʔaeŋ tʁu na:?
yùp meɲ khɲom tʁu mʁ:l lkhaon.

(3) kè: lè:ŋ rùəŋ ʔʁy?
lè:ŋ rùəŋ prèəh lèəksenəvùəŋ(s) taŋ-pì: prèəh prù(h)m mò:k pò:(r) nì:əŋ.

(4) lʔɔ: mʁ:l tè:?
yì:! lʔɔ: mʁ:l nas!

(5) lkhaon rò:ŋ na:?
rò:ŋ phsa:(r)-kap-kò:. (6) ʔì:! ʔaɲ thlɔŋ ʔʁ:y thlɔŋ! mənùs(s) mʁ:l cɔɲʔiət nas. vì:ə nìyì:əy knì:ə lù: so:(r) ʔù:-ʔù:. sdap kè: crìəŋ mùm lù: soh. (7) ʔaɲ saəc ʔʁ:y saəc. pù:ək tlok kɔmplaeŋ lʔɔ: mʁ:l nas. (8) ʔaɲ lù: nèək mnèək nìyì:əy knì:ə kha:ŋ kraoy ʔaɲ tha: 'yì:! khɲom lù: tha: kè: mʁ:l kon ʔɔŋkùy cùt mùm lʔɔ: mʁ:l tè:, prùəh vì:ə ɲ̀əə(r). kè: mʁ:l tae pì: cɔmɲa:y. ʔae lkhaon mèc mùm ɲ̀əə(r)? (9) kè: mʁ:l cùt-cùt thnak le:k(h) mù:əy ba:n lʔɔ: mʁ:l.' (10) ʔaɲ nùk knoŋ cʁt(t) tha: nèək nìh prəhael-cì:ə nèək-srae, mùm-dael skɔ̀əl lkhaon skɔ̀əl kon, ba:n-cì:ə nìyì:əy ʔɔɲcʁŋ. (11) lùh dɔl maoŋ dɔp-pì:(r), kè: va: rò:ŋ. ʔaɲ daə(r) mò:k sì: bəbo:(r) ʔɔs mù:əy ca:n. rù:əc ʔaɲ mò:k de:k ʔae phtèəh vèɲ.

(2) *bɔ:ŋ ʔaeŋ*. See Lesson 42.1 for this use of *ʔaeŋ* as **post n.p.**

(4) *yì:* or *ʔì:*, as in (6) express the same idea of great surprise. For them and *ʔʁ:y* in (6), see this lesson, above.

(6) *lù:*. Impersonal use of *lù:* as part of a major verbal sequence.

Re 'change of subject' in the middle of the construction, see Lesson 37. *lùː soː(r)* is often followed by a further verb which describes the sound, e.g. *baek kɔŋ lùː soː(r) krùk-krùk.* 'Something went wrong with the bike and it made a clicking sound over and over'.

(7) *pùːək tlok kɔmplaeŋ lʔɔː mỳːl nas.* **N V V V f.** There is, however, a close connection between the last two verbs which sometimes characterizes a sequence, attributive verb-operative verb, cf. *chŋaɲ sìː* tasty to eat, *pìːrùəh sdap* delightful to hear, *pìbaːk thvỳː* difficult to do.

(8) *tae.* General dependent particle, which does not affect the construction of the whole sentence: **N V (p) A** . *cɔmŋaːy.* cf. *chŋaːy.* See Lesson 45.

> **n v p pN**
> **n v p pn**

ʔae lkhaon. Separated from the rest of the sentence. In plain prose style *mëc, mëc-kɔː* or *häet(o)-ʔvɤy-baːn-cìːə* usually occupy first position but in lively speech the sentence subject or another construct may be emphasized by preceding the rest of the sentence and being pronounced as a separate phrase. See Lesson 38.3.

(9) *thnak leːk(h) mùːəy.* A limited **A.**; **pre n.p.** *pìː* or *nỳu* could be used before it.

baːn. Here used in its first, essential sense of 'get'. *lʔɔː mỳːl*, good-to-see, 'a good view'. A noun is required in translation but no nominalizing particle is present in the Cambodian to suggest an *ad hoc* nominalization of the verbal sequence, *lʔɔː mỳːl.* One must be content with a sequence of verbs which may be compared with *bat kdau*, 'become cooler' (lose to be hot), *mìːən thủm krəʔoːp* 'there is a delightful scent' (there is to smell to be pleasant-to-smell).[1]

(11) *ʔɔs mùːəy caːn. ʔɔs* **pre n.p.** see Lesson 36.3.

ʔae phtɛ̀əh. The speaker is not now at home and may therefore say *ʔae phtɛ̀əh*, not *nỳu phtɛ̀əh.*

Exercise 53 B

Mr. — and his two friends went to the theatre last night. It was not very crowded because many people preferred the play at the Meat Market Theatre. Also, there was a very good film at the Ciné Luxe, to which many people no doubt went.

LESSON 44

PREFIXES

44.1. *Prefixes in monosyllables*

Many of the monosyllables with 2- or 3-place extended initials (discussed above in Lesson 4.3), may be analysed into two parts, a prefix, consisting of one or two consonants, and a partner word which occurs elsewhere alone.

e.g. *phdac* to break (string, thread) (tr.), *dac* to break (string, thread) (intr.)

tətùk to be wet	*tùk* water
prədoːc to compare	*doːc* to be like
prəchlùəh to squabble together	*chlùəh* to quarrel

---

[1] See footnote to Lesson 21.1, No. 1.

If the partner word begins with a liquid or nasal, a first register prefixed consonant will change the register of the vowel:—

kraːp to prostrate oneself	*rìːəp* to be flat, low-lying
krevɔŋ circular	*vùəŋ* circle

The aspiration (*h*) and the short neutral vowel (*ə*) which may occur as features of junction between consonants in extended monosyllables[1] are not taken into account when the prefixes are being discussed. Thus the prefixes illustrated in the pairs of words given above would be listed as *p*, *t*, *pr*, *pr*, *k*, and *kr*. Where a single prefixed consonant is the same as the initial consonant of the partner word (as in *tətùk* above), it is called a reduplicative prefix.

44.2. *Prefixes in restricted disyllables*

Many restricted disyllables may similarly be analysed into two parts, the first syllable being a prefix and the second being a partner word which elsewhere occurs alone.

e.g. *bəndaə(r)* to cause to walk	*daə(r)* to walk
sɔnsaəm dew	*saəm* wet

Again a change of register takes place if the partner word has an initial liquid or nasal consonant and the first prefix consonant is first register,

e.g. *bɔŋriən* to teach	*rìən* to learn
bɔŋvɤl to turn round (tr.)	*vùl* to turn round (intr.)

These prefixes consist of *k*, *c*, *d*, *b*, *s*, *r* and *ʔ*, followed by short inherent vowel and a nasal which varies according to the nature of the following consonant. They may be represented for convenience as *bN*, *sN*, etc., on the understanding that *N* represents any nasal consonant and that the short inherent vowel occurs as a link between the first consonant and the nasal.

The term 'partner word' is used to mean 'word of related meaning'.

44.3. *The structure of prefixes*

This may be summarized as follows:—

1. A single consonant different from the initial consonant of the partner word.

2. A single consonant reduplicating the initial consonant of the partner word.

3. A consonant + *r* (*kr*, *cr*, *tr*, *pr*, *sr*).

4. A consonant + *N* (*kN*, *cN*, *tN*, *dN*, *bN*, *pN*, *rN*, *lN*, *sN*, *ʔN*).

The meaning conveyed by the prefixes is in many instances not clearcut. The prefixing processes are not to any extent alive now (i.e. being used freely by Cambodian speakers to make new words). Either the partner word or the prefixed form, or both, may therefore have undergone a change of meaning, since the prefixing process became obsolete.

Some generalizations may however be made:—

---

[1] See Lesson 4.

1. Single consonant, different from the initial of the partner word.

k, *c*, *s* restrict the meaning; form words of lower frequency.

e.g. *tɔ̀ət* to kick away   *khtɔ̀ət* to rebound
    mùːl round   *chmoːl* to roll into a ball
    rỳːs to pick out   *crỳːs* to take one's choice
    tɔ̀ət in *tìəŋ-tɔ̀ət* exact   *stɔ̀ət* to be thorough (of knowledge)

p. Turns the partner word into a causative verb.

e.g. *kùː* a pair   *phkùː* to pair off
    deːk to lie down   *phdeːk* to cause to lie down

r. Often forms an attributive verb.

e.g. *dɔːk* to uproot   *rədɔːk* uprooted
    dɔh to free   *rədɔh* freed, free

2. Single consonant reduplicated. Adds the idea of repetition or intensification to the meaning of the partner word.

e.g. *keh* to scratch   *kəkeh* to scratch constantly
    thɛ̀ək to kick   *təthɛ̀ək* to kick repeatedly
    srt to comb   *səsrt* to pick, clean, sift
    ɲɔ̀ə(r) to tremble   *ɲəɲɔ̀ə(r)* to tremble constantly

3. Consonant + *r*.

kr, *sr*, restrict the meaning.

e.g. *pùl* poison   *krəpùl* nauseating
    vɔ̀ət to throw from the horns   *krəvɔ̀ət* to throw to a short distance
                                  from oneself
    lìːəp to paint   *srəlaːp* to put on ointment or lotion

pr gives an idea of reciprocity, to be translated as 'each other', 'together'.

e.g. *mùːl* round   *prəmoːl* to gather together

4. Consonant + *N*.

All the prefixes except *bN* may form either a verb of restricted meaning or a noun:—

    rỳːs to choose   *cùmrỳːs* choice
laek in the phrase
    daoy laek different   *cɔmlaek* strange
    vɛ̀ːŋ long   *sɔŋvaeŋ* widely separated
    saəm damp   *sɔnsaəm* dew
    vɔ̀əs to measure extent   *rùəŋvɔ̀əs* an instrument for measuring extent
    lòːp(h) greed   *rùmlòːp(h)* to usurp
    tɛ̀ək to trap   *ʔɔntɛ̀ək* a snare

bN turns the partner word into a causative verb.

e.g. *kaən* to increase (intr.)   *bɔŋkaən* to increase (tr.)
    chùp to stop (intr.)   *bɔɲchùp* to stop (tr.)

Exercise 54 A

(1) rùɨəŋ hɔ̰ŋ(s) nɨ̀ŋ ʔɔndaək

(2) nɤ̀u-knoŋ srah mù:əy mì:ən ʔɔndaək thom mù:əy nɤ̀u-knoŋ srah nùh. mì:ən hɔ̰ŋ(s) mù:əy kù: tɤ̀u rɔ̀:k-sì: knoŋ srah nùh rɔ̀əl thŋay. (3) dɔl khae praŋ tɤ̀k srah nùh rì:ŋ ʔɔs tɤ̀u, ʔɔndaək kùt nɨ̀ŋ kəka:y rù:ŋ, thvɤ̀: kɔnlaeŋ nɤ̀u cì:ə thmɤ̀y tìət. srap-tae hɔ̰ŋ(s) tɛ̀əŋ pì:(r) co:l tɤ̀u nìyì:əy tha:, (4) 'bo:ŋ ʔɔndaək, bo:ŋ ʔɔndaək! bo:ŋ ʔaeŋ nɤ̀u (h)nɤ̀ŋ pìba:k nas. tɤ̀k srah rì:ŋ ʔɔs haəy. ba:n ʔɤ̀y sì:ʔ bo:ŋ ʔaeŋ tɤ̀u nɤ̀u srok ʔae nɔh, tɤ̀:p sɔp̂ba:y, mì:ən cɔmnɤ̀y sì: krùp mùk(h)'. (5) ʔɔndaək tha: 'khɲom tɤ̀u mùm kaət tè:. bo:ŋ hɔ̰ŋ(s) ʔɤ̀:y, khɲom kmì:ən sla:p haə(r) tè:.' (6) hɔ̰ŋ(s) chlaəy tha:, 'ʔaə! baə bo:ŋ ʔaeŋ tɤ̀u, khɲom yɔ̀:k tɤ̀u ba:n, tae ʔaoy bo:ŋ ʔaeŋ kham mɔ̀ət ʔaoy cùt. nɛ̀ək na: tha: mɛ̌c kom-ʔaoy to: nɨ̀ŋ vì:ə'. (7) ʔɔndaək tha:, 'ba:n' haəy hɔ̰ŋ(s) tɛ̀əŋ pì:(r) tɤ̀u pɔ̀əm mɛ̀:k chɤ̀: mù:əy kɔmnat mɔ̀:k. rù:əc prap tha: 'ʔaoy bo:ŋ ʔɔndaək ʔaeŋ kham cɔm kɔnda:l, khɲom pɔ̀əm sɔ:ŋ̂kha:ŋ' haəy kɔ: haə(r) tɤ̀u. (8) lùh dɔl srok mù:əy mì:ən mənù̀s(s) cì:ə craən. kè: lè:ŋ nɤ̀u-mùk(h) phtɛ̀əh. ba:n khɤ̀:ɲ hɔ̰ŋ(s) tɛ̀əŋ pì:(r) haəy, kè: sraek tha:, 'mɤ̀:l hɔ̰ŋ(s) pɔ̀əm ʔɔndaək vɤ̀:y!' (9) ʔɔndaək lùɨ: sɔmle:ɲ mənù̀s(s) tha: do:c⁼nɔh, kɔ: kùt nìyì:əy tha:, 'coh-baə sɔmlaŋ ʔa̰ɲ pɔ̀əm nɔ̀əm ʔa̰ɲ tɤ̀u, ʔaeŋ cam bac nìyì:əy ʔɤ̀y?' (10) krɔ̀ən-tae kùt tha: poɲ̂ɲɤ̀ŋ, kɔ: rəbo:t mɔ̀ət thlɛ̀ək baek sno:k slap tɤ̀u.

(2) The second *nɤ̀u-knoŋ srah nùh* is redundant, but this is acceptable.

(3) *ʔɔs.* Here the verb, *ʔɔs.* (**A N V V v**) *kùt nɨ̀ŋ kəka:y rù:ŋ.* cf. *ʔa:c nɨ̀ŋ yɔ̀:k* in Exercise 51, (5).

cì:ə thmɤ̀y. **A.** *ad hoc* nominalization of verb, *thmɤ̀y.*

srap-tae immediately.

tɛ̀əŋ. Here the dependent general particle. See Lesson 36.

co:l tɤ̀u. co:l is here a main verb.

(4) Repetition of terms of address is very common in Cambodian narratives. For use of *bo:ŋ* and *ʔaeŋ*, see Lessons 41 and 42.

bo:ŋ ʔaeŋ nɤ̀u (h)nɤ̀ŋ pìba:k nas. Change of subject from one verb to the next, since the second verb is used impersonally. (One cannot say *bo:ŋ ʔaeŋ pìba:k nas.*)

(6) *ʔaə.* See Lesson 39.

khɲom. Each swan says 'I'. *nɛ̀ək na: tha: mɛ̌c.* A clause with no **m**.

(7) *bo:ŋ ʔɔndaək ʔaeŋ.* For use of *ʔaeŋ*, expressing greater friendship towards the tortoise, see Lesson 41.

sɔ:ŋ̂kha:ŋ 'both sides'. First syllable is a Thai loanword, meaning 'two'.

haəy kɔ:. Two markers do occur sometimes. 'and so'. *haə(r) tɤ̀u. tɤ̀u* here occurs as a minor verb of motion but, being the last word in the sentence it has stress.

(8) *dɔl.* Main verb.

mù:əy 'a certain'.

cì:ə craən. ad hoc nominalization of numeral.

vɤ̀:y. See Lesson 43.

(9) *rəbo:t mɔ̀ət, baek sno:k. ʔɔndaək* is still the sentence topic but is the subject of only two of the four verb constructs, i.e. of *thlɛ̀ək* and *slap.* The verbs *rəbo:t* and *baek* are used impersonally with the nouns of reference

following, giving a more vivid narrative effect. Analysis of the last clause:

m   (N)   V V V V v
m (mooted subject) vN v vN v v
                        vn v vn v v

Exercise 54 B

This is a story about a pair of geese and a tortoise. The latter was living near a lake which had dried up in the dry season and where there was little food. The geese offered * to carry the tortoise to another place; the tortoise was to grasp in his mouth the middle part of a branch while the geese held an end each. * The tortoise agreed and the geese, holding a branch in their mouths, carried him up with them. However, the tortoise heard people below talking and laughing about him and opening his mouth to reply fell to his death.

* . . . . * Translate by direct speech.

Exercise 55 A

(1) rəbiəp thvɤ̀: skɔː(r) tnaot

(2) khae naː kè: thvɤ̀: skɔː(r) tnaot? khae praŋ. (3) kè: thvɤ̀: skɔː(r) tnaot nùh doːc tɔ:-tɤ̀u nìh. kaːl-naː: daəm-tnaot mìːən phka: haəy kè: cɔːŋ bɔŋʔaoŋ pìː kraom dol lɤ̀: haəy kè: laəŋ tɤ̀u cɤt phkaː-tnaot trɔŋ mùk(h) vìːə pìː(r) bɤ̀y kambɤt. rùːəc kè: yɔ̀:k khnìːəp kìːəp phkaː-tnaot bɔntec-bɔntec mùm-ʔaoy khlaŋ tèː. (4) kè: laəŋ tɤ̀u cɤt mùk(h) vìːə pìː(r) bɤ̀y prùk haəy kìːəp phoːŋ. kè: yɔ̀:k bɔmpùəŋ mɔ̀:k ʔɔp kom-ʔaoy thùm klɤn cùː(r) haəy yɔ̀:k tɤ̀u trɔːŋ taŋ-pìː lɲìːəc prəhael maoŋ pram rəhoːt-dɔl phlùː:, tɤ̀:p kè: tɤ̀u dak tùk-tnaot. (5) knɔŋ mùːəy daəm mìːən pram pram-mùːəy bɔmpùəŋ. kè: mùm-mɛ̀ːn thvɤ̀: tae mùːəy daəm tèː. kè: thvɤ̀: pram pram-mùːəy daəm. (6) lùh kè: dak mɔ̀:k dɔl dɤ̀y haəy, kè: tətùːəl tìːən khlah, kè: lùək khlah. (7) cùːən-kaːl kè: yɔ̀:k tùk-tnaot mɔ̀:k cak knɔŋ khtɛ̀əh thom mùːəy haəy kè: yɔ̀:k tɤ̀u dak knɔŋ lɔː, rùːəc dot phlɤ̀:ŋ ʔaoy pùh rìːɲ nɤ̀u tae skɔː(r). (8) kè: thvɤ̀: skɔː(r) coh ʔos nas. kè: dam mùːəy khtɛ̀əh mùːəy thŋay, tɤ̀:p rìːɲ baːn cìːə skɔː(r). lùh rìːɲ haəy kè: dak cɛɲ pìː phlɤ̀:ŋ, kè: koː(r) vùk ʔaoy sʔɤt haəy kè: yɔ̀:k kʔoːm rùː: pìːəŋ mɔ̀:k cak tùk lùək rùː: tùk tətùːəl tìːən.

(1) *rəbiəp*, like the noun-formers, *kaː(r)*, *sĕckdɤy*, *rùəŋ*, forms a **N** with a **V** (**vN**) used attributively. cf. Exercise 45, (1).

(2) *khae naː*. The **A** which forms the question-sequence is placed more vividly at the beginning of the sentence, with a rise in pitch on *naː*. The more pedestrian word-order would be, as set out in Lesson 18.2 (last example) with the **A** at the end. *khae naː* and *khae praŋ* are not made specifically singular or plural grammatically but semantically (and therefore in English translation) the plural is required since there are several 'dry' months in the dry season.

(3) *skɔː(r) tnaot nùh*. 'The palm sugar of which we have just made mention'. In Lesson 14 (footnote to Exercise 1 B, 1) it was stated that English definite and indefinite articles had no counterpart in Cambodian except under special circumstances. Here is the kind of context in which English 'the' is represented in Cambodian; *nùh*, and not *nìh*, is used. This usage is particularly

common when a character or object in a story is referred to for a second or further time, e.g. *mənùs(s) nùh*, the man (about whom we are telling the tale), *seh nùh*, the horse (which was mentioned just now). The English indefinite article is represented in a narrative by *mùːəy*. e.g. 'They came to a house . . . .' *mɔ̀ːk dɔl phtɛ̀əh mùːəy*. *mùːəy* may also represent English 'a certain'. e.g. *mìːən mənùs(s) mnɛ̀ək*, 'There was a certain man . . . .' *dɔːc tɔː-tr̃u nìh. tɔː-tr̃u*, which has been met as a compound final particle, 'from then onwards, continuing' is here nominalized by the preceding **pre n.p.** *dɔːc* and the following **post n.p.** *nìh*. 'as follows'.

kraom and *lr̃ː* are similarly nominalized here by being preceded by *pìː* and *dɔl* respectively.

trɔŋ = 'to move directly towards', as well as 'to be upright, straight'.

pìː(r) br̃y kambr̃t **X** (**xxc**). It will be remembered that **xx** may represent a series of two numerals comprising a number when added together, e.g. *mùːəy-rɔ̀ːy haːsr̃p* (**xx**) 150. Here **xx** represents two numerals which are never added together to form a number and which are therefore understood to be alternatives, 'two or three'. *pìː(r) rùː br̃y* is possible but less usual and more precise. Sometimes in the orthography a short line or hyphen separates the alternative numerals. The numerals *buːən dɔp* are frequently used together in this way to mean 'several' (literally 'four or ten'). The **X** here under discussion has the verb, *cr̃t*, as headword.

khnìːəp kìːəp. Instance of an infix which forms a name of a utensil from a verbal root. See Lesson 45.

mùn-ʔaoy khlaŋ tèː. This reinforces the '*bɔntec-bɔntec*'. 'So as not to be violent, not overdoing it.'

(5) *knoŋ mùːəy daəm*. *knoŋ* nominalizes the **X**.

(6) *khlah* functioning as a pronoun as in Exercise 52, (2).

(7) *pùh rìːŋ nr̃u tae skɔː(r)* **V V V**. The first two verbs refer to the mooted subject, *tùk tnaot*, while the last is used impersonally.

(8) *kèː thvr̃ː skɔː(r) coh ʔos nas*. **N V V f**. The second verb here is used
            n vN vN f
with no reference to the independent **N**, *kèː*. For *coh ʔos*, cf. Lesson 26, impersonal uses of verbs 'with much firewood' (literally 'goes down the firewood very much'.

Exercise 55 B

How do they climb the sugar-palms?

By means of scaffolding which they fix round each tree from top to bottom.

What do they use for scraping the sugar-palm flower?

They use a knife to do this.

For how long do they leave the node of bamboo to catch the juice?

From evening until dawn.

How is the sugar made?

The juice of the sugar-palm is put on a stove to reduce by boiling and turn to sugar.

LESSON 45

INFIXES

45.1. *Infixes in monosyllables*

Many monosyllables with 2- or 3-place extended initial sequences may be analysed into two parts, an infix, consisting of one or two consonants, and a partner word which occurs elsewhere alone.

e.g. *smoːm* beggar   *soːm* to ask, beg
     chnok stopper   *cok* to stop up, to cork
     trənỳː means of lateral support   *tỳː* to be supported laterally
     trənùm perch   *tùm* to perch

The aspiration (*h*) and the short neutral vowel (*ə*) which may occur as a feature of junction between consonants in extended monosyllables are again not taken into account. Thus the infixes present in the above four words are listed as *m, n, rn, rn*.

45.2. *Infixes in restricted disyllables*

Many restricted disyllables may similarly be analysed into two parts, an infix and a partner word.

e.g. *kùmrùp* to complete   *krùp* all
     cɔmŋaːy distance   *chŋaːy* distant[1]
     tùmlɔ̀əp custom   *thlɔ̀əp* to be accustomed
     kɔmnat a cut piece   *kat* to cut
     dɔmneːk sleep   *deːk* to sleep

These infixes consist of either one nasal consonant or *mn*, preceded by the short inherent vowel (either *ɔ, ùə* or *ù*, according to the register of the initial consonant and the nature of the nasal).

45.3. *The commonest infixes (n, m and mn)*

The following examples illustrate their meanings:—

n Utensil, means   *kìːəp* to pinch   *khnìːəp* pincers
     rìːəp flat   *rənìːəp* floor
     rɔ̀əs to rake   *rənɔ̀əs* a rake
     rὲəŋ to keep off   *rənὲəŋ* a screen
     doː(r) to barter   *thnoː(r)*[2] price

m 1. Agent

     i. (where partner word has a simple initial consonant)
         soːm to beg   *smoːm*[3] a beggar
         cùːəp to do business   *chmùːəɲ*[3] business-man

     ii. (infixed between the two consonants of the initial sequence)
         khlau ignorant   *kɔmlau*[3] ignoramus
         khsɔt destitute   *kɔmsɔt*[3] a destitute person
         khlaːc to fear   *kɔmlaːc*[3] a timid person

---

[1] Note that the aspiration which marks the junction between the initial sequences in these partner words is absent in the infixed form.

[2] Note that simple initial *d* loses voice and implosion when followed by a nasal infix.

[3] In modern Khmer these words are chiefly used in conjunction with *nὲək* or *mənùs(s)*, which have already replaced the **m** infix as a live noun-forming device.

2. Noun-former *tbaːɲ* to weave   *dɔmbaːɲ*[1] equipment for weaving

> *khos* to be wrong   *kɔmhos* a wrong
> *khɤŋ* to be angry   *kɔmhɤŋ* anger
> *sdɤy* to speak   *sɔmdɤy* speech

3. Causative (for words whose initials may not take the prefixes, *p*, or *pN*)

> *rəlùət* extinguished   *rùmlùət* to extinguish
> *slap* to die   *sɔmlap* to kill
> *thlɛ̀ək* to fall   *tùmlɛ̀ək* to let fall

mn Noun-former (often an abstract noun)

> *saːp* to sow   *sɔmnaːp* seedling
> *kaət* to be born   *kɔmnaət* birth
> *daə(r)* to walk, travel   *dɔmnaə(r)* journey (n.)
> *kɔ̀ː(r)* to heap up   *kùmnɔ̀ː(r)* a heap

45.4. *Less common infixes*

b Noun-former (object achieved by action of verb)

> *rìən* to learn   *rəbìən* method
> *lèːŋ* to play   *lbaeŋ* game
> *lùən* to be quick   *lbùən* speed

rn   *tɤ̀ː* to be supported   *trənɤ̀ː* or *thnɤ̀ː* a shelf
          laterally
          pɛ̀ək to hang on,   *prənɛ̀ək* to carry on back or
          (tr.), to wear   shoulder
          sok(h) happy   *srənok(h)*, *srənok* easy
          tùm to perch   *trənùm* a perch

Exercise 56 A

                 (1) **cùːəp-cùm pùː nùŋ mìːŋ**

(2) *nɛ̀ək saːrùən*   cùmrìːəp-suːə(r), lòːk-pùː, nɛ̀ək-mìːŋ. sok(h)-sɔp̄baːy cìːə tèːʔ

(3) *pùː*   pùː mìːŋ sok(h)-sɔp̄baːy tèː. pùː dɤŋ thaː ʔaeŋ cùːt tɤ̀u srok kèː haəy tɤ̀ːp pùː mìːŋ khɔm chlìət mɔ̀ːk lèːŋ ʔaeŋ bontec.

(4) *nɛ̀ək saːrùən*   khɲom tɤ̀ːp-nùŋ tətùːəl sɔmbot(r) lòːk-pùː pìː prùɨk meŋ (h)nə. khɲom sɔp̄baːy nas daoy lòːk-pùː nɛ̀ək-mìːŋ baːn ʔɔŋcɤ̀ːɲ-mɔ̀ːk cùːəp-cùm knìːə tɛ̀əŋ-ʔɔs doːcᵓneh.

(5) *mìːŋ*   ʔaeŋ troːv tɤ̀u rìən poɱmaːn chnam tìət?

(6) *nɛ̀ək saːrùən*   ʔao! yùː(r) dae(r), nɛ̀ək-mìːŋ, prəhael pram, pram-mùːəy chnam.

(7) *pùː*   ʔaeŋ tɤ̀u rìən khaːŋ ʔɤy?

(8) *nɛ̀ək saːrùən*   khaːŋ sɔŋ phtɛ̀əh, sɔŋ thnol, sɔŋ spìːən ʔɤy-ʔɤy ʔɔs (h)nɤŋ, lòːk-pùː.

(9) *pùː*   ʔaeŋ troːv laəŋ kɔpal-hɔh nɤ̀u maoŋ poɱmaːn?

---

[1] Or *tɔmbaːɲ*.

(10) *nèək saːruən*   sʔaek maoŋ buːən kɔnlah, lòːk-pùː. lòːk-pùː cɔŋ cùːn khɲom
                       tʳu rùːʔ kom ʔʳy. nɔ̀əm tae ʔɔmpùəl lòːk-pùː tèː.

(11) *pùː*   mùn ʔʳy tèː. pùː nùŋ mìːŋ ʔaeŋ cɔŋ tʳu mʳːl ʔaeŋ laəŋ
                       kɔpal-hɔh dae(r).

(12) *nèək saːruən*   khɲom ʔɔː(r) kùṇ craən haəy daoy lòːk-pùː nèək-mìːŋ baːn
                       ʔɔɲcʳːɲ-mɔ̀ːk, rùːəc cùːn khɲom tʳu cɔmnɔːt yùən(t)-hɔh
                       tiət.

(13) *pùː*   mùn ʔʳy tèː. tùmrɔ̀əm khʳːɲ ʔaeŋ mdɔːŋ tiət, pram, pram-
                       mùːəy chnam. mleh pùː mìːŋ cas ʔɔs haəy tùmrɔ̀əm ʔaeŋ
                       mɔ̀ːk vèɲ.

(1) cf. Exercise 51, (1). The title is a verb, to be translated by a verbal
noun (-ing) in English.

(2) *cùmrìːəp suːə(r)*. A correct form of greeting for any time of day.
Alternative form: *suːəsdʳy*.

lòːk-pùː, nèək-mìːŋ. The choice of pronoun or title to be used in addressing
a person is a delicate matter, since the chosen term must combine the proper
degree of respect with the desired degree of friendliness. The terms *lòːk* and
nèək which one might expect to have the same degree of elevation as their
respective partners, *lòːk-srʳy* and *nèək-srʳy* are in fact less elevated than the
corresponding female terms. Thus the speaker in this passage was being only
slightly more familiar to his aunt in using the term, *nèək-mìːŋ*.

(3) *sok(h)-sɔpbaːy tèː* or *sok(h)-sɔpbaːy cìːə tèː* is the usual reply to (2).
tèː here occurs in an affirmative sentence, as in Exercise 48, (15).
srok kèː 'a foreign country' (literally 'someone's country').

(4) *(h)nə*. See Lesson 43.

(8) *khaːŋ* acts like *sëckdʳy*, *kaː(r)*, *rùəy* here in expressing the abstract
idea from a verb. The verb constructs, *sɔŋ phtèəh*, *sɔŋ thnɔl* and *sɔŋ spìːən*
ʔʳy-ʔʳy are attached attributively to *khaːŋ* in a developed **N**.

(10) *kom ʔʳy*. 'Don't do anything.' 'Don't trouble.' cf. *mùn ʔʳy tèː*.
(11) 'It's nothing.' 'Not at all.' *kom* gives a command. *ʔʳy* is here catalysed
as an *ad hoc* verb.
tae . . . . tèː. *tèː* is frequently associated with affirmative sentences in which
tae occurs.

(12) *ʔɔː(r) kùṇ* 'to thank' (literally 'be glad at the good deed'). Cambodians
do not express thanks in words as often as English people do. Thanks for
small services are expressed by a smile and/or by the *sɔmpèəh* (placing of
palms together as in greeting). This is accompanied by bowing to a superior
or by prostration to an august personage. The words, *ʔɔː(r) kùṇ*, form a very
decided expression of gratitude; if the foreigner uses the words when a letter
is handed to him or food is put in front of him he will only cause amusement.

(13) *pram pram-mùːəy chnam*. *tùmrɔ̀əm* introduces a clause in a composite
sentence, **m (N) V a f** (,|), and the **X** is a whole clause by itself, verbalized by
its context. A contradictory response to this sentence might be, *mùn-mèːn
pram pram-mùːəy chnam tèː*, *lòːk-pùː. prəhael-cìːə pram-bʳy chnam, tʳːp
khɲom mɔ̀ːk vèɲ*.

Exercise 56 B

Goodmorning, Mr. —!
Ah! Hello, Mrs. —!
Did you go to Phnom Penh to see your nephew off?
Yes, we just got back this lunch-time.
What is he going to study?
He's studying to be a doctor.
Oh! Will he be away a long time?
Yes, about six years.
What a long time! Was your sister in Phnom Penh well?
Very well thank you.

Exercise 57 A

(1) kaː(r) tɛ̀ək dɔmrʋy

(2) nʋu srok khmae(r) mìːən prèy phnùm cìːə craən dael pɛ̀ɲ tʋu daoy (h)voːŋ
dɔmrʋy prèy. (3) baə troːv kaː(r) cɔŋ tɛ̀ək dɔmrʋy, kɛ̀ː troːv yɔ̀ːk trəmɛ̀ək dael ceh
prəsop haəy kɛ̀ː bəbuːəl knìːə prəhael mphèy nɛ̀ək cìh tùːk toːc-toːc. (4) knoŋ
tùːk mùːəy-mùːəy kɛ̀ː cìh pìː(r) nɛ̀ək haəy kɛ̀ː laəŋ daə(r) tʋu knoŋ prèy kiəŋ
sạt(v)-dɔmrʋy tɛ̀əŋ (h)voːŋ. (5) mənùs(s) tɛ̀əŋ-ʔos troːv mìːən prədap sɔmrap
kaː(r)pìːə(r) khluːən, mìːən daːv, lùmpɛ̀ːŋ, kambʋt, cìːə daəm. (6) lùh kɛ̀ː khʋ̀ːɲ
(h)voːŋ dɔmrʋy haəy, kɛ̀ː daə(r) kiəŋ ʔaoy vìːə coh knoŋ tùːk stùŋ, tùənlɛ̀ː, bʋŋ,
haəy kɛ̀ː coh tʋu cìh tùːk tɛ̀əŋ-ʔos knìːə. (7) kɛ̀ː ʔom tùːk kiəŋ coh kiəŋ laəŋ haəy
kɛ̀ː bɔmrɔŋ thaː nùŋ tɛ̀ək yɔ̀ːk tae mùːəy. (8) trəmɛ̀ək dɔmrʋy sraek prap nɛ̀ək
tɛ̀əŋ-ʔos knìːə ʔaoy dɛ̀ŋ dɔmrʋy laəŋ tʋu lʋ̀ː kòːk haəy kɛ̀ː kiəŋ yɔ̀ːk tae mùːəy.
(9) trəmɛ̀ək dɔmrʋy troːv laəŋ cìh lʋ̀ː kɔː[1] dɔmrʋy mùːəy nùh kap kbaːl nùŋ
pùːthau. (10) dɔmrʋy thvʋ̀ː ʔʋy kɔː mùm baːn, prùəh nʋu knoŋ tùːk crʋu phot
cʋ̀ːŋ phot day. (11) lùh kɛ̀ː dʋŋ thaː vìːə ʔos kɔmlaŋ nas haəy, tʋ̀ːp kɛ̀ː yɔ̀ːk mɔ̀ːk
coːŋ tùːk nùŋ bɔŋkòːl mùːəy dael kɛ̀ː bɔh knoŋ tùːk crʋu ʔaoy phot day cʋ̀ːŋ
dɔmrʋy, haəy kɛ̀ː tʋu phtɛ̀əh tɛ̀əŋ-ʔos knìːə. (12) prəhael-cìːə mùːəy ʔaːtùt(y),
kɛ̀ː yɔ̀ːk smau mùːəy koːŋ mɔ̀ːk ʔaoy sìː. dɔl ʔaːtùt(y) kraoy, kɛ̀ː yɔ̀ːk tʋu phtɛ̀əh
bɔŋhat ʔaoy ceh sdap pìːək(y) mənùs(s) khlah. (13) daoy kaː(r) lùmbaːk tɛ̀ək
doːc-ᵈneh baːn-cìːə kɛ̀ː lùək dɔmrʋy mùːəy-mùːəy thlay nas. (14) kɛ̀ː troːv ʔaoy
chmùəh dɔmrʋy taːm cʋt(t) kɛ̀ː.

(1) In this title *kaː(r)* the noun-construct-former is used. Contrast the
titles of Exercises 51 and 56.

(2) *prèy phnùm.* No linking particle required. **N** (**nn**) may be noun with
noun attribute (possession), noun (title) with name, as in *nɛ̀ək saːruən*, or
noun with further noun as a list, as here.

cìːə craən **A.** A little more emphatic than *craən* (**x**) as above.

pɛ̀ɲ .... tʋu. **V ← v** *tʋu* adds meaning to *pɛ̀ɲ*, 'full in various directions'.

(3) *troːv kaː(r) cɔŋ.* The use of two verbs, 'to need' and 'to wish' seems at
first sight contradictory but, as often in Cambodian, the two verbs comple-
ment each other, giving in this case the meaning expressed in our one verb,
'to require'.

bəbuːəl knìːə. bəbuːəl is very often used with *knìːə.* It can convey the sense

---

[1] The word *kɔː* 'neck' here is spelt regularly and is thus distinguished from the particle *kɔː.

'urge each other to', 'spur each other on' but often has the less strong sense 'get together to do'.

cìh tù:k to:c-to:c. Here the reduplicative can only mean 'small and numerous' and not 'very small', as the subject is known to be plural.

(4) *mù:əy-mù:əy* **v.** Used attributively with a noun, this reduplicative has the meaning 'each'; used as the second verb in a major verbal sequence it has the meaning 'slowly, one by one'.

(7) *kiəy coh kiəy laəy.* See Lesson 47 for this type of phrase. 'go up and down, driving them' (literally drive up drive down).

tha: m.

(8) *lȳ: kò:k. ad hoc* nominalization of *kò:k*, **v.**

(9) *lȳ: kɔ: dɔmrɤy mù:əy nùh* **A** . Here the attribute of the noun *kɔ:* is

        pN
          nN
            nxp

itself a **N** (*dɔmrɤy mù:əy nùh*).

(10) *dɔmrɤy thvȳ: ʔɤy kɔ: mùn ba:n.* **N V V.** *mùn* catalyses the second verb as a second position main verb and takes away the possibility of construing *kɔ: ba:n* as the final phrase particle. Nevertheless the effect of *kɔ:* is to give the stressed 'any' meaning to the question word, *ʔɤy.*

phot cȳ:ŋ phot day. Reduplication in syntax. See Lesson 47. For the sequence **vn**, not translated as verb-object, see Lesson 38.5. 'free, slipping, without a good grip, in respect of hands and feet'.

(11) A composite sentence consisting of six clauses:—

m N V (,|) m N V a f (,|) m N V ← v V V A (,|) m N V A (,|) m V N (,|) m N V aa (\\)

tha:, **m.** or **f.** and *haəy*, **m.** or **f.** are construed in accordance with the recording of the passage.

(12) *prəhael-cì:ə mù:əy ʔa:tùt(y).* **g.X.** *mù:əy ʔa:tùt(y).* There is no **f.**, such as *mɔ̀:k, haəy* or *kraoy*, to indicate its relationship in time to the action expressed by the verb, *yɔ̀:k.* One is left to assume that it is 'about a week later'.

(13) The marker *ba:n-cì:ə*, 'reason why, that is why', is very often used to introduce one clause while *pì:-prùəh* 'because' introduces another. Here *daoy ka:(r)* 'because of the fact . . . .' is used instead of *pì:-prùəh.*

daoy ka:(r) lùmba:k tèək do:c⁼neh **A** . Here a sequence which could

        pN
          nVa
           vva

function as a sentence in a mooted context, (**vva**), is used attributively with *ka:(r)* to form a **N.**

(14) Indirect object expressed without a minor verb. See Lesson 20.

Exercise 57 B

Sometimes a party of men from our village go to trap an elephant. They separate one elephant from the herd; then the elephant driver mounts on his neck and strikes his head. When the elephant is exhausted they tie him to a stake fixed in a pool or river. Then they go back home. The week after, they bring him some grass to eat. When he has been there two whole weeks they take him home to train him to obey commands.

LESSON 46

REDUPLICATIVE WORDS

46.1. *Formation*

The process of reduplication is encountered both in the formation of words and in syntax. In this lesson we are concerned with word-formation. The effect of reduplication on lexical meaning varies but there is a strong tendency towards either the intensification or the restriction of the meaning of an unreduplicated partner-word. The following examples may be regarded as fairly typical:—

kaːy to scratch (the surface of the earth), *kəkaːy* (with reduplicative prefix) to scratch constantly.

khpùəs high, *khpùəŋ-khpùəs* (alliterative compound) high-ranking.

A high proportion of reduplicative compounds are attributive verbs. These often convey the idea of plurality to the noun with which they are associated.

1. *Reduplication in the formation of simple words*

This occurs when a homorganic consonant is prefixed to a simple word as in *təthὲək* 'to kick repeatedly', cf. *thὲək* 'to kick'. Such words were discussed in Lesson 44.3.

2. *Reduplication in the formation of compound words*

This, the commonest form of reduplication, occurs chiefly in compounds which have two components[1]; any reduplicatives with three components which have been noted are given below in the appropriate section. One or more elements (initial consonant, vowel or final consonant) of the first component are repeated in the second. There are four types of reduplicative compound, as follows:—

Alliterative compounds (A.C.)

Here either (i) the initial consonant (or sequence of consonants) of a simple word-form are repeated in the second component or (ii) both the initial consonant or consonant sequence and the vowel are repeated.

e.g. (i) repeated initial consonant or sequence.

(simple monosyllable) *cat-caeŋ* 'to organize', *tὲək-tìːəm* 'to be inter-related'

(extended monosyllable) CC *khsɤk-khsuːəl* 'to sob quietly', CCC *trəmùŋ-trəmɤ̀ːy* 'to be gloomy', *srənok-srənaːn* 'to be happy, comfortable'

(restricted disyllable) *bɔŋʔuːət-bɔŋʔɔ̀ː* 'to boast, to try to impress', *səmruːəc-səmraŋ* 'to try to finish (a piece of work) with care'

Note. The two components usually have the same register.

(ii) repeated initial consonant or sequence and vowel.

(simple monosyllable) *biət-biən* 'to oppress', *yùəŋ-yùəl* 'to understand thoroughly'

---

[1] These may be simple monosyllables, extended monosyllables or restricted disyllables. Usually the two components have the same structure as each other.

(extended monosyllable) CC *prɤm-prɤy* 'to be beautiful', *skɔp-skɔl* 'to be satiated', CCC *prɔɲap-prɔɲal* 'to be in a great hurry'
(restricted disyllable) *bɔɲcaɔc-bɔɲcaə* 'to flatter and coax immoderately'

Chiming compounds (C.C.)

The initial consonant or sequence of consonants and the final consonant of the first component are repeated in the second.

e.g. (simple monosyllable) *kaeŋ-kaoŋ* 'to be pretentious'
(extended monosyllable) CC *phde:s-phda:s* 'to be careless', CCC *srəmo:m-srəma:m* 'to be hairy to the point of untidiness'
(restricted disyllable) *kɔntre:k-kɔntra:k* 'to hang in tatters'

Rhyming compounds (Rh.C.)

The vowel and the final consonant of the first component are repeated in the second. Here the initial consonants or sequences of consonants of the two components are not important to the reduplication and frequently have different structures; the only word-form of which the structure tends to be repeated exactly is the simple monosyllable.

e.g. (simple monosyllable) (*h*)*mɔt-cɔt* 'to be precise, net', *rì:əy-mì:əy* 'to be mentally confused', *caeŋ-vaeŋ* 'to be criss-cross', *caəŋ-maəŋ* 'to be snooty'
(other combinations of simple word-forms) *sɔ̀:s-krəlɔ̀:s* 'to be ugly, vulgar' (of things), *ca:n-kba:n* 'crockery', *srəlaŋ-kaŋ* 'to be stupified, to swoon'

A three-syllabled word belongs to this section: *slaŋ-kaŋ-phɛ̀əŋ* 'to swoon' (a literary word). Rhyme in Khmer poetry may cut across register.[1] One-fifth of the rhyming compounds collected have components on different registers, e.g. *rùŋ-prɤŋ* 'to do with all one's might', *rùt-tbɤt* 'to spend with care', *rùŋ-tʔɤŋ* 'to be obstinate', *ka:(r)-ɲì:ə* 'duties', *sɔndap-thnɔ̀əp* 'method, order'. Sometimes alternative forms are current, e.g. *smɔ̀:k-krò:k* and *smaok-krò:k* 'messy and dirty'; *sop-trop* and *sùp-trùp* 'growing thickly with overhanging branches'.

Repetitive compounds (Rep.C.)

The entire simple word-form is repeated to form a compound.

e.g. (simple monosyllable) *ŋo:v-ŋo:v* 'to make sounds of pleading and protest', *tù:t-tù:t* 'to pop, toot'
(extended monosyllable) *khvɤ̀:c-khvɤ̀:c* 'to limp, hobble', *plaom-plaom* 'to lick the lips', *pdaom-pdaom* 'to bow and scrape', *mhɔ:p-mhɔ:p* 'to have a gaping mouth', *rəyù:t-rəyù:t* 'to do slowly with great effort'
(restricted disyllable) *rùəŋvɤ̀:l-rùəŋvɤ̀:l* 'to be not close together, not often', *ʔɔntrɤ̀:t-ʔɔntrɤ̀:t* 'to step on tiptoe, walk stealthily'

Some three-syllabled words belong to this section: *mɤ̀:k-mɤ̀:k-mɤ̀:k* 'to be slow-moving, sluggish', *phlɤ̀:k-phlɤ̀:k-phlɤ̀:k* (id.), *rəŋɤ̀:k-rəŋɤ̀:k-rəŋɤ̀:k* (id.), *tù:c-tù:c-tù:c* 'very small' (and plural); *ʔɤy-ʔɤy-ʔɤy* 'whatever things, any things'. These forms have been observed in colloquial speech.

---

[1] See J. M. Jacob, 'Some features of Khmer versification', in *In Memory of J. R. Firth*, London, 1966, pp. 227–241.

46.2. *Grammatical analysis of reduplicative compounds*

1. *Categories of speech*

Reduplicatives belong chiefly to the category of verb and especially of attributive verb. There is, however, a small number of nouns in each of the four sections. Some examples of nouns and verbs in each section are given below.

A.C. Nouns. *səmlɔː-səmlok* (name of a dish made by the *slɔː-slok* method of cooking) 'a stew, soup', *lop-lae* 'screen' (for door), *peːŋ-pɔh* 'tomato', *cak-can* (name of a kind of cake), *bʋŋ-buːə* 'ponds', *bɔŋ-bɔt* 'spirit' (animist), *ʔəmpùl-ʔəmpèːk* 'glow-worm'.

Verbs. *kɔŋcèəh-kɔŋcìːəy* 'to scatter objects disrespectfully', *khvɔl-khvaːy* 'to be busy, to be in a whirl of activity', *cùːəs-cùl* 'to patch up, to mend', *tùəntěŋ-tùəntùːt* 'to speak redundantly', *tèək-tùn* 'to be interlaced', *bɔŋcaəc-bɔŋcaə* 'to flatter immoderately, to coax', *prəyát(n)-prəyaeŋ* 'to pay great attention', *phdeːk-phdʋl* 'to stick loyally to one's friends', *skùh-skìːəy* 'open and white' (of flower).

C.C. Nouns. *keːŋ-kɔːŋ* (name of a legendary snake), *krəlìːŋ-krəlòːŋ* (name of a variety of bird) Gracupeia nigricollis, *chùː-chìː* (name of a culinary dish), *thùən-thìːən* (Sanskrit words) 'belongings', *ʔəŋkreːm-ʔəŋkrɔːm* (name of a creeper).

Verbs. *kdoŋ-kdaŋ* 'to make a repeated clanging sound', *kʔeːŋ-kʔɔːŋ* 'to be impudent', *ŋae-ŋɔː* 'to be indecisive', *tətìːm-tətìːəm* 'to be confused, not clear', *pəplʋk-pəplɔk* 'to have the sound of soft waves lapping', *phoːŋ-phaːŋ* 'to have the sound of kicking, breaking, to crash, bang, thud', *phlìː-phlʋ̀ː* 'to be very stupid'.

Rh.C. Nouns. *kɔntae-rae* (name of a country dance), *kɔndiə-tiə* (name of an extinct animal), *kaː(r)-ŋìːə* (Sanskrit words) 'duties', *caːŋ-(h)vaːŋ* 'director, boss', *caːn-kbaːn* 'crockery', *caeŋ-vaeŋ* (name of a grass), *chmaː-baː* 'large owl', *trəlùŋ-tùŋ* (name of a tree whose fruit is used to give a sour flavour in cooking).

Verbs. *chao-lao* 'to make a hubbub', *tʋŋ-rʋŋ* 'to compel by force', *pěŋ-lěŋ* 'to do with might and main', *rəkhaːk-rəyìːək* 'to be in tatters', *sùːk-krəlùːk* 'to be in a muddle', *slɔːt-bɔːt* 'to be affable', *ʔiən-priən* 'to be bashful'.

Rep.C. Nouns. The number of nouns and verbs in this section is unlimited since the formation of repetitive nouns is a live process, applicable to any noun or verb, though perhaps more commonly applied to simple words. *pros-pros* 'men in general', *srʋy-srʋy* 'women in general', *taː-taː* 'old men in general'.

Verbs. *krak-krak* 'to bubble', *krùːəp-krùːəp* 'to crunch', *taək-taək* 'to wriggle', *tùk-tùk* 'to put away' (numerous objects), *ploŋ-ploŋ* 'to be seen intermittently, to flicker', *rəpaoy-rəpaoy* 'to float', *vèːŋ-vèːŋ* 'to be long (and numerous), very long'.

2. *Free and bound forms*

Reduplicative compounds may be composed of either (i) two free forms or (ii) one free and one bound form or (iii) two bound forms.

(i) Here two free forms which have certain features of initial consonant or consonantal sequence, vowel or final consonant in common are used together to form a compound. Such compounds as these could be reduplicative merely by chance, but their high frequency rate seems to justify their inclusion in the category of reduplicative compound.[1]

e.g. A.C. *khcat-khca:y* (to be scattered, broken up/to be diffused)[2] 'to be scattered, sprinkled all over', *cat-caeŋ* (to send/to explain) 'to organize, administer', *bɔŋchr̆t-bɔŋchiəŋ* (to cause to pass close by, to brush past/to cause to deviate slightly) 'to make a remark which one intends to be overheard by someone not addressed directly', *rəvì:əs-rəvèy* (to hurry/to turn) 'to bustle about', *rəlr̆:p-rəlùəŋ* (to be damp/to be shining and wet, to glisten) 'to be shining and wet', *phsah-phsa:* (to heal/to be in anguish) 'to make up a quarrel', *prì:ət-prɔ̀:ŋ* (to appear in flashes/to radiate light) 'to flash here and there'.

C.C. *rùt-rùət* (to be tight/to grasp) 'to be drawn tightly round', *rəhaek-rəhaok* (to be torn/to have holes, to be full of holes) 'to be thoroughly tattered', *srəmo:m-srəma:m* (to be hairy/to have a spreading beard or whiskers) 'to be untidily hairy'.

Rh.C. *kɔmsɔt-tù:rəkùət* (to be poor/to be destitute) 'to be wretched', *ka:(r)-ŋì:ə* (work/duty) 'duties', *chʔaəm-khpr̆:m* (to be disdainful/to be disgusted) 'to despise', *sʔa:t-ba:t* (to be clean/soles of feet) 'to be spick and span'.

(ii) It is felt that strictly speaking only this type of reduplicative compound can be said to be genuinely reduplicative. In these instances one can point to the simple partner-word and show that some element or elements in it have been reduplicated to form the compound.

e.g. A.C. *bɔŋʔae-bɔŋʔɔŋ* (—/to delay) 'to dilly-dally', *rəlɔ̀ət-rəlɔ̀:c* (to be split, cut as to the skin or flesh/—) 'to be split, cut in several places', *sɔmcaə-sɔmcay* (—/to save) 'to hoard secretly'.

C.C. *kmeːŋ-kma:ŋ* (young/—) 'small children', *prəlùəŋ-prəlèəŋ* (spirit/—) 'spirit' (one's own; used in a limited number of expressions), *rùmcì:-rùmcì:ə* (—/to pretend) 'to tease, to pretend', *lùmbe:k-lùmba:k* (—/to be difficult) 'to be very difficult'.

Rh.C. *crəlaəs-baəs* (to be rude/—) 'to be vulgar, lawless', *mè:n-tè:n* (to be true/—) 'to be true', *bu:əŋ-su:əŋ* (to pray/—) 'to implore, to beg and pray'.

Rep.C. *pros-pros* (man) 'men in general', *phse:ŋ-phse:ŋ* (to be different) 'to be various, to be different (and numerous)', *phtɔ̀əp-phtɔ̀əp* (to be near together) 'to be very near together'.

(iii) Compounds of which both components are bound forms have probably been formed long ago on the same principles as either (i) or (ii). The simple words have now become obsolete.

e.g. A.C. *rəpec-rəpr̆y* 'to be of slight consequence, unimportant (and plural)', *rəvr̆:-rəvì:əy* 'to be unable to concentrate, unable to speak coherently, incoherent'.

C.C. *səsre:k-səsra:k* 'to slop (water)', *rʔeh-rʔoh* 'to be diffident', *ve:v-va:v* 'to rattle'.

Rh.C. *so:m-məmo:m* 'to grow in great profusion', *saəy-məmaəŋ* 'to be bewildered on waking', *srəlaŋ-kaŋ* 'to swoon'.

---

[1] Alternatively they might be classified as compounds by the methods set out in Lesson 48.
[2] Meanings of the components are given in parentheses, separated by a sloping line.

Rep.C. Many repetitive compounds fit into this group, since the component occurs only in the repetitive compound and is therefore to be regarded as a bound form. Phonaesthetic words are particularly common in this group. e.g. *krop-krop* 'to champ, nibble', *krùːt-krùːt* 'to give or have the sound of dragging', *preh-preh* 'to crackle', *sỳːk-sỳːk* 'to be sluggish, inert'.

Sometimes a free form or another bound form may be directly compared with a bound form in a reduplicative compound in respect of both lexical meaning and phonological structure. Examples of such forms thus related to components of reduplicative compounds are:—

vùəl 'to turn, revolve' (cf. *krəvɔl-krəvaːy* 'to be disturbed, troubled'. *krəvɔl* is a prefixed form, with change of register, of *vùəl*).

tron, bound form occurring in *tron-tron*, 'to shiver with fear or cold'. (cf. *son-tron* 'to retreat in fear').

3. *Affixation in reduplicative compounds*

Some prefixed and infixed forms of reduplicative compounds occur.

e.g. *leh-lɔh* 'to be frivolous', *pleh-plɔh* 'to tease', *pəpleh-pəplɔh* 'to be constantly teasing (naughtily)'.

　　doh-daːl 'to grow rapidly', *bɔndoh-bɔndaːl* 'to bring up or look after someone else's child'.

　　dɔh-day 'to avoid a situation, try to get out of a situation', *bɔndɔh-bɔnday* 'to give good excuse'.

46.3. *Analysis of reduplicative compounds from a lexical point of view*

1. *Nouns*

Nouns in the alliterative, chiming and rhyming sections are, as may be seen from the examples given on the previous pages, the names of plants, animals, dances, culinary dishes and other objects. A striking contrast is seen in the meanings of nouns in the repetitive section; these are general plurals of the singular forms.

2. *Verbs*

A very large number of verbs in all sections are phonaesthetic. Those which represent sounds are found chiefly in the chiming and repetitive sections (e.g. *tɔːŋ-taːŋ* 'to clatter down', *tətùː(r)-tətɔ̀ə(r)* 'to echo', *prèc-prèc* 'drip-drip'), while in the rhyming section there is a high proportion of words describing manner, distribution of objects, appearance (e.g. *chao-lao* 'to be in disorder', *sùp-trùp* 'to grow thickly and with overhanging branches'). The alliterative section has the greatest number of words which do not seem to be phonaesthemes (e.g. *prɔŋ-priəp* 'to prepare', *praə-prah* 'to use').

3. *Comparison of meanings with related words*

When reduplicative compounds are composed of either a free form and a bound form or two free forms[1] it is interesting to compare the meanings of

---

[1] The other possible combination, that of two bound forms (see 2 (iii) in 46.2 above), does not concern us here.

the free forms with the meanings of the compounds which are based on them. The meaning of the compound in comparison with that of the simple word is generally speaking one of the following:—

(i) Plural, suggesting repetition, intensified.

e.g. A.C. *bɔmphlec-bɔmphlaːɲ* (—/to destroy) 'to destroy utterly'. C.C. *phsaːr-phsao* (market/—) 'all kinds of markets', *rəheːm-rəhaːm* (—/overflowing, abundant) 'to be excessive (especially of tears)'. Rep.C. *kmeːɲ-kmeːɲ* (young) 'children in general', *kraːs-kraːs* (thick) 'thick and numerous'.

Sometimes both a plural (or repetitive) and an intensified meaning occur. e.g. *khpùəs* 'high', *khpùəs-khpùəs* 1. 'high and numerous', 2. 'very high'. The context shows which meaning is intended. e.g. *prəsaːt mùːəy khpùes-khpùəs* 'a very high temple' but *daəm-chɤ̀ː khpùəs-khpùəs* 'high trees'.

(ii) Restricted, specific, metaphorical, slightly different from the simple word.

e.g. A.C. *pɤːt-paoŋ* (—/inflated) 'pretentious'. Rh.C. *rùuŋ-pɤŋ* (firm/—) 'making every effort, with all one's might'. Rep.C. *mùːəy-mùːəy* (one) 'one at a time, slowly', *rùːəy-rùːəy* (close together) 'often'.

Compounds composed of two free forms fit into this group. e.g. *rəhaek-rəhaoy* (to be torn, pierced) 'to be tattered, worn'.

(iii) The same (lexically) as for the simple word. The difference is stylistic. The reduplicative is the livelier, more interesting word and is more suitable for narrative, written or spoken, or for poetry.

e.g. Rh.C. *sräc-bac* (finished/—) 'finished'. Rep.C. *lɔːp-lɔːp* (to proceed stealthily) 'to proceed stealthily'.

Exercise 58 A

(1) **rùːəŋ mèːmaːy mnɛ̀ək**

(2) 'khɲom mìːən koːn krəmom mnɛ̀ək kè: dɔndɤŋ haəy. kɔmnɔt coːl ròːŋ nɤ̀u thɲay kraoy. (3) ʔɤyloːvꞁnìh kùɨt phɲaə sɔmbot(r) tɤ̀u prap bɔːŋ-pʔoːn cùɨt chɲaːy ʔaoy mɔ̀ːk sì: kaːˑ(r)' haəy kɔ̀ət kɔː phɲaə sɔmbot(r) tɤ̀u krùp bɔːŋ-pʔoːn tɛ̀əŋ-ʔos. (4) nɛ̀ək nɤ̀u knoŋ phtɛ̀əh tɛ̀əŋ-ʔos knìːə tɤ̀u tèŋ rùssɤy yòːk mɔ̀ːk thvɤ̀ː ròːŋ. (5) lùh dɔl prùɨk thɲay coːl ròːŋ mìːən phɲiəv ʔɔɲcɤ̀ːɲ mɔ̀ːk cìːə craən. mìːən phlèːŋ lèːŋ lùɨː soːˑ(r) trəhùɨŋ. (6) khlah nìyìːəy knìːə lèːŋ sɔpbaːy. (7) khlah suːə(r) thaː, 'pùː nɤ̀u srok naːʔ' kè: chlaəy thaː, 'khɲom nɤ̀u srok kɔmpùəŋ-chnaŋ.' (8) 'mìːŋ mùɨm ʔɔɲcɤ̀ːɲ-mɔ̀ːk tèːʔ' 'mɔ̀ːk dae(r)' 'pùː nɤ̀u srok nùh skɔ̀əl pùː hìːən tèːʔ' 'skɔ̀əl' (9) 'kɔ̀ət sok(h)-sɔpbaːy tèːʔ' 'baːt, kɔ̀ət sok(h)-sɔpbaːy tèːˑ'. (10) nɤ̀u kɔnlaeŋ coŋphɤ̀u, nɛ̀ək khlah chaː sac crùːk lùɨː cheːv-chaːv; khlah han bɔnlae; khlah ceɲcram sac crùːk lùɨː poːk-paːk-poːk-paːk. (11) nìːəŋ mcas-phtɛ̀əh dae(r) coh dae(r) laəŋ baek ɲɤ̀ːs hoːˑ(r) səsrak. (12) bɔntec mìːən phɲiəv cɔmnuːən dɔp-pram nɛ̀ək; mìːən kmeːŋ toːc-toːc bɤy buːən nɛ̀ək. (13) phɲiəv nùh troːv cìːə bɔːŋ bɔŋkaət kɔ̀ət bɤy nɛ̀ək, pros mnɛ̀ək, srɤy pìːˑ(r) nɛ̀ək nùŋ bɔːŋ-pʔoːn cìːˑ-doːn mùːəy khlah phoːŋ. (14) kaːˑl-naː mɔ̀ːk dɔl phtɛ̀əh, nìːəŋ mcas phtɛ̀əh kɔː stùh tɤ̀u cùmrìːəp suːə(r) lɤ̀ːk day sompɛ̀əh haəy suːə(r) thaː 'bɔːŋ sok(h)-sɔpbaːy tèːʔ' kè: chlaəy thaː 'sok(h)-sɔpbaːy tèːˑ'. (15) haəy kɔː hau phɲiəv ʔaoy laəŋ tɤ̀u lɤ̀ː phtɛ̀əh nìyìːəy knìːə thaː 'mənùs(s) pros dael kè: dɔndɤŋ koːn ʔaeŋ nɤ̀u srok naːʔ ròːk-sìː thvɤ̀ː ʔɤyʔ' nìːəŋ nùh thaː 'nɤ̀u srok kɔmpùəŋ chnaɲt ròːk-sìː thvɤ̀ː cùmnùːəɲ'. (16) nìːəŋ mcas-phtɛ̀əh nìyìːəy thaː 'pùː laːŋ mĕc kɔ̀ə.

193

mùm ʔɔɲcɤ̀ːɲ-mɔ̀ːkʔ prəhael sombot(r) tɤu mùm dɔl rùːʔ' haəy kɔ̀ət ɲì:ək tɤu yɔ̀:k nùm pì:(r) bɤy mɔ̀:k ʔaoy kmù:əy kɔ̀ət haəy thaː 'kmù:əy ɲam tɤu! prəhael-cì:ə mùm skɔ̀əl mì:ɲ tèː, mɤ̀:l tɤuʔ'.

(2) *thɲay kraoy*. *kraoy*, 'after, behind, next'. Here, not 'the next day', a meaning which these words do often have, but 'a day in the near future'.

co:l rò:ɲ, i.e. enter the specially constructed marriage-room.

cùt chɲa:y. Note the use of opposites together, with no 'and'. See Lesson 47.

(3) *sì: ka:(r)*. *ka:(r)* n. 'work', e.g. *thvɤ̀: ka:(r)* 'to work', *kec(c) ka:(r)* 'procedure'; *ka:(r)* v. 'to marry'; *sì: ka:(r)* (to eat the wedding) 'to attend the wedding'.

krùp bɔ:ɲ-pʔo:n tèəɲ-ʔɔs. Two words, *krùp* and *tèəɲ-ʔɔs*, each of which may be translated as 'all'. 'all . . . . without exception'.

(4) *nèək*, the agent-former. See Lesson 48. *nèək . . . . knì:ə* **N** . As in

nvAaa

Exercise 57, (13) a limited sentence form, **V A a a**, is used attributively with a noun to form a **N**.

(5) *dɔl* may here be construed as a main verb. **m V**

vN

nN

nV

vn

(10) Note the liveliness achieved by the use of reduplicatives, *che:v-cha:v, po:k-pa:k-po:k-pa:k*, and in (11) *daə(r) coh daə(r) laəɲ* and in (12) *to:c-to:c*.

(12) *bɔntec*, a. 'soon, a little later'. Often *bɔntec tìət* is used.

(13) *bɔ:ɲ-pʔo:n cì:-do:n mù:əy*. **N** . *mù:əy* with no numeral coefficient is

nnx

what one would expect here. There is no counting of grandmothers; *mù:əy* = 'one and the same'.

(15) *laəɲ tɤu lɤ̀: phtèəh*. Not only does one normally *laəɲ phtèəh* 'climb up to the house' rather than *co:l phtèəh* 'enter the house'; one may even 'climb up on to the house' as here 'come up into.'

(16) Prominence is given to *pù: la:ɲ*, in that it is placed first before the marker, *mëc*. cf. Exercise 55, (2) where the more vivid word order is used.

prəhael and *prəhael-cì:ə* both used as markers.

Exercise 58 B

(Elderly person to young) Everyone seems busy in your house today!

Yes, tomorrow is my elder sister's wedding.

Are many guests coming?

Twelve.

Are they coming from far away?

My grandfather and grandmother come from Battambang and my mother's older brother comes from far away in Kratie.

Do you know all the relatives who are coming?

I know both my grandparents and all my uncles and aunts but there are two cousins whom I don't know.

Lesson 47

Reduplication in Syntax

47.1. *Simple reduplication*

The reduplication may consist of the straightforward repetition of a word or sequence of words once or twice.

1. Repetition of a word. Potentially a repeated intonation tune is in operation here.

e.g. *chùp* (\) *chùp* (\)*!* Stop!

   baːl (ˌ) *baːl* (ˌ). Yes (quite right, carry on).

   pìːm (ˌ)-*pɤ̀ːm* (.) *pìːm* (ˌ)-*pɤ̀ːm* (.) *pìːm* (ˌ)-*pɤ̀ːm* (.) groping and creeping about.[1]

Semantically the effect of the repetition is to intensify the meaning of the single word.

2. Repetition of a sequence of words.

e.g. *mùːəy bɔ̀l mùːəy bɔ̀l mìːən poñmaːn tuːə?* How many syllables has each verse (lit. 'one verse one verse has how many syllables?').

   dak daoy laek daoy laek. Mix them up for variety (lit. 'put according to difference according to difference').

47.2. *Interpolated reduplication*

1. Interpolation of a single word. This occurs with the interpolation of the word *ʔɤy/ʔɤːy* or *kɔː*.

e.g. *kdau ʔɤy kdau!* Isn't it hot! *craən ʔɤːy craən!* What a lot!

   lʔɔː kɔː lʔɔː! Isn't it beautiful! *slɔːt kɔː slɔːt!* How very kind!

The unusual words, *ʔuːəti̤ːnùːə*, 'horrible' and *sùːpətrùː*, 'big and roomy', alternative form of *sùː-trùː*, might be regarded as a syntactical form of rhyming reduplication with an interpolated syllable or prefix; other instances of interpolated *tìː* or *pə* are lacking however.

2. Interpolation of a word or sequence of words. A word or sequence is repeated in positions 2 and 4 of a series; sequences in positions 1 and 3 are nearly alike.

e.g. *pɔ̀ə(rŋ) svaːy daoy laek, phlae svaːy daoy laek.* The colour mango (mauve) and the fruit mango are different.

   bɔ̀l nùh mìːən pram-bɤy tuːə kɔː-mìːən, pram-buːən tuːə kɔː-mìːən. Some of these verses have eight syllables and some nine (lit. these verses have eight syllables possible, nine syllables possible).

47.3. *Interpolated reduplication with opposites*

1. Interpolation of words. This occurs with words of opposite meanings such as *coh* with *laəŋ*, *mùk(h)* with *kraoy*, etc. The reduplicated word may occur in positions 1 and 3 of a sequence of four words.

---

[1] The repeated intonation tune with potential pause in the middle helps to catalyse these sequences of syllables as 2 (or 3) words and not repetitive compounds.

e.g. *tr̃u vèɲ tr̃u mɔ̀ːk* to and fro (go back go come).

tìːəs tr̃u tìːəs mɔ̀ːk to turn to and fro.

pah mùk(h) pah kraoy to mend, patch in front and behind.

stùh coh stùh laəɲ to leap up and down.

lah coh lah laəɲ to scurry up and down.

pìː nìh pìː nùh hither and thither.

str̃ː rùəs str̃ː slap ⎫ at death's door (on the point of living, on the
prəvaː slap prəvaː rùəs ⎭ point of dying).

mdɔːŋ haəy mdɔːŋ tìət once again (once already, once more).

duːəs nìːəy duːəs ʔaːɾy ⎫ to pick and choose (to skim this side, skim that
kìəs nìːəy kìəs ʔaːɾy ⎭ side, to scrape this side, etc.

Literary examples (with words which are not true opposites):—

pìːən traok pìːən traŋ ⎫
pìːən traok pìːən prèy ⎭ to act thoughtlessly, careless of right and wrong
(literally, 'to climb on mounds of earth, to climb on *traŋ*' (alliterative
syllable) and 'to climb on mountains, to climb in the forest').

khos phloːv khos kùənlɔ̀ːŋ having lost the way (wrong as to the way,
wrong as to the place).

Sometimes an interpolated reduplication of words or sequences of words
with opposites has the reduplicated word in positions 2 and 4:—

thom kdɤy toːc kdɤy both big and little (big thing little thing).

nìh kɔː-daoy nùh kɔː-daoy This on the one hand and that on the other
hand.

2. Interpolation of sequences of words. In Cambodian repetition is sought
rather than avoided. Successive clauses with similar constructions and only
one or two word-changes are a feature of the language.

e.g. *khlah kèː thv̀ːː nìh, khlah kèː thv̀ːː nùh.* Some do one thing, some another.

cɔŋ dɤŋ nèək naː chnèəh, nèək naː caɲ. I want to know who won (lit.
'I want to know who won, who lost').

Opposites are also used together without reduplication and without a
linking word. Similar combinations have been met already: *ʔoːpùk-mdaːy,*
parents, *cìː-doːn-cìː-taː,* grandparents.

e.g. *pros srɤy,* male and female; *khos troːv,* right and wrong; *coh laəŋ,* up and
down; *coːl cèɲ,* in and out; *sëckdɤy kùːə(r) pụm kùːə(r),* anything polite
or impolite.

Exercise 59 A

(1) mìːək̀(h)-boːcìːə vìsaːk̀(h)-boːcìːə

(2) thŋay-ʔaːtùt(y) mphèy khae-ʔosəphìːə, krùp vɔ̀ət(t) tèəŋ-ʔos knoŋ srok-
khmae(r), pèːl maoŋ buːən rəsiəl, kèː rìəp-com phkaː nùɱ tùɾk phè:səcèə
phse:ŋ-phse:ŋ, mìːən tùɾk-tae cìːə daəm, bɔmroŋ nùɱ prəkèːm lòːk. (3) kèː kùəh
rəkèəŋ prəcụm lòːk-sɔ̀ŋ(k̀h) tèəŋ-ʔos knoŋ vɔ̀ət(t) prəkèːm tùɾk phè:səcèə lòːk
chan. (4) lùh maoŋ pram-bɤy haəy, kèː prəcụm pùːək ʔobaːsɔ̀k ʔobaːsekaː soːt(r)
thɔ̀ə(rm) thvaːy bɔŋkùm, rùːəc haəy kèː nìmùən(t) lòːk-sɔ̀ŋ(k̀h) ʔaoy coːl knoŋ
vìhìːə(r) haəy soːt(r) thɔ̀ə(rm). (5) vɔ̀ət(t) khlah mìːən cak maːsìːn-pùəŋrìːk-
sɔmleːŋ ʔaoy lùː chŋaːy. (6) vɔ̀ət(t) khlah kmìːən maːsìːn-criəŋ pùəŋrìːk tèː.
(7) lùh lòːk soːt(r) thɔ̀ə(rm) rùːəc haəy kèː nìmùən(t) lòːk mùːəy ʔɔŋ(k̀) rùː pìː(r)

ʔɔŋ(k̊) somdaeŋ thə̀ə(rm) tèːsnaː. (8) cùːən-kaːl kè: tèːsna: pìː(r) dɔːŋ, taːm coːl cɤt(t). (9) lùh tèːsna: cɔp haəy kè: thvɤ̀ː bɔ̀t̊ phseːŋ-phseːŋ ʔɔmpì: prè̀əh-ʔɔŋ(k̊) prəsoːt(e) rùː: cëɲ buːəs rùː: p̪arenìp̊(v)ìːən. (10) rəbiəp thvɤ̀ː boɲ(y) mìːək(h)-boːcìːə nùɲ vìsaːk(h)-boːcìːə, doːc khɲom baːn nìyìːəy mɔ̀ːk nìh, kè: thvɤ̀ː tae knoŋ thŋay dɔp-pram kaət khae-mìːək̊(h) nùɲ khae-vìsaːk(h). (11) baə thvɤ̀ː khae-mìːək̊(h) hau tha: mìːək̊(h)-boːcìːə. baə thvɤ̀ː khae-vìsaːk(h) hau tha: vìsaːk(h)-boːcìːə. (12) boɲ(y) nìh kè: thvɤ̀ː rùmlùk dɔl pìːək̊(y) dael prè̀əh-ʔɔŋ(k̊) baːn prap ʔaːnɔn(t̊) tha: 'nèː, ʔaːnɔn(t̊)! tə̪thaːk̊ùət̊ nɤu tae buːən khae tè: nùɲ coːl nìp̊(v)ìːən haəy.' prè̀əh pùt̊t̪həɗɤyka: nìh baːn prap ʔaːnɔn(t̊) knoŋ thŋay dɔp-pram kaət khae-mìːək̊(h). (13) lùh dɔl thŋay dɔp-pram kaət khae-vìsaːk(h) prè̀əh-ʔɔŋ(k̊) p̪arenìp̊(v)ìːən. (14) ʔobaːsɔk ʔobaːseka: mìːən sĕckdɤy saok-sdaːy srənoh prè̀əh-ʔɔŋ(k̊) nas baːn-cìːə thvɤ̀ː boɲ(y) nìh rìəŋ-mɔ̀ːk taŋ-pìː yù̀ː(r) haəy rəhoːt-mɔ̀ːk-dɔl sɔp̊(v) thŋay nìh. (15) kè: thvɤ̀ː bɔ̀t̊ phseːŋ-phseːŋ doːc baːn nìyìːəy mɔ̀ːk khaːŋ lɤ̀: nìh ʔɔs mù̀əy yùp. cùːən-kaːl kè: thvɤ̀ː tae pìː(r) bɤy maoŋ tèː. (16) lùh prùk laəŋ kè: nìmù̀ən(t̊) lòːk chan bəbɔː(r), thŋay trɔŋ chan baːy. (17) ʔɔs kec(c) boɲ(y) mìːək̊(h)-boːcìːə nùɲ vìsaːk(h)-boːcìːə tae poññeh.

(1) The Indian compounds, with components in the opposite order from Cambodian, are retained, even though *mìːək̊(h)*, *vìsaːk(h)* and *boːcìːə* are current as separate words in Cambodian. Only in a very formal context, however, would the inherent vowels which have been dropped in *mìːək̊(h)* and *vìsaːk(h)* be heard, e.g. *mìːəkhə̪əboːcìːə* or *mìːəkhəboːcìːə*. In the recording of this passage the speaker aspirated the two final velar consonants but uttered no vowel-sound.

(5)–(6) There is some confusion in the text here, due to the writer's unfamiliarity with Western machines. *cak* 'to pierce' is currently used in Cambodia to mean 'to put the needle on a record' but the writer uses it in (5) to mean 'connect up, use (a microphone)'. In (6) he wishes to refer again to microphones but uses the word, *maːsìːn-criəy*, which really means 'gramophone'.

(9) Translate as if *prè̀əh-ʔɔŋ(k̊)* *(kèː)* *prəsoːt(e)*. *cëɲ buːəs* 'come out from being a novice'.

(10) *mɔ̀ːk nìh*, 'up to here, up to now'.

(12) Sentence form III. *dɔl* towards (of feelings).

nɤu tae buːən khae tèː. Note *tèː* in affirmative sentence, preceded as often, by *tae*. The same sequence occurs in (15).

(14) *yù̀ː(r)* catalysed as an *ad hoc* noun by use with *pìː*.

(15) *ʔɔs*. For this use of this form see Lesson 36.

(17) Here *ʔɔs* may be taken as the main verb of the sentence. 'It is the whole of the procedure . . . . just like this' (i.e. 'as I have said'). Alternatively one might take *ʔɔs* as the **pre n.p.**, as in (15) and regard *poññeh* as being verbalized in this sentence. A denial of the statement might be '*mù̀n-mèːn tae poññeh tèː*'.

Exercise 59 B

What is the festival which is being held today?
It is called the *mìːək̊(h)-boːcìːə*.
What does it commemorate?
It commemorates the Buddha's entry into Nirvana.
What do people do?

They invite the clergy to recite prayers and preach during the whole of one night and in the morning they offer food to the monks. They celebrate this festival to mourn the Buddha.

Does this festival take place in all the monasteries in Cambodia tonight? Yes, in every one.

LESSON 48

COMPOUND WORDS

48.1. *Definition of compound words*

Words consisting of two simple word-forms (the full disyllables of Lesson 4) may be foreign loanwords which either happen to fit or have been naturalized to fit the Cambodian word-structure, e.g.

cì:vùt life (Skt. and Pali jīvita)   *kausù:* rubber (French caoutchouc)
ʔa:ha:(r) food (Skt. and Pali āhāra)   *sa:bù:* soap (Portuguese sabão)
nèaŋkɔ́əl plough (Pali naṅgala)
sa:la: hall (Skt. and Pali sālā)
kò:rùp̀ to respect (Skt. gaurava)

Native disyllables may fall into one of the following categories:—

1. Neither word-form conveys lexical meaning to the whole word and there is no reduplication in the structure of the two syllables. e.g. *ka:roŋ* 'a bag'. Such words may be loanwords which have not been recognized as such or may be compounds of which both components have fallen out of use.

2. One word-form is current as a free form while the other is not. There is no reduplication. e.g. *sëckdɤy* 'matter', *kdɤy* 'thing, item'. Such words are probably old compound formations of which one component has fallen out of use.

3. The components are reduplicative.[1] In this case either one or both or neither of them may be current as a free form. e.g. *bɤŋ-bu:ə* 'numerous little lakes', *bɤŋ* 'lake' (*bu:ə* does not occur), *rəpeh-rəpɔh* 'small and numerous' (neither form occurs separately). Such words are regarded as compounds in that each component contributes by its form to the meaning of the whole word.

In this lesson we are chiefly concerned with yet another type of word-sequence which may be regarded as a compound and which has as far as possible been so treated in this book. In this type of compound both components are in current use as words and there is no reduplication. e.g. *lò:k-srɤy* 'Mrs., madam'. Such compounds are composed in accordance with one of the patterns already met in the make-up of constructs. Thus the compound noun may be **n** + **n**, the second noun denoting possession as in *rò:ŋ-kon* (building of film) 'cinema'; or being in apposition as in *lò:k-krù:* (Mr. teacher) 'teacher'. A compound verb may be **v** + **v** expressing purpose, as in *rò:k-sì:* (to seek to eat) 'to earn a living' or expressing two simultaneous actions as in *lùək-do:(r)* (to sell to barter) 'to do business'. Sequences such as these might well have been left in the transcription as two words but, since formal criteria can be found to catalyse many of them as compounds, these

---

[1] See Lesson 46.

have been hyphenated and entered in the vocabulary as one word, thereby reducing the number of entries required. Care has been taken not to mark sequences of words as compounds merely because of the frequency of their occurrence together or because of their English translation as one word. It is rather the case that some word-sequences, which might justifiably[1] have been hyphenated, have been left unmarked, e.g. the 'language' sequences, *phìːəsaː baːraŋ*, *phìːəsaː khmae(r)*, etc. The chief formal criteria which have been used are set out below as each kind of compound is discussed.

48.2. *Compound nouns* (n + n) (n + v)

The framework of the noun construct is used to catalyse the compound noun. A compound noun may occur in place of **n** in a noun construct, e.g. *koːn-pros lòːk pìː(r) nèək nùh*, 'those two sons of yours'. The compound noun is characterized by the following special feature in this usage that the two components may not be separated by the occurrence of a numeral construct, as may a succession of two nouns or of noun with attributive verb,

e.g. *siəvphɤ́u khɲom mùːəy* a book of mine (**nnx**)

or   ,,   *mùːəy khɲom*   ,,   ,,   (**nxn**)

   ʔaːv sɔː mùːəy   a white shirt   (**nvx**)

or *ʔaːv mùːəy sɔː*   ,,   ,,   (**nxv**)

Contrast *lòːk-krùː mnèək* a teacher
       rətèh-phlɤ́ːŋ mùːəy train

lòːk mnèək krùː or *rətèh mùːəy phlɤ́ːŋ* are not possible.

Examples

(**n + n**) *nèək-srɤy* madam, Mrs., *ʔoːpùk-mdaːy* parents, *khao-ʔaːv* suit, *sbaek-cɤ̀ːŋ* (skin of foot) shoe.

(**n + v**) *yùən(t)-hɔh* (machine fly) aeroplane, *sat(v)-haə(r)* (animal fly) bird, *daəm-chɤ̀ː* (trunk made of wood) tree, *lòːk-thom* important person.

By the use of this criterion to catalyse the compound noun, certain abstract expressions such as *sĕckdɤy sok(h)*, 'happiness', which are translated into English by a noun and which one feels 'should' be compounds are not classed as compounds, because they cannot be counted. Such expressions must be regarded as sequences of words in a noun construct. There is no doubt, however, that the development of the Cambodian language in respect of abstract expressions is slighter than that of Western languages and it may therefore be in fact a reasonable point at which to halt the compound noun.

Further characteristics of the compound noun are:—

(i) that the two components may, in an initiating context, have only one stress, e.g. *daəm-'tnaot*, *khao-'ʔaːv*, as contrasted with *'koːn 'lòːk*, *'ʔaːv 'khɲom*.

---

[1] i.e. by the use of the criteria set out below or by the use of further criteria which may be found.

(ii) that a second reference includes both components in contrast to a second reference to one of two nouns.

e.g. *rətèh-phlɤ̀ːŋ naː tɤ̀u bat-dɔmbɔːŋ? baːl, rətèh-phlɤ̀ːŋ nìh tɤ̀u bat-dɔmbɔːŋ.*
    Which train goes to Battambang? This train goes to Battambang.
    kaːsaet thmɤy nɤ̀u ʔae naː? khɲom mùn dɤŋ kaːsaet nɤ̀u ʔae naː tèː.
    Where is the new newspaper, Mr. —? I don't know where it is. (i.e.
    kaːsaet thmɤy is not repeated.)

48.3. *Compound verbs* (v + v)

The framework of the verb construct is used to catalyse compound verbs. A succession of two verbs in a Cambodian sentence may be (i) an initiating verb with a following verb used in a verb construct, e.g. *khɲom cɔŋ səseː(r) sɔmbot(r).* 'I want to write a letter.' (ii) a minor verb following a main verb in a verb construct, e.g. *khɲom phɲaə(r) tɤ̀u haəy.* 'I've sent it off already.' (iii) Two major verb constructs, in which both verbs receive stress, e.g. *vìːə 'rùət 'dëɲ cao(r).* 'He ran to chase the thief.'

The characteristics of the compound verb are:—

(i) The first component is not an initiating verb.

(ii) The second component is not a minor verb.

(iii) In first reference the two components do not necessarily both have stress.

(iv) In contrast to the utterance of a sequence of major verbs, the components may not be phrased separately.

(v) No other word may intervene between the two components, as is possible with two major verbs, e.g. *vìːə rùət dëɲ cao(r).* 'He ran to chase the thief.' One might equally say, *vìːə rùət tɤ̀u dëɲ cao(r).* 'He ran off to chase the thief.' Contrast *vìːə daə(r)-lèːŋ.* 'He was going for a walk.' There is no possibility of *vìːə daə(r) tɤ̀u lèːŋ.* 'He went off for a walk.' Only *vìːə daə(r)-lèːŋ tɤ̀u* might be possible.

(vi) A second reference includes both components, e.g. *daə(r)-lèːŋ rùːəc haəy, vìːə trəlɔp tɤ̀u phtèəh vèɲ.* 'When he had finished his walk, he went back home.'

Examples

Two operative verbs: *slìək-pèək* (to wear below the waist/to wear above waist or on legs and arms) 'to wear in general'; *dɤk-nòəm* (to lead animals or a cart/to lead people) 'to transport'; *sɔmpèəh-suːə(r)* (to place palms together in greeting/to ask questions, visit) 'to greet'.

Two attributive verbs: *khlaːc-kraeŋ* (to fear/to be afraid) 'to be afraid'; *ʔìən-khmaːs* (to be shy/to be ashamed) 'to be very shy'.

Operative verb/attributive verb: *rìəp-cɔm* (to prepare/to be direct, straight) 'to prepare'.

By the use of these criteria to catalyse the compound verb certain sequences of v + n, which are translated by one English word and which one feels 'should' be compound verbs are left out, e.g. *dac cɤt(t)* 'to decide', *sok(h) cɤt(t)* 'to consent', *thvɤ̀ː kaː(r)* 'to work', *hael tùk* 'to swim', *sruːəl khluːən* 'to be well'. Between such verbs and the following noun there is a very close junction; the two words are always pronounced in one phrase and no other word may intervene between them. This close connection is no closer, however, than that between any verb and the noun which follows it expressing the object of an action or the destination of a movement. A further reason against including these sequences among the compounds is that the noun component is sometimes part of a noun construct, e.g. *nèək thvɨ̀ː kaː(r) ʔɤy?* What work do you do?

48.4. *Compound numerals*

These were introduced in Lesson 22. Two or more words form a compound which represents one number, e.g. *pram-bɤy* 8; *mphèy-pìː(r)* 22; *saːmsɤp-pram-buːən* 39. Such compounds have the characteristics of the compounds discussed above in having only one essential stress, no possibility of interruption and complete repetition in second reference. The higher numbers, from 100, are each catalysed as a series of compound words, by the fact that part can be phrased separately (with rising pitch and pause) a feature which could not occur in the middle of a word.[1]

48.5. *Compound particles*

A set of general principles has been followed in establishing the compound particles. Thus they all have the following characteristics:—

(i) They may be pronounced, like any other particle, with no stress and with low or mid level pitch.[2]

(ii) They may be substituted for a simple particle in a characteristic construct or position in a sentence. Often one component of the compound particle is itself a simple particle of comparable meaning.

(iii) When they do receive stress and change of pitch the components form one phrase or part of a phrase; i.e. there is no pause between the components.

The following sentences illustrate points (i) and (ii).[3]

nèək nìh tɤu thvɨ̀ː kaː(r) nɤu (.) phnùm-pèɲ (\\).
This person is going to work in Phnom Penh.

The compound pre-nominal particle *nɤu-ʔae* may be substituted for the simple particle *nɤu*; it may also be pronounced with low pitch and no stress.

nèək nìh tɤu thvɨ̀ː kaː(r) nɤu(.)-ʔae (.) phnùm-pèɲ (\\).

The following sentences illustrate point (iii).

baə khɲom tɤu siəm-rìːəp (,|), khɲom nùŋ nɤu mùːəy ʔaːtùt(y) (\\).
If I go to Siem Reap I shall stay a week.

baə-sɤn-naː-cìːə khɲom tɤu siəm-rìːəp (,|), khɲom nùŋ nɤu mùːəy ʔaːtùt(y) (\\).

The second sentence suggests a slightly more vague possibility.

khɲom prɔ̀ːm tɤu siəm-rìːəp (,|), tae khɲom mùn nɤu ʔɔs mùːəy ʔaːtùt(y) tèː (\\).
I agree to go to Siem Reap but I shall not stay a week.

---

[1] Some compound numerals have been recorded on the tapes. See Part VII, Appendix 4.
[2] Particles may also in some contexts receive stress and be pronounced with a change of pitch but here we are concerned only with their potential lack of such features.
[3] Some sentences illustrating these points have been recorded on the tapes. See Part VII, Appendix 4.

khɲom prɔːm tɤ̀u siəm-rìːəp (,|), *kɔː(ˉ)-poñtae* (,|), *khɲom mùn nɤ̀u ʔɔs mùːəy ʔaːtùt(y) tèː* (\).
I agree to go to Siem Reap *but* I shall not stay a week.

kɔː-poñtae receives stress and separate phrasing but no pause may occur between *kɔː* and *poñtae*. The last sentence illustrates point (ii) as well as point (iii).

The above criteria have been applied to all compound particles. Special methods may be applied to some individual categories of particle, as follows:—

1. Pre-nominal particles

Compound pre-nominal particles must be substitutable for a simple particle in an adverbial construct pronounced as a separate phrase at the beginning of a sentence, e.g.

lɤ̀ː tok (,|), *mìːən ʔɤyvan craən rəbɔs lòːk.*
nɤ̀u-lɤ̀ː tok (,|), *mìːən ʔɤyvan craən rəbɔs lòːk.*
There are a lot of your things on the table.
This avoids possible confusion with minor verbs following the main verb.

2. Pre-verbal particles

Compound pre-verbal particles must be able to occur without stress between one of the pre-verbal particles, *mùn, nùŋ, kom* and *kɔː* and the verb construct, e.g.

lòːk nùh kɔː troːv-tae thvɤ̀ː kaː(r) tìət.
He then had to do some more work.

3. Final phrase particles

Again an adverbial construct occurring as a separate phrase at the beginning of a sentence is used as a catalyser. It must be a construct rounded off by a post-nominal particle. Then any word which follows in the same phrase is a final phrase particle, e.g.

pìː thɲay nùh tɤ̀u, ... 'From that day onwards, ... '
There is still the possibility of the occurrence of two independent final phrase particles together, e.g.

pìː chnam nùh tɤ̀u haəy, ... 'Already from that year on, ... '

A check must be made, therefore, that the component could not be present alone (as could either *tɤ̀u* or *haəy* in the example above), e.g.

pìː chnam nùh tɔː-tɔː-tɤ̀u . . . . 'Ever since that year . . . . '
tɔː-tɔː could not occur alone in such a position. The sequence is thus catalysed as a compound final phrase particle.

Note that in the context taken here, that of the separately phrased adverbial construct at the beginning of the sentence, the particle cannot be pronounced with low or mid level pitch; it has to follow the trend of the intonation of the phrase.[1] However, particles thus catalysed are capable also of being pronounced at the end of a sentence with low or mid level pitch,[1] e.g.

---

[1] This feature may be heard on the tape recordings. See Part VII, Appendix 4, 'Intonation of final phrase particles, *kɔː-baːn* and *kɔː-daoy*'.

kɔ̀ət mùn troːv nx̌u phtèəh nìh tɔː (.)-tx̌u (.) tèː (\\).
He does not have to stay in this house from now on.

4. Responding particles[1]

These have the special feature of being pronounced either (i) on a low note before the beginning of the sentence-tune or (ii) as a complete sentence-tune. They are catalysed by the context in which they occur, i.e. always preceding a reply.

5. Initiating particles[1]

These are exceptions to the general rule in that they may not be substituted for a simple particle. All initiating particles are compounds. They are, however, clearly catalysed by the context in which they occur, i.e. always preceding an initiated utterance.

6. Adverbial and post-nominal particles

Two sequences of simple word-forms, *tèəŋ ʔɔs* and *ʔae tìət*, each of considerable frequency, having the respective meanings, 'all' and 'other', seem to be most easily handled if regarded as compounds, *tèəŋ-ʔɔs* and *ʔae-tìət*. Both occur in situations where one would expect a post-nominal particle. *tèəŋ-ʔɔs* also occurs independently in such a way as to fit into the category of adverbial particle.

48.6. *Indian loanwords in Khmer compounds*

Here one is not concerned with the complete compounded Indian borrowing, such as *kɔmpùcèərɔ̀ət(th)*, 'kingdom of Cambodia', in which Indian rules of structure apply and the resulting form is polysyllabic. One is concerned to draw attention to the occurrence of compounds formed on the Cambodian pattern but with naturalized Indian loanwords as one or both components.

Compounds are formed as follows:—

(i) With two borrowed components and the borrowed word-order.

rìːəc-kaːr(r) (rāja royal/kāra work) state administration, civil service
rìːəc-sap(t) (rāja royal/sapta speech) royal vocabulary
prèəh-ʔɔŋ(k) (vara revered/aṅga body) eminent person **c.**

(ii) With two borrowed components and Cambodian grammatical form (**nn** with no link).

yùəs-sak(te) (yasa reputation/sakti honours) prestige
pèːl-vèːlìːə (vela/vela time—two separately developed forms) times

(iii) With one borrowed component and Cambodian grammatical structure.

yùən(t)-hɔh (yanta machine/*hɔh* to fly) aeroplane
rùːp-rìːəŋ (rūpa form/*rìːəŋ* form) form, shape, person
saːlaː-rìən (sālā hall/*rìən* to learn) school

---

[1] Compound responding and initiating particles are words required in religious and royal society. They are given in Lessons 39 and 40.

Exercise 60 A

(1) kec(c)-kaː(r) rəbɔs nɛ̀ək-srae

(2) dɔl khae-vìsaːk(h) mìːən phlìəŋ craən rɔ̀əl thŋay. (3) tə̀k dɔk nɤ̀u-knɔŋ srae tɛ̀əŋ-ʔɔs. nɛ̀ək-srae rìəp-cɔm prədap-prədaː sɔmrap thvɤ̀ː srae, kə̀ː nɛ̲̀əŋkɔ́əl, rənɔ̀əs, cɔːp-kap cìːə daəm. (4) kɛ̀ː tə̀m kòː mùːəy nə̀m tɤ̀u phcùːə(r) thnaːl mùːəy haəy kɛ̀ː rɔ̀əs yòːk smau cɛ̀ɲ ʔaoy sʔaːt pìː thnaːl nùh. rùːəc kɛ̀ː yòːk sroːv dael tram tùk pìː(r) bɤy thŋay mùn, dael mìːən pùənlɔ̀ːk lmɔ̀ːm, tɤ̀u saːp knɔŋ thnaːl nùh. kɛ̀ː prəya̲t(n) mùːm-ʔaoy kòː rə̀ː sa̲t(v) sìː tèː. (5) lùh sɔmnaːp nùh dos baːn kɔmpùəs lmɔ̀ːm haəy, kɛ̀ː dɔːk cɛ̀ɲ, cɔːŋ cìːə kɔndap toːc-toːc haəy kɛ̀ː tɤ̀u phcùːə(r) srae phseːŋ tìət daoy yòːk kɔndap dael dɔːk nùh tɤ̀u stùːŋ knɔŋ srae. (6) lùh kɛ̀ː stùːŋ srae nùh pɛ̀ɲ haəy kɛ̀ː tɤ̀u stùːŋ srae dətèy tìət. knɔŋ krùːəsaː(r) mùːəy-mùːəy mìːən srae pram, pram-mùːəy, cùːən-kaːl dɔp rə̀ː dɔp-pram kɔː-mìːən dae(r). (7) nɛ̀ək-srae trɔ̀əm nas daoy cùːən-kaːl kdau pèːk, cùːən-kaːl rəɲìːə pèːk. tae mùːm tʔoːɲ-tʔae(r) thaː kdau rə̀ː rəɲìːə laəy. (8) lùh stùːŋ krùp srae ʔɔs haəy kɛ̀ː chùp sɔmraːk pìː(r) bɤy khae, tae pros-pros troːv tɤ̀u mɤ̀ːl srae cìːə rùːəy-rùːəy kraeŋ srae kmìːən tùːk rə̀ː tùːk craən pèːk. baə kmìːən tùːk kɛ̀ː kap bɔŋhoː(r) tùːk taːm prəlaːy bɔɲcoːl tɤ̀u knɔŋ srae. baə mìːən tùːk craən kɛ̀ː bɔŋhoː(r) cɛ̀ɲ khlah. (9) baːn mùːəy khae sroːv nùh lɔ̀əs lʔɔ nas. (10) mùːm yùː(r) poɲ̃maːn, sroːv phaəm krùp srae tɛ̀əŋ-ʔɔs. (11) kɛ̀ː mùːm-mɛ̀ːn stùːŋ sroːv khsaːy tɛ̀əŋ-ʔɔs tèː. kɛ̀ː stùːŋ sroːv dɔmnaəp khlah dae(r). sroːv dɔmnaəp kɛ̀ː tùːk thvɤ̀ː nùm phseːŋ-phseːŋ. (12) lùh sroːv cɛ̀ɲ phlae ʔɔs haəy kɛ̀ː cat mənùs(s) ʔaoy tɤ̀u dɛ̀ɲ caːp rɔ̀əl thŋay. cùːən-naː kɛ̀ː cɔːŋ rəyìːəl caːp pɛ̀ɲ srae; cùːən-naː kɛ̀ː thvɤ̀ː tìːŋmòːŋ dak kɔndaːl srae ʔaoy caːp khlaːc. (13) kɛ̀ː lə̀ː soː(r) mɔ̀ət mənùs(s) sraek dɛ̀ɲ caːp voːs-vaːs-voːs-vaːs rɔ̀əl-tae prùːk. (14) srae naː nɤ̀u cə̀rt prèy kmìːən mcas tɤ̀u cam sroːv nùh sa̲t(v)-caːp sìː nɤ̀u tae srəkɤy. (15) lùh sroːv tùm khlah haəy kɛ̀ː bɔŋhoː(r) tùːk cɛ̀ɲ ʔaoy ʔɔs pìː srae haəy kɛ̀ː yòːk chɤ̀ː tɤ̀u phdeːk ʔaoy sroːv duːəl rìːəp srənok croːt. (16) kɛ̀ː rìəp-cɔm kɔndiəv sɔmrap croːt sroːv krùp knìːə tɛ̀əŋ-ʔɔs. (17) lùh kɛ̀ː phdeːk sroːv haəy kɛ̀ː croːt cɔːŋ cìːə kɔndap dak dɔɲhae knìːə. (18) rùːəc kɛ̀ː dɤk sroːv nùh yòːk mòːk tùk mùk(h) phtɛ̀əh. baə nɛ̀ək naː mìːən srae craən kɛ̀ː troːv yòːk vèː(r) knìːə tɤ̀u croːt khaːŋ neh mùːəy thŋay, khaːŋ nɔh mùːəy thŋay. (19) baə troːv lɤ̀ː vèː(r) nɛ̀ək naː, nɛ̀ək nùh troːv rìəp-cɔm baːy tùːk phoːŋ. (20) lùh dɤk sroːv yòːk mòːk tùk knɔŋ lìːən haəy kɛ̀ː baok nùːŋ kdaː(r) ʔaoy crùh krɔ̀əp sroːv rə̀ː kɔː baen rə̀ː kɔː bɔɲcɔ̀ən kɔː-mìːən. (21) cùːən-naː kɛ̀ː yòːk vèː(r) knìːə kɔː-mìːən dae(r). (22) lùh kɛ̀ː baen baok bɔɲcɔ̀ən rùːəc haəy kɛ̀ː cùəŋcùːn cɔmbaəŋ tɤ̀u kɔ̀ː(r) tùːk nɤ̀u kɔnlaeŋ mùːəy. rùːəc kɛ̀ː yòːk sroːv tɤ̀u rɔ̀ːy kɔndaːl vìːəl srae dael mìːən khyol ʔaoy crùh sɔndɤy cɛ̀ɲ, yòːk tae sroːv dael mìːən krɔ̀əp lʔɔ tɤ̀u tùk knɔŋ cùəŋrùk haəy kɛ̀ː troːv lùək khlah phoːŋ, tùk khlah phoːŋ. (23) knɔŋ krùːəsaː(r) mùːəy-mùːəy baːn sroːv hoksɤp cɤtsɤp thaŋ, cùːən-kaːl mùːəy-rɔ̀ːy thaŋ, mùːəy-rɔ̀ːy-haːsɤp thaŋ kɔː-mìːən.

(24) nɤ̀u srok-khmae(r) mìːən maːsìːn kɤn sroːv dae(r), tae mùːm mìːən krùp-krɔ̀ən tèː. nɛ̀ək-srae troːv yòːk sroːv tɤ̀u kɤn nùːŋ tbal, kɤn ʔaoy crùh ʔɔŋkaːm haəy yòːk ʔɔŋkɔː(r) nùh mòːk bok rə̀ː cɔ̀ən nùːŋ tbal-kdɯəŋ. (25) lùh ʔɔŋkɔː(r) sɔː haəy kɛ̀ː baː(r) cɛ̀ɲ pìː tbal yòːk mòːk ʔom yòːk kɔntùk ʔaoy crùːk sìː, yòːk ʔɔŋkɔː(r) mòːk dam baːy tətùːəl tìːən.

(26) nɛ̀ək-srae mùːm-mɛ̀ːn thvɤ̀ː tae srae tèː. srok khlah thvɤ̀ː sroːv praŋ dae(r). rəbiəp thvɤ̀ː sroːv praŋ mùːm khos knìːə pìː thvɤ̀ː srae va̲(s)saː tèː.

204

(1) *rəbɔs nɛ̀ək-srae* **A**.

(2) *rɔ̀əl thɲay* **A**.

(3) *kùːr.* Here **v**.

(4) *sʔaːt* 'to be clean', but with the sense of 'cleaned up, freed from dirt or anything that can spoil'. Hence it can be followed by *pìː. sʔaːt* can be used of people with the sense 'smart, well-turned out'.

dael . . . . , dael . . . . Both clauses introduced by *dael* interrupt the third clause of the sentence. See Lesson 24.5.

tr̀u. Initiating verb here and in (5).

baːn. Second verb of a major sequence but not with the sense 'can', referring back to the first verb. The sense of 'achievement' refers forward to *kɔmpùəs*.

(5) *dael dɔːk.* This short clause (**m (N) v**) is used in so subsidiary a way that it is included in the **N** as an attribute of *kɔndap*, with *nùh* to round up the whole **N** at the end. The use of *nùh* in this position is quite common even when the descriptive *dael* clause is a longer one.

(8) *craən,* **x**. Here to be taken as fulfilling the verbal function.

(10) *mùən yùː(r) poñmaːn. mùən* indicates the main verb. The clause has no marker. *yùː(r)* is used impersonally. For *mùən . . . . poñmaːn,* see Lesson 32.2.

(12) *sroːv cëɲ phlae.* cf. *bɔmpùəɲ cëɲ tùk,* discussed in Lesson 38.3. *pḛɲ* 'throughout'.

(14) *srae naː . . . . sroːv nùh.* There is no *dael* here to help to clarify the particular use of *naː.* The meaning is the same as if it were *srae naː dael nr̀u . . . . , sroːv knoɲ srae nùh . . . .*

sroːv nùh sɑt(v)-caːp sìː nr̀u tae srəkŕy. sroːv nùh is the sentence topic, object of the first verb, *sìː,* but loosely connected with the second, impersonal verb, *nr̀u.* See Lesson 38.3.

(15) *khlah.* Here *khlah* is **a**.

ʔɔs, here **v**.

ʔaoy sroːv dùːəl rìːəp srənok croːt. Although in the present analysis this clause (**m N V V V V**) consists of a major verbal sequence of four verbs, these are in fact grouped in twos, *dùːəl rìːəp* and *srənok croːt.* Attributive verbs often occur in close second position to operative verbs having, as was shown in Lesson 21.1, an adverbial sense in translation (here 'to fall flat'), while, as was mentioned in the note on Exercise 53, A (7), an attributive verb closely preceding an operative one tends to need in translation, an adjective followed by an infinitive (here 'easy to harvest').

(16) *krùp knìːə tɛ̀əɲ-ʔɔs.* Could be analysed as **pre n.p. n. post n.p.** or **v. a. a.**

(18) *mùk(h) phtɛ̀əh. mùk(h)* here functions as a **pre n.p.**

baə . . . . naː. Indefinite clause; translation of the question word is therefore as in grammatical context 2, see Lesson 32.

neh . . . . nɔh. These are alternative forms of *nìh* and *nùh.* If one considers the spelling, they are first register equivalents of *nìh* and *nùh. neh* and *nɔh* are used particularly in colloquial speech and have, in the colloquial, a special use, meaning 'here' and 'there', without the word *tìː* or *kɔnlaeɲ,* e.g. *mɔ̀ːk neh!* Come here! *tr̀u nɔh!* Go there! They are used with a colloquial form of *ʔae, ʔìː,* e.g. *ʔìː neh,* 'here', *ʔìː nɔh,* 'there'.

yɔ̀ːk vèː(r). *vèː(r)* is a word specially connected with help given in harvesting. In some parts of the country, *vèː(r)* is used alone as a verb, 'to help in turn'; in other parts the phrase is '*yɔ̀ːk day vèː(r) knìːə*' and in others, the short version which occurs here.

(19) *troːv lɨ̀ː* 'to hit upon, have a turn at'. *troːv* is basically 'to go direct to, to go straight, to hit a target' and hence it has the meaning 'to be right', as opposed to *khos*, 'to be wrong' and the further sense, 'to have to'.

(20) *ʔaoy crùh krɔ̀əp sroːv* **m V N**. *crùh krɔ̀əp sroːv* and *crùh sɔndɣy* in (22) and *crùh ʔɔŋkaːm* in (24) are regarded as instances of the impersonal use of a verb since no independent noun construct precedes. 'There-is-a-shedding (in respect of) seeds', etc. This construction occurring with a following noun is used particularly in connection with accidents and natural events. See Lesson 26.3.

(22) *kɔndaːl vìːəl srae*. A limited **A**. The **pre n.p.** *nɨ̀u* could occur before it. . . . . *phɔːŋ* . . . . *phɔːŋ* both . . . . and . . . . too.

(24) *krùp-krɔ̀ən* sufficient (i.e. for everyone to have one).

(25) Analysis:—

m N V f   N V ← v A   V ← v V V   m N V V   ← v V V
m n v f   n v ← v pn   v ← v v vn   m n v vn ← v vnv

Three clauses, the third interrupting the second, if one regards *ʔaoy* as a marker here. *ʔaoy* could be taken as a verb, 'take the dust to give to the pigs to eat'. This would give two clauses, the second of which needs to be phrased into at least three phrases. Nine verbs have stress if *ʔaoy* is treated as a marker, ten, if it is treated as a verb.

(26) *srok khlah*. Another limited **A**, once again connected lexically with time or place.

Exercise 60 B

Paddy is soaked for two or three days, until it has shoots. Then it is sown in a seed-bed. Later, when the seedlings have grown enough, they are transplanted into the ricefields. When the paddy is ripe it is harvested and tied in sheaves. Then it is beaten or trodden and winnowed in an open space in the rice field.

PART IV

ORTHOGRAPHY

1. KEY TO EXERCISE IN USE OF SCRIPT, PART I, LESSON 10.6

The keys to the first part of each exercise will be found in Part V, Keys.

1.

ក ក ច ឆ ឥ ធ គ យ យ ឈ ល ស ហ ណ ច ម
អ ង ឌ ញ ទ ន ព រ វ ឡ ឍ ឋ ថ ផ

2.

កា ប្ដ គ ងា ជ្ឈ ញ្ញ ដ៏ ណា តោ ទី ន បេ ពេ
មោ យ្ឈ រ ល វ៊ ស ហា ឡ្ អោ ខ ឆ ឝ យោ ផៅ
ភ្ ឈ ឋ តេ កើ

3.

បា៉ យ៉ុ ម៉ុ ស៉ុ វ៉ា ប៉ុ ហ៉ា អ៊ឺ រ៉ា

4.

កក ចារ ទូល សាច លុះ សាម ចាស លាន សុក ទុក ពុះ
ព្ញ រៀល សីង ហើរ

5.

កៃ កាយ កៅ កៅ តារ ជាយ ខៃ តៅ ដៅ ចារ ដារ ដៅ ថៃ

6.

ចក ជំ កក់ ចាង ចាង់ ឆាត ចាត់ បង បង់ ហាម ហា ព្ញ
កៈ ឡៈ សំ តក តក់ ជាត ជាក់ ជាត់ ទ្ញ ទាន់ ពង កំ
ពាត់ ណាស់ រង រាង រាល់ ជំ កក់

209

7.

ដុះ កោះ បះ គោះ រះ ទះ ពុះ តះ គេះ

8.

គោក ឡាន កង់ ស្តួប សេះ ពូរ មាក់ ទង ដោះ លង់ រះ
នាម រាំ ចាំ ប៉ាក់ សើង

9.

បើប ខុស ធូរ ឈាម ភួ ផៅន គាប់
ដួត លួង ក្តម ពុះ
ប្រើន ស្វា គ្រូ ត្រាប់ ស្រក់ ឈ្ញួញ
ឆ្លក់ ថុ ផ្លុស ល្វី ខ្វ
ពពក ដដែល ទនៀល រដក

10.

ប្រសប់ ស្រពោន ត្រជាក់ ប្រជាប់
ជង្គក់ ត្រណោត ពលប់ ស្រមោច ក្រឡា
ជ្រុល ទទាក់ ស្រិច ពព្រាយ
កក្លក សង្ស្លា រនេង ប៉ផ្ល់ក់

11.

ដគ្លាក់ កញ្ចាស់ ទន្ទេញ ពន្លក
ទំពែក រដ្បុល កំប៉ាំង ចំបក់
ចំណង ចំឡាក់ សំរប់ ដំតាន
បន្តិង អណ្ឋេក បន្លុ សណ្ឋេក
សង្ឃ្រាក ទ្រ្ថោម បំភ្លាំ បង្និត

210

2. 'IRREGULAR' SPELLINGS

List of words of which the spelling could not be deduced from the transcription or described easily, as in the case of e.g. *vay*, spelt *vìːəy*. The words given below have been marked by an asterisk at their first occurrence and are so marked wherever they occur in the vocabulary, Part VI. Here they are given in the same word-order as that used for the vocabulary with the correct orthography.

kɔndol, កណ្ដុរ

kɔː, ក៏

kaulʀy, កៅអី

krom, ក្រុម

krəʔɔːp, ក្រអូប

klʀŋ(k), ក្លិង្គ

khsʀp, ខ្សិប

kənaʔ, គណៈ

kənaː, ករុណា

kìːlɔːmaet(r), គីឡូម៉ែត្រ

cɔŋkʀh, ចង្កេះ

cah, ចាស់

ceːdʀy, ចេតិយ

dɔː, ដ៏

däc, ដែជ

tok, តុ

thom, ធំ

thɔɔm-mədaː, ធម្មតា

nèək, អ្នក

nìh, នេះ

nùh, នោះ

bùyrɔː, ប៊ីរ៉ូ

pakkaː, បក្ខ

pyaɲcɔnèə, ពាំជ្ឈាន

prampùl, ប្រាំពីរ

prəcìːəthìpdʀy(y), ប្រជាធិបតេយ្យ

mìkèəseː(r), មិតសិរ

rùt, រិត

rùssʀy, ឫស្សី

rùː, ឫ

lʀp, ទ្បិប

lec, លិច

lùː, ឡ

vìhìːə(r), វិហារ

vìət-mìɲ, វេ]កមិញ

sʀŋ(h), សិង្ហ

sₐmaːcùk, សមាជិក · ʔaːmeːrìːkaŋ, អាម៉េរីកាំង

soː(h)vəə(r), សូហ្វុរ · ʔʋyloːv, ឥឡូវ

seːnaːpₐdɤy, សេនាបតិ · ʔʋyloːʋnìh, ឥឡូវ នេះ or ឥឡូវនេះ

səseː(r), សរសេរ · ʔʋyvan, ឥ៝វ៉ាន់

səsay, សរសៃ · ʔoːn, អូន

ʔɔŋklèːs, អង់គ្លេស · ʔaep, ឥអប

ʔaːnɔn(l), អានន្ទ · ʔaoy, ឲ្យ

ʔaːmeːrìːk, អាម៉េរីក

3.   ORTHOGRAPHY OF EXERCISES 1–60 A

Exercise 1 A

ៗពុកជំនួយ ។ ម្ដាយធ្វើម្ហូប ។ បងនៅផ្ទះ ។ ប្អូនលេងល្បែង ។ ខ្ញុំ
ទៅសាលារៀន ។ នាធ្វើទូ ។ ប្អូនទៅ ។ ខ្ញុំនៅ ។

Exercise 2 A

បងធំ ។ ប្អូនតូច ។ នាចាស់ ។ ឡានតូច ។ ល្បែងថ្មី ។ ខ្ញុំក្មេង ។

Exercise 3 A

ទួលណាស់ ។ បងទៅសាលារៀន ។ មិននៅផ្ទះ ។ ម្ចបក្ដៅពេក ។
ពួមានឡាន ។ នាជំនួយ ។

Exercise 4 A

ប្អូនលេងល្បែងថ្មី ។ មិនធ្វើម្ហូបក្ដៅ ។ ៗពុកធ្វើទូធំ ។ ពួមានឡានល្អ ។
ខ្ញុំទៅសាលារៀនតូច ។ នាទៅផ្ទះទុលាយ ។

Exercise 5 A

ឯពុកខ្ញុំនៅផ្ទះ ។ បង្គរំវាទៅសាលារៀន ។ ប្អូនអ្នកគួបណ្ណាស់ ។ ផ្ទះពួន-

លាយ ។ ឯពុកវាចាស់ណាស់ ។ សាលារៀនខ្ញុំល្អ ។

Exercise 6 A

ខ្ញុំឃើញឯពុកខ្ញុំ ។ ឯពុកម្ដាយមានផ្ទះធំ ។ បង្គប្អូនវានៅផ្ទះ ។ បង្គស្រីអ្នក

ទៅសាលារៀន ។ ប្អូនប្រុសឃើញឆ្ពុំ ។ ផ្ទះថ្មីល្អណាស់ ។

Exercise 7 A

វាមិនទៅផ្ទះរធំ ។ ផ្ទះខ្ញុំមិនជិតផ្ទះរទេ ។ ម្ដាយមិនទិញគ្រីទេ ។ ប្អូន

ប្រុសខ្ញុំលក់គ្រីឆ្ងៃ)ត ។ បង្គស្រីវាមិនល្អទេ ។ ខ្ញុំមិនមានបង្គប្អូនទេ ។

Exercise 8 A

វានៅបន្ទប់ វាឬទេ? ។ អ្នកមានកន្ទេលល្អទេ? ។ មីងមិនទិញគ្រីគូចទេ ។

មួបក្ដៅឬទេ? ។ បង្គប្អូនអ្នកនៅផ្ទះទេ? ។ ឯពុកមានកន្ទេលទេ? ។

Exercise 9 A

បានទេ បន្ទប់ខ្ញុំគ្មានបន្ទុចធំទេ ។ ចាំទេ ឯពុកម្ដាយមិននៅផ្ទះទេ ។ ពុផ្ទៃទេ?

បាន គាត់ផ្ទៃ ។ បង្គជិះឡានឯពុកឬទេ? បាន ។ ឡានវាថ្មីទេ? ចាំ ថ្មី ។

Exercise 10 A

ប្អូនអ្នកមានផ្ទះប៉ុន្មាន? បាន វាមានផ្ទះពីរ ។ អ្នកមានបង្គប្អូនប៉ុន្មាននាក់? ចាំ

ខ្ញុំមានបង្គបីនាក់ ។ ឯពុកអ្នកមានបង្គប្អូនប៉ុន្មាននាក់? បាន ខ្ញុំមិនដឹងទេ គាត់

មានគ្រីបីនាក់ ។ អ្នកមានគូប៉ុន្មាន? បាន ខ្ញុំមានគូពីរ ។ នាមានចៅប៉ុន្មាន

នាក់? បាន មានចាំនាក់ ។ មីងទិញគ្រីប៉ុន្មាន? គាត់ទិញប្អូន ។

Exercise 11 A

មិនមានបន្ទប់ប៉ុន្មាននាក់ ? ។ តាយេីញឡ្យានខ្ញុំទេ ? ។ ចៅទៅសាលារៀនទេ ? ។

អ្នកដឹងទេ ? ។ ឫូនទិញករភ្លេលទេ ? ។ ឥឡូវអ្នកនៅផ្ទះទេ ? ។

Exercise 12 A

មិនទិញមានធំឫូននោះទេ ? ។ អ្នកយេីញស្អប់ផ្ទូកនោះឫូទេ ? ថ្ងៃណាស់ ។

ព្យមានកូនប៉ុន្មាននាក់ ? បាទ តាត់មានបីនាក់ ។ ផ្ងងៗទៀតប្រក់ស្ងូកភ្លេតទេ ?

បាទទេ ប្រក់ស្យូវ ។ ផ្ងងនាមានបន្ទូបប៉ុន្មាន ? បាទ មានពីរ ។ តាទិញស្អប់

ផ្ទូកនេះឫូទេ ? ទេ ថ្ងៃណាស់ ។

Exercise 13 A

អ្នកបំរើពីរនាក់នោះទៅផ្សារ ។ វាទិញស្អប់ផ្ទូកជាក ។ ស្អប់ជាកនេះមិនល្អទេ ។

ឥឡូវម្តាយខ្ញុំមិនប្រើអ្នកបំរើទេ ។ ទុំនោះល្អណាស់ ។ បងឫូនអ្នកចាំអ្នកទេ ? ។

Exercise 14 A

មិនទិញសំពត់ឫូទេ ? ចាំ ខ្ញុំស្ដ្បាញ្ញពណិ៌កហមនោះ ។ បងស្វៀកខោសទេ ?

ទេ បងស្វៀកខោខ្ចៅ ។ ព្យពាក់អាវថ្ងៃ ។ ផ្ងូមានអាវសទេ ? ចាំ ផ្ងូន

មានអាវសពីរ ។ ឫូនស្វៀកពាក់ខោអាវបារាំងឫូទេ ? បាទទេ ឫូនស្វៀកសំពត់ ។

សំពត់នេៃថ្ងៃណាស់ តាមានសំពត់ជាកឫូទេ ? បាទទេ ខ្ញុំគ្មានសំពត់ជាកទេ ។

Exercise 15 A

ឥឡូវនៅក្នុងបន្ទប់ តាត់មេីលសៀវភៅអំពីស្រុកកូម៉ា ។ ក្ងួយស្រីខ្ញុំមិនទៅស្រុក

អន់គ្លេសទេ តាត់នៅក្នុងស្រុកសៀម ។ ថ្ងៃនេះបងស្រីអ្នកពាក់អាវល្អណាស់ ។

ឥឡូវយើនមកពី ﹇ស្រុកយួន ﹈ស្ងែកយើនទៅ ﹇ស្រុកសេ ﹈ម ។ យើនគ្មានសេ ﹈រ-
ភៅបៃតតនេះក្នុងសាលារ ﹈នយើនទេ ។ សំពត់ភួមាអ្នកនៅលើតុថ្មី ។

Exercise 16 A

យប់មិញចារម្លាក់ចូលផុះតា តាត់មិនដីនទេ ។ ខ្ញុំនិនទៅស្ងរមឹនខ្ញុំក្នុងផុះពេទ្យ
ល្ងាចនេះ តាត់ឈឺពីមិៗល ។ ឆ្នំនេះចៅនិនវ ﹈នភាសាបារាំងសៃស ។ បន្តិច
ទៅ ﹈តពូនិនទិញទុកមួយ ។ ពេលនោះបន ﹇សិអ្នកឈឺបន្តិច ។ ក្នុងទីនេះគេមិន
លក់ ﹇តិនៃ ﹈តទេ ។

Exercise 17 A

ម៉េចក៏លោក ﹇គូទៅសាលារ ﹈នថ្ងៃនេះ? ថ្ងៃនេះយើនមិនវ ﹈នទេ ។ តាមានផុះ
នៅឯណា? បាទ ខ្ញុំមានផុះឯភ្នំពេញ ។ លោកចេះភាសាបារាំងសៃសឬទេ?
បាទ ខ្ញុំចេះបន្តិចបន្តួច ។ អ្នកទៅ ﹇ស្រុកសេ ﹈មផុចម្ងេច? បាទ ខ្ញុំជិះយន្តហោះ ។
មឹនចូលផុះពេទ្យពីអន្ងាល់? ចាះ មឹនចូលពី ﹇ពឹកមុិៗ ។ ពីម្ងិលមុិញពូអ្នកជិះទូក
តាត់ទៅណា? ចាះ ពូទៅកំពង់ចាម ។

Exercise 18 A

គេលក់ខ្ច្ងៃឯណា? ។ អ្នកណាទៅទី ﹇ក្រុន ﹇ពឹកនេះ? ។ ក្នុងសាលារ ﹈ននោះគេ
បរ ﹇នៃ ﹈នភាសាអន់គ្លេសយ៉ាន់ណា? គេ ﹇បើសេ ﹈រនៅណាខ្ងះ? ។ ﹇ពឹកមុិញ
អ្នកឃើញអ្នកណាក្នុងទី ﹇ក្រុន? ។ លោក ﹇គូមានកូនសិស្សប៉ុន្មាននាក់ក្នុងថ្នាក់នេះ? ។
យប់មិញចារប៉ុន្មាននាក់ចូលផុះពូ? ។

Exercise 19 A

កូនខ្មែរលេងល្បែងណាខ្លះ? ។ បងមកពី[សុករសេ]មពីអន្លាល់? ។ ផ្ទះប្អូន
ជិតផ្សារឬទេ? ។ ខ្ញុំគ្មាន[តិនេ]តថ្ងៃនេះទេ ។ ស្ពាននេះដូនតាលោកៅណា? ។
ឧពុកវាចិញ្ចឹមកូន[ប្ញាំនាក់យ៉ាងដូចម្តេច? ។

Exercise 20 A

ឆ្នាំនោះរៅខ្ញុំស្លូវតែស្លាប់ ។ លោកបំណាំតែធ្វើការក្នុងបន្ទប់ណា? ។ អ្នកដែល
ទៅកិព៌ចាមទេ? បាទ ដែល ។ លោកមិនសូវ[ស្រួលទេ ។ ម្នាយចេញ
ពីផ្ទះ ចារពីរនាក់[សាប់តែចូលបន្ទប់ ។ មិនមិនដែលទៅ[សុករសេ]មទេ ។
កូនសិស្សម្នាក់[គ្មានតែចេះអក្សរ ។ ក្នុងថ្នាក់នេះកូនទេីបតែនិន[បច្បេង ។
ម្តេចក៏ដៅបេះតែឈឺ? ។ នៅផ្សារខ្មែរ[ចិនតែស្លេ]កសំពត់ ។ ក្នុងផ្សារ[តិ
នេ]តតែនិនតែជៅក ។ សំពត់ល្អនោះសុទ្ធតែថ្មៃ ។

Exercise 21 A

អ្នកណាចង់មេីលកូននេះ? ម្នាយខ្ញុំចង់មេីលកូននេះស្នែក ថ្ងៃនេះគាត់[ត្រូវនៅបន្ទប់
គាត់ ។ ពេលនោះនាង មិនបាននៅក់អារវ៉េ]រ៉ៃទេ ។ ម្នាយរវល់ធ្វើការក្នុងផ្ទះ ។
ឧពុកតែនិនតែជៈទ្ធាន ។ ចៅតែ[ចបសប់រៀនភាសាបារាំងសែសរទេ? ។ លោក
[ត្រូវខ្ញុំឈប់នៅផ្ទះនេះ ។ ខ្ញុំបានមេីលកូនបារាំងសែសរនោះ ។ លោកមិន[ត្រូវទៅ
[ក្នុងភ្នំពេញឬទេ? ។ សំពត់សរនេះសំរាប់ធ្វើអាវ ។ កូនយេីងសូមលេងល្បែង
នោះ ។ ម៉េចក៏ចៅវិវ៉រ៉េ]ភាសាអង់គ្លេស? ចៅតិតទៅ[សុកអាម៉េរិកទេ? ។

216

ខ្ញុលចិត្តទិញសំពត់លេ]ងនោះ ។ បនលោកចង់មើលកូនខ្មែរនោះទេ? ។

លោក[ចញ្ចាប់ទៅណា? ។

Exercise 22 A

នាងមិនទាន់ចេះដក់ប៉ារី ។ អាម៉េរិកាំងចេះតែចង់ទិញសំពត់សេ]មនេះ ។ ឪពុក

យើងតែងតែរវល់សរសេរសំបុ[ត ។ កូនមិនសូវហ៊ានចូលបន្ទប់នាទេ ។ មិង

សិនតែនិង[ពមទៅ[ស្រុកប៉ារិស ។ កូនសិស្សនោះសុទ្ធតែខំរៀនភាសាអង់គ្លេស ។

Exercise 23 A

ហិបអ្នកនៅ[ក្រោម[គុ]វ្ញុំ ។ អារនាងបែតនង់នោះដូចអារលោក[សិ ។ មនុស្ស

ម្នាក់[គូវមកតាមខ្ញុំ ។ ស្មែកលោកនិងយកសំបុ[តនេះឆេញពីថតតុ ។ ចារវត់

ចេញពីបន្ទប់ ។ លោកដេញវាដល់កន្លែងណា? ។ អ្នកណាធ្វើកញ្ចាប់នោះមក? ។

នាងបានដក់ថាសការហ្វេលើតុតូច ។

Exercise 24 A

ចៅមកដុះយើនជិនលា ។ ខ្ញុំមិនសូវស្បាយធ្វើការក្នុងទីនេះទេ ។ អ្នកបក់ដែ

ហៅស៊ីក្លូ ។ មេប៉ុបានអញ្ជើញលោក[គូមកដុះ ។ នានោះចង់ទៅមើលបុណ្យ

ក្នុងភូមិយើនស្មែក ។ ដូនអ្នក្រា្ញកន្ទួលរហ័សណាស់ ។ លោក[សិ[ថិ

អ្នកបំរើដុះទេ? ។ កូនលោកសុទ្ធតែ[ឲ]ន់ពីរោះណាស់ ។ សេ]មប្ផូនាក់

នោះបានមក[ស្រុកខ្មែរនាមផ្លូវអាកាស ។ វារត់ដេញចារ ។ ករ[ញ្ញានលោត

ខាំកមាន់ ។ កូននោះនិយាយខ្លាំងពេក ។

Exercise 25 A

ក្មេងម្នាក់បានយកសំបុ[តទៅ ។ ឯពួកមិនទិញ្ញទុកធំទេ ។ មិនដាំបាយជូនលោក
ឬទេ? ។ ម្ជួយខ្ញុំធ្វើមួយបន្លាព្ញាណាស់ ។ អ្នកប៉ែ[សដក[ស្រូវចេញពីដី ។ លោក
ដិនទ្បានធ្មី ។

Exercise 26 A

គាត់បានជូនទិកតែមកយើនមួយពៃនម្នាក់ ។ កូន[ប្រុសខ្ញុំមិនទាន់[បឡ្បឯចូលជ្វាក់ទីបី
ទេ ។ ដ្ខ្ញុំបណ្តោយដប់ព្ រ្តម ។ ឯឪ្ពុ រ្ដ៏នេលោកមានសេបុ៉ឪ្ឋាន? ពាន
ខ្ញុំមានថ្លៃ ។ ក្ដុនជ្វាក់ទីពីរកូនសិស្ស[ចិនតៃនអាយុ[ប្រាំពីរឆ្នាំ ។ មួយឆ្នាំទ]ត
ខ្ញុំទៅ[ស្រុកអន់ឯត្គេស ។ [សីនោះបានជូនបារីពីរវ៉ដណ្ដាប់ដើមមកខ្ញុំ ។ លោក
សឪ្ជ្បពីរអឪ្ឋនេះ[ចិនតៃទកស[តារពេលល្ងាច ។ ចៅពីរនាក់ទៃចបឯិន[ប្រឡ្បឯ ម្នាក់
[គាន់តៃជាប់ ម្នាក់ធ្លាក់ ។ វ៉ាមិន[ពមដើរពីរគីឡ្បម៉ែ[តទ]ត ។ [ស្ងូវ
មួយហាបថ្ងៃដប់រ]ល ។ [តីនេះថ្ងៃប៉ុ៉ឪ្ឋានវ]ល? ពាទ មួយឪ្ឋផ្លាក់ពីរវ]ល ។

Exercise 27 A

គាំឪ្ញពីខ្ញុំមកប៉ាត់ដឯបឯខ្ញុំល្ធីបន្ដិច ។ ទោះបីកូនសិស្សនេ៎វំរ]នវ៉ាឪ្ឋ៏មិនចេះ[ចិន
ទេ ។ បឪ្ឋ[ប្រុសខ្ញុំ[បឡ្ឯបីដឯប៉ុ៉ឯតៃគាត់ចេះតៃធ្លាក់ ។ វ៉ាបានដាក់ដីមួយដុំនោះ
ដើម្ផ្យ្ញ្ការុឪ្ឋន៎ ។ បើ[បសិនជាសំបុ[តនោះមិនបានមកដល់ឯពួកឪ្ឋ៏មិនចេញ
ពីប៉ែ[ពតករថ្ពៃនេះទេ ។ ក្ដុនពេលដែលលោក[សីមកស្ដួរខ្ញុំឪ្ឋ៏ផ្ដួរចោរម្នាក់ចូលផ្ដួរលោក
[សីល្ងចន៎វ៉ាន់[ចិន ។ នាមខ្ញុំស្ងានគណៈ[បជាធិបតេយ្យឪ្ឋ៏មិនឈ្មួរទេ ។

ម្ចាយបានធ្វើមួប រូបគាត់ចេញទៅផ្សារ ។ ខ្ញុំចង់មើលសំបុ[ត្រដែលម្ចាយធ្វើពី[ស្រុក សេ]ម ។ កាលណាបើលោកមកកំពង់ចាមម្តងទេ]តលោក[ត្រូវពិសាបាយងផ្ទះខ្ញុំ ។

Exercise 28 A

មីន[តឡប់ពី[ស្រុកសេ]មមករវិញ្ជហើយឬ? ។ តាបានធ្វើការពី[ពលឹមហើយឥ- ទ្យូ រ្ងិនគាត់[ត្រូវបធ្វើ្យកៅអីនេះផន ។ ទ! ជូនឥតឈឺទេតើ? ពីម្ងៃលគាត់ បាន្ចូលផ្ទះពេ្យ ។ អ្នកទៅបានដំបងជីខរទេនភ្លើនថ្ងៃនេះក៏បាន ខ្ញុំជិទ្ឡានស្លេក ក៏បាន ។ ខ្ញុំមិនឃេ្ញកខ្នួងណាល្បួសាះឡេីយ ។ នាងមិន[ពមជូតផ្ទះទេ]តទេ ។

Exercise 29 A

គេមិនទាន់ទុំស្បួរទេឬ? ។ កាលណាចន្ឌ្ឌនអ្នកមកមេីលបុណ្យអុំទុកអ្នកនីនទៅទទួល ងកប៉ាល់បួទេ? ។ យើនបានចួបគ្នាហើយឬ? ។ មីនអ្នកមិនបានដាប់ចិត្តទិញ្ជផ្ទះថ្មី នោះទេឬ? ។ លោក[គូចង់ធ្វើទោសកូនសិស្ស[កាចនោះឬ? ។

Exercise 30 A

ងឥឡេីងផ្ទះសិន អញ្ចងនិយាយជាមួយនីងងឥភ្ក្លាម ។ ពីម្ងៃលមុិញ្ជឆ្លាក់ភ្លេ]ឥ មកវ[ចិន ។ ក្ឌឥកុំវៃ[ស្រក [គូមិនមៃនថ្ឌឥទេ ។ ក្ឌនស្ងួនលោកកៃពេល[ព លប់ផ្ឌកិនផ្សារ[កអូបណាស់ ។ ៃនេះភ្ក្ជណាស់ពេលយប់ ។ កូយកុំដេីរ រ្ហាសដូច្ងេះ មីនមិនឧចង់ទៅ ផល់មុនម៉ាងទេ ។ ក្ឌនបនួប់នេះ[តជាក់ណាស់ នាងអាឈាតបិទផ្ដិតឡ្យខ្ញុំ ។ ៃថ្ងនេះកៃតរ[ឱិមួយប្ពែក ខ្ញុំនិឥនិទានទៅលោក [សី ។ ក្ឌនវៃ[ពនេះពេល[ពលឹមពួស្បួរឥត្បុហៃរវ[ចិន ។ នៅសល់នំពីរដុំទេ]ត អ្នកអញ្ជ្ញោ្ញពិសាមួយចុះ ។

Exercise 31 A

ពេល[ពឹកដល់ម៉ោង[បាំបីខ្ញុំ[បាំដណ្តប់នាទី   លោក[គ្រូទុន្សូរទាល់តែកូនសិស្សច្រូល
សាលារៀនទាំងអស់គ្នា ។   ក្នុងកន្លែងនេះ   ទោះជាហ្លួសម៉ោង[ពីរដណ្តប់យប់ក៏
ដោយ[ពួ្សរមនុស្ស[ចិននាក់សើបតាមផ្លូវ ។   មានហេតុមួយទេ[រតបានជាខ្ញុំមិនចង់
ទៅផ្ញើការរងកំពង់តាម   ពី[ពោះខ្ញុំទើប នឹងទិញ្ញផ្ទុះនៅ ភ្នំពេញ ។   រទេះភ្លើងចេញ
ម៉ោងប៉ុន្មាន?   បាទ ចេញទៅម៉ោង[បាំពីរ[ពឹក   ទៅដល់បាត់ដំបងម៉ោងប៉ុន្មាន?
បាទ ទៅដល់ម៉ោង[បាំមួយ ល្ងាច ។   លោក[គ្រូនពីអាទិត្យមុនប៉ុន្តែលោកមិន[ពម
ហៅ[គ្រូពេទ្យទេ ។   ថ្វីពុនខ្ញុំចេញពីផ្ទុះពី[ពលឹមទៅចាប់[តី   ដល់ម៉ោង[បាំមួយ
ល្ងាចខ្ញុំ[តឡប់មកវិញ្ញ   ឃ្លានអីឃ្លាន! ។

Exercise 32 A

អ្នកនាក់ស៊ីក្លូនោះនឹង[បាប់ខ្ញុំជាមានផ្លូវសំណាក់នៅឯណា ។   ខ្ញុំមិនដឹងជាគាត់រកស៊ី
ផ្ញើការអីទេ ។   ទៅ[គ្រូវជំរាបលោក[គ្រូថាទៅបានមើលទំពីរណាខ្ខ ។   តាមិនទាន់
ដឹងជាឡ្បានឈ្មួលនឹងមកដល់ភ្នំពេញ ម៉ោងប៉ុន្មានទេ ។   ពីអាទិត្យមុនមួយ ខ្ញុំឈឹយ៉ាង
ខ្លាំង   បន[សី ខ្ញុំចង់ព្យាបាលគាត់នៅផ្លូ:   [គ្រូពេទ្យក៏[បាប់ថា[គ្រូវផ្ញើអ៊ូខ្ខ ។
ខ្ញុំសូមស្ងួរលោក[សីតើលោក[សី នឹងអញ្ញើញ្ញទៅស្ងួរលោកដូនអធ្យាល ។   អ្នកបំរើ
នោះមិន[ពមជាក[ន្តែលោក[សីបាត់ទៅណាទេ ។   លោក[គ្រូមិនដែល[បាប់ខ្ញុំជាមាន
កូនសិស្សប៉ុន្មាននាក់នៅថ្មាក់ទីពីរវ ។   សូមឲ្យនាង[បាប់ខ្ញុំជាដល់ម៉ោង[បាំបីបីហើយ
ឬនៅ ។   ខ្ញុំចង់ជំរាបលោក[សីជាម៉េចបានជាខ្ញុំមិនបានទៅស្ងួរគាត់នៅផ្លូនពេទ្យ ។

Exercise 33 A

ចៅទៅលេងផុះមិត្តសំឡាញ់ចៅមិនបានទេ ចៅដេីរមិនកេីតពី[ពោះឈឺដេីង ។ [ចារ

ព័រនាក់ចេញទៅតាមបន្តូចហេីយជិះឡានទៅយ៉ាងរហ័ស ។ របស់ធ្ងន់ណាស់ គោ

អូសរទេះមិនរួច ។ សេចក្តីនោះពិព្ភាកណាស់ តាគិតមិនយេីញទេ ។

លោកសង្ឃ្រូបួនអង្គនោះបាននិមន្តទៅមិនទាន់ឡានឈ្នួល ហេតុនេះហេីយបានជាលោក

និមន្តតាមផ្លូរ ។ មិនអីទេ ខោអាវខ្ញុំទទឹកមិនសូវរជោកទេ ។ រាល់ថ្ងៃអគ្គារ

មិត្តសំឡាញ់ខ្ញុំព័រ-បីនាក់មកលេងផុះខ្ញុំនៅម៉េ៉ង[ប៉ាម្ពួយកន្លះមិនខាន ។ សព្ទថ្ងៃនា

ថ្ងៃបន្តិច តាត់ស្តាប់វិទ្យុមិនញ្ញទេ ។ ឯពួកមេីលកាសែតមិនទាន់រួច អ្នក[ស្រូវ

ចាំបន្តិច ទេីបអ្នកមេីលបាន ។ នាងនោះ[កុនយ៉ាងខ្លាំង មុខនាងចេះតែ[កហាម

មិន[សាក ។

Exercise 34 A

កូនសិស្ស[ទាំងអស់រ[ៀនភាសាបារាំងឬ? ទេ មានកូនសិស្សប៉ុ៉ន្ឋាននាក់ដែរវដែល

មិនរ[ៀនភាសាបារាំង ។ យប់មិញខ្ញុំចេះតែយល់សព្ទយេីញអី ។ ដួចជាមនុស្ស ។

ខ្ញុំដឹងជាមានបុណ្យរអីមួយក្នុងវត្តនេះ ។ មនុស្សប៉ុ៉ន្ឋាននាក់នោះចេះបារាំង ។ [ប-

ហេលជាថៃ្ងណាមួយយេីងនឹងឃួបគ្នា[ៀតមេីលទៅ ។ មនុស្ស[ខ្លះឆ្លាប់មេីលកុនមួយ

ភាទិត្យបីដង ។ [គូ[ប្រាប់កូនសិស្សជាមាន[ស្រុកណាខ្លះវដែលគេមិនដាំ[ស្រូវទេ ។

ប៉ូលិសបាន[ប្រាប់ជាចោរនោះ មុននឹងស្លាប់ បាននិយាយអ្វីខ្លះអំពីរ[ៀននេះ ។

មានកព្ទប់អ្វីក្នុងបន្ទប់ទទួលភ្ញ[ៀវ ។ ខ្ញុំមិនដឹងកព្ទប់នោះមកពីណាទេ ។ លោក

តាចេះតែឲ្យយេីងធ្វើការអី ។ ។

Exercise 35 A

គាត់មិនបានជាអីទេ ។ ស្រុកអផ្គេសមិនឆ្ងាយប៉ុន្មានពីស្រុកបារាំងទេឫ? ។ ខ្ញុំឲ្យ
យាយនោះរបស់អ្វីដែលខ្ញុំមិនត្រូវការ ។ បើអ្នកមានរបស់អ្វី ៗ មានដម្លៃសូមឲ្យ
អ្នកទុករបស់នោះក្នុងថតតុ ។ ខ្ញុំមិនស្គាល់កូនសិស្សណាក្នុងថ្នាក់នេះដែលអាចធ្វើ
ដូចឯងទេ ។ គ្មានកន្លែងណាដែលយើងលាក់ក្បូននេះបានទេ ។ ឯងធ្វើការអី ៗ
ត្រូវធ្វើឲ្យព្រោះ ។ អ្នកចង់ទៅកន្លែងណាខ្ញុំបើកឡានជូនអ្នកទៅកន្លែងនោះ ។
អ្នកណាវាយគេ ៗ និងវាយអ្នកនោះវិញ ។ គ្មានប្រដាប់ប្រដាសម្រាប់ធ្វើស្ងួន
អ្វីឡួយនៅក្នុងស្ងួននោះ ។

Exercise 36 A

ត្រូវអានពាក្យអ្វីមួយ សិស្សក៏អានពាក្យនោះតាម ។ សំពត់នេះថ្លៃប៉ុន្មាន ក៏ខ្ញុំ
យកដែរ ។ លោករូបើខ្ញុំធ្វើអី ខ្ញុំក៏មិនព្រមធ្វើដែរ ។ អ្នកស្រឡាញ់សំពត់
ណាមួយ ខ្ញុំក៏ស្រឡាញ់សំពត់នោះដែរ ។ អ្នកទៅណា ខ្ញុំក៏ទៅនោះដែរ ។
គ្រូជាធ្វើអី កូនសិស្សក៏ធ្វើតាម ។ ទោះបីឪពុកវាយកូននោះដូចម្តេច កូននោះ
ក៏មិនយំដែរ ។ ម្តាយធ្វើបបរអ្វីមួយ កូនក៏និងដួយធ្វើដែរ ។ បងធ្វើការនេះ
ដូចម្តេច ខ្ញុំក៏ធ្វើដូចធម្មតា ។ ភ្លៀងដូចម្តេច ខ្ញុំក៏ទៅ ។

Exercise 37 A

ខ្ញុំគិតទៅស្រុកខ្ញុំ ៗ ទៅថៃណុកក៏បាន ។ ស្វាយនេះមកពីស្រុកណាក៏ដោយ
ខ្ញុំចូលចិត្តទាំងអស់ ។ អ្នកត្រូវនែកត់ស្ងីក៏ដោយនៅពេលដែលវានិយាយ ។ ម្តាយ
មកពេលណាក៏ដោយ កូនមានកន្លែងដួយជានិច្ច ។ អ្នកស្រីអញ្ជើញមកលេងផ្ទះខ្ញុំ

ពេលណាក៍បាន ។ អ្នកធ្វើយ៉ាងណាក៍ដោយ ឲ្យតែឆាប់ហើយ ។ ដូចម្តេចក៍
ដោយ ឯងត្រូវធ្វើឲ្យទាន់មុនពេលយប់នេះ ។ អ្នកធ្វើអ្វីក៍បាន ខ្ញុំនឹងមិនជាអី
ទេ ។ មិនទិញសេ្រវកៅណាមួយឲ្យក្មួយក៍បានដែរ ។ ថ្ងៃប៉ុន្មានក៍ដោយ ខ្ញុំ
ក៍ទិញ ។

Exercise 38 A

ប៉ុន្មានឆ្នាំទៀតទេ ខ្ញុំនឹងធ្វើការរកស៊ីដូចពួកខ្ញុំដែរ ។ គ្មានលោកគ្រូណាមួយ
សោះដែលបានមើលសេ្រវកៅទាំងអស់នោះ ។ ឲ្យពុកស្តាប់អ្នកណាដែលតថ្ងៃវ៉ាន់
ពេក ។ អ្នកណាធ្វើបាបគេយ៉ាងណា គេធ្វើបាបអ្នកនោះវិញយ៉ាងនោះដែរ ។
មិនទៅជិះយន្តហោះកាលណាក៍បាន ក្មួយជួនមិនទៅកន្លែងបំណត ។ វ៉ាន់ទៅ
កន្លែងណាមួយដែលវ៉ាទៅពីរ-បីឆ្នាំមុននោះ ។ មានអីខ្លះនៅក្នុងឆ្នូរតីនេះ? គ្មាន
ស្ករថ្មៃកទេ ។ ឯងទិញទឹកដោះគោឲ្យខ្ញុំមួយកំប៉ុង ទឹកដោះគោបែបបណា? បែប
ណាក៍ដោយ ។

Exercise 39 A

ឯចំណែកលោកពូ គាត់ឆ្លាតជានគេក្នុងគ្រួសាររបស់យើង ។ ពីថ្ងៃនោះហូតមក
ដល់ថ្ងៃនេះ ប៉ុលិសពិនិត្យមើលមនុស្សទាំងអស់ដែលចូលក្នុងផ្ទះវ៉ា ។ អ្នកទៅ
ជិះកប៉ាល់ក៍បានជិះឡានក៍បាន ខ្ញុំនឹងទៅដល់មុនអ្នក ។ តាំងពីថ្ងៃនោះមកខ្ញុំបំរុងនឹង
ទៅស្រុកជប៉ុនមិនខាន ។ កូនសិស្សនោះហាត់រៀវាល់ថ្ងៃប៉ុន្តែមានតែពីរនាក់ទេដែល
ចេះវ៉ាយ៉ាងទន់ភ្លន់ ។ យន្តហោះសម័យថ្មីទៅបានមួយម៉ោងជានមួយពាន់គីឡូម៉ែត្រ ។

223

ខ្ញុំខ្លួចចូលចិត្តពិសាការហូរជាន់ទឹកតែ ។ ឯពួកនាងធ្វើគូរពេទ្យនៅភ្នំពេញប្រវែល ដប់ឆ្នាំហើយ ។ មុខជាអ្នកគួរឱ្យអ្នកបំរើដូរផ្សះមុន ។ គួរកត្យន់នោះគប់ កន្លែនឥតឃេញ ។ មិត្តសំឡាញ់ចៅនឹងទៅអត្ថុរវត្តអស់មួយអាទិត្យ ។ ពីឆ្នាំ នោះត ៗ មកទៅត ស្តេចខ្មែរសុទតែសោយរាជនៅភ្នំពេញ ។

ឥវ៉ាន់នោះ ខ្ញុំលើកមិនរួច ។ លោកច្រុស គាត់លឺយ៉ាងខ្លាំង យើនគួរ តែនៅស្ងៀម ។ កន្លែលនោះ លោកយាយតប្រាញ់ខ្លួនឯង ។ ស្រីនោះ ពីរ-បីខែមុន ថ្មីស្លាប់ទៅ ។ គេហស្ថានថ្មីនោះសង់នឹងឥដ្ឋទាំងអស់ ។ ទ្វារនេ ចាក់សោរហើយ ក៏ចិទមិនជិតដែរ ។ លោកនោះចូលមកប៉ុស្ត៊ិផ្ទើកញ្ចប់មួយទៅ ស្រុកឥន់ត្គោស ។ អ្នកណាក៏ដោយ លោកក៏មិនព្រមទួលព្រឹកនេះដែរ ។ ចារជិទទុកក្អួននេះទៅណា ប៉ូលិសនឹងជិះកណ្តាតទៅតាមដែរ ។ ទ្បាននេ បរ ទៅ ពួសូរគ្រឹក ៗ ។

ផ្ទះចៅហៅ

ផ្ទះចៅហៅពីដើមអំពីលើ ច្រក់ស្ពឹកត្គោត សង់លើចន្លុ់ មានទ្វារមួយហើយនឹង បន្ទូចបីខ្ទប ៗ ។ ខ្មែរមិនធ្វើទ្វារបន្ទូចច្រើនទេ ។ គេឡើងផ្ទះតាមជណ្ដើរ ។ នៅក្នុងផ្ទះមានបន្ទប់ពីរ ឬមួយ ហើយនឹងគុមួយ ។ នៅក្នុងផ្ទះគ្មានកៅអីនឹងគែ ទេ គេដេកលើកន្លែលគ្រាលលើរនាប ។

Exercise 42 A

ផ្សេរចៅហ្វាន ត

ផ្សេរចៅហ្វានមានរបងបង្គោលបូស្រ្តៃទ្វៃដុំវិញ ។ នៅក្នុងរបងនោះមានដើមបេក ផូន ស្លា ។ នៅកេ្រ}មានក្រាលគោ នៅក្រោមម្លប់ដើមស្បាយមាន ទុន ជ្រូកហើយ និង ទុនមាន់ ។ នៅមុខផ្សេរមានក្នុងលេនសប្បាយ ។

Exercise 43 A

ផ្សារក្នុងភូមិចៅហ្វាន

ផ្សារក្នុងភូមិចៅហ្វាន ច្រក់ក្បៀៀនមានសសរវង្ស ចំហាតឧជព័ញ្ជាន ។ នៅផ្សារនោះ អ្នកស្រុកដាក់ទំនិញលក់ ។ ផ្សារមាន ចវៃន ប៉ាំបីម៉េ ត បៃកជាច្រើនល្បែន ។ ក្នុងល្បែនមួយមានចិនលក់សាច់គោ នៅល្បែនមួយទេ}តមាន សីលក់ គីអន្តុយចៅង ហ្វានដាក់កញ្ជ្រោព័មុខ មាន គីរ័ស់ គី ស្រស់ គី ន៉ាប់ គី ន្លៃ}ត គីឆ្លៃ ។ កៃ ន្លៃនលក់សាច់ហើយ និង គីនេនគេ ពួសលាន រាល់ថ្ងៃ ។

Exercise 44 A

ភ្នំដួន ពេញ

នៅទី ក្នុង ភ្នំពេញ មានភ្នំមួយ មានវត្តតាំននៅលើ ភ្នំនោះ ដែលជាលិអ ដល់ទី ក្នុន ។ ច្បៃហ្វលជាមានភ្នំនេ ះ ហើយ បានជាគេ ហៅថា ភ្នំពេញ រហូត មកដល់សព្វ ថ្ងៃ នេ ះ ។ នៅ ភ្នំ នេ ះ ខាង លិច ព ះ វិហារវន}ន ខាង ត្បូន មាន ចេតិយ មួយ ធំ ដែលខ្លង់ ស្បួរ ព័ មៃក ឈើ ផេ្ទ ន ។ នៅ ខាង ជើន ព័ ដើម មាន ទុន ខ្លារ វិន ខ្លាធំ ខ្លាយ៉ុ ។ និង នៅ ខាង ត្បូន មាន ក ៃ ន្លន គេ ចិ ញ្ចឹ ម ក ព័ ស្បា

ពស់ ប្រើស និងមានសត្វផ្សេង ៗ ទៀត ។ សទ្យវនេះ រាជការយករបស់
នេះបេញអស់ហើយ នៅតែទឹកខ្លែងបន្តិចបន្តួច ។

ការធ្វើគីធ្នៀត

គេយកគីរ៉ស់ គីផ្សេង ៗ មកយកស្រការបេញ ហើយវះពោរជ្រកជា
ប្ូនដំរៀក ។ ឮូនកាលគេកាត់ក្បាលបោលហើយគេយកទុនុង ឃុំងបេញដែរ ។
គេបុកអំបិលឲ្យស្ថិត យកទៅប្របង្ហក់គី ហើយគេ ត្រិទុកប្របហលបី-ប្ូនម៉ោង ។
គេយកមកលាងទឹក ហាលថ្ងៃ ប្របហលពីរ-បីថ្ងៃ ឮ្ចហាលលើស្ពាក់ ។

គ្រួសាររបស់ចៅហេង

គា នៅ ក្នុង គ្រួសារចៅមានមនុស្សប្ុំ ឆ្នានាក់ ?

ចៅ ពាទ ខ្ញុំមិនដឹងទេ ប្របហលជា ប្ំពីរនាក់ ។

គា ៩! ចៅមិនដឹងប្ុំ ឈ្ន័ន ចៅមានឪពុកម្ដាយទេ ?

ចៅ ពាទ ខ្ញុំមាន ។

គា ចៅមានបងប្ូនទេ ?

ចៅ ពាទ ខ្ញុំមានបងប្ុសបីនាក់ បងស្រីពីរនាក់ និងប្ូនប្ុសម្នាក់ ។

គា ដីដូនដីតាចៅនៅជាមួយចៅឬទេ ?

ចៅ ពាទទេ ប្ុំ ឆ្នែឪពុកខ្ញុំចិញ្ចឹមក្មួយ ស្រីម្នាក់ ។

226

តា ដូរខ្លះរចៅមានឧបុកម្ពាយ បន្ថួន ្រ្បាំមួយនាក់ និន្ក្ខ្ឈយម្ពាក់ គឺ ្រ្បាំមួយនាក់ទាំងអស់ ។

ចៅ បាទទេ នារភ្លេច្ខ្ញុំ ។

តា ទ! អញ្ចឹងមានដប់នាក់ ។

Exercise 47 A

ភ្នំពេញថ្ងៃ ៣ ខែមេសា ១៩៦៤

សំឡាញ់

ថ្ងៃនេះជាថ្ងៃអាទិត្យ យើននិនបបូលសំឡាញ់ដើរលេងកំសាន្តតាមមាត់ទន្លេ ហើយនិនមើលកូនដេីម្ប៊ីឲ្យសប្បាយចិត្ត ។ ហេតុនេះ ខ្ញុំសូមអញ្ជើញសំឡាញ់ មកជួបនិន ខ្ញុំនៅផ្ទះខ្ញុំថ្ងៃរសៀ]លម៉ោន ៤ កុំខាន ។

សួស្ត៊ី

សំឡាញ់

Exercise 48 A

ភ្នំពេញថ្ងៃ ៣ ខែមេសា ១៩៦៤

មក រស់សារ]ន ជាទីរ៉ពក

ជាយូរៗនែហើយ យើនមិនដែលបានជួបពាក្យរស័ដ៏ឲ្យមុនរបស់សំឡាញ់ងនសោះ ។ តាំងពីថែកគ្មួមក ្របហែលជា ៤-៥ ខែហើយ ឲ្យមួយសំឡាញ់ថែកចិត្តអំពីយើន បានជាមិនឃេីញផ្ដើសំបុ្រតមកសោះ ។ យើនមិនបានដិនទ៊ីកនៃន្ននសំឡាញ់ងនឲ្យពិត

227

ព្រាកដ ទើបតែសួរគេដឹងជា សំឡាញ់ឯងចេញពីវៃ ព្រែតករទៅនៅប៉ារីស ។

សព្វថ្ងៃសំឡាញ់ឯងសុខសប្បាយទេឬ? ។ ឬមួយមានសេចក្ដីឃ្លាំងណា? ។

បើសំឡាញ់ឯងបានសេចក្ដីសុខហើយ យើងមានចិត្ត ត្រេកអរណាស់ ។ រកឯ
ប្រៀ ច ផ្ទឹមគ្នា ចំណែកខាងខ្ញុំវិញ សុខសប្បាយទេ ។

សូមទទួលដោយមេត្រីភាព

Exercise 49 A

ភ្នំពេញថ្ងៃ ៣ ខែមេសា ១៩៦៦

ខ្ញុំសូមជំរាបមកលោកធំ ទីចាត់ការនៃ ក្រុមផ្សាយដំណឹងល្អ

ខ្ញុំមិនបានមកផ្ដល់ខ្លួនខ្ញុំ ព្រោះថ្ងៃនេះខ្ញុំមិនស្រួល ស្រួល ខ្លួនបេះតែវិលមុខឈឺ
ក្បាល ។ ហេតុនេះ ខ្ញុំសូមឈប់ឈប់ធ្វើការពីរថ្ងៃ ទំរាំដល់ខ្ញុំ ស្រួលខ្លួន
ឡើងវិញ ។ សូមមេត្តាដោយសេចក្ដីអនុ ត្រោះ ។

សេចក្ដីគួរ ព្រួ យ សូមអភ័យទោស ។

Exercise 50 A

ម៉ាស៊ីនអក្ខរលិលេខ

កាលពីថ្ងៃ ១ ខែមិថុនា ឆ្នាំ ១៩៦២ ខ្ញុំ ត្រូវបួលរៀ នរ៉ាយម៉ាស៊ីនអក្សរ ។

នៅក្នុងកន្លែងរៀ នមានគុ ពីរផ្សេ មាន គ្រូ ស្រីជាតិយួនម្នាក់ និងសិស្សជា ច្រើននាក់ ។

ខ្ញុំលទៅសួរជាភាសា ខ្មែរថា មានសល់កន្លែងទេ? ។ ខ្ញុំ ផ្ដ់លរៀ នដែរ ។

ស្រីនោះឆ្លើយថា កន្លែងចន្លើ តណាស់ ។ បើ អ្នកចង់រៀន រៀ នបាន តែ

228

ពេល ្រ ពីកម្ដួយម៉ោន និន ស្ដាបម្ដួយម៉ោន ។ ខ្ញុំក៏សុខចិត្ត ហើយគេឲ្យ ខ្ញុំកត់ឈ្នោះ ទ ីលំ នៅ និន បន់ ្រ ពាក់ ៦០០ រ ៀ ល មុន ។ ពេល ខ្ញុំ ចូល រ ៀ ន ខ្ញុំ ពិបាក ចិត្ត និ ន ដ ែ ខ្ញុំ ណាស់ ្រ ពោះ ដែ ខ្ញុំ រ ៀ ន មិន ទាន់ ស្ដាត់ ។ ជូ នកាល វា យ ទាំ ្រ មាម ្រ ពាំ ។ ឥ ឡ ូ វ នេះ ខ្ញុំ រ ៀ ន យ ្រ គាន់ បើ ហើយ ដ ល់ ថ ៃ ្រ ក្រោយ ខ្ញុំ និ ន ្រ ប ដ្ឋ ន យ ក សញ្ញាប់ ្រ ត ពេ ញ ធ្វើការ ក្ន ុ ង ក ្រ ន្ត ណាម្ដួយ មិន ខាន ។

Exercise 51 A

ទ ិ ញ សំ ប ុ ្រ ត ឡ្ងាន ឈ្មួល

អ្នកលក់សំប ុ ្រ ត	លោក អ ញ្ជ ើ ញ ទៅ ណា?
លោកសំរិត	ខ្ញុំ ចង់ ទៅ កំ ពង់ ចាម នៅ ម៉ោ ង ម្ដួយ ក ន្ល ង ថ្ង ្រ ត្ង ់ នេះ ។
អ្នកលក់សំប ុ ្រ ត	លោក ចង់ បាន ប៉ុ ន ណា?
លោកសំរិត	ខ្ញុំ ចង់ បាន ខាង មុ ខ ជិត ស្ង ប ្ហ ័ រ ។
អ្នកលក់សំប ុ ្រ ត	១ ! នៅ ស ល់ ក ្រ ន្ត ម្ដួយ លោក លោក អា ច និ ន យ ក បាន ។
លោកសំរិត	ហ្ង ៊ ន ហើយ តើ ថ្ង ៃ ប៉ុ ន្ម ាន?
អ្នកលក់សំប ុ ្រ ត	ហាសិប ្រ ប ៉ាំ រ ៀ ល លោក ។
លោកសំរិត	១ ! ខ្ញុំ មាន ត ែ ្រ ក ដា ស ម្ដួយ រ យ រ ៀ ល ទ ។
អ្នកលក់សំប ុ ្រ ត	មិន អ ី ទ លោក ខ្ញុំ មាន ដ ុ រ ដ ូ ន លោក បាន ។
លោកសំរិត	អ ី ម៉ោ ង ប៉ុ ន្ម ាន បាន ឡ្ងាន ទៅ ដ ល់ កំ ពង់ ចាម?
អ្នកលក់សំប ុ ្រ ត	្ហ ទ ្រ ប ហែ ល ជា ម៉ោ ង ប ីក ន្ល ះ ប្ង ូ ន ។

Exercise 52 A

ល្ខោនខ្មែរ

នៅក្រុងភ្នំពេញ មានល្ខោនខ្មែរ ៣ កណ្ដែង រោងថ្ម ១ រោងផ្សារស៊ីវិប ១ និងរោងផ្សារកាប់គោ ១ ។ ពេលយប់ម៉ោង ៨ នៅមុខរោងគប់ល្ខោនទាំងអស់ មានមនុស្សច្រើនណាស់ ខ្លះលក់បំណរផ្សេងៗ ខ្លះទិញសំបុត្រល្ខោន ខ្លះសួររកគ្នាថាគេលេងរឿងអី ខ្លះនិយាយគ្នាពីរឿងអ្វីផ្សេងៗ ពួកសួរទីហាន់អ៊ីនកន ។ ដល់ម៉ោង ៩ អ្នកលេងភ្លេងល្ខោន គេលេងភ្លេងគំនាប់ពេកករុណារូបហើយ គេចាប់លេងរឿងផ្សេង ៗ តទៅ ។ អ្នកមើល ខ្លះនិយាយគ្នាថា ល្ខោនស្រេចនិងអ្នកត្តុក បើអ្នកត្តុកមិនសួរកំប្លែងទេ មិនល្អមើលទេ ។ ខ្លះថា អញមើលល្ខោនមិនសួរចាំរឿងសោះ អ្នកទៀត អញមិនចូលចិត្តមើលល្ខោនរោងថ្មទេ អញចូលចិត្តមើលល្ខោនរោងផ្សារកាប់គោ ព្រោះស្រី ៗ ល្អ ៗ ណាស់ ហើយរបៀនពីរោងផន ។

Exercise 53 A

ក្នុងរោងល្ខោន

យប់មុិញបានឯងទៅណា? យប់មុិញខ្ញុំទៅមើលល្ខោន ។ គេលេងរឿងអី? លេងរឿងព្រះលក្សណវង្ស គាំពីព្រះព្រហ្មកពរនាង ។ ល្អមើលទេ? យី! ល្អមើលណាស់ ។ ល្ខោនរោងណា? រោងផ្សារកាប់គោ ។ អី! អញ ថ្ដន់អ៊ីយថ្ដន់ មនុស្សមើលបផ្ញៀតណាស់ វានិយាយគ្នាពួសួរអ្ញ ៗ ស្ដាប់គេរបៀនមិនញញសោះ ។ អញសើងអ៊ីយសើង ពួកអ្នកត្តុកកំប្លែងល្អមើលណាស់ ។

អញ្ញញ អ្នកម្នាក់និយាយគ្នាខាន្រ្គាយអញ្ញជា យី! ខ្ញុំញជា គេមើលកុនអន្តួយជិត មិនល្បមើលទេ ្រ្ពះវាញ្រ្គរ គេមើលតែពីរបម្ងាយ ងល្ងោនម៉េចមិនញ្ញ្គរ? គេ មើលជិត ៗ ថ្នាក់លេខ ១ បានល្ងមើល ។ អញ្ញិកក្នុងចិត្តជា អ្នកនេះ្របហែល ជាអ្នករ្ងែស មិនដែលស្គាល់ល្ងោនស្គាល់កុន បានជានិយាយអញ្ញ៉ិន ។ លុះ ដល់ម៉េ៉ាន ១២ គេរ៉ាវាង អញ្ញដើរមកសូ៉ចបរអស់ ១ បានរួបគ្រេ្ញមកដេកងផ្ងុះវិញ ។

Exercise 54 A

រ្ ៀងហាន្រ្ងនិងអណ្ណើក

នៅក្នុង្រ្គេះមួយ មានអណ្ណើកធំមួយ នៅក្នុង្រ្គេះនោះ មានហាន្រ្ងមួយគូ ទៅរកស៉ូក្នុង្រ្គេះនោះរាល់ថ្ង ។ ដល់ខែ្បុំ៉ានទឹក្រ្គេះនោះវិនអស់ទៅ អណ្ណើកគិតនិងកកាយរួន ផ្ងើកខ្ងែនទៅជា ថ្ងេ្ ៀត ្រ្គាប់តែហាន្រ្ង្ងាំន៍ពីរ ចូល ទៅនិយាយជា បន៍អណ្ណើក ៗ បន៍ងងនៅ៉្មុន៍ពីបាកណាស់ ទឹក្រ្គេះវិន អស់ហើយ បានអ៉ីស្ឞ? បន៍ងងទៅ៍នៅ្រ្សុកងណេះទៃបសប្ប៉ាយ មាន ចំណ៉ីស៉ី្រ្គប៉ម្ងុ ។ អណ្ណើកជា ខ្ញុំទៅមិនកើតទេ បន៍ហាន្រ្ងអ៉ើយ ខ្ញុំគ្គាន ស្ងាបហើរទេ ។ ហាន្រ្ងន្ងើយជា អ៉ើ បើបន៍ងងទៅខ្ញុំយកទៅបាន តែ្ឞ៉ុបន៍ ងង៍ខ៉ាម៉ាត់្ឞ៉ុជិត អ្នកណាជាម៉ែចកុំ្ឞ៉ុតនិង៍វ ។ អណ្ណើកជាបាន ហើយហាន្រ្ង ្ងាំន៍ពីរទៅ៉ៅ៉ែមកលើមួយកំណាត់មក រួ៉ុ្រ្ឞ៉ាប់ជា ្ឞ៉ុបន៍អណ្ណើកងង៍ខ៉ាបំកណ្ងាល ខ្ញុំ៉ៅ៉សន៍ខ៉ាន ហើយ៉ក៉ហើរទៅ ។ លុះដល់្រ្សុកមួយ មានមនុស្ឞជារ្បើន

231

គេលេននៅមុខផ្ទះ បានឃើញហង្សទាំងពីរហើយ គេរ៉ិសេកជា មើលហង្សព្រាំ អណ្ដើករ៉ុយ អណ្ដើកញ្ញសំទ្បេងមនុស្សជាដូច្នោះ ក៏គិតនិយាយជា ចុះបើសំ-ទ្បាញ់អញ្ញេញនាំអញ្ជេ។ ឯឯចាំបាប់និយាយអី? ក្រាន់តែគិតជាប៉ុណ្ណាន ក៏ឬបូតមាត់ធ្លាក់បៃកស្លកស្លាប់ទៅ ។

Exercise 55 A

រប៉ៀបធ្វើសូរវត្ថោត

ខែណាគេធ្វើសូរវត្ថោត? ខែ្រ ចុ៉ា្ន ។ គេធ្វើសូរវត្ថោតនោះដូចគតទៅនេះ ។ កាលណាដើមត្ថោតមានផ្ការហើយ គេឋនបឆ្នោងពីក្រាមដល់លើ ហើយគេឡ្បើនទៅចិតផ្កាត្ថោតត្រង់មុ៑ូវ ៦-៣ កាំបិត រួចគេយកហ្ឃូចគាតផ្កាត្ថោតបត្តិច ។ មិនឱ្យ្ខ្លាំនទេ ។ គេឡ្បើនទៅចិតមុ៑ូវ ៦-៣ ពីកហើយគាតបជឋ ។ គេយកចំពឆ់មកអប់ឱ្យជុំក្តិនដូរ ហើយយកគេទៅ ្រតនតាំនពីល្ឃ៊ូវ ្រចបៃលម៉េ ្រៃ ្ររ៉ាហ្ឃូតដល់ភ្តី ទើបគេទៅដាក់ទិកត្ថោត ។ ក្នុនមួយដើមមាន ៤-៦ បំពឆ់ ។ គេមិនមៃន ធ្វើតៃ ១ ដើមទេ គេធ្វើ ៤-៦ ដើម ។ លុះគេដាក់មកដល់ជីហើយ គេ ទ ទួលទានខ្មះ គេលក់ខ្មះ ។ ទូនកាលគេយកទិកត្ថោតមកចាក់ក្នុនខ្ម៑ូធំ ១ ហើយគេយកទៅដាក់ក្នុនឡ្ យ រួចដុតភ្ឃ៊នឱ្យពុះរ៉ិ្ចេនៅតៃសូរ ។ គេធ្វើសូរ្ខ៑ះ ឧសណាស់ គេដាំ ១ ខ៑ះ ១ ថ្ឃ ទើបរ៉ិ្ចេបានជាសូរ ។ លុះរ៉ិ្ចេហើយគេ ដាក់ចេញពីភ្ឃ៊ន គេក្ខ៑ូវ៉ិកឱ្យស្ងួតហើយគេយកក្ខមឬពាងមកចាក់ទុកលក់ឬទុក ទ ទួលទាន ។

Exercise 56 A

ឆួប ជុំពូនីនមីន

 អ្នកសារ៉ែន ជំរាបសួរលោកពូ អ្នកមីន សុខសប្បាយជាទេ?

ពូ ពូមីនសុខសប្បាយទេ ។ ពូដឹងថាងន់ជិតទៅស្រុកគេហើយទើបពូ
មីនឋិន្ឫ្យឪតមកលេងងន់បន្តិច ។

អ្នកសារ៉ែន ខ្ញុំទើបនឹងទទួលសំបុត្រលោកពូពីព្រឹកមិញុ៎ ។ ខ្ញុំសប្បាយ
ណាស់ដោយលោកពូអ្នកមីនបានអញ្ជើញមកឆួបជុំគ្នាទាំងអស់ដូចធ្ងៈ ។

មីន ងន់ត្រូវទៅរៀនប៉ុន្មានឆ្នាំទៀត?

អ្នកសារ៉ែន ៣! យូរដែរអ្នកមីន ប្រហែល ៥-៦ ឆ្នាំ ។

ពូ ងន់ទៅរៀនខាងអី?

អ្នកសារ៉ែន ខាងសង់ផុៈ សង់ផុល សង់ស្ពានអី ៗ អស់ហ្ន៎ីន លោកពូ ។

ពូ ងន់ត្រូវឡើងកប៉ាល់ហោះនៅម៉ោងប៉ុន្មាន?

អ្នកសារ៉ែន ស្អែកម៉ោងឆួបកន្លះលោកពូ ។ លោកពូចង់ជូនខ្ញុំទៅឬ? កុំអី
នាំតែអំពល់លោកពូទេ ។

ពូ មិនអីទេ ពូនឹងមីនងន់ចង់ទៅមើលងន់ឡើងកប៉ាល់ហោះដែរ ។

អ្នកសារ៉ែន ខ្ញុំអរគុណច្រើនហើយដោយលោកពូអ្នកមីនបានអញ្ជើញមកជួបជុនខ្ញុំទៅ
ចំណាតយន្តហោះទៀ ត ។

ពូ មិនអីទេ ទំរាំយើញងន់មុននទៀ ត ៥-៦ ឆ្នាំ ម្លេះពូមីនចាស់
អស់ហើយទំរាំងន់មកវិញ ។

Exercise 57 A

ការទាក់ដំរី

នៅ ស្រុកខ្មែរ មានព្រៃភ្នំជាច្រើនដែលពេញទៅដោយហ្វូងដំរីច្រើន ។ បើ ត្រូវការបង់ទាក់ដំរី គេត្រូវយកទមាក់ដែលបេះច្របសប់ហើយគេបចូលគ្នាច្របហែល ម្តងនាក់ ជិះទូកត្បូង ។ ក្នុងទូកមួយ ។ គេជិះពីរនាក់ ហើយគេឡើងដេរទៅ ក្នុងព្រៃ កេ ៀនសត្តូដំរីទាំងហ្វូង ។ មនុស្សទាំងអស់ត្រូវមាន ច្របាប់សម្រាប់ ការពារខ្លួន មានដាវ លំពែង កាំបិតជាដើម ។ លុះគេយើញហ្វូងដំរីហើយ គេដេរកេ ៀនឲ្យវាចុះក្នុងទឹកស្ទីន ទន្លេ បឹង ហើយគេចុះទៅជិះទូកទាំងអស់គ្នា ។ គេអុំទូកកេ ៀនចុះកេ ៀនឡើន ហើយគេបំរុងថានឹងទាក់យកតែមួយ ។ ទមាក់ ដំរីវៃ ស្រកច្បាប់អ្នកទាំងអស់គ្នាឲ្យដេញដំរីឡើននៅលើគោក ហើយគេកេ ៀនយក តែមួយ ។ ទមាក់ដំរីត្រូវឡើនជិះលើកដំរីមួយនោះ កាប់ក្បាលនឹងព្យហោ ។ ដំរីផ្ទើអ៊ីមិនបាន ព្រោះនៅក្នុងទឹកចេ ជាជុតដេីនជុតដែ ។ លុះគេជីនជា វាអស់កំឡាំងណាស់ហើយ ទើបគេយកមកបនទុកនឹងបផ្គេលមួយដែលគេបោះក្នុង ទឹកចេ ជាឲ្យជុតដែដេីនដំរី ហើយគេទៅផ្ដុះទាំងអស់គ្នា ។ ច្របហែលជាមួយ អាទិត្យគេយកស្មៀមួយកនមកឲ្យស៊ី ដល់អាទិត្យច្រាយគេយកទៅផ្ដុះបផ្គត់ឲ្យបេះ ស្តាប់ពាក្យមនុស្សខ្លួ ។ ដោយការលំបាកទាក់ដូរច្ងេះ បានជាគេលក់ដំរីមួយ ។ ថ្លៃណាស់ ។ គេត្រូវឲ្យឈ្លោះដំរីតាមចិត្តគេ ។

Exercise 58 A

រឿងមេមាយម្នាក់

ខ្ញុំមានកូនក្រមុំម្នាក់ គេដណ្ដឹងហើយ កំណត់ចូលរោងនៅថ្ងៃក្រោយ ។ ឥឡូវរូវគិតផ្ញើសំបុត្រទៅប្រាប់បងប្អូនជិតឆ្ងាយ ឲ្យមកស៊ីការ ហើយភាគ់ក៏ផ្ញើ សំបុត្រទៅគប់បងប្អូនទាំងអស់ ។ អ្នកនៅក្នុងផ្ទះទាំងអស់គ្នា ទៅទិញ្ចប្រស្ប្រី យកមកផ្ញើរោង ។ លុះដល់ពីកថ្ងៃចូលរោង មានភ្ញៀវអញ្ជើញមកជាច្រើន មានភ្ញួនលេនពួស្បួរ្ទប៉ាន ។ ខ្លះនិយាយគ្នាលេនសប្បាយ ។ ខ្លះសួរថា ពួនៅស្រុកណា? គេឆ្លើយថា ខ្ញុំនៅស្រុកកំពន់ឆ្នាំង ។ ម៉ឺងមិនអញ្ជើញមក ទេ? មកដែរ ។ ពួនៅស្រុកនោះស្គាល់ពួហ៊ានទេ? ស្គាល់ ។ គាត់សុខ សប្បាយទេ? បាទ គាត់សុខសប្បាយទេ ។ នៅកន្លែងបុនកៅ អ្នកខ្លះនា សាប់ផ្សែកញនេរនាវ ខ្លះហាន់បថៃ ខ្លះចិព្រ្ងាំសាប់ផ្សែកញ្ញូកប៉ាក ។ ។ នាន ម្ដាស់ផ្ទះ ដេររុះដេររឡ្ទីង បៃកញ្រៀសប្ពួរស្រាក់ ។ បន្តិចមានភ្ញៀវ ចំនួន ១៥ នាក់ មានក្នុនតូប ។ ៣-៤ នាក់ ។ ភ្ញៀវនោះត្រូវជាបងបធ្ងឹតគាត់ ៣ នាក់ប្រុសម្នាក់ស្រី ៦ នាក់ និនបងប្អូនជីដូនមួយ ខ្លះឆន ។ កាលណាមកដល់ ផ្ទះ នានម្ដាស់ផ្ទះក៍សួរទៅជីវាបស្ពួរ លើកដៃសំពះ ហើយសួរថា បន សុខសប្បាយទេ? គេឆ្លើយថា សុខសប្បាយទេ ។ ហើយក៏លោរភ្ញៀវឲ្យ ឡ្ទីនទៅលើផ្ទះ និយាយគ្នាថា មនុស្សប្រុសដែលគេដណ្ដឹងកូនឯន នៅ ស្រុកណា? រកស៊ីធ្វើអី? នាននោះថា នៅស្រុកកំពន់ឆ្នាំង រកស៊ីធ្វើជំនួញ ។

នាងម្ចាស់ផ្នូនិយាយថា   ពួឡានម៉េចគាត់មិនអញ្ជើញមក? ឬបែបលសំបុ[តទៅ
មិនដល់ឬ?   ហើយគាត់នាកទៅយកនំ ៦-៣ មកឲ្យកូយគាត់ហើយថា   កូយ
ញ្ញាំទៅ ។   ឬបែបលជាមិនស្គាល់ម៊ីតទេមើលទៅ? ។

Exercise 59 A

មាយប្ជូជា-វិសាខប្ជូជា

ថ្ងៃអាទិត្យ ២០ ខែឧសភា   [គប់វត្តទាំងអស់   ក្នុង[ស្រុកខ្មែរ   ពេល
ម៉ោង ៦ រសៀ]ល   គេរ]ចបំផ្ល   នឹងទិករេសជផ្សេង ៗ   មានទឹកតែ
ជាដើម   បំរុននឹ[ងបគេនលោក ។   គេគោរវគាំ[ងដុំលោកសង្ឃ]ទាំងអស់
ក្នុងវត្ត   [បគេនទឹករេសជលោកនាត់ ។   លុះម៉ោង ៨ ហើយ   គេ[ចដុំ
ពួកឧបាសក-ឧបាសិកា   សូ[តធមិ៉ថ្វាយបឋ្គំ   រួចហើយគេនិមន្តលោកសង្ឃ]ឲ្យចូល
ក្នុងវិហារ   ហើយសូ[តធមិ ។   វត្តខ្លះ   មានចាក់ម៉ាស៊ីនព[ឝិកសំឡេងឲ្យឮ
ឆ្ងាយ ។   វត្តខ្លះ   គ្មានម៉ាស៊ីន[ឝ]នព[ឝិកទេ ។   លុះលោកសូ[តធមិរួច
ហើយ   គេនិមន្តលោក ១ អង្គឬ ២ អង្គសំដែងធមិទេស្ណា ។   ផ្នកាលគេ
ទេស្ណា ៦ ៨៩   តាមឥូលចិត្ត ។   លុះទេស្ណាចប់ហើយ   គេធ្វើឆទផ្សេង ៗ អំពី
[ពះអង្គ[បស្ខុតិ   ឬបេញ្ញឥូស   ឬបវិនិព្ទាន ។   រូបេ]បធ្វើបុណ្យមាយប្ជូជា
នឹងវិសាខប្ជូជា   ដូចខ្ញុំបាននិយាយមកនេះ   គេធ្វើតែក្នុងថ្ងៃ ១៥ កើតខែមាយនឹង

ខែវិសាខ ។ បើធ្វើខែមាយហៅថាមាយបូជា បើធ្វើខែវិសាខហៅថាវិសាខបូជា ។ បុណ្យនេះគេធ្វើរំឭកដល់ពាក្យដែល ព្រះអង្គបាន ប្រាប់ អានន្ទជា នៃអានន្ទ គជា-គតនៅតែ ៤ ខែទៀ និងចូលនិព្វានហើយ ។ ព្រះពុទ្ធ ជាការនេះបាន ប្រាប់ អានន្ទ ក្នុងថ្ងៃ ១៥ កើតខែមាយ ។ លុះដល់ថ្ងៃ ១៥ កើតខែវិសាខ ព្រះអង្គ បរិនិព្វាន ។ ឧបាសក ឧបាសិកាមានសេចក្ដីសោកស្ដាយ ស្រណោះ ព្រះអង្គណាស់ បានជាធ្វើបុណ្យនេះរឿងមក តាំងពីយូរហើយ រហូតមកដល់សព្វថ្ងៃនេះ ។ គេធ្វើបទ ផ្សេង ៗ ដូចបាននិយាយមកខាងលើនេះ អស់ ១ យប់ ដូចកាលគេធ្វើ តែ ២–៣ ម៉ោងទេ ។ លុះ ព្រឹកឡើង គេនិមន្តលោកឆាន់បបរ ថ្ងៃគង់ ឆាន់បាយ ។ អស់កិច្ចបុណ្យមាយបូជានិងវិសាខបូជាតែប៉ុណ្ណោះ ។

Exercise 60 A

កិច្ចការរបស់អ្នកស្រែ

ដល់ខែវិសាខ មានភ្លៀងធ្លាក់ចើនរាល់ថ្ងៃ ។ ទឹកដក់នៅក្នុងស្រែទាំងអស់ អ្នកស្រែរៀបចំ ប្រដាប់ ប្រដាសប្រមប់ធ្វើស្រែ គឺ នង្គ័ល រនាស់ ចបកាប់ ជាដើម ។ គេទិមគោ ១ និមទៅភ្ជួលមួយហើយគេរាស់យកស្មៅ បេញ ឲ្យស្អាតពីភ្ជួលនោះ រួចគេយក ស្រូវ ដែល ត្រាំ ទុក ពីរបីថ្ងៃ មុនដែលមានពន្លក ល្មម ទៅ សាបក្នុងភ្ជួលនោះ គេ ប្រយ័ត្ន មិនឲ្យគោ ឬ សត្វ ស៊ី ទេ ។ លុះសំណាបនោះ ដុស បានកំ ពស់ ល្មម ហើយ គេដកបេញ ចងជាកណ្ដាប់ ទុក ។ ហើយគេ ទៅ ភ្ជួរ ស្រែ

ផ្សេងទៅ]តដោយយកកណ្ដាប់ដែលជកនោះទៅស្ងួតក្នុង[ស ។ លុះគេស្ងួត[ស

នោះពេញហើយ   គេទៅស្ងួត[សជទៃទៅ]ត ។   ក្នុង[គ្គុសារម្មយ ៗ មាន

[ស ៥-៦ ដួនកាល ១០ ឬ ១៩ ក៏មានៃដរ ។   អ្នកៃ[ស[ទិណាស់ដោយ

ដួនកាលក្ដៅពេកដួនកាលរងាពេកៃតមិនតព្ញាត្ត្រូវជាក្ដៅឬរងាឡើយ ។   លុះស្ងួត[គប់

ៃ[សអស់ហើយ   គេលប់ស[មាក ២-៣ ៃ២   ៃតប្ុស ៗ ត្រូវទៅមើល

ៃ[សជារ]យ ។   ៃ[កឆៃ[សគ្មានទិកឬទិក[ចិនពេក   បើគ្មានទិកគេកាប់បន្ថុរ

ទិកតាម[ចឆ្លាយបញ្ចូលទៅក្នុងៃ[ស   បើមានទិក[ចិនគេបន្ថុររបេញខ្លះ ។

បាន ១ ៃ២[ស្រូវនោះលាស់ល្ណុណាស់ ។   មិនយូរប៉ុន្នាន   [ស្រូវផ្ដើម[គប់ៃ[ស

ទាំងអស់ ។   គេមិនៃមនស្ងួន[ស្រូវខ្យាយទាំងអស់ទេ   គេស្ងួន[ស្រូវជំណ៉ុប ខ្លះ

ៃជ្រ ។   [ស្រូវជំណ៉ុបគេទុកធ្វើនំផ្សេង ៗ ។   លុះ[ស្រូវបេញៃផ្នអស់ហើយ

គេចាត់មនុស្ស]ឲ្យៅជេញចាប[វាល់ៃថ្ង   ដួនណាគេបឋរយាលចាបពេញៃ[ស   ដួនណា

គេផ្ដើមមោឆ[ដាក់កណ្ដាល[ស   ឲ្យបាឆខ្លាឆ ។   គេព្ញស្ងរមាត់មនុស្ស[ស្រក

ជេញចាប រ៉ុសវ៉ាស ៗ វាល់ៃត[ពិក ។   ៃ[សណាគេនៅជិតៃ[ជ   គ្មានម្ណស់ទៅចាំ

[ស្រូវនោះសត្ូចាបស្ុ៉នៃត[សកី ។   លុះ[ស្រូវទិខ្លះហើយ   គេបន្ថុរទិកបេញ

ឲ្យអស់ពីៃ[ស   ហើយគេយកឆលើទៅផ្នកឲ្យ[ស្រូវដួលរាប[សណ្ុក[ច្ុត ។

គេរ]ឆបំកណ្ណ៉]វស[មាប់[ច្ុត[ស្រូវ[គប់គ្នាទាំងអស់ ។   លុះគេផ្នក[ស្រូវ

238

ហើយ គេច្រូតចងជាកណ្តាប់ដាក់ដង្ហែរគ្នា ។ រួចគេដឹកស្រូវនោះយកមកទុកមុខផ្ទះ ។ បើអ្នកណាមានស្រែច្រើន គេត្រូវយកវេរគ្នាទៅច្រូតខាងណោះមួយថ្ងៃ ខាងណោះមួយថ្ងៃ ។ បើត្រូវលើវេរអ្នកណា អ្នកនោះត្រូវរៀបចំបាយទឹកផង ។ លុះដឹកស្រូវយកមកទុកក្នុងលានហើយ គេបោកនឹងក្តារឲ្យជ្រុះគ្រាប់ស្រូវ ឬក៏បែនឬបញ្ជាន់ក៏មាន ។ ជួនណាគេយកវេរគ្នាក៏មានដែរ ។ លុះគេបែន បោក បញ្ជាន់រួចហើយ គេជញ្ជូនចំបើងទៅគរទុកនៅកន្លែងមួយ រួចគេយកស្រូវទៅរោយកណ្តាលវាលស្រែ ដែលមានខ្យល់ឲ្យជ្រុះសណ្តីចេញ យកតែស្រូវដែលមានគ្រាប់ល្អ ទៅទុកក្នុងជង្រុក ហើយគេត្រូវលក់ខ្លះផង ទុកខ្លះផង ។ ក្នុងគ្រួសារមួយ ៗ បានស្រូវ ៦០-៧០ ថាំង ជួនកាល ១០០ ថាំង ១៥០ ថាំងក៏មាន ។

នៅស្រុកខ្មែរ មានម៉ាស៊ីនកិនស្រូវដែរ តែមិនមានគ្រប់គ្រាន់ទេ អ្នកស្រែត្រូវយកស្រូវទៅកិននឹងត្បាល់ កិនឲ្យជ្រុះអង្កាមហើយយកអង្ករនោះមកបុកឬជាន់នឹងត្បាល់ក្តៀង ។ លុះអង្ករសហើយ គេបារចេញពីត្បាល់យកមកអុំយកកន្ទកឲ្យជ្រូកស៊ី យកអង្ករមកដាំបាយទទួលទាន ។ អ្នកស្រែមិនមែនធ្វើតែស្រែទេ ស្រុកខ្លះធ្វើស្រូវប្រាំងដែរ របៀបធ្វើស្រូវប្រាំងមិនខុសគ្នាពីធ្វើស្រែវស្សាទេ ។

4. ORTHOGRAPHY OF EXERCISES 1–60 B (KEYS)

Exercise 1 B

តាលេនរៃល្បៀន ។ ម្ពួយទៅផ្ទះ ។ បនធ្វើមួប ។ ឯពុកទៅ ។ ប្អូនទៅ

សាលារៀន ។ ឯពុកធ្វើទ ។ ខ្ញុំជិះឡាន ។ តាទៅ ។

Exercise 2 B

សាលារៀនថ្មី ។ ឯពុកធំ ។ បនចាស់ ។ ទុប្ស ។ ផ្ទះទុលាយ ។

ខ្ញុំតូច ។

Exercise 3 B

ខ្ញុំមានទុ ។ ប្អូនធំណាស់ ។ ម្ពួយនៅផ្ទះ ។ ខ្ញុំក្មៅពេក ។ ឡាន

ថ្មីណាស់ ។ មិនធ្វើមួប ។

Exercise 4 B

មិនមានផ្ទះថ្មី ។ តាជិះឡានធំ ។ បនទៅសាលារៀនធំ ។ ប្អូនមានទុតូច ។

ផ្ទះតូចណាស់ ។ ពួមានឡានទុលាយ ។

Exercise 5 B

ឡានមិនតូចណាស់ ។ ផ្ទះរាំធំពេក ។ សាលារៀនប្អូនល្អណាស់ ។ ពួរាំ

ទៅផ្ទះ ។ ទុឯពុកតូចពេក ។ ម្ពួយអ្នកធំ ។

Exercise 6 B

ឯពុកម្ពួយអ្នកនៅផ្ទះ ។ បន ប្រុស រាំមានឡានធំ ។ ទុធំថ្មី ។ ប្អូន ស្រី ខ្ញុំ

យើញអ្នក ។ បនប្អូនរាំទៅសាលារៀន ។ តាធ្វើផ្ទះថ្មី ។

Exercise 7 B

ផ្ទះនាមិនល្អទេ ។   សាលារៀនបង់ប្រុសមិនធំទេ ។   ៥ពុកម្តាយអ្នកមិនជិះឡាន ទេ ។   ខ្ញុំមិនទិញ(តីផ្ទៃ)ត ។   ទូធំមិនល្អ ។   ពូវាមិនលក់ឡានទេ ។

Exercise 8 B

អ្នកលក់(តីផ្ទៃ)តទេ? ។   កន្ទេលល្អនៅបន្ទប់អ្នកឬទេ? ។   អ្នកឃើញ៥ពុកម្តាយ វាឬទេ? ។   ប្ដូន(ប្រុសវាទៅសាលារៀនល្អ ។   ផ្ទះពូធំទេ? ។   វាមានឡាន ប៉ុឬទេ? ។

Exercise 9 B

អ្នកមានបន្ទប់ធំទេ?   បាទទេ បន្ទប់ខ្ញុំតូច ។   មិនទៅផ្សារឬទេ?   បាទ គាត់ទៅ ផ្សារ ។   នាជិះឡានឬទេ?   បាទ គាត់ជិះឡាន ។   ម្ចួបក្តៅឬទេ?   ចាះ ក្តៅណាស់ ។   ពូធ្វើទូធំទេ?   ចាះទេ គាត់មិនធ្វើទូទេ ។   វាលក់(តីផ្ទៃ)តឬទេ?   ចាះទេ វាមិនលក់(តីផ្ទៃ)តទេ ។

Exercise 10 B

ពូមានលៅប៉ុន្មាននាក់?   បាទ គាត់មានពីរនាក់ ។   ម្ចាយមានទូប៉ុន្មាន?   បាទ គាត់ មានទូមួយ ។   អ្នកមាន(តីប៉ុន្មាន?   បាទ ខ្ញុំមាន(បាំ ។   គាត់មានតូប៉ុន្មាន?   ចាះ គាត់មានតូបី ។   គាត់មានបង់ប្ដូនប៉ុន្មាននាក់?   ចាះ ខ្ញុំមិនដឹងទេ ។   អ្នក មានមិនប៉ុន្មាននាក់?   ចាះ ខ្ញុំមាន(ចីននាក់ ។

Exercise 11 B

ម្ចាយធ្វើមបទេ? ។   ពូធ្វើទូទេ? ។   នាជិងឬទេ? ។   បងនៅផ្ទះទេ? ។   មិន ទិញ(តីផ្ទៃ)តឬទេ? ។   មិនទៅផ្សារឬទេ? ។

Exercise 12 B

ពួមានមាន់ប៉ុន្មាន? ។ ឲ្យសីគាត់ទិញសាប់ជ្រូក ។ កូនច្រូស ខ្ញុំពីរនាក់ទៅសាលា រៀនផ្ទះជ្ជុំនោះ ។ ខ្ញុំមានពួបីនាក់ អ្នកមានមីងឲ្យនាក់ ។ ឲ្យស្រីទិញត្រី ផ្ទៀតងទៀតឬទេ? ។ បនស្រីតាពីរនាក់នៅផ្ទុះនេះ ។

Exercise 13 B

ឯពុកហៅអ្នកបំរើបីនាក់នោះ ។ កូនពីរនាក់ចាំមីងវា ។ ផ្ទះនោះច្រក់ស្ម្រវ័ ទេ? ។ ពួជិះឡានក្ងួចនោះទេ? ។ ជ្រូកពីរនេះមិនថ្ងៃទេ ។ ឯពុកពួចាំអ្នក ឬទេ? បាទទេ គាត់ទៅផ្ទះកូនស្រីគាត់ ។

Exercise 14 B

ពួស្ម្រៀកខោសនោះឬទេ? បាទទេ គាត់ស្ម្រៀកសំពត់ ។ មីងទៅផ្ទរុធំឬទេ? ចាំសទេ ខ្ញុំទៅផ្ទុរក្ងួច ។ ម្ដាយទិញសំពត់លៀងនោះទេ? ចាំស ។ បនច្រូស អ្នកស្ម្រៀកខោបារាំងទេ? បាទទេ គាត់ស្ម្រៀកសំពត់ ។ ចៅម្ដក់ពាក់អាវទ្រៀវ ចៅម្ដក់ស្ម្រៀកខោខ្លៅ ។ ម្ដាយគាត់ពាក់អាវ្រ្កហមឬទេ? បាទទេ គាត់មិនពាក់ អាវ្រ្កហមទេ ។

Exercise 15 B

ផ្ទុនៅផ្ទុះធំសនោះឬទេ? បាទទេ គាត់នៅផ្ទុះនេះ ។ ពួមានសៀរៀកៅរ្ចើនអំពី ស្រុកអន់គ្គួស សៀរៀកៅរនោះនៅក្ងួងបន្ទប់គាត់ឬទេ? ចាំស នៅក្ងួនទុក្ងួ ។

បនទៅផ្សារភ្លាមឬទេ? បាទ ខ្ញុំទៅភ្លាម ។ ម្ដាយទិញសំពត់ថ្ងៃ[កហាមនោះពី

[ស្រុកសេ]ម ល្អណាស់ ។ អ្នកយើញសំពត់សលើតុទេ? ជាកណាស់ ។

មិនទិញសំពត់ខ្សៅនោះនៅមុខសំពត់សទេ? ចាះទេ ថ្ងៃណាស់ ។

Exercise 16 B

[ពកនេះខ្ញុំនឹងទិញសេ]វិកៅពីរនោះអំពី[ស្រុកសេ]ម ។ ចៅគាត់មិនចូលផ្ទះថ្ងៃ

នោះទេ ។ ចៅរបីនាក់ចូលផ្ទះពីខាងនោះឬទេ? ។ ពីថ្ងៃនោះច្បូន[ប្បុសវានៅផ្ទះពេទ្យ

នេះ ។ យូរ ៗ ម្ដនយើនទៅស្ងួរគាត់ ។ ពីម្ព្រលកានោះលក់[តិក្នុងទីនេះ ។

Exercise 17 B

ម៉េចក៏ដូននៅក្នុងផ្ទះពេទ្យ? ពូជីនទេ? ។ អ្នកដាក់សេ]វិកៅនោះនៅងណា?

បាទ ខ្ញុំដាក់នៅឬឬនោះ ។ គាត់មកពី[ស្រុកអនំគ្លេសយ៉ាងដូចម្ដេច? គាត់ជិះយនួ

ហោះឬទេ? ។ ចៅច្បូននាក់នោះនឹងស្ងួរដូនអ្ផ្កាល់? ។ ខ្ញុំនឹងបានកន្លែងក្នុង

សាលារ]ននោះយ៉ាងដូចម្ដេច? ។ ហេតុអ្វីបានជាកប៉ាល់នោះមកកំពង់ចាមពីភ្នំពេញ? ។

Exercise 18 B

កូនសិស្សរណាខ្ទុះរ]នភាសាបារាំងសែសឆ្នាំនេះ? ។ ឯពុកអ្នកសូរអ្នកណានៅផ្ទះ

ពេទ្យពីម្ព្រលមុិញ? ។ លោក[ប្បូជាយ៉ាងម៉េចអំពីកូន[ប្បុសអ្នក? ។ ចៅទិញ

សេ]វិកៅប៉ុន្មាន[ពកមុិញ? ។ អ្នកណាយើញលោក[ក្នុងទី[ក្នុងពីម្ព្រល? ។

យួននោះលក់ផ្ទះណាមួយ឵ទ្យុរ? ។

243

Exercise 19 B

លោក[គូនេះមានកូនសិស្សប៉ុន្មាននាក់ក្នុងថ្នាក់គាត់? គាត់មានដប់នាក់ ។ គាត់
សរសេរសេ]វិកៅងទេ]តអំពី[ស្រុកខ្មែរឬ្យូទេ? បាទ ខ្ញុំមិនដីងទេ ។ នាងិន
ពាក់អាវវេ]វិថ្មីនៅកាលណា? ។ លោកជិះកប៉ាល់លណា? ។ ហេតុអ្វីបានជា
អាវលេ]ងនៅខ្វៃ? មិនល្អទេ ។ ដូនអ្នកចិញ្ចឹម[ជ្រូកប៉ុន្មាន? ចាះ គាត់
ចិញ្ចឹមបី ។

Exercise 20 B

គាត់កំពុងតែសង់ផ្ទះថ្មីមួយ ។ ពួមិនទាន់ទៅផ្សារ ។ កូនសិស្សណាបេះតែលេន
នៅលើផ្ទូរ? ។ ម៉េចក៏[ចូរនោះវិកតៃកាច? ។ មីនរាកំពុងតែធ្វើអ្វី? ។
នាទៃបនិងមើលសេ]វិកៅណាមួយ? ។ យើនរ[ថិនតៃយើញលោកកៃនៅផ្ទូរនេះ ។
មនុស្សនេះមិនមៃនខ្ញុចទេ ។ កូនសិស្សខ្មែរសុទៃទៅបុណ្យនេះនៅប៉ារីស ។
ខ្ញុំទៃបតៃនិងយើញលោក[គូយើនក្នុង[កុន ។ នាខ្ញុចនោះស្មើតៃនិងដុតផ្ទះនេះ ។
គាត់មិនដៃលទៅ[ស្រុកអន់ក្លួសឆ្នាំនេះទេ ។ ក្នុង[ចូសកាចនេះមិនទាន់បេះអក្ស ។
យើន[គូរតៃផ្ញើសំបុ[តនេះទៅប៉ារីស ។

Exercise 21 B

យើនបងងិទិញ្សំពៃតៃបៃតន សំពៃត់នេះខ្វៃពៃក ។ ម្តាយបាន[ពមទៅក្នុនផ្ទូនេះ
ឬទេ? ។ គាត់មិនឡៃប់ធ្វើការនៅទៃ[កុន ។ បាទ គេ[គូរស្មៃ]កពាក់ខោអាវនៅ
ទៃនេះ ។ គាត់មិនហ៊ានទៅផ្ទូនោះទេ ។ អ្នកដាក់អាវជៃាកនៅវ៉ណា? ។ ទូនេះ

244

សំរាប់ទុកខោអាវលោក ។ កូន ប្រុសពីរនាក់មិនចេះបើកឡានទេ ។ សេ វ្រិកៅ នេះសំរាប់រ ៀនភាសាអង់គ្លេស ។ វាមិនឆ្អាប់ចាប់ ត្រីទេ វាមិនចេះផ្ទើទេ ។ ចៅ ប្រុសអ្នកឆាប់រ ៀន ។ ម៉េចក៏ពួងន៍ទៅ ស្រុកបារាំង? ។ កូយ ស៊ី ខ្ញុំតិត រ ៀនភាសាអង់គ្លេស ។ ឯពុក ត្រូវសួរអ្នកណានៅផ្ទះពេទ្យ? ។

Exercise 22 B
មីឌមិនមែនឧឌង់នៅភូមិនោះ ។ ចោរ ស្រាប់តែរត់ជិះឡាន ។ ចិន ប្រិនតែទិញ គេ ៀមនោះ ។ ខ្ញុំទើបនឹងសូមមើលសេ វ្រិកៅអង់គ្លេសនោះ ។ ពួមិនដែល រ ៀននិយាយភាសាខ្មែរទេ ។ គាត់មិនសួរបេះសរសេរអក្សរ ។

Exercise 23 B
សេ វ្រិកៅបារាំងសែសឧអ្នកនៅ កាយម៉ាស៊ុនអន្ឌលិលេខ ។ យើងបានផ្ទើសំបុ ត្រ បីទៅពួអ្នក ។ គាត់បានទិញសេ វ្រិកៅនោះឲ្យកូនសិស្សញ្ញាក់នេះ ។ ខ្ញុំនឹងផ្ទើ កញ្ចប់នេះទៅ ស្រុកអង់គ្លេសដួចម្ដេច? ។ ហេតុអ្វីបានជាអ្នកបាននាំមនុស្សនោះមក ចូលផ្ទះ? ។ កូន ប្រុសឃ្លួននាក់និឌមកដល់ស្អែក ។ គាត់ឡើងជណ្ដើរមកកសទ្បុរ ។ អ្នកណាយកជាសទៅចូលបន្ទប់តា? ។ អ្នកណាឲ្យសំបុ ត្រនោះទៅលោ? ។ ពួគាត់ បន្ឲ្យបូ្បយើង ។

Exercise 24 B
ក្មួនសប្បាយ ꞉[០] ꞉ឌចំរ ៀន ។ គាត់បានឧឌ់ទិញសេ វ្រិកៅរ ៀនភាសាបារាំង- សែស ។ មេហ៊ុំនាំចៅទៅដាក់គុក ។ មីឌ ត្បា្រញកព្ធោល់ឌផ្សរ ។ គាត់

បានផ្ញើសំបុ{្ត[្ចាប់យើនអំពីសេចក្តីនោះ ។ កូនសិស្ស{ទ្ុកសេ]វរគោតគត់សប្បាយ
ណាស់ ។ នាងបានរេ]នល្ប្ាញសំពត់ផ្ញើក្រ្ាប់ ។ ខ្ញុំទិញសំពត់ផ្ញើអារពីរ ។
ក្មេន ច្ួស[្ចាំនាក់ទៅផ្ងុះជំរាបមេប៉ុំ ។ មនុស្សប្ូននាក់ជិះទូកពីរនោះរ្ូចជីវិត ។
អ្នកបំរើនោះរ[ច]នពីរោះណាស់ ។ លោក[្ចបិ ខ្ញុំផ្ញើអ្វី? ។

Exercise 25 B

ខ្ញុំបានយេិញ្ញកញ្ញប់ផំនោះ មិនធ្ងន់ពេកទេ ។ អ្នក{ស្ែកំពុន្តែរ]បជំសាប
[ាប់[្ស្ូវ ។ វាយកបបជីកជី ។ អ្នក{ស្ែខ្ែរ[្ចិបបធ្ងន់ ។ គាត់សរ-
សេរសំបុ{្តវ្ែនទៅលោក[្គ្ូ ។ យើនបន៍លក់ផ្ងុះចាស់ ។

Exercise 26 B

កូនសិស្សជប់[្ចាំបិនាក់[្ចឡ្ងន្ឆ្ំនេះ ដប់នាក់ជាប់ ។ យើនទៅស្ូរដួនខ្ញុំមួយ
ខែបិ៍ដន ។ ស្ងេចបិ[ពះអង្គបានៅ្ក្ុនរាជវាំននេះ ។ ចៅអង្ទិ្ការមានស[្នាពីរ
គំពីក្ុនវត្ត ។ អ្នកនិនពិសាផ្ួនមួយចំហ]ន្ឬទេ? ៤ពុកខ្ញុំទេបនិនទិញ្ញមួយផ្ងន ។
ខ្ញុំទិញ[្គិផ្ែ]តនៅ៍ងណា? ទីនេះ ប៉ុំ៍្ងានចផ្ងក់ លោក? មួយចផ្ងក់ប៉ុំ៍្ងាន
រ[ល? មួយចផ្ងក់[្ចាំរ[ល ។ ក្ុនបំការនេះ ខ្ញុំមាន[្មេបច្ួនជនួន ។ កូន
សិស្សាមសិបនាក់រ[ន៍ភាសាអង់គ្លេសៅ្ក្ុនផ្ងក់ទិមួយ ។ នាផ្ទាប់ជិះស្ុ៍ក្ូ
មួយភាទិ្ម្ូន ។ លោកបានផ្ញើ[្តសក់ប្ូននៅទៅ៍ងនទិ្ការ ។ យើនរ[្ចិន៍ត
[្ត្ូវ៍ចាំរទេ៍ភ្លិន៍អ្នកពីរបិមិនុត ៍ថ្ងនេះយើនបានចាំពីរម៉ាង ។ ហេតុអ្វីបានជាមិន
បានលេចផ្ំពីរ[្គាប់នោះ៍ថ្ងនេះ? ។

Exercise 27 B

ក្មេងម្នេបីនាក់បាន[បច្ឆ្លងហើយនឹង[ប៉ាប្ងូនដណ្ដប់នាក់ជាប់ ។   ឫន្លៃមិន[ព្រះឫ
ខ្ញុំមិនឲ្យ ។   លោកបានជាផ្ងុះគាត់នៅផ្សូរផំទេ? ។   កាលណាលោក[គូទូដ្ឋុួរ
ក្មេងនឹងបេញ្ញមក ។   មនុស្សនោះបាន[ប្រាប់ ខ្ញុំជាផ្ងុះ ខ្ញុំនេះ ។   [ក្រាយពីមេហុំ
ទៅដល់ទាហានបេញ្ញពីផ្ងុះ ។   បន្ទប់ទួលាយណាស់ប៉ុន្ថៃយើងមិនដាក់ឲ្យមួយ[ទ]តទេ ។
បន្ឥឈ្ងួនបានមកក្ឫុំពេញ្ញមើលបុណ្យអុំ[ឫួប៉ុន្ថៃគាត់បាននៅបីអាទិត្យ ។   កាលណាគាត់
ទៅ[ស្រុកបារាំងគាត់នឹងស្ទ្យេ]កសំពត់មួង ។ ។ ឬ[ទ? ។   [ក្រាយពីមនុស្សពីរនាក់បាន
ជួបគ្នានៅផ្ងុះ   គាត់បេញ្ញពីកំពង់ចាមតាមនាមទូក ។

Exercise 28 B

លោក[គូបានជាចៅខ្ញុំមិនរ[]នភាសាបារាំងនៃសេសសោះឡើយ ។   ខ្ញុំឥដ្ឋនឹងបើលោក
ដាប់ចិត្តបេញ្ញពីក្ឫុំពេញ្ញ ។   នៅ[តេ]មនោះគេលក់សំពត់ពី[ស្រុកក្ឫម្ភ្ងៃដៃរ ។   ពួ
លោក[តឈ្ងួប់មកផ្ងុះហើយ ។   ស្ងៃកឯងនៅក្ឫុំពេញ្ញផ្ងើ? ។ ខ្ញុំទៅទិញ្ញាវរ៉ាន់ហើយ
នឹងទៅស្ងួរមិត្តសំឡ្ងាញ្ញខ្ញុំឥង ។   ចៅអន្ទុ ការនឹងគិតសេចក្ដីទ]ត ។

Exercise 29 B

កាលអ្នកបានចូលបន្ទប់ៗពុកអ្នកមិនបានឃើញ្ញក[ឥ្ង ខ្ញុំទេឫ? ។   បើ ខ្ញុំទៅជ័ុះរទេះ
ភ្ងើនលោកពូនឹងទៅជាមួយនឹង ខ្ញុំទេ? ។   តាំងពីនាគាត់ស្ងាប់គាត់បានលឿឫ? ។
ទេះបីនាងនោះបានលួចសេ[]រនៅក៏ដោយនាងនោះមិនភិតភ័យជួ[ច្ងួនទេឫ? ។   អ្នកមិន
បានលាក់សំបុ[តនោះដើម្ប្ងី]ឲ្យបព្ញ្ងាតគាត់ទេឫ? ។

247

Exercise 30 B

យកសេ]រភៅពីរនោះទៅជូនលោកកែ ។ ហ្លួសម៉ាងហើយ យើងមិន[ត្រូវទៅ

ដល់យឹត ។ ខ្ញុំមិនបង់ដេីរលេឌ ក្តេពោកថ្ងៃនេះ ។ ធ្លាក់ភ្ល]ៀងមកហើយ

យើង[ត្រូវ[បញ្ជាប់ហៅសុ្កូ ។ ព្រសួរក្នុងយឹរ[កាយផុះ ។ ហ្លួកុំទិញ[គី

នេ]តងស្ករធំ ថ្ងៃពោកនៅទីនោះ ។ ធុំក្លិនផ្កាកុលាប ក្នុងបន្ទប់ប៉ុន្តែ ខ្ញុំអត់យេីញ

ផ្កាសោរ ។ អញ្ចេីញញអ្គុយនៅទីនេះ រវានៅជីតទ្វារ ។ ថៃកបានបីហើយនឹង

ពេ]បថាសដន ។ ធ្លាក់ក្បៀ់ងមួយដុប្លលវិហារ ។

Exercise 31 B

កូនពេលដែលធ្លាក់ភ្ល]ៀងមករ[ចិនយើងបានចាំនៅ ក្នុនវត្ត ។ កុំមកថ្ងៃ[ពហស្បតិ

យើងទៅមេីលកុនអាមេរិកាំននៅរោងកុនថ្មី ។ ដ]ៀតតៃម៉ាង[ប៉ាំពីរបហើយនាាហើយ

នឹងកូនគាត់មិនបានបរ ង្វៀយកៅអីរ ទេ ។ លោកៃកធ្លាប់ទទូលទានដំណោកពេលរសេ]ល

ប៉ុន្តៃ ខ្ញុំមិនស្មានថាគាត់លក់ទេ ។ បេីបង[សិ ខ្ញុំទៅរ]នៅ[ស្រុកអន់គ្លេសខៃតុលា

គាត់នឹងនៅ ប្លូនឆ្នាំ ។ ថៃពិសាខនឹងក្ពៅណាប់ [ត្រូវបេីកផ្ញិតពេលយប់ ។

Exercise 32 B

ខ្ញុំសួរលោកតេីគាត់ចូលចិត្តទៅមេីល[ស្រុកណាខ្លះ ។ គេនឹងសួរខ្ញុំតេីយប់នេះខ្ញុំចង់

បរិភោគនៅផ្ទះប្លូទេ ។ អាណិត[ប៉ាប់ ខ្ញុំតេីរទេរភ្លេីននេះទៅណា ។ លោកនេះ

មិនបង់[ប៉ាប់ ខ្ញុំថាគាត់បានសួរអ្នកណានៅ ភ្ញុំពេញ្ញទេ ។ ខ្ញុំនឹងសួរលោកពូថាគាត់នឹង

មកកំពង់ចាមកាលណា ។ យើងបានគិតជាតេី[ពៃកឡ្ជៀងប្លូន[ប្រុសនាងនឹងផ្ញើអ្វី

ទៀត ។ គាត់មិនប្រាប់ថាចោរបានចូលបន្ទប់យ៉ាងដូចម្ដេចទេ ។ ខ្ញុំសួរចៅថាហេតុអ្វីបានជាចៅព្រួយព្រឹកនេះ ។ លោកស្រីមិនបានថាមានមនុស្សប៉ុន្មាននាក់នៅក្នុងផ្ទះទេ ។ ចោរដឹងថាលោកទុកប្រាក់នៅកន្លែងណា ។

Exercise 33 B

ដូនរកសៀវភៅអំពីវិហារនោះមិនឃើញ ។ គាត់មើលខោអាវមិនឃើញថារហែកទេ ។ នៅកន្លែងនេះឮសូរក្មេងស្រែកច្រើននាក់ពេក ខ្ញុំស្ដាប់អ្នកមិនឮសោះ ។ មនុស្សខូចនោះដេញតាមទាហានចាស់នោះមិនទាន់ ។ ខ្ញុំទទួលទានចំណីអាហារមិនកើតព្រោះខ្ញុំឈឺ ។ ដូនមើលទូកមិនឃើញពីព្រោះគាត់ទាបពេក ។ បើប៉ូលីសបានជិះកាណូតដេញតាមចោរនោះគេនឹងបានទាន់ចោរនោះមិនខាន ។ ខ្ញុំទិញកាសែតអង់គ្លេសនៅឯណាបាន? ។ ខ្ញុំបានសួរក្មេងស្រីនេះថាម៉េចក៏សំលៀកបំពាក់ទទឹកជោកប៉ុន្តែវានិយាយមិនកើតសោះ ។ យើងបានឮតាមវិទ្យុថាគេរកយន្តហោះឃើញនៅកន្លែងណាប៉ុន្តែខ្ញុំថាឈ្មោះកន្លែងនោះមិនត្រូវ ។

Exercise 34 B

គេបានប្រាប់ខ្ញុំថាអ្នកនឹងអង្គុយកន្លែងណា ។ ខ្ញុំចូលចិត្តគិតការអ្វីមួយនឹងលោក ។ ឯងដឹងថារបស់ខ្ញុំនៅឯណាទេ? បាទ ខ្ញុំមិនដឹងទេប៉ុន្តែមានរបស់អ្វីខ្លះនៅលើតុ ។ គាត់បានទិញសៀវភៅយួនខ្លះហើយ ។ ជួនកាលប្អូនប្រុសខ្ញុំសរសេរសំបុត្រទៅម្ដាយនៅស្រុកខ្មែរ ។ ក្មេងស្រីនោះមានរឿងអ្វីមួយជំរាបលោកស្រី ។

ងផ្សារមានគីបែបបណាខ្ពុំថ្ងៃគ្គីគីគីនោរថ្លៃណាស់ ។ មានគេចាំរាជកុនពេលយប់ ។ ខ្ញុំស្មានថាចៅមានបេ្រ]ឥអ្វីមួយប្រាប់ខ្ញុំមើលទៅ? ។ លោកស្រីនៅផ្ទុះនោះឬទេ? ។ ទេ ប៉ុន្តែមានរបស់អ្វីជាច្រើននៅក្នុងផ្ទុះ ។

Exercise 35 B

ខ្ញុំមិនបេ៉ីញវ៉ាត់រវ៉ាត់របស់អ្នកណាក្នុងកន្លែងនេះទេ ។ ថ្ងៃនេះគ្មានទូកក្តេ្តឯប៉ុន្មាននៅលើទន្លេទេ ។ ឬ្ឬនណាងមិនលេងល្បេ្យឯណាសោះឡើយ ។ គ្មានអ្នកណាជីឥជាអ្នកណាធ្វើនោះ ។ គ្រូសារសេ]មនោះមិនបឥជីរវទេះភ្ជើនទៅណាទេ ។ បើ់ចៅយករបស់បេញពីឯតតុនោះសូននឥវិឥណាស់ ។ គ្មានច្រ្រាប់ច្រាត្រអ្វីក្នុងផ្ទុះពួ ។ តាចូលចិត្តនៅផ្ទុះ គាត់មិនពេ្រាមទៅណាទេ ។ ខ្ញុំមិនបានបេ៉ីញកព្ញប់អ្វីនៅកន្លែងនោះ ។ ចៅអ្វីការនោះមិនដែលទៅកន្លែងណាកេ្រ៉ាពីកំពឥចាម ។

Exercise 36 B

លោកស្រីនៅកន្លែងណា ខ្ញុំក៏នឥមកស្រូវមិនខាន ។ អ្នកណាបានថានោះ អ្នកនោះក៏មិនជីឥអ្វីអំពីសេចក្តីនោះទេ ។ កូនទៅទីកន្លែងណា មួយក៏ទៅទីកន្លែងនោះ ដែរ ។ លោកគ្រូរើសអ្នកណា អ្នកនោះគ្ត្រាវអានរ]ឥ ។ ឫពុកម្ត៉ាយយើឥទិញវិទ្យុបែបណា កូនក៏ចូលចិត្ត ។ លោកគ្រូមានសេ]រភៅណា ខ្ញុំក៏នឥទិញសេ]រភៅនោះដែរ ។ កូ្យធ្វើអ្វីមួយ មិនក៏នឥជួយធ្វើដែរ ។ អ្នកដេរ ប៉ុន្មានគឫ្យម៉ៃត្រ ខ្ញុំក៏នឥដេរតាម ។ ខ្ញុំធ្វើអ្វី ក៏គាត់មិនគ្ត្រាវចិត្តដែរ ។ សមាជិករើសអ្នកណា យើឥក៏សុខចិត្តដែរ ។

250

Exercise 37 B

អ្នកចូលផ្ទះពេទ្យណាក៍ដោយ   គេនិងព្យាបាលអ្នកដោយសេចក្ដីប្រយ័ត្នប្រយែន ។

គាត់រៀនវិជ្ជាណាក៍ដោយ   គាត់និងប្រឡងជាប់ ។   លោកមកពេលណាក៍

ដោយ   យើងចេះតែសុខចិត្តទទួលលោក ។   អ្នកជាម៉េចក៍ដោយ   យើងនិងមិន

រើសតាំងអ្នកនោះ ។   គាត់តថ្លៃយ៉ាងណាក៍ដោយ   ខ្ញុំនិងមិនបន់ព្រាក់ហាសិប

រៀលទេ ។   លោកស្រីទ្យខ្ញុំទៅផ្សារណាមួយ?   ឯងទៅផ្សារណាក៍បាន ។

កូនអ្នកណាក៍ដោយ   គួរតែធ្វើទាហាន ។   គេធ្វើឲ្យាននេះដូចម្ដេចក៍ដោយ   ក៏ប៉ុន្ដៃ

ម៉ាស៊ីនមិនដើរ ។   គួរពេទ្យចាក់ថ្នាំអ្វីក៍ដោយ   អ្នកជំងឺនេះនិងមិនជាទេ ។   ដូច

ម្ដេចក៍ដោយ   អ្នកត្រូវមកជួបនិង ខ្ញុំនៅម៉ោងប្រាំពីរល្ងាចនេះមិនខាន ។

Exercise 38 B

មានម្ងាស់តៃម៉ខ្ញុំនៅកៃខ្នើននេះដៃលលក់ទិនិញ្ញយូន ។   គ្មានអ្នកណាមួយដៃល

ខ្ញុំស្គាល់ក្នុងភូមិនេះ ។   កាលយាយនោះចូលមកលោកមិនជាអ្វីទេ ។   យាយ

នោះគ្មានបងប្អូនសោះឡើយ ។   ខ្ញុំស្គាប់មិនស្ងួរព្យទេព្រោះខ្ញុំថ្ងន់ប៉ុន្មានឆ្នាំទៅហើយ ។

តាំងពីថ្ងៃគត់ងដល់ពេលព្រលប់   គ្មានអ្នកណាចូលផ្ទះយើង ។   រាជការនិង

រើសស្រុកណាក៍ដោយ   ថ្មីខ្ញុំនិងគ្រូវទៅស្រុកនេះ ។   របស់នោះនៅកៃខ្នើនណា

មួយក្នុងផ្ទះប៉ុន្ដៃ ខ្ញុំរកមិនឃើញ ។

Exercise 39 B

ហោរាយកត្រ្ងនពីជាមួយនិងប្រាក់ដៃលនៅក្នុងថតु ។   ពីថ្ងៃបន្ទុកក្នុង អាទិត្យមុនដល់

ថ្ងៃសុគ្រកក្នុងអាទិត្យគ្រោយលោកនៅវៃព្រនគរ   ។   ម្ងាស់តៃម៉ប្រាប់ប៉ូលិស

251

ជាល្អូបនោះមិនឃើញក្មួន ប្រុសណាក្នុងគេ ម ។ នៅផ្ទះប៉ូន ប្រុស ខ្ញុំនិយាយ ច្រើនប៉ុន្តែនៅប៉ុររ៉ូគាត់នៅស្រេ ម ។ ម៉េចក៏សំឡាញ់អ្នកមានផ្ទះជិតភ្នំផូវធ្លេះ? ។ ដល់ថ្ងៃសៅររ កាយ ខ្ញុំនឹងបានរកស៊ីអស់មួយអាទិត្យ ។ ងាំវំណែកគាគាត់បេញពីភ្នំពេញ ទៅនៅបាត់ដំបង ។ ផ្ទះរបស់ដួនអ្នកនៅជិតកំពង់ចាមជាង ។ សូមអ្នកសររសរ សំបុ្តតនេះជំនួស ខ្ញុំ ខ្ញុំមិនស្គាល់លោកនេះសោះ ។ លោកនោះបានជាគាត់នឹង នៅកវែន្តនផដែលដល់ខ្ញុំនឹង គឤ្ចប់មករវិញ ។ ពីថ្ងៃទីបីតទៅផ្ទេបឡុំលោក ស្រីមួយ ថ្ងៃតែមួយ គាប់ហើយ ។ នៅ រកាមផ្ទះមានកវែន្តនដែល ស្រី ។ គ្យាញ់សំពត់ ។

Exercise 40 B

ដីនេះបញ្ចូលទឹកតាំងពីឆ្នាំមុន ។ រាល់ពេល ពលប់ដំរីនោះមករហូតដល់ស៊ីននេះ ដើម្បីនឹងដឹកទឹក ។ ក្មួយ ប្រុសគាត់ជាគេចូលចិត្តទៅជិនទូកក្តានជាងកប៉ាល់ ។ គ្មានអ្នកណាក្នុងភូមិនេះដែលចាក់សោររពេលយប់ទេ ។ គេជាម្ចាស់គេ ម នោះជា មនុស្សរប្រាយជាងគេនៅកំពង់ចាម ។ ប្ដី សព្វថ្ងៃគាត់ធ្វើការណាស់ជា គូរពេទ្យ នៅខាងជើន ស្រុក ។ រដូម ្ត្រ ដឹងជាមនុស្សខ្លះរួមតំនិតនឹងចាប់បន ពេះអង្កម្ចាស់ ។ អាទិត្យ រកាយពីថ្ងៃអង្គារដល់ថ្ងៃ ពហស្បតិ៍គេធ្វើបុណ្យចូលឆ្នាំ ។ យើនសុទតែ ស្រឡាញ់គេហស្ថានចាស់ ៗ ជាងគេហស្ថានថ្មី ៗ នៅក្នុងទី ក្ងុននោះ ។ តវ៉ាន់ ទាំងអស់នេះខ្ញុំនឹងផ្ញើទៅ ស្រុកអាម៉េរិកតាមជើនសមុ ្ទ ។

Exercise 41 B

ដំបូលផ្ទះអ្នក ប្រក់ស្លឹកត្នោតទេ? បាទទេ ផ្ទះយើន ប្រក់ក្បឿន ។

Exercise 42 B

អ្នកចិព្ចឹមសត្វណាខ្លះក្នុងរ[កាលរបស់ អ្នក? បាទ យើងចិញ្ចឹម[ជូកនិងមាន់[ចើន ។
របងធ្វើអំពីអ្វី? បាទ ធ្វើអំពីឬស្សី ។

Exercise 43 B

ឧ្ពុក អ្នកដាក់ទិនិញ្ញនៅឯណា? បាទ ក្នុងឡ្បែននោះខាងស្តាំ ឥឡូវរ្ងូមិនស្បូរ
ស្ថាតតែគិចទេ]តគេនិឪលាឪ ។

Exercise 44 B

កន្លែឪ ដែលគេចិញ្ចឹមសត្វ ជូ ងជាសត្វសិ ្ហ និងសត្វ ខ្លាជាដើមគេ ហៅយ៉ាឪ ម៉េ ច? បាទ
ហៅ ជាសួនសត្វ ។ ម៉េ ចក៏មិននៅ មានស្លួនសត្វ នៅ ជិតភ្នំ? បាទ ម៉ើ ល ទៅ[៦ ហ៊ុ ៦ បហល
ជាដោយ[តូវការ សឪ ្ផុ វ ទូលាយ នៅ កន្លែ ឪ នេះ ឥ ៣ ្ផុ ៖ គ្នា កន្លែ ឪ ដាក់ ស្ទួ នសត្វ
ទេ] ត ។

Exercise 45 B

លោកអាណិ ត[ប្ញប់ ខ្ញុំ គឺ[តី ដែ លហាល ថ្ងៃ នោះ ជា[តី ហៅ អ្វី? បាទ [តី នោះ ហៅ
[តី រ័ ស់ ។ នោះ ហើ យ និ ឪ[តី បែ បបឪ ទ]ត ហាល ថ្ងៃ ពី របី ថ្ងៃ ទៅ រួ ចហៅ
ជា[តី ន្]ត ។

Exercise 46 B

អ្នកមានបឪ ប្ញ ួ ន ទេ? បាទ ទេ ច៎ ៖ ទេ ខ្ញុំ គ្មា នបឪ ប្ញ ួ ន ទេ ។ បាទ ច៎ ៖ ខ្ញុំ មានបឪ
[ប្ញ ុ ស—នាក់ បឪ[ស៊ី—នាក់ ប្ញ ួ ន[ប្ញ ុ ស—នាក់ ប្ញ ួ ន[ស៊ី—នាក់ ។ មាន
មនុ ស្ស ប៉ុ ្គ នានាក់ នៅ ផ្ទ ៖ អ្នក? បាទ ច៎ ៖ មាន—នាក់ នៅ ផ្ទ ៖ ខ្ញុំ ។

Exercise 47 B

សំឡាញ់

ខ្ញុំចង់អញ្ជើញអ្នកជួបនិង ខ្ញុំងហាន——នៅម៉ោង ប្រាំបីល្ងាចថ្ងៃ ដប់ ៃ នេះ ពិសាបាយ ។

Exercise 48 B

ជំរាបមកហេងសូម ជាប

ខ្ញុំនិងបង សី ខ្ញុំមានសេចក្ដីស្តាយ យ៉ាង ធ្ងន់ដោយ ៅ បុណ្យ ៃ ្ង សៅរ៍ មុនមិនបានហើយ និង ដោយបានខានជួបនិង អ្នក យើងមិន ៃ ដ លជួប គ្នាជាយូរ ៃ ្ង ហើយ អ្នកអញ្ជើញមក ស្អែក យើង ពេល ្ង ាច ៃ ្ង ណាមួយ បានឬទេ? ។

Exercise 49 B

ខ្ញុំសូមជំរាបមក លោក——

កូន ្ប ុស ខ្ញុំ ្ធ ើ ការ ៃ ្ង នេះ មិនបានព ៃ ្រ ្ពះឈឺ ្គ ុន ខ្ញុំមានស ្ង ្ឃ ឹមជាភ្លាមទិត ្រ ្ក ាយ ៏ វានិង ៅ ្ធ ើ ការ ្ព ុំ ខាន ។

Exercise 50 B

សំឡាញ់ខ្ញុំ កំពុង ៃ ត រ] នវាយម៉ា ៊ ស ុ ន អក្សរ ៅ សាលា រ] ននោះ គាត់ជាពិបាកនិងបាន ក ៃ ្ខ ន បន ្ត] តណាស់ ។ មួយ ៅ] ត ្ត ្រ វ បន់ ្ប ្រ ាក់បីរយ រ] លមុន ។

Exercise 51 B

ស ព ្វ ៃ ្ង ៅ សេ] មវាចជ៉ិះ ្ខ ្ល ានឡ្មើ លបានឬ ទេ?
បាន មានឡ្ម ្ល ្ម ើ ល ៅ វាល់ ៃ ្ង ។

ថ្លៃប៉ុន្មាន?

បាន មួយរយថ្មែរៀល ។

ខ្ញុំចូលចិត្តទៅវៃស្មុក មានសល់កន្លែងទេ?

បានមានសល់កន្លែងមួយខាងក្រោយ ។

ហ្នឹងហើយ ខ្ញុំយកកន្លែងនោះ ឲ្យានបេញម៉ោងប៉ុន្មាន?

នៅម៉ោង ប្រាំពីរព្រឹក លោក ។

Exercise 52 B

យប់នេះយើន និន ទៅមើលល្ខោនមើលទៅ ពួមិនអស់កំឡុំងទេឬ?

បានទេ ខ្ញុំមិនអស់កំឡុំងទេតើ យើននិនទៅរោនណា?

ស្រោចនិនពួ ពួអញ្ញើញរីសរកពីព្រោះពួមកលេន ភ្នំពេញ ខ្ញុំគន់តៃនៅភ្នំពេញ

ទៅមើលល្ខោនល្ខបណាក៏បាន ។

ទេ ក្មួយស្គាល់រោនល្ខោនជាន់ ខ្ញុំ ក្មួយស្រឡាញ់ល្ខោនណាជាន?

ខ្ញុំ ស្រឡាញ់រោន ឋ ជាន គេ អ្នកគ្លុកកំឡៃនណាស់ ។

បើអញ្ញើនយើនទៅរោនឋ ។

Exercise 53 B

ពីយប់មុ្ញ្ញលោកនិនមិត្តសំឡាញ់ពីរនាក់ទៅមើលល្ខោន មិនបន្ទ្រៃតប៉ុន្មានពីរព្រោះគេ

ច្រើនទៃស្រឡាញ់ល្ខោននៅរោនកាប់គោជាន មួយទៃតមានកុនប៉ារាំនៃសេសល្ខ

ណាស់នៅស៊ីណេល្ខ មុខជាមនុស្សរច្រើននាក់ទៅមើលកុននេះ ។

Exercise 54 B

រ]ៀងនេះនិទានអំពីហាន្ស្រមួយគូនិងអណ្ដើកមួយ   អណ្ដើកនោះនៅជិត[សរមួយ ខៃ[ប៉ាន្[សរនោរវិងអស់ទៅមិនសូវរមានចំណាស្ថិ   ហាន្ស្រក៏និយាយថា   បងអណ្ដើក អើយ !   ចុះបើយើងយកងងទៅកខៃ្លនមួយទេ]ត?   [គូរវឹងចាប់ទាំមៃកឈើបំ កណ្ដាល   យឹននិឝពាំសឆ្ពាន   អណ្ដើកក៏[ពមធ្វើដូច្ឈេះ ។ ហាន្ស្រក៏ពាំមៃកឈើ យកអណ្ដើកឡើងជាមួយប៉ុ ខៃនអណ្ដើកញមនុស្ស្រខានរ[កាមនិយាយសើ ចៗ អំពី$\overset{\ddot{u}}{ន}$ក៏គិតនិង ធ្លើយបើកមាត់ស្ពាប់ទៅ ។

Exercise 55 B

គេទ្បៀងដើមត្នោតយ៉ាងម៉េ ច?

 បាទ ឝនបផ្នោនពើ[កាមដល់លើជំវិញ្ញដើមមួយ ៗ សិមទ្បៀង ។

គេយក[ចដាប់[ចដាអ្វីមកចិតផ្សារត្នោត?

បាទ គេយកកាំបិតមកធ្វើនោះ ។

បំពង់ឬស្រសំរាប់[តងទិកផ្សារនោះគេទុកឃ្យរប៉ុ ឆ្ឈាន?

ពិល្ឈ វឝ ល់[ពលិម ។

គេធ្វើស្ឆុយ៉ាងម៉េ ច?

បាទ គេឝាក់ទិកត្នោតក្ងុ ឧ្ឈ $ ឝ$ ៗ ពុះ វិ[ព្ញ ទៅ ជាស្ឆុ ។

Exercise 56 B

ជំរាបសួរ លោក ។

១ ! សូរស្ដី លោក[សី ។

លោកបានទៅ ភ្នំពេញជួនក្ដួយទៅឬទេ?

បាទ យើងទើបនិង្គតឡូប់មករវិញ្ពេលថ្ងៃ្គតង់ម៉ុញ ។

គាត់ទៅរ]ិនខាងអី?

រ]ិនធ្វើជា្គូពេទ្យ ។

៩! គាត់្គូវនៅ្ស្រុកគេឃ្យូរទេ?

បាទ ្ចបហាល្ប្រាំមួយឆ្នាំ ។

ឃ្យូរដែរ លោក ។ បងៗ្សីលោកដែលនៅ ភ្នំពេញសុខសប្រ្បាយជាឬទេ?

បាទ សុខសប្រ្បាយជារទេ ។

Exercise 57 B

ជួនកាលពួកមនុស្សៗពីភូមិយើងទៅទាក់ដំរី លុះគេគេ]ិងដំរីមួយពីហ្វូងហើយ្ទ-
មាក់ដំរីឡ្យើងលើកដំរីនោះគាប់ក្បាលរា កាលណាដំរីអស់កំឡុំងហើយគេបង់រាននិង
បង្ខោលមួយបោះក្នុងទឹក្សរៈឬូទឹកស្ទិន រូបគេ្តឡូប់ទៅផ្ទុះវិញ ។ មួយ
អាទិត្យ្រគាយគេយកស្ពេ]ៀ្យរាស្ដុ ។ ដល់រានៅកន្លែងនោះអស់ពីរអាទិត្យហើយគេ
នាំរាទៅផ្ទុះបង្ខាត់ធ្វើតាមបង្ខាប់មនុស្ស ។

Exercise 58 B

ថ្ងៃនេះគេសុទដែររល់ក្នុងផ្ទុះចៅមើលទៅ ។

បាទ ស្លេកស្ងុ៎ការបង្គ្សី ខ្ញុំ ។

មានភ្ញ]ិវ្ចិននាក់មកឬទេ?

បាទ មានដប់ពីរនាក់ ។

មកពីឆ្ងាយឬពីជិតខាង?

បាទ ជីដូនជីតាខ្ញុំមកពីបាត់ដំបងហើយឯឯងច្រើសរបស់ម្ដាយមកពីឆ្ងាយនៅខែគ្រ
ក្រចេះ ។

ចៅស្គាល់បងប្អូនទាំងអស់ដែលមកឬទេ?

ខ្ញុំស្គាល់ជីដូនជីតាពីរនាក់ហើយនឹងពូមីងទាំងអស់ប៉ុន្តែក្មួយពីរនាក់ខ្ញុំអត់ស្គាល់ទេ ។

Exercise 59 B

ថ្ងៃនេះគេធ្វើបុណ្យអ្វី?

បុណ្យនេះហៅថាមាយបូជា ។

គេធ្វើបុណ្យនេះរំឭកដល់អ្វី?

គេរំឭកដល់ព្រះអង្គបរិនិព្ពាន ។

គេធ្វើយ៉ាងម៉េច?

គេនិមន្តលោកសង្ឃស្ងូត្រធម៌និងទេស្នាអស់មួយយប់ហើយព្រឹកឡើងគេបគេបងផ្កាន់
លោកនានំ ។ គេធ្វើបុណ្យនេះដោយសោកស្ដាយព្រះ ។

បុណ្យនេះធ្វើយប់នេះនៅវត្តទាំងអស់នៅស្រុកខ្មែររឬទេ?

បាទ នៅវត្តទាំងអស់ ។

Exercise 60 B

ស្រូវត្រាំទុកពីរបីថ្ងៃដល់មានពន្លកហើយ សឹមគេសាបក្នុងថ្នាល ។ ដល់តិច
ទៀតសំណាបនោះបានកំពស់លុមគេស្ងួនទៅក្នុងស្រែ ។ កាលណាស្រូវទុំហើយ
គេច្រូតឯងជាកណ្ដាប់ រួចគេបោកប្បែនហើយនឹងរោយក្នុងវាលស្រែ ។

258

PART V

KEYS

1.   Key to Dictations in Part I, Lessons 1–4

References are to the numbered paragraphs.

1. sɔː naː soː hɔː hoː maː leː roː yaː haː seː lɔː
2. loːy soːm sɔːm yaːŋ saːs heːl saːŋ heːm sɔːy soːn heːs saːm
3. laŋ saːy hoːs noːy lɔːy hoy haːs haŋ hay haːy laːn rɔŋ
5. say haːm sɔː hɔl hol neh maŋ leːs hoːl nɔh maːs sɔːŋ
6. kɔːŋ taːm kɔŋ cɔm poːl taŋ pan kɔh cɔh toːŋ caŋ peːs
7. sak haːp toːc kaːk soc lak hoːk meːt kaːc kɔːp cɔp
9. kaː naek saəp hay haek haəy taək keːŋ laəŋ kaəŋ haep raːy
10. haoŋ laəy saoy pay paek pau taol taok saoc taəc paːy cay
11. paːŋ vau ŋɔk voːŋ mɔŋ viək noːk naen val ŋak nuːəc vaːp
12. taŋ laːŋ haːm paːv san toːŋ pau laːn cao maoc kuːəc hoŋ
13. daəm ʔaoy baek ʔaon ʔaek dɔː ʔɔːl baŋ baoy dael ʔɔt diəm
14. kaːy hɔk cʏk ʔaːŋ dʏy hɔːk sɔl dʏt hɔŋ pʏn lʏk paəm
15. sʏt dʏk kʏt dʏy buəŋ bʏːt ʔʏːy kʏy nʏt lʏy cuəŋ sʏl
17. rùːk pèːk rìək nìh pìːək cèːs cùːk cìːət
18. kèː mèː lèːŋ mèː pèːt teː pèːk nèːp
19. pèŋ leh tèː pèːŋ lèːŋ meŋ tèy ceh vèy vèːŋ lèŋ deː
20. toːŋ kɔːk cùːn ròːc tɔːŋ pòːl pɔ̀ː rɔ̀ːl loːy poːy tùː lɔ̀ːm
21. tɔ̀ət tɔ̀ːt lùək rɔ̀əp pùːək kùət pèək kɔ̀ət cùəh cèːk cèək lùp
22. kùt lùəŋ rùəy kùː buəŋ pùəŋ nùŋ kùən suəŋ rùk lùː kùm
23. rùəŋ kùːəl rʏ̀ː tʏ̀u pùː nʏ̀u kùːl lùːək ŋùː cùə ŋʏ̀ːp rùː
25. prak trɔŋ crùl prùːəs kraːl crɔ̀ːk truːət srɔŋ krùn prùəh srac prùh
26. kɔːŋ phɔːŋ thɔːt kat thèək pah tèək paoŋ tak khɔːŋ chap thaok
27. snaːm kbʏn mcùl slɔː tbaːŋ kʔaek sdap mdaːy spùː mlɔh lʔʏt stʏ̀ː
28. khcùl thvìːə khpom chmaː thnɔl thmèn phloːv phcap
29. rəcol kəkìːət səsɔː rəmìːəs pəpèː kəkoː cəceːs tətùm
30. crəbac krəmom trələp srənok tətrèək cəcrùl pəpʔaep pəphtɔk
31. sondaek kɔndaːl tùəŋkʏ̀ː cəŋvaː bɔŋʔɔs kəmpreːv bɔmpèəm ʔɔmpùl
32. sɔmnak kɔmnɔt cɔmnam ʔɔmnaːc kùmnɔ̀əp dɔmneːk pùmnùt bɔmnol
34. cəcrɔ̀ːk-məmɔ̀ːk pəprèəŋ-pəprʏ̀ːt phlìs-phlèh caːn-kbaːn skɔp-skɔl sruːəl-buːəl rùmʔae-rùmʔuːəy lhʏt-lhae

2.   Key to Exercise in Use of Script, Part I, Lesson 10.6

The keys to the second part of each exercise will be found in Part IV, Orthography.

1. pɔ̀ː pɔ̀ː phɔ̀ː ŋɔ̀ː phɔ̀ː tɔː kɔː chɔː thɔ̀ː yɔ̀ː khɔ̀ː sɔː lɔː thɔː dɔː cɔ̀ː mɔ̀ː bɔː ʔɔː rɔ̀ː hɔː lɔ̀ː khɔː vɔ̀ː cɔː kɔː nɔ̀ː tɔ̀ː nɔː chɔ̀ː
2. taː cuːə cìː thù laə suːə bao nùù rèː pìːə phèː kiə pì nao haː lìːə cheː thèː seː phau phùùə chù khiə thʏ khʏ̀ː
3. rʏy pao hìː yaː moː ʔʏ̀u veː

4. *dae(r) rìːəy hoːp lìːət hael rùːŋ kaːs kɔ̀ːm baos tɤ̀ːp tùːk mìən baːc tìːəɲ saen*
5. *ŋɤ̀u ɲìːəy ɲìːəv kaːv tau day baːy*
   ʔae rùː dù ʔao ʔɤt ʔɔː(r) lùː ʔaon
6. *kɔ̀əm sɔŋ bɔm kam kaːc dac pɔ̀əm rɔ̀ət rìːəy lìːəc vèəŋ rɔ̀ːŋ saŋ dɔk bɔt pùm*
7. *bɔh coh rèəh pùəh lùh ceh pah cìh tèh*
8. *poːk dak beh pèəh lùp rìəm cɔ̀əm kùəh bak rùh sɔk hùp sah*
9. *chap thɔːt khoːc phəəm chùːk khɤ̀u*
   (h)vaːy (h)leːv (h)mɔːp
   lpɤ̀u stùːŋ sdap tbaːɲ
   kraːp trùː krè slap krɔː smaːn
   chɲaɲ khlaːc khlìːət thnùː phlùk
   cəcèːk rəboːt tətèː lələ̀ːk səsòh
10. *prətèəh krəpɤ̀ː srətùm krədaːs*
    crəmoh prəmoːl trələp prəhɤ̀ːn krəvael
    kəkrìːət cəcrɔ̀ːk tətrɤ̀ːt pəprah
    pəphʔoːk səslɔk rəphoy kəkhùk
11. *bɔŋkac dɔmbɔːŋ cɔŋkak sɔnsɔm*
    səmʔap rùmpèc dɔmbaːɲ kɔmpɔ̀ːt
    ʔɔmnaoy kùmnùt lùmnɤ̀u səmleːŋ
    dɔndam ʔɔndaet kɔntaːɲ bɔntoːc
    bɔŋkhaːt kɔɲciəv cɔŋkrìːəŋ bɔŋkraːp

3.   KEYS TO EXERCISES 1–60

The translations given below (particularly for Exercises 1–40) are not the only possible correct ones. A Cambodian sentence, taken out of its context, as sentences in exercises must be, is not as precise as an English sentence in respect of number, time, definiteness or indefiniteness of nouns, reference of titles to first or third person. An English sentence is not as precise as a Cambodian one in respect of status and sex of the person speaking and the person addressed. The method used in presenting the keys has been to give alternatives, separated by /, where it has been thought necessary or helpful, and particularly where a new possibility of alternatives has just been presented in a lesson. As the work advances, alternatives of a recurrent nature are gradually omitted. Parentheses are used occasionally to indicate words which may perfectly well be left out without making the translation wrong or for which there is no word in the sentence in the exercise. The reader is reminded that the orthography of the keys to Exercises 1–60 B is available in Part IV. Alternative translations are not, however, given in the orthography.

Exercise 1

A.1. Father gets into/goes in the car. 2. Mother is making the meal. 3. Elder brother/sister is at home. 4. Younger brother/sister is playing a game. 5. I am going to school. 6. Grandfather/the old man is making a cupboard. 7. Younger brother/sister is going. 8. I am staying.

B.1. *taː lèːŋ lbaeŋ.* 2. *mdaːy tɤu phtèəh.* 3. *bɔːŋ thvɤ̀ː mhoːp.* 4. *ʔɔːpùk nɤ̀u.* 5. *pʔɔːn tɤu saːlaː-rìən.* 6. *ʔɔːpùk thvɤ̀ː tùː.* 7. *khɲom cìh laːn.* 8. *taː tɤ̀u.*

Exercise 2

A.1. Elder brother/sister is tall. 2. Younger brother/sister is small. 3. Grandfather is old. 4. The car is beautiful. 5. The game is new. 6. I am going.

B.1. *saːlaː-rìən thmʁy. 2. ʔɔːpùk thom. 3. bɔːŋ cas. 4. tùː lʔɔː. 5. phtèəh tùːlìːəy. 6. khɲom tɔːc.*

Exercise 3

A.1. The cupboard is very nice. 2. Elder brother/sister goes to school. 3. Aunt is at home. 4. The meal is too hot. 5. Uncle has a car. 6. Grandfather/the old man rides in/is getting into the car.

B.1. *khɲom mìːən tùː. 2. pʔɔːn thom nas. 3. mdaːy nɤ̆u phtèəh. 4. khɲom kdau pèːk. 5. laːn thmʁy nas. 6. mìːŋ thvɤ̀ː mhoːp.*

Exercise 4

A.1. Younger brother/sister is playing a new game. 2. Aunt is making a hot meal. 3. Father is making a big cupboard. 4. Uncle has a lovely car. 5. I go to a small school. 6. Grandfather/the old man lives in a roomy house.

B.1. *mìːŋ mìːən phtèəh thmʁy. 2. taː cìh laːn thom. 3. bɔːŋ tʁu saːlaː-rìən thom. 4. pʔɔːn mìːən tùː tɔːc. 5. phtèəh tɔːc nas. 6. pùː mìːən laːn tùːlìːəy.*

Exercise 5

A.1. My father is at home. 2. His elder brother/sister goes to school. 3. Your younger brother/sister is very small. 4. Uncle's house is roomy. 5. His father is very old. 6. My school is lovely.

B.1. *laːn mìːŋ tɔːc nas. 2. phtèəh vìːə thom pèːk. 3. saːlaː-rìən pʔɔːn lʔɔː nas. 4. pùː vìːə tʁu phtèəh. 5. tùː ʔɔːpùk tɔːc pèːk. 6. mdaːy nèək thom.*

Exercise 6

A.1. I see my father. 2. Father and mother have a big house. 3. His brothers and sisters are at home. 4. Your elder sister goes to school. 5. (Our/my)/the younger brother sees the new cupboard. 6. The new house is very nice.

B.1. *ʔɔːpùk-mdaːy nèək nɤ̆u phtèəh. 2. bɔːŋ-pros vìːə mìːən laːn thom. 3. tùː thom thmʁy. 4. pʔɔːn-srʁy khɲom khɤ̆ːɲ nèək. 5. bɔːŋ-pʔɔːn vìːə tʁu saːlaː-rìən. 6. taː thvɤ̀ː tùː thmʁy.*

Exercise 7

A.1. He isn't going to the big market. 2. My house is not near the market. 3. Mother doesn't buy fish. 4. My younger brother sells dried fish. 5. His/her/their elder sister is not beautiful. 6. I haven't brothers and sisters/I haven't (any) brothers or sisters.

B.1. *phtèəh taː mùən lʔɔː tèː. 2. saːlaː-rìən bɔːŋ-pros mùən thom tèː. 3. ʔɔːpùk-mdaːy nèək mùən cìh laːn tèː. 4. khɲom mùən tèɲ trʁy-ŋìət. 5. tùː thom mùən lʔɔː. 6. pùː vìːə mùən lùək laːn tèː.*

Exercise 8

A.1. Is he/she/are they in his/her/their room(s)? 2. Have you a nice mat? 3. Aunt doesn't buy small fish. 4. Is the meal hot? 5. Are your brothers and sisters at home? 6. Has father a mat?

B.1. *nèak lùak trɤy-ŋìat tèː? 2. kɔntèːl lʔɔː nɤ̀u bɔntùp nèak rùː tèː? 3. nèak khɤ̀ːp ʔoːpùk-mdaːy vìːa rùː tèː? 4. pʔɔːn-pros vìːa tɤ̀u saːlaː-rìan lʔɔː. 5. phtèah pùː thom tèː? 6. vìːa mìːan laːn thmɤy rùː tèː?*

Exercise 9

A.1. No, my room hasn't big windows. 2. Yes, he/she/they goes/go to a big school. 3. No, (my) parents are not at home. 4. Is Uncle making a cupboard? Yes, he is. 5. Is elder brother going in father's car? Yes. 6. Is his/her/their car new? Yes, it is.

B.1. *nèak mìːan bɔntùp thom tèː? baːl tèː, bɔntùp khɲom tɔːc. 2. mìːŋ tɤ̀u phsaː(r) rùː tèː? baːl, kɔ̀at tɤ̀u phsaː(r). 3. taː cɯ̀h laːn rùː tèː? baːl, kɔ̀at cɯ̀h laːn. 4. mhoːp kdau rùː tèː? cah, (mhoːp) kdau nas.* (Subject may be absent since it is not a person at all.) *5. pùː thvɤ̀ː tùː thom tèː? cah tèː, kɔ̀at mùn thvɤ̀ː tùː tèː.*

Exercise 10

A.1. How many houses has your younger brother/sister? He has two. 2. How many brothers and sisters have you? I have three elder siblings/brothers and sisters. 3. How many brothers and sisters has your father? 4. I don't know. He has several/quite a number/many. 4. How many tables have you? I have two. 5. How many grandchildren has the old man? Five. 6. How many fish is aunt buying? Four/She is buying four.

B.1. *pùː mìːan cau pɔnmaːn nèak? baːl, kɔ̀at mìːan pùː(r) nèak. 2. mdaːy mìːan tùː pɔnmaːn? baːl, kɔ̀at mìːan (tùː) mùːay. 3. nèak mìːan trɤy pɔnmaːn? baːl, khɲom mìːan (trɤy) pram. 4. vìːa/kɔ̀at mìːan tok pɔnmaːn? cah, vìːa/kɔ̀at mìːan tok bɤy. 5. vìːa/kɔ̀at mìːan bɔːŋ-pʔoːn pɔnmaːn nèak? cah, khɲom mùn dɤŋ tèː. 6. nèak mìːan mìːŋ pɔnmaːn nèak? cah, khɲom mìːan craən nèak.*

Exercise 11

A.1. How many older brothers and sisters has aunt?/How many older brothers and sisters have you, aunt? 2. Does the old man see my car?/Do you see my car, grandfather? 3. Does grandson go to school?/Do you go to school, grandson? 4. Do you know? 5. Is younger brother/sister buying a mat? Are you buying the mat, younger brother/sister? 6. Is your father at home?

B.1. *mdaːy thvɤ̀ː mhoːp tèː? 2. pùː thvɤ̀ː tùː tèː? 3. taː dɤŋ rùː tèː? 4. bɔːŋ nɤ̀u phtèah tèː? 5. mìːŋ tèɲ trɤy-ŋìat rùː tèː? 6. mìːŋ tɤ̀u phsaː(r) rùː tèː?*

Exercise 12

A.1. Is aunt/Are you . . . . , aunt, buying those four big fowls? 2. Do you see that pork? It's very dear! 3. How many children has uncle? He has three. 4. Are the other houses roofed with palm-leaf? No, they are roofed with thatch/have thatched roofs. 5. How many windows has grandfather's house?/How many windows has your house, grandfather? Two.

6. Is the old man buying this pork?/Are you buying this pork, grandfather? No, it's very dear.

B.1. *pùː mìːən mə̀ən poñmaːn?* 2. *pʔɔːn-srɤy vìːə/kə̀ət tèɲ sac-crùːk.* 3. *kɔːn-pros khɲom pìː(r) nèək tɤu saːlaː-rìən thom thmɤy nùh.* 4. *khɲom mìːən pùː bɤy nèək. nèək mìːən mìːŋ buːən nèək.* 5. *pʔɔːn-srɤy tèɲ trɤy-ŋìət ʔae-tìət rùː tèː?* 6. *bɔːŋ-srɤy taː pìː(r) nèək nɤu phtèəh nìh.*

Exercise 13

A.1. Those two servants are going to the market. 2. He/she/they buys/buy cheap pork. 3. This cheap meat is not (at all) good. 4. My parents do not have servants/don't have (any) servants. 5. That big cupboard is very nice! 6. Are your brothers and sisters waiting for you?

B.1. *ʔɔːpùk hau nèək-bɔmraə bɤy nèək nùh.* 2. *kɔːn pìː(r) nèək cam mìːŋ vìːə.* 3. *phtèəh thom nùh prɔk sbɔːv rùː tèː?* 4. *pùː cùh laːn tɔːc nùh tèː?* 5. *crùːk pìː(r) nìh mùən thlay tèː.* 6. *ʔɔːpùk pùː cam nèək rùː tèː? baːl tèː/cah tèː, kə̀ət (not vìːə) tɤu phtèəh kɔːn-srɤy kə̀ət.*

Exercise 14

A.1. Are you buying a sarong/material, aunt? Yes, I like that red colour. 2. Is elder brother wearing white trousers? No, (he is wearing) black (ones/trousers)/Are you wearing white trousers, elder brother? No, (I am wearing) black (ones/trousers). 3. Uncle is wearing an expensive shirt/ You are wearing an expensive shirt, uncle. 4. Has grandmother a white blouse? Yes, (she has) two (white blouses)/Have you a white blouse grandmother? Yes, (I have) two (white blouses). 5. Is younger brother wearing a European suit? No, (he is wearing) a sarong/Are you wearing a European suit, younger brother? No, (I am wearing) a sarong. 6. This material/sarong is very dear. Have you (some) cheap material/a cheap sarong? No, I haven't (any) cheap material/a cheap one/sarong.

B.1. *pùː sliək khao sɔː nùh rùː tèː? baːl tèː, kə̀ət sliək sɔmpùət.* 2. *mìːŋ tɤu phsaː(r) thom rùː tèː? cah tèː, khɲom tɤu phsaː(r) tɔːc.* 3. *mdaːy tèɲ sɔmpùət lùəŋ nùh tèː? cah.* 4. *bɔːŋ-pros nèək sliək khao baːraŋ tèː? baːl tèː, kə̀ət sliək sɔmpùət.* 5. *cau mnèək pèək ʔaːv khìəv. cau mnèək sliək khao khmau.* 6. *mdaːy vìːə/kə̀ət pèək ʔaːv krɔhɔːm rùː tèː? baːl tèː, kə̀ət mùn pèək ʔaːv krɔhɔːm tèː.*

Exercise 15

A.1. Father is in (his) room. He is reading a book about Burma. 2. My niece is not going to England. She is staying in Siam. 3. Today your elder sister is wearing a very beautiful blouse. 4. Now we are coming from Vietnam. Tomorrow we are going to Siam. 5. We haven't this green book in our school. 6. Your Burmese material is on the new table.

B.1. *dɔːn nɤu phtèəh thom sɔː nùh rùː tèː? baːl tèː, kə̀ət nɤu phtèəh nìh.* 2. *pùː mìːən siəvphɤu craən ʔɔmpìː srok-ʔɔŋklèːs. siəvphɤu nùh nɤu knoŋ bɔntùp kə̀ət rùː tèː? cah, nɤu knoŋ tùː tɔːc.* 3. *bɔːŋ tɤu phsaː(r) phlìːəm rùː tèː? baːl, (khɲom tɤu) phlìːəm.* 4. *mdaːy tèɲ sɔmpùət thlay krɔhɔːm nùh pìː srok siəm. lʔɔː nas.* 5. *nèək khɤːŋ sɔmpùət sɔː lɤː tok tèː? thaok nas.* 6. *mìːŋ tèɲ sɔmpùət khmau nùh nɤu-mùk(h) sɔmpùət sɔː tèː? cah tèː, thlay nas.*

265

Exercise 16

A.1. Last night a thief entered grandfather's house. He didn't know. 2. I shall go to visit my aunt in the hospital this afternoon. She has been ill since yesterday/She was (taken) ill yesterday. 3. This year grandson will learn French. 4. Soon uncle will buy a boat. 5. That time your elder sister was rather ill/not very well. 6. They don't sell dried fish here.

B.1. *prùk nìh khɲom (nùŋ) tèɲ siəvphŕu pì:(r) nùh ʔɔmpì: srok-siəm. 2. cau vì:ə/kɔ̀ət mùn co:l phtèəh thŋay nùh tè:. 3. cao(r) bŕy nèək co:l phtèəh pì: kha:ŋ nùh rù: tè:? 4. pì: thŋay nùh pʔo:n-pros vì:ə nŕu phtèəh-pèːl̃(y) nìh. 5. yù:(r)-yù:(r) mdɔ:ŋ yŕ:ŋ tŕu su:ə(r) vì:ə/kɔ̀ət. 6. pì: msŕl ta: nùh lùək trŕy knoŋ tì: nìh.*

Exercise 17

A.1. Why does the teacher go to school today?/Why are you going to school today, sir? Today we don't learn/study. 2. Where have you a/Where is your house, grandfather? (I have a house/My house is) in Phnom Penh. 3. Do you know French, Mr. —? Yes, I know a little. 4. How do you/did you go to Siam? I go/went by plane. 5. When did aunt go into hospital?/ When did you go into hospital, aunt? She/I went in yesterday morning/ this morning (depending on whether one is speaking during the morning or a later part of 'today'; literally 'last morning'). 6. Yesterday your uncle got into the boat. Where did he go? He went to Kompung Cham.

B.1. *mëc-kɔ:/häet(o)-ʔvŕy-ba:n-cì:ə do:n nŕu knoŋ phtèəh-pèːl̃(y)? pù: dŕŋ tè:? 2. nèək dak siəvphŕu nùh nŕu-ʔae na:/nŕu kɔnlaeŋ na:? ba:l̃, khɲom dak nŕu tù: pù: nùh. 3. vì:ə/kɔ̀ət mɔ:k pì: srok-ʔɔŋklè:s do:c-mdëc/ya:ŋ mëc/ya:ŋ do:c-mdëc? vì:ə/kɔ̀ət cìh yùən(t)-hɔh rù: tè:? 4. cau bu:ən nèək nùh nùŋ su:ə(r) do:n (vì:ə) ʔɔŋkal/ka:l na:? 5. khɲom nùŋ ba:n kɔnlaeŋ knoŋ sa:la:-rìən nùh ya:ŋ mëc/do:c-mdëc/ya:ŋ do:c-mdëc? 6. mëc kɔ:/häet(o)-ʔvŕy-ba:n-cì:ə kɔpal nùh mɔ:k kɔmpùəŋ-ca:m pì: phnùm-pèɲ?*

Exercise 18

A.1. Where do they sell string? 2. Who is going to the town/city this morning? 3. In that school, how do they teach English? What books do they use? 4. Yesterday morning/this morning (i.e. now past) whom did you see in the town/city? 5. How many pupils has the teacher in this class? 6. How many thieves entered uncle's house last night?

B.1. *ko:n-sŕs(s) na:/na:-khlah rìən phì:rəsa: ba:raŋsaes chnam nìh? 2. ʔo:pùk nèək tŕu su:ə(r) nèək na: nŕu phtèəh-pèːl̃(y) pì: msŕl/pì: msŕl meɲ? 3. lò:k-krù: tha: ya:ŋ mëc/ya:ŋ do:c-mdëc/do:c-mdëc ʔɔmpì: ko:n-pros nèək? 4. cau tèɲ siəvphŕu poṅma:n prùk meɲ? 5. nèək na: khŕ:ŋ lò:k-krù: knoŋ tì:-kroŋ pì: msŕl meɲ/msŕl meɲ/pì: msŕl/msŕl? 6. yù:ən nùh lùək phtèəh na:/na:-mù:əy ʔŕylo:v?*

Exercise 19

A.1. What games do Cambodian children play? 2. When did elder brother/ sister come from Siam?/When did you come from Siam, elder brother/ sister? 3. Is younger brother's/sister's house near the market?/Is your house near the market, younger brother/sister? 4. I haven't (any) dried fish today. 5. Where are your grandparents going this afternoon? 6. How does his father keep/bring up five children?

B.1. *lòːk-krùː nìh mìːən koːn-sʋs(s) poñmaːn nèək knoŋ thnak kòət? kòət mìːən dɔŋ nèək. 2. vìːə/kòət səseːr(r) siəvphʋu ʔae-tìət ʔɔmpìː srok-khmae(r) rùː tèː? baːt, khɲom mùn dʋŋ tèː. 3. taː nùŋ pèək ʔaːv khiəv thmʋy nùh ʔɔŋkal/kaːl naː? 4. lòːk cìh kɔpal naː/naː-mùːəy? 5. mɛc kɔ/häet(o)-ʔvʋy-baːn-cìːə ʔaːv lùəŋ nùh thlay? mùn lʔɔː tèː. 6. doːn nèək ceñcʋm crùːk poñmaːn? cah, (kòət ceñcʋm) bʋy.*

Exercise 20

A.1. That year my grandchild nearly died/was at death's door/was about to die (but didn't). 2. Which room do you usually work in, sir? 3. Have you (ever) been to Kompung Cham? Yes, I have. 4. Mr. — is not very well. 5. The mother went out of the house. Two thieves immediately went into the room. 6. Aunt has never been to Siam. 7. One pupil hardly knows his alphabet. 8. In this class the children have just sat the examination. 9. Why is grandson always ill? 10. At home, Cambodians usually wear a sarong. 11. In the market smoked fish is usually cheap. 12. Those nice sarongs/materials are all dear.

B.1. *vìːə/kòət kɔmpùŋ-tae sɔŋ phtèəh thmʋy mùːəy. 2. pùː mùn-tòən tʋu phsaːr(r). 3. koːn-sʋs(s) naː ceh-tae lèːŋ nʋu-lʋː phloːv? 4. mɛc-kɔ pros nùh rùt-tae kaːc? 5. mìːŋ vìːə kɔmpùŋ-tae thvʋː ʔvʋy? 6. taː tʋːp-nùŋ mʋːl siəvphʋu naː-mùːəy? 7. yʋːŋ craən-tae khʋːŋ lòːk kae nʋu phloːv nìh. 8. mənùs(s) nìh mùn-mèːn khoːc tèː. 9. koːn-sʋs(s) khmae(r) sɔl-tae tʋu bon(y) nìh nʋu paːrìːs. 10. khɲom tʋːp-tae-nùŋ khʋːŋ lòːk-krùː yʋːŋ knoŋ kroŋ. 11. taː nùh stʋː-tae nùŋ dot phtèəh nìh. 12. vìːə/kòət mùn-dael tʋu srok-ʔɔŋklèːs chnam nìh tèː. 13. kmeːŋ-pros nìh mùn-tòən ceh ʔɔksɔː(r). 14. yʋːŋ troːv-tae phɲaə sɔmbot(r) nìh tʋu paːrìːs.*

Exercise 21

A.1. Who wants to see this film? My mother wants to see this film tomorrow; today she has to stay in her room. 2. That time she did not wear the blue dress. 3. Mother is busy working in the house. 4. Father usually (goes) by car. 5. Is young Kê good at (learning) French? 6. My teacher no longer lives at/has ceased to live at this house. 7. I have seen that French film. 8. Must you go to Phnom Penh, aunt?/Does aunt have to go to Phnom Penh? 9. This white material is used for making shirts/blouses/dresses. 10. Our children are asking to play that game. 11. Why are you trying hard to learn English, grandson? Are you thinking of going to America?/ Why is grandson .... Is he thinking .... 12. I (would) like to buy that yellow material/sarong. 13. Does your elder brother/sister want to see that Cambodian film? 14. Where are you rushing away to?

B.1. *yʋːŋ cɔŋ tèŋ sɔmpùət baytɔːŋ. sɔmpùət nìh thlay pèːk. 2. mdaːy baːn prɔːm nʋu knoŋ phtèəh nìh rùː tèː? 3. vìːə/kòət mùn thlɔəp thvʋː kaː(r) nʋu tìː kroŋ. 4. baːt, kèː troːv sliək-pèək khao-ʔaːv tìː nìh/nʋu tìː nìh/knoŋ tìː nìh. 5. vìːə/kòət mùn hìːən tʋu phtèəh nùh tèː. 6. nèək dak ʔaːv thaok nʋu-ʔae naː? 7. tùː nìh sɔmrap tùk khao-ʔaːv lòːk. 8. koːn-pros pìː(r) nèək mùn ceh baək laːn tèː. 9. siəvphʋu nìh sɔmrap rìən phìːəsaː ʔɔŋklèːs. 10. vìːə/kòət mùn*

thlɔəp cap trʁy tèː. vìːə/kɔ̀ət ʔɔt/mùən ceh thvʁ̀ː tèː. 11. *cau-pros nɛ̀ək chap rìən.*
12. *mëc-kɔː pùː cɔŋ tʁu srok-baːraŋ?* 13. *kmuːəy-srʁy khɲom kùt rìən*
phìːəsaː ʔɔŋklèːs. 14. *ʔɔːpùk troːv suːə(r) nɛ̀ək naː nʁu phtɛ̀əh-pɛ̀ːl(y)?*

Exercise 22

A.1. The young lady doesn't yet (know how to) smoke. 2. Americans always
want to buy this Siamese material. 3. Our father is constantly busy writing
letters. 4. The children hardly dare to go into grandfather's/the old man's
room. 5. Aunt is on the point of agreeing to go to Europe. 6. Those pupils
are all working/trying hard to learn English.

B.1. *mìːŋ mùən-mɛ̀ːn cɔŋ nʁu phùːm(ì) nùh.* 2. *cao(r) srap-tae rùət cìh laːn.*
3. *cʁn craən-tae tèɲ tiəm nùh.* 4. *khɲom tʁ̀ːp-nùəŋ soːm mʁ̀ːl siəvphʁu ʔɔŋklèːs*
nùh. 5. *pùː mùən-dael rìən nìyìːəy phìːəsaː khmae(r) tèː.* 6. *vìːə/kɔ̀ət mùən-*
soːv ceh səseː(r) ʔɔksɔː(r).

Exercise 23

A.1. Your trunk is under my bed. 2. That green blouse of yours/hers is like
Mrs. —'s/yours, Mrs. —. 3. One man must follow me along/come after me.
4. Mr. —/you will take this letter out of the drawer tomorrow. 5. The thief
ran out of the room. 6. Where did you/Mr. — pursue them/him/her to?/
How far did you chase them/him/her? 7. Who sent that parcel? 8. She/
The young woman put the tray of coffee on the little table.

B.1. *siəvphʁu baːraŋsaes nɛ̀ək nʁu kraoy maːsìːn-ʔɔŋkùlìːleːk(h).* 2. *yʁ̀ːŋ*
baːn phɲaə sɔmbot(r) bʁy tʁu pùː nɛ̀ək. 3. *vìːə/kɔ̀ət baːn tèɲ siəvphʁu nùh*
ʔaoy koːn-sʁs(s) thnak nìh. 4. *khɲom nùəŋ phɲaə kɔpcɔp nìh tʁu srok-ʔɔŋklèːs*
doːc-mdëc/yaːŋ mëc/yaːŋ naː? 5. *häet(o)-ʔvʁy-baːn-cìːə/mëc-kɔː nɛ̀ək baːn*
nɔ̀əm mənùs(s) nùh mɔ̀ːk coːl phtɛ̀əh? 6. *koːn-pros buːən nɛ̀ək nùəŋ mɔ̀ːk dɔl*
sʔaek. 7. *vìːə/kɔ̀ət laəŋ cùəndaə(r) mɔ̀ːk ʔʁyloːv.* 8. *nɛ̀ək naː yɔ̀ːk thaːs tʁu*
coːl bəntùp taː? 9. *nɛ̀ək naː ʔaoy sɔmbot(r) nùh tʁu/mɔ̀ːk cau?/nɛ̀ək naː ʔaoy*
cau sɔmbot(r) nùh? 10. *pùː vìːə/kɔ̀ət bɔŋhaːŋ tùː ʔaoy yʁ̀ːŋ/yʁ̀ːŋ tùː.*

Exercise 24

A.1. The grandson/He came to our house on a donkey. 2. I am not very
happy working here. 3. You wave your hand to call a cyclo. 4. The village
chief invited the teacher home/to come to (his) house/to (his) house.
5. That old man wants to go to see/watch the fête in our village tomorrow.
6. Your grandmother weaves mats very quickly. 7. Do you/does Mrs. —
have servants to clean the house? 8. Your/Mr. —'s children all sing very
well/delightfully. 9. Those four Thais came to Cambodia by air. 10. He
ran after the thief. 11. The fox grasped/bit the fowl's neck. 12. Those
children talk too loudly.

B.1. *kmeːŋ sɔpbaːry criəŋ cɔmriəŋ.* 2. *vìːə/kɔ̀ət baːn cɔŋ tèɲ siəvphʁu rìən phìːəsaː*
baːraŋsaes. 3. *mèː khùm nɔ̀əm cao(r) tʁu dak kùk.* 4. *mìːŋ tbaːŋ kɔŋcʁ̀ː lùək*
ʔae/knɔŋ/nʁu phsaː(r). 5. *vìːə/kɔ̀ət baːn phɲaə sɔmbot(r) prap/cùmrìːəp*
yʁ̀ːŋ ʔɔmpìː sëckdʁy nùh. 6. *koːn-sʁs(s) tùk siəvphʁu vìːə/kɔ̀ət sɔpbaːry nas.*
7. *kɔ̀ət/nìːəy/vìːə baːn rìən tbaːŋ sɔmpùət thvʁ̀ː kbac.* 8. *khɲom tèɲ sɔmpùət*
thvʁ̀ː ʔaːv pìː(r). 9. *kmeːŋ-pros pram nɛ̀ək tʁu phtɛ̀əh cùmrìːəp mèː khùm.*

10. *mənùs(s) buːən nèək cìh tùːk pìː(r) nùh rùːəc cìːvùt.* 11. *nèək-bəmraə nùh criəŋ pìːrùəh nas.* 12. *lòːk praə khɲom thvɤ̀ː ʔvɤy?*

Exercise 25

A.1. A child took the letter away. 2. Father isn't buying the big boat. 3. Is aunt cooking rice for you? 4. My mother makes very good/tasty meals. 5. The farmers uproot the paddy (from the earth). 6. Mr. — is getting into a new car.

B.1. *khɲom baːn khɤ̀ːɲ kɔɲcɔp thom nùh. mùn thɲùən pèːk tèː.* 2. *nèək-srae kəmpùŋ-tae rìəp dɤy saːp krɔəp sroːv.* 3. *vìːə/kɔ̀ət yɔ̀ːk cɔːp cìːk dɤy.* 4. *nèək-srae khmae(r) praə cɔːp thɲùən.* 5. *vìːə/kɔ̀ət səseːr(r) səmbot(r) vèːŋ tɤ̀u lòːk-krùː.* 6. *yɤ̀ːŋ cɔŋ lùək phtèəh cas.*

Note on sentence analysis. The sentences in A. are alternately **N V V** and **N V**. Those in B. are all **N V** except nos. 2 and 3.

Exercise 26

A.1. They offered us a cup of tea each. 2. My son has not yet sat for the examination for going into the third class. 3. My land is twenty yards long. 4. How many horses have you now, sir? I have twenty. 5. In the second class the pupils are mostly/usually seven years old. 6. In another year I am going to England. 7. That woman offered me twelve cigarettes! 8. Those two monks usually read manuscripts in the afternoon. 9. The two grandchildren have just sat for the examination. One has just passed, one has failed. 10. He refuses to walk two more kilometres. 11. Sixty kilograms of paddy cost 10 riels.

B.1. *kɔːn-sɤs(s) dɔp-pram-bɤy nèək prəlɔːŋ chnam nìh. dɔp nèək cɔ̀əp.* 2. *yɤ̀ːŋ tɤ̀u suːə(r) doːn khɲom mùːəy khae bɤy dɔːŋ.* 3. *sdăc bɤy prèəh-ʔɔ̀ŋ(k) baːn nɤ̀u knoŋ rùːəc-vèəŋ nìh.* 4. *cau ʔàtthìkaːr(r) mìːən sa̱traː pìː(r) kùmpìː knoŋ vɔ̀ət(t).* 5. *nèək nùŋ pìsaː doːŋ mùːəy cəmhiəŋ rùː tèː? ʔoːpùk khɲom tɤ̀ːp-nùŋ tèŋ mùːəy phloːŋ!* 6.a. *khɲom tèŋ trɤy-ŋìət nɤ̀u-ʔae naː?* b. *tùː nìh/ʔae neh. poňmaːn cɔŋkak, lòːk?* a. *mùːəy cɔŋkak poňmaːn rìəl?* b. *mùːəy cɔŋkak pram rìəl.* 7. *knoŋ cəmkaːr(r) nìh khɲom mìːən mrèc buːən cùənlùəŋ.* 8. *kɔːn-sɤs(s) saːmsɤp nèək rìən phìːəsaː ʔɔŋklèːs nɤ̀u-knoŋ thnak tùː mùːəy.* 9. *taː thlɔ̀əp cìh sùːkloː mùːəy ʔaːtùt(y) mdɔːŋ.* 10. *lòːk baːn phɲaə trəsok buːən tɤ̀u cau ʔàtthìkaːr(r).* 11. *yɤ̀ːŋ craən-tae troːv cam rətèh-phlɤ̀ːŋ nèək pìː(r) bɤy mìːnùt. thɲay nìh yɤ̀ːŋ baːn cam pìː(r) maoŋ!* 12. *häet(o)-ʔvɤy-baːn-cìːə/mëc-kɔː mìːŋ baːn lèːp thnam pìː(r) krɔəp nùh thɲay nìh?*

Exercise 27

A.1. Ever since I came to Battambang, I have not been very well/I have been rather off colour. 2. Even if this student studies hard, he will not know a great deal. 3. My elder brother sat for the examination three times but he always failed. 4. They/he/she put (in) that piece of earth so that the bag would be heavy. 5. If that letter hasn't arrived, father will not leave Saigon today. 6. While Mrs. —/you came to visit me at my house, a thief entered Mrs. —'s/your house and stole many things. 7. In my opinion/According to my guess the democratic party will not win. 8. The mother made the meal; then she went out to the market. 9. I wish to read the letter which mother sent from Thailand. 10. If ever you/Mr. — come/ comes to Kompung Cham again, you/he must eat at my house.

B.1. *kmeːŋ mphèy-bɤy nèək baːn prəlɔːŋ haəy-nùŋ pram-buːən-dɔndɔp nèək cɔ̀əp.* 2. *rùː chkae mùn/ʔɔt/ʔɤt prùh rùː khɲom mùn/ʔɔt/ʔɤt lùː.* 3. *lòːk baːn thaː phtèəh vìːə/kɔ̀ət nɤ̌u phsaː(r) thom tèː?* 4. *kaːl-naː lòːk-krùː tùːŋ skɔ̀ː(r), kmeːŋ nùŋ cə̆ɲ mɔ̀ːk.* 5. *mənùs(s) nùh baːn prap khɲom thaː phtèəh khɲom cheh.* 6. *kraoy-pìː mè: khùm tɤ̌u/mɔ̀ːk dɔl, tùːəhìːən cə̆ɲ pìː phtèəh.* 7. *bɔntùp tùːlìːəy nas poñtae yɤ̌ːŋ mùn dak tùː mùːəy tìət tèː.* 8. *bɔːŋ-pʔoːn baːn mɔ̀ːk phnùm-pə̆ɲ mɤ̌ːl bɔɲ(y) ʔɔm tùːk poñtae vìːə/kɔ̀ət baːn nɤ̌u bɤy ʔaːtùt(y)!* 9. *kaːl-naː kɔ̀ət/vìːə tɤ̌u srok-baːraŋ kɔ̀ət/vìːə nùŋ slìək sɔmpùət mdɔːŋ-mdɔːŋ rùː tèː?* 10. *kraoy-pìː mənùs(s) pìː(r) nèək baːn cùːəp knìːə nɤ̌u phtèəh vìːə/kɔ̀ət cə̆ɲ pìː kɔmpùəŋ-caːm taːm tùːk.*

Exercise 28

A.1. Aunt has returned from Thailand, hasn't she? 2. The old man/Grandfather has worked since dawn and now he has to finish this chair. 3. Oh! Grandmother isn't ill, then? Yesterday she had gone into hospital! 4. One possibility is for you to go to Battambang by train; another is for me to go tomorrow by car. 5. I can't see a single nice place! 6. She/The girl refuses to clean the house again.

B.1. *lòːk-krùː baːn thaː cau khɲom ʔɔt/mùn/ʔɤt rìən phìːəsaː baːraŋsaes sɔh laəy.* 2. *khɲom cɔŋ dɤŋ baə lòːk dac cɤt(t) cə̆ɲ pìː phnùm-pə̆ɲ.* 3. *nɤ̌u tìəm nùh kè: lùək sɔmpùət pìː srok-klɤŋ(k̆) dae(r).* 4. *pù: lòːk trəlɔp mɔ̀ːk phtèəh haəy.* 5. *sʔaek ʔaeŋ tɤ̌u phnùm-pə̆ɲ thvɤ̌ː ʔvɤy? khɲom tɤ̌u tèɲ ʔɤyvan haəy-nùŋ tɤ̌u suːə(r) mùt (t)-sɔmlaɲ khɲom phɔːŋ.* 6. *cau ʔaìthìkaː(r) nùŋ kùt sĕckdɤy tìət.*

Exercise 29

A.1. They haven't yet rung the bell/beaten the gong, have they? 2. When your relatives come to see the Water Festival, will you go to meet them at the quay (lit. 'boat')? 3. We have met before, haven't we? 4. Your aunt hasn't decided to buy that new house, has she? 5. The teacher wants to punish those naughty pupils, doesn't he?

B.1. *kaːl nèək baːn coːl bɔntùp ʔoːpùk nèək mùn baːn khɤ̌ːɲ kɔntray khɲom tèː rùː? 2. baə khɲom tɤ̌u cìh rətèh-phlɤ̌ːŋ lòːk-pù: nùŋ tɤ̌u cùːə-mùːəy-nùŋ khɲom tèː?* 3. *taŋ-pìː taː vìːə/kɔ̀ət slap, vìːə/kɔ̀ət baːn chùː rùː?* 4. *tùəhbɤy nìːəŋ nùh baːn lùːəc sìəvphɤ̌u kɔː-daoy, nìːəŋ nùh mùn phùt-phéy doːcɂneh tèː rùː?* 5. *nèək mùn baːn lèək sɔmbot(r) nùh daəmbɤy-ʔaoy bɔɲchaot vìːə/kɔ̀ət tèː rùː?*

Exercise 30

A.1. Off you go, up into the house! I want to speak to you immediately. 2. Yesterday a lot of rain fell. 3. Don't shout, children! I'm not/Your teacher is not actually deaf! 4. At dusk there is a delightful scent of flowers in Mr. Kê's garden. 5. It is very hot at night during this month. 6. Don't walk so quickly, (niece)! I don't want to arrive before the time. 7. It is very cool in this room. Please turn off the fan for me, (young lady/Miss).

8. An interesting thing/incident happened today. I will tell you, Mrs. —/
I will tell Mrs. —. 9. At dawn in this forest there is a sound of many birds/
many birds may be heard. 10. There are two pieces of cake left. Do
have one!

B.1. *yɔ̀ːk siəvphʏ̀u pìː(r) nùh tʏ̀u cùːn lòːk kae!* 2. *huːəs maoŋ haəy. yʏ̀ːŋ mùŋ
troːv tʏ̀u dɔl yùːt.* 3. *khɲom mùn/ʔɔt cɔŋ dao(r)-lèːŋ. kdau pèːk thŋay nìh.*
4. *thlèək phlìəŋ mɔ̀ːk haəy. yʏ̀ːŋ troːv prəɲap hau sìːkloː.* 5. *lùː soː(r) kmeːŋ
yùm kraoy phtèəh.* 6. *pʔɔːn kom tèɲ trʏy-ɲìət ʔae/knoŋ phsaː(r) thom!
thlay pèːk nʏ̀u tìː nùh.* 7. *thùm klʏn phkaː-kolaːp knoŋ bɔntùp pontae khɲom
ʔɔt khʏ̀ːɲ phkaː sɔh.* 8. *ʔɔɲcʏ̀ːɲ ʔɔŋkùy nʏ̀u tìː nìh. rəŋ̀ːə nʏ̀u-cùːt tvìːə(r).*
9. *baek caːn bʏy haəy-nùŋ pìəc thaːs phɔːŋ.* 10. *kbuəŋ mùːəy thlèək pìː
dɔmboːl vìhìːə(r)./thlèək kbuəŋ (mùːəy) pìː dɔmboːl vìhìːə(r).*

Exercise 31

A.1. In the morning at a quarter to eight the teacher beats the gong until
all the pupils have gone into the school together. 2. Even after midnight
there is plenty of noise here of people laughing in the street. 3. There is
another reason why I do not want to go and work in Kompung Cham:
I have just bought a house in Phnom Penh. 4. At what time does the
train leave? It leaves at seven in the morning. What time does it get to
Battambang? At six in the evening. 5. Mr. — had a fever last week but
he wouldn't call a doctor. 6. On Wednesday I left home at dawn to go
fishing. At six o'clock in the evening I came back. How hungry I was!

B.1. *knoŋ-pèːl-dael thlèək phlìəŋ mɔ̀ːk craən yʏ̀ːŋ baːn cam nʏ̀u-knoŋ vɔ̀ət(t).*
2. *kom mɔ̀ːk thŋay prəhɔ̀əs(p + tè). yʏ̀ːŋ tʏ̀u mʏ̀ːl kon ʔaːmeːrìːkaŋ nʏ̀u
ròːŋ-kon thmʏy.* 3. *dɓʏt-tae maoŋ prampùəl haəy, taː haəy-nùŋ koːn kɔ̀ət
mùn baːn bɔŋhaəy kauʔʏy tèː.* 4. *lòːk kae craən-tae/thlɔ̀əp tətùːəl tìːən
dɔmneːk thŋay rəsiəl/pèːl rəsiəl pontae khɲom mùn smaːn thaː kɔ̀ət lùək tèː.*
5. *baə bɔːŋ-srʏy khɲom tʏ̀u rìən nʏ̀u srok-ʔɔŋklèːs khae-tola: kɔ̀ət nùŋ nʏ̀u
buːən chnam.* 6. *khae-pìsaːk(h) nùŋ kdau nas. troːv baək phlʏt pèːl yùp.*

Exercise 32

A.1. That cyclo-driver will tell me where there is a hotel. 2. I don't know
what he does for a living. 3. You must tell the teacher what pages you have
read, grandson. 4. The old man/Grandfather doesn't yet know what time
the bus will get to Phnom Penh. 5. Last week my mother was very ill.
My elder sister wanted to look after her at home. The doctor therefore
told her what she had to do/what things had to be done/what it was
necessary to do. 6. I want to ask Mrs. —/you, Mrs. —, when she/you will
go to visit grandmother. 7. That servant will not say where madam's
scissors have disappeared to. 8. The teacher never told me how many
students there are/were in the second class. 9. Please tell me, (Miss),
whether it is yet eight o'clock? 10. I should like to tell Mrs. —/you,
Mrs. —, why it was that I didn't go to see him/her in hospital.

B.1. *khɲom suːə(r) lòːk taə kɔ̀ət coːl cʏt(t) tʏ̀u mʏ̀ːl srok naː-khlah.* 2. *kè: nùŋ
suːə(r) khɲom taə yùp nìh khɲom cɔŋ bɔrephòːk nʏ̀u phtèəh rùː tèː?* 3. *ʔaːnʏt
prap khɲom taə rətèh-phlʏ̀ːŋ nìh tʏ̀u naː?* 4. *lòːk nìh mùn cɔŋ prap khɲom
thaː kɔ̀ət baːn suːə(r) nèək naː nʏ̀u phnùm-pèɲ tèː.* 5. *khɲom nùŋ suːə(r)*

271

lòːk-pùː thaː kòət nùŋ mòːk kɔmpùəŋ-caːm kaːl naː? 6. yɤ̀ːŋ baːn kùt thaː taə prùk laəŋ pʔoːn-pros nìːəŋ nùŋ thvɤ̀ː ʔvɤy tìət. 7. vìːə/kòət mùn prap thaː cao(r) baːn coːl bɔntùp yaːŋ doːc-mdëc tèː. 8. khɲom suːə(r) cau thaː häet(o)-ʔvɤy-baːn-cìːə cau prùːəy prùk nìh? 9. lòːk-srɤy mùn baːn thaː mìːən mənùs(s) poñmaːn nèək nɤ̀u-knoŋ phtèəh tèː. 10. cao(r) dɤŋ thaː lòːk tùk prak nɤ̀u kɔnlaeŋ naː.

Exercise 33

A.1. Grandson cannot go to play/visit at the house of his friend. He cannot walk because he has hurt his leg. 2. The two thieves went out through the window, got into the car and went off rapidly. 3. The things are very heavy. The ox cannot pull the cart. 4. That matter/question/problem is very difficult. The old man/I can't solve it! 5. Those four monks have missed the bus; that is why they are walking along the road. 6. That's all right! My suit is not actually wet through. 7. Every Tuesday two or three friends of mine come and visit me at half past six without fail. 8. Grand-father/The old man is a bit deaf nowadays. He can't hear the radio. 9. Father hasn't finished reading the newspaper. You must wait a bit and then you may read it. 10. This girl has a high fever; her face is constantly red.

B.1. *doːn ròːk siəvphɤu ʔɔmpìː vìhìːə(r) nùh mùn khɤ̀ːɲ. 2. kòət mɤ̀ːl khao-ʔaːv mùn khɤ̀ːɲ thaː rəhaek tèː. 3. nɤ̀u kɔnlaeŋ nìh lùː soː(r) kmeːŋ sraek craən nèək pèːk. khɲom sdap nèək mùn lùː sɔh. 4. mənùs(s) khoːc nùh dëp taːm tìːəhìːən cas nùh mùn tɔ̀ən. 5. khɲom tətùːəl tìːən cɔmnɤy-ʔaːhaː(r) mùn kaət prùəh khɲom chùː. 6. doːn mɤ̀ːl tùːk mùn khɤ̀ːɲ pìː-prùəh kòət tìːəp pèːk. 7. baə poːlìːs baːn cìh kaːɲoːt dëp taːm cao(r) nùh kèː nùŋ baːn tɔ̀ən cao(r) nùh mùn khaːn. 8. khɲom tèp kaːsaet ʔɔŋklèːs nɤ̀u-ʔae naː baːn? 9. khɲom baːn suːə(r) kmeːŋ-srɤy nìh thaː mëc-kɔ səmliək-bɔmpèək tətùk còːk poñtae vìːə nìyìːəy mùn kaət sɔh. 10. yɤ̀ːŋ baːn lùː taːm vìtyù thaː kèː ròːk yùən(t)-hɔh khɤ̀ːɲ nɤ̀u kɔnlaeŋ naː poñtae khɲom thaː chmùəh kɔnlaeŋ nùh mùn troːv.*

Exercise 34

A.1. All the students learn French, don't they? No, there are some who don't learn French. 2. Last night I constantly dreamed that I saw something or other like a human being. 3. I know there is some festival in this monastery. 4. Those few men know French. 5. Perhaps some day we shall meet again. 6. Some people are used to going to the cinema three times a week. 7. The teacher told the students that there are some countries where paddy is not grown. 8. The police gave the information that that thief said a few things about the incident before he died. 9. There are some parcels in the sitting-room. I don't know where they came from. 10. Grandfather is always giving us some work or other to do.

B.1. *kèː baːn prap khɲom thaː nèək nùŋ ʔɔŋkùy kɔnlaeŋ naː. 2. khɲom coːl cɤt(t) kùt kaː(r) ʔvɤy-mùːəy nùŋ lòːk. 3. ʔaey dɤŋ thaː rəbɔs khɲom nɤ̀u ʔae naː tèː? baːl, khɲom mùn dɤŋ tèː. poñtae mìːən rəbɔs ʔvɤy-khlah nɤ̀u-lɤ̀ː tok. 4. kòət baːn tèp siəvphɤu yùːən khlah haəy. 5. cuːən-kaːl/cuːən-naː/mdɔːŋ-mdɔːŋ pʔoːn-pros khɲom səseː(r) sɔmbot(r) tɤu mdaːy nɤ̀u srok-khmae(r).*

6. *kmeːŋ-srɤy nùh mìːən rùəŋ ʔvɤy-mùːəy cùmrìːəp lòːk-srɤy.* 7. *ʔae phsaː(r) mìːən trɤy baep naː-khlah poñtae trɤy nùh thlay nas.* 8. *mìːən kèː cam ròːŋ-kon pèːl yùp.* 9. *khɲom smaːn thaː cau mìːən rùəŋ ʔvɤy-mùːəy prap khɲom, mɤ̀ːl tɤ̀u?* 10. *lòːk-srɤy nɤ̀u phtèəh nùh rùː tèː? tèː, poñtae mìːən rəbɔs ʔvɤy cìːə craən nɤ̀u-knoŋ phtèəh.*

Exercise 35

A.1. He didn't say anything. 2. England isn't very far from France, is it? 3. I give that old lady any things which I don't need. 4. If you have any things of value, please put them in the drawer/a drawer. 5. I don't know any student(s) in this class who would dare to do this/to act like this. 6. There is no place where we can hide this jewel. 7. If you do anything/ Whatever work you do/you should do it properly. 8. If you want to go anywhere/Wherever you want to go I will give you a lift (there/to that place). 9. Anyone who hits a person is hit in return. 10. There is not a single garden tool in that garden.

B.1. *khɲom mùn khɤ̀ːŋ ʔɤyvan rəbɔs nèək naː knoŋ kɔnlaeŋ nìh tèː.* 2. *thŋay nìh kmìːən tùːk-kdaoŋ poñmaːn nɤ̀u-lɤ̀ː tùənlèː tèː.* 3. *pʔoːn nìːəŋ mùn lèːŋ lbaeŋ naː sɔh laəy.* 4. *kmìːən nèək naː dɤŋ cìːə nèək naː thvɤ̀ː nùh.* 5. *krùːəsaː(r) siəm nùh mùn cɔŋ cìh rətèh-phlɤ̀ːŋ tɤ̀u naː tèː.* 6. *baə cau yɔ̀ːk rəbɔs cèŋ pìː thɔːt-tok nùh dɔːn nùŋ khɤŋ nas.* 7. *kmìːən prədap-prədaː ʔvɤy knoŋ phtèəh pùː.* 8. *taː cɔːl cɤt(t) nɤ̀u phtèəh. kɔ̀ət mùn prɔːm tɤ̀u naː tèː.* 9. *khɲom mùn baːn khɤ̀ːŋ kɔɲcɔːp ʔvɤy nɤ̀u kɔnlaeŋ nùh.* 10. *cau-ʔaltthìkaː(r) nùh mùn-dael tɤ̀u kɔnlaeŋ naː krau-pìː kɔmpùəŋ-caːm.*

Exercise 36

A.1. Whatever word the teacher pronounces, the students pronounce after him. 2. Whatever this material costs I shall take it/buy it. 3. Whatever you/he/Mr. — wants me to do/asks me to do/tells me to do, I shall refuse. 4. I like whatever material you like. 5. I shall go wherever you go. 6. Whatever the teacher says to do, the child does/the children do. 7. However much the father beats that child, he still doesn't cry. 8. Whatever dish you prepare, mother, I shall help you. 9. You may do the work how you like, (elder); I shall do it the usual way. 10. However much it rains, I shall go.

B.1. *lòːk-srɤy nɤ̀u kɔnlaeŋ naː, khɲom kɔː nùŋ mɔ̀ːk suːə(r) mùn khaːn.* 2. *nèək naː baːn thaː nùh, nèək nùh kɔː mùn dɤŋ ʔvɤy ʔɔmpìː sĕckdɤy nùh tèː.* 3. *koːn tɤ̀u tùː-kɔnlaeŋ naː, mdaːy kɔː tɤ̀u tùː-kɔnlaeŋ nùh dae(r)!* 4. *lòːk-krùː rɤ̀ːs nèək naː, nèək nùh troːv ʔaːn/mɤ̀ːl rùəŋ.* 5. *ʔoːpùk-mdaːy yɤ̀ːŋ tèŋ vìtyù baep naː, koːn kɔː cɔːl cɤt(t).* 6. *lòːk-krùː mìːən siəvphɤ̀u naː, khɲom kɔː nùŋ tèŋ siəvphɤ̀u nùh dae(r).* 7. *kmuːəy thvɤ̀ː ʔvɤy-mùːəy, mìːŋ kɔː nùŋ cùːəy thvɤ̀ː dae(r).* 8. *nèək daə(r) poñmaːn kìːlòːmaet(r), khɲom kɔː nùŋ daə(r) taːm.* 9. *khɲom thvɤ̀ː ʔvɤy kɔː kɔ̀ət mùn troːv cɤt(t) dae(r).* 10. *samaːcùk rɤ̀ːs nèək naː, yɤ̀ːŋ kɔː sok(h) cɤt(t) dae(r).*

Exercise 37

A.1. I am thinking of going home/to my country. I can go *any* day. 2. Whatever region those mangoes come from, I like them all! 3. You must note down *any*thing he says. 4. When*ever* you come, mother, I always have room for you. 5. You may come and visit me at *any* time. 6. Do it any way you like, so long as you finish it quickly. 7. You must do it before tonight *some*how. 8. You may do what you like. I shall say nothing. 9. Buy *any* book for me, aunt/It doesn't matter which book you buy for me, aunt. 10. I shall buy it whatever the cost.

B.1. *nèək cɔːl phtèəh-pèːɫ(y) naː kɔː-daoy, kèː nùəŋ pyìːəbaːl nèək daoy sëckdɤy prəyát(n)-prəyaeŋ. 2. kɔ̀ət rìən vìɔ̀cìːə naː kɔː-daoy, kɔ̀ət nùəŋ prəlɔːŋ cɔ̀əp. 3. lòːk mɔ̀ːk pèːl naː kɔː-daoy, yɤ̀ːŋ ceh-tae sok(h) cɤt(t) tətùːəl lòːk. 4. nèək thaː mëc kɔː-daoy, yɤ̀ːŋ nùəŋ mùən rɤ̀ːs-taŋ nèək nùh. 5. kɔ̀ət tɔː thlay yaːŋ naː kɔː-daoy, khɲom nùəŋ mùən bɔŋ prak haːsɤp rìəl tèː. 6. lòːk-srɤy ʔaoy khɲom tɤ̀u phsaː(r) naː-mùːəy? ʔaeŋ tɤ̀u phsaː(r) naː kɔː-baːn. 7. kɔːn nèək naː kɔː-daoy troːv-tae thvɤ̀ː tìːəhìːən. 8. kèː thvɤ̀ː laːn nìh doːc-mdëc kɔː-daoy, kɔː-poñtae maːsìːn mùən daə(r). 9. krùː-pèːɫ(y) cak thnam ʔvɤy kɔː-daoy, nèək-cùmŋùː nìh nùəŋ mùən cìːə tèː. 10. doːc-mdëc kɔː-daoy nèək troːv mɔ̀ːk cùːəp nùəŋ khɲom nɤ̀u maoŋ prampùəl lɲìːəc nìh mùən khaːn.*

Exercise 38

A.1. In a few years' time, I shall work for a living like my father. 2. There is not a single teacher who has read all those books. 3. Father hates anybody who bargains a great deal. 4. If a person harms another in a certain way, the other does harm back to that person in the same way. 5. Whatever time you go for the plane, aunt, I will give you a lift to the airport. 6. He/They want(s) to go to a (certain) place to which he/they went two or three years ago. 7. What is there in this fish market? There's nothing interesting. 8. a. Go and buy a tin of milk for me. b. What sort of milk? a. *Any.*

B.1. *mìːən mcas-haːŋ khlah nɤ̀u kɔnlaeŋ nìh dael lùək tùmnèɲ yùːən. 2. kmìːən nèək naː-mùːəy dael khɲom skɔ̀əl knoŋ phùːm(ì) nìh. 3. kaːl yìːəy nùh cɔːl mɔ̀ːk, lòːk mùən/ʔɤt thaː ʔvɤy tèː. 4. yìːəy nùh kmìːən bɔːŋ-pʔoːn sɔh laəy. 5. khɲom sdap mùən-soːv lùː tèː prùəh khɲom thlɔŋ poñmaːn chnam tɤ̀u haəy. 6. taŋ-pìː thŋay trɔŋ dɔl pèːl prəlùp, kmìːən nèək naː cɔːl phtèəh yɤ̀ːŋ. 7. rìːəc̀-kaː(r) nùəŋ rɤ̀ːs srok naː kɔː-daoy, pdɤy khɲom nùəŋ troːv tɤ̀u srok nìh. 8. rəbɔs nùh nɤ̀u kɔnlaeŋ naː-mùːəy knoŋ phtèəh poñtae khɲom rɔ̀ːk mùən khɤ̀ːɲ.*

Exercise 39

A.1. As for uncle, he is the cleverest in our family. 2. From that day right up to this, the police have scrutinized everyone who has entered his/her/their house. 3. You may/Whether you go by aeroplane or car I shall arrive before you. 4. Ever since that day, I have (never) failed to want to go to Japan. 5. Those students practise dancing every day but there are only two who can dance well/with supple movements. 6. Modern aeroplanes can go at more than a thousand kilometres per hour. 7. Some Cambodians prefer to drink coffee rather than tea. 8. Her father has been a doctor in Phnom Penh for about ten years. 9. It looks as though/Perhaps you had better get a servant to clean the house beforehand. 10. We/They looked for that jewel everywhere but couldn't find (it). 11. His/Her/The grand-child's friend is going to/will go to Angkor Wat for a whole week. 12. From that year onwards, Cambodian kings all ruled the kingdom from Phnom Penh.

B.1. *cao(r) yɔ:k tbo:ŋ pì: tù: cì:ə-mù:əy-nùŋ prak dael nɣu knoŋ thɔ:t-tok.* 2. *pì: thŋay cán(t̀) knoŋ ʔa:tùt(y) mùn dɔl thŋay sok(r) knoŋ ʔa:tùt(y) kraoy lò:k nɣu prèy-nəkɔ̀:(r).* 3. *mcas tiəm prap po:lì:s tha: lŋì:əc nùh mùn khɣ̀:ŋ kme:ŋ-pros na: knoŋ tiəm.* 4. *nɣu phtèəh pʔo:n-/bo:ŋ-pros khŋom nìyì:əy craən poñtae nɣu bùyro: kə̀ət nɣu sŋiəm.* 5. *mëc-kɔ: səmlaŋ nèək mì:ən phtèəh cùt phnùm do:c=neh?* 6. *dɔl thŋay sau(r̀) kraoy khŋom nùŋ ba:n rò:k-sì: ʔɔs mù:əy ʔa:tùt(y).* 7. *ʔae (-cɔmnaek) ta:, kə̀ət cëp pì: phnùm-pèŋ tɣu nɣu bat-dɔmbo:ŋ.* 8. *phtèəh rəbɔs do:n nèək nɣu cùt kɔmpùəŋ-ca:m cì:əŋ.* 9. *so:m nèək səse:(r) sɔmbot(r) nìh cùmnù:əs khŋom. khŋom ʔɣt skɔ̀əl lò:k nìh sɔh.* 10. *lò:k nùh ba:n tha: (kə̀ət nùŋ) nɣu kɔnlaeŋ dədael dɔl khŋom nùŋ trəlɔp mò:k vèŋ.* 11. *pì: thŋay tì: bɣy tɔ:-tɣu, cù:n thnam lò:k-srɣy mù:əy thŋay tae mù:əy krɔ̀əp haəy.* 12. *nɣu-kraom phtèəh mì:ən kɔnlaeŋ dael srɣy-srɣy/srɣy tba:ŋ sɔmpùət.*

Exercise 40

A.1. I can't lift *those* things. 2. My *husband* is seriously ill. We absolutely must keep quiet. 3. As for that mat, the old lady wove (it) herself. 4. *That* woman lost her husband two or three months ago. 5. Those new buildings are all built of brick. 6. This *door!*—even when it's locked it isn't tightly closed! 7. That gentleman came into the post office and sent a parcel to England. 8. Whoever (it is), Mr. — is not willing to receive him this morning/Mr. — will receive *no-one* this morning. 9. If the thieves get into this sailing boat and go anywhere/If the thieves get away in this sailing-boat, the police will still follow them in a motor-boat. 10. This car—you drive off and there's a clanking sound/This car makes a clanking sound as you set off.

B.1. *dɣy nìh, bɔŋco:l tùk taŋ-pì: chnam mùn.* 2. *rɔ̀əl pè:l prəlùp dɔmrɣy nùh mò:k rəho:t-dɔl stùŋ nìh daəmbɣy-nùŋ phɣk tùk.* 3. *kmu:əy-pros kə̀ət tha: kè: co:l cɣt (t) tɣu cìh tù:k-kdaoŋ cì:əŋ kɔpal.* 4. *kmì:ən nèək na: knoŋ phù:m(ì) nìh dael cak sao(r) pè:l yùp tè:.* 5. *kè: tha: mcas tiəm nùh cì:ə mənù:s(s) sɔpba:ry cì:əŋ kè: nɣu kɔmpùəŋ-ca:m.* 6. *pdɣy, sɔp̀(v) thŋay kə̀ət khɔm thvɣ̀: ka:(r) nas cì:ə krù:-pè:l(y) nɣu kha:ŋ-cɣ̀:ŋ srok.* 7. *rɔ̀ət(th)-mùəntrɣy dɣŋ tha: mənù:s(s) khlah rù:əm kùmnùt nùŋ cap-cɔ:ŋ prèəh-ʔɔŋ(k̀)-mcas.* 8. *ʔa:tùt(y) kraoy pì: thŋay ʔɔŋkì:ə(r) dɔl thŋay prəhɔ̀ɔs(p + tè) kè: thvɣ̀: bon(y) co:l chnam.* 9. *yɣ̀ŋ soi-tae srəlaŋ kè:hɔ̀(s)tha:n cas-cas cì:əŋ kè:hɔ̀(s)-tha:n thmɣy-thmɣy nɣu-knoŋ tù:-kroŋ nùh.* 10. *ʔɣyvan tèəŋ-ʔɔs nìh khŋom nùŋ phŋaə tɣu srok-ʔa:me:rì:k ta:m cɣ̀:ŋ sɔmot(r).*

Exercise 41

A.   Young Heng's House (1)

Young Heng's house is made of wood. It has a palm-leaf roof (and) is built on stilts. It has one door and three very small windows. Cambodians don't make many doors and windows. One goes up into the house by means of a stairway. In the house (there) are two rooms, a cupboard and a big table.

275

In the house there is no armchair or (lit. 'and') bed at all. People sleep on mats spread on the floor.

B.   *dɔmbo:l phtὲəh nὲək prɔk slɤk-tnaot tὲ:? ba:l tὲ:, phtὲəh yɤ̀:ŋ prɔk kbuəŋ.*

Exercise 42

A.   Young Heng's House (2)

Young Heng's house has a fence of bamboo paling round (it). Within the fence there are banana, coconut and areca trees. In a corner there is an enclosure for a cow. Beneath the shade of a mango is a pig-stye and hen-pen. In front of the house there are young people playing happily.

B.   *nὲək ceɲɕɤm sa̱t(v) na:-khlah knoŋ kraol rəbɔs nὲək? ba:l/cas, yɤ̀:ŋ ceɲɕɤm crù:k nùŋ mɔ̀ən craən. rəbo:ŋ thvɤ̀: ʔɔmpì: ʔvɤy? ba:l/cas, thvɤ̀: ʔɔmpì: rùssɤy.*

Exercise 43

A.   The Market in Young Heng's Village

The market in young Heng's village has a tiled roof and brick pillars; it is open with no walls. In the market the country people put their goods to sell. The market is 8 metres long (and) about 20 metres wide. It is divided into many sections. In one (section) is a Chinese selling beef; in another (section) there are women selling fish, squatting on their heels, having put (their) baskets in front (of them). There are *rɔs* fish, fresh fish, dead fish, salted fish and smoked fish. The area (in which) meat and fish are sold is swept and washed every day.

B.   *ʔo:pùk nὲək dak tùmnὲ̀ŋ nɤu-ʔae na:? ba:l, knoŋ lvὲ:ŋ nùh kha:ŋ sdam. ʔɤylo:v≈ǹih mùn-so:v sʔa:t tae tec tὲ̀ət kὲ: nùŋ lì:əŋ.*

Exercise 44

A.   The Phnom Daun Penh (= *phnùm do:n pὲ̀ɲ*)

In the city of Phnom Penh there is a hill (which) has a monastery built on it, which is an embellishment to the city. Perhaps this hill was there already and for this reason they called it Phnom Penh right up to the present day. On this hill, to the west of the temple (and) slightly to the south is a big stupa which rises high above the branches of the various trees. To the north, there were originally cages of leopards and two kinds of bears, and to the south there was a place where crocodiles, monkeys, snakes, deer and various other animals were kept. Nowadays, the Government has taken away all these things. There remains only a small area.

B.   *kɔnlaeŋ dael kὲ: ceɲɕɤm sa̱t(v) do:c-cì:ə sa̱t(v)-*sɤŋ(h) nùŋ sa̱t(v)-khla: cì:ə daəm kὲ: hau ya:ŋ mὲ̀c? ba:l, hau tha: su:ən-sa̱t(v). mὲ̀c-kɔ: mùn nɤu mì:ən su:ən-sa̱t(v) nɤu-cùt phnùm? ba:l, mɤ̀:l tɤ̀u prəhael-cì:ə daoy tro:v ka:(r) sɔŋ phlo:v tù:lì:əy nɤu kɔnlaeŋ ǹih. do:c≈neh kmì:ən kɔnlaeŋ dak su:ən-sa̱t(v) tὲ̀ət.*

Exercise 45

A.   The Procedure of Salting and Drying Fish (= work of doing
dried-and-salted fish)

One takes *rɔs* fish or some other kind of fish (and) removes the scales. Cutting (the fish) open one divides (it) into four sections. Sometimes the head is cut off and thrown away, and the backbone is also taken out. Salt is finely ground and sprinkled on the fish. Then one soaks the fish for approximately three to four hours. It is washed in water and put in the sun for about two or three days. Then it is spread out on racks.

B. *lòːk ʔaːnɤt prap khɲom taə trɤy dael haːl thɲay nùh cɨːə trɤy hau ʔvɤy? baːl, trɤy nùh hau trɤy-rɔs. trɤy-rɔs nùh haəy-nùŋ trɤy baep ʔae-tìət, haːl thɲay pìː(r) bɤy thɲay tɤ̀u, rùːəc hau thaː trɤy-ŋìət.*

Exercise 46

A. Young Heng's Family

Old man	How many people are there in your family?
Heng	I don't know! About seven.
Old man	Well! You don't know, eh? Have you a father and mother?
Heng	Yes, I have.
Old man	Have you sisters and brothers?
Heng	Yes, I have three elder brothers, two elder sisters and a younger brother.
Old man	Do your grandfather and grandmother live with you?
Heng	No—but my father is bringing up a niece.
Old man	Well then, you have (your) father and mother, six brothers and sisters and the niece; that's nine all together.
Heng	No! You forgot me!
Old man	Oh! Then there are ten.

B. *nèək mìːən bɔːŋ-pʔoːn tèː? baːl/cas tèː. khɲom kmìːən bɔːŋ-pʔoːn tèː.*

or *baːl/cas, khɲom mìːən bɔːŋ-pros — nèək, bɔːŋ-srɤy — nèək, pʔoːn-pros — nèək nùŋ pʔoːn-srɤy — nèək. mìːən mənùs(s) ponmaːn nèək nɤ̀u phtèəh nèək? baːl/cas, mìːən — nèək nɤ̀u phtèəh khɲom.*

Exercise 47

A. Phnom Penh, 3rd March, 1964.

Dear Friend,

Today is Sunday—We are going to encourage you to come for a pleasant walk along the riverside and to see a film and so to enjoy yourself.

May I then invite you to come and meet me at my house this afternoon at 4 p.m.? Do be there (without fail).

Goodbye,
(Your) Friend.

B. *sɔmlaɲ!*

khɲom cɔŋ ʔɔɲcɤ̀ːɲ nèək cùːəp nùŋ khɲom ʔae haːŋ — nɤ̀u maoŋ pram-bɤy lŋìːəc thɲay dɔp khae nìh pìsaː baːy.

· · · · · ·

Exercise 48

A. Phnom Penh, 3rd March, 1964.

To Ros Sarœun, as a token of regard.

It is already several months (since) I heard a word (from you) or saw your face. It is already about four or five months since we parted from each other. Have you changed your mind about me? Is that why no letter has come? I didn't know your address exactly. I have only just found out from someone that you have left Saigon and gone to live in Paris. Are you in good health, these days? Or have you troubles of some sort? If you are happy, I am delighted. I can't find anything to compare. For my part, I am fine.

Please receive (this) in friendship.

B. *cùmrìəp mòːk heːŋ soːm crìəp*

khɲom nùŋ bɔːŋ-/pʔoːn-srɤy khɲom mìːən sëckdɤy sdaːy yaːŋ thɲùən daoy tɤu bon(y) thɲay sau(ř) mùn mùn baːn haəy-nùŋ daoy baːn khaːn cùːəp nùŋ nɛ̀ək. yɤ̌ːŋ mùn-dael cùːəp knìːə cìːə yùː(r) khae haəy. nɛ̀ək ʔɔɲcɤ̌ːɲ-mòːk suːə(r) yɤ̌ːŋ pèːl lɲìːəc thɲay naːmùːəy baːn rùː tèː?

. . . . . .

Exercise 49

A. Phnom Penh, 3rd March, 1964.

I beg to inform the Manager, Mr. —, of the office for distributing information (lit. 'good news').

I haven't been able to come (to work) because I am not well today. I am dizzy and have a headache all the time. I ask permission, therefore, to be absent from work for two days until I am better again.

Please forgive (me) in (your) indulgence.

Please excuse anything impolite.

B. *khɲom soːm cùmrìːəp mòːk lòːk —*

koːn-pros khɲom thvɤ̌ː kaː(r) thɲay nìh mùn baːn pìː-prùəh chùː krùn. khɲom mìːən soŋkhùm thaː ʔaːtùt(y) kraoy vìːə nùŋ tɤu thvɤ̌ː kaː(r) pùm khaːn.

. . . . . .

Exercise 50

A.   The Typewriter

On the 1st January, 1962, I was to begin learning typewriting. In the classroom were two rows of desks. There was a Vietnamese lady teacher and a crowd of students. I went in and asked in Cambodian, 'Is there a place left? I should like to begin to learn too.' The lady replied, 'The class is very crowded. If you want to learn, you may do so only an hour in the morning and an hour in the afternoon.' I agreed. Then I had to put down my name and address and pay 200 r. in advance. When I began to learn, I had great difficulty with my hands because they were stiff and not yet capable. Now I can type fairly well. Next month I shall sit for the examination and take a certificate and leave to work somewhere.

B. *sɔmlaɲ khɲom kɔmpùŋ-tae rìən vay maːsìːn ʔɔksɔː(r) nɤu saːlaː-rìən nùh. kɔ̀ət thaː pìbaːk nùŋ baːn kɔnlaeŋ. cɔɲʔìət nas. mùːəy tìət, troːv bɔŋ prak bɤy rɔ̀ːy rìəl mùn!*

278

Exercise 51

A.   Buying a bus ticket

Ticket-seller   Where are you going, sir?
Mr. Samret   I want to go to Kompung Cham at 1.30 today (= this
                mid-day).
Ticket-seller   What row of seats would you like to have?
Mr. Samret   I would like to have (a seat) at the front near the driver.
Ticket-seller   Well, there is this one left, sir, (which) you can have.
Mr. Samret   Right! How much is it?
Ticket-seller   Fifty-five riels, sir.
Mr. Samret   Oh! I have only a 100 riel note.
Ticket-seller   That's all right, sir! I have change to give you/I can give you
                the change.
Mr. Samret   Er—At what time does the bus get to Kompung Cham?
Ticket-seller   About half-past three or four o'clock.

B.   *sɔp̀(v) thŋay tr̆u siəm-rìːəp cìh laːn-chnùːəl baːn rùː tèː?*
     baːl̀, mìːən laːn-chnùːəl tr̆u rɔ̀əl thŋay.
     thlay poǹmaːn?
     baːl̀, mùːəy-rɔ̀ːy mphèy rìəl.
     khɲom coːl cr̆t(t) tr̆u sʔaek. mìːən sɔl kɔnlaeŋ tèː?
     baːl̀, mìːən sɔl kɔnlaeŋ mùːəy khaːŋ kraoy.
     (h)nr̆ŋ haəy! khɲom yɔ̀ːk kɔnlaeŋ nùh. laːn cèŋ maoŋ poǹmaːn?
     nr̆u maoŋ prampùəl prùk, lòːk.

Exercise 52

A.   The Cambodian Theatre

In Phnom Penh there are 3 Cambodian theatres, the stone one, the petty
thieves market one and the meat-market one. At eight o'clock in the evening
there are crowds of people outside (in front of) all the theatres. Some sell
various things to eat, some are buying tickets, some are asking each other
what play is being acted; some are talking together about various matters.
There is a hum of chattering. At nine o'clock when the theatre orchestra
has played the national anthem they begin to act the (various) plays (from
then onwards). Some of the audience say to each other, 'The show depends
on the comedians. If the comedians are not very funny, it isn't worth seeing.'
Some say, 'When I watch a play I hardly remember the story at all'. Others
say, 'I don't like going to the Stone Theatre; I like to go to the theatre at the
meat-market because the girls are very pretty and they sing well too'.

B.   *yùp nìh yr̆ːŋ nùəŋ tr̆u mr̆ːl lkhaon, mr̆ːl tr̆u. pùː mùn ʔɔs kɔmlaŋ tèː rùː?*
     baːl̀ tèː. khɲom mùn ʔɔs kɔmlaŋ tèː taə! yr̆ːŋ nùəŋ tr̆u rɔ̀ːŋ naː?
     sräc nùəŋ pùː. pùː ʔɔŋcr̆ːŋ rr̆ːs-rɔːk pùː-prùəh pùː mɔ̀ːk lèːŋ phnùm-pèɲ.
     khɲom kùəy-tae nr̆u phnùm-pèɲ, tr̆u mr̆ːl lkhaon lɲìːəc naː kɔː-baːn.
     tèː. kmùːəy skɔ̀əl rɔ̀ːŋ-lkhaon cìːəŋ khɲom. kmùːəy srəlaŋ lkhaon naː cìːəŋ?
     khɲom srəlaŋ rɔ̀ːŋ thmɔː cìːəŋ kèː. nèək-tlok kɔmplaeŋ nas.
     baə ʔɔŋcr̆ːŋ yr̆ːŋ tr̆u rɔ̀ːŋ thmɔː.

Exercise 53

A. In the Theatre

'Where did you go last night?' 'I went to the theatre last night.' 'What was the play?' 'Preah Laksanavongs from where Brahma comes to greet the girl.' 'Was it good?' 'It certainly was!' 'Which theatre was it?' 'The theatre at the meat-market. Ooh! Was I deafened! The audience was packed. They were jabbering to each other. You couldn't hear the singers at all. I laughed and laughed. The comedians were really very funny. I heard someone speaking behind me, say "You know, I heard that if one watches a film sitting near it, it isn't satisfactory (lit. good to see) because it shakes. People only watch from a distance. What about the theatre? Why doesn't it shake? People watch (it) (from) very close, the first row, and can see well!" I thought to myself, "This person is perhaps a farmer and he never came across the theatre and films; that's why he talks like this." At 12 o'clock they finished the performance. I walked along, had a bowl of soup and then came back home to sleep.'

B. *pìː yùp meɲ lòːk nùɲ mùt(t)-sɔmlaɲ pìː(r) nèək tʀ̌u mʀ̌ːl lkhaon. mùn cɔɲʔiət poṅmaːn pìː-prùəh kèː craən-tae srəlaɲ lkhaon nʀ̌u ròːɲ phsaː(r)-kap-kòː cìːəɲ. mùːəy tìət mìːən kon baːraɲsaes lʔɔː nas nʀ̌u sìːneːlùk(s). mùk(h)-cìːə mənùs(s) craən nèək tʀ̌u mʀ̌ːl kon nìh.*

Exercise 54

A. The Story of the Swans and the Tortoise

In a certain pool there lived a large tortoise. A pair of swans went every day to get food in that pool. When, in the dry season, the water in the pool was all dried up, the tortoise was just considering digging a hole and making a new place to live when the two swans arrived. 'Friend tortoise,' they said, 'It is very hard for you to stay here; the water in the pool is all dried up. What do you get to eat? Go and live in the land over there and you will be happy. There is food to eat, of all kinds.' The tortoise said, 'I cannot go, friend swans, I have no wings for flying.' 'If you will go,' the swans replied, 'we can take you. Only bite firmly with your mouth. If someone says "What's that?", don't reply to him.' 'Right,' said the tortoise, and the two swans proceeded to take in their mouths the branch of a tree. They told the tortoise, 'Take hold of the middle in your mouth. We shall hold both ends.'— And off they flew. When they arrived at a certain country there were many people at leisure in front of their houses. When they saw the two swans they called out, 'Look! Swans carrying a tortoise!' The tortoise heard (the sound of the) people saying such things. He thought of saying, 'What if my friends (do) carry me along? Do you have to say anything?' He only just thought of saying this and his mouth came open. He fell to his death with a broken shell.

B. *rùəy nìh nìtìːən ʔɔmpìː hɔɲ(s) mùːəy kùː nùɲ ʔɔndaək mùːəy. ʔɔndaək nùh nʀ̌u cùt srah mùːəy. khae praɲ srah nùh rìːɲ ʔɔs tʀ̌u, mùn-soːv mìːən cɔmnʀ̌y sìː. hɔɲ(s) kɔː nìyìːəy thaː 'bɔːɲ ʔɔndaək ʔəəy! coh-baə yʀ̌ːɲ yɔːk ʔaeɲ tʀ̌u kɔnlaeɲ mùːəy tìət. troːv ʔaeɲ cap kham mèːk chʀ̌ː cɔm kɔndaːl; yʀ̌ːɲ nùɲ pɔ̀əm sɔːɲkhaːɲ.' ʔɔndaək kɔː prɔ̀ːm thvʀ̌ː dɔːc=neh. hɔɲ(s) kɔː pɔ̀əm mèːk chʀ̌ː*

yɔ̀ːk ʔɔndaək laəɲ cìːə mùːəy poǹtae ʔɔndaək lừː mənừs(s) khaːɲ kraom nìyìːəy saəc ʔɔmpừː khluːən kɔː kừt nừɲ chlaəy baək mɔ̀ət slap tr̃u.

Exercise 55

A.   Method of Making Toddy

In what season is toddy made? In the dry season. It is made as follows. When the sugar-palm has got its flowers scaffolding is fixed up from top to bottom (of the tree). People climb up and make two or three slight incisions in the flower at the end. Then they squeeze the flower slightly with pincers—not too strongly. For two or three mornings they climb up to make an incision and squeeze (the flower). They take nodes of bamboo, scent them to avoid any sour smell and put them to catch the drips (from the flowers) from about 5 p.m. until dawn. Then they go and bring (down) the toddy. There are five or six nodes of bamboo in one tree. They don't do only one tree. They do five or six. When they have finished putting the toddy down, they drink some (and) sell some. Sometimes they pour the toddy in a big stew-pan and put it on a stove. Then they light a fire so that it boils down and only the sugar remains. Much wood is used in making the sugar. One pan is boiled per day; then it can be reduced to sugar. When it has been reduced it is taken away from the fire. It is stirred and so becomes sticky and then poured into a pitcher or cup and put for sale or for drinking.

B.   *kèː laəɲ daəm-tnaot yaːɲ mëc?*
   baːl, cɔːɲ bɔɲʔaoɲ pìː kraom dɔl lr̃ː cùmvèɲ daəm mùːəy-mùːəy, sr̃m laəɲ.
   kèː yɔ̀ːk prədap-prəda: ʔvr̃y mɔ̀ːk cr̃t phkaː-tnaot?
   baːl, kèː yɔ̀ːk kambr̃t mɔ̀ːk thvr̃ː nừh.
   bəmpừəɲ rùssr̃y səmrap troːɲ tùk phka: nừh kèː tùk yừː(r) poǹmaːn?
   pìː lɲìːəc dɔl prəlùm.
   kèː thvr̃ː skɔː yaːɲ mëc?
   baːl, kèː dak tùk-tnaot knoɲ lɔː ʔaoy pùh rìːɲ tr̃u cìːə skɔː(r).

Exercise 56

A.   A Meeting with Uncle and Aunt

Sarœun   Hello, Uncle and Aunt! How are you?
Uncle   We are well. I knew you were almost off to foreign parts so we made the effort to come and pay you a short visit.
Sarœun   I just got your letter this morning, Uncle. I am delighted that you and Aunt have come so that we could all meet together like this.
Aunt   How many more years do you have to go and study for?
Sarœun   Oh, for a long time, Aunt! About 5 or 6 years.
Uncle   What subject are you going to study?
Sarœun   The construction of houses, roads, bridges and all those things, Uncle.
Uncle   What time do you have to get on board the 'plane?
Sarœun   Tomorrow at half-past four, Uncle. You want to see me off, then, Uncle? Don't bother! It will only give you trouble.
Uncle   It's no trouble. Your Aunt and I want to go and see you get in the 'plane too.

Sarœun   I do thank you and Aunt very much for coming and also for going
with me to the airport too!

Uncle   Not at all! It will be 5 or 6 years before we see you again. So your
Aunt and I will be really old when you come back again.

B.   *cùmrìːəp-suːə(r), lòːk.*
ʔao! suːəsdǰy, lòːk-srǰy!
lòːk baːn tǰu phnùm-pèɲ cùːn kmuːəy tǰu rùː tèː?
baːl, yǰːŋ tǰːp-nùŋ trələp mòːk vèɲ pèːl thŋay trɔŋ meɲ.
kòət tǰu rìən khaːŋ ʔǰy?
rìən thvǰː cìːə krùː-pèːl(y).
ʔao! kòət troːv nǰu srok kèː yùː(r) tèː?
baːl, prəhael pram-mùːəy chnam.
yùː(r) dae(r), lòːk! bɔːŋ-/pʔoːn-srǰy lòːk dael nǰu phnùm-pèɲ sok(h)-sɔp͡baːy cìːə rùː tèː?
baːl, sok(h)-sɔp͡baːy cìːə tèː.

Exercise 57

A.   Trapping Elephants

In Cambodia there are many wooded hills which are full of herds of wild
elephant. If an elephant is to be trapped it is necessary to take a really
experienced elephant-driver and to go in a party of about 20 people. They
go in small boats; two people to a boat. They go on foot up into the forest
to drive a complete herd of elephant before them. Each man has to have
weapons to defend himself: swords, javelins, knives, etc. When they have
spotted a herd of elephant they walk along shepherding them down into a
stream, big river or lake. The men go down and all get into their boats.
They row up and down herding (the elephants). Their aim is to capture only
one. The elephant-driver has to climb up on to the neck of the elephant and
strike his head with an axe. The elephant can do nothing because he is in
deep water and his feet slip. When they are sure that he is at the end of his
strength they (take him and) tie him to a stake sunk into deep water so
that his feet are not on firm ground and then they go home. About a week
(later) a bale of hay is brought for him to eat. The week after that they take
him home and train him to understand some words of humans. It is because
of this difficulty of capturing (elephants) that their individual cost is high.

B.   *cùːən-kaːl pùːək mənùs(s) pìː phùːm(ì) yǰːŋ tǰu tèək dɔmrvy. lùh kèː kiəŋ
dɔmrvy mùːəy pìː (h)voːŋ haəy, trəmèək dɔmrvy laəŋ lǰː kɔː dɔmrvy nùh kap
kbaːl vìːə. kaːl naː dɔmrvy ʔɔs kɔmlaŋ haəy kèː cɔːŋ vìːə nùŋ bɔŋkòːl mùːəy bɔh
knoŋ tùk srah rùː tùk stùŋ. rùːəc kèː trələp tǰu phtèəh vèɲ. mùːəy ʔaːtùt(y)
kraoy kèː yòːk smau ʔaoy vìːə sìː. dɔl vìːə nǰu kɔnlaeŋ nùh ʔɔs pìː(r) ʔaːtùt(y)
haəy kèː nòəm vìːə tǰu phtèəh bɔŋhat thvǰː taːm bɔŋkòəp mənùs(s).*

Exercise 58

A.   A Widow's Story

'I have a grown-up daughter; she's engaged. The date for the wedding is
soon. (We) are first sending letters to tell (our) relatives (both) near and far
to come to the feast.' She then sent letters to all the relatives. All the people
who lived in the house went to buy bamboo to make a pavilion. In the

morning on the day of the wedding guests came in great numbers; there was a hum of music playing. Some people were talking together happily. Someone asked, 'What part of the country do you live in, sir?' 'I live in Kompung Chnang' was the answer. 'Your wife didn't come, did she?' 'Yes she came too.' 'As you live in that district, do you know Mr. Hean?' 'I do.' 'Is he well?' 'Yes, he's well.'

In the kitchen the pork is sizzling; someone is chopping vegetables; another person is dicing pork with a chopping noise. The mistress of the house walks to and fro perspiring freely. Soon there are 15 guests. There are 2 or 3 small children and some cousins too. As they arrive at the house the mistress of the house jumps up to say 'Hello' to them, raising her hands in greeting. She asks, 'How are you, (elder)?' and the reply is 'Very well, (thank you).' Then she calls the guests (up) into the house; they chat together, as follows: 'What part of the country does he live in (your fiancé)? What does he do for a living?' The girl says, 'In Kompung Chnang. He earns his living in business.' The mistress of the house says, 'Why didn't Uncle Lang come? Perhaps the letter didn't arrive' and bends to pick up two or three cakes to give to her niece. 'Eat these,' she says. 'I suppose you don't know your aunt at all!'

B. *thŋay nìh kèː soł-tae rəvùəl knoŋ phtèəh cau, mỳːl tr̃u?*
baːł, sʔaek sìː kaːʔr) bɔːŋ-srvy khɲom.
mìːən phɲiəv craən nèək mɔːk rùː tèː?
baːł, mìːən dɔp-pìːʔr) nèək.
mɔ̀ːk pìː chɲaːy rùː pìː cùt khaːŋ?
baːł, cìː-doːn-cìː-taː khɲom mɔːk pìː bat-dɔmbɔːŋ haəy bɔːŋ-prɔs rəbɔs mdaːy mɔ̀ːk pìː chɲaːy nr̃u khaet(r) krəceh.
cau skɔ̀əl bɔːŋ-pʔoːn tèəy-ʔɔs dael mɔ̀ːk rùː tèː?
khɲom skɔ̀əl cìː-doːn-cìː-taː pìːʔr) nèək haəy-nùŋ pùː-mìːŋ tèəy-ʔɔs poñtae kmuːəy pìːʔr) nèək khɲom ʔɔt skɔ̀əl tèː.

Exercise 59

A. The Offerings of January–February and April–May

On Sunday the 20th May, in all the monasteries in Cambodia, at 4 o'clock in the afternoon, flowers (are arranged) and various soft drinks are prepared, such as tea, etc., in order to offer them to the monks. The gong is beaten and all the monks in the monastery are assembled and offered drinks. At 8 o'clock the laymen and laywomen are assembled; when the prayer of adoration has been recited, the monks are invited to enter the temple and recite prayers. In some monasteries they use a microphone to diffuse the sound so that it may be heard far away. Other monasteries have no machine to relay (the sound). After the monks have finished reciting prayers, one or two monks are invited to expound the Law. Sometimes there are two expositions, according to preference. When the expositions are ended, various chants are performed, about the Buddha's birth or leaving the (life of a) novice or death. The procedure for celebrating the festival of the offerings of January–February and April–May which I have described up to now are held only on the 15th of the waxing moon of January–February and April–May. If it is held in January–February it is called *mìːəkh-bòːcìːə* and if in

April–May, *vìsa:kh-bo:cì:ə*. This festival is held to commemorate the words which the Buddha spoke to Ananda. 'Ah, Ananda,' he told him, 'I stay only four months and (then) shall enter Nirvana.' These words of the Buddha were said to Ananda on the 15th of January–February. On the 15th of the waxing moon of April–May the Buddha died. Laymen and laywomen mourn the loss of the Buddha and it is for this reason that they have held this festival continuously from long ago right up to the present day.

Various chants are performed, as I have said above, during the whole of one night. Sometimes this goes on only for two or three hours. In the morning, the monks are invited to have soup and at mid-day, rice. The entire procedure of the festival of the *mì:əkh* offering and *vìsa:k(h)* offering is just like this.

B.   *thŋay nìh kè: thvỳ: boṇ(y) ʔʋy?*
   boṇ(y) nìh hau tha: mì:ək(h)-bo:cì:ə.
   kè: thvỳ: boṇ(y) nìh rùmlùk dol ʔʋʋy?
   kè: rùmlùk dol prèəh-ʔɔŋ(k̆) bɔrenìp̆(v)ì:ən.
   kè: thvỳ: ya:ŋ mëc?
   kè: nìmùə̱n(t) lò:k-sɔ̱ŋ(k̆h) so:t(r) thɔ̱ə̱(rm) nùəŋ tè:sna: ʔɔs mù:əy yùp haəy pruk laəŋ kè: prəkè:n cɔŋhan lò:k chan. kè: thvỳ: boṇ(y) nìh daoy saok-sda:y prèəh.
   boṇ(y) nìh thvỳ: yùp nìh nʋu vɔ̱ə̱t(t) tèəŋ-ʔɔs nʋu srok-khmae(r) rù: tè:?
   ba:t̆, nʋu vɔ̱ə̱t(t) tèəŋ-ʔɔs.

Exercise 60

A.   The Work of the Rice-grower

By April–May there is abundant rain every day. The water collects in all the rice-fields. The farmers get ready the tools used for the rice-field: ploughs, rakes, hoes, etc. A team of oxen is yoked to plough a seed-bed and the grass is raked out clean from it. Then paddy which has been left to soak for two or three days beforehand and which has shoots of the right size is (taken and) planted in the furrow. Care is taken that oxen and (other) animals do not eat it. When the seedlings grow to a suitable height they are uprooted and tied in small bundles. Further rice-fields are ploughed and these uprooted bundles (of seedlings) are transplanted into them. When all the rice fields are planted out still others are planted. In each family there are five or six or sometimes ten rice-fields or even fifteen. Rice-growers are very tough because sometimes it is too hot (and) sometimes too cold; (but) they don't make a fuss about the heat or cold at all. When they have transplanted into all the rice-fields, they stop and rest for two or three months, except that the men have to go constantly to watch the rice-fields in case they have no water or too much water. If there is no water they cut (a way) to cause water to flow in along channels into the rice-field. If there is a lot of water, they cause some to flow out. By the end of one month the paddy has sprung up beautifully. A little later, the paddy in all the fields is swollen.

Not all the rice planted is common rice by any means; some sticky rice is planted too. This is kept for making various items of confectionery. When all the paddy has produced its fruit, men are sent daily to chase away the sparrows. Sometimes devices to scare the sparrows are tied up all over the rice-fields. Sometimes a scarecrow is made and placed in the middle of the rice-field to frighten the sparrows. The sound of people calling to chase away the sparrows, 'shoo! shoo!' is heard every morning. Rice-fields which are near the forest and have no owner going to keep watch—the paddy there is eaten by the sparrows and only the husks are left. When some paddy is ripe, the water is taken off entirely from the rice-field. Then, with sticks, the paddy is flattened down so as to be easy to harvest. Together people prepare the scythes ready for cutting down the paddy. When it has been flattened it is cut and tied in bundles, which are placed in rows. Then the paddy is brought in front of the house. Where people have a lot of rice-fields, they have to help each other in turn, going to harvest here one day and there another. The person who happens to be receiving help has to prepare food and drink. When the paddy has been conveyed to the threshing floor it is beaten with a board so that the grains of rice fall off or else it is trodden on or cattle are made to trample it. Sometimes people help each other. When the treading or trampling by cattle and beating are finished the chaff is carried away and put on one side in a heap in some place. Then the paddy is winnowed in the middle of a flat place in the rice-field when there is a breeze to make the husks come off. Only the paddy which has good grains is taken and put in the granary; some to be sold and some kept. Each family obtains 60 or 70 bushels, sometimes 100 or even 150.

In Cambodia there are machines for crushing the rice but not enough (of them). The rice-growers have to crush the paddy with a mortar to (make the) husk drop off and pound or beat the white rice with a mortar and pestle. When the rice is white they sweep up the mortar and pestle and blow to take the dust for pigs to eat (while) the husked rice is cooked as food to eat.

The rice-growers don't do only rice-fields. In some areas dry season rice is grown too. The method of doing rice in the dry season is no different from in the wet season.

B. *sroːv tram tùk pìː(r) bɤy thŋay dɔl mìːən pùənlɔ̀ːk haəy. sɤm kèː saːp knoŋ thnaːl. dɔl tec tìət sɔmnaːp nùh baːn kɔmpùəs lmɔ̀ːm, kèː stùːŋ tr̆u knoŋ srae. kaːl-naː sroːv tùm haəy, kèː croːt cɔːŋ cìːə kɔndap. rùːəc kèː baok rùː baen haəy-nùŋ ròːy knoŋ vìːəl srae.*

PART VI

VOCABULARY

CAMBODIAN–ENGLISH

ENGLISH–CAMBODIAN

1. Lexical content.

The aim has been to cover all words introduced in Parts II and III either in the exercises or in the examples, giving them both from Cambodian to English and *vice versa*, even though in fact they may have occurred only one way. It was found practical, however, to allow the following exceptions to this principle:—

(i) reduplicative words introduced in the lesson on reduplication of which the meaning is complex,

e.g. *bɔndɔh-bɔndaːl* 'look after or bring up someone else's child'.

Here 'foster' was not suitable since the Cambodian word may refer to a period of a few hours only. In such cases the word is given only in the Cambodian–English part.

(ii) numerical compounds above 20. These are not entered either way since their components are entered both ways separately.

(iii) exclamations. These are not necessarily entered in the English–Cambodian part since the translations from Cambodian are not simple and require some explanation.

2. Grammatical content. Cambodian.

The principle followed is that each Cambodian word which by itself translates an English word is given a grammatical designation,

e.g. *tùː* n., cupboard/cupboard, *tùː* n.

The grammatical designations are those introduced in Parts II and III. They are listed and defined in Part VII. In 4 below a complete list of the terms, with the abbreviations used for them, is given.

Several different Cambodian words may be given to translate one English word; in this case it may be found that the grammatical designation is given at the end of the list, if it applies to all.

e.g. whatever n., *ʔvɤy*, (sing.) *ʔvɤy-mùːɔy*, (plur.) *ʔvɤy-khlah* n.

Where a sequence of Cambodian words is needed to translate an English word, no grammatical designation is given for the Cambodian words,

e.g. bolt v., *cak sao(r)*

Both the words *cak* and *sao(r)* may, however, be found as separate entries in the Cambodian–English part.

Where homonyms occur, they are placed so that the abbreviated forms of their grammatical designations are in alphabetical order.

289

3. Grammatical content. English.

English grammatical designations are given only where there is ambiguity, e.g. 'wave v.', since 'wave n.' is also possible; and 'which, relative pronoun', since 'which, interrogative adjective', is also possible. A list of abbreviations used is given below. In the vocabularies to the exercises English verbs have always been given in the infinitive, e.g. '*mə̀ːl* — to look'; and Cambodian attributive verbs have always been translated with the verb to be, e.g. '*thom* — to be big'. In the vocabulary this practice is dropped in favour of 'look v.' and '*thom* v. — big'.

4. Abbreviations and signs.

(i) Those used with reference to Cambodian:—

a. adverbial particle	n. noun
c. numeral coefficient	p. particle
e. exclamatory particle	p.v.p. pre-verbal particle
f. final phrase particle	post n.p. post-nominal particle
g. general particle	pre n.p. pre-nominal particle
i. initiating particle	r. responding particle
lit. literary	v. verb
m. marker	x numeral

(ii) Those used with reference to English:—

adj. adjective	n. noun
adv. adverb	p. part. past participle
conj. conjunction	prep. preposition
excl. exclamation	rel. relative
interrog. interrogative	tr. transitive
intr. intransitive	v. verb

(iii) Those used with reference to either:—

pron. pronoun	plur. plura
sing. singular	

5. Transcription.

The transcription is as set out in Lesson 11.4.

Certain conventions observed in connection with the transcription should be borne in mind, e.g. that *ə̀/ùə* represents a pair of vowels which are spelt one way before final *k*, *ŋ* and *m* and another way before other finals[1]; and that glottal stop plus vowel are expected to be spelt with the Indian initial vowel-sign where possible. *rùt* and *ʔaep* are for these reasons respectively 'irregular'.

6. Use of the asterisk.

Words like *rùt* and *ʔaep*, of which the 'irregular' spelling cannot be deduced from the transcription, have been marked by an asterisk at their first occurrence in Part II or III and are asterisked in vocabularies to exercises (which constitute the first occurrence of some words) and in the following vocabulary. The asterisk indicates that the orthography of the word is given in the list in Part IV 2. Asterisked words are still written in the transcription with all possible diacritics, e.g. *dàc*, in order to help the memory, in subsequent occurrences. The position in the vocabulary of words of 'irregular' spelling is that which their transcription spelling would indicate for them

---

[1] See Lesson 5.2.24 and 5.3.47.

(see below). Where a component of a compound word is spelt 'irregularly', only the component is asterisked and given in the orthography list.

7. Order of consonant- and vowel-symbols.

The Cambodian syllabary order is adhered to fairly closely. Thus the consonant-symbol order is:—

k $k\grave{}$ η $\eta\grave{}$ c $c\grave{}$ $\tilde{n}$ $\tilde{n}\grave{}$ d $d\grave{}$ t $t\grave{}$ n $n\grave{}$ b $b\grave{}$ p $p\grave{}$ m $m\grave{}$ y $y\grave{}$ r $r\grave{}$ l $l\grave{}$ v $v\grave{}$ s $s\grave{}$ h $h\grave{}$ $ʔ$ $ʔ\grave{}$

The vowel-symbol order is:—

ɔ ɔː a aː ɤ ɤː o oː uːə aə uə iə e eː ae ao au ùə ɔ̀ː ɔ̀ ɛ̀ə ìːə ì ìː ù ùː ùːə ɤ̀ː ùə ìə è èː ɛ̀ː ɔ̀ː ɤ̀u

For the purpose of the vocabulary the register of the whole word is decided by the register of its first vowel or diphthong (ə is not counted as a vowel). Thus *kɔmpùŋ* is a 'first register word' and *cùəndaə(r)* is a 'second register word'. As is indicated in the consonant list above, all words which are by this criterion first register words and of which the first letter in the transcription is *k* are entered before second register words having the same initial. Similarly, for words of which the first letter in the transcription is *ŋ*, all first register words precede second register words. e.g. *kɔmnɔt, kat, kɔ̀ət, ŋìət.* This principle is followed throughout the consonant list above. e.g. *dɔp tae tìət nas nìh yaːŋ yùp laːn lòːk sɔː häet(o) ʔaoy ʔùː.*

Words having an initial consonantal sequence (*pram, khɲom, khɔm, rəhoːt, prəɲap*) are entered under the section devoted to words having the same first consonant[1] and the same register. Thus *pram, phot* and *prəɲap* are all before *pùː, phùːm(ì)* and *prəcìːrəthìpdɤ̀y(y)*; and *rəhoːt* is in the first register *r* section, thus coming before *rìən.* Within each section the word-order is:

(i) the words with a simple initial, e.g. *kɔt* to *kau,* following the vowel-order set out in the list above.

(ii) words having a complex initial sequence in which no junction feature (*h* or *ə*) is recorded. These are arranged with their second consonants in the consonantal order set out above, except that *h* is omitted. e.g. *kɲoŋ kbac kmeːŋ kroŋ klɤ̀ŋ(k) kʔɔːm.*

(iii) the words in whose initial sequence *h* is a second (functional) consonant. e.g. *kham khaːt khos.*

(iv) words in whose consonantal initial sequence *h* is recorded as a feature of junction. The third letters of the transcription are then in the consonantal order set out above. e.g. *khɲom khnɔːŋ khmae(r) khlaŋ khsae.*

(v) words having *ə* written between the first two consonants. The second consonants are in the order set out above. e.g. *rətèh rəmɛ̀ːŋ-tae rəvùəl.*

Note that words having a 3-place initial sequence are placed according to the first two; thus they come under (ii) or (v) above, following all other vowels. e.g. *kroŋ krəʔoːp klɤ̀ŋ(k), troːv trəsɔk, thnùː təthèək, lkak lkhaon.*

Final consonants are taken in syllabary order, e.g. *caːn caːp caːm.* Letters in parentheses are for this purpose treated like other letters. e.g. *kaːc kaː(r) kaːl.*

---

[1] This applies even where the first consonant is in parentheses. Thus *(h)mɔt* and *(h)voːŋ* are entered in the *h* first register section.

k

kɔŋcɔp n., parcel
kɔŋcèəh-kɔŋcìːəy v., scatter objects disrespectfully
kɔŋcɤ̀ː n., basket
kɔŋcròːŋ n., fox
kɔt v., note down
kɔndap c. n., sheaf
kɔndaːl n., middle
kɔndiə-tiə n., name of an extinct mammal
kɔndiəv n., scythe
kɔntaŋ c. n., basket (capacity ¼, ⅓ or ½ bushel)
kɔntae-rae n., name of a country dance
kɔntray n., scissors
kɔntreːk-kɔntraːk v., hang in tatters
kɔntùk n., dust which falls off husked rice when it is riddled to clean it (used as pig-food)
kɔntùy c. n., tail
kɔnlah c. n., half
kɔntèːl n., mat
kɔnlaeŋ c. n., place n.; kɔnlaeŋ na: (in negative or indefinite context), anywhere
kɔnsiəv n., kettle
kɔnsiəv c., kettleful
kɔmnɔt v., fix v.
kɔpal n., steamer
kɔpal-hɔh n., aeroplane
kɔmnat c. n., cut piece
kɔmnaət n., birth
kɔmpoŋ c. n., tin
kɔmplaeŋ v., funny
kɔmpùəŋ-caːm n., Kompung Cham
kɔmpùəŋ-chnaŋ n., Kompung Chnang
kɔmpùəs n., height
kɔmpùŋ-tae p.v.p., in the middle of —ing, just now
kɔmpùcèəròət(th) n., Kingdom of Cambodia
kɔmrɔːŋ c. n., garland
kɔmrɔːŋ-phkaː n., garland of flowers
kɔmsɔt v., destitute
kɔmsɔt-tùːrəkùət v., wretched
kɔmsaːn(t) v., relax (= be at leisure)
kɔmhɤ̀ŋ n., anger
kɔmhos n., wrong n.
kɔmlaŋ n., strength; ʔɔs kɔmlaŋ, tired
kɔmlaːc v., timid
kɔmlau v., ignorant
kɔrùna: r., see *kəna:
kɔrùna:-pìseːs r., yes (or polite introduction to reply; male speaker to prince or princess)
*kɔː p.v.p. m., so, therefore, accordingly;— ʔɤy kɔː —! How very —! What a lot of —!
kɔː n., neck
*kɔː-daoy f., even if (referring to what precedes); *kɔː-daoy—*kɔː-daoy, possible— possible (emphasizes one possibility as contrasted with another)
*kɔː-baːn—*kɔː-baːn f., either—or (re possibilities, potential only)
*kɔː-pɔñtae m., however, but
*kɔː-mìːən—*kɔː-mìːən f. (definite alternatives) either—or
kɔːŋ c., bale
kɑkda: n., July
kɑɲɲaː n., September

kat v., cut; kat sëckdɤy, to decide (make a legal decision)
kɑtdɤk n., October–November
kan v., hold v.
kan pre n.p., towards
kan c. n., book
kan-tae p.v.p., increasingly
kap v., strike with pointed or sharp weapon; kap—cak v.—v., stab, attack with dagger
kambɤt c., stroke of a knife
kambɤt n., knife
kaːc v., naughty
kaːɲɔːt n., motor-boat
kaːy v., scratch (the surface of the earth)
kaː(r) n., work n., matter, business
kaː(r) v., marry v. tr.
kaː(r)-ɲìːə n., duties
kaː(r)-pìːə(r) v., protect
kaːroŋ c. n., hemp sack (capacity: 3 bushels)
kaːl m., when
kaːl n., time
kaːl-dael m., when (in past) conj.
kaːl-naː m., when, whenever, conj.
kaːl-naː-baə m., if ever, whenever
kaːl-baə m., if, whenever, when
kaːl-pìː pre n.p., at, on (of time)
kaːlɤy c. n., set of 20 sarong lengths
kaːsaet n., newspaper
kɤn v., crush v.
kɤy c., loomful, 20-yard length (of material)
kɤy n., loom
kon n., film
kom p.v.p., not, do not
kom-tae m., unless
komphèə n., February
kom-ʔaoy m., so that—not, so as not to, in order that—not, in order not to, let—not
kol n., pig (in names of years)
koːn n., child
koːn-pros n., son
koːn-sʀy n., daughter
koːn-sʀs(s) n., pupil, student
koː(r) v., stir v. tr.
koːrəna: r., see *kəna:
kaən v., increase v. intr.
kaət v., be born; arise, happen, wax (of moon); kaət 2nd v., be able, manage
kaət c., period of the waxing moon
kiəŋ v., herd v., drive (animals) before one
kiən n., corner
kiəs v., scrape
kec(c) n., procedure
kec(c)-kaː(r) n., procedure, work
keh v., scratch v.
keːŋ-koːŋ n., name of a legendary snake
kae n., Kê (proper name)
kaeŋ-kaoŋ v., pretentious
kaoɲ(e) x, ten million
kausɤp x, ninety
kausù: n., rubber, tar macadam
*kauʔɤy n., chair
kda(r) n., plank
kdɤy—kdɤy f., either—or, and—and (referring to what precedes)
kdoŋ-kday v., make a repeated clanging sound
kdau v., hot
knoŋ pre n.p., in

knoŋ-pèːl-dael m., when conj. (in past); while
kbac n., design n.
kbaːl c., pair (of horns); volume (= book)
kbaːl n., head
kbuəŋ n., tile
kmuːəy n., nephew, niece
kmuːəy-srʋy n., niece
kmeːŋ n., young person, child
kmeːŋ v., young
kmeːŋ-kmaːŋ n., small children
kmeːŋ-kmeːŋ n., children in general
kmeːŋ-pros n., boy, child
kmeːŋ-srʋy n., girl, child
krɔː v., poor
krak-krak v., bubble v.
kraːp v., prostrate oneself
kraːp-tùːl i. (introduces polite conversation; female speaker to royalty)
kraːl v., spread out
kraːs-kraːs v., thick and numerous
kroŋ n., town
krop-krop v., champ, nibble
*krom n., group, department
kraeŋ v., fear (mild word. cf. 'I'm afraid I can't come—')
kraom pre n.p., under
kraom v., be under
kraom-prèəh-baːt n. pron., you (female speaker to royalty other than the King or Queen)
kraoy m., after
kraoy pre n.p., behind, after
kraoy v., behind, after (of place and time), next
kraoy-pìː m., after conj.
kraol n., enclosure
krau-pìː pre n.p., outside, apart from
krəkhvɔk v., dirty
krədaːs n., paper; (monetary) note
krəbʋy n., buffalo
krəmom n., girl of marriageable age
krəvɔŋ v., circular
krəvɔl-krəvaːy v., disturbed, troubled
krəhɔːm v., red
*krəʔoːp v., having a pleasant scent
*klʋŋ(k) v., Indian
klʋn n., scent n.
kʔɔːm c., pitcherful n.
kʔɔːm n., pitcher (¾ pint)
kʔeːŋ-kʔɔːŋ v., impudent
khɔm v., try hard (to)
khap c. n., jar for water (earthenware with same size base and top, with lid)
kham v., bite v.
khaːŋ n., side, direction
khaːŋ pre n.p., on the part of, in the direction of
khaːŋ-cʋːŋ n., north
khaːŋ-tboːŋ n., south
khaːŋ-*lec n., west
khaːn v., miss v. (1st or 2nd v.)
khaːl n., tiger (in names of years)
khʋŋ v., angry
khos v., wrong, different; *kùt—khos* v.—v., be wrong (incorrect); *smaːn—khos* v.—v., guess wrongly
khoːc v., wrong, go wrong; break down; wicked

khuːəp c., year's cycle
khiəv v., blue
khae c. n., month
khae-kakdaː n., July
khae-kaŋŋaː n., September
khae-katdʋk n., October–November
khae-komphèə n., February
khae-cäet(r) n., March–April
khae-cèːs(th) n., May–June
khae-tolaː n., October
khae-thnù n., December
khae-bos(s) n., December–January
khae-phɔlkun n., February–March
khae-pìsaːk(h) or *khae-vìsaːk(h)* n., April–May
khae-phʒətrèəbʒì n., August–December
khae-mìthona n., June
khae-mèəkara n., January
khae-mìːək(h) n., January–February
khae-*mìkèəseː(r) n., November–December
khae-mìːnìːə n., March
khae-mèːsaː n., April
khae-vìsaːk(h), *khae-pìsaːk(h)* n., April–May
khae-vìccheka n., November
khae-sʋyha n., August
khae-sraːp(+ ṅ) n., July–August
khae-ʔassoc n., September–October
khae-ʔaːsaːḷ(h) n., June–July
khae-ʔosaphìːə n., May
khao n., trousers
khao-ʔaːv n., suit n.; clothes (= 'washing')
khcat-khcaːy v., scattered, sprinkled all over
khɲom n. pron., I
khɲom-*kəna:, *khɲom-koːrəna:* n. pron., I (to monk)
khɲom-koːrəna:, see *khɲom-kəna:*
khɲom-baːt n. pron., I (male to superior)
khɲom-prəbaːt-tìːən, see *khɲom-prèəh-baːt-tìːən*
khɲom-prəbaːt-mcas, see *khɲom-prèəh-baːt-mcas*
khɲom-prèəh-baːt-tìːən n. pron., I (servant to master)
khɲom-prèəh-baːt-mcas n. pron., I (of lesser mandarin to higher)
khɲom-mcas n. pron., I (female speaker to royalty)
khnɔːŋ c., back (of houses)
khnɔːŋ n., back
khnəət n., period of waxing moon
khmae(r) n., Cambodian n.
khmau v., black
khyɔl n., wind n.
khlaŋ v., strong, loud
khlah post n.p., n. pron., some, certain (plur.)
khlaː n., tiger
khlaː-khmùm n., bear n.
khlaː-*thom n., royal tiger
khlaː-rəkhʋn n., panther
khlaːc v., fear v.
khlaːc-kraeŋ v., afraid
khlʋy v., short
khluːən n., body, person, self, you (to equal); *khluːən ʔaeŋ*, oneself, himself, herself, etc.; *khluːən yʋːŋ*, ourselves; *khluːən kɔət*, him-, her-, themselves; *khluːən vìːə*, himself, herself, itself, themselves; *khluːən khɲom*, myself

khlau v., ignorant
khvɔl-khvaːy v., busy (in a whirl of activity)
khvah v., lack v.
khsɔt v., destitute
khsac n., sand
khsaːy v., common
khsɤk-khsuːəl v., sob quietly
*khsɤp v., whisper
khsae c., bundle of palm-leaf manuscript pages
khsae n., string
kəkaːy v., dig, scratch constantly at the earth's surface
kəkeh v., scratch constantly v.
*kəŋaʔ n., party (political); *kəŋaʔ **prəciːəthìpdɤy(y)*, Democratic Party
*kənaː and *koːrənaː* or *kɔrùnaː*, yes (or merely a polite introduction to a reply by layman to monk)

k̇

kùəŋ v., stay, sit (of monk)
kùəŋ-tae p.v.p., continually, still
kùənlɔːŋ (lit. word) n., place
kùəl c. n., trunk of tree (with branches removed)
kùəh v., kick away, knock away, beat (gong)
kɔː(r) v., heap (up)
kɔ̀ət n. pron., he, she, they (respectful), you (friendly)
kiːloː c., kilogramme
kiːloːmaet(r) c., kilometre
kiːəp v., squeeze v.
kùt v., think, consider, ponder, discuss, wonder, think of (—ing); *kùt—khɤ̀ːɲ* v.—v., realize, conclude, solve a problem
kùːː m., that is, viz.
kùːː v., consist of, be by nature, be essentially
kùk n., prison; *phtὲəh kùk* (id.)
kùmnɔ̀ː(r) c. n., heap
kùmnɔ̀əp v., salute
kùmnùː n., drawing
kùm(p̀) c. n., clump n.
kùmpìː c. n., collection of books or papers
kùmrùp v., complete v.
kùs v., strike (matches)
kùː c. n., pair n. (male and female)
kùː v., draw v.
kùːə(r) v., proper
kὲː n. pron., one, someone, people, a person, he, she, they
kὲːhə(s)thaːn n., building
kòː n., ox, cow
kòːk n., dry land
kòːrùp v., respect v.
knìːə a., together, each other, reciprocally
knìːə n. pron., I, we, they, he, she (familiar)
knìːə-yɤ̀ːŋ n. pron., we
kmìːən = mùn mìːən v., have not, there is not, there are not
krɔ̀ən-tae p.v.p., only just, hardly
krɔ̀ən-baə v., enough, quite well, quite
krɔ̀əp c., pill
krɔ̀əp n., seed
krìːə-dael m. (lit.), when conj.
krìːstəsəkraːὲ n., Christian Era

krùːt-krùːt v., give or have the sound of dragging
krùn v., have a fever
krùp v., pre n.p., every, all
krùp-krɔ̀ən v., sufficient
krùː n., teacher
krùː-bɔɲrìən n., teacher
krùː-pὲːt̀(y) n., doctor
krùːəp-krùːəp v., crunch
krùːəsaː(r) n., family
krὲː n., bed
krəp̀ùl v., nauseating
krəpɤ̀ː n., crocodile
krəlìːŋ-krəlòːŋ n., name of a variety of bird (Gracupeia nigricollis)
khùm n., district (an administrative area)
khɤ̀ːɲ v., see, perceive
khcùl v., lazy
khtɔ̀ət v., rebound v.
khtὲəh n., pan
khnìːəp n., pincers
khpùəŋ-khpùəs v., high-ranking
khpùəs v., high
khpùəs-khpùəs v., very high, high and numerous
khlìːən v., hungry
khvɤ̀ːc-khvɤ̀ːc v., limp, hobble

ŋ

ŋoːv-ŋoːv v., with sounds of pleading and protest
ŋae-ŋoː v., indecisive

ŷ

ŋɔ̀əp v., dead
ŋìːək v., bend v. intr.
ŋìːəy v., easy; *tὲəŋ ŋìːəy*, easily, with ease
ŋìət v., dried and salted
ŋəŋùt v., dark

c

cɔŋ v., wish (to)
cɔŋkak c. n., large skewer
*cɔŋkɤh n., chopsticks
cɔŋkaom c. n., cluster (e.g. of fruit)
cɔŋvaːy c. n., skein
cɔŋhan n., food (of monks)
cɔɲìət v., confined (= lacking space), narrow
contùəl n., stilt n.
contìːəs c. n., small bundle (of paddy, cane, etc.)
cɔp c. v., get to the end
cɔm pre n.p., directly on
cɔm v., direct
cɔmkaː(r) n., market-garden
cɔmŋaːy n., distance
cɔmnɔːt n., station; *cɔmnɔːt yùən(t)-hɔh*, airport
cɔmnam-tae p.v.p., usually, habitually
cɔmnɤy n., food
cɔmnɤy-ʔaːhaː(r) n., food
cɔmnùːəp n., business (= trade, commerce)
cɔmnùːən n., number
cɔmnὲɲ n., profit n.

cɔmnaek c. n., type, social class

cɔmnaek pre n.p., with regard to, as to, as for

cɔmnaek-khaːŋ pre n.p., on the part of

cɔmbaəŋ n., chaff

cɔmpùːk (or cùmpùːk) c. n., chapter

cɔmraən-pɔ̀ː(r) r., yes (or polite introduction to reply; monk's word to a general)

cɔmriək c. n., lengthwise section

cɔmriəŋ n., song

cɔmlaek v., strange, interesting

cɔmhɔː v., open-sided

cɔmhiəŋ c. n., half of a symmetrically-shaped object

cɔmʔɔːk v., mock

cɔmʔaːm c., handspan

cɔː n., dog (in names of years)

cɔːŋ v., tie v.

cɔːp n., fork, spade, hoe

cɔːp-kap n., hoe n.

cak v., stab at; pour, shoot (bolt); put needle on record; cak—mùt v.—v., inflict a stab-wound; cak maːsìːn-pùəŋrìːk-sɔmleːŋ, use a microphone

cak-can n., name of a kind of cake

cat v., dispense; cat kaː(r), administer

cat-caeŋ v., organize, administer

catvaːsák n., fourth of the cycles of twelve years

cap v., catch; begin to

cap-cɔːŋ v., capture v.

cam v., await, wait for, guard, remember

cam-bac, take the trouble to; ʔaeŋ cam-bac . . . . do you have to . . . . ?

cas v., old, grown up

*cah r., yes (or merely a polite introduction to a reply by female speaker)

caːŋ-(h)vaːŋ n., boss, director

caːn c., plateful, bowlful; 'plate' or sheet of wax

caːn n., plate, bowl; 'plate' or sheet of wax

caːn-kbaːn n., crockery

caːp n., sparrow

caːy v., pay out, spend

cɤk v., bite v. (of snake)

cɤt v., scrape

cɤt(t) n., heart (= feelings), mind

cɤtsɤp x, seventy

cɤn n., Chinese n.

cok v., 1. hurt adj., 2. stop up, cork

coŋ c., weight measurement (= 30 kgms)

coŋphɤu n., cook

coh f., go on! do!

coh v., go down

coh-baə m., what if . . . . ?

cɔːl v., enter; cɔːl cɤt(t), like to

cɔːl (spelt cɔːr) m., come now (exhortation)

cuːən-kaːl, see cùːən-kaːl

cuːən-naː, see cùːən-naː

cuːəp, see cùːəp

caəŋ-maəŋ v., snooty

cëɲ v., go out; cëɲ pìː, leave (a place)

ceɲcɤm v., nourish, keep, bring up

ceɲcram v., cut up in small pieces by chopping

ceh v., know, know how (to)

ceh-tae p.v.p. (before attributive verb), con-stantly, always; (before operative verb) still, in spite of something

*ceːdɤy n., stupa

cae n., (title used to Chinese or Vietnamese female shopkeeper)

caek v., divided

caeŋ-vaeŋ n., name of a grass

caeŋ-vaeŋ v., criss-cross

cäet(r) n., March—April

caoŋ-haoŋ v., squat on heels

cao(r) n., thief, burglar

caol v., throw away

cau n., grandchild, 'young' (as title)

cau-pros n., grandson

cau-srɤy n., grand-daughter

cau-ʔatthìkaː(r) n., abbot

cdao(r) c., lingot

cbap n., permission

cbap c. n., copy n.

cbas v., clear

crɔːt v., cut down with a scythe

craən x, many, much

craən-tae p.v.p., mostly, usually, nearly all

criəŋ v., sing

crɔlaəs-baəs v., vulgar, lawless v.

chɔːsák n., sixth of the cycles of twelve years

chan v., eat or drink (of monks)

chap v., quick (to)

chaː v., fry v. tr.

cheh v., on fire, catch fire

cheːv-chaːv v., sizzling

chiəŋ v., inclining towards

chao-lao v., make a hubbub

chkae n., dog

chŋɔl v., surprised

chŋaɲ v., tasty

chŋaːy v., distant

chnaŋ c. n., metal cooking pot

chnam c. n., year

chnam-kol n., year of pig

chnam-khaːl n., year of tiger

chnam-cɔː n., year of dog

chnam-cùːt n., year of rat

chnam-chlɔːv n., year of ox

chnam-thɔh n., year of hare

chnam-msaɲ n., year of serpent

chnam-məmì n., year of horse

chnam-məmɛ̀ n., year of goat

chnam-rò:ŋ n., year of dragon

chnam-rɔka: n., year of cock

chnam-vɔ̀ːk n., year of monkey

chnok n., stopper, cork

chnaot n., lottery; poll

chmaː n., cat

chmaː-baː n., large owl

chmoːl v., roll into a ball

chlaːt v., clever

chlɔːv n., ox (in names of years)

chlaəy v., reply v.

chliət v., persist

chʔaəm-khpɤ̀ːm v., despise

chʔaə(r) v., roasted

c

cùək v., to smoke (tr.) (of tobacco)

cùəŋcèəŋ n., wall

cùəŋcùːn v., transport, take

cùəndaə(r) n., stairway, staircase

cùənlùəŋ c. n., trellis (on which pepper-trees are grown)

cɔ̀ən v., tread on; pound rice with pestle and mortar

cɔ̀əp v., stick v. intr.; pass (examination) v.

cì:ə m., that (followed by reported speech)

cì:ə pre n.p., as, being; (with following nominalized attributive verb, in a — manner)

cì:ə v., 1. be, be as, 2. be well

cì:ə-mù:əy a., together

cì:ə-mù:əy pre n.p., together with

cì:ə-mù:əy-nùŋ pre n.p., together with

cì:əŋ a., to a greater extent, more

cì:əŋ pre n.p., more, in excess of, exceeding, to a greater extent than

cì:ət(e) n., race (= nationality, kind)

cì:əl c. n., basket (meshed, with narrow neck and handle; capacity ½ bushel)

cìh v., mount; get into, onto; ride in or on; go in, by

cì: c., weight measurement (3·75 grms.)

cì:-do:n n., grandmother

cì:-ta: n., grandfather

cì:-do:n-cì:-ta: n., grandparents

cì:k v., dig v.

cì:vùt n., life

cùt pre n.p., near

cùt v., near, close

cùt-cùt v., very near

cùt-dɔl p.v.p., almost (of time and place)

cùəŋrùk n., granary

cùəpcèəŋ n., wall

cùm c., round n.

cùmnù:əs n., replacement (object used to replace)

cùmnù:əs p.v.p., instead of

cùmpù:k, see cɔmpù:k

cùmrì:əp v., inform

cùmrì:əp-su:ə(r) v., good morning, good-afternoon, etc. (more formal than 'hello' but applicable to any time of day); greet

cùmrìək, see cɔmrìək

cùmrɤ̀:s n., choice

cùmvèɲ pre n.p., round

cù:t n., rat (in names of years)

cù:t v., wipe; dust v.

cù:n v., to offer; cù:n (kè:) tɤu, give a lift to, see off

cù:(r) v., bitter, sour

cù:əŋ v., do business v.

cù:ən v., happen v.

cù:ən-ka:l, cu:ən-ka:l a., sometimes

cù:ən-na:, cu:ən-na: a., sometimes

cù:əp, cu:əp v., meet, meet with v.

cù:əp-cùm v., meet together

cù:əy v., help v.

cù:ə(r) c. n., line, row

cù:əs pre n.p., instead of

cù:əs v., replace v. tr.

cù:əs-cùl v., patch up, mend

cɤ̀:ŋ n., leg, foot; north

cìəs v., avoid; cìəs—phot v.—v., escape from, get free from

cèy-yò:(è) e., long live . . . . ! hurrah!

cè:(r) v., rebuke v.

cè:s(th) n., May–June

cò:k v., soaked

crùŋ c. n., corner

crùh v., shed past part.

crù:k n., pig

crìək v., split into lengthwise sections

cròːŋ c. n., criss-cross pile

crɤ̀:s v., take one's choice

crɤu v., deep

chù: v., ill

chùp v., cease (to), stop

chù:-chì: n., name of a culinary dish

chɤ̀: n., (piece of) wood

chɤ̀: v., wood; of a tree

chɤ̀:kùs n., match

chò:ŋ v., extend the hand

chnèəh v., win v.

chnù:əl n., cost of hiring a person's services

chmùəh n., name

chmù:əɲ n., business man

chlùəh v., quarrel v.

chvè:ŋ v., left (as opposed to right)

ɲ

ɲam v., eat (family word)

ɲ̀

ɲɔ̀ə(r) v., shake v. intr., tremble

ɲɤ̀:s n., perspiration

ɲəɲɔ̀ə(r) v., tremble constantly

d

dɔk v., collect (of water forming a pool)

dɔŋhae(r) v., in an ordered sequence

dɔndɤ̀ŋ v., ask in marriage, ask to marry

dɔp x, ten

dɔp-bɤy x, thirteen

dɔp-bu:ən x, fourteen

dɔp-pram x, fifteen

dɔp-pram-bɤy x, eighteen

dɔp-pram-bu:ən x, nineteen

dɔp-*prampùl x, seventeen

dɔp-pram-mù:əy x, sixteen

dɔp-pì:(r) x, twelve

dɔp-mù:əy x, eleven

dɔmnam n., plant n.

dɔmnɤŋ n., news; dɔmnɤŋ l?ɔ:, information

dɔmnaəp v., sticky (of rice, maize, etc.)

dɔmne:k n., sleep, rest

dɔmnaə(r) n., journey

dɔmbɔ:(r) c., four (used in counting fruit and vegetables)

dɔmba:ɲ n., equipment for weaving

dɔmbot c. n., small skewer

dɔmbo:l n., roof

dɔmrɤy n., elephant

dɔmlay n., value n.

dɔmlɤ̀ŋ c., ounce

dɔmlo:ŋ n., potato

dɔl m., until, when (definite and future)

dɔl pre n.p., until, as far as, towards (of feelings)

dɔl v., arrive

dɔl-ka:l-na: m., when (in future)

296

dɔl-pèːl-dael m., until, when (in future)
dɔh v., free v. tr.
dɔh-day v., avoid a situation, try to get out
   of a situation
*dɔː g., the one which, the . . . .
dɔːk v., uproot, pull out
dɔːŋ c. n., time, occasion
dɔːŋ-*pakkaː n., pen
dɔːp c. n., jar
dak v., put, put in
dac v., break v. intr.; torn (of string, thread);
   dac cɤt(t) decide
dam v., 1. cook v. 2. grow, plant
day n., hand, arm
daːv n., sword
dɤk c., a man-load
dɤk v., lead (animals or cart)
dɤk-nɔəm v., transport v.
dɤŋ f., do you know?
dɤŋ v., know; dɤŋ khluːən, conscious, aware
dɤy n., earth, ground, land
dot v., set fire to
dom c., lump, piece
doh v., grow v. intr.
doh-daːl v., grow rapidly
doːŋ n., coconut
doːc v. pre n.p., like
doːc-cìːə p.v.p., as though
doːc-cìːə v., seem as though, be like
doːc⁼neh a., thus, like this
doːc⁼noh a., like that
doːc-mdĕc a., (in question) how; (in emphatic
   context) in whatever way
doːn n., grandmother
doːn-taː n., grandparents
doː(r) n., change
doː(r) v., barter, give change
duːəl v., fall over
duːəs v., skim
daəm c., (used for counting cylindrically-
   shaped objects)
daəm n., tree, tree trunk, beginning; cìːə daəm,
   etcetera
daəm-ceːk n., banana-tree
daəm-chɤː n., tree
daəm-tnaot n., sugar-palm
daəm-svaːy n., mango-tree n.
daəmbɤy m., so that (expressing purpose)
daəmbɤy-kom-*ʔaoy m., so that . . . . not
   (expressing purpose)
daəmbɤy-nùŋ m., so that (expressing purpose)
daəmbɤy-nùŋ-mùn-*ʔaoy m., so that . . . .
   not (expressing purpose)
daəmbɤy-mùn-*ʔaoy m., so that . . . . not
   (expressing purpose)
daəmbɤy-*ʔaoy m., so that (expressing
   purpose)
daə(r) v., walk, travel v.
daə(r)-lèːŋ v., go for a walk
dëɲ v., pursue, chase (away); dëɲ thlay,
   bargain v.
deːk v., lie down, sleep, rest
deː(r) v., sew
deːsìːmaet(r) c., decimetre
dae(r) f., too, also, as well, indeed, even so
dael m., who, whom, which; of, at, in, about,
   with reference to whom, which

dael p.v.p., already; has/have ever at some
   time in the past
daoy m., because
daoy pre n.p., along, by, in a — manner
daoy-saː(r) m., because
daoy-häet(o) m., because
dbɤt m., because, although
dbɤt-tae m., although
dədael v., alike, the same
dəraːp, in cìːə dəraːp, always

ɗ

dətèy v., other

t

tɔː v., continue; reply; tɔː thlay, bargain v.
tɔː-tɔː-tɤu f., all the time from then, since
tɔː-tɔː-mɔːk f., all the time up to now, ever
   since
tɔː-tɤu f., continually, from then
tɔː-pìː pre n.p., ever since
tɔː-mɔːk f., continually until now
taŋ v., set, place, set to, begin to
taŋ-pìː m., ever since
taŋ-pìː pre n.p., ever since, from
tatha:kùət n. pron., I (of a Buddha)
taː n., grandfather, old man
taː-taː n., old men in general
taːm m., as, according to what, in accordance
   with what
taːm pre n.p., following, through, by, along
taːm v., follow, go along
taːraŋ n., notice n.
tɤŋ-rɤŋ v., compel forcibly
*tok n., table
tola: n., October
toːc v., small, little
toːc-toːc v., very small, small and numerous
toːŋ-taːŋ v., clatter down
tuːə c. n., (used for counting upright objects)
   letter (in writing), syllable, character in
   play, person
taə f., then, after all (used in exclamations)
taə m., (a question follows), tell me:
taək-taək v., wriggle
tiəm n., shop
tae g., only, not more than, just
tae m., however, but
taeŋ v., have the habit of
taeŋ-tae p.v.p., usually, habitually
tau c., bushel
tnaot n., sugar-palm
tbal n., mortar
tbal-kduəŋ n., mortar with pestle
tbaːɲ v., weave
tbɤt-tbiət v., bargain v.
tboːŋ n., jewel
tboːŋ c. n., 5-yard length (of material)
tbiət v., pinch
trɔŋ v., verticle, direct, move directly towards; thɲay trɔŋ mid-day
trɔːŋ v., catch drips, as when filtering a liquid
tram v., soak v. tr.
trɤy n., fish
trɤy-ŋiət n., dried, salted fish
trɤy-rɔs n., name of kind of fish

trɤysák n., third of the cycles of twelve years
tron-tron v., shiver with fear and cold
tro:v v., have to, must, coincide, be necessary (impersonal use); right, correct, deserve; *kùt—tro:v* v.—v., be right; *sma:n—tro:v* v.—v., guess rightly; *tro:v cɤt(t)*, satisfied; *tro:v tò:s*, deserve punishment; *tro:v chnaot*, win a lottery; *tro:v ci:ə*, be, happen to be, coincide with; *tro:v ka:(r)*, need v.
tro:v-tae p.v.p., absolutely must
tre:k-?ɔ:(r) v., delighted, pleased
traok n. (lit. word), hillock
trəciək n., ear
trənaot c. n., skewer, anything used as a skewer
trəbo:k c. n., wrapper, packet
trələp v., turn round v. intr., turn back, return; *trələp—mò:k*, come back; *trələp—tɤu*, go back
trəsok n., cucumber
tlok n., comedian
t?o:ɲ-t?ae(r) v., grumble
*thom v., big, tall
thɔh n., hare (in names of years)
thɔ:t-*tok n., drawer (in table)
thaŋ c., 2 bushels
thaŋ n., zinc barrel (capacity 2 bushels)
tha: f., (indicates that direct or lively indirect speech follows)
tha: m., that (followed by reported speech)
tha: v., say
tha:s n., tray
thao-kae n., shopkeeper (prosperous)
thaok v., cheap
thŋay n., day; late morning, lunch-time; *sɔp̀(v) thŋay*, nowadays
thŋay-cɑn(t̀) n., Monday
thŋay-pùt̀(h) n., Wednesday
thŋay-prəhɔ̀əs(p + tè) n., Thursday
thŋay-sok(r) n., Friday
thŋay-sau(r̀) n., Saturday
thŋay-?ɔŋki:ə(r) n., Tuesday
thŋay-?a:tùt(y) n., Sunday
thnɔl n., road
thnak c. n., level, class in school, row in theatre or cinema
thnaŋ c. n., node of bamboo
thnam n., medicine; *thnam x krɔ̀əp*, x pills
thna:l n., seed-bed
thno:(r) n., price
thmɔ: n., stone
thmɤy v., new
thlɔŋ v., deaf, deafened
thlay n., cost n.
thlay v., dear, expensive, cost v.; *tɔ: thlay*, bargain v.
thva:y v., offer (to the Buddha or to royalty); *thva:y bɔŋkùm*, greet (respected persons) by placing palms together
thva:y-prèəh-pɔ̀:(r) r., yes (or introduction to polite reply, monk to royalty)
thvɤy-dbɤt-tae m., although

ì

tùən-phlùən v., supple
tùəntèɲ-tùəntù:t v., speak redundantly

tùənlè: n., river, the Tonle
tùəh m., even if
tùəh-ci:ə m., even if
tùəhbɤy m., even if
tɔ̀:t v., read (of monks)
tɔ̀ət v., kick away
tɔ̀ən v., catch, be in time for, catch up with
tɔ̀əl-dɔl m., until, when (in future)
tɔ̀əl-tae m., until, when (in future), so that (result)
tɔ̀əl-tae-dɔl m., until, when (in future)
tèək v., trap v.
tèək-tì:əm v., inter-related
tèəŋ pre n.p., with, together with, all, including all
tèəŋ-la:y post n.p. a., all
tèəŋ-?ɔs post n.p. a., all
tèəh v., hit with flat of hand
ti:ən n., gift, favour
ti:əp v., small (in height), low
tì:əs v., turn away (intr.)
ti:əhì:ən n., soldier
tì: n., place; *tì:* + numeral forms ordinal number
tì:-kɔmlaeŋ n., place
tì:-kroŋ n., city, town
tì:-cat-ka:(r) n., management
tì:-lùmnɤu n., address
tì:ŋmò:ŋ n., scarecrow (made to look like a man)
tùk c., round (of boxing match)
tùk n., water
tùk-tae n., tea (ready to drink)
tùk-tnaot n., toddy (in unfermented juice)
tùk-dɔh-kò: n., milk
tùm v., yoke v.
tùk v., put away, keep, put on one side
tùk-dak v., put, (to work) (= apply)
tùk-tùk v., put away (numerous objects)
tùm v., ripe
tùm v., perch v. intr.
tùmnèɲ n., goods
tùmnè: v., free (at leisure, for leisure)
tùmpɔ̀ə(r) c. n., page
tùmrɔ̀əm m., before conj.
tùmrɔ̀əm-dɔl m., before conj.
tùmlèək v., let fall
tùmlɔ̀əp n., custom
tì: n., cupboard
tù:k n., boat
tù:k-kdaoŋ n., sailing-boat
tì:ŋ v., beat (drum) (= cause to resound)
tù:c-tù:c-tù:c v., very small
tù:t-tù:t v., toot, pop (of sound)
tù:l v., carry on head
tì:l-bɔŋkùm n. pron., I (male speaker to lower-ranking prince or princess)
tì:l-bɔŋkùm-ci:ə-khɲom n. pron., I (male speaker to lower-ranking royalty)
tì:l-prèəh-bɔŋkùm-ci:ə-khɲom n. pron., I (male speaker to high-ranking royalty)
tì:lì:əy v., large and roomy, wide
tìəŋ-tɔ̀ət v., exact
tìət f., further, again, more
tèɲ v., buy
tè: f., (not)—at all, indeed; indeed; (in a question) or not?

tè:sna: n., exposition (of the Buddhist law)

tè:sna: v., expound (the Buddhist law)

tò:s n., punishment; *ʔaphéy tò:s* v., take away fear of punishment

tò:sák n., second of the cycles of twelve years

tɤ: v., be supported laterally

tɤ:p m., then, next, (after fulfilment of condition)

tɤ:p-tae p.v.p., have just

tɤ:p-tae-nùŋ p.v.p., have just

tɤ:p-nùŋ p.v.p., have just

tɤu f., forth, from then

tɤu v., go, go (to)

tɤu-tìət f., longer (of time)

trɔəm v., endure (= put up with)

trùəŋ n. pron., you (monk, male speaker or female speaker to lower-ranking male royalty)

trùəŋ-prèəh-kɔrùna:-pìse:s n. pron., you (male layman or monk to royalty of high or medium rank)

trùŋ n., cage, pen, small enclosure

trɔcèək v., fresh, cool

trɔnùŋ-khnɔ:ŋ n., back-bone

trɔnùm n., perch v.

trɔnɤ: n., shelf, means of lateral support

trɔmèək n., elephant-driver

trɔmùŋ-trɔmɤ:y v., gloomy

trɔlùŋ-tùŋ n., name of variety of tree, whose fruit is used to give a sour flavour in cooking

trɔhùŋ v., humming

trɔhùŋ-ʔɤ:ŋ-kɔ:ŋ v., humming, buzzing

tvì:ə(r) n., door, entrance

thùən-thìən n., belongings n.

*thɔ̀əm-mɔda: v., usual

thɔ̀ə(rm) n., prayers

thèək v., kick v.

thùm v., smell v. tr.

thù:(r) v., slack, soft

thŋùən v., heavy

thnɔəp c., finger's width

thnù: n., December

thnɤ: n., shelf

thmèŋ n., tooth

thlèək v., fall (from a height); fail (an examination)

thlɔəp v., used to, accustomed to

thvɤ: v., do, make, do the work of; *thvɤ: cì:ə,* become, be as; *thvɤ: boŋ(y),* celebrate a festival; *thvɤ: ka:(r),* work v.; *thvɤ: tò:s (kè:),* punish (a person); *thvɤ: ba:p,* harm v., do a wrong

tɔtùk v., wet; *tɔtùk—cò:k* v.—v., wet through

tɔtùŋ n., width

tɔtì:m-tɔtì:əm v., confused, not clear

tɔtù:(r)-tɔtɔ̀ə(r) v., echo v.

tɔtù:əl v., receive; agree (to); meet (e.g. a person at a station); *tɔtù:əl tì:ən,* eat; take (as food or drink); *tɔtù:əl tì:ən dɔmne:k,* rest v.

tɔtù:əl-prèəh-rì:əc-savɑnɤy(y)-cì:ə-mcas r., yes (or polite introduction to reply; female speaker to high-ranking princess)

tɔthèək v., kick repeatedly

nɔh n., that, over there, there

nas a., very

na: n., (in a question) where, what place; (negative or indefinite context) anywhere; (emphatic context) wherever, anywhere; *ʔae na:,* to what place, to any place (according to context)

na: post n.p., (in a question) which (Eng. interrog. adj.); (indefinite, negative or emphatic context) any; *kɔnlaeŋ na:,* (in a question) where; (negative, indefinite or emphatic context) anywhere; *ya:ŋ na:,* (in a question) how; (negative, indefinite or emphatic context) anyhow

na:-khlah post n.p., (in a question) which (plur.) (Eng. interrog. adj.); (affirmative context) some, certain (plur.); (indefinite or emphatic context) any (plur.)

na:-na: post n.p., (lit. chiefly) various (indefinite)

na:-mù:əy post n.p., (in a question) which (sing.) (Eng. interrog. adj.); (affirmative context) a certain; (negative or indefinite context) any(one), (not) .... a single; (emphatic context) whichever (sing.)

neh a., here

neh post n.p., this

nɔ̀əm v., lead, take (a person)

nèək c., person

*nèək n., you (to equal), person; **nèək na:,* (in a question) who, whom (Eng. interrog. pronoun); (in affirmative context) some-one; (in negative or indefinite context) anyone

*nèək-krù: n., teacher

*nèək-cùmŋù: n., patient n.

*nèək-tlok n., comedian

*nèək-thèək-sì:klo: n., cyclo-driver

*nèək-nì:əŋ n., you (familiar yet polite to young lady)

*nèək-bɔmraə n., servant

*nèək-mɤ:l n., spectator

*nèək-lùək-sɔmbot(r) n., person selling tickets

*nèək-lè:ŋ-phlè:ŋ-lkhaon, theatre orchestra

*nèək-srɤy n., Mrs., madam

*nèək-srok n., country people, people of the area

*nèək-srae n., farmer

*nèək-ʔɔŋ(k)-mcas n., princess or prince (of whom either both parents are of royal blood but distantly removed from the sovereign or one parent is of royal blood and one not)

nèəŋkɔəl n., plough n.

nì:ə (lit.) pre n.p., with, and, of

nì:əŋ n., young lady, Miss, young Mrs.

nì:əŋ-khɲom n. pron., I (female to superior)

nì:ətì: c., minute

nì:əl c., pound (weight) (= 600 grms.)

nitì:ən v., relate, tell (a story)

nìppì:ən n., Nirvana

nìmùən(t) v., invite (monks)

nìmùən(t)-tr̀u v., go (of monks)
nìmùən(t)-mɔ̀:k v., come (of monks)
nìmù:əy post n.p., each
nìyì:əy v., speak
*nìh post n.p., this
nùk v., think about, rack one's brains;
    nùk—khr̀:ɲ v.—v., realize, come to a
    conclusion
nùŋ pre n.p., and, with (= by means of)
nùŋ p.v.p., shall, will (future), intend to
nèc(c) v., frequent
nùm c. n., team, yoke (of buffalo, oxen)
nùppèəsák n., ninth of the cycles of twelve
    years
nùm n., cake
*nùh n. post n.p., that (demonstrative noun
    or adj.)
nù:v, see *nr̀u*
nè: e., now! come now!); oh (preceding name
    or title in addressing equals or inferiors,
    to gain attention of addressed person)
nèy (lit.) pre n.p., of
nr̀u v., remain, stay in, at; live at, in, on;
    be in, at, still
nr̀u pre n.p., at
nr̀u (written *nù:v*) (lit.) pre n.p., with, and
nr̀u-knoŋ pre n.p., in
nr̀u-kraom pre n.p., under
nr̀u-cùt pre n.p., near
nr̀u-tae p.v.p., continually, still
nr̀u-pè:l-dael m., while
nr̀u-mùk(h) pre n.p., in front of
nr̀u-lr̀: pre n.p., on, above
nr̀u-ʔae pre n.p., at

b

bɔk v., wave v.
bɔŋ v., pay v.; *bɔŋ prak* x *rìəl*, pay x riels
bɔŋ-bot n., spirit (animist)
bɔŋkaət v., related by blood
bɔŋkaən v., increase v. tr.
bɔŋkùm v., greet (respected persons) by
    placing palms of hands together
bɔŋkò:l n., stake
bɔŋrìən v., teach
bɔŋvr̀l v., turn round tr.
bɔŋhat v., train v. tr.
bɔŋha:ɲ v., show v. tr.
bɔŋho:(r) v., cause to flow; *bɔŋho:(r) tùk co:l*,
    irrigate
bɔŋhaəy v., finish
bɔŋʔu:əc n., window
bɔŋʔu:ət-bɔŋʔɔ̀: v., boast, try to impress
bɔŋʔae-bɔŋʔɔŋ v., dilly-dally
bɔŋʔaoŋ n., scaffolding
bɔŋco:l v., cause to enter
bɔŋcaəc-bɔŋcaə v., flatter immoderately, coax
bɔŋchaot v., deceive
bɔŋchr̀t-bɔŋchìəŋ v., make a remark which
    one intends to be overheard by someone
    other than the person addressed
bɔŋcɔ̀ən, have (oxen or buffalo) walk round
    one treading on (sheaves of rice, to loosen
    grains)
bɔŋchùp v., stop v. tr.
bɔ̀l n., metre (poetical); verse

bɔndɔh-bɔnday v., give good excuse
bɔndɔh-bɔnda:l v., look after or bring up
    someone else's child
bɔndo:l n., proper name
bɔndaə(r) v., cause to walk
bɔndaoy v., long, have length
bɔntec a., a little, a little while; *bɔntec tìət*,
    a little later
bɔntec-bɔntec a., a very little
bɔntec-bɔntu:əc a., a little, to a small extent
bɔntùp n., room
bɔntùp-tətù:əl-phɲìəv n., sitting room
bɔnlae n., vegetable
bɔmphlec-bɔmphla:ɲ v., destroy utterly
bɔmpùəŋ n., pipe, node (of bamboo)
bɔmroŋ v., set one's mind on; *bɔmroŋ nùŋ
    thvr̀:*, *bɔmroŋ tha: nùŋ thvr̀:*, intend to do
bɔrenìppì:ən v., enter *nirvana*
bɔrephò:k v., eat, have dinner
bɔh v., drive in (e.g. a stake)
bɔ:ŋ n., elder sibling, elder brother or sister;
    you (to elder sibling or wife to husband)
bɔ:ŋ-pros n., elder brother
bɔ:ŋ-sr̀y n., elder sister
bɔ:ŋ-plo:n n., brothers and sisters; relatives,
    relations
bɔ:(r) v., drive v. tr. (= cause to move
    forward by riding, leading, driving,
    propelling)
baŋ n., row of seats
bac v., bother to
bat v., disappear, lost
bat-dɔmbɔ:ŋ n., Battambang
baytɔ:ŋ v., green
ba:c v., sprinkle, scatter
ba:l r., yes (or merely a polite introduction
    to a reply by male speaker); *ba:l tè:*, no
ba:n v., get, obtain; have already (+ Eng.
    past part.) be able (2nd v.)
ba:n-cì:ə m., the reason why . . . .; that is
    why . . . ., wherefore
ba:y n., cooked rice, food
ba:(r) v., sweep up
ba:raŋ n., French (the language), Frenchman,
    European
ba:raŋ v., European, French
ba:raŋsaes v., French; French (the language)
ba:rr̀y n., cigarette
ba:v c. n., sack of meshed china-grass or
    bark-cloth (capacity 100 lbs. of raw cotton)
br̀ŋ n., lake
br̀ŋ-bu:ə n., ponds
br̀l v., shut v. tr.; turn off (electrical appli-
    ances)
br̀y x, three
br̀y-dɔndɔp x, thirteen
bok v., pound v.
bon(y) n., celebration
bos(s) n., December–January
bu:ən x, four
bu:əŋ-su:əŋ v., implore, beg and pray
bu:ən-dɔndɔp x, fourteen
bu:əs v., be a novice (enter the religious life)
baə m., if
baə-ka:l-na: m., if (at any time, present or
    future)
baə-prəsr̀n-cì:ə m., if (by any chance)

baə-sɤn-na: m., if (by some possible chance)
baə-sɤn-na:-cì:ə m., if (by some possible chance)
baək v., open, v. tr.; turn on, put on (electrical appliances); drive (a car)
biət v., be near
biət-biən v., oppress
beh v., pluck, gather
baek v., break, v. intr.; separate v. intr.; *baek knì:ə*, separate from each other; *baek cɤt(t)*, fall out of friends; *baek pɤ̀:s*, perspire
baen v., tread on (sheaves of rice to loosen grains)
baep c. n., kind, sort
baok v., beat (against a fixed plank, etc.); beat with flat of hand; wash (clothes)
baos v., sweep
bəbɔ:(r) n., soup
bəbu:əl v., invite, suggest
*bùyro: n., office

p

paɲcəsák n., fifth of the cycles of twelve years
pan c., teapotful
pan n., teapot
pah v., mend by patching
pa:rì:s n., Paris
pɤ:t-paoɲ v., pretentious
poññɔh a., like that
poññɤ̀ɲ a., like that, so, is that so?
poññeh a., like this, so
poñlae m., but, however
poñma:n x, (in a question) how many, how much; (affirmative context) a certain number, some, a few, to a certain extent; (negative or indefinite context) (not) many, any great number, to any extent; (emphatic context) however much, however many, to whatever extent; *pì: poñma:n chnam mɔ:k haəy*, for many years
pos(te) n., post, post office, letter-box
po:k-pa:k v., clattering, banging
po:lì:s n., police
po:vthau n., axe
pe:ɲ-poh n., tomato
paetsɤp x, eighty
pdɤy n., husband
pdaom-pdaom v., bow and scrape
*pyaɲcənɛ̀ə c. n., syllable, consonant
prɔk v., be roofed with
prak n., money
praɲ v., dry (rainless); *sro:v praɲ*, paddy (grown in) dry season
prap v., tell
pram x, five
pram-dɔndɔp x, fifteen
pram-bɤy x, eight
pram-bɤy-dɔndɔp x, eighteen
pram-bu:ən x, nine
pram-bu:ən-dɔndɔp x, nineteen
*prampùl x, seven
*prampùl-dɔndɔp x, seventeen
pram-mù:əy x, six
pram-mù:əy-dɔndɔp x, sixteen
pra:kɔ̀t v., exact

prɤm-prɤy v., beautiful
proɲ-priəp v., prepare
proɲ-prəyát(n) v., careful
pros-pros n., boys, men (plural), men in general
praə v., use, use the services of, have (servants)
praə-prah v., use v.
praəs n., deer
priəp v., compare
priəp-phtɯ̀m v., compare, make equal
preh-preh v., crackle
prəka:(r) c. n., item
prənap v., be in a hurry (to), hurry
prənap-prənal v., in a great hurry
prədap n., utensil
prədap-prəda: n., utensil, tool
prədo:c v., compare
prəba:l̀-tìən, see *prɛ̀əh-ba:l̀-tì:ən*
prəba:l̀-mcas, see *prɛ̀əh-ba:l̀-mcas*
prəmo:l v., gather together
prəyát(n) v., take care
prəyát(n)-prəyaeɲ v., careful, pay great attention
prəlɔ:ɲ v., sit for an examination
prəlak v., sprinkle
prəla:y n., channel (for irrigation)
prəva: v., be on the point of
prəvaeɲ n., length
prəsop v., to be clever (at)
prəsɤn-cì:ə m., if, supposing
prəsɤn-baə m., if (by any chance)
prəso:t(e) v., bear (a child)
prəhael g., about (approximately)
prəhael m. p.v.p., see *prəhael-cì:ə*
prəhael-cì:ə, *prəhael* m. p.v.p., perhaps, it is possible that
prəʔɔp c. n., box
ploɲ-ploɲ v., seen intermittently, flicker v.
pleh-plɔh v., tease
plaek v., different, interesting
plaom-plaom v., lick the lips
pʔo:n n., younger brother or sister, younger sibling
pʔo:n-pros n., younger brother
pʔo:n-srɤy n., younger sister
phəlkùn n., February—March
pho:ɲ f., too, as well, also
phɤk v., drink v.; *phɤk tɯ̀k*, have a drink (of animals)
phot v., free from (uncluttered, unhampered by)
pho:ɲ-pha:ɲ v., bang (expresses sound of kicking, breaking, crashing, thudding)
phaəɲ c. n., earthenware basin
phaəm v., swollen, pregnant
phaen c., tablet
phaen n., disc
phka: n., flower n.
phka:-kola:p n., rose
phka:-tnaot n., flower of the sugar-palm
phka:-thmɔ: n., coral
phɲaə v., send
phɲiəv, see *phɲìəv*
phdac v., break (string, thread) tr.
phde:k v., cause to lie down, flatten
phde:k-phdɤl v., stick loyally to one's friends

phde:s-phda:s v., careless
phdaəm v., begin (to)
phlɤt n., fan
phlo:n c., forty (used in counting fruit and vegetables)
phlo:v n., road, street
phlo:v-thnəl n., main road (raised road)
phlae n., fruit
phlae-chɤ: n., fruit
phsah-phsa: v., make up a quarrel
phsa:-phsao n., all kinds of markets
phsa:y v., diffuse v. tr.
phsa:(r) n., market
phsa:(r)-kap-kò: n., meat-market
phse:ŋ v., different
phse:ŋ-phse:ŋ v., various; different and numerous
ph?aem v., sweet (of taste)
pəplɤk-pəplɔk v., have the sound of soft waves lapping
pəpleh-pəplɔh v., constantly teasing naughtily

p̀

pùəŋrì:k v., diffuse v. tr.
pùənlɔ:k n., shoot (= new growth of plant)
pùəs n., snake
pùəh n., stomach
pɔ̀:(r) n., blessing
pɔ̀:(r) r., yes (or polite introduction to reply; monk to lay persons and women to lowest rank of prince)
pɔ̀:(r)-mcas r., yes (or polite introduction to reply; women to high or medium rank of prince)
pɔ́əl(lh) v., go round
pɔ̀ən c., see ho:pɔ̀ən
pɔ̀ən x, thousand
pɔ̀əm v., carry in mouth
pɔ̀ə(rɲ) n., colour
pɛ̀ək v., wear (above waist or on feet and legs); hang on
pì:ək(y) n., word, speech
pì:əŋ c. n., tall earthenware pitcher for water
pì:ən v. (lit. word), climb
pìnùlt(y) v., examine
pìnùlt(y)-mɤ̀:l v., scrutinize
pìba:k v., difficult; pìba:k cɤt(t), depressed
pìsa:, pì:sa: v., eat or drink (polite of other people)
pìsa:k(h), vìsa:k(h) n., April–May
pì: pre n.p., from (of place or time), at (of past time), about, concerning
pì:-prùəh m., because
pì:-prùəh pre n.p., because of
pì:m-pɤ̀:m v., groping and creeping about
pì:(r) x, two
pì:rùəh v., good to hear, beautiful to hear
pì:(r)-dɔndɔp x, twelve
pì:sa:, see pìsa:
pùt v., true
pùlthḛəṣạkra:č n., Buddhist Era
pùm p.v.p., not (literary alternative of mùn)
pùm(ph) c. n., sheet
pùl v., poisonous
pùh v., boil v.

pù: n., uncle (younger brother of parent)
pù:kae v., clever
pù:thau, po:vthau n., axe
pù:ək c. n., group
pìəc v., dented
pĕ̀ɲ v., full; pĕ̀ɲ cɤt(t), like v. tr.
pĕ̀ɲ-lĕ̀ɲ v., do with might and main
pè:k a., too, too much
pè:l n., time
pè:l m., when
pè:l-dael m., when conj.
pè:l-na:-dael m., whenever
pè:l-vè:lì:ə n., time
pè:ŋ c., cupful
pè:ŋ n., cup
pè:ŋ-cɔ:k c. n., small cup
pyì:əba:l v., look after
pyì:əm c., fathom
prùəh m., because
prùəh-tae m., because
prɔ̀:m v., agree (to)
prɔ̀:m-tḛəŋ m. pre n.p., and, at the same time as, together with
prɛ̀əh-kərùna: n., His Majesty
prɛ̀əh-kərùna:-cì:ə-?ɔŋ(k)-mcas-cì:vùt n. pron., you (monk speaking to King or Queen)
prɛ̀əh-kərùna:-cì:ə-?ɔŋ(k)-mcas-cì:vùt-lɤ̀:-tbo:ŋ n. pron., you (male or female speaker to King or Queen)
prɛ̀əh-kərùna:-thlay-pìse:s r., yes (or polite introduction to reply, male speaker to King or Queen)
prɛ̀əh-kərùna:-pìse:s r., yes (or polite introduction to reply; male speaker to male or high-ranking royalty)
prɛ̀əh-*däč-prɛ̀əh-kùɲ n. pron., (title used when speaking to mandarin, monastery chief, general, etc.)
prɛ̀əh-ba:l-tì:ən, prəba:l-tì:ən n., I (servant to master)
prɛ̀əh-ba:l-mcas, prəba:l-mcas i., (to initiate conversation, lesser mandarin to higher)
prɛ̀əh-pɔ̀:r-cì:ə-mcas r., yes (or polite introduction to a reply, female speaker to King)
prɛ̀əh-pùllhḛdɤyka: n., utterance of the Buddha
prɛ̀əh-prù(h)m n., Brahma
prɛ̀əh-mè:-cì:ə-mcas r., yes (or polite introduction to a reply, female speaker to Queen or princess)
prɛ̀əh-lḛəksenəvùəŋ(s) n., Laksanavamsa (name of a play)
prɛ̀əh-vḛ(s)sa: c., year (as spent by monk)
prɛ̀əh-*vìhì:ə(r) n., temple
prɛ̀əh-?ɔŋ(k) c., person (royal)
prɛ̀əh-?ɔŋ(k) n., the Buddha
prɛ̀əh-?ɔŋ(k)-mcas n., prince, princess (of whom both parents are close blood relations of the sovereign)
prɛ̀əh-?ɔŋ(k)-mcas-ksatra: n., King
prɛ̀əh-?ɔŋ(k)-mcas-ksatrɤy n., Queen
prɛ̀əh-?ɔŋ(k)-mcas-ksatrɤya:nì: n., Queen
prɛ̀əh-?ɔŋ(k)-mcas-cì:vùt-lɤ̀:-tbo:ŋ n. pron., you (female speaker to King or Queen)
prì:ət-prɔ̀:ŋ v., flash here and there
prì:əp n., pigeon
prùk n., morning

prùh v., bark v.

prù:əy v., sad, miserable; *prù:əy cɤt(t)*, very sad, miserable

prèc-prèc v., drip-drip

prèy n., forest

prèy-nəkɔ:(r) n., Saigon

prəkè:n v., offer (to monk)

*prəcì:əthìpdɤ̀y(y) n., democrat

prəcừm v., assemble v. tr.; **nèək prəcừm*, meeting n.

prəchlùəh v., squabble together

prənèək v., carry on back or shoulder

prəpừ̀ən(lh) n., wife

prəlùŋ-prəlèəŋ n., spirit (one's own) Used in a limited number of expressions

prəlùm n., dawn

prəlùp n., dusk

phɔ̀ətrèəbɔ̀l n., August–September

phì:ək c. n., part

phì:əsa: n., language

phùt-phéy v., terrified

phù:mì:ə v., Burmese

phù:m(ì) n., village

phùən-phìən n., group of friends

phè:səcèə n., herb (medicine, tobacco, areca, betel, etc.); *(tùk) phè:səcèə*, soft drinks

phkù: v., pair off

phɲèəv, phɲèəv n., guest

phtɔ̀əp-phtɔ̀əp v., very near together

phtɔ̀əl v., present (oneself) v. tr.

phtèəh n., house, home

phtèəh-pè:l(y) n., hospital

phtèəh-səmnak n., hotel

phtùm v., parallel, comparable

phnùm n., hill; the Phnom in Phnom Penh on which there is a monastery

phnùm-pèɲ n., Phnom Penh

phnè:k n., eye

phlì:əm a., immediately

phlì:-phlɤ̀: v., very stupid

phlù: n., dawn

phlɤ̀:k-phlɤ̀:k-phlɤ̀:k v., slow moving, sluggish

phlɤ̀:ŋ n., fire

phlìəŋ n. v., rain

phlèc v., forget

phlè:ŋ n., music

phlè:t c., moment

pəprì:əy v., twinkle, sparkle v.

m

ma:sì:n n., machine

ma:sì:n-crìəŋ n., gramophone

ma:sì:n-pùəŋrì:k-səmle:ŋ n., microphone

ma:sì:n-ʔəŋkùlì:le:k(h) sp. *lè:k(h)* n., typewriter

mɤ:n x, ten thousand

mëc a., how; (after verb of saying) what, anything

mëc m., why; *mëc ba:n-cì:ə*, how is it that, what is the reason why

mëc post n.p., (occurs only in *ya:ŋ mëc*) how

mëc-*kɔ: m., why

meɲ, mèɲ post n.p., last (in time), previous, just past

maet(r) c., metre

maoŋ c. n., hour, o'clock

mkha:ŋ a., at one side

mcas n., owner; you (monk to lowest rank of female royalty)

mcas-ksɑtra: n., you (male speaker to King or Queen)

mcas-tìəm n., shop-keeper

mcas-phtèəh n., householder

mdɔ:ŋ a., once

mdɔ:ŋ-mdɔ:ŋ a., sometimes, every time

mda:y n., mother

mdëc m., how, why

mdëc-*kɔ: m., how, why

mleh a., thus, so

msaɲ n., serpent (in names of years)

msɤl n., yesterday; *pì: msɤl*, (id.)

mhɔ:p-mhɔ:p v., have a gaping mouth

mhɔ:p n., meal

m̊

mɔ̀:k f., forth from then till now

mɔ̀:k v., come, come (to)

mɔ̀:k-dɔl pre n.p., by (of future time)

mɔ̀ət n., mouth, edge (of water)

mɔ̀ən n., fowl, hen, cock

mè̀əkəra: n., January

mì:ək(h) n., January–February

mì:əkh-bo:cì:ə n., offering in month of *mì:ək h* (January–February)

mì:ən v., have, there is, there are

*mìkèəse:(r) n., November–December

mìthona: n., June

mì:ŋ n., aunt (strictly the younger sister of one's parent)

mì:nì:ə n., March

mì:nùt c., minute

mì:lì:maet(r) c., millimetre

mùt(t)-səmlaɲ, mùt(r)-səmlaɲ n., friend

mùt(r)-səmlaɲ n., see *mùt(t)-səmlaɲ*

mùn p.v.p., not

mùn-dael p.v.p., never (in past or present)

mùn-tɔ̀ən p.v.p., not yet

mùn-mè:n p.v.p., not really

mùn-so:v p.v.p., hardly; (with attributive verb) not very

mùn-*ʔaoy m., so that . . . . not, so as not to, in order that . . . . not, in order not to, let . . . . not

mùk(h) c., item, course (of a meal), kind

mùk(h) n., front, face

mùk(h) pre n.p., in front of

mùk(h)-cì:ə m. p.v.p., perhaps, it is possible that, it is probable that, probably

mùk(h)-tae p.v.p., probably

mùt v., cut, pierced at the surface

mùn a. pre n.p., before

mùn-nùŋ m., before conj.

mù:l v., round

mù:əy x, one, a certain

mù:əy-dɔndɔp x, eleven

mù:əy-mù:əy v., one at a time, slowly, each

mɤ̀:k-mɤ̀:k-mɤ̀:k v., slow moving, sluggish

mɤ̀:l f., it looks as though, probably, perhaps; *mɤ̀:l lɤ̀u*, probably, perhaps, do you think?

mɤ̀:l v., look, look at; read

mèɲ, see *meɲ*

mè: n., chief

303

mè:tta: v., forgive
mè:trɤyphì:əp n., friendship
mè:ma:y n., widow
mè:sa: n., April
mè: r., yes (or polite introduction to reply; female speaker to lowest rank of female royalty)
mè:-cì:ə-mcas r., yes (or polite introduction to reply; female speaker to high rank of female royalty)
mè:-mcas r., yes (or polite introduction to reply; female speaker to medium rank of female royalty)
mè:k n., branch
mè:n-tè:n v., true
mtè:s n., seasoning
mnɔ̀əl e., all (followed by title of persons addressed)
mnèək post n.p. a., alone, one person
mnùs(s), see *mənùs(s)*
mphèy x, twenty
mrì:əm n., finger
mrĕc n., pepper
mlùp n., shade
mlù: n., betel
mənì: n., Mani (proper name)
mənùs(s), mnùs(s) n., man, people, person
məmì: n., horse (in names of years)
məmè: n., goat (in names of years)

y

ya:ŋ c. n., way, method, kind; *ya:ŋ na:, ya:ŋ mëc, ya:ŋ do:c-mdëc,* how

ỳ

yùəy-yùəl v., understand thoroughly
yùən(t)-hɔh n., aeroplane
yùəl v., understand; *yùəl sɔp(t),* dream v.
yùəs-sək(te) n., prestige
yɔ̀:k v., take, carry
yì:əy n., old lady, grandmother
yì: e., see *ʔì:*
yùù:t v., be late
yùù:t-yùù:t v., slowly
yùp n., night, evening after dark
yùm v., cry, call (of animals) v.
yù:(r) v., long (of time)
yù:ən v. n., Vietnamese (n. and adj.)
yɤ̀:ŋ n. pron., we, us, I
yɤ̀:ŋ-khɲom n., we (speaker stresses his own inclusion in the group) Used to superiors
yè:, see *ʔì:*

r

rʔeh-rʔoh v., diffident
rəka: n., cock (in names of years)
rəkha:k-rəyì:ək v., in tatters
rədɔh v., freed, free
rədɔ:k v., uprooted
rədo:v n., season
rəbɔs n., thing, object, belonging
rəbɔs pre n.p., of, belonging to
rəbɔ:ŋ n., fence
rəbo:t v., slip out of position v.

rəbiən n., method
rəbiəp n., method
rəpec-rəpɤy v., of slight consequence, unimportant (and pl.)
rəpeh-rəpɔh v., small and numerous
rəpaoy-rəpaoy v., float v.
rəsiəl n., early afternoon, noon–2 p.m.
rəhás v., be quick
rəho:t-dɔl pre n.p., until, all the time until, as far as, all the way to
rəho:t-mɔ̀:k-dɔl pre n.p., all the time until
rəhe:m-rəha:m v., excessive (especially of tears)
rəhaek-rəhoy v., tattered, worn
rəhaek-rəhaok v., thoroughly tattered

r̀

rùəŋvɔ̀əs n., instrument for measuring extent
rùəŋvɤ̀:l-rùəŋvɤ̀:l v., not close together, not often
rùət c. n., tier
rùət v., run
rùəs v., alive
rùəs-sa:rùən n., Ros Sarœun (proper name)
rɔ̀:k v., seek, look for; *rɔ̀:k—khɤ̀:ɲ,* find
rɔ̀:k-sì: v., earn a living
rɔ̀:y x, hundred
rɔ̀ət(th)-mùəntrɤy n., minister
rɔ̀əp, hɔ̀əp e., stop! wo!
rɔ̀əm v., dance v.
rɔ̀əl pre n.p., every, all; *rɔ̀əl knì:ə,* all together
rɔ̀əl-tae pre n.p., absolutely every
rɔ̀əs v., rake v.
rèəŋ v., keep off
rì:əc̀ n., kingdom
rì:əc̀-ka:(r) n., administration, government
rì:əc̀-vèəŋ n., palace
rì:əc̀-səp̀(t) n., royal vocabulary
rì:əp v., flat, low-lying
rì:əy-mì:əy v., mentally confused
rì:-ʔae (lit.) pre n.p., with regard to, as to, as for
rì:k v., fully open (of flowers)
rì:ŋ v., dried up
rì:ɲ v., having boiled down to a semi-solid state
rùŋ v., hard, stiff
rùŋ-tʔɤŋ v., obstinate
rùŋ-pɤŋ v., do with all one's might
rùt-tbɤt v., spend with care
rùt-tae p.v.p., increasingly
rùt-rùət v., drawn tightly round
rùp e., off! go!
rùssɤy n., bamboo
rùù: f., or, or isn't that so? *rùù: tè:,* or not? *tè: rùù:* surely?
rùù: pre n.p., or
rùù: m., or; *rùù: .... rùù: ....* either .... or ....
rùɲ v., push v.
rùmŋɤ̀:k (phlɤ̀:ŋ) n., embers
rùmcì:-rùmcì:ə v., tease, pretend
rùmpĕc c., moment
rùmlùət v., extinguish
rùmlùk v., commemorate
rùmlɔ̀:p̀(h) v., usurp

rù:ŋ n., burrow n.

rù:p c., person (in philosophical or literary context)

rù:p-rì:əŋ n., form, shape, person

rù:əc m., then, after that, next (next step in story)

rù:əc v., finish, achieve, get through to the end; 2nd v., be able; *mùn rù:əc* 2nd v., be unable; *mùn-tɔ̀ən rù:əc* 2nd v., have not yet finished

rù:əc-haəy m., then, next, after that (next step in story)

rù:əc-pì: pre n.p., after

rù:əm-kumnùt v., plot v.

rɤ̀:s v., pick out, choose

rɤ̀:s-taŋ v., elect

rɤ̀:s-rɔ̀:k v., choose

rùəŋ n., story, matter, event, play

rùəy-rùəy v., often, frequent

rìəŋ-mɔ̀:k f., continually up to now

rìən v., learn (to), study; *rìən—ceh* v.—v., know by learning, have learned, have managed to learn

rìəp v., prepare; *rìəp khlu:ən*, prepare oneself, get oneself ready

rìəp-cɔm v., prepare

rìəl c., riel

rè:ŋ-tae p.v.p., usually, habitually

rɔ̀:ŋ n., 1. dragon (in names of years) 2. building, hall, pavilion

rɔ̀:ŋ-kon n., cinema

rɔ̀:c v., wane (of moon)

rɔ̀:y v., sift

rəkèəŋ n., gong

rəyì:ə v., cold

rəyɤ̀:k-rəyɤ̀:k-rəyɤ̀:k v., slow moving, sluggish

rətèh c., cartload

rətèh n., cart

rətèh-phlɤ̀:ŋ n., train n.

rənɔ̀əs n., rake n.

rənèəŋ n., screen n.

rənì:əp n., floor

rənɔ̀:c n., period of the waning moon

rəmè:ŋ-tae p.v.p., usually, habitually

rəyì:əl n., scarecrow (any device which scares birds, not necessarily a device resembling a person)

rəyù:t-rəyù:t v., slowly and with great effort

rəlùət v., extinguished

rəlɔ̀ət-rəlɔ̀:c v., split, cut in several places

rəlùk v., miss (= be sad without)

rəlɤ̀:p-rəlùəŋ v., shining and wet

rəvùəs-rəvèy v., bustle about

rəvùəl v., be busy (—ing), concerned

rəvɤ̀:-rəvì:əy v., incoherent, unable to concentrate, unable to speak coherently

lɔndɔn n., London

lɔ: n., stove

lah v., scurry

la:ŋ n., Lang (proper name)

la:n n., car

la:n-chnu:əl n., bus

lop-lae n., screen for door

laəy v., rise up, climb, go up, enter (house)

laəy f., at all (almost always after a negative verb. Adds emphasis. Suggests argument)

leh-lɔh v., frivolous

laek v., different

lbuən n., speed

lbaeŋ n., game

lʔɔ: v., beautiful, nice, lovely, good

lʔɔ:ŋ-thù:lì:-prèəh-ba:t n. pron., you (male speaker to male prince of high or medium rank)

lʔɤt v., fine (i.e. finely cut or ground)

ì

lùək v., 1. sell, 2. be asleep

lùək-do:(r) v., do business

lɔ: v., try (to)

lɔ:p-lɔ:p v., proceed stealthily

lɔəs v., spring up (of plants)

lèək v., hide v. tr.

lì:ə n., donkey

lì:ə v., goodbye (= I depart); *so:m lì:ə*, say goodbye

lì:əŋ v., wash v.

lì:ən n., threshing-floor

lì:ən x, million

lì:əp v., paint v.

likhɤt n., letter, certificate

likhɤt-chlɔ:ŋ-daen n., passport

*lù: v., hear

lùmba:k v., difficult

lùmbe:k-lùmba:k v., be very difficult v.

lùmpè:ŋ n., javelin

lùmʔɔ:(r) n., embellishment

lùh m., when (and not before) conj.

lùh-tae m., when conj., only if, provided that

lùh-tra:-tae m., when conj., only if, provided that

lù:əc v., steal

lɤ̀: v. pre n.p., on, above; *tro:v lɤ̀:*, have a turn at

lɤ̀:k v., lift v.

lɤ̀:k-tae m., unless

lɤ̀:s v., above, exceeding

lùəŋ v., yellow

lùən v., quick

lè:ŋ v., play v.; act v.; visit socially, visit for pleasure

lè:p v., swallow v.

lè:ŋ v., cease (to)

lò:k n., sir, Mr., you (polite, formal)

lò:k-krù: n., teacher (polite, in speaking to or about the teacher)

lò:k-ta: n., grandfather (very polite); you (polite to elderly man)

lò:k-*thom n., important person

lò:k-pa: n., father

lò:k-pros n., husband (polite term, often used by wife of own husband)

lò:k-pù: n., uncle, you (polite)

lò:k-mì:ŋ n., aunt, you (= aunt) (very polite to real aunt or polite to older female friend)

lò:k-yì:əy n., old lady

lò:k-sɔŋ(kh) n., monk

lò:k-srɤy n., Mrs., madam

lò:t v., jump v.

lò:p(h) n., greed

lɲi:ɔc n., afternoon (2 p.m.–dusk), evening (if time stated)

lmɔ̀:m v., be just right, just enough

lvè:ŋ c. n., section

v

vay (spelt and read as *vì:ɔy*) v., strike, hit; type v.

vɔ(s)sa: n., rainy season

va: in *va: rò:ŋ*, end the show

vɤy, see *vɤ:y*

vɤ:y, *vɤy* e., look!, hey! (calls attention)

vo: e., shoo! be off!

vo:s-va:s-vo:s-va:s e., shoo!

v̇

vùəŋ c. n., circle, group, company

vùəŋvè:ŋ v., bewildered

vùəl v., turn, revolve v. intr.

vɔ̀:k n., monkey (in names of years)

vɔ̀ət v., throw from the horns v.

vɔ̀ət(t) n., monastery

vɔ̀əs v., measure extent

vèəh v., cut open v. tr.

vi:ə n. pron., he, she, they (familiar), it (re animal)

vì:ɔy, see *vay*

vì:əl n., plain, flat place

vìcci:ə n., subject of study

vìccheka: n., November

vìtyù n., radio

vìsa:k(h), *pìsa:k(h)*, April–May

vìsa:k(h)-bo:cì:ə n., offering in month of April–May

vìhì:ə(r) n., temple

vùk v., stir v. tr.

vùl v., turn round v. intr.; *vùl mùk(h)* v., dizzy

vù:s-va:s e., shoo! be off!

vɤ:y e., look!

viət-mìɲ n. (sp. *yìək-mìɲ*), Viet Minh

vèɲ f., back adv., back again

vè:(r) v., help each other with work (special word particularly used in connection with harvesting)

vè:k c., ladleful

vè:k n., ladle

vè:ŋ v., long

vè:ŋ-vè:ŋ v., long (and numerous), very long

s

sɔŋ v., build

sɔŋkhùm n., hope n.; *mì:ən sɔŋkhùm tha:* .... hope v. that ....

sɔŋtì:maet(r) c., centimetre

sɔŋvaeŋ v., widely separated

sɔndap-thnɔ̀əp n., method, order

sɔndɤy, *sɔmdɤy* n., husk

sɔntùh c., moment

sɔnlɤk c., leaf, sheet

sɔnsaəm n., dew

sɔpba:y v., be happy; *sɔpba:y cɤt(t)*, be pleased

sɔp(v) v. pre n.p., every, all; *sɔp(v) thŋay*, nowadays

sɔp(v)-krùp v., all, complete, without exception

sɔmcaə-sɔmcay v., hoard secretly

sɔmdăc n., prince, princess (parent or sibling of sovereign)

sɔmdɤy n., 1. speech, 2. see *sɔndɤy*

sɔmdaeŋ v., explain

sɔmna:p n., seedling

sɔmbot(r) n., letter

sɔmbot(r)-la:n-chnu:əl n., bus ticket

sɔmpùət n., material, cloth, sarong

sɔmpèəh v., place palms together in greeting

sɔmpèəh-su:ə(r) v., greet v.

sɔmrap c. n., set (necessary parts or equipment)

sɔmrap v., be used for

sɔmra:k v., rest v.

sɔmra:n(t) v., rest v. (formal elevated style)

sɔmrɤt n., Samret (proper name)

sɔmrɤ̀tthìsák n., tenth and last of the cycles of twelve years

sɔmru:ɔc-sɔmraŋ v., try to finish (a piece of work) with care

sɔmlɔ: n., stew, soup

sɔmlɔ:-sɔmlok n., dish made by the *slɔ:-slok* method of cooking, mixture, stew, soup

sɔmlaŋ n., friend

sɔmlap v., kill

sɔmle:ŋ n., sound

sɔmʔa:t v., clean v. tr.

sɔl v., remain, be left over

sɔh f., at all; (exclamation, almost always after a negative verb)

sɔ: v., white

sɔ:ŋkha:ŋ a., both sides

sák n., cycle of 12 years

sɑk(te) n., insignia

sɑkra:c̀ c. n., century

sac n., flesh, meat

sac-crù:k n., pork

sac-kò: n., beef

sɑɲɲa:bɑt(r) n., certificate, degree

sɑt(v) n., animal

sɑt(v)-kɔndol n., rat

sɑt(v)-khla: n., tiger

sɑt(v)-ca:p n., sparrow

sɑt(v)-dɔmrɤy n., elephant

sɑt(v)-sɤŋ(h) n., lion

sɑt(v)-haə(r) n., bird

sɑtra: n., palm-leaf manuscript

sɑptɑsák n., 7th of the cycles of 12 years

sɑma:cùk n., member

sa:bù: n., soap

sa:p v., sow (grain, rice)

sa:msɤp x, thirty

sa:ra:y n., seaweed

sa:ruən n., Sarœun (proper name)

sa:la: n., hall, pavilion

sa:la:-thom n., University

sa:la:-rìən n., school

sɤŋ-tae p.v.p., almost all, almost always, almost

*sɤŋ(h) n., lion
sɤt v., comb v.
sɤn f., do! get on with it immediately!
sɤm m., then, next (after something else has been done for a short time)
sɤyha: n., August
sɤs(s) n., pupil
sok(h) v., happy; sok(h) cɤt(t), pleased
sok(h)-sɔpba:y v., well, content; sok(h)-sɔpba:y cì:ə tè:? Are you happy and in good health? How are you?
soł-tae p.v.p., all, without exception
son-tron v., retreat in fear
sop-trop v., growing thickly with overhanging branches
so:t(r) n., silk
so:t(r) v., recite
so:n(y) v., zero
so:m v., ask, ask (to), ask a favour; so:m lì:ə, say goodbye
so:m-trùəŋ-prèəh-mè:tta:-praos i., (introduces a new conversation politely; male speaker to male royalty of very high rank)
so:m-trùəŋ-mè:tta:-praos i., (introduces a new conversation politely; male speaker to royalty of medium rank)
so:m-məmo:m v., grow in great profusion
so:m-mè:tta:-praos i., (introduces a new conversation politely; male speaker to lowest rank of royalty)
so:mbɤy g., even
so:(r) n., sound
*so:(h)vòə(r) n., driver
su:ən n., garden
su:ən-phka:(r) n., flower-garden
su:ən-sɑt(v) n., zoo
su:ə(r) v., ask a question; visit (a person)
su:əsdɤy e., hello! goodbye!
saəŋ-məmaəŋ v., bewildered on waking
saəc v., laugh v.
saəm v., damp
siəm v., Siamese, Thai
siəvphɤu n., book
sëckdɤy n., matter; sëckdɤy tùk(h), misery; sëckdɤy sok(h), happiness; sëckdɤy ʔanùkrùəh, indulgence (= kind forgiveness)
seh n., horse
se:n c., cent
*se:na:pɑdɤy n., general n.
saen x, hundred thousand
saesɤp x, forty
saok-sda:y v., mourn
saot f., moreover, in addition, too
saoy v., rule v.
sao(r) n., bolt n.
skɔp-skɔl v., satiated
skɔ:(r) n., sugar
ska:k n., shelf
sŋiəm v., silent
sdăc n., king
sdap v., listen; understand (spoken language)
sdam v., right (as opposed to left)
sda:y v., sorry
sdɤy v., speak
sno:k n., shell (of tortoise)
sbo:v n., thatch
sbaek-cɤ̀:ŋ n., shoe

sma:n v., guess, think, be of the opinion; sma:n—tro:v v.–v., guess correctly; sma:n—khos v.–v., guess wrongly
smo:m n., beggar
smaok-krò:k, see smò:k-krò:k
smau n., grass
srɔs v., fresh
srɔ:k v., abate
srak c. n., stack n.
sräc v., sräc nùŋ depend upon
sräc-bac v., finished
srap-tae p.v.p. m., immediately, suddenly
srah n., lake
sra:p̀(+ ṅ) n., July–August
srɤy n., woman
srɤy v., female
srɤy-srɤy n., women in general
srok n., country
srok-khmae(r) n., Cambodia
srok-*klɤŋ(k̀) n., India
srok-cɛ̀əpon n., Japan
srok-ba:raŋ n., Europe, France
srok-ba:raŋsaes n., France
srok-phù:mì:ə n., Burma
srok-yù:ən n., Vietnam
srok-siəm n., Thailand, Siam
srok-*ʔɔŋklè:s n., England
srok-*ʔa:me:rì:k n., America
sro:v n., paddy
sru:əl v., comfortable, be well; sru:əl khlu:ən, well adj.
srae n., ricefield
sraek v., shriek, cry out
srəka: n., scale (of fish)
srəkɤy n., husk
srənɔh v., miss (= be sad at the lack of)
srənok(h), srənok v., easy
srənok-srəna:n v., happy, comfortable
srəmo:m-srəma:m v., untidily hairy v.
srəlaŋ-kaŋ v., swoon v.
srəlaŋ v., like, love
srəlah v., clear, free
srəla:p v., put on ointment or lotion
slɔ: v., make a stew, soup
slaŋ-kaŋ-phɛ̀əŋ v., swoon v.
slap v., die
sla: n., areca
sla:p n., wing
sla:p-prì:ə c., spoonful
sla:p-prì:ə n., spoon
slɤk c., four hundred (with reference to counting fruit and vegetables. Not now used.)
slɤk n., leaf
slɤk-tnaot n., leaf of sugar-palm
slo:t-bo:t v., affable
sliək v., wear (below the waist)
sliək-pèək v., wear (a suit or clothing in general), see sliək and pèək
sva: n., monkey
sva:y n., mango
sva:y v., mauve
sʔɔp v., hate
sʔa:t v., cleaned
sʔa:t-ba:t v., spick and span
sʔɤt v., sticky
sʔɤy, see ʔvɤy

sʔɤy-khlah, see ʔvɤy-khlah
sʔɤy-mùːəy, see ʔvɤy-mùːəy
sʔɤy-sʔɤy, see ʔvɤy-ʔvɤy
sʔaek a., tomorrow
səmoì(r) n., sea
səsɔː(r) n., pillar
səsɤt v., pick, clean, sift
*səse:(r) v., write
*səsay c., blade (of grass), strand (of hair), etc.
*səsay n., sinew
səsrak v., freely
səsreːk-səsraːk v., flowing freely

ŝ

sɔ̀ːŝ-krəlɔ̀ːŝ v., ugly, vulgar (of things)
sìː v., eat (of animals and, familiarly, of
people); sìː kaː(r), attend a marriage feast
sìː-*lɤp v., do petty thieving
sìːkloː n., 'cyclo', cyclo-pousse
sùp-trùp, see sop-trop
sùː-trùː v., large and roomy
sùː-pətrùː v., big and roomy
sùːk-krəlùːk v., in a muddle
sɤ̀ːk-sɤ̀ːk v., sluggish, useless
skɔ̀ː(r) n., drum
skɔ̀əl v., know (a person), recognize
skùs-skìːəy v., open and white (of flower)
stɔ̀ət v., thorough, accomplished
stùŋ n., mountain stream
stùh v., leap up
stùːŋ v., transplant
stɤ̀ː v., be on the point of
stɤ̀ː-tae p.v.p., on the point of, about to
stɤ̀ː-tae-nùŋ p.v.p., on the point of, about to
spìːən n., bridge
smɔ̀ːk-krɔ̀ːk, smaok-krɔ̀ːk v., messy and dirty

h

hɔ̀ŋ(s) n., swan
hoːŋ, lit. form of phɔːŋ, q.v.
hat v., practise
hạt(th) n., cubit
han v., cut up into small pieces
haːŋ n., store, big shop
haːp c., weight measurement = 60 kgrms.
haːm v., forbid, restrict
haːl v., spread out (in the air); haːl thŋay,
spread in the sun
haːsɤp x., fifty
hɤp n., trunk (luggage-container)
hoksɤp x., sixty
hoŋ c. n., reel n.
hoːpɔ̀ən, pɔ̀ən c., honour (of military insignia)
hoː(r) v., flow v.
huːəs v., pass, go beyond
haəy f., already
haəy m., then, after that, next
haəy-nùŋ m. pre n.p., and, with
haə(r) v., fly v.
hìəp-tae p.v.p., almost
hǎet(o) n., reason
hǎet(o)-ʔvɤy-baːn-cìːə m., why
hǎet(o)-tae m., because
heːŋ n., Heng (proper name)
hao c. n., packet, box (small)

hau v., call v. tr.; summon; be named, have
the name
(h)nɤŋ post n.p. (colloquial only), this;
(h)nɤŋ haəy! that's right! (I accept what
you say)
(h)nə, spelt (h)nɔː e., (used at end of sentence)
isn't that so?
(h)mɔt-cɔt v., precise, net
(h)voːŋ c. n., herd

ȟ

hɔ̀əp, see rɔ̀əp
hìːə n., (title used to Chinese or Vietnamese
male shopkeeper)
hìːən n., Hean (proper name)
hìːən v., dare (to)
hùp c. n., log (with bark and branches
removed)

ʔ

ʔ ̣ksɔː(r) (pronounced also ʔaksɔː) n., writing,
alphabet
ʔɔŋkɔː(r) n., husked rice
ʔɔŋkɔː(r)-vɔ̀ət(t) n., Angkor Vat
ʔɔŋkal a., when? (colloquial)
ʔɔŋkaːm n., bran
ʔɔŋkreːm-ʔɔŋkrɔːm n., name of a creeper
ʔɔ̀ŋ(k) c., (for monks)
ʔɔŋkùy v., sit
*ʔɔ̀ŋklèːs v., English
ʔɔ̀ŋcɤy a., so, if so, well then; baə ʔɔ̀ŋcɤŋ (id.)
ʔɔ̀ŋcɤ̀ːp v., invite to; please do
ʔɔ̀ŋcɤ̀ːŋ-tɤ̀u v., go (of respected person)
ʔɔ̀ŋcɤ̀ːŋ-mɔ̀ːk v., come (of respected person)
ʔɔt, ʔɤt p.v.p., not (colloquial)
ʔəndaək n., tortoise
ʔɔntrɤ̀ːt-ʔɔntrɤ̀ːt v., step on tiptoe
ʔɔnlùːŋ c., stroke of a mallet
ʔɔnlùːŋ n., mallet
ʔɔntèək n., snare n.
ʔɔnlɤ̀ː n., place
ʔɔp v., burn (leaves or petals) in order to
scent the container or in order to make
perfume
ʔɔmbɤl n., salt
ʔɔmpùəl v., trouble v. tr.
ʔɔmpì: pre n.p., about, concerning, of, from,
(made) of
ʔɔmpùl-ʔɔmpèːk n., glow-worm
ʔɔs pre n.p., the whole of, all the (single unit
of time)
ʔɔs v., all, whole, be at the end (of), (— have
exhausted supply (of)); ʔɔs kɔmlaŋ, tired
ʔɔː(r) (kùn) v., thank v.
ʔaɲ n. pron., I (familiar)
ʔạtthasák n., eighth of the cycles of twelve
years
ʔaphéy (tɔ̀ːs) v., take away (fear of punishment), forgive
ʔay-yaː e., help! crash!
ʔay-yoːy e., ooh! ouch!
ʔạssoɔ̀ n., September–October
ʔaː e., (familiar or derogatory effect on
following noun)
ʔaːkaːs n., air; phloːv ʔaːkaːs, air

ʔaːkrɔk v., bad
ʔaːc v., have the power to, dare to
ʔaːtùt(y) c. n., week
ʔaːtma: n. pron., I (monk to layman)
ʔaːtmaːphìːəp̀ n. pron., I (monk speaking to royalty)
ʔaːn v., pronounce, read aloud
*ʔaːnɔn(ì) n., Ananda
ʔaːnʁt v., be so kind as to, please
*ʔaːmeːrìːkaŋ n., American n.
*ʔaːmeːrìːkaŋ v., American
ʔaːyù v., aged —; be — years old
ʔaːv n., dress, blouse, shirt
ʔaːsaːì(h) n., June–July
ʔaːhaː(r) n., food
ʔʁt pre n.p., without
ʔʁt(th) n., brick
ʔʁy, ʔʁːy e., (occurs between two reduplicated words, with or without *kɔː); — ʔʁy —! or — ʔʁy *kɔː —, What a lot of —! How very —!
ʔʁy n. post n.p., see ʔvʁy
ʔʁy-khlah, see ʔvʁy-khlah
ʔʁy-mùːəy, see ʔvʁy-mùːəy
ʔʁy-ʔʁy, see ʔvʁy-ʔvʁy
*ʔʁyloːv a., now
*ʔʁyloːv=nìh a., now
*ʔʁyvan n., things, luggage
ʔʁː e., er (expressing hesitation)
ʔʁːy, see ʔaəy and ʔʁy
ʔobaːsɔk n., layman
ʔobaːsekaː n., laywoman
ʔom n., uncle (strictly the elder brother of one's parent)
ʔom v., riddle v. (i.e. to clean grain)
ʔom v., row v.
ʔom-pros n., uncle (strictly the elder brother of one's parent)
ʔom-sʁy n., aunt (strictly the elder sister of one's parent)
ʔos n., firewood
ʔosaphìːə n., May
*oːn n., you (husband to wife)
ʔoːpùk n., father
ʔoːpùk-mdaːy n., parents
ʔoːs v., pull along
ʔuːràːnùːə v., horrible
ʔaə r., yes (or merely a polite introduction to a reply by a person of superior rank)
ʔaəy, ʔʁːy e., oh! hail! hello! (used after title or name of person addressed)
ʔiən-khmaːs v., very shy
ʔiən-priən v., bashful
ʔeː e., hurray!
ʔeːp e., hey there!
ʔae pre n.p., to, at, as to, as for

ʔae-cɔmnaek pre n.p., with regard to, as to, as for
ʔae-tiət post n.p., other, another
ʔaekɑsák n., first of the cycles of twelve years
ʔaeŋ n. pron. post n.p., you (familiar), self
*ʔaep pre n.p., near
ʔao e., oh! (expressing surprise)
*ʔaoy m., so that, so as to, in order that, in order to
*ʔaoy pre n.p. (with a following attributive verb), for, in a — manner
*ʔaoy v., give, let (someone do . . . .), have (someone do . . . . for one)
*ʔaoy-tae m., so long as, provided that
ʔvʁy, ʔʁy or sʔʁy n., (in a question) what (English interrogative noun); (affirmative context) something; (negative, indefinite or emphatic context) anything
ʔvʁy, ʔʁy or sʔʁy post n.p., (in a question) what (English interrogative adjective); (affirmative context) some or other; (negative, indefinite or emphatic context) any
ʔvʁy-khlah, ʔʁy-khlah or sʔʁy-khlah n. (plur.), (in a question) what things, what (English interrogative noun); (affirmative context) some things; (negative, indefinite or emphatic context) any things
ʔvʁy-khlah, ʔʁy-khlah or sʔʁy-khlah post n.p. (plur.), (in a question) what (plur.) (English interrogative adjective); (affirmative context) some (plur.); (indefinite or emphatic context) any (plur.)
ʔvʁy-mùːəy, ʔʁy-mùːəy or sʔʁy-mùːəy n. (sing.), (in a question) what (English interrogative noun); (affirmative context) something; (negative, indefinite or emphatic context) anything
ʔvʁy-mùːəy, ʔʁy-mùːəy or sʔʁy-mùːəy post n.p. (sing.), (in a question) what (English interrogative adjective); (affirmative context) some; (negative, indefinite or emphatic context) any
ʔvʁy-ʔvʁy, ʔʁy-ʔʁy or sʔʁy-sʔʁy n. (plur.), (affirmative context) something or other, some things or other
ʔvʁy-ʔvʁy, ʔʁy-ʔʁy or sʔʁy-sʔʁy post n.p. (plur.), (affirmative context) some or other, various; (indefinite context) any at all, any whatever

ʔ

ʔìː, yìː, yèː e., oh! well! (expressing surprise)
ʔùː r., yes (or introduces a reply to inferior)
ʔùː-ʔùː v., murmuring

abate, *srɔːk* v.

abbot, *cau-ʔalthɨkaː(r)* n.

about, (= concerning) *ʔɔmpɨː, pɨː* pre n.p.; (= approximately) *prəhael* g.; about to, *stɨː-tae, stɨː-tae-nùŋ* p.v.p.

above, *lɨ̀ː* pre n.p. v., *nɨ̀u-lɨ̀ː* pre n.p.; (= exceeding) *lɨ̀ːs* v.

absent-minded, *tɔːy-nɔːy* v.

absolutely must, *troːv-tae* p.v.p.

accomplished, *stɘ̀t* v.

accordance, in accordance with what *taːm* m.

accordingly, **kɔː* m. p.v.p.

accustomed, *thlɔ̀əp* v.

achieve, *rùːəc* v.

act v. (in theatre), *lèːŋ* v.

addition, in addition *saot* f.

address n., *tɨ̀ː-lùmnɨ̀u* n.

administer, *cat kaː(r)*; *cat-caey* v.

administration, *rìːəc̀-kaː(r)* n.

aeroplane, *yùən(t)-hɔh, kɔpal-hɔh* n.

affable, *slɔ̀ːt-boːt* v.

afraid, *khlaːc-kraey* v.

after, (of time) *kraoy, kraoy-pɨː* m., *rùːəc-pɨː* pre n.p.; (of place and time) *kraoy* v. pre n.p.; after that, *rùːəc, haəy, rùːəc-haəy* m.

afternoon (2 p.m.–dusk), *lŋìːəc* n.; early afternoon (noon–2 p.m.), *rəsìəl* n.

again, *tìət* f., *mdɔːŋ tìət*; back again, *vèɲ* f.

aged, *ʔaːyù* v.

agree, *prɔ̀ːm, tətùːəl* v.

air, *ʔaːkaːs* n., *phloːv ʔaːkaːs*

airport, *cɔmnɔːt yùən(t)-hɔh*

alike, *dədael* v.

alive, *rùəs* v.

all, *sɔl-tae* p.v.p., *tɕəŋ-ʔɔs* post n.p. a., *tɕəŋ* pre n.p., *sɔ̀p̀(v), krùp, ʔɔs* v. pre n.p., *sɔ̀p̀(v)-krùp* v., *tɕəŋ-laːy* (lit.) post n.p. a., *mnɛ̀əl* e. (followed by title at beginning of speech); nearly all, *craən-tae* p.v.p.; at all, *(mùn) . . . . tèː, sɔh, laəy* f.

almost, *hìəp-tae* p.v.p.; (of time and place) *cùt-dɔl* pre n.p.; almost all, almost always, almost altogether, *sɨy-tae* p.v.p. (not colloquial)

alone, *mnɛ̀ək* post n.p. a., *mnɛ̀ək ʔaey*

along, *taːm, daoy* pre n.p.; go along, *taːm, daoy* v.

alphabet, *ʔɔksɔː(r)* n.

already, *haəy, rùːəc* f.; has/have already, *dael* p.v.p.

also, *dae(r), phoːŋ* f.

although, *dɓɨt, dɓɨt-tae, thvɨːy-dɓɨt-tae* m.

always, *ceh-tae* p.v.p., *cìːə nèc(c), cìːə dəraːp*

America, *srok-*ʔaːmeːrìːk* n.

American, **ʔaːmeːrìːkaŋ* v. n.

Ananda, **ʔaːnɔn(t)* n.

and, *haəy-nùŋ* m. pre n.p., *nɨ̀u* (written *nùːv*), *nìːə* (both lit.) pre n.p., *prɔ̀ːm-tɕəŋ* m. pre n.p., *nùŋ* m.; and then (next step in story) *haəy, rùːəc-haəy* m.; and . . . . and, *kdɨy . . . . kdɨy* f. (referring to what precedes)

anger, *kɔmhɨ̀ŋ* n.

Angkor Vat, *ʔɔŋkɔː(r)-vɔ̀ət(t)* n.

angry, *khɨ̀ŋ* v.

animal, *sɔt(v)* n.

another, *mùːəy tìət*

any, (indefinite, negative or emphatic context) *ʔvɨy, naː* post n.p.; (sing.) *ʔvɨy-mùːəy, naː-mùːəy* post n.p.; (indefinite or emphatic context) (plur.) *ʔvɨy-khlah, naː-khlah* post n.p.; any of any kind, any at all, (indefinite context) *naː-naː, ʔvɨy-ʔvɨy* post n.p.; at any time, (indefinite or emphatic context) *kaːl naː, pèːl naː*; to any extent, (negative, indefinite or emphatic context) *poɲmaːn* x; in any way, (emphatic context) *mĕc, dɔːc-mdĕc, a. yaːŋ naː, yaːŋ mĕc*

anyhow, (emphatic context) *dɔːc-mdĕc, a. yaːŋ mĕc, yaːŋ naː*

anyone, (negative, indefinite or emphatic context) *nɛ̀ək naː*

anything, (in negative or indefinite context) *ʔvɨy, ʔɨy* or *sʔɨy, ʔvɨy-mùːəy* n.; anything at all, (indefinite context) *ʔvɨy-ʔvɨy, ʔɨy-ʔɨy* n.

anywhere, (in negative, indefinite or emphatic context) *naː* n., *kɔnlaeŋ naː*; (= to any place) (negative, indefinite or emphatic context) *ʔae naː*

apart (from), *krau-pɨː* pre n.p.

April, *mèːsaː, khae-mèːsaː* n.

April–May, *pìsaːk(h)* or *vìsaːk(h), khae-pìsaːk(h)* or *khae-vìsaːk(h)* n.

areca, *slaː* n.

arise (impersonal v. = happen), *kaɘt* v. (used impersonally)

arm n., *day* n.

arrive, *dɔl* v.

as (= being), *cìːə* v. pre n.p.; as to, as for, *ʔae, cɔmnaek, ʔae-cɔmnaek, rɨ̀ː-ʔae* pre n.p.; as though, *dɔːc-cìːə* p.v.p.

ask, *sùːə(r)* v.; ask to, *sɔːm* v.; ask a favour, ask to do, *sɔːm* v.; ask in marriage, ask to marry, *dɔndɨ̀ŋ* v.

asleep, *lùək* v.

assemble v. tr., *prɔcùm* v.

at (of place), *ʔae, nɨ̀u, nɨ̀u-ʔae* pre n.p.; (of past time), *pɨː, kaːl-pɨː* pre n.p.; (= arriving at, as far as), *dɔl* v. pre n.p.; at all, *(mùn) . . . . tèː* f.

attack (with dagger), *kap—cak* v.—v.

attend, attend a marriage feast *sɨ̀ː kaː(r)*

attention, pay great attention, *prɔyɔt(n)-prɔyaeŋ* v.

August, *sɨyhaː, khae-sɨyhaː* n.

August–September, *phɔ̀ətrɛ̀əbɔ̀t, khae-phɔ̀ətrɛ̀əbɔ̀t* n.

aunt, *mìːŋ* (strictly the younger sister of a parent); *lòːk-mìːŋ* (very polite); *ʔom-sɨy* (strictly the elder sister of a parent) n.

avoid, *cìəs* v.; avoid a situation, *dɔh-day* v.

await, *cam* v.

aware, *dɨ̀ŋ khluːən*

axe, *pùːthau, pɔːvthau* n.

back, *khnɔːŋ* n.; *vèɲ* a.; turn back, *trəlɔp—mɔ̀ːk/tɨ̀u* v.

back-bone, *trənùŋ-khnɔːŋ* n.

bad, *ʔaːkrɔk* v.

bale, *kɔːŋ* c.

bamboo, **rùssɨy* n.; node of bamboo, *thnaŋ* c. n.

banana tree, *daəm-ceːk* n.
bang, *phoːŋ-phaːŋ* v.
banging, *poːk-paːk* v.
bargain, *dëŋ thlay, toː thlay*
bark v., *prùh* v.
barrel (of zinc, capacity 2 bushels), *thaŋ* c. n.
barter v., *doː(r)* v.
bashful, *ʔiən-priən* v.
basin (earthenware), *phaəŋ* c. n.
basket (capacity 1 bushel), *kɔɲcɤː* c. n.;
    small meshed basket with narrow neck
    and handle (capacity ½ bushel), *ciːəl* c. n.;
    basket (capacity ¼, ⅓ or ½ bushel), *kɔntaŋ*
    c. n.
Battambang, *bat-dɔmbɔːŋ* n.
be, *ciːə* v.; be as, *ciːə* v., *thvɤː ciːə*; be in, at,
    nɤu v.; being, *ciːə* pre n.p.; be, essentially,
    kùː v.; happen to be, be, *troːv ciːə*
bear n., *khlaː-khmùm* n.
bear (a child), *prəsoːt(e)* v.
beat = strike with fist or stick, *kùəh* v.;
    = cause gong to resound, *tùːŋ* v.; = against
    a firm surface, *baok* v.; = with flat of hand,
    baok v.; = beat each other with flat of
    hand, *prəbaok* v.
beautiful, *lʔɔː, prɤm-prɤy* v.; beautiful to
    hear, *pìːrùəh* v.
because, *pìː-prùəh, prùəh, prùəh-tae, daoy-
    saː(r), daoy-häet(o), häet(o)-tae, dɤt* m.
become, *thvɤː ciːə*
bed, *krèː* n.; bed of stream, *cɔŋhoː(r)* n.
beef, *sac-kòː* n.
before (of time), *tùmrɔəm, tùmrɔəm-dɔl, mùn-
    nuŋ* m. pre n.p.; *mùn* v. a. pre n.p.
beggar n., *smoːm* n.
begin, *phdaəm, taŋ, cap* v.
beginning, *daəm* n.
behind, *kraoy* v. pre n.p.
belonging n., *rəbɔs* n.; (plur.) *thùən-thìːən* n.
belonging to, *rəbɔs* pre n.p.
bend v. intr., *ŋìːək* v.
betel, *mlùː* n.
bewildered, *vùəŋvèːŋ* v.; (on waking) *saəŋ-
    maəŋ* v.
big, **thom* v.
bird, *sat(v)-haə(r)* n.
birth, *kɔmnaət* n.
bite v., *kham* v.; (of snake) *cɤk* v.
bitter, *cùː(r)* v.
black, *khmau* v.
blade, **səsay* c.
blessing, *pɔ̀ː(r)* n.
blouse, *ʔaːv* n.
blue, *khiəv* v.
boast (try to impress), *bɔŋʔuːət-bɔŋʔɔ̀ː* v.
boat, *tùːk* n.; sailing-boat, *tùːk-kdaoŋ* n.
boil v., *pùh* v.; boiled down to a semi-solid
    state, *rìːŋ* v.
bolt n., *sao(r)* n.
bolt v., *cak sao(r)*
book, *siəvphɤu* n., *kan* c. n.
born, be born, *kaət* v.
boss (master) n., *caːŋ-(h)vaːŋ* n.
both, *tèəŋ pìː(r)*; both sides, *soːŋkhaːŋ* a.
bow, bow and scrape, *pdaom-pdaom* v.
bowl, *caːn* n.
bowlful, *caːn* c.

box n., (small) *hao, prəʔɔp* c. n.; (big) *hɤp* n.
box v., *dal* v.
boy, *kmeːŋ-pros* n.; boys, men (plural),
    pros-pros n.
Brahma, *prèəh-prù(h)m* n.
brain, rack one's brains, *nùk* v.
bran, *ʔɔŋkaːm* n.
branch, *mèːk* n.
break v. intr., *baek* v.; (of string, thread)
    dac v.; break down, *khoːc* v.; break (string,
    thread) v. tr., *phdac* v.
brick, *ʔɤt(th)* n.
bridge, *spiːən* n.
bring, (things) *yɔ̀ːk—mɔ̀ːk*; (people) *nɔəm—
    mɔ̀ːk* v.—v.; bring up, *ceɲcɤm* v.
brother (older), *bɔːŋ-pros* n.; (younger),
    pʔoːn-pros n.; brothers and sisters, *bɔːŋ-
    pʔoːn* n.
brush past (nearly touch in passing), *pah* v.
bubble v., *krak-krak* v.
buffalo, *krəbɤy* n.
build, *sɔŋ* v.
building, *kèːhə(s)thaːn, ròːŋ* n.
bundle (of paddy, cane, etc.) small, *cɔntìːəs*
    c. n.; large, *bac* c. n.; (of palm-leaf manu-
    script pages), *khsae* c. n.
burglar, *cao(r)* n.
Burma, *srok-phùːmìːə* n.
Burmese, *phùːmìːə* v.
burn (leaves or petals in making perfume or
    to scent a container), *ʔɔp* v.
burrow, *rùːŋ* n.
bus, *laːn-chnuːəl* n.
bushel, *tau* c.; 2 bushels, *thaŋ* c.
business, *kaː(r)* n.; (= trade, commerce),
    cɔmnuːəŋ n.; do business, *cùːəŋ* v., *lùək
    doː(r)*; business-man, *chmùːəŋ* n.
bustle about, *rəvìːəs-rəvèy* v.
busy, *rəvùəl* v.; busy (in a whirl of activity),
    khvɔl-khvaːy v.
but, **kɔː-pontae, pontae, tae* m.
buy v., *tèɲ* v.
buzzing, *trəhuŋ-ʔɤːŋ-kɔːŋ* v.
by (= by means of or along by), *daoy, taːm*
    pre n.p.; (of future time), *mɔ̀ːk-dɔl* pre n.p.

cage, *trùŋ* n.
cake, *nùm* n.; name of a cake, *cak-can* n.
call v., *hau* v.; be called, have the name,
    hau v.; (of animals), *yùm* v.
call n., *mɔət* c.
Cambodia, *srok-khmae(r)* n.
Cambodian n. adj., *khmae(r)* n. v.
capture v., *cap-coːŋ* v.
car, *laːn* n.
careful, *prəyát(n)-prəyaeŋ, proŋ-prəyát(n)* v.
carefully, *daoy sëckdɤy prəyát(n)-prəyaeŋ*
careless, *phdeːs-phdaːs* v.
carry, *yɔ̀ːk* v.; (on head), *tùːl* v.; (in mouth),
    pɔ̀əm v.; (on back or shoulder), *prənèək* v.
cart, *rətèh* n.
cartload, *rətèh* c.
cat, *chma:* n.
catch v., *cap* v.; (= be in time for), *tɔən* v.;

catch up with, *tɔən* v.; catch drips (as in filtering a liquid), *trɔːŋ* v.
cease, *chùp, lɛ̀ːŋ* v.
celebrate, *thvɤː (boŋ(y))* v.
celebration, *boŋ(y)* n.
cent, *seːn* c.
centimetre, *sɔŋtìːmaet(r)* c.
century, *sakraːc̀* c. n.
certain (plur.), *khlah* post n.p.; a certain number, *poñmaːn* x (affirmative context); a certain, *mùːɔy* x, *naː-mùːɔy, ʔvɤy-mùːɔy* post n.p. (affirmative context)
certificate, *saɲɲaːbɑt(r), likhɤt* n.
chaff, *combaɔŋ* n.
chair, **kauʔɤy* n.
champ, *krop-krop* v.
change n., *doː(r)* n.; give change, *doː(r)* v.
channel (for irrigation), *prəlaːy* n.
chapter, *cɔmpùːk* or *cùmpùːk* c. n.
character (in a play), *tuːə* c.
chase v., *dëɲ* v.
cheap, *thaok* v.
chief n., *mèː* n.
child, *koːn, kmeːŋ; kmeːŋ-pros* (male); *kmeːŋ-srɤy* (female) n.; small children, *kmeːŋ-kmaːŋ* n.
Chinese, *cɤn* n.
choice, *cùmrɤ̀ːs* n.
choose, *rɤ̀ːs, rɤ̀ːs-rɔ̀ːk* v.
chopsticks, **cɔŋkɤh* n.
cigarette, *baːrɤy* n.
Ciné Luxe, *sìːneːlùk(s)* n.
cinema, *ròːŋ-kon* n.
circle, *vùəŋ* j.
circular, *krəvɔŋ* v.
city, *tìː-kroŋ* n.
clang, make a repeated clanging sound, *kdoŋ-kdaŋ* v.
class (in school), *thnak* c. n.; social class, *cɔmnaek* c. n.
clattering, *poːk-paːk* v.; clattering down, *toːŋ-taːŋ* v.
clean v. tr., *sɔmʔaːt* v.; (by picking, sifting), *sɑsɤt* v.
cleaned, *sʔaːt* v.
clear adj., *cbas* v.; (= free from), *srəlah* v.
clever, *prəsɔp, pùːkae, chlaːt* v.
climb v., *laəŋ* v.
close adj. adv., *cùt* v.
cloth, *sɔmpùət* n.
clothes, (= what one wears) *sɔmliək-bɔmpèak*; (= what one washes) *khao-ʔaːv* n.
clump n., *kùm(p̀)* c. n.
cluster (e.g. of fruit), *cɔŋkaom* c. n.
coax, *bɔŋcaɔc-bɔŋcaɔ* v.
cock, *mɔ̀ən; rəkaː* (in names of years) n.
coconut, *doːŋ* n.
coincide, coincide with, *troːv cìːə*
cold, *rəŋìːə* v.
collect (of water forming a pool), *dɔk* v.
collection (of books or papers), *kùmpìː* c.
colour, *p̀ɔ̀ə(rn)* n.
comb v., *sɤt* v.
come, *mɔːk* v.; (of respected persons), *ʔɔŋcɤ̀ːɲ-mɔːk* v.; (of monks), *nìmùən(t)-mɔːk* v.; come in (house), *laəŋ* v.; come now—*coːl* (sp. *coːr*) m.

comedian, *nèək-tlok, tlok* n.
comfortable, *sruːəl, srənok-srənaːn* v.
commemorate, *rùmlùk* v.
common, *khsaːy* v.
company (e.g. theatrical), *vùəŋ* c.; in company with, *cìːə-mùːəy-nùŋ* pre n.p.
compare, *priəp-phtùm, prədoːc* v.
compel forcibly, *tɤŋ-rɤŋ* v.
complete, *sɔp̀(v)-krùp, kùmrùp* v.
completion, to completion *rùːəc* v. (2nd v.)
concerned with, *rəvùəl dɔl*
concerning, *ʔɔmpìː, pìː* pre n.p.
conclude, *kùt—khɤ̀ːɲ* v.—v.
conclusion, come to a conclusion *nùk—khɤ̀ːɲ* v.—v.
confined (lacking in space), *cɔŋʔiət* v.
confused (not clear), *tətìːm-tətìːəm* v.
consider, *kùt* v.
constantly, *ceh-tae̲* p.v.p.
content, *sok(h)-sɔ̲pbaːy* v.
continually, *kùəŋ-tae, nɤu-tae* p.v.p.; from then continually, *tɔː-tɤu, tɔː-tɔː-tɤu* f.; from then continually until now, *tɔː-mɔ̀ːk, tɔː-tɔː-mɔ̀ːk; rìəŋ-mɔ̀ːk* f.
continue, *tɔː* v.
cook n., *cɔŋphɤ̀u* n.
cook v., *dam* v.
cool, *trəcèak* v.
copy, *cbap* c. n.
coral, *phkaː-thmɔː* n.
cork (stopper), *chnok* n.
cork v., *cok* v.
corner, *kiən* n., *crùŋ* c. n.
correct adj., *troːv* v.
correctly, *troːv* v.
cost n. v., *thlay* n. v.
country, *srok* n.; country people, *nèək-srok* n.
course (of a meal), *mùk(h)* c. n.
cow, *kòː* n.
crackle, *preh-preh* v.
crash! *ʔay-yaː* e.
creeper (name of a variety of creeper), *ʔɔŋkreːm-ʔɔŋkrɔːm* n.
criss-cross, *caeŋ-vaeŋ* v.
crockery, *caːn-kbaːn* n.
crocodile, *krəpɤ̀ː* n.
cross, *khɤŋ* v.
crunch, *krùːəp-krùːəp* v.
crush v., *kɤn* v.
cry n., *mɔ̀ət* c.
cry v., *yùm* v.; cry out, *sraek* v.
cubit, *hɑt(th)* c.
cucumber, *trəsok* n.
cup, *pèːŋ* n.; (small), *pèːŋ-coːk* n.
cupboard, *tùː* n.
cupful, *pèːŋ* c.; (small), *pèːŋ-coːk* c.
custom, *tùmlɔ̀əp* n.
cut v., *kat* v.; cut open v. tr., *vèəh* v.; cut down with a scythe, *croːt* v.; cut up in small pieces v. tr., *han, ceñcram* v.; be cut, *mùt* v.; be cut in several places, *rəlɔ̀ət-rəlɔ̀ːc* v.; a cut piece, *kɑmnat* c. n.
cycle (of one year), *khuːəp* c.
cycle (of 12 years), *sák* c.
cyclo, *sìːklo* n.
cyclo-driver, *nèək-thèək-sìːkloː* n.

damp, *saəm* v.
dance v., *rɔəm* v.; name of a dance, *kɔntae-rae* n.
dare v., *hì:ən*, *ʔa:c* v.
dark, *ŋəŋùt* v.
daughter, *kɔ:n-srʏy* n.
dawn, *prəlùm*, *phlù:* n.
day, *thŋay* c. n.
dead, *ŋɔ̀əp* v.
deaf, *thlɔŋ* v.
deafened, *thlɔŋ* v.
dear (= expensive), *thlay* v.
deceive, *bɔɲchaot* v.
December, *thnù:*, *khae-thnù:* n.
December–January, *bos(s)*, *khae-bos(s)* n.
decide, *dac cʏt(t)*; (= make a legal decision), *kat sëckdʏy*
decimetre, *de:sì:maet(r)* c.
deep, *crɤu* v.
deer, *praəs* n.
degree certificate, *saɲɲa:bạt(r)* n.
delighted, *tre:k-ʔɔ:(r)* v.
democrat, **prəcì:əthìpdʏy(y)* n.
democratic party, **kəŋạʔ-*prəcì:əthìpdʏy(y)* n.
dented, *pìəc* v.
department, **krom* n.
depend on, *sräc nùŋ*
depressed, *pìba:k cʏt(t)*
deserve, *tro:v* v.
design n., *kbac* v.
despise, *chʔaəm-khpʏ̀:m* v.
destitute, *khsɔt*, *kɔmsɔt* v.
destroy utterly, *bɔmphlec-bɔmphla:ɲ* v.
dew, *sɔnsaəm* n.
die v., *slap* v.
different, *khos*, *phse:ŋ*, *laek* v.; (and therefore of interest), *plaek* v.; (and numerous), *phse:ŋ-phse:ŋ* v.
difficult, *pìba:k*, *lùmba:k* v.; (very), *lùmbe:k-lùmba:k* v.
diffident, *rʔeh-rʔoh* v.
diffuse v. tr., *phsa:y*, *pùəŋrì:k* v.
dig, *cì:k* v.; (scratch the earth's surface), *kəka:y* v.
dilly-dally, *bɔŋʔae-bɔŋʔɔŋ* v.
dine, *bərephò:k* v.
direct adj., *cɔm* v.
direction, *kha:ŋ* n.; in the direction of, *kha:ŋ pre n.p.*
directly, *cɔm*, *trɔŋ pre n.p.*; move directly towards, *trɔŋ* v.
director, *ca:ŋ-(h)va:ŋ* n.
dirty, *krəkhvɔk* v.
disappear, *bat* v.
disc, *phaen* n.
discuss a matter, *kùt ka:(r)*
disperse, *cat* v.
distance, *cɔmŋa:y* n.
district, (administrative group of villages), *khùm*; (wider area), *srok* n.; people of the district, *nɛ̀ək-srok* n.
disturbed (troubled), *krəvɔl-krəva:y* v.
divided, *caek* v.
dizzy, *vùl mùk(h)*
do, *thvʏ̀:* v.; do not, *kom* p.v.p.; do, go on! *cɔh*, *tʏ̀u*, *sʏn!* f.; do with might and main, *pɛ̀ɲ-lɛ̀ɲ*, *rùŋ-pʏ̀ŋ* v.

doctor, *krù:-pɛ̀:t̀(y)* n.
dog, *chkae*; (in names of years), *cɔ:* n.
donkey, *lì:ə* n.
door, *tvì:ə(r)* n.
down, go down, *coh* v.
dragging (of sound), *krùt:t-krùt:t* v.
dragon (in names of years), *rò:ŋ* n.
draw (pictures), *kù:* v.
drawer (in table), *thɔ:t-*tok* n.
drawing, *kùmnù:* n.
dream v., *yùəl sɔp(t)*
dress n., *ʔa:v* n.
dried up, *rì:ŋ* v.; dried and salted, *ŋìət* v.
drink (soft), *tùk-phè:sạcɛ̀ə*
drink v., *phʏ̀k* v.; *phʏ̀k tùk*; (of monks), *chan* v.; have a drink (animals), *phʏ̀k tùk*
drip-drip, *prèc-prèc* v.
drive v., (a car), *baək*; (any vehicle or animal), *bɔ:(r)*; (animals before one), *kìəŋ* v.; drive in (e.g. a stake), *bɔh* v.
driver, **sɔ:(h)vɔ̀ə(r)* n.
drum, *skɔ̀:(r)* n.
dry (rainless), *praŋ* v.; dry land, *kò:k* n.
dusk, *prəlùp* n.
dust n. (which falls off from husked rice when it is riddled to clean it), *kɔntùək* n.
dust v., *cù:t* v.
duties, *ka:(r)-ŋì:ə* n.

each, *mù:əy-mù:əy* v., *nìmù:əy post n.p.*; each other, *knì:ə* a.
ear, *trəcìək* n.
earn, earn a living, *rɔ̀:k-sì:* v.
earth, *dʏy* n.
ease, with ease, *tɛ̀əŋ ŋì:əy*
easily, *tɛ̀əŋ ŋì:əy*
easy, *ŋì:əy*, *srənok* v.
eat v., *tətù:əl tì:ən*, *bərephò:k* v.; (polite of other people), *pìsa:*, *pì:sa:* v.; (family word), *ɲam* v.; (of animals or persons very familiarly), *sì:* v.; (of monks), *chan* v.
echo, *tətù:(r)-tətɔ̀ə(r)* v.
edge (of water), *mɔ̀ət* n.
eight, *pram-bʏy* x
eighteen, *pram-bʏy-dɔndɔp*, *dɔp-pram-bʏy* x
eighty, *paetsʏp* x
either (conj.), **rù:* m.; **kɔ:-daoy*, **kɔ:-ba:n*, **kɔ:-mì:ən* f.; either .... or **rù:* .... **rù:* m.; (emphasizing the possibilities), **kɔ:-daoy* .... **kɔ:-daoy* f.; (potential possibilities), **kɔ:-ba:n* .... **kɔ:-ba:n* f.; (definite alternatives), **kɔ:-mì:ən* .... **kɔ:-mì:ən*, *kdʏy* .... *kdʏy* f.
either adv., (not) .... either, *dae(r)* f.
elder (brother or sister), *bɔ:ŋ* n.; elder brother, *bɔ:ŋ-pros* n.; elder sister, *bɔ:ŋ-srʏy* n.
elect, *rʏ̀:s-taŋ* v.
elephant, *dɔmrʏy*, *sạt(v)-dɔmrʏy* n.
elephant-driver, *trəmɛ̀ək* n.
eleven, *mù:əy-dɔndɔp*, *dɔp-mù:əy* x
embellishment, *lùmʔɔ:(r)* n.
embers, *rùmŋʏ̀:k phlʏ̀:ŋ*
enclosure (enclosed space), *kraol* n.; small enclosure, *trùŋ*, n.

end, end the show, *va: rò:ŋ*; get to the end, *cɔp* v. c.; *rù:ɔc* v.; be at end of (= have exhausted supply of), *ʔɔs* v.

endure (= put up with), *trɔ̀ɔm* v.

England, *srok-*ʔɔŋklè:s* n.

English, **ʔɔŋklè:s* v.

enough, *lmɔ̀:m, krɔ̀ɔn-baɔ* v.

enquire, *dɔndɣŋ* v.

enter, *co:l* v.; (house), *laɔy* v.; cause to enter, *bɔŋco:l* v.

entrance, *tvì:ə(r)* n.

era, Buddhist era, *putthɛ̀ɔsɑkra:č* n.; Christian era, *krì:stɑsɑkra:č* n.

escape, *ciɔs—phot* v.—v.; *rù:ɔc* v. (*pì:* from); escape with one's life, *rù:ɔc cì:vùt*

etcetera, *cì:ə daɔm*

Europe, *srok-ba:raŋ* n.

European, *ba:raŋ* v.

even, *so:mbɣy* g.; even if, *tùəh, tùəh-cì:ə, tùəhbɣy* m.; **kɔ:-daoy* f. (refers to what precedes); even so, *dae(r)* f.

evening, (if still light or if time stated), *lŋì:ɔc* n.; (if at dusk), *prəlùp* n.; (if dark), *yùp* n.

event, *rùɔy* n.

ever, *dael* p.v.p. (has/have ever); if ever, *ka:l-baɔ, ka:l-na:-baɔ* m.; ever since, *tɔ:-pì:, taŋ-pì:* m. pre n.p.; *tɔ:-tɔ:-mɔ̀:k* f.; *rɔ̀ɔl* pre n.p.; *sɔ́p̀(v)* pre n.p.; *krùp* v. pre n.p.; absolutely every, *rɔ̀ɔl-tae* pre n.p.

exact, *pra:kɔ̀t, tìɔŋ-tɔ̀ɔt* v.

examination, sit for an examination, *prəlɔ:ŋ* v.; pass an examination, *cɔ̀ɔp* v.; fail an examination, *thlèɔk* v.

examine, *pìnùut(y)* v.

exceeding, *cì:ɔy* pre n.p.

exception, without exception, *sol-tae* p.v.p., *sɔ́p̀(v)-krùp* v.

excess, in excess of, *cì:ɔy* pre n.p.

excessive (especially of tears), *rəhe:m-rəha:m* v.

excuse, give a good excuse, *bɔndɔh-bɔnday* v.

expensive, *thlay* v.

explain, *sɔmdaeŋ* v.

exposition (of the Buddhist Law), *tè:sna:* n.

expound, *tè:sna:* v.

extend (the hand), *chò:ŋ* v.

extent, to a small extent, *bɔntec-bɔntu:ɔc* a.; to a greater extent, *cì:ɔy* a.; to a greater extent than, *cì:ɔy* pre n.p.; to whatever extent, to any extent, *poñma:n* x (negative or emphatic context)

extinguish, *rùmlùɔt* v.; extinguished, *rɔlùɔt* v.

eye, *phnè:k* n.

face n., *mùk(h)* n.

fall (from a height), *thlèɔk* v.; fall over, *du:ɔl* v.; fall out of friends, *baek cɣt(t)*; let fall, *tùmlèɔk* v.

family, *krù:ɔsa:(r)* n.

fan, *phlɣt* n.

far, *chŋa:y* v.; as far as, *dɔl* v. pre n.p.; *rəho:t-dɔl* pre n.p.

farmer, *nèɔk-srae* n.

father, *ʔo:pùk, lò:k-pa:* n.

fathom, *pyì:ɔm* c.

favour n., *tì:ɔn* n.; ask a favour, *so:m* v.

fear v., *kraeŋ* v. (mild fear as in 'I am afraid I can't come'); *khla:c* v.

feast, attend a marriage feast, *sì: ka:(r)*

February, *komphɛ̀ɔ, khae-komphɛ̀ɔ* n.

February–March, *phɔlkùn, khae-phɔlkùn* n.

fence, *rəbo:ŋ* n.

festival, *bon(y)* n.; Water Festival, *bon(y) ʔom tù:k* (row boat)

fête, *bon(y)* n.

fever, have a fever, *krùn* v.

few, a few, *poñma:n* x (affirmative context)

fifteen, *pram-dɔndɔp, dɔp-pram* x

fifty, *ha:sɣp* x

film, *kon* n.

find v., *rɔ̀:k—khɣ̀:ŋ* v.—v.

fine (finely cut or ground), *lʔɣt* v.

finger, *mrì:ɔm* n.; finger's width, *thnɔ̀ɔp* c.

finish v., *rù:ɔc* v. (+ v.); *haɔy* v.; (= complete v. tr.), *bɔŋhaɔy* v.; finished, *sräc-bac* v.; try to finish a piece of work with care, *sɔmru:ɔc-sɔmraŋ* v.

fire, *phlɣ̀:ŋ* n.; be on fire, catch fire, *cheh* v.; set fire to, *dot*

firewood, *ʔɔs* n.

fish, *trɣy* n.; dried fish, *trɣy-ŋìɔt* n.

five, *pram* x

fix v., *kɔmnɔt* v.

flash here and there, *prì:ɔt-prò:ŋ* v.

flat, low-lying, *rì:ɔp* v.; flat place, *vì:ɔl* n.

flatten, *phde:k* v.

flatter, immoderately, *bɔŋcaɔc-bɔŋcaɔ* v.

flesh, *sac* n.

flicker, *ploŋ-ploŋ* v.

float, *rəpaoy-rəpaoy* v.

floor, *rənì:ɔp* n.

flow, *ho:(r)* v.; cause to flow, *bɔŋho:(r)* v.; flowing freely, *sɔsrak, sɔsre:k-sɔsra:k* v.

flower n., *phka:* n.

flower-garden, *su:ɔn-phka:* n.

fly v., *haɔ(r)* v.

follow, *ta:m* v.; following, *ta:m* pre n.p.

food, *ʔa:ha:(r), cɔmnɣy, cɔmnɣy-ʔa:ha:(r), ba:y* (cooked rice) n.; (of monks), *cɔŋhan* n.; name of a culinary dish, *chù:-chì:* n.

foot, *cɣ̀:ŋ* n.

for, **ʔaoy* v. (2nd) p.v.p.; *cù:n* v. (2nd) (polite)

forbid, *ha:m* v.

forest, *prèy* n.

forget, *phlèc* v.

forgive, *mè:tta:* v.

fork, n., *cɔ:p* n.

form, *rù:p-rì:ɔŋ* n.

forth, *tɣ̀u* f.; (until now), *mɔ̀:k* f.

forty, *saesɣp* x; *phlo:n* c. (used in counting fruit and vegetables)

four, *bu:ɔn* x; *dɔmbɔ:(r)* c. (used in counting fruit and vegetables)

four hundred, *slɣk* c. (used in counting fruit and vegetables)

fourteen, *bu:ɔn-dɔndɔp, dɔp-bu:ɔn* x

fox, *kɔŋcrò:ŋ* n.

fowl, *mɔ̀ɔn* n.

France, *srok-ba:raŋsaes* n.

free v. tr., *dɔh* v.; free (uncluttered, unhampered), *phot* v.; free (for leisure, at leisure), *tùmnè:* v.; get free from, *cìəs—phot* v.—v.; free (clear of), *srəlah* v.; freed, *rədɔh* v.

French adj. and n. (people and languages), *ba:raŋsaes, ba:raŋ* v.

frequent, *nèc(c), rùəy-rùəy* v.

fresh, *srɔs* v.; (of atmosphere), *trəcèək* v.

Friday, *thŋay-sok(r)* n.

friend, *mùt(t)-sɔmlaɲ* or *mùt(r)-sɔmlaɲ, sɔmlaɲ* n.; fall out of friends, *baek cɤt(t)*

friendship, *mè:trɤyphi:əp* n.

frivolous, *leh-lɔh* v.

from (of place or time), *pì:, ʔɔmpì:* pre n.p.; (of time), *taŋ-pì:* pre n.p.

front, *mùk(h)* n.; in front of, *mùk(h), nʌu-mùk(h)* pre n.p.

fruit, *phlae, phlae-chʌ:* n.

fry v. tr., *cha:* v.

full, *pèɲ* v.

funny, *kɔmplaeŋ* v.

further, *tìət* f.

game, *lbaeŋ* n.

gaping, with gaping mouth, *mhɔ:p-mhɔ:p* v.

garden, *su:ən, su:ən-phka:* n.

garland, *kɔmrɔ:ŋ* c. n.; garland of flowers, *kɔmrɔ:ŋ-phka:* n.

gather (= pluck), *beh* v.

gather together, *prəmɔ:l* v.

general n., **se:na:pədɤy* n.

get, *ba:n* v.; get in, on (vehicle of any kind), *cìh* v.

gift, *tì:ən* n.

girl, *kme:ŋ-srʌy* n.; girl of marriageable age, *krəmom* n.

give, **ʔaoy* v.

gloomy, *trəmùŋ-trəmʌ:y* v.

glow-worm, *ʔɔmpùl-ʔɔmpè:k* n.

go, *tʌu* v.; (of monks), *nimùən(t)-tʌu* v.; (of respected persons), *ʔɔɲcʌ:ɲ-tʌu* v.; go in, *cɔ:l* v.; go in, by (vehicle), *cìh* v.; go in (house), *laəŋ* v.; go out, *cèɲ* v.; go round, *pɔ̀ət(ìh)* v.; go up, *laəŋ* v.

goat, *məmè:* n. (in names of years)

gong, *rəkèəŋ* n.

good, *lʔɔ:* v.; good to hear, *pì:rùəh* v.; good afternoon, good morning, *cùmri:əp-su:ə(r)* v. (general greeting, used at any time of day)

goodbye, *su:əsdɤy* e., *lì:ə* v. (= depart); say goodbye, *sɔ:m lì:ə*

goods, *tùmnèɲ* n.

Government, *rì:əc-ka:(r)* n.

gracupeia nigricollis, *krəlè:ŋ-krəlò:ŋ* n.

gram, 3·75 grams, *cì:* c.; 600 grams, *nì:əl* (= 1 lb.) c.

gramophone, *ma:sì:n-crìəy* n.

granary, *cùəŋrùk* n.

grandchild, *cau* n.

grand-daughter, *cau-srʌy* n.

grandfather, *cì:-ta:, ta:* n.

grandmother, *cì:-do:n, do:n, yì:əy* n.

grandparents, *cì:-do:n-cì:-ta:, do:n-ta:* n.

grandson, *cau-pros* n.

grass, *smau* n.; name of a grass, *caeŋ-vaeŋ* n.

greed, *lò:p̀(h)* n.

green, *baytɔ:ŋ* v.

greet, *cùmri:əp-su:ə(r)* v.; (by placing palms together as a salute), *sɔmpèəh, sɔmpèəh-su:ə(r)* v.; (to elevated persons), *thva:y bɔŋkùm*

groping, *pì:m-pʌ:m* v.

ground, *dɤy* n.

group, *pù:ɔk, vùəŋ* c. n., **krom* n.; (of friends), *phùən-phìən* n.

grow v. intr., *dɔh* v.; grow rapidly, *dɔh-da:l* v.; grow profusely, with overhanging branches, *sùp-trùp* v.

grow v. tr., *dam* v.

grown up, *cas* v.

grumble, *tʔɔ:ɲ-tʔae(r)* v.

guard v., *cam* v.

guess v., *sma:n* v.

guest, *phɲìəv* or *phɲìəv* n.

habit, have the habit of, *taeŋ* v.

habitually, *cɔmnam-tae, taeŋ-tae, rè:ŋ-tae, rəmè:ŋ-tae* p.v.p.

hairy (untidily), *srəmo:m-srəma:m* v.

half, *kɔnlah* c. n.; (of a symmetrically-shaped object), *cɔmhìəŋ* c. n.

hall, *rò:ŋ, sa:la:* n.

hand, *day* n.

handspan, *cɔmʔa:m* c.

hang, hang in tatters, *kɔntre:k-kɔntra:k* v.; hang on (tr.), wear, *pèək* v.

happen, *cù:ən, kaət* v. (both used impersonally)

happiness, *sèckdɤy sok(h)* n.

happy, *sɔp̀ba:y, sok(h), srənok-srəna:n* v.

hard, *rùŋ* v.; try hard, *khɔm* v.; work hard, *khɔm thvʌ̀: ka:(r)*

hardly, *mùn-so:v* p.v.p.; (= only just), *krɔ̀ən-tae* p.v.p.

hare, *thɔh* n. (in names of years)

harm, do harm to, *thvʌ̀: ba:p*

hate, *sʔɔp* v.

have, *mì:ən* v.; have (to), *trɔ:v* v.; have (someone do something for one), **ʔaoy* v. (*kè: thvʌ̀: . . . .*)

he (familiar), *vì:ə, knì:ə* n. pron.; (respectful), *kɔ̀ət, kè:* n. pron.

head n., *kba:l* n.

heap, *kùmnɔ̀:(r)* c. n.; heap up, *kɔ̀:(r)* v.

hear, **lùː* v.; hear (intentionally), manage to hear, be able to hear, *sdap—*lùː* v.—v.

heart (= feeling), *cɤt(t)* n.

heavy, *thɲùən* v.

height, *kɔmpùəs* n.

hello! *su:əsdɤy* e.

help, *cù:əy* v.; help each other with work (special word particularly used in connection with harvesting), *vè:(r)* v.; help! *ʔay-ya:* e.

hen, *mɔ̀ən* n.

herb, *phè:səcèə* n.

herd, (h)*vo:ŋ* c. n.

herd v., *kìəŋ* v.

herself, *khlu:ən vì:ə, khlu:ən kɔ̀ət, khlu:ən nì:əŋ*

hide, *lèək* v.

high, *khpùəs* v.

high-ranking, *khpùəŋ-khpùəs* v.

hill, *phnùm* n.
hillock, *traok* (lit. word) n.
himself, *khlu:ən vì:ə, khlu:ən kɔ̀ət*
hit, *vay* (spelt and read as *vì:əy*) v.; (with flat of hand), *tɛ̀əh* v.
hoard secretly, *sɔmcaə-sɔmcay* v.
hobble, *khvɤ̀:c-khvɤ̀:c* v.
hoe, *cɔ:p-kap* n.
hold, *kan* v.
home, *phtɛ̀əh* n.
honour, *hɔ:pɔ̀ən* c. (of military insignia)
hope, *sɔŋkhùm* n. v.; *mì:ən sɔŋkhùm .... tha: ....* (hope *....* that *....*)
horrible, *ʔu:əti:nù:ə* v.
horse, *seh; məmì:* (in names of years) n.
hospital, *phtɛ̀əh-pɛ̀:l̀(y)* n.
hot, *kdau* v.
hotel, *phtɛ̀əh-sɔmnak* n.
hour, *maoŋ* c. n.
house, *phtɛ̀əh* n.
householder, *mcas-phtɛ̀əh* n.
how, *ya:ŋ na:; mɛ̆c, do:c-mdɛ̆c* a.; how *....!* (exclamation), — *ʔɤy* —*! — *ʔɤy *kɔ:* —*! (with same verb before and after); how many, much, *poñma:n* x
however, *kɔ:-poñlae, poñlae, tae* m.; however many, much, *poñma:n* (emphatic context) x
hubbub, making a hubbub, *chao-lao* v.
humming, *trəhùŋ-ʔɤ:ŋ-kɔ:ŋ* v.
hundred, *rɔ̀:y* x; hundred thousand, *saen* x; four hundred (of fruit and vegetables), *slɤk* c.
hungry, *khlì:ən* v.
hurrah! *čéy-yò:(č)* e.
hurry, *prəɲap* v.; in a great hurry, *prəɲap-prəɲal* v.
hurt adj., *cok* v.
husband, *pdɤy, lò:k-pros* n.
husk, *srəkɤy, sɔmdɤy* or *sɔndɤy* n.

I, *khɲom, yɤ̀:ŋ*; (familiar), *ʔaɲ*; (male to superior), *khɲom-ba:l̀*; (female to superior), *ni:əŋ-khɲom*; (layman or laywoman to monk), *khɲom-*kəna:, khɲom-kɔ:rəna:*; (a Buddha speaking), *təthaːkùət*; (monk speaking), *ʔa:tma:*; (monk's word to royalty), *ʔa:tma:phì:əp*; (male speaker to high-ranking royalty), *tù:l-prɛ̀əh-bɔŋkùm-ci:ə-khɲom*; (male speaker to lower-ranking royalty), *tù:l-bɔŋkùm-ci:ə-khɲom* (to lowest rank of royalty or female low-ranking royalty), *tù:l-bɔŋkùm*; (female speaker to royalty), *khɲom-mcas*; (lesser mandarin to higher), *khɲom-prɛ̀əh-ba:l̀-mcas*; (servant to master), *khɲom-prɛ̀əh-ba:l̀-tì:ən, khɲom-prəba:l̀-tì:ən, prəba:l̀-tì:ən* or *prɛ̀əh-ba:l̀-tì:ən* n. pron.
if, *baə, baə-sɤn-na:, baə-sɤn-na:-cì:ə, baə-ka:l-na:, ka:l-baə, prəsɤn-baə, prəsɤn-cì:ə, baə-prəsɤn-cì:ə* m.; if ever, *ka:l-na:-baə* m.; even if, *tùəh, tùəh-cì:ə, tùəhbɤy* m.
ignorant, *khlau, kɔmlau* v.
ill, *chù:* v.
immediately, *phlì:əm* a.; *srap-tae* p.v.p. m.; get on with it immediately, *sɤn* f.

important (person), *(lò:k)* **thom*
impudent, *k̀le:ŋ-k̀lɔ:ŋ* v.
in, *knoŋ, nɤ̀u-knoŋ* pre n.p.
inclining towards, *chiəŋ* v.
include, including all, *tɛ̀əŋ* pre n.p.
incoherent, *rəvɤ̀:-rəvì:əy* v.
increase (v. intr.), *kaən* v.
increase (v. tr.), *bɔŋkaən* v.
increasingly, *kan-tae* p.v.p.; **rùt-tae* p.v.p. (less colloquial)
indecisive, *ŋae-ŋɔ:* v.
indeed, *tɛ̀:* f. (giving emphasis to a preceding verb usually negative); *dae(r)* f. (giving emphasis to a preceding verb usually affirmative)
India, *srok-*klɤŋ(k̀)* n.
Indian, **klɤŋ(k̀)* v.
indulgence (= kind forgiveness), *sɛ̆ckdɤy ʔanùkrùəh* n.
inert, *sɤ̀:k-sɤ̀:k* v.
inform, *cùmrì:əp* v.
information, *dɔmnɤŋ lʔɔ:*
insignia, *sak(te)* n.
instead of, *cù:əs, cùmnù:əs* pre n.p.
intend (to), *nùŋ* p.v.p.
interesting, *plaek, cɔmlaek* v.
inter-related, *tɛ̀ək-tì:əm* v.
invite, *ʔɔpcɤ̀:p, bəbu:əl* v.; (monks), *nimùən(t)* v.
irrigate, *bɔŋhoː(r) tùk cɔ:l*
it, *vì:ə* n. pron. (chiefly for animals; for objects, noun is repeated or all reference absent)
item, *mùk(h), prəka:(r)* c. n.
itself, *khlu:ən vì:ə*

January, *mɛ̀əkɐra:, khae-mɛ̀əkɐra:* n.
January–February, *mì:ək̀(h)* n.; Festival held in January–February, *mì:əkh-bo:cì:ə* n.
Japan, *srok-cɛ̀əpon* n.
jar, *dɔ:p* c. n. (earthenware, for water, with lid); *khap* c. n.
javelin, *lùmpɛ̀:ŋ* n.
jewel, *tbo:ŋ* n.
journey, *dɔmnaə(r)* n.
July, *khae-kɐkda:* n.
July–August, *sra:p̀(+ ǹ)* n.
jump v., *lò:t* v.
June, *mìthona:, khae-mìthona:* n.
June–July, *ʔa:sa:l̀(h), khae-ʔa:sa:l̀(h)*
just, *tae*, g.; have just, *tɤ̀:p-tae, tɤ̀:p-tae-nùŋ, tɤ̀:p-nùŋ* p.v.p.; just now, *kɔmpùŋ-tae* p.v.p.; only just, *krɔ̀ən-tae* p.v.p.; be just right, just enough, *lmɔ̀:m* v.

keep (nourish), *ceñcɤm* v.; keep in a certain place, *tùk* v.; keep off, *rɛ̀əŋ* v.
kettle, *kɔnsiəv* n.
kettleful, *kɔnsiəv* c.
kick, *thɛ̀ək* v.; kick away, *tɔ̀ət, kùəh* v.; kick repeatedly, *təthɛ̀ək* v.
kill, *sɔmlap* v.
kilogram, *kì:lo:* c.; 60 kgm, *ha:p* c.; 30 kgm, *coŋ* c.
kilometre, *kì:lo:maet(r)* c.

316

kind adj., be so kind as to, *ʔaːnɤt* v.
kind n., *yaːŋ, baep, mùk(h)* c. n.
king, *sdäc* n.
kingdom, *rìːəč* n.; kingdom of Cambodia, *kɔmpùcèərɔ̀ət(th)* n.
kitchen, *kɔnlaeŋ coŋphɤu*
knife, *kambɤt* n.; stroke of a knife, *kambɤt* c.
knock away, *kùəh* v.
know, *dɤŋ* v.; know (a person), *skɔ̀əl* v.; know how (to), *ceh* v.; do you know? *dɤŋ* f.
Kompung Cham, *kɔmpùəŋ-caːm* n.
Kompung Chnang, *kɔmpùəŋ-chnaŋ* n.
Kratie, *krəceh* n.

lack v., *khvah* v.
ladle n., *vèːk* n.
ladleful, *vèːk* c.
lady, old lady, *lòːk-yìːəy, yìːəy* n.
lake, *srah, bɤŋ* n.
land n., *dɤy* n.; dry land, *kòːk* n.
language, *phìːəsaː* n.
lap, have the sound of soft waves lapping, *pəplɤk-pəplɔk* v.
large, big, **thom* v.; large and roomy, *sùː-trùː, tùːlìːəy* v.
last (in time = just past), *meɲ* or *mèɲ* post n.p.
late, *yùːt* v.
laugh v., *saəc* v.
lawless, *crəlaəs-baəs* v.
layman, *ʔobaːsɔ̀k* n.
laywoman, *ʔobaːsekaː* n.
lazy, *khcùl* v.
lead v., *nɔ̀əm* v.; (animals or cart), *dɤk* v.
leaf, *slɤk* n.; leaf of sugar-palm, *slɤk-tnaot* n.; leaf (of paper), *sɔnlɤk* c.
leap up, *stùh* v.; leap up and jump about, *phnaːl-phnaːl* v.
learn, *rìən* v.; learn to, *rìən* (+ v.)
leave (a place), *cèɲ pìː*
left (as opposed to right), *chvèːŋ* v.
left over, *sɔl* v.
leg, *cɤ̀ːŋ* n.
length, *prəvaeŋ* n.; 5 yard length (of material), *tbɔːŋ* c. n.; 20 yard length (of material), *krɤy* c. n.; set of 20 sarong-lengths, *kaːlɤy* c. n.; have length, *bɔndaoy* v. (length then specified)
let v. (let someone do something), *ʔaoy* v. (*kèː thvɤ̀ː : ....*)
letter, *sɔmbot(r), lìkhɤt* n.; letter (of alphabet), *tuːə* c.
level n., *thnak* n.
lick the lips, *plaom-plaom* v.
lie down, *deːk* v.; cause to lie down, *phdeːk* v.
life, *cìːvùt* n.; escape with one's life, *rùːəc cìːvùt*
lift v., *lɤ̀ːk* v.; give a lift to, *cùːn (kèː) tɤu* (*v.—v.*)
like (prep.), *dɔːc* pre n.p.; like this, *dɔːc=neh, poɲɲeh* a.; like that, *dɔːc=nɔh, poɲɲɔh, poɲɲɤŋ* a.
like v., *srəlaɲ* v., *cɔːl cɤt(t), pɛ̀ɲ cɤt(t)*; be like, *dɔːc, dɔːc-cìːə* v.
limp v., *khvɤ̀ːc-khvɤ̀ːc* v.
lingot, *cdao(r)* c.

lion, **sɤŋ(h), sɑt(v)-*sɤŋ(h)* n.
listen, *sdap* v.
little, *tɔːc* v.; a little, *bɔntec, bɔntec-bɔntec, bɔntec-bɔntuːəc* a.
live in, at, *nɤu* v.
local people, *nèək-srok* n.
London, *lɔndɔn* n.
long, *vèːŋ* v.; (= have a certain length, which is specified), *bɔndaoy* v.; (of time), *yùː(r)* v.; (= long and numerous or very long), *vèːŋ-vèːŋ* v.
longer (of time), *tɤu-tìət* f.
look v., *mɤ̀ːl* v.; look at, *mɤ̀ːl* v.; look for, *rɔ̀ːk* v.; look after, *pyìːəbaːl* v.; look! *vɤy, vɤːy!* e.
loom, *krɤy* n.
loomful (20-yard length of material), *krɤy* c.
lost, *bat* v.
lot, what a lot! — *ʔɤy *kɔː —!* (with the same noun before and after)
lottery, *chnaot* n.
loud, *khlaŋ* v.
love v., *srəlaɲ* v.
lovely, *lʔɔː* v.
low, *tìːəp* v.
loyal, stick loyally to one's friends, *phdeːk-phdɤl* v.
luggage, **ʔɤyvan* n.
lump, *dom* c.
lunch-time (late morning), *thŋay* n.

madam, *nèək-srɤy*; (more elevated), *lòːk-srɤy* n.
main road, *phlɔːv-thnɔl* n.
Majesty (His Majesty), *prèəh-kɔrùnaː* n.
make, *thvɤ̀ː* v.
mammal (name of), *kɔndìːə-tìə* n.
man, *mənùs(s)* n.; men, boys (plural), *pros-pros* n.
management, *tìː-cat-kaː(r)* n.
mango, *svaːy* n.
Mani (proper name) n., *məɲìː* n.
man-load, *dɤk* c.
manner, in a — manner, *cìːə, *ʔaoy* pre n.p. with following nominalized attributive verb
many, *craən* x; how many, *poɲmaːn* x; (not) — many, *poɲmaːn* x; for many years, *pìː poɲmaːn chnam mɔ̀ːk haɤy*
March, *mìːnìːə, khae-mìːnìːə* n.
March–April, *cäet(r), khae-cäet(r)* n.
market, *phsaː(r)* n.; meat market, *phsaː(r)-kap-kòː* n.; market garden, *cɔmkaː(r)* n.; market of mixed goods, *phsaː-phsao* n.
marry v. tr., *kaː(r)* v.
mat, *kɔntèːl* n.
match n., *chɤ̀ː-kùs* n.
material, *sɔmpùət* n.
matter, *sëckdɤy, rùəŋ, kaː(r)* n.
mauve, *svaːy* v.
May, *ʔosaphìːə, khae-ʔosaphìːə* n.
May–June, *cèːs(th), khae-cèːs(th)* n.
meal, *mhoːp* n.
measure, measure extent, *vɔəs* v.; instrument for measuring extent, *rùəŋvɔəs* n.
meat, *sac* n.

medicine, *thnam* n.

meet, *cù:əp, cu:əp* v.; (a person at a station), *tətù:əl* v.; meet together, *cù:əp-cụm* v.

meeting, **nèək-prəcụm* n.

member, **sạma:cùuk* n.

men (a general plural), *pros-pros* n.

mend, *cù:əs-cùl* v.; (by patching), *pah* v.

method, *ya:ŋ* c. n., *rəbiən, rəbiəp, sɔndap-thnɔ̀əp* n.

metre, (= verse), *bɔ̀l*; (measurement), *maet(r)* c.

microphone, *ma:sì:n-pùəŋrì:k-sɔmle:ŋ* n.

mid-day, *thŋay trɔŋ*

middle, *kɔnda:l* n.; in the middle of —ing, *kɔmpùŋ-tae* p.v.p.

milk, *tùuk-dɔh-kò:* n.

millimetre, *mì:lì:maet(r)* c.

million, *lì:ən* x; ten million, *kaoṭ(e)* x

mind n., *cʏt(t)* n.

minister, *rɔ̀ęt(th)-mùəntrʏy* n.

minute, *nì:əṭì:, mì:nùt* n.

miserable, *prù:əy* v., *prù:əy cʏt(t)*

misery, *sĕckdʏy tùk(h)*

Miss, *nì:əŋ* n.

miss v., *kha:n* v. (1st or 2nd v.); (= be sad without), *rəlùuk, srənɔh* v.

mock v., *cɔmʔɔ:k* v.

moment, *phlèːt, rùmpĕc, sɔntùh* c.

monastery, *vɔ̀ęt(t)* n.

Monday, *thŋay-cạn(t)* n.

money, *prak* n.

monk, *lò:k-sɔ̣ŋ(kh)* n.

monkey, *sva:*; (in names of years), *vɔ̀:k* n.

month, *khae* c. n.

moon, period of the waxing moon, *khnaət*; period of the waning moon, *rənò:c* n.

more, *tìət* f.; *cì:əŋ* a. pre n.p.; not more than, only, *tae g*.

moreover, *saot* f.

morning, *prùuk* n.; late morning, lunch-time, *thŋay* n.

mortar, *tbal* n.; mortar with pestle, *tbal-kduəŋ* n.

mostly, *craən-tae* p.v.p.

mother, *mda:y* n.

motor-boat, *ka:ṇo:t* n.

mount v., *cìh* v.

mourn, *saok-sda:y* v.

mouth, *mɔ̀ət* c. n.

Mr. *lò:k* n.

Mrs., *nèək-srʏy; lò:k-srʏy* (more elevated) n.; young Mrs., *nì:əŋ* n.

much, *craən* x

muddled, in a muddle, *sù:k-krəlù:k* v.

murmuring, *ʔù:-ʔù:* v.

music, *phlè:ŋ* n.

must, *tro:v* v.; absolutely must, *tro:v-tae* p.v.p.

myself, *khlu:ən khṇom*

name, *chmùəh* n.

namely, *kùu:* v. m.

narrow, *cɔŋʔiət* v.

nature, be by nature, *kùu:* v.

naughty, *ka:c* v.

nauseating, *krəpùl* v.

near, *bìət, cùut* v.; *nʏu-cùut, *ʔaep* pre n.p.;

very near, *cùut-cùut, phtɔ̀əl-phtɔ̀əl* v.; place near, *phcùut* v.

nearly, *hìəp-tae* p.v.p.

necessary, *tro:v* v. (used impersonally)

neck, *kɔ:* n.

need v., *tro:v ka:(r)*

nephew, *kmu:əy* n. (or niece); *kmu:əy-pros* n.

never (past or present), *mùun-dael* p.v.p.

new, *thmʏy* v.

news, *dɔmnʏŋ* n.

newspaper, *ka:saet* n.

next, *kraoy* v.; (then next, after fulfilment of condition), *sʏm, tʏ̀:p* m.; (next step in story), *rù:əc, haəy, rù:əc-haəy* m.

nibble, *krop-krop* v.

nice, *lʔɔ:* v.

niece, *kmu:əy* n. (or nephew); *kmu:əy-srʏy* n.

night, *yùp* n.

nine, *pram-bu:ən* x

nineteen, *pram-bu:ən-dɔndɔp, dɔp-pram-bu:ən* x

ninety, *kausʏp* x

nirvana, *nìppì:ən* n.; enter nirvana, *bɔre-nìppì:ən* v.

node (of bamboo), *thnaŋ* c. n.

north, *kha:ŋ-cʏ̀:ŋ* n.

not, *mùun* p.v.p.; *pùm* p.v.p. (literary); *kom* p.v.p. (in commands)

note (monetary), *krəda:s* n.

note down, *kɔt* v.

notice n., *ta:raŋ* n.

nourish, *ceñcʏm* v.

November, *viccheka:, khae-viccheka:* n.

November–December, **mìkɛ̀əse:(r), khae-*mìkɛ̀əse:(r)* n.

novice, be a novice (i.e. enter the religious life), *bu:əs* v.

now, **ʔʏ́ylo:v꞊nìh* a.

nowadays, *sạp̀(v) thŋay*

number, *cɔmnu:ən* n.; a certain number, *poñ̀ma:n* (affirmative context) x

object (thing), *rəbɔs* n.

observe, *nùuk—khʏ̀:ŋ* v.—v.

obstinate, *rùuŋ-tʔʏŋ* v.

obtain, *ba:n* v.

occasion, *do:ŋ* c. n.

occasionally, *mdo:ŋ-mdo:ŋ* a.

o'clock, *maoŋ* c. n.

October, *tola:, khae-tola:* n.

October–November, *kạtdʏk, khae-kạtdʏk* n.

of, *rəbɔs, nì:ə* (lit.) pre n.p.; *nèy* (lit.) pre n.p.; out of, made of, *ʔɔmpì:, nùuŋ* pre n.p.

offer v., *cù:n*; (to monks), *prəkè:n*; (to the Buddha or royalty), *thva:y* v.

offering (religious), *bo:cì:ə* n.; offering in January–February, *mì:ək(h)-bo:cì:ə* n.; offering in April–May, *vìsa:k(h)-bo:cì:ə* n.

office, **bùyro:* n.

often, *rùuəy-rùuəy* v.; not often, *rùəŋvʏ̀:l-rùəŋvʏ̀:l* v.

ointment, put on ointment, *srəla:p* v.

old, *cas* v.; (= x years old), *ʔa:yù* (x *chnam*) v.; old man, *ta:, lò:k-ta:* n.; old men (general plural), *ta:-ta:* n.; old lady, *yì:əy, lò:k-yì:əy* n.

318

on, *lɤ:* pre n.p. v., *nɤu-lɤ:* pre n.p.; (of time), *ka:l-pi:* pre n.p.

once, *mdo:ŋ* a.

one, *mù:əy* x; one (= someone), *kè:* n. pron.; one at a time, *mù:əy-mù:əy* v.

only, *tae* g.; only just, *krɔən-tae* p.v.p.; then only (then after fulfilment of condition), *sɤm, lɤ:p* m.

onwards, *tɤu, to:-tɤu, to:-to:-tɤu* f.

open adj. (of flower), *ri:k* v.; open and white (of flower), *skù:s-ski:əy* v.

open v., *bəək* v.

open-sided, *cɔmho:* v.

opinion, be of the opinion, *sma:n* v.

oppress, *biət-biən* v.

or, *rù:* pre n.p. m.

orchestra, *phlè:ŋ mù:əy vùəŋ*; theatre orchestra, *nèək-lè:ŋ-phlè:ŋ-lkhaon* n.

order, *sɔndap-thnɔ̀əp* n.; in order to, in order that, *ʔaoy, daəmbɤy, daəmbɤy-ʔaoy, daəmbɤy-nùŋ* m.; in order not to, *daəmbɤy-kom-ʔaoy, kom-ʔaoy, mùn-ʔaoy* m.; in ordered sequence, *dɔŋhae(r)* v.

organize, *cat-caeŋ* v.

other, (different), *dətèy* v.; (in addition), *ʔae-tiət* post n.p.

ounce, *dɔmlɤŋ* c.

ourselves, *khlu:ən yɤ:ŋ*

out, go out, *cëɲ* v.

outside prep., *krau-pi:* pre n.p.

owl (large variety), *chma:-ba:* n.

owner, *mcas* n.

ox, *kò:*; (in names of years), *chlo:v* n.

packed (crowded), *cɔŋʔiət* v.

packet, *hao; trəbo:k* (e.g. of cigarettes) c. n.

paddy, *sro:v* n.

page, *tùmpɔ̀ə(r)* c. n.

paint v., *li:əp* v.

pair n., *kù:* c. n.; (of horns), *kba:l* c. n.

pair off v., *phkù:* v.

palace, *ri:əc-vèəŋ* n.

palm-leaf manuscript, *sɑtra:* n.

pan n., *khtèəh* n.

panther, *khla:-rəkhɤn* n.

paper, *krəda:s* n.

parcel n., *kɔɲcɔp* n.

parents, *ʔo:pùk-mda:y* n.

Paris, *pa:rì:s* n.

part, on the part of, *kha:ŋ, cɔmnaek-kha:ŋ* pre n.p.

party (political), *kɑɲaʔ* n.

pass v., *hu:əs* v.; (an examination), *cɔ̀əp* v.

passport, *likhɤt-chlo:ŋ-daen* n.

past adj. = just past in time, *meɲ* or *mèɲ* post n.p.

past (a certain time), be past (in time), *hu:əs* v.

patch up, *cù:əs-cùl* v.

pavilion, *sa:la:, rò:ŋ* n.

pay v., *bɔŋ prak*

pen, *do:ŋ-pɑkka:* n.

pen (e.g. hen-pen), *trùŋ* n.

people, *kè:* n. pron.; *mənùs(s)* n.; people of the district, local people, *nèək-srok* n.

pepper, *mrèc* n.

perceive, *khɤ:ɲ* v.

perch n., *trɔnùm* n.

perch v. intr., *tùm* v.

perhaps, *prəhael, prəhael-cì:ə, mùk(h)-cì:ə* p.v.p. m.; *mɤ:l* f.; *mɤ:l tɤu*

permission, *cbap* n.

persist, *chliət* v.

person, *nèək* c.; *prèəh-ʔɔŋ(k)* c. (for royalty); *ʔɔŋ(k)* c. (for monks); *rù:p* c. (for people in philosophical or literary context); one person, alone, *mnèək* a.; (considered as upright object, figure), *tu:ə* c.; someone, a person, *kè:* n., *mənùs(s) mnèək*; the person who . . . ., *nèək* n. (+ v.); person = shape, form, *rù:p-rì:əŋ* n.

perspiration, *ŋɤ:s* n.

perspire, baek *pɤ:s*

petty-thieving, do, *sì:-lɤp* v.

Phnom (the 'hill' in Phnom Penh on which a monastery is situated), *phnùm* n.

Phnom Penh, *phnùm-pèɲ* n.

pick out, *rɤ:s* v.

piece, *dom* c. n.; cut piece, *kɔmnat* c.

pierced at the surface, *mùt* v.

pig, *crù:k* n.; (in names of years), *kol* n. (spelt *kor*)

pigeon, *prì:əp* n.

pile n. (criss-cross construction of planks, logs, etc.), *crò:ŋ* c. n.

pill, *krɔ̀əp* c.

pillar, *sɑsɔ:(r)* n.

pincers, *khnì:əp* n.

pinch, *tbiət* v.; (with pincers), *kiəp* v.

pipe, *bɔmpùəŋ* n.

pitcher, *kʔo:m* n.; with stopper, *tho:* n.; earthenware, for water, *pì:əŋ* n.

pitcherful, *kʔo:m, tho:, pì:əŋ* c.

place n., *ti:, kɔnlaeŋ,* c. n.; *ʔɔnlɤ:, tì:-kɔnlaeŋ* n.; (lit. word), *kùənlɔ̀:ŋ* n.

place v., *taŋ* v.

plain n., *vì:əl* n.

plank, *kda:(r)* n.

plant n., *dɔmnam* n.

plant v., *dam* v.

plate, *ca:n* n.; 'plate' or sheet of wax, *ca:n* c. n.

plateful, *ca:n* c.

play n., *rùəŋ* n.

play v., *lè:ŋ* v.

plead, sounds of pleading and protest, *ŋo:v-ŋo:v* v.

pleasant, to hear, *pì:rùəh* v.; to smell, *krɑʔo:p* v.

please, (+ verb), *ʔa:nɤt* v. (+ v.); *ʔɔɲcɤ:ɲ* v. (+ v.); please do! *ʔɔɲcɤ:ɲ!*; pleased, *sɑpba:y cɤt(t), sok(h) cɤt(t); tre:k-ʔo:(r)* v.; please may I? (+ v.), *so:m* v. (+ v.)

plot v. (to . . . .), *rù:əm kùmnùt (nùŋ)*

plough n., *nèəŋkɔ̀əl* n.

plough v., *phcù:ə(r)* v.

pluck v., *beh* v.

point, on the point of, *stɤ:, prəva:* v.; *stɤ:-tae, stɤ:-tae-nùŋ* p.v.p.

poisonous, *pùl* v.

police, *po:lì:s* n.

ponder, *kùt* v.

ponds, *bɤŋ-bu:ə* n.

poor, *krɔː* v.
pop (of sound), *tùːt-tùːt* v.
pork, *sac-crùːk* n.
possibility, have the possibility, *baːn* v. (2nd v.)
possible, it is possible that.... *prəhael, prəhael-ciːə, mùk(h)-ciːə* m.
post, post office, post box, *pos(te)* n.
pot, metal cooking pot, *chnaŋ* n.
potato, *dɔmloːŋ* n.
pound n. (weight), *niːəl* c.
pound v., *bok* v.; by means of a pestle and mortar, *cɔən* v.
pour, *cak* v.
power, have the power to, *ʔaːc* v.
practise, *hat* v.
pray, beg and pray, *buːəŋ-suːəŋ* v.
prayers, *thɔ̀ə(rm)* n.
precise, *(h)mɔt-cɔt* v.
pregnant, *phaəm* v.
prepare, *prɔŋ-priəp, rìəp, rìəp-cɔm* v.; prepare oneself, *rìəp khluːən*
present (oneself) v. tr., *phtɔ̀əl (khluːən)* v.
prestige, *yùəs-sak(te)* n.
pretend, *rùmcìː-rùmcìːə* v.
pretentious, *pʏːt-paoŋ* v., *kaey-kaoŋ* v.
previous (= last of time), *meŋ, mèŋ* post n.p.
price, *thnoː(r)* n.
prince, *prèəh-ʔɔŋ(k̀)-mcas, sɔmdäc* n.
princess, *nèək-ʔɔŋ(k̀)-mcas* n.
prison, *kùk, phtèəh-kùk* n.
probable, it is probable that, *mùk(h)-ciːə* m.
probably, *mùk(h)-tae* p.v.p.; *mùk(h)-ciːə* p.v.p. m.; *mʏːl* f.; *mʏːl tʏu*
problem, solve a problem, *kùt—khʏ̀ːŋ* v.—v.
procedure, *kec(c), kec(c)-kaː(r)* n.
profit n., *cɔmnɛ̈ŋ* n.
pronounce, *ʔaːn* v.
proper, *kùːə(r)* v.
properly, *ʔaoy praːkɔt*
prostrate oneself, *kraːp* v.
protect, *kaː(r)-pìːə(r)* v.
provided that, *ʔaoy-tae* m., *lùh-tae, lùh-traː-tae* m.
pull, pull along, *ʔoːs* v.; pull out by roots, *dɔːk* v.
punish, *thvʏ̀ː tòːs (kèː)* v.
punishment, *tòːs* n.; take away fear of punishment, *ʔaphéy tòːs*
pupil, *koːn-sʏs(s), sʏs(s)* n.
pursue, *dɛ̈ŋ* v.
push v., *rùŋ* v.
put, *dak* v.; put away, put on one side, *tùk* v.; put in, *dak* v.; put on (electrical appliances), *baək* v.; put on ointment, *lìːəp* v.; put (to work) = apply, *tùk-dak* v.; put away (numerous objects), *tùk-tùk* v.

quarrel v., *chlùəh* v.; make up a quarrel v., *phsah-phsa:* v.
quick, *chap, rəhás, lùən* v.; be quick (to), *chap* v. (+ v.)
quickly, *daoy rəhás*
quite, quite well, *krɔən-baə* v.

race (= nationality, kind), *ciːət(e)* n.
rack one's brains, *nùk* v.
radio, *vìtyù* n.
rain n., *phlìəŋ* n.
rake n., *rənɔ̀əs* n.
rake v., *rɔ̀əs* v.
rank, degree of military rank, *hoːpɔ̀ən* c.
rat, *sat(v)-kɔndol*; (in names of years), *cùːt* n.
read, *mʏːl* v.; (of monk), *tɔ̀ːt* v.; read aloud, *ʔaːn* v.
ready, get oneself ready, *rìəp khluːən*
realize, *nùk—khʏ̀ːŋ, kùut—khʏ̀ːŋ* v.—v.
really, *mɛ̀ːn* v.; not.... really, *mùn-mɛ̀ːn* p.v.p.
reason n., *häet(o)* n.; the reason why...., *baːn-ciːə* m. (followed by *pìː-prùəh* = is that....)
rebound v., *khtɔ̀ət* v.
rebuke v., *cèː(r)* v.
receive, *tətùːəl* v.
reciprocally, *knìːə* a.
recite, *soːt(r)* v.
recognize, *skɔ̀əl* v.
red, *krəhoːm* v.
redundantly, speak redundantly, *tùəntɛ̈ŋ-tùəntùːt* v.
reel n., *hoŋ* c. n.
regard, with regard to, *cɔmnaek, ʔae-cɔmnaek, rìː-ʔae* (lit.) pre n.p.
related by blood, *bɔŋkaət* v.
relations (relatives), *bɔːŋ-pʔoːn* n.
relatives, *bɔːŋ-pʔoːn* n.
relax (= be at leisure), *kɔmsaːn(t)* v.
remain (in, at), *nʏu* v.; (= be left over), *sɔl* v.
remember, *cam* v.
replace v. tr., *cùːəs* v.
replacement (object used to replace), *cùmnùːəs* n.
reply v., *chlaəy, tɔː* v.
respect v., *kòːrùp̀* v.
rest n., *dɔmneːk* n.
rest v., *deːk, sɔmraːk, sɔmraːn(t)* v.; *tətùːəl tìːən dɔmneːk*
restrict, *haːm* v.
retreat in fear, *son-tron* v.
return v., *trɔlɔp—tʏu/mɔ̀ːk* v.
revolve v., *vùəl* v.
rice (cooked), *baːy* n.; husked rice, *ʔɔŋkɔː(r)* n.
ricefield, *srae* n.
rice-seed, *krɔ̀əp sroːv*
riddle v. (i.e. to clean grain), *ʔom* v.
ride v., *cih* v.
riel, *rìəl* c.
right (as opposed to left), *sdam* v.
right (correct), *troːv* v.; be just right, *lmɔ̀ːm* v.; be right (think correctly), *kùut—troːv* v.—v.; right! (= I accept what you say), *(h)nʏŋ haəy!*
ripe, *tùm* v.
rise v., *laəŋ* v.
river, *tùənlè:* n.
road, *phloːv* n.; main road, *thnɔl, phloːv-thnɔl* n.; *phloːv *thom*
roasted, *ch?aə(r)* v.
roll into a ball v., *chmoːl* v.
roof, *dɔmboːl* n.; roofed with, *prɔk* v.
room, *bɔntùp* n.

roomy, *tù:lì:əy* v.; big and roomy, *sù:-pətrù:* v.

rose, *phka:-kola:p* n.

round n., *cùm* c.; of boxing match, *tùk* c.; go round, *pôəl(lh)* v.; turn round v. intr. (ready to return), *trələp* v.; round prep., *cùmvèɲ* pre n.p.; round adj., *mù:l* v.

row n. (= line), *cù:ə(r)* c. n.; in theatre or cinema, *thnak* n.

row v., *ʔom* v.

rubber, *kausù:* n.

rule v., *saoy* v.

run v., *rùət* v.

sack, *ba:v* c. n.; hemp sack (capacity 3 bushels), *ka:roŋ* c. n.

sad, *prù:əy* v., *prù:əy cɤt(t)*

Saigon, *prèy-nəkɔ:(r)* n.

sailing-boat, *tù:k-kdaoŋ* n.

salt, *ʔəmbɤl* n.; salted and dried, *ɲiət* v.

salute, *kùmnɔəp* n.

same, *dədael* v.; at the same time as, *prɔ:m-tɛ̀əŋ* m. pre n.p.

sand, *khsac* n.

sarong, *səmpùət* n.; set of 20 sarong-lengths, *ka:lɤy* c. n.

satiated, *skɔp-skɔl* v.

satisfied, *tro:v cɤt(t)*

Saturday, *thŋay-sau(t)* n.

say v., *tha:* v.

scaffolding, *bəɲʔaoŋ* n.

scale (of fish), *srəka:* n.

scarecrow (any device which scares birds), *rəyì:əl* n.; (one made to resemble a man), *tì:ŋmɔ:ŋ* n.

scatter v., *ba:c* v.; scatter objects disrespectfully, *kɔpcèəh-kɔpcì:əy* v.; scattered, *khcat-khca:y* v.

scent n., *klɤn* n.; having a pleasant scent, *krəʔo:p* v.

school, *sa:la:-rìən* n.

scissors, *kɔntray* n.

scrape, *cɤt, kìəs* v.

scratch v., *ka:y* v.; scratch oneself, *keh* v.; scratch constantly, *kəka:y* v.; scratch oneself constantly, *kəkeh* v.

screen n., *rənèəŋ* n.; screen for door, *lop-lae* n.

scrutinize, *pìnùət(y)-mɤ̀:l* v.

scurry, *lah* v.

scythe, *kəndiəv* n.

sea, *səmòt(r)* n.; by sea, *ta:m cɤ̀:ŋ tùk*

season, *rədo:v* n.; rainy season, *və(s)sa:* n.

seasoning, *mtè:s* n.

seat, row of seats, *baŋ* n.

seaweed, *sa:ra:y* n.

section, *lvè:ŋ* c. n.; lengthwise section, *cɔmrìək* c. n.

see, *khɤ̀:ŋ* v.; see someone off, *cù:n (kè:) tɤ̀u*

seed, *krɔəp* n.

seed-bed, *thna:l* n.

seedling, *səmna:p* n.

seek, *rɔ:k* v.

seem, *do:c-cì:ə* v.

self, *khlùən* n.; oneself, *khlù:ən ʔaeŋ*

sell v., *lùək* v.

send, *phɲaə* v.

separate v. intr., *baek* v.; separated widely, *sɔɲvaeŋ* v.

September, *kaɲɲa:, khae-kaɲɲa:* n.

September–October, *ʔassòc, khae-ʔassòc* n.

serpent (in names of years), *msaɲ* n.

servant, *nèək-bəmraə* n.

set n. (= necessary parts or equipment), *səmrap* c. n.; set of 20 sarong-lengths, *ka:lɤy* c. n.

set one's mind on, *bəmroŋ (nùŋ)* v.

seven, *prampùl* x

seventeen, *prampùl-dəndɔp* x, *dɔp-prampùl* x

seventy, *cɤtsɤp* x

several, *craən* x

sew, *de:(r)* v.

shade, *mlùp* n.

shake v. intr., *ɲɔ̀ə(r)* v.

shape, *rù:p-rì:əŋ* n.

she (familiar), *vi:ə, knì:ə*, n. pron.; (respectful), *kɔ̀ət, kè:* n. pron.

sheaf, *kəndap* c. n.

shed past part., *crùh* v.

sheet (of paper), *sənlɤk, pùm(ph)* c. n.; (of wax), *ca:n* c. n.

shelf, *ska:k, trənɤ̀:, thnɤ̀:* n.

shell (of tortoise), *sno:k* n.

shining and wet, *rəlɤ̀:p-rəlùəŋ* v.

shirt, *ʔa:v* n.

shiver with fear and cold, *tron-tron* v.

shoe, *sbaek-cɤ̀:ŋ* n.

shoo! be off! *vo:, vù:s-va:s, vo:s-va:s-vo:s-va:s* e.

shoot (= new growth of plant), *pùənlɔ̀:k* n.

shop, *tiəm, ha:ŋ* n.

shop-keeper, *mcas-tiəm, mcas-ha:ŋ* n.; prosperous shop-keeper, *thao-kae* n.

short, *khlɤy* v.

show v., *bəɲha:ɲ* v.

shriek v., *sraek* v.

shut v. tr., *bɤt* v.

shy, very shy, *ʔiən-khma:s* v.

Siam, *srok-siəm* n.

Siamese, *siəm* v.

sibling, (older), *bo:ŋ*, (younger), *pʔo:n* n.

side, *kha:ŋ* n.; at one side, *mkha:ŋ* a.; both sides, *sɔ:ŋkha:ŋ* a.

sift, *rò:y* v.

silent, *sɲiəm* v.

silk, *so:t(r)* n.

since, *taŋ-pì:, tɔ:-pì:* m. pre n.p.; all the time from then, *tɔ:-tɔ:-tɤ̀u* f.; all the time since until now, *tɔ:-tɔ:-mɔ̀:k* f.; ever since, *taŋ-pì:, tɔ:-pì:* m. pre n.p.; *tɔ:-tɔ:-mɔ̀:k* f.

sinew, *səsay* c. n.

sing, *criəŋ* v.

single, *na:-mù:əy* (in negative or indefinite clause) post n.p.

sir, *lò:k* n.

sister (older), *bo:ŋ-srɤy* n.; (younger), *pʔo:n-srɤy* n.; brothers and sisters, *bo:ŋ-pʔo:n* n.

sit, *ʔəŋkùy* v.; sit (of monk), *kùəŋ* v.; sit for an examination, *prəlɔ:ŋ* v.

sitting room, *bəntùp-tətù:əl-phɲiəv* n.

six, *pram-mù:əy* x

sixteen, *pram-mù:əy-dəndɔp, dɔp-pram-mù:əy* x

321

sixty, *hoksɤp* x

sizzling, *che:v-cha:v* v.

skein, *cɔŋva:y* c. n.

skewer n. (large), *cɔŋkak* c. n.; (small), *dɔmbot* c. n.; anything used as a skewer, *trɘnaot* c. n.

skim, *du:ɘs* v.

slack, *thù:(r)* v.

sleep (rest) n., *dɔmne:k* n.

sleep (rest) v., *de:k* v.

slip out of position, *rɘbo:t* v.

slowly, *mù:ɘy-mù:ɘy* v., *yù:t-yù:t* v.; slowly and with great effort, *rɘyù:t-rɘyù:t* v.

slow-moving v., *mɤ̀:k-mɤ̀:k-mɤ̀:k* v., *rɘŋɤ̀:k-rɘŋɤ̀:k-rɘŋɤ̀:k* v., *phlɤ̀:k-phlɤ̀:k-phlɤ̀:k* v.

sluggish, *sɤ̀:k-sɤ̀:k* v., *mɤ̀:k-mɤ̀:k-mɤ̀:k*, *rɘŋɤ̀:k-rɘŋɤ̀:k-rɘŋɤ̀:k*, *phlɤ̀:k-phlɤ̀:k-phlɤ̀:k* v.

small, *to:c* v.; (in height), *tì:ɘp* v.; very small, *to:c-to:c*, *tù:c-tù:c-tù:c* v.; small and numerous, *rɘpeh-rɘpoh*, *to:c-to:c* v.; small, unequal and numerous, *kɔmpɤk-kɔmpok* v.

smell v. tr., *thừm* v.

smoke v. tr. (tobacco), *cừɘk* v.

snake, *pùɘs* n.; (name of a legendary snake), *ke:ŋ-ko:ŋ* n.

snare, *ʔɔntèɘk* n.

snooty, *caɘy-maɘy* v.

so conj., *kɔ:* m.; adv., *do:c⸗neh*, *poп̃п̃ɤy*, *ʔɔпcɤŋ*, *mleh* a.; so that (result), *tɔ̀ɘl-tae* m.; so that, so as to (purpose), *ʔaoy, daɘmbɤy-*ʔaoy, daɘmbɤy-nùŋ, daɘmbɤy* m.; so that .... not, so as not to, *kom-*ʔaoy, mùɘn-*ʔaoy, daɘmbɤy-kom-*ʔaoy, daɘmbɤy-mùɘn-*ʔaoy, daɘmbɤy-nùŋ-mùɘn-*ʔaoy* m.; so long as, *ʔaoy-tae, lùh-tra:-tae, lùh-tae* m.; isn't that so? *rù:* f. tè: *rù:*; if so, *ʔɔпcɤŋ* a.

soak v. tr., *tram* v.

soaked (wet through), *cò:k* v.

soap, *sa:bù:* n.

sob quietly, *khsɤk-khsu:ɘl* v.

soft (of earth), *thù:(r)* v.; soft drinks, (*tùk*) *phè:sɘcèɘ*

soldier, *tì:ɘhì:ɘn* n.

solve a problem, *kừt—khɤ̀:p* v.—v.

some adj., (sing.), *na:-mù:ɘy, ʔvɤy-mù:ɘy* post n.p. (affirmative context); (plur.), *poп̃ma:n* x, *na:-khlah, ʔvɤy-khlah* post n.p. (affirmative context); *khlah* post n.p.; some or other, *na:-na:, ʔvɤy-ʔvɤy* post n.p.

some n., *khlah* v.

somehow, *ya:ŋ na:-mù:ɘy* (affirmative context)

someone, *kè:* n.

something (affirmative context), *ʔvɤy, ʔɤy, sʔɤy* n.; *ʔvɤy-mù:ɘy, ʔɤy-mù:ɘy, sʔɤy-mù:ɘy* n.; some things, *ʔvɤy-khlah, ʔɤy-khlah, sʔɤy-khlah* n.; something or other, *ʔvɤy-ʔvɤy, ʔɤy-ʔɤy, sʔɤy-sʔɤy* n.

sometime, *mdɔ:ŋ* a.

sometimes, *mdɔ:ŋ-mdɔ:ŋ, cu:ɘn-ka:l, cu:ɘn-na:* a.; *yù:(r)-yù:(r) mdɔ:ŋ*

somewhere (affirmative context), *kɔnlaeŋ na:-mù:ɘy*; to, at some place (affirmative context), *ʔae na:*

son, *ko:n-pros* n.

song, *cɔmriɘŋ* n.

sorry, *sda:y* v.

sort, *baep* c. n.

sound, *so:(r), sɔmle:ŋ* n.

soup, *bɘbɔ:(r), sɔmlɔ:* n.

sour, *cù:(r)* v.

sow (grain, rice), *sa:p* v.

spade, *cɔ:p* n.

sparrow, *ca:p, sɑt(v)-ca:p* n.

speak, *nìyì:ɘy, sdɤy* v.

spectator, *nèɘk-mɤ̀:l* n.

speech, *sɔmdɤy* n.; (= words), *pì:ɘk(y)* n.

speed, *lbuɘn* n.

spend, *ca:y* v.; spend with care, *rùt-tbɤt* v.

spick and span, *sʔa:t-ba:t* v.

spirit (animist), *bɔŋ-bot* n.; one's own, *prɘlùŋ-prɘlɘŋ* n.

split adj., *rɘlɔ̀ɘt-rɘlò:c* v.; split into lengthwise sections v. tr., *crìɘk* v.

spoon, *sla:p-prì:ɘ* n.

spoonful, *sla:p-prì:ɘ* c.

spread out in the sun p. part., *ha:l thŋay*

spread out v. tr., *kra:l* v.

spring up (of plants), *lɔ̀ɘs* v.

sprinkle, *prɘlak, ba:c* v.; sprinkled all over, *khcat-khca:y* v.

squabble together, *prɘchlùɘh* v.

squeeze, *kì:ɘp* v.

stab at, *cak* v.

stack n., *srak* c. n.

staircase, *cùɘndaɘ(r)* n.

stairway, *cùɘndaɘ(r)* n.

stake n., *bɔŋkò:l* n.

stay v., *nɤu* v.; stay in, at, *nɤu* v.; (of monks), *kùɘŋ* v.

steal, *lù:ɘc* v.

stealthily (of walk), *ʔɔntrɤ̀:t-ʔɔntrɤ̀:t* v.; proceed stealthily, *lɔ̀:p-lɔ̀:p* v.

steamer n., *kɘpal* n.

step on tiptoe, *ʔɔntrɤ̀:t-ʔɔntrɤ̀:t* v.

stew n., *sɔmlɔ:* n.; dish made by the *slɔ:-slok* method of cooking, *sɔmlɔ:-sɔmlok* n.

stew v., *slɔ:* v.

stick v., *cɔ̀ɘp* v.

sticky, *sʔɤt* v.; (of rice, maize, etc.), *dɔmnaɘp* v.

stiff, *rùŋ* v.

still, *kùɘŋ-tae, nɤu-tae* p.v.p.; *nɤu* v.

stilt, *cɔntùɘl* n.

stir v. tr., *vùk, ko:(r)* v.

stomach, *pùɘh* n.

stone, *thmɔ:* n.

stop v. tr., *bɔпchừp* v.; stop v. intr., *chừp* v.; stop up, *cok* v.; stop! wo! *rɔ̀ɘp* or *hɔ̀ɘp* e.

stopper, *chnok* n.

store (big shop), *ha:ŋ* n.

story, *rùɘŋ* n.

stove, *lɔ:* n.

strand, *sɘsay* c.

strange, *cɔmlaek* v.

stream (mountain), *stùŋ* n.

street, *phlo:v* n.

strike v., *vay*, spelt and read as *vì:ɘy* v.; (with pointed weapon), *kap* v.; (matches), *kùs* v.

string, *khsae* n.

strong, *khlaŋ* v.

student, *ko:n-sɤs(s)* n.

study v., *rìən* v.
stupa, *ceːtɤy* n.
stupid (very), *phlìː-phlɤ̀ː* v.
stupified, *srəlaŋ-kaŋ* v.
subject (of study), *vìccìːə* n.
suddenly, *srap-tae* p.v.p. m.
sufficient, *krùp-krɔ̀ən* v.
sugar, *skɔː(r)* n.
sugar-palm, *tnaot, daəm-tnaot* n.
suggest (an action to someone), *bəbuːəl* v.
suit n., *khao-ʔaːv* n.
summon, *hau* v.
Sunday, *thŋay-ʔaːtùut(y)* n.
supple, *tùən-phlùən* v.
support n., means of lateral support, *trənɤ̀ː* n.
supported laterally, *tɤː* v.
surely (in exclamation), *taə* f.; (in question), *tèː rùː*
surprised, *chŋɔl* v.
swallow v., *lèːp* v.
swan, *hɔ̀ŋ(s)* n.
sweep, *baos* v.; sweep up, *baː(r)* v.
sweet, *phʔaem* v.
swollen, *phaəm* v.
swoon v., *srəlaŋ-kaŋ, slaŋ-kaŋ-phɛ̀əŋ* v.
sword, *daːv* n.
syllable, *pyaɲcɤnɛ̀ə* c. n.; syllable (as written), *tuːə* c. n.

table, *tok* n.
tablet, *phaen* c.
tail, *kəntùy* c. n.
take, *yɔːk* v.; (persons), *nɔ̀əm* v.; (in food or drink, i.e. to eat or drink), *tətùːəl tìːən* v.; (= transport in fairly large quantities), *cùəpcùːn* v.; take one's choice, *crɤːs* v.
talk, *nìyìːəy* v.
tall, *thom* v.
tar macadam, *kausùː* n.
tasty, *chŋaɲ* v.
tattered, *rəhaek-rəhoy* v.; in tatters *rekhaːk-reyìːək* v.; thoroughly tattered v., *rəhaek-rəhaok* v.
tea (ready to drink), *tùk-tae* n.
teach, *bəŋrìən* v.
teacher, *krùː, lòːk-krùː, nɛ̀ək-krùː* n.
team n., *nùm* c. n.
teapot, *pan* n.
teapotful, *pan* c.
tease, *rùmcìː-rùmcìːə, pleh-plɔh* v.; tease constantly and unkindly, *pəpleh-pəplɔh* v.
tell, *prap* v.; (superior), *cùmrìːəp* v.; (a story), *nìtìːən* v.; tell me (introducing a question), *taə* m.
temple, *prɛ̀əh-vìhìːə(r), vìhìːə(r)* n.
ten, *dɔp* x; ten thousand, *mɤːn* x; ten million, *kaot(e)* x
terrified, *phùt-phéy* v.
Thai, *sìəm* v.
Thailand, *srok-sìəm* n.
thank, *ʔɔː(r) kùn*
that dem. adj., *nùh* post n.p.; (colloquial), *nɔh* post n.p.; that (conj.), *thaː, cìːə* m.; that is, viz., *kùː* m. v.; like that, *dɔːc⁼nɔh* a.
thatch, *sbɔːv* n.

theatre, *lkhaon* n.; theatrical company, *lkhaon mùːəy vùəŋ*
themselves, *khluːən vìːə, khluːən kɔ̀ət*
then (next, after fulfilment of conditions, then only), *tɤ̀ːp* m.; then (after that, next step in story), *rùːəc, haəy, rùːəc-haəy* m.; from then, *tɤu* f.; from then until now, *mɔːk* f.
there, *tìː nùh, ʔae nɔh*; there is, are, *mìːən* v.
therefore, *kɔː* m. p.v.p.
thereupon, *srap-tae* m.
they (familiar), *vìːə, knìːə* n. pron.; (respectful), *kɔ̀ət, kèː* n. pron.
thick, *kraːs* v.; thick and numerous, *kraːs-kraːs* v.
thief, *cao(r)* n.
thing, *rəbɔs* n.; things, luggage, *ʔɤyvan* n.
think (ponder), *kùt* v.; (guess), *smaːn* v.; do you think? *mɤːl tɤu*; think about, rack one's brains, *nùk* v.
thirteen, *bɤy-dɔndɔp, dɔp-bɤy* x
thirty, *saːmsɤp* x
this, *nìh, neh* post n.p.; like this, *dɔːc⁼neh* a.
thorough, correct, *stɔ̀ət* v.
thoroughly, *ʔaoy praːkɔt*
thousand, *pɔ̀ən* x; ten thousand, *mɤːn* x; hundred thousand, *saen* x
three, *bɤy* x
threshing-floor, *lìːən* n.
through, *taːm* pre n.p.
throw (from the horns), *vɔ̀ət* v.; throw away, *caol* v.
Thursday, *thŋay-prəhɔ̀əs(p + té)*
thus, *dɔːc⁼neh* a.
ticket, *sɔmbot(r)* n.; bus ticket, *sɔmbot(r)-laːn-chnuːəl* n.; person selling tickets, *nɛ̀ək-lùːək-sɔmbot(r)* n.
tie v., *cɔːŋ* v.
tier, *rùət* c. n.
tiger, *sɑt(v)-khlaː* n.; (in names of years), *khaːl* n.; royal tiger, *khlaː-thom* n.
tight, drawn tightly round, *rùt-rùət* v.
tile, *kbuəŋ* n.
time, *pèːl, kaːl* n.; (= occasion), *dɔːŋ* c. n.; all the time since, *tɔː-tɔː-tɤu* f.; all the time since up to now, *tɔː-tɔː-mɔːk* f.; all the time until, *rəhoːt-dol, rəhoːt-mɔːk-dol* pre n.p.; at the same time as, *prɔːm-tɛ̀əŋ* pre n.p. m.; by the time that, *tùmrɔ̀əm* m.
times, *pèːl-vèːlìːə* n.
timid, *kɔmlaːc* v.
tin, *kɔmpoŋ* c.
tired, *ʔɔs kɔmlaŋ*
to (direction towards), *ʔae* pre n.p.; *tɤu, mɔːk* v. (depending on position of speaker in relation to main verb)
toddy (unfermented), *tùk-tnaot* n.
together, *knìːə, cìːə-mùːəy* a.; all together, *rɔ̀əl knìːə*; together with, *prɔːm-tɛ̀əŋ* m. pre n.p.; (= in company with), *cìːə-mùːəy, cìːə-mùːəy-nùŋ* pre n.p.
tomato, *peːŋ-pɔh* n.
tomorrow, *sʔaek* a.
Tonle (Sap), *tùənlèː* n.
too, too much, *pèːk* a.; (= also), *dae(r), phɔːŋ, saot* f.
tool, *prədap-prəda* n.

323

toot (horn), *tùːt-tùːt* v.

tooth, *thmɛ̀ɲ* n.

torn, *dac* v.

tortoise, *ʔɔndaək* n.

towards, *trɔŋ, kan,* pre n.p.; (of feelings), *dɔl,* pre n.p.; move directly towards, *trɔŋ* v.

town, *krɔŋ, tìː-krɔŋ* n.

train n., *rətèh-phlɤ̀ːŋ* n.

train v. tr., *bɔɲhat* v.

transplant, *stùːŋ* v.

transport v., *dɤk-nɔ̀əm* v.

trap v., *tɛ̀ək* v.

travel v., *daə(r)* v.

tray, *thaːs* n.

tread v., *cɔ̀ən* v.; tread on (sheaves of rice to loosen grains), *baen* v.; have (oxen or buffalo), walk round treading on (sheaves of rice to loosen grains), *bɔɲcɔ̀ən* v.

tree, *daəm-chɤ̀ː* n.; variety of tree, *trəlùːŋ-tùːŋ* n.

tree-trunk, *daəm* c. n.

trellis (on which pepper trees are grown), *cùənlùəŋ* c. n.

tremble v., *ɲɔ̀ə(r)* v.; tremble constantly, *ɲəɲɔ̀ə(r)* v.

trouble v. tr., *ʔɔmpùəl* v.; don't trouble! *kom ʔɤy!*; take the trouble to, *cam-bac* v.; troubled, *krəvəl-krəvaːy* v.

trousers, *khao* n.

true, *mèːn-tèːn, pùt* v.

trunk (= luggage-container), *hɤp* n.; (of tree), *daəm* c. n.; (of tree with branches removed), *kùəl* c. n.; trunk-shaped object, *daəm* c.

try v., *lɔ̀ː* v.; try hard (to), *khɔm* v.

Tuesday, *thŋay-ʔɔŋkìːə(r)* n.

turn v. intr., *vùəl* v.; turn round (intr.), *vùəl* v.; turn away (intr.), *tìːəs* v.; turn round, turn back (intr.), *trəlɔp—tɤu/mɔ̀ːk* v.—v.; turn round (tr.), *bɔɲvɤl* v.; turn off (electrical appliances), *bɤt* v.; turn on (electrical appliances), *baək* v.; have a turn at, *troːv lɤ̀ː*

twelve, *pìː(r)-dɔndɔp, dɔp-pìː(r)* x

twenty, *mphèy* x

twinkle, *pəprìːəy* v.

two, *pìː(r)* x

type n. (= kind), *cɔmnaek* c. n.

type v., *vay* v. (spelt *vìːəy*)

type-writer, *maːsìːn-ʔɔŋkùlìːleːk(h)* n. (*leːk(h)* spelt *lèːkh*)

ugly (of things), *sɔ̀ːs-krəlɔ̀ːs* v.

unable, *mùn baːn, mùn kaət, mùn rùːəc* v. (2nd v.)

uncle, *pùː* n. (strictly the younger brother of one's parent); *ʔom, ʔom-pros* (strictly the elder brother of one's parent)

under, *kraom* v. pre n.p.; *nɤu-kraom* pre n.p.

understand, *yùəl* v.; understand spoken language, *sdap* v.; understand thoroughly, *yùəŋ-yùəl* v.

unimportant (of slight consequence), *rəpec-rəpɤy* v.

University, *saːlaː-*thom* n.

unless, *lɤ̀ːk-tae, kom-tae* m. *baə . . . . mùn*

until, *dɔl, dɔl-pèːl-dael, tɔ̀əl-dɔl, tɔ̀əl-tae-dɔl, tɔ̀əl-tae,* m.; *dɔl, rəhoːt-dɔl, rəhoːt-mɔ̀ːk-dɔl,* pre n.p.

up, *laəŋ* v.; go up, *laəŋ* v.

uproot, *dɔːk* v.; uprooted, *rədɔːk* v.

use v., *praə-prah, praə* v.; use the services of, have (a servant), *praə* v.; used to (= accustomed), *thlɔ̀əp* v.; used for, *sɔmrap* v.

usual, **thɔ̀əm-mədaː* v.

usually, *craən-tae, cɔmnam-tae, taeŋ-tae, rəmèːŋ-tae, rèːŋ-tae* p.v.p.

usurp v., *rùmlòːp(h)* v.

utensil, *prədap, prədap-prədaː* n.

utterance, *mɔ̀ət* c.; (of the Buddha), *prèəh-pùlthɛ̀ədɤyka:* n.

value n., *dɔmlay* n.

various, *naː-na:* post n.p.; *phseːŋ-phseːŋ* v.

vegetable, *bɔnlae* n.

verse, *bɤt* n.

very, *nas* a.; not very (with attributive verb), *mùn-soːv* p.v.p.

Viet Minh, **vièt-mìɲ* (spelt *yìək-mìɲ*) n.

Vietnam, *srok-yùːən* n.

Vietnamese, *yùːən* v. n.

village, *phùːm(ì)* n.

visit v. (a person), *suːə(r)* v.; (at a house, visit for pleasure), *lèːŋ* (+ noun) v.; pay a social call, *lèːŋ (phtèəh kèː)* v.

viz., *kùː* m. v.

vocabulary (royal), *rìːəc-sap(t)* n.

volume (= book), *kbaːl* c. n.

vulgar v., *crəlaəs-baəs* v.; (ugly, in bad taste), *sɔ̀ːs-krəlɔ̀ːs* v.

wait v., *cam* v.; wait for, *cam* v.

walk v., *daə(r)* v.; (of monks), *nìmùən(t)* v.; cause to walk, *bɔndaə(r)* v.; go for a walk, *daə(r)-lèːŋ* v.

wall, *cùəɲcèəŋ* n.

wane (of moon) v., *ròːc* v.; period of waning moon, *rənòːc* n.

wash v., *lìːəŋ* v.; (clothes), *baok* v.

water, *tùk* n.

wave v., *bɔk* v.

wax v. (of moon), *kaət* v.; period of waxing moon, *khnaət* n.

way (= method), *yaːŋ* c. n.; all the way to, *rəhoːt-dɔl* pre n.p.

we, *yɤːŋ, knìːə, knìːə-yɤːŋ, yɤːŋ-khɲom* n.

wear v., (below the waist), *slìək* v.; (above waist or on feet and legs), *pèək* v.; (in general), *slìək-pèək* v.

weave, *tbaːɲ* v.; equipment for weaving, *dɔmbaːɲ* n.

Wednesday, *thŋay-pùt(h)* n.

week, *ʔaːtùt(y)* c. n.

well adj., *sruːəl, sok(h)-sɔ̀pbaːy* v., *sruːəl khlùːən*

well excl., *ʔìː, yìː, yèː* e.; well then, *ʔɔŋcɤŋ* a., *baə ʔɔŋcɤŋ*; as well, *dae(r), phɔːŋ* f.

West, *khaːŋ-*lec* n.

wet, *tətùk, saəm* v.; wet through, *tətùk—còːk* v.—v.; wet and shining, *rəlɤ̀ːp-rəlùəŋ* v.

what (interrog. pronoun), *ʔvɤy, sʔɤy, ʔɤy* n.; (sing.), *ʔvɤy-mùːəy, sʔɤy-mùːəy ʔɤy-mùːəy*; (plur.), *ʔvɤy-khlah, sʔɤy-khlah, ʔɤy-khlah,* n.; (interrog. adj.), *ʔvɤy, ʔɤy sʔɤy* post n.p.; (sing.), *ʔvɤy-mùːəy, sʔɤy-mùːəy, ʔɤy-mùːəy* post n.p.; (plur.), *ʔvɤy-khlah, sʔɤy-khlah, ʔɤy-khlah* post n.p.; what if . . . .? *cohbaə* . . . . m.; what (interrog. adj.), *ʔvɤy* post n.p.

whatever adj., *ʔvɤy*; (sing.), *ʔvɤy-mùːəy*; (plur.), *ʔvɤy-khlah* post n.p. (emphatic context); of whatever sort, *ʔvɤy-ʔvɤy, naː-naː* post n.p.; in whatever way, *yaːŋ naː; doːc-mdёc, doːc-mёc* a. (emphatic context); whatever number, *poñmaːn* x (emphatic context); whatever things (numerous), *ʔɤy-ʔɤy-ʔɤy* n. (emphatic context)

whatever n., *ʔvɤy*; (sing.), *ʔvɤy-mùːəy*, (plur.), *ʔvɤy-khlah* n. (emphatic context)

when conj., (present or future colloquial), *ʔɔŋkal* a.; past (colloquial), *pìː ʔɔŋkal*; past, *pìː kaːl naː; lùh, kaːl, kaːl-naː, kaːl-dael, pèːl-dael, pèːl, krìːə-dael* (literary) m.; future, *dɔl, dɔl-kaːl-naː, dɔl-pèːl-dael, tɔəl tae* m.

whenever, *pèːl-naː-dael, kaːl-naː-baə, kaːl-naː, kaːl-baə* m.; (in emphatic context), *kaːl naː*

where (= what place), *naː* n., *kɔnlaeŋ naː*; (= at, in what place), *nɤu-ʔae naː*; (= to what place), *ʔae naː*

wherefore, *baːn-cìːə* m.

wherever, *naː* n. (emphatic context)

which (interrog. adj.), *naː* post n.p.; (sing.), *naː-mùːəy* post n.p.; (plur.), *naː-khlah* post n.p.; (rel. pron.), *dael* m.

while, *knoŋ-pèːl-dael, nɤu-pèːl-dael* m.; a little while, *bɔntec* a.

whisper v., **khsɤp* v.

white, *sɔː* v.

who, **nèək naː*; (rel. pron.), *dael* m.

whom, **nèək naː*; (rel. pron.), *dael* m.

whoever, **nèək naː*

whole, *ʔɔs* v.; the whole of, *ʔɔs* pre n.p.

why, *mёc, mdёc, mёc-*kɔː, mdёc-*kɔː, häet(o)-ʔvɤy-baːn-cìːə* m.; and that is why, *baːn-cìːə* m.

wicked, *khoːc* v.

wide, *tùːlìːəy* v.

widow, *mèːmaːy* n.

width, *tɔtùŋ* n.; finger's width, *thnɔəp* c.

wife, *prɔpùən(tìh)* n.

win v., *chnèəh* v.; win a lottery, *troːv chnaot*

wind n., *khyɔl* n.

window, *bɔŋʔuːəc* n.

wing, *slaːp* n.

wipe v., *cùːt* v.

wish v., *cɔŋ* v.

with (= in company with), *cìːə-mùːəy-nùŋ; nɤu* (written *nùːv*), *nìːə* (both lit.), *haəy-nùŋ* pre n.p.; (= by means of), *nùŋ* pre n.p.; together with, *tèəŋ* pre n.p.

without, *ʔɤt* pre n.p.

woman, *srɤy* n.; women in general, *srɤy-srɤy* n.

wonder v., *kùt* v.

wood n. (= piece of wood), *chɤː* n.; of wood, *chɤː* v.

word, *pìːək(y)* n.

work n., *kaː(r), kec(c)-kaː(r)* n.

work v., *thvɤː kaː(r)*

worn, *rəhaek-rəhoy* v.

wrapper, *trəboːk* c. n.

wretched, *kɔmsɔt-tùːrəkùət* v.

wriggle, *tɔək-tɔək* v.

write, **səseː(r)* v.

writing n., *ʔɔksɔː(r)* n.

wrong, *khoh* v.; be wrong, go wrong, *khoːc* v.; do a wrong to, *thvɤː baːp* v.

wrong n., *kɔmhoh* n.

year, *chnam* c. n.; year spent by monk, *prèəh-vɔ(s)sa:* n.; for many years, *pìː poñmaːn chnam mɔːk haəy*

yellow, *lùəŋ* v.

yes (male speakers), *baːɫ*; (female speakers), **cah*; (person of superior rank speaking), *ʔaə, ʔùː*; (layman to monk), **kənaː, koːrənaː*; (monk to ordinary layman), *pɔː(r)*; (monk to superior), *cɔmrəən-pɔː(r)*; (monk to royalty), *thvaːy-prèəh-pɔː(r)*; (male speaker to King or Queen), *prèəh-kɔrùnaː-thlay-pìseːs*; (male speaker to high-ranking royalty), *prèəh-kɔrùnaː-pìseːs*; (male speaker to lower-ranking royalty), *kɔrùnaː-pìseːs*; (female speaker to King), *prèəh-pɔː(r)-cìːə-mcas*; (female speaker to Queen), *prèəh-mèː-cìːə-mcas*; (female speaker to high- or medium-ranking prince), *pɔː(r)-mcas*; (female speaker to low-ranking prince), *pɔː(r)*; (female speaker to high-ranking princess), *tɔtùːəl-prèəh-rìːəc-sɔvanɤy(y)-cìːə-mcas*; (female speaker to medium-ranking princess), *mèː-mcas, prèəh-mèː-cìːə-mcas*; (female speaker to lower-ranking princess), *mèː* r.

yesterday, *msɤl, pìː msɤl*

yet, (not) yet, *mùn-tɔən* p.v.p.

yoke (= team), *nùm* c. n.

yoke v., *tùm* v.

you (to equal), **nèək* n.; (to superior (male)), *lòːk* n.; (to superior (female)), *lòːk-srɤy, *nèək-srɤy* n.; (to inferior, familiar), *ʔaeŋ* n. pron.; (to equal (friendly)), *khluːən* n.; (between close but polite male friends), *kɔət* n. pron.; (monk to King or Queen), *prèəh-kɔrùnaː-cìːə-ʔɔŋ(k)-mcas-cìːvùt* n. pron.; (monk to high-ranking prince), *trùəŋ-prèəh-kɔrùnaː-pìseːs* n. pron.; (monk to prince), *trùəŋ* n. pron.; (monk to princess), *mcas* n.; (male or female speaker to King or Queen), *prèəh-kɔrùnaː-cìːə-ʔɔŋ(k)-mcas-cìːvùt-lɤː-tboːŋ* n. pron.; (male speaker to royalty of high or medium rank), *trùəŋ-prèəh-kɔrùnaː-pìseːs* n. or *lʔɔːŋ-thùːlìː-prèəh-baːɫ* n. pron.; (male speaker to lower-ranking male royalty), *trùəŋ* n. pron.; (female speaker to royalty other than King or Queen), *kraom-prèəh-baːɫ* n. pron.

young, *kmeːŋ* n.; young lady, *nìːəŋ* n.; young person, *kmeːŋ* n.

younger (brother or sister), *pʔoːn* n.

zero, *soːn(y)* v.

zoo, *suːən-sat(v)* n.

PART VII

Y*

APPENDICES AND GENERAL INDEX

The following appendices are contained in Part VII:—

1. List of abbreviations used for grammatical terms (Cambodian).
2. Index to words belonging to each category of particle.
3. Notes on the grammatical terms used in this book, with an account of the catalysis of the word categories.
4. Text of recorded material illustrating sentence-tunes 1 and 2; some features of phrasing, intonation and stress; and colloquial forms of words.
5. Bibliography of dictionaries and readers.
6. List of diacritics and signs which are used in connection with the transcription.

These are followed by a general index to topics discussed in all previous parts of the book.

1. LIST OF ABBREVIATIONS AND SIGNS USED FOR GRAMMATICAL TERMS (CAMBODIAN)

a. adverbial particle
A. adverbial construct
c. numeral coefficient
e. exclamatory particle
f. final phrase particle
g. general particle
i. initiating particle
m. marker
n. noun
N. noun construct

p. particle
p.v.p. pre-verbal particle
post n.p. post-nominal particle
pre n.p. pre-nominal particle
r. responding particle
S.F. sentence-form
v. verb
V. verb construct
x numeral
X numeral construct

2. INDEX TO WORDS BELONGING TO EACH CATEGORY OF PARTICLE

For each category of particle listed below alphabetically, is given either a list of the particles in that category (as occurring in this book) or a reference to the Lesson where such a list may be found.

a. adverbial particle

No list is given elsewhere. The following adverbial particles occur in this book:—

kniːə together, each other, reciprocally
ciːə-mùːəy together
ciːəŋ to a greater extent
cùːən-kaːl sometimes
cùːən-naː sometimes
doːc-mdëc how
doːc=nɔh like that
doːc=neh like this
tèəŋ-laːy all
tèəŋ-ʔɔs all
nas very
bɔntec a little
bɔntec-bɔntec a very little
bɔntec-bɔntuːəc very little
poṅṅɔh like this

poṅṅɤŋ like this
poṅṅeh like this
pèːk too, too much
phlìːəm immediately
mëc how
mkhaːŋ one side
mdɔːŋ once
mdɔːŋ-mdɔːŋ sometimes
mleh so, like this
mùn before
mnèək alone
sɔːŋkhaːŋ both sides
*ʔɤyloːv now
*ʔɤyloːv=nih now

e. exclamatory particle
List is in Lesson 43

f. final phrase particle
List is in Lesson 25.2

329

g. general dependent particle
Listed in Lesson 36.4

i. initiating particle
See table, Lesson 40

m. marker
List is in Lesson 24.2

p.v.p. pre-verbal particle
List is in Lesson 19.1

post n.p. post-nominal particle
No list is given elsewhere. The following post-nominal particles occur in this book:—
khlah some
tὲəŋ-laːy all
tὲəŋ-ʔɔs all
naː which, any, whichever

naː-mùːəy which, some, any, whichever (sing.)
neh this
nimùːəy each
nìh this
nùh that
meɲ just past, last (of periods of time)
mnὲək one (counting human beings)
ʔae-tìət other
ʔvʀy, sʔʀy, ʔʀy what, some, any, whatever
ʔvʀy-khlah, sʔʀy-khlah, ʔʀy-khlah what, some, any, whatever (plur.)
ʔvʀy-mùːəy, sʔʀy-mùːəy, ʔʀy-mùːəy what, some, any, whatever (sing.)
mὲc Only in *yaːŋ mὲc* 'how?'

pre n.p. pre-nominal particle
List is in Lesson 35.1

r. responding particle
See tables in Lessons 39 and 40

3. Notes on the Grammatical Terms Used in This Book, With an Account of the Catalysis of the Word Categories

The analysis on which the treatment of Cambodian grammar in this book is based is summarized and explained here. The word categories are listed in full in the order in which they may be arrived at by the methods used. The methods themselves are outlined for each category. A résumé of constructs, sentence-forms, etc., follows the list of categories.

1. *The catalysis of the four main word-categories, verb, noun, numeral and numeral coefficient*

Verb, **v.**—Four words are taken as catalysers, *mùn, nùŋ, kom* and *kɔː*. Any word which occurs regularly immediately following one or more of these catalysers is held to belong to the category of verb. e.g. *nùŋ tʀu* 'will go', *kom sraek* 'don't call out!'.

Noun, **n.**—The words *knoŋ, ʔae* and *ʔɔmpὶː* are taken as catalysers. Any word which occurs regularly immediately following one or more of these catalysers is held to belong to the category of noun. e.g. *knoŋ tùː* 'in the cupboard', *ʔae khɲom* 'as for me'.

Pronouns are a sub-class of nouns. They are not followed by attributive verbs in close junction or by *rɔbɔs*, **pre n.p.** and a further noun.

Numeral, **x.**—The words *tὶː* and *cɔmnuːən* are taken as catalysers. Any word which occurs regularly immediately following these words is held to belong to the category of numeral. All numerals except *craən* 'many' and *poñmaːn* 'how many' might equally have been catalysed by their representation by the written figures 1–9 and 0 in one or other of their combinations. e.g. *tὶː mùːəy* 'first', *cɔmnuːən poñmaːn* 'what number?'

Numeral coefficient, **c.**—Any word which occurs following a numeral in close junction is held to belong to the category of numeral coefficient. e.g. *pram nὲək* 'five persons', *mùːəy thnɔəp* 'one finger's-width'. Many word-forms belong to both the categories of noun and numeral coefficient.

2. *Particles*

All words which cannot be catalysed as **v**, **n**, **x** or **c** are regarded as particles. Particles may be dependent, i.e. occurring with potential lack of stress and only preceding or following a **n**, **v** or **x**[1] or independent, i.e. occurring without reference to the word which precedes or follows and capable of being pronounced as a separate phrase. Before the individual catalysis of particles, definitions of sentence-form I and the noun construct are needed:—

(i) Sentence-form I, S.F.I. A simple initiating sentence may consist of **nvn** uttered either as one phrase, **nvn(\)**, or as two, **n(,|)vn(\)**. **nvn** may also occur as a question, being uttered either as one phrase, **nvn(')**, or as two, **n(,|)vn(')**.

(ii) Noun construct, **N**. The noun element of a sentence may consist of **n** alone, or of **n** with attributive **v** or **n** (**nv**, **nn**) or of **n** with **x** or **xc** (**nx(c)**) or of **n** with all of these attributes, **nvnxc**. Finally it may be followed, still within the same phrase (checked by sentence-tune 1b or 2b), by a dependent particle, which, by its occurrence in this context, is catalysed as a post-nominal particle. The whole sequence, or a noun used alone or with any of the possible attributes or with the post-nominal particle, is called a noun construct.

Dependent particles

Post-nominal particles, **post n.p.**—These are catalysed as stated in (ii) above. See list in alphabetical list of categories of particle in VII 2.

Pre-nominal particles, **pre n.p.**—These cannot occur without a **n** immediately following. Once a large **n** class has been established by means of the particles *knoŋ*, *ʔae* and *ʔɔmpìː*, the nouns may in turn catalyse as **pre n.p.** various other dependent particles. See list in Lesson 35.1.

Pre-verbal particles, **p.v.p.**—These cannot occur without a **v** immediately following. Once a large **v** class has been established by means of the particles, *mùn*, *nùŋ*, *kom* and *kɔː*, the verbs themselves may in turn catalyse as **p.v.p.** various other dependent particles. See list in Lesson 19.1.

General dependent particles, **g.**—A few words, e.g. *tae*, *prɔhael*, **dɔː* and *sɔːmbɤy*, which, though dependent on a following word, do not require that word to belong to any particular one of the four main word categories, have been called 'general dependent particles'; they are catalysed as such by the fact that they are dependent particles but not of any of the above categories.

Independent particles

These are catalysed as such by the fact that they are not **v**, **n**, **x** or **c** and that they do not occur in association with any particular word. Many of them may form complete utterances alone. They may be assigned to categories in the following order.

Responding particles, **r.**—These are catalysed by the fact that they may occur in both of the following ways: they may be uttered with low pitch and no stress at the beginning of a response, before the beginning of the

---

[1] i.e. a dependent particle cannot be pronounced as a separate phrase.

sentence-form and its sentence-tune; they may form a complete response and be uttered with a complete sentence-tune. See tables, Lessons 39 and 40.

Initiating particles.—These are catalysed by the fact that they occur in the first way in which responding particles occur but not the second and that the utterance is an initiating one. See table, Lesson 40.

Markers, **m.**—These are catalysed by their occurrence at the beginning of a sentence-form as part of the sentence-tune, i.e. not, like responding and initiating particles, before and separate from the sentence-tune. See Lesson 24.2 for list.

Final phrase particles, **f.**—These are catalysed by their occurrence at the end of phrases. They are distinguished from post-nominal particles by the fact that the phrase need not include a noun. See Lesson 25.2 for list.

Exclamatory particles, **e.**—These may be catalysed by the fact that they alone, or the short sentences in which they occur, are uttered with the vigour, range of pitch and steepness of fall or rise in pitch associated with exclamatory utterances. Many of them may also be catalysed by their occurrence, like responding and initiating particles, before the sentence-form and separate from the sentence-tune, with the difference that unlike responding particles they need not occur in responses, and unlike initiating particles they need not be followed by a sentence. See Lesson 43 for list.

Adverbial particles, **a.**—These are catalysed by the fact that they do not fit into any other category. See list in alphabetical list of categories of particle, VII 2.

3. *The constructs*

Noun construct, **N.**—This is either a noun with no other word occurring in close junction with it or a noun closely followed in one phrase by one or more of the following: (i) a verb (usually attributive); (ii) another noun; (iii) a numeral with numeral coefficient if required; (iv) a post-nominal particle (which is normally the last word in the sequence).

Verb construct, **V.**—This is either (i) a verb (operative or attributive) with no noun following it in close junction or (ii) a verb followed by a noun construct in close junction or (iii) a verb preceded by an initiating verb in close junction or (iv) a verb both followed by a noun construct and preceded by an initiating verb.

A minor verb construct (←**v**) is one composed like **V** but with a minor verb and no possibility of an initiating verb as **v**. It follows a major verb construct.

Adverbial construct, **A.**—This is a noun construct preceded by a pre-nominal particle. In a limited form of the adverbial construct there may be no pre-nominal particle but a pre-nominal particle before the construct may be used in the same sentence without altering the meaning of the sentence.

Numeral construct, **X.**—This consists of one or more numerals, forming a number, followed if required by a numeral coefficient: **x(x)(c)**. It may occur as part of a noun construct. When it occurs independently it may occupy the same range of sentence-positions as **A**.

4. *Sequence and phrase*

Close verbal sequence.—This consists of an initiating verb followed by a verb in close junction.

Major verbal sequence.—This term is applied to the major verbs of a series of major verb constructs in a sentence.

Phrase.—By 'phrase' is meant part of a sentence separated from the other part or parts by potential pause and by rise in pitch on the last syllable (except for the last syllable of the last phrase in a statement; this has a steep fall). A phrase has no direct relationship with the sentence-forms. It may consist of one independent particle, one construct or several, a whole sentence-form, etc.

5. *Sentence-forms*

Sentence-form I 1   **N V** or **(r) (m) (A/a/X) N (A/a/X) (p)V (A/a/v/X) (f)**

Sentence-form I 2   **N V V** or **(r) (m) (A/a/X) N (A/a/X) (p)V (A/a/v/X) (p)V (A/a/v/X) (f)**

Sentence-form II 1   **V** or **(r) (m) (A/a/X) (p)V (A/a/v/X) (f)**

Sentence-form II 2   **V V** or **(r) (m) (A/a/X) (p)V (A/a/v/X) (p)V (A/a/v/X) (f)**

Sentence-form III 1   **N N V** or **(r) (m) N (A/a/X) N (A/a/X) (p)V (A/a/v/X) (f)**

Sentence-form III 2   **N N V V** or **(r) (m) N (A/a/X) N (A/a/X) (p)V (A/a/v/X) (p)V (A/a/v/X) (f)**

6. *Sentence-tunes*

Sentence-tune 1 *a*   . . . . (\\)

Sentence-tune 1 *b*   . . . . (,|) . . . . (\\)

Sentence-tune 1 *c*   . . . . (,|) . . . . (,|) . . . . (\\)

Sentence-tune 2 *a*   . . . . (')

Sentence-tune 2 *b*   . . . . (,|) . . . . (')

Sentence-tune 2 *c*   . . . . (,|) . . . . (,|) . . . . (')

4. TEXT OF RECORDED MATERIAL ILLUSTRATING SENTENCE-TUNES 1 AND 2; SOME FEATURES OF PHRASING, INTONATION AND STRESS; AND COLLOQUIAL FORMS OF WORDS

(This follows Exercise 60 on the tape-recordings.)

Sentence-tune 1 (statements)[1]

1 *a.* **khɲom tɤu phtɛ̀əh.** I am going home.
     khɲom mùɨn tɤu phtɛ̀əh tɛ̀:. I am not going home.
     phtɛ̀əh nìh thom nas. This house is very big.

1 *b.* **ʔo:pùk khɲom (,|) nɤu phtɛ̀əh thom.** My father lives in a big house.
     nɤu phnùm-pĕɲ (,|) nɛ̀ək khɤ̀:ɲ phtɛ̀əh thmɤy craən nas. In Phnom Penh you see very many new houses.
     taŋ-pì: thɲay-ʔa:tùɨt(y) mɔ̀:k (,|) lò:k chùɨ: bɔntec. Ever since Sunday he has not been very well.
     vì:ə tɛ̀ɲ sìəvphɤ̀u nìh (,|) ʔaoy khɲom. He bought these books for me.[2]

---

[1] See Lessons 14.1; 16.4; 17.5; 20.2; 28.
[2] This sentence illustrates Lesson 20.2.

1 *c.* **pìː thŋay nìh (,|) bɔːŋ-pros khɲom (,|) mùn tʁu saːlaː-rìən tèː.** From that day my brother didn't go to school.

pìː msʁl meɲ (,|) dɔl thŋay ʔɔŋkìːə(r) (,|) kèː chùp thvʁ̀ː kaː(r). From yesterday until Tuesday they stop working.

nʁu srok khmae(r) (,|) ʔaːtùt(y) nìh (,|) kèː thvʁ̀ː boɲ(y) coːl chnam. In Cambodia this week it is the New Year Festival.

Sentence-tune 2 (questions)[1]

2 *a.* **nɛ̀ək tʁu phsaː(r) tèːʔ** Are you going to market?

nɛ̀ək tʁu phsaː(r) rùː tèːʔ Are you going to market?

dɔl maoŋ bʁy haəy rùː nʁuʔ Is it three o'clock yet?

2 *b.* **ʔaːtùt(y) nìh (,|) lòːk troːv tʁu thvʁ̀ː kaː(r) tèːʔ** Do you have to go to work this week?

dɔl khae-kắɲɲaː (,|) nɛ̀ək nùŋ ceh-tae tʁu saːlaː-thom tèːʔ In September will you still go to the University?

prùk meɲ (,|) ʔaeŋ baːn cù:t tok nìh tèːʔ Did you dust this table this morning?

2 *c.* **yùp meɲ (,|) prəhael maoŋ pìː(r) (,|) nɛ̀ək baːn lùː chkae prùh tèːʔ** Last night at about three o'clock did you hear a dog barking?

pèːl lŋìːəc (,|) knoŋ rədoːv kdau (,|) taə lòːk ceh-tae tətùːəl tìːən domneːk rùː tèːʔ Do you always have a rest in the afternoons in the hot season?

Phrasing in relation to clauses[2]

1 *phrase, 1 clause*   **lòːk-krùː cɔŋ tʁu kɔmpùəŋ-caːm dae(r).** The teacher wants to go to Kompung Cham too.

2 *phrases, 1 clause*   **siəvphʁu nùh saot (,|) kɔː mùn lʔɔː mʁ̀ːl tèː taə!** That book's not worth reading either, then!

2 *phrases, 2 clauses*   **kaːl-naː cau səseː(r) sɔmbot(r) rùːəc haəy (,|) khɲom nùŋ yɔ̀ːk sɔmbot(r) tʁu dak pos(te).** When you have finished writing the letter I will take it to the post.

Intonation of responding particles[3]

'ʔoːpùk nʁu ʔae-naːʔ' 'baːt̪, ʔoːpùk nʁu phtɛ̀əh.' 'Where is father?' 'He is at home.'

'ʔoːpùk nɛ̀ək nʁu phtɛ̀əh tèːʔ' 'baːt̪.' 'Is your father at home?' 'Yes.'

'pʔɔːn tʁu phsaː(r) tèːʔ' 'baːt̪ tèː.' 'Are you going to market?' 'No.'

Intonation of markers[4]

Phrased separately. **kɔ̀ət tʁu rɔ̀ːk-sìː thvʁ̀ː cìːə smiən nʁu-ʔae kɔmpùəŋ-caːm, rùːəc (,|) pìː(r) bʁy chnam kraoy (,|) kɔ̀ət trəlɔp mɔ̀ːk phnùm pɛ̀ɲ vɛ̀ɲ.** He went to work as a secretary in Kompung Cham; then, two or three years afterwards, he came back to Phnom Penh.

---

[1] See Lessons 15.1,2; 16.4; 17.5; 28.
[2] See Lessons 24.1; 25.4; 28.
[3] See Lessons 15.2; 28.
[4] See Lesson 24.4.

ko:n-sʁs(s) khmae(r) craən-tae tʁu sa:la:-rìən nʁu srok ba:raŋ; ko:-poñtae (,|) sɔp̣(v) thŋay (,|) mì:ən ko:n-sʁs(s) craən nὲək tʁu srok-ʔɔŋklὲ:s dae(r). Cambodian students often go to college in France, but nowadays many go to England too.

Included in another phrase. khɲom tʁu phtὲəh. rù:əc khɲom tʁu su:ə(r) mì:ŋ. I'm going home. Then I'll go and visit aunt.

kɔ̀ət chlaəy tha: 'ba:n', tʁ̀:p kɔ̀ət de:k lùək tʁu. He answered 'Yes' and then fell asleep.

ka:l-na: khɲom mʁ̀:l siəvphʁu nìh cɔp haəy, tʁ̀:p khɲom tʁu daə(r)-lὲ:ŋ. When I have finished reading this book, I'll go for a walk.

Intonation of final phrase particles, **kɔ:-ba:n** and **kɔ:-daoy**, after an emphasized question word[1]

kɔnlaeŋ na: kɔ:-daoy, ta: de:k lùək dae(r). Grandfather can sleep *any*where.

'nὲək cɔŋ ba:n baŋ na:ʔ' 'na: kɔ:-daoy kɔ:-ba:n dae(r).' 'Which seat do you want?' '*Any* will do.'

'so:m lò:k-ta: ʔɔɲcʁ̀:ɲ ʔɔŋkùy.' 'ʔɔŋkùy nʁu-ʔae na:, cauʔ' 'ʔae na: kɔ:-ba:n dae(r).' 'Do sit down, grandfather.' 'Where shall I sit, grandson?' 'Where you like.'

ʔaeŋ tha: mὲc kɔ:-ba:n. kὲ: mùm prɔ̀:m tʁu tὲ:. Say what you like. He won't go.

Intonation of exclamatory particles[2]

ʔʁ:, nìh thlay poñma:nʔ Er, what price is this?

yì:! ʔaeŋ tha: mὲcʔ *What* did you say? (implying surprise and disapproval).

ʔao! khɲom ʔɔt khʁ̀:ɲ lò:k tὲ:. Oh! I didn't see you!

nʁu sɲiəm (h)nə! Be quiet!

tʁu na: (h)nəʔ Where are you going, then?

kdau ʔʁy kdau! How hot it is!

phlìəŋ ʔʁy kɔ: phlìəŋ! What rain!

Intonation and phrasing of compound numerals[3]

pram-mù:əy lì:ən, mù:əy-rɔ̀:y-ha:sʁp-bʁy-pɔ̀ən, pì:(r)-rɔ̀:y kausʁp-pì:(r). mù:əy-rɔ̀:y sa:msʁp-bu:ən rìəl.

Compound particles[4]

nὲək nìh tʁu thvʁ̀: ka:(r) nʁu phnùm-pĕɲ. (Repeated with *nʁu-ʔae* instead of *nʁu*.) This person is going to work in Phnom Penh.

pì: thŋay dɔp-bu:ən khae kɑɲɲa: dɔl thŋay pram-mù:əy tola:, khɲom nùŋ tʁu bat-dɔmbo:ŋ. (Repeated with *rəho:t-dɔl* instead of *dɔl*.) I shall be in Battambang from the 14th of September until the 6th of October.

kɔ̀ət tʁu su:ə(r) ʔo:pùk kɔ̀ət rɔ̀əl ʔa:tùt(y). (Repeated with *rɔ̀əl-tae* instead of *rɔ̀əl*.) He goes to visit his father every week.

nὲək-srae cas-cas, dael thvʁ̀: ka:(r) lùmba:k do:c-cì:ə ʔo:pùk khɲom, mì:ən ʔa:yù vὲ:ŋ. (Repeated with *do:c* instead of *do:c-cì:ə*.) Old farmers who do hard work like my father are long-lived.

---

[1] See Lessons 34.2; 48.5.
[2] See Lesson 43.
[3] See Lessons 22.1; 48.4.
[4] See Lesson 48.5.

ʔoːpùk khɲom haəy-nùŋ bɔːŋ khɲom nɤ̀u prèy-nəkɔ̀ː(r). (Repeated with *nùŋ* instead of *haəy-nùŋ*.) My father and my brother live in Saigon.

Emphasis of one word in excited or argumentative speech style[1]

'soːm tòːs. ʔɔt khɤ̀ːɲ.' 'ʔaeŋ kmìːən *phnèːk* tèː rùːʔ' 'Sorry. I didn't see it.' 'Haven't you any eyes, then?'

'khɲom mùn prɔ̀ːm thvɤ̀ː.' 'ʔaeŋ nìyìːəy *doːc⁼neh* mùn troːv tèː.' 'I won't do it.' 'It's not right to talk like that.'

'phtèəh nùh *thom* ʔɤy thom!' 'mùn thom poɱ̃aːn tèː, kɔː-poɱ̃ae mìːən bɔntùp craən.' 'What a big house it is!' 'It's not very big but it has a lot of rooms.'

Colloquial forms of words[2]

1. Extended monosyllables

   rəlùət, ʔəlùət; rənaː(r), ʔənaː(r); bəbɔː(r), pəbɔː(r); dədael, tədael; səsɔː(r), təsɔː(r); səseː(r), təseː(r).

2. Restricted disyllables

   kondaːl, kədaːl; kùmnɔ̀əp, kənɔ̀əp; cɔmbaŋ, cəbaŋ; cùmtìːəv, cətìːəv; tùmnèɲ, tənèɲ; sɔmnaːp, sənaːp; sɔndaek, sədaek.

   dɔndɤŋ, tədɤŋ; bɔŋʔuːəc, pəʔuːəc.

   sɔmnaːp, srənaːp; bɔŋʔuːəc, prəʔuːəc; kɔmnat, krənat.

   ʔɔntùəŋ, ntùəŋ; ʔɔmbaɲ, ɱbaɲ; kɔŋkaeɲ, ŋkaeɲ; cùəɲcùːn, ɲcùːn; cùəɲcìːŋ, ɲcìːŋ; sɔnsaəm, ŋsaəm.

5.   BIBLIOGRAPHY OF DICTIONARIES AND READERS

The following dictionaries and reading materials have been found useful during the teaching of the course contained in this book:—

Dictionaries

S. TANDART. *Dictionnaire français–cambodgien*. Hongkong, 1910–11. 2 vols.

J. GUESDON. *Dictionnaire cambodgien–français*. Paris, 1930. 2 vols.

S. TANDART. *Dictionnaire cambodgien–français*. Phnom Penh, 1935. 2 vols.

Dictionnaire cambodgien. 2nd edition. Phnom Penh, 1951. 2 vols. (1st edition, Tome 1, 1938, Tome 2, 1943).

PREAP SOKH. *Dictionary English–Cambodian*. Phnom Penh, 1957.

SAM THANG. *Lexique Franco–Khmer*. Phnom Penh, 1961.

SAM THANG. *Lexique Khmer–français*. Phnom Penh, 1962. [Deals with newly acquired vocabulary only.[3] Cambodian text with a one-word French translation for each article.]

TEP-YOK and THAO-KUN. *Dictionnaire français–khmer*. Phnom Penh. Vol. 1, 1962, Vol. 2, 1964.

R. KOVIN. *Mots culturels Khméro–français expliqués*. Phnom Penh, 1964. [Deals with newly acquired vocabulary only.[3] Cambodian text with a one-word French translation for each article.]

---

[1] See Lessons 25.2 and 25.4, no. 5 in each case.

[2] See Lesson 5.6.

[3] In the last few years a new vocabulary of about 3,000 words has been invented by borrowing from the Sanskrit and Pali languages. Cambodians used to use French words to refer to many abstract ideas and features of Western culture. The new vocabulary includes words of this kind as well as modern scientific terminology. The student will meet this vocabulary if he reads the conversations in Sonolet and Pa Pheng 'Le Cambodge . . .', cited below as reading material.

Reading materials, arranged in order of difficulty

MANIPOUD, CCHIM SOT, KHEM PENG. *Viccheakhemarapheasa. Kumaratthan.* [Cambodian school reader. Infant class.] Phnom Penh, 1965. [Orthography followed by easy reading passages.]

Viccheakhemarapheasa. Atikatthan. [Cambodian school reader. Elementary class.] Phnom Penh, 1950. [Reading passages.]

J. F. SONOLET and PA PHENG. *Le Cambodge Guide Franco–Khmer.* Phnom Penh, 1963. [Conversations and vocabularies classified according to subject matter concerned with a large variety of topics. The orthography, a transcription and a French translation are given side by side. The book also contains tourist information, maps, etc., and a few pages on pronunciation and grammar.]

C. CHUM. *Morceaux Choisis. Lecture. Dictée. Rédaction Traduction.* Cours primaire complementaire et examens. 10th edition, 1964. [Contains passages of Cambodian often with French translation alongside.]

Commission des mœurs et des coutumes du Cambodge. Recueil des contes et légendes cambodgiens. Fasc. 1–5, Phnom Penh, 1963. [Cambodian text throughout.]

6. LIST OF DIACRITICS AND SIGNS WHICH ARE USED IN CONNECTION WITH THE TRANSCRIPTION

` indicates second register (either in the pronunciation of a vowel or in the orthography of a consonant). See Lessons 3.1 and 11.4.

. indicates that a sound is written with an Indian cerebral consonant. See Lesson 11.4.

′ indicates that the vowel so marked is written by means of the inherent vowel and the *saɲɲòːksaɲɲaː*.

⌃ indicates that the initial consonant of a syllable is written subscript to the final consonant of the preceding syllable. See Lesson 11.4.

ı indicates that the *tɔɔndəkhìːət* occurs over the consonant in the orthography. See Lesson 11.4.

ı indicates that the vowel is written with the vowel-sign, *ù*, and not by means of the inherent vowel and the *bɔntɔk*. See Lesson 11.4.

- indicates that the two or more syllables or restricted disyllables so joined form a compound word. See Lessons 11.4 and 48.

* indicates that the following word, or component of a compound word, has an irregular spelling which will be found in a list in Part IV.

(\) indicates that the preceding syllable is pronounced with a steep fall in pitch to low level.

(,) indicates that the preceding syllable is pronounced with a rise from fairly low level.

(|) indicates that pause potentially occurs after preceding syllable.

(,|) indicates that both the last two features occur.

(′) indicates that the preceding syllable is pronounced with a rise in pitch from mid to high level.

(.) indicates that the preceding syllable is pronounced with fairly low, level pitch and no stress.

(ˌ) indicates that the preceding syllable is pronounced with a fall in pitch from mid to low level.

(¯) indicates that the preceding syllable is pronounced with moderately high pitch.

GENERAL INDEX

Most references relate to Parts I–III of the book, which are divided into lessons. The references are therefore to the lessons or to their numbered sub-sections. e.g. **32** means 'Lesson 32' and **42**.1,3 means 'Lesson 42.1 and Lesson 42.3'. If a reference relates to Part IV, V, VI or VII, the Part number is given and may be followed by an arabic numeral indicating the section concerned, e.g. VII 3, 'Part VII, section 3'. n. = 'footnote' or 'note to exercise'. nn. = 'notes'. Ex. = Exercise.

statement	affirmative —, **14**.2 negative —, **14**.6
stress	— in restricted disyllables, **4**.5 — in full disyllables, **4**.6 n. — of major verb, **21**.1 — in compound nouns, **48**.2 — in compound verbs, **48**.3 — in compound numerals, **48**.4 — in compound particles, **48**.5 VII 4
style	formal reading —, **5**.5 colloquial —, **4**.5 **5**.6 VII 4
subject	sentence —, **14** sentence — emphasized, **14**.1 **38**.1 — not expressed in responding sentence, **15**.2 — of verb varying in one clause, **37**.7
syllabary	**7–9**
syntax	reduplication in —, **47**
taə	in indirect question, **29**.1
terms	summary of grammatical — used in **14–27** with definitions, **28** tables of — of address, i.e. responding and initiating particles and titles, used in addressing laymen, monks and royalty, **39 40** additional notes on common — of address, **41** notes on grammatical — used in this book, VII 3
tha:	use of — in indirect question, **29**.1
time	expressions of —, **17**.3 **26**.3 context of —, **17**.7 — difference between two clauses, **25**.5 vocabulary for telling the —, **27**.1 grammatical processes for expressing the —, **27**.2 indication of — in two-clause sentences, **29**.4
title	**39**.3,4,5 **40 41** — used as a form of address, **42**.2 note on choice of —, **45** Ex. 56 A (2) n.
tɔəndəkhi:ət	**11**.2
topic	sentence —, **38**.3
transcription	origin and aims of the — used in this book; account of additional signs used from **11** onwards, **11**.4
translation	— of 'you', **15**.4 — of 'I', **16**.5 — of 'it', **17**.6 — of English preposition by verbs of motion and position, **20**.4 — of 'some', **31** — of 'any', **32–34** — of 'all', **36**.3 — of English passive voice, **38**.4 — of 'self', **42**.1
trisyllable	**4**.6 n. **10**.5 n.
trʏysəp̀(ł)	**7**.3
verb	**14 28** attributive —s, **14**.3 operative —s, **14**.3 definition of main —, **17**.1 — construct, **17**.1 full — construct, **19**.2 initiating —, **19**.2,3 two initiating —s used together, **45** Ex. 57 A (3) n. initiating — used with compound pre-verbal particle, **19**.4 minor —, **20**.1 list of minor —s, **20**.3 sentences illustrating the use of minor —s, **20**.3 minor — construct, **20**.1 more than one initiating or minor — in one sentence, **37**.1 limitation of minor — construct, **37**.2 close verbal sequence, **19**.2 major verbal sequence, **21**.1 **30**.1 impersonal use of —, **26**.3 2nd position main —, **30**.1,2 relation of — to noun or subject, **37**.7 analysis of reduplicative —s from lexical point of view, **46**.3 compound —, **48**.3
visarga	**7**.4 **8**.3
voice	— quality, **1**.1 translation of English passive —, **38**.4
vocabulary	special — for addressing various ranks of person, **39 40 41**
vowel	pronunciation of 1st register —s, **1 2** pronunciation of 2nd register —s, **3** neutral — occurring in initial consonant sequence, **4**.3 résumé of pronunciation of 1st and 2nd register —s, **5**.2,3 inherent —, **5**.2 (No. 18) orthography of —s, **8**.1,2 Sanskrit initial — -signs, **8**.2 orthography of short —s, **8**.3 orthography of inherent —, **8**.3
vowel-signs	see vowels, orthography
weather	expression of ideas connected with —, **26**.3
word	interrogative —s, **18**.1 question —s in indirect question, **29** sentences illustrating uses of question —s, **29**.2 question —s in various grammatical contexts, **31 32 33 34** indefinite —s, **31**.1,4 **32**.3 reduplicative —s, **46** compound —s, see compound
word-form	pronunciation of the various —s, **4** orthography of the various —s, **10** résumé of pronunciation and orthography of —s, **5**.5 variant forms in rapid colloquial speech, **5**.6 VII 4
word-order	**14**.2 **15**.1
you	translation of 'you', **15**.4